NANCY CUNARD

Nancy, at twenty (1916)

Lois Gordon

NANCY CUNARD

Heiress, Muse,
Political Idealist

Columbia
University
Press •
New York

Columbia University Press

Publishers Since 1893

New York   Chichester, West Sussex

Copyright © 2007 Columbia University Press

Library of Congress Cataloging-in-Publication Data

Gordon, Lois G.

    Nancy Cunard : heiress, muse, political idealist / Lois Gordon.

      p. cm

    Includes bibliographical references and index.

    ISBN 0-231-13938-1 (alk. paper)

    ISBN 0-231-51137-x (electronic)

    1. Cunard, Nancy, 1896–1965.   2. Authors, English—20th century—
Biography.   3. Women political activists—England—Biography.
4. Women journalists—England—Biography.   I. Title.

PR6005.U6Z65 2007

821'.912—dc22

[B]

                                2006026710

∞

Columbia University Press books are printed
on permanent and durable acid-free paper.
Printed in the United States of America

Designed by Lisa Hamm

c 10 9 8 7 6 5 4 3 2 1

To Alan and Robert

Contents

Illustrations

Preface

About fifteen years ago, I went into a small shop in Paris to buy a few mementos. My eye was instantly drawn to a picture postcard near the door and the image of a beautiful woman wearing dozens of distinctive and handsome African bracelets on both arms, from her wrists to her shoulders. The African rings on both her hands emphasized her delicate fingers, which were clasped at her left shoulder. Although the bracelets seemed to dominate the photo, I couldn't take my eyes from her face. She was looking away from the camera, as though reticent to detract from her adornments and the unusual fashion and cultural statement she was making. But her face was mesmerizing; it looked like that of a child with perfect features, and her enormous, light eyes were highlighted by dark makeup. When I noticed that the photo had been taken by the great Man Ray, I realized that the young woman identified as Nancy Cunard must have been posed in this way. As I much later learned, Ray, a good friend of Nancy's in Paris, understood her well: he had captured her beauty, intensity, and, above all, her commitment to her ideals—in this instance, the brilliance of African art.

I bought the card of this still-mysterious woman for myself, and it has remained on my dresser, where I have looked at it daily over all these years. During this time, I wrote two books on Samuel Beckett, and, as I had written in my Beckett biography and forgotten, Nancy Cunard was the first person to publish Beckett. For whatever reason, it had never occurred to me to associate the author of *Waiting for Godot* with the woman on my dresser. If anything, I associated the name "Cunard" with majestic ships. Later, when writing a book on *Godot*, I realized that the word "Cunard" appeared several times in a long, climactic speech in Beckett's play. The full significance of the Nancy–Beckett relationship occurred to me only after another Beckett scholar related my convictions about Beckett's politics to the articles Beckett had translated for Miss Cunard's anthology, *Negro*.

Yes, Nancy Cunard was a publisher, but that's just the tip of the iceberg.

Nancy Cunard (1896–1965) was one of the most unusual women of the twentieth century and perhaps of all time. Great-granddaughter of the founder of the Cunard Line and child of an American beauty and a British aristocrat, Nancy abandoned the life of a celebrated socialite for a lifelong battle against social injustice. Her astonishing beauty, intelligence, and seductive powers led to romances with many of the greatest writers of the era, including three Nobel Prize winners. Indeed, she might have become the queen of England had she returned the ardent interest of the Prince of Wales. She became a popular icon and trend setter of the Jazz Age, and she was the model for major characters in the works of writers such as Ezra Pound, T. S. Eliot, Aldous Huxley, Evelyn Waugh, Samuel Beckett, Ernest Hemingway, Louis Aragon, Tristan Tzara, Pablo Neruda, and the first modern super best-seller, Michael Arlen. Greta Garbo, Constance Bennett, Tallulah Bankhead, and Katharine Cornell played Nancy's character in films and on stage.

Nancy was also a prolific poet, publisher, translator, and journalist. Her long poem *Parallax* (1925) was favorably compared with Eliot's *The Waste Land*. She originated the Hours Press and was the first to publish, in her own hand-printed editions, Beckett, Laura Riding, and Pound's *A Draft of the XXX Cantos*. In 1927, she fell in love with a black American jazz pianist who educated her about racism in the United States. She closed her press and after extensive research and travel published *Negro* (1934), a mammoth work that was the first comprehensive study of the achievement and plight of blacks throughout the world. Her contributors included Langston Hughes, W. E. B. Du Bois, Zora Neale Hurston, Theodore Dreiser, and Beckett, among scores of other admired figures. She was ridiculed and rejected by both family and friends.

Her courage as a journalist and humanitarian aid worker during and following the Spanish Civil War transformed her into a hero of that war. As the only eyewitness reporter for the *Manchester Guardian*, she trudged to battlefronts in the midst of artillery fire; she later walked through aerial bombardment alongside the refugees in their exodus to France. She subsequently exposed the atrocities of the French concentration camps, the "holding centers," for Spanish refugees and Republican soldiers. In *Authors Take Sides*, she created a unique political literary genre, calling on famous writers to take a side for or against fascism. She continued her anti-fascist efforts during World War II as a writer and broadcaster of coded material for the Supreme Headquarters, Allied Expeditionary Force (SHAEF). After the war, she fought tirelessly to rescue Spanish refugees from the Franco regime and to find them a homeland in Latin America; she eventually joined a guerrilla movement to restore democracy in Spain. Throughout, she continued writing poetry, essays, and news reports.

Because of her involvement in the life of her times, exploring Nancy Cunard's life allows one an opportunity to revisit some of the major historical, social, and artistic events and movements of the first half of the twentieth century. At the same time, one learns from diaries and extensive correspondence that Nancy's public achievements and vivacious demeanor belied a lifelong struggle with loneliness, insecurity, and physical illness. Her many letters to and from friends also reveal an immense kindness, wit, and stoicism, as well as an often flamboyant, determined defiance of prejudiced social conventions that made her headline news on both sides of the Atlantic.

The great poet William Carlos Williams called Nancy "one of the major phenomena of history"; another friend said that "to be in the presence of Nancy was more like coming to grips with a force of nature. . . . It was impossible for her to work quietly for the rights of man; Nancy functioned best in a state of fury in which, in order to defend, she attacked every windmill in a landscape of windmills." My goal is to give Nancy Cunard what seems to me to be her rightful place in history.

Acknowledgments

I am enormously grateful to many curators, archivists, and librarians in both the United States and England for making available Nancy Cunard's diaries, scrapbooks, manuscripts, and extensive correspondence. I also thank Anthony R. A. Hobson, who collected the bulk of Nancy's papers and arranged for their deposit at the Harry Ransom Humanities Center (HRC), University of Texas at Austin. I thank him, as well as the representatives of Nancy Cunard's heirs, for permission to quote from this material. Of the many helpful people at the HRC, I warmly acknowledge Linda Briscoe Myers, Patrice Fox, and Eric Lupfer.

Other generous curators from American libraries include Katie Salzman and her assistant Anthony Barger at the Morris Library, Southern Illinois University; Iris Snyder at the University of Delaware; Laila Vejzovic at Washington State University; Michael Basinski at the Edward H. Butler Library, State University of New York at Buffalo; Kathryn Rawdon at the Beinecke Rare Book and Manuscript Library at Yale University; and various unnamed specialists on rotation at the reference desks at the Library of Congress and New York Public Library, particularly its Schomberg Center for Research in Black Culture.

I am also grateful to those on the other side of the Atlantic, especially Dr. James N. Peters at the John Rylands Library, University of Manchester; Oliver House at the New Bodleian Library and Tricia Buckingham at the Bodleian

Library, University of Oxford; Dr. Richard Price and Gareth Barker at the British Library; and Julia Creed at the Hyman Kreitman Research Centre, Tate Library and Archive.

While my research has led me to a different understanding and portrait of Nancy Cunard, I owe thanks to three people who have previously written about her: Hugh Ford, the first academic to champion her work and life and the editor of an invaluable collection of essays (1968); Daphne Fielding, the author of an elegant memoir of Nancy and her mother (1968); and Anne Chisholm, who published a highly informative biography of Nancy (1979), the first and only one to date.

For their close reading of the book in manuscript, I want to thank Warren French, Kimball King, and Alan W. Friedman, and, for their expertise and commentary on the Spanish Civil War, I am particularly indebted to Paul Preston, as well as Peter Carroll, George Eisenwein, Sebastiaan Faber, and Stanley Payne. Jacqueline Hurtley, at the University of Barcelona, offered vital information regarding Nancy's life during and after the Spanish Civil War.

Once again, I must acknowledge my librarian-friends, whose goodwill and expertise I have relied on over many years: Eileen MacIlvaine, Sarah Witte, Bob Scott, and Junko Stuveras at Butler Library, Columbia University; and Kathy Stein Smith, Laila Rogers, and Judy Katz at Weiner Library, Fairleigh Dickinson University. Barbara Merdler, Monica Hinosa, and Adhi Kesavan were helpful in solving computer problems in the preparation of the manuscript. I also thank my friends for their encouragement and reliable good cheer: Edna Charles, Barbara Deblat, Ilene Engelmayer, Mary Farrell, Michael T. Garodnitz, Claire Goodlin, Vivian and Georges Gottlib, Anita Hicks, Barbara Kaplan, Sybil Maimin, Irwin Radezky, and Marvin Rechter. Above all, for his enthusiastic support and insightful comments throughout this project, I am deeply grateful to my friend and college dean, John R. Snyder.

Finally, I must express my appreciation to the talented people at Columbia University Press for the extraordinary care and skill with which they worked on this book, especially Anne McCoy, Lisa Hamm, and Elizabeth Cosgrove. I owe a special debt of gratitude to Jennifer Crewe, associate director of the press, for her enthusiastic support of this project. She offers an author the wonderful combination of a highly responsive, intellectually imaginative editor and an empathic and generous colleague.

My greatest debt is to my family, my always-inspiring son, Robert, and most essential of all, my husband, Alan, an incredible source of ideas and comfort.

NANCY CUNARD

1

Golden Girl

[It is] a low thing—the lowest.

—NANCY'S MOTHER, ON MOTHERHOOD

Nancy Cunard was the great-granddaughter of Samuel Cunard, the founder of the renowned transatlantic steamship line, and she was brought up with all the privileges of the aristocracy. As a child, she showed precocious intelligence and an insatiable desire to learn, but she was often lonely because of the frequent absence of her parents. When the Cunards were at home, the young Nancy was often bewildered by their ambiguous moral values. She was expected to obey strict rules and prohibitions, while her father passively watched her mother break the most elemental bonds of married life—mutual trust and respect. Nancy grew up to despise everything her parents and their class represented. As an adult, she returned to the palatial estate of her youth three times, on each occasion finding it increasingly "dehydrated" of meaning and feeling.[1]

Queen Victoria had dubbed Samuel Cunard a baronet, the title that was passed on to succeeding generations. The Cunard family also had eminent American roots: Nancy's father, Bache (pronounced "beach") Cunard, the third baronet, was a direct descendant of Benjamin Franklin; the Bache family (rhyming with "match" in the United States) moved from Franklin's Philadelphia to Staten Island, New York, and resided there for several decades;[2] one street still bears the family name. The American Cunards are now scattered throughout the United States and Canada.

Bache Cunard, dark-haired, heavyset, and distinguished by his bushy moustache, was forty-three when he married Maud Burke, a highly spirited blonde and blue-eyed American beauty of twenty-three. Although her fortune was even greater than his, her California family was regarded as well off but not well born. The marriage was arranged according to a practice common at the time: wealthy American daughters were paired with European men of high social standing. The women arrived in their new homelands with dowries that substantially enriched their spouses—in Maud's case, a titled member of the English establishment. Other affluent migrant-brides of the time included Lady Ribblesdale, Lady Granard, Lady Curzon, and Lady Astor—all eventually among Maud's good friends.

In Maud and Bache's arrangement, a $2 million dowry was exchanged for the bride's residence at (and presumably a share of) Bache's 13,000-acre estate, Nevill Holt, in rural Leicestershire; Maud also became a "Lady." Holt was located in a remote area of the Midlands that remains best known for its foxhunting and Stilton cheese, rather than its mineral (ironstone, coal, lead, slate), agricultural (turnips, cabbage, carrots, grain), and knitting industries. The sparsely populated countryside is also notable for its medieval castles (one of which Bache owned) and beautiful wildflowers that fill the meadows by the banks of the local rivers and small brooks.

The bride was vivacious and well educated, and her appetite for cultural and social advancement was voracious. However, her bridegroom, while educated at Cambridge, had neither cultural nor intellectual interests; nor was he outgoing or interested in the world of finance. Before their wedding, one of Bache's sisters, it is said, begged Maud to break off the engagement. She realized that Maud required the excitement and glamour of the city and society and that her brother would be happy only if he continued his quiet life in the country.[3]

Bache's home was, in every way, his castle. It dated back to about 1210, the time of King John, although it had been altered over the years with Georgian and early Victorian additions. Constructed of gray and yellow stone, one end ·of it was attached to a church. The living area alone covered more ground space than, say, the New York Public Library. The Great Hall, two stories high, was famous for its exquisitely carved arched window and gigantic Elizabethan fireplace, but Bache took pride in its every appendage—its towers, cloisters, crenelated walls, and stables; great beamed roofs; dark wood paneling, stone floors, curving staircases, and stained-glass windows; tapestries, swords, stuffed heads, and armor. Nancy grew up in this fabulous castle set among tall beeches, oaks, elms, and yews (nourished with bulls' blood); manicured lawns and walled gardens; and birds, ferrets, and fish ponds. At the front of the estate, which bordered on miles of magnificent wildflowers and trees, an iron gate bore the Nevill arms—a bull's head rising out of a crown.

Bache had forsaken the family business in order to live the life of a country gentleman honing his various hobbies: hunting, fishing, horseback riding, and metalworking. He spent most of his time in a tower workroom creating objects in gold, silver, and wrought iron. Nancy was always proud of her father's artistry, writing many years later that most of her recollections of him were at this loft where, with his "able hands," he hammered silver and carved coconuts into beautiful cups. To her, he was an "ingenious and gifted" man.[4]

While Bache's family history was highly respectable, Maud's resembled the plot of a racy late Victorian novel. To begin, the identity of Maud's father was questionable (as the identity of Nancy's would be). Although her half-French mother's husband and her legal father was James Burke (related to the great Irish rebel-patriot Robert Emmet, whom Nancy called her great-grand-uncle), it was rumored that her true father was a blond, blue-eyed millionaire and mine explorer named William O'Brien.[5] One way or the other, Maud was half Irish, a most agreeable idea to the adult Nancy.

So, too, as Nancy was to be, Maud was raised by servants, and after her father died during her adolescence, Maud's mother had many suitors. One of her wealthy admirers, Horace Carpentier, a former Civil War general and highly cultured man, adopted young girls as their "uncle"; in this case, he adopted the widow's daughter, Maud. Of Carpentier's collection of "nieces," a family friend explained that besides being a book collector, "he was also a collector of young girls, preferring those comparable to first editions, in mint condition, with leaves uncut."[6] Of all of Carpentier's "nieces," little Maud Burke was his favorite.

Both mother and daughter shared Uncle Horace's interest in Greek and Latin poetry, Shakespeare, and Balzac (*Pamela*, about a virtuous young girl cleverly eluding the lecherous advances of her wealthy employer's son until he marries her, would remain Maud's favorite English novel), and his amorous attention, as well. Carpentier introduced Maud not only to the pleasures of reading and piano playing, which became lifelong interests, but also to opera. After *The Valkyrie*, the first performance she attended, the excited child said, "It was as if a new world had opened out, revealing a race of men and women, very Titans of humanity endowed with superb gifts."[7] She was twelve years old. Maud would later meet Thomas Beecham, the legendary impresario of London opera, and become a patron of the musical arts, especially opera. Their love affair would last for thirty years, until Beecham married another woman.

After Maud's mother remarried a wealthy stockbroker, Maud, then eighteen, retained as a second residence her home with Carpentier, whom she now called her guardian. She occasionally traveled to the Continent with her mother (as Nancy would with her), and she most enjoyed France (as Nancy would as well). Maud was a voracious reader, and she became a passionate advocate of Emile Zola and George Moore because of their free thinking and zealous efforts to liberate art from bourgeois notions of propriety. She so strongly believed that the word could change the world (as Nancy would later believe) that when invited to a luncheon at the Savoy Hotel, which Moore was to attend, she changed the place cards so she could sit next to him. To Moore, befriended by Mallarmé, Huysmans, Manet, and Degas, and the famous author of *Esther Waters* and esteemed art critic, her impassioned "George Moore, you have a soul of fire!" was "the compliment of his life, the remembrance of which," Nancy later wrote, he constantly cherished.[8] Maud was twenty-one, and he was in his forties, also about twice her age like Carpentier and Bache Cunard, the man she would later marry. Maud became Moore's lover and muse, a woman to whom he would be devoted for forty years.

Moore, or G. M., as he was called, said that most appealing about Maud was her "independence [and] intellectual audacity." He openly admitted his idealization of her: "I loved but an immortal goddess descended once more among men. . . . Her sensuality was so serene and so sure of its divine character that it never seemed to become trivial or foolish." That he viewed her as a spirit free to descend anywhere at will may explain his toleration, or rationalization, of her many infidelities. Their romantic liaisons were always dictated by Maud's moods: "While walking in the woods with one, she would say, 'Let us sit here,' and after looking steadily at one for a few seconds, the pale marmoreal eyes glowing, she would say, 'You can make love to me now, if you like.'" G. M. admits that she captivated him with "her cold sensuality, cold because it was divorced from tenderness and passion."[9]

G. M. re-created Maud in his fiction; in *Memoirs of My Dead Life* she is Elizabeth:

> Again I hear the soft sound of the door opening over the velvet pile of carpet. It does not follow that because a woman sometimes reminds one of a dryad that she does not at other times remind one of Boucher or Fragonard, and that night [she] seemed to me a very Fragonard, a plump Fragonard maiden as she sat up in bed reading, her gold hair in plaits and a large book in her hands. I asked her what she was reading, and might have talked literature for a while, but throwing the vain literature aside she revealed herself, and in that moment of august nakedness the mortal woman was forgotten. I saw the eternal spirit shining through her like a lamp hidden in an alabaster vase. That night the mortal woman glowed with intensity.[10]

He never asked Maud to marry him; one does not marry La Belle Dame sans Merci.

G. M.'s romantic idealization of Maud, in life and art, lasted until the end of his life. During one of their separations, he lamented that "only a month ago, [I beheld] the most beautiful thing that had ever appeared in my life, an ideal which I knew from the first I was destined to follow. . . . Thinking of her my senses grow dizzy, a sort of madness creeps up behind the eyes, what an exquisite despair."[11] Idealizing the beloved and dictating the terms of the liaison were qualities that G. M. and Maud passed on to Nancy.

It was rumored that G. M. was Nancy's father, but she was never certain about the matter. She once asked him, and he replied, "My dear, I fear I cannot say. . . . You must ask your mother," but she never did. Agitated by his comment, he soon afterward asked her, "Nancy, you haven't mentioned this to your mother have you?" and she reassured him that she had not. A friend of Nancy's once remarked: "I may have been influenced by suggestion, but it did seem to me that George Moore's eyes and Nancy's had the same blue intensity and . . . droop of lid."[12]

Nancy loved G. M. as her "first friend," a frequent and sole companion during most of her childhood. He defended her against the strict authority of her mother and governesses; he introduced her to the beauty of language, literature, art, and nature; he was a role model of the artist consecrated to his craft and to improving society. Nancy would become a romantic and social idealist like G. M., and this manifested itself in her passionate commitment to social and political causes, as well as in her highly unorthodox commitment to many lovers. In addition, like G. M., her mother, and her grandmother, Nancy would be sexually promiscuous—with a vengeance. While presumably in love with one man, she would run off with another, sometimes for an afternoon. (She was, in G. M.'s words, another "immortal goddess descending once more among men.") This is undoubtedly related, in part, to the highly unconventional behavior she witnessed at Nevill Holt when her mother invited one admirer after another for a weekend, both when her father was away fishing and when he was at home. Nancy's promiscuity may also be related to G. M.'s behavior, when he was not acting in a paternal or mentor role.

G. M. considered himself something of a roué, and he frequently bragged about his amorous adventures in Nancy's presence. He was not just boastful about his sexual prowess; he was also often vulgar about his sexual conquests. Generally, his attitude to women was, as he bluntly, if artfully, put it, "I would lay aside the wisest book to talk to a stupid woman."[13] When Nancy was in her late teens and he was over sixty, he asked her to tell him about her lovers, and he later repeatedly begged her to undress for him (which she finally did)— all of which suggest a relationship parallel to the triangle of her mother and grandmother with Carpentier. Nancy's unusual relationship to her mother's lovers undoubtedly influenced her own adult relationships with men.

Maud's affair with G. M. was interrupted when she traveled with her mother to the United States. During their stay in San Francisco, she misinterpreted the intentions of a wealthy and handsome Polish prince who had been writing to her, and the press reported that she and André Poniatowski, grandson of the late king of Poland, were to be married. When the gentleman in question learned of this (he was more a frog than a prince: his attentions were attracted to an even wealthier, more socially prominent woman), he coerced her into a public refutation. To avoid additional embarrassment, Maud and her mother announced that Maud's guardian, Horace Carpentier, had objected to the engagement. Unable to face the mounting gossip, Maud agreed to marry Bache Cunard, whom she had recently met in New York. Although they first announced a June wedding, the date was moved ahead, and on April 17, 1895, the bride took her vows wearing a gray cloth gown. Three days later, the newlyweds left for Nevill Holt, which Maud would gracefully negotiate as a gilded stepping-stone toward becoming one of Britain's most admired social hostesses.

The Lonely Child

Nancy Clara Cunard, an unwanted only child, was born less than a year later, on March 10, 1896. The role of motherhood was alien to Maud: "She had never really wished to have a child and had no maternal instinct. Motherhood to her was merely the fulfillment of a wifely duty." She maintained that no great woman had ever had a child: "Elizabeth had none, and how about George Eliot [and] George Sand?" After her confinement, she moved into a separate bedroom and read the classics and contemporary French and English literature late into the night. The child was brought up by nurses and governesses, as well as by a staff of forty servants. Among the many family photos taken during her youth, strikingly few are of Nancy, compared with the many of her parents, their estate, and their servants and pets.[14]

Nancy spent a great deal of her early childhood by herself in the nursery—except for her visits with G. M., which she cherished. "I suppose I was about four years old," she later wrote, "when I first remember G. M. and I suppose I may, in some sort, even call him 'my first friend.' . . . If I knew him first when I was four, he must have seen me first in a nurse's arms." But even before she was four, she adds, her "desire to read was acute and there was an early reverence in me for those who wrote books." She continues, again referring to her earliest years: "Easy words like 'dog' and 'cat' . . . had been mastered, but the longer phrases and abstract terms still gave me so much trouble that I feared I should never read properly. A book in my hands . . . was my evening pleasure." When she was four, G. M. said to her, "Can you really enjoy it at your age? Let me see. . . . Oh! *The Violet Fairy Book!* So you have gotten beyond *Reading Without Tears!*"[15]

Beside G. M., the only person she recalls with love during her childhood was her first governess, a girl from Toulon. Nancy adored and depended on her young mentor, who disappeared one day after caring for Nancy for two years, and the "sullen-hearted" child was given no explanation. The sense of loss at never again seeing this cheerful, forgiving, adventuresome girl remained with Nancy for many years. In her volume of poems *Sublunary*, she wrote of her in "Toulonnaise":

> She was a rebel governess
> Who came from Toulon in the south,
> Red cherries tumbling on her hat,
> Loud laughter breaking on her mouth.

> Came to the Midlands there to teach
> A girl of seven sullen-hearted—
> Her voice was full of life's adventure,
> Her eye too gay, so she departed.

The next governess, whose name and personality might be out of a Dickens novel, was Miss Scarth, a mean-spirited harridan. The cold but highly intelligent woman had been Vita Sackville-West's tutor. A strict disciplinarian, Miss Scarth reigned with an iron ruler, and Nancy never complained when she was whacked on her hands, perhaps an early source of her later identification with those who were unempowered or unjustly punished.

Miss Scarth's rules included a cold bath every morning, regardless of how chilly the house was, and Nancy grew to hate and even fear the cold. Miss Scarth also forced the child to eat porridge daily, which she could barely swallow. Nancy's dislike of food continued throughout her life, and as an adult she remained model-thin in figure. Miss Scarth's prohibitions were many: there could be no bathing in the pond; picnicking was forbidden. A family friend recalls that Nancy "soon stopped asking permission to join in the simplest pleasures vouchsafed to other children, knowing in advance that her request would be refused."[16] Once Nancy left Holt, she would follow her own rules.

Whenever she made entries in her diaries, of horseback riding and reading, she never revealed her feelings, since she knew that Miss Scarth read her diary. "I remember my *odious* governess sometimes added things here," she wrote many years later on top of the July 14, 1910, entry, explaining: "Her writing is discernable."[17] The earliest of the diaries on record begins on January 1, 1909, but it is likely that the child began these earlier. Rather than the usual earnest vows of commitment and candor with which most children inaugurate diaries, Nancy writes as if continuing a narrative (and she writes on calendars from the Northern Assurance Company, rather than on bound blank sheets, with advertisements of fire, accident, life, and burglary insurance on each page). Inserted into the calendars are postcards, photos, invitations, elegant menus, riddles, and magazine clippings of glamorous women (one in a "Gown of Transient Gloom"). For the rest of her life, Nancy kept diaries and detailed date books, and she frequently used the backs of old ads or bills—any receipt she had—as her stationery; her letters often overflowed with photos, clippings, and other miscellaneous items.

Her first two brief entries in 1909 reveal the rigor of her activities, her youthful insecurity, and her creative inclinations: "Today we traveled to Grendon by train. Play rehearsing after lunch until bed time. Snow melting all around. Lovely costumes. . . . In the afternoon some people (about fifty) came to see a dress rehearsal, which went well? Did they think so? Harewood does not know his speeches in the last act. He broke down and laughed." The next day, she continues: "Today we acted the play. The Grand Duke and his family were present"; after this: "We motored home. Mother inquired at all the inns if there was any La Seoten [?] broth." Nancy then composes "Ode to the Motor Car," praising many discoveries, including "Archimedes' law," and concludes

But praise from us here and families from afar
To the man who invented the motorcar.[18]

With Miss Scarth always watching over her, Nancy became increasingly lonely and secluded, and the only place she could escape was in her daydreams. Fifty years later, her recollection of her childhood caretaker remained vivid: "How out of place was Miss Scarth with so juvenile a child. She should never have been a governess . . . least of all to me, who had every reason to hate her and her detestable temper, her punishments and outrageous discipline."[19]

Maud was pleased that the extremely bright Miss Scarth was cultivating her daughter's talents and unusual intelligence. Nancy practiced the piano regularly and earnestly, and she always finished her strenuous assignments: she never misconjugated an irregular French verb or failed to memorize and write out her lines from Shakespeare, like Clarence's fearful "Methoughts that I had broken from the Tower" speech in *Richard III*.[20] Nancy never objected to the subjects she had to master: if anything, enriching her mind was another diversion from reality. Becoming well educated, she knew, would also enhance her relationship with G. M. As an adult, Nancy followed the pattern of escaping from personal distress by moving from one ambitious creative project to another and one major social cause to another. But the busy-ness of her life—from her work and madcap romances to her rigorous travels around the world—belied a desperate, frenetic, and lonely quality. The isolation of her early years would leave a lifelong imprint.

Perhaps Maud preferred that her daughter have a Miss Scarth instead of an "uncle"; perhaps she did not know, or care to know, her daughter well enough to recognize her distress. Some have said that Maud would have been happier if she had had a son, and it is curious and unfortunate that, as a child, Nancy believed that her parents would have preferred a boy and she often wished that she were a boy:[21] after all, if she were going to perpetuate the family line, perhaps she would have been given more love and attention. Whatever the reasons for Maud's indifference to Nancy's unhappiness, the child was forgiving, and her accounts of her youth, both at the time and until her late twenties, convey considerably more affection than anger toward her mother. The most dramatic example that Nancy cites of youthful rebellion, in fact, involved her refusal to take a chocolate from her mother and her subsequent "daring" flight, later that night, into the morning room, where she helped herself to the sweets.

Throughout her early childhood, Nancy saw her parents only briefly and at specific hours. She was always presented to them in perfect dress, in well-starched embroidered or lace-trimmed frocks, although on occasion her mother asked that she be dressed in the colors and style of a painter. Nancy would then appear in dark velvets with lace at her wrists and neck, like a Velázquez child. Or, in the colors of G. M.'s favorite artist, Edouard Manet, she wore black and white, with predictable white socks and black patent-leather shoes.

She was unhappy in these clothes, for they made her flights out of doors and into the woods difficult. She always feared tearing her dress as she climbed trees or crawled through briars in search of magical new hills and beautiful wildflowers. She had no local friends of her own age, but she loved playing with her Uncle Gordon's sons Edward and Victor, who became lifelong friends. Bache's nieces, Riette and Jean, visited rarely, because they hated the overbearing Miss Scarth. Nancy recalls in her diary how "Miss Scarth crawled out today and leaned on my arm. She wanted to get me out of the garden." Nancy had wanted to play with "a puppy, two guinea pigs, and a little chicken."[22] On any of these occasions, her mother was unsympathetic to Nancy and her guests. Whether it was natural, acquired (from her intensive practice of French), or a childhood tic, Nancy began to speak in sentences that rose at the end—with a vocabulary that sounded unusually stilted.

Her parents were often away—her father pursuing one of his sporting interests; Maud shopping or socializing in London or on the Continent. Her postcards, like Nancy's later in life, were filled with details about ruins and antiquities; but unlike Nancy's, very few included a personal or an affection-ate note. (None ends with "Love, Mother.") Maud did, however, occasionally take Nancy to London to shop or to see an opera, a concert, or the theater. One unkind friend of Maud's wrote of them to a mutual friend: "Do you know Lady Cunard's little girl aged eleven? I went to *Figaro* the other day with them and between the acts, Nancy said in her high little squeakly toneless voice, 'The count is exactly like George the Second. The countess I should put a little later—about 1790.' What are children coming to?"[23]

Nancy also spent time alone with her father, joining him at the Haycock Inn, in Wansford, where he took rooms. She stayed with him for long stretch-es of time. She took an interest in his foxhunting and tore these lines from a local newspaper to keep in her diary:

> May everyone do his endeavor,
> Hounds, horses, and foxes in plenty be found
> And fox-hunting flourish forever.[24]

The diaries of 1909 and 1910 indicate that Nancy's parents included her on one of their trips to the capital cities of Europe. On April 2, 1909, she writes: "Here begins my diary of what happened abroad"; she speaks of "Mother's shopping" and of how much she enjoyed "when we tried on dresses and bought some new hats at Galleries Lafayette, and such lovely things too! This afternoon we went to the Louvre to see the Fragonards and had chocolate at a café." When she got sick in Rome, she wrote: "What's the use of coming to Rome to be ill! . . . I was at such a temper at being ill"—an early but lifelong response to any physical incapacity.

Although many of her entries are typical of a child's responses—"the chicken I had to eat"; "This is such a beautiful setting!"—others are more precocious. When they reached Genoa, for example, she described the "deli-cious" quality of "the very blue coast" and drew a picture of the sea with its "lovely plains with cork trees in the distance." After arriving in Rome, she wrote several poems, one on a thunderstorm and the serene evening that fol-lowed; another was called "The Shepherd and His Love":

> The sky was blue, the earth was green
> and many golden stars were seen
> and daisies pied and violets blue
> and Cuckoo pints of greenish hue.
> As on the grass beneath a tree
> there did I lie with sweet Mearie.
> The birds did sing above her head,

the sun on crimson poppies glowed
And there I asked her for to wed
And many a glance on her bestowed.

Nancy's lifelong interest in art developed on these trips: "We went to the Kaiser Friedriech [*sic*] gallery, which has Rembrandts and two Vermeers, glorious ones . . . Botticellis, Velasquezes, . . . one Giorgione, one Holbein. . . . We also saw Voltaire's room adorned with parrots and storks."

When they returned to Holt, her parents again went their separate ways. Since Bache regularly spent the month of August fishing in Scotland, this became Maud's favorite month to entertain. It was clear to the child that her parents had little in common. Her mother's conversation with her father and his friends was limited to county politics, the breeding of horses and hounds, and matters regarding foxes.

Ever since her arrival, Maud had found Nevill Holt tedious and almost unbearable. So she devised an odd hobby that she found endlessly appealing. After removing the former residents' Victorian furniture and replacing it with solid oak pieces in order to restore the castle's original "feudal grandeur," she began rearranging everything. She wanted to enhance the glowing colors of the silk and satin fabrics, as well as the muted colors of the oriental rugs. Nancy recalled that "moving the furniture was [her] constant occupation" and went so far as to praise her mother's "genius for beautifying, . . . creating, transforming, humanizing."[25] To the child, both her parents were artists.

Because Maud found the countryside and outdoors dull, Bache tried to entice her out of the house. He designed a garden gate consisting of several pony-size horseshoes with "Come into the Garden Maud" incorporated into the design. Maud may have been touched by the gesture, but she remained within, playing Beethoven and Chopin or reading. On Sundays, Bache traveled by himself to church in his elegant coach with four gray horses. One is not surprised that Nancy said, "Somehow I felt—and was—entirely detached from both [parents], admiring and critical of them by my own standards, those of a solitary child wondering much in silence how life was going to be."[26]

G. M. had been writing to Maud since her marriage, and his notes, such as "When shall I see you again?" often included intimate gifts, like scented flannel for perfuming her undergarments. His letters began "Dearest Maud, Dearest Primavera!"; "Dearest and Best of Women"; or "Dear Vision, Dear and Divine," continuing: "Come down to me through many generations from the time when there were gods upon the earth." They had, in fact, seen each other a few months after the wedding when Maud invited him to the country and Bache was away fishing. But she rejected his advances, since her body was beginning to bear the signs of pregnancy: "Every night," he lamented, "she locked her door, and the sound is and will ever be in my ears."[27] Not long after Nancy was born, G. M. became a frequent guest at Nevill Holt, and as the years passed and Nancy approached her teens, he visited when Bache was at home. Although the host always seemed unaware of G. M.'s feelings for his wife, one suspects that both Nancy and her father knew that Maud no longer locked her door. G. M. continued to idolize Maud: "Very few have possessed all they were capable of desiring of beauty and grace; I have possessed more, for the reality has exceeded the desire."

With or without G. M. present, Maud hosted elegant weekend parties. Once it became clear that young members of the royal family had taken an interest in her, both the local people and the fashionable London set looked forward to her invitations. As Elsa Maxwell later phrased it, it became "a social benediction" to travel to Leicestershire, and Lady Cunard became universally recognized as a vivacious, intelligent, and interesting woman. The London press reported her parties regularly, and even the *New York American* took an interest in her celebrity and how quickly she set trends. She had, for one, invented a three-week "milk cure," evaluated as "far better than the continental cure" to "recover from the dissipations of the London season": the "regime is to rise early in the morning and walk a distance to where two glasses of warm milk from the cow are drunk. Then a stroll in the kitchen-garden, picking a little fruit from the trees and eating it on the spot. Then a quiet walk, and breakfast consisting of very little fish, more fresh milk at midday, and then a little light lunch, mostly fruit."[28]

As Nancy approached adolescence and was no longer sequestered in her room, she wandered around the house but was neither seen nor heard, except by G. M., and she chronicled Maud's weekend parties with a mature eye for detail. Her father is noticeably absent on all but two occasions. She recalls, for example, the "constant arrivals and departures, . . . elaborate long teas on the lawn with tennis and croquet, . . . [and] people playing bridge there for hours. Beautiful and exciting ladies moved about in smart tailor-mades; they arrived in sables or long fox stoles, a bunch of Parma violets pinned into the fur on the shoulder."[29]

The house parties eventually brought together diverse and sophisticated people who were witty, bright, and fashionable—diplomats and politicians, writers and artists: Somerset Maugham, Max Beerbohm, Mrs. Charles Hunter (the subject of Sargent's great portrait), the Duchess of Rutland, the Asquiths, the Balfours, and Lady Randolph Churchill (then Jennie Cornwallis-West). As Nancy recalls, "The men . . . became more intellectual as . . . the autumns proceeded and the host was away shooting and fishing lengthily in Scotland."[30] She remembers their interesting conversations (on W. B. Yeats's collaboration with G. M. on a play); special visits (Ezra Pound's arrival to request financial assistance for James Joyce); and, most of all, G. M.'s outrageous debates (on the hypocrisy of using fig leaves on Roman statuary). Typical of the times, the family kept "Visitor Books," and Nancy kept an autograph album (signed by guests like Fyodor Chaliapin, Lenin, and Ford Madox Ford). In either one, they wrote notes, made sketches or caricatures, or composed poems. On one occasion, Beerbohm drew an "entirely cruel" image of G. M., like a "late black berry in the hedge, swollen with suns and rains and near collapse."[31]

Since the playground of Nancy's youth was her mother's tireless social life, she wrote in her diary on January 8, 1909: "I am not going to write a diary while mother is in America as nothing amusing or interesting happens. I begin again my scrawl of our events under this date of Saturday, 2 April."

Nancy missed her parents during this three-month trip, and her crowded schedule of lessons was only temporarily distracting. She was aware of her loneliness, starting a new "Fox Hunter's Diary" on November 1, 1910: "This diary begins with dancing. May it end as happily! For I went to dancing class at Harbor's as I do every Tuesday afternoon. . . . We are all alone since Father and Mother have not returned yet." Once her parents returned, Nancy could resume her special activities: making sure there were flowers throughout the house and walking with the housemaids into each room to verify that everything was in order, including a sufficient supply of Russian cigarettes, books, sweets, and, of course, notepaper and ink pens for the distinguished calligraphy that was in vogue. When Nancy was allowed to place blossoms in small vases by the beds, she learned the names of the many wildflowers in the region as she collected them. She always remembered an experience that occurred with the Holt gardener involving the inequities of social class: she had asked him if he might like to take a bunch of flowers home to his young daughter. It surprised and angered her when he said he had no right to take his employer's flowers. The young girl wrote in her diary: "How I *hate* tyrants. Down with 'em, devils enter them."[32]

Maud's parties were unique. If conversation lagged, the guests were asked to provide some entertainment—a parlor trick, song, or poetry reading. Some of their games were rather spicy. Nancy recalls one that was played when the host was at home. It was "a sort of Truth game in which every man was bound to say whom he was in love with, if only from afar." Everyone wondered if the fabulously rich and charming Prince M., Maud's most recent conquest, "would dare out with the truth—which meant the hostess." A true prince charming, the "paladin of masculinity" stopped the game with gales of laughter: "Oh, *I* am in love with the page-boy at the St. James's Club." Another of Maud's lovers was Lord Alexander Thynne, son of the fourth Marquess of Bath, a dashing and interesting man about town and member of Parliament. (Long after their affair, Maud remarked to a member of his family that the "witty and handsome" Alexander was one of the world's "great lovers.") As the ever-smitten G. M. explained: "She liked not continuity."[33]

Maud often planned her parties around romantic intrigues. She invited beautiful, ardent, and voluptuous women in gowns designed by Poiret, Worth, or Reville. Her women friends—all confidantes of one another's deepest secrets—made a cult of beauty, and all of them had suitors. On more than one occasion, Maud became involved in a nasty scandal. One, for instance, involved Jennie Cornwallis-West, previously Jennie Jerome and later Lady Randolph Churchill, who sued her husband when he had an affair with the great actress Mrs. Patrick Campbell.

Nancy knew that her parents didn't care for each other; she also knew that on certain weekends many guests at Holt were in love with her mother. If this was not apparent to Bache during the "Truth" game, it became so one very warm evening when he returned home to find the house full of music lovers gone berserk. One of them had opened his bedroom window to sing the cry of the Valkyries, after which voice after voice responded with another Wagnerian melody. Maud said of this occasion to the photographer Cecil Beaton, "When my husband came back, he noticed an atmosphere of love." Bache had remarked: "I don't understand what is going on in this house, but I don't like it."[34]

Her First Friend

Nancy adored G. M. from her early childhood until his death in 1933, and she mourned him for the rest of her life. He may have been the most important influence in her life, although their relationship was distinctly complex. She often said, "If I were his daughter it seems to me I should become quite a different personality and a much more contented one."[35]

As a child, Nancy considered G. M.'s devotion to her to be absolute. He was, to begin, her protector. She recalls an early explosion in the household when she was discovered reading a book, aptly bound in purple, by the "audacious" Elinor Glyn (whose term "the It Girl" later symbolized the open sexuality of the movie star Clara Bow and the 1920s). The book, *Three Weeks*, was about a "beautiful, perfidious, dashing" temptress, and it was "exactly what I wanted to know about!" The heroine "blazed awhile across the repressions of my childhood" in this, the first novel Nancy read; the second, which she read immediately afterward, was Montague Eliot's parody of upper-class manners, *Too Weak*. Nancy was eleven years old at the time; she had smuggled the books into her room and devoured them into "the clandestine hours of dawn."

As she discussed the books with G. M., Miss Scarth was passing the study, and when she expressed her indignation, G. M. said, "I strongly advise you not to thwart her curiosity, which is a natural thing, for you will only drive it underground. What possible ha-arm can there be? She is not a silly girl." Ignoring G. M., Miss Scarth promptly reported the event to Maud, and both G. M. and Nancy "were in disgrace together," which was a great comfort to the child. G. M. then told Nancy that he, too, as a young boy, had surreptitiously and passionately read such a book, which "gave him confidence in his instincts."

On yet another occasion, when Nancy "misbehaved," G. M. came to her defense. Her dog, Buster (G. M. referred to him as "Boxer, or Brewster, whatever the beastly dog is called"), nipped him while he was demonstrating his waltzing skills. G. M. kicked the dog, which, to Nancy's horror, began to howl excruciatingly, and Nancy's response was instinctual: "It must have been like a stone from a sling that I hurled myself at G. M. and gave him a furious slap in the face." Maud became enraged, and the nonplussed G. M.'s efforts to calm her were to no avail. Nancy was "confined to the schoolroom for two days in disgrace." When Nancy remarked, "I don't like Her Ladyship," G. M.'s response was insightful. He thought it would have been much more healthy if she had said "I hate my mother."[36] Nancy was already associating the upper class with the arbitrary abuse of power.

Nancy and G. M. spent most of their time exploring the countryside, a beloved pastime throughout her life. He would send her scampering in the fields to bring back unusual flowers and rocks, which they would scrutinize and identify; they also made up stories about the trees and birds after identifying them. Nancy's love of natural beauty, of rocks and "objets trouvés," may have inspired her love of Pre-Columbian and African art and contemporary sculpture—all of which eventually filled her homes. Wildflowers, subtle changes in the colorations of fields and the sun—and the arboreal discoveries of her childhood—would fill her later poetry as well. Nature would also provide her with a dependable refuge from the hardships and loneliness of everyday life.

G. M. was not just an adventurer, geographer, historian, poet, and philosopher. He was also a teacher, and he shared his knowledge, philosophy, and poet's eye and ear with Nancy. He might begin: "'Flowers, like us, Nancy, have their season,'" and then continue: "'But that is the yaffle's cry! I am not mistaken. *He* is with us the whole year round.' As the bright wing flashes across the rise, G. M. bids me remember that 'yaffle' is a much prettier word than 'woodpecker.'"

When they began a hike, G. M. would ask Nancy which villages they should visit. Nancy said "the rhyming ones," even if they were miles away:

Ayston and Glaston
Ooston and Glooston.

An art critic and a devotee of opera, he shared his sensitivity to colors and words with her. Her poetry would be filled with the synesthetic responses he cultivated in her; Nancy recalls: "A pause in front of a new perspective revealed 'a field like an early Corot' . . . the shepherd resting under a tree, his sheep all about him, a landscape from the Bible! Or it might be the very sunset that held us, recalling the Götterdämmerung, full of unheard trumpets."

G. M. encouraged her fantasies and creativity. A hollow in a ditch on the side of the road "became my house," and she furnished it with "works of art"—an "oddly curved root, a stick stripped of its bark, the wood gleaming with polishing, a few . . . fierce sea-green flints, a beautiful shard of pottery, a small blue, medicine-bottle." (Nancy later decorated her homes with wood, flints, pottery, and bottles.) When G. M. asked her why she wanted a house, "I told him that I liked to make or invent things of my own," prepared that he "should mock me." However, she quickly discovered: "No sneerer at fancies was he—the flints attracted him too—and [he] murmur[ed] that I was a funny child of nine."

At times he shared his romantic travel plans with her, which undoubtedly played a part in her love of traveling. Before he went to what he anticipated as the "highly exotic" Holy Land, he was overwhelmed by images and questions: "The monastery is in the wilderness. Is there a river there? . . . There is sure to be a spring or well; if so, what sort of spring? Can you see the Dead Sea or can't you? These are the questions I must get answered."

Although they often spoke in French, G. M. insisted that English was the most beautiful of languages. He was rhapsodic in his yearning that it be protected from its imminent state of decline: he lamented the loss of "thee" and "thou" from contemporary usage and feared that the language would become a "dry shank bone . . . lying . . . on the dust-heap of empire." Sometimes he began a conversation with the etymology or usage of a word. "No," he once said, a "tallboy" was not exactly a *chiffonier*, a *fourre-tout*, a *sous-main*. And why, he once asked, "Should one use the word 'corset,' a French word, instead of the excellent 'stay'?" Proper English was required even when a not-so-proper joke was told.

Nancy became multilingual (and as an adult was as adept in writing poetry in French—and Spanish, Italian, and German—as in English), and she had an uncommon appreciation of formal language. In daily speech, for example, she never abbreviated words, saying "luncheon" for "lunch," and she often used archaic constructions like "No sneerer . . . was he [G. M.]" and the formal "one" rather than "I" or "he." In writing poetry, as well as in much of her correspondence, she was obsessed with the music and rhythms of all languages.

Both Nancy and G. M. left Nevill Holt, more or less permanently, in 1911. G. M., already angered by the "jingo-imperialism" of the Boer War, joined the Celtic Revival in Ireland, an early influence, perhaps, on Nancy's later anticolonialist politics. Until then, they carried on with their intense intellectual conversations, on subjects as esoteric as Maurice Barrès's *Les Déracinés* and as complex as Nietzsche's *Thus Spake Zarathustra*. They parsed the styles and ideas of many artists and writers, from Whistler and Manet to Wagner and Debussy and Flaubert and Turgenev. When Nancy visited G. M. in London, they turned to the more modern Proust and D. H. Lawrence. (Later asked if he had read Joyce's "novel of genius, *Ulysses*," he said, yes, but it "cannot be a novel, for there isn't a tree in it.")[37] They also discussed poetry and read it aloud to each other, an evening's activity that Nancy would most enjoy with her closest friends and her lovers. Nancy had begun writing when she was ten, and she shared her poems with G. M., including "The First Sonnet," which begins:

> My soul is frozen, but the tears fall fast
> From these sad eyes that cannot understand
> Why they should weep except for sorrows past
> Or longing memories of some lovèd land
> Once seen in dreams beyond the reach of most,
> A vision of some scented southern clime
> Now past for ever and for ever lost
> In the arcades of everlasting time.

If Nancy's earliest recollections regarding the inequities in human affairs included her comment to the gardener, she had a number of experiences with G. M. that heightened this awareness. When they visited a nearby potter, she always became sad, because he was "a very old man, blind from birth, who worked at his wheel in a hut." She also never forgot the hoboes in the countryside—those "generally dirty, slouchy men with stubby chins"—and even as a child, she observed the anger in their eyes. Still, these tramps excited her, and "I told G. M. I wanted to run away and be a vagabond." Not just aware of social inequalities, Nancy had begun to identify with the needy.

G. M. encouraged her to share her deepest feelings, and she did so because she trusted him: "'Nancy,' he once said, 'You were a funny child. Do you remember what you said to me in the churchyard at Holt? You bade me come to it with you and we sat on one of the beautiful old gravestones, you and I. Then you said to me, I often come here alone. And I often wonder where we go after we are dead. You were about five years old then. Don't you remember, Nancy?'" But she did not. On another occasion, at an ancient spa on Nevill Holt, Nancy commented: "Look at all the rust," which moved him to say: "You *are* a romantic child, Nancy."[38]

There was also a vulgarity in G. M.'s demeanor with Nancy. Whether or not she wanted to hear this (and one assumes not), from the time Nancy could understand language, she heard G. M. relate anecdotes and express opinions about sexual matters that might make an adult blush. Once, for example, he reported a female friend's attempt to become a better wife: "She went to Paris and took lessons from some of the ladies in the Chabanel. A French cocotte has a good deal to teach, you may be sure. When she returned she began to put these lessons into practice in bed with her husband. Oh, it must have been a dreadful moment when she heard him say: 'Dora, *ladies never move.*' Khk, Khk, Khk." Another time, when asked how he liked American widows, she heard him reply, "Well, there they are, . . . heavily scented sirens. . . . Why should they try to play bridge when they can sit on sofas and be made love to by gallants, arousing jealousy in other gallants? . . . They are not averse to a *sidestep* now and then, and what is the ha-arm in that?"

Of even greater importance, Nancy observed that G. M. and her mother were unfaithful to each other (in addition to Bache). Reminded of one of her mother's glamorous friends, wearing "a resplendent dog-collar of pearls and diamonds," Nancy recalled: "How often I [saw] G. M. whispering some saucy, racy tid-bits into her delighted ear." G. M. was equally indiscreet in lecturing Nancy on love and revealing his own predilections: "From talking to me about the Love Courts of the Middle Ages and the love-tenets of those times, he would pass on to wonder at the strange forms that love has ever taken, a man or a woman lying in one lover's arms, his thoughts or hers on those of another. Well, said he, one may be unfaithful and yet constant—a great truth many people were unwilling to recognize." He would later be inappropriately and overtly jealous of Nancy's boyfriends. In a surprisingly naïve fashion, Nancy relates how, many years later, he visited her home in Normandy. After he realized that she had a "very cultured young man" staying with her "alone for two days," he sulked and exhibited a "ridiculous malaise over nothing at all."[39]

When G. M. became involved in the Celtic Revival, he felt as if he had been called to revive Irish culture, reinstitute the Irish language, and provide Ireland with a literature of its own. W. B. Yeats, also deeply involved in the Revival, wanted to be G. M.'s partner in one event. They would collaborate on a play, *Diarmuid and Grania*, which would ultimately be translated into folk dialect. Enraptured by this possibility, Yeats appeared at G. M.'s home in the middle of the night and awakened him with a complicated plan: the play would be written in French by G. M. and then translated into English, then Irish, and finally local dialect. Yeats would add poetic flourishes along the way. G. M. agreed and went to France "to be in the proper atmosphere" to write in French. Suddenly aware of how silly the plan was, he stuffed the scene he had written into his pocket as a reminder of "what a damned fool a clever man like Yeats could be when he was in the mood to be a fool."[40] G. M. realized that the most he could do was support the translation of *The Arabian Nights* into Irish.

• • •

Her beloved G. M.'s initial political idealism may have run amok, but twenty years later, Nancy would seek to revive another culture's language, myths, and history. Her publication of *Negro* would be a first step in her effort to enlighten the world about the past and present achievements of an extraordinary culture too long denied its rightful recognition and, more important, denied the most rudimentary elements of social justice.

2

Coming of Age During a
Revolution in the Arts

She really did know about poetry and really did love it. . . . She thought,
felt and held that being a poet conferred a standing and a dignity, and
that poetry should be rightfully placed at the center of social living.

—EWART MILNE

Maud took Nancy, just fifteen, to London in 1911 when she separated from
Bache and enrolled her in Miss Woolf's elite school for girls. Then she set
out to pursue the great love affair of her life with Thomas Beecham—at
thirty-two, six years her junior—and to become one of London's most successful hostesses. She had already caught the eye of the notoriously gregarious King Edward VII at Nevill Holt. In the years to come, Maud would become a trusted confidante of his grandson, the Prince of Wales, and his bride,
Wallis Simpson.

At about the same time that Maud rented the flat at 20 Cavendish Square
from Prime Minister Herbert Asquith (now at 10 Downing Street), G. M. returned to London, compelled to live near his goddess. He took a flat on Ebury
Street, unaware that Maud had fallen in love with the upcoming musical genius and future great conductor, the charismatic, wealthy heir to the liver pill
empire. The prodigiously gifted and energetic Beecham could recite lengthy
scenes of Shakespeare from memory, and he played the piano beautifully.
Still married, Beecham had just survived a major scandal involving another
married Maud, a woman named Maud Foster.

Nancy's mother was soon involved with musicians as well as artists, diplomats, and politicians, and she spent her days indefatigably furnishing her
apartment in the magnificent fabrics, colors, and designs inspired by Diaghilev's Ballets Russes productions, with which Beecham had been closely

associated. Maud rested from her labors by meeting Beecham and Diaghilev at the Savoy for supper. Her weekend parties of romantic intrigue were over, even though many of her friends still called her "the Lollipop" or "Pocket Venus" (G. M.'s endearment) and pondered whether Boucher or Fragonard would have been the ideal artist to have painted her.

As Maud grew expert in planning her dinner parties, she sifted through her guest lists as if she were preparing the most delicate soufflé. She mixed and measured choice politicians, royalty, artists, musicians, and writers. Eventually, she would be inviting cabinet ministers and their wives like the Churchills or Anthony Edens, the Prince of Wales or one of his brothers, and one or two savories such as Yeats, Pound, Shaw, Maugham, and Evelyn Waugh. After deciding on a smart blend of guests, she mailed out her signature purple party invitations. An always reliable assemblage, assuming each was in London, included the Baldwins, Simpsons, and Mountbattens; Prince Edward; and Lady Diana and Duff Cooper. This was the milieu in which Nancy grew up.

Although Maud served majestic food on a circular table made of lapis lazuli, the consummate attraction at her gatherings was the witty, intelligent, and brisk conversation that she skillfully choreographed. Maud was highly (self-)educated and well spoken on everything from the history of cockfighting to Jacobean drama (she knew a number of plays by heart). She was also adept in making the most reticent guests feel so comfortable that they could become the most articulate voices in a conversation. One observer called Maud "a spiritual dowser in a desert"; she "could flick her guests into animation like a practiced ring-master." Famous as well for her "throwaway shockers," she often made provocative statements and asked embarrassing questions with such aplomb that all heads instantly turned toward her. "Christ had a very unpleasant face," she once said casually; in the mid-1930s, she cooed at Joachim von Ribbentrop, the German ambassador: "Tell us, dearest Excellency, *why* does Herr Hitler dislike the Jews?"[1]

Osbert Sitwell tried to explain how this bookish, talented, and quick-witted woman's mind worked. He concluded that she had a unique use of the syllogism and that it was impossible beforehand to guess at what conclusion she would arrive. Although, as he put it, the majority of ill-read London hostesses loved dullness for its own sake, Maud wanted to be amused, and toward that end she developed a method: she would "goad the conversation, as if it were a bull, and she a matador, and compel it to show a fiery temper." In awe of her impact on the British cultural scene, he also remarked that in the world of music, Lady Cunard "reigned alone, enabling" the opera and ballet seasons to materialize: "Her passion for music [was] fervent enough to make opera almost compulsory for those who wished to be fashionable."[2]

Not only was Nancy away from Nevill Holt, but she was also away from her estranged father. Although her teachers found her highly intelligent and affable, and the studious girl won several academic awards, she was bored with her classes and homesick for the country and her father. In the autumn of 1913, she asked her mother if she could go to Germany to study language and music. Maud located a proper family for her to stay with in Munich and arranged for a governess. A new acquaintance described first meeting Nancy, "a raw Scotch-looking girl of about sixteen . . . dowdily dressed, simple, straightforward and quite unconscious of herself and her alert governess. . . . She was going to be—a poetess."[3] Whatever the presumed responsibilities of her overseer, Nancy was given extensive freedom, and it was here, as she said, that she "became a woman."

When Maud heard about her lack of supervision, she insisted that Nancy leave at once, and the next spring she was enrolled in a Paris finishing school run by the Demoiselles Ozanne, the three unmarried daughters of a minister. One, Marie Ozanne, became Nancy's friend. G. M. asked Nancy if she was as discontented there as she appeared, and she replied, "Indeed, yes. . . . Having worked hard in Munich at music and German the autumn before, I had tasted of adult life, had been taken away from it and put in a place where I could go ahead at nothing, the lessons being almost infantile." For a time, she told him, "music saved me, . . . three concerts a week, the Opera, [and] the further discovery of César Franck." But for the most part, Nancy amused herself by experimenting with language, writing entries in her diary in her own version of Old English ("Fathere dyde leave today forr Ye Holte") and designing a form of Old French ("G. M. et moys allones fayre une promenade a Sohoe"). For Nancy, paying attention to variations in sound and rhythm was satisfying; the act of recording daily activities and feelings was also cathartic. This kind of writing would become the avocation of a lifetime. Finally, "school changed with the litera[ture] of Professeur Bellessort. . . . The Russians and Scandinavians . . . were of great interest to me."[4]

Nancy pored over her new authors, especially Turgenev, and was irritated when she had to put her books aside to join the school's mandatory extracurricular outings. They were as tedious as the classes—chaperoned sightseeing tours to churches and museums. She preferred the small streets she could associate with specific writers and painters. She subsequently replied to G. M., who asked if she had had "a crise de mysticisme": "No—certain old churches in Paris were a delight and I lingered long in them [and] in the old streets near the Rue Mouffetard. . . . My mysticisme was in those streets." Whenever Nancy returned to London, she visited her first mentor and they renewed their conversations: "Did I not like Villon?" G. M. asked.

"Almost more than any other poet, I told him, along with Baudelaire, and the contrast made him smile."[5]

During the summers, Nancy went to Venice, where her mother rented a palazzo, and in 1913 became friendly with Lady Diana, the daughter of Maud's frequent guest, the Duchess of Rutland. The strikingly beautiful, chic, and clever Diana Manners was three years older than Nancy, and Nancy immediately came under her spell and acquired a social defiance that would last a lifetime. Since Diana referred to her mother as "Her Grace," Nancy began to regularly call hers "Her Ladyship." Diana and her daring group of friends, the "Corrupt Coterie" as they called themselves, were fearless but polite rebels, committed to the ostentatious defiance of convention. Nancy had never known anyone like them. Children of the very rich and famous—of the Asquiths, Grenfells, and Beerbohms, all of whom reprimanded their children for their unseemly behavior—they nevertheless did as they pleased. They had all-night parties, created and performed plays for one another, bathed naked in the Adriatic in the moonlight, wrote one another witty and wanton love letters, and, since they were in Venice, did as the Venetians do: dressed as gondoliers and sang in Italian as they rowed up the canals.

In the spring of 1914, Maud began to plan the reluctant Nancy's presentation as a debutante. There were dances to be arranged and clothes to be bought. Nancy had become astonishingly beautiful: she had an elegant demeanor regardless of what she was wearing or where she was wearing it. She was tall and very slim, with long, shapely legs and a graceful sway in her walk that was like a delicate dance. Her "lion-like mane" of hair was ashen blond; her skin, flawless and fair; her features, finely chiseled. Her eyes were "like glimpses of the sea"—at times, light blue; at other times, the color of turquoise. Her voice was distinctive: "She spoke in high piping notes, punctuated by odd stresses and pouncing exclamations of jubilance or rejection: 'Ohhh!' 'Ahhh!' The obstinate, staccato 'No!' An inward mirth simmered through [her] sentences." Her manner might be unpredictable and one of extremes, but she was most frequently vivacious and even flamboyant: "She was both delicate and shocking, perceptive and always surprising."[6]

For this important social season, Maud bought Nancy everything from unnecessary corsets, an excessive number of Poiret ball gowns (for which they traveled to Paris), and leopard furs to a variety of morning, afternoon, and evening frocks; she also insisted on four different outfits for the Ascot races. Even then, Nancy disliked haute couture, preferring berets and turbans to Marthe Callot's broad-brimmed, flowery hats.

Although she grew increasingly depressed by the inevitable, forthcoming social rituals, she dutifully attended the obligatory balls. When she was at last presented at court, she wore a pale pink dress with a train of rose petals on tulle. She was invited to a garden party at Buckingham Palace but not to a court ball because Queen Mary did not approve of her mother. At her own ball, the Prince of Wales was one of her partners, soon to become one of her suitors.

Two years older than Nancy, Edward was, to the world, the storybook prince: handsome, blond, blue-eyed, high-colored, and the most eligible bachelor in Great Britain. Wherever he traveled, he was wooed by royal families as the potential husband for their maiden daughters—for the German Victoria Louise (a friend observed: "wholly without good looks but with much sweetness") and for Princess May (to another friend: "such a nice girl . . . but an awkward job. . . . Her teeth were in need of attention and her nose was too red").[7]

Edward, like Nancy, was the child of cold, unaffectionate parents, but he had responded to them differently, even though he ultimately gave up family (as she would) and rank when he abdicated the throne and married Wallis Simpson. To the young prince, however, King George V, with his hair-trigger temper and abrasive manner, was frightening, and his mother, Mary ("May"), who shared Maud's conviction that childbearing insulted the female body, also kept her first son at a distance. Whenever his father was sarcastic, insensitive, or unkind, his mother was afraid to stand up for him. Edward once remarked to his brothers: "She's as frightened of Papa as we are."[8]

Unlike Nancy, Edward took little interest in the life of the mind, and neither of his parents encouraged him to study. As Lady Frances Donaldson remarks, George V lacked "what Henry James has termed 'the deeper sense,' and his children were conditioned to disregard things of the intellect and spirit, because, the king believed, they would stunt the moral sense." Queen Mary was surprisingly uncultured: she saw *Hamlet* for the first time when she was twenty-seven and first read Tolstoy and Dostoevsky when she was in her eighties. The prince was brought up with his back to one of the finest art collections in the world; his ear was tuned only to the bagpipe, and he lived in total ignorance of English literature.[9] Not unlike Bache Cunard, Edward's tastes ran elsewhere: in his case, to clothing, horsemanship, guns, and golf. He was happy to leave Oxford to join the army in late 1914, when he was commissioned in the Twenty-second Battalion of the Grenadier Guards and sent to France.

Before this, he had gained a reputation for his sartorial independence, and he was certainly unique, if not a trendsetter, in wearing loud, checkered suits and every combination of bright clothing in large patterns and two-toned shoes. To those in the court and undoubtedly to Nancy, he had vulgar taste. Like Nancy, however, he had an enormous amount of energy. He slept only eight out of seventy-two hours, and he drank a great deal and suffered bouts of depression, as she would after the war. He felt imprisoned in his monarchical status and wrote with self-pity about the miseries of being a royal.[10]

The prince was also "physically slow to mature." Nancy had already become a woman, as she phrased it, several years before he showed any sexual interest in women. He admitted to friends—and it became well known—that he enjoyed the companionship of women but felt no strong urge to consummate a relationship. He later wrote a friend that in 1916 he had visited a brothel and watched naked girls in erotic poses but had found all of it "filthy and revolting."[11] The prince invited Nancy to dance with him at numerous parties between 1914 and the 1920s, which led to speculation that he was smitten with her. He also sent her lavish gifts. But when Nancy was asked about him, she always repeated the same word: "boring." Even if he could offer a royal title, his lack of cultural interests, sophistication, and aristocratic ways were not to her liking.

As Nancy attended the parties of 1914, she found them so tedious that champagne became her most appealing companion. She later wrote of the London season that it was "my first and last, I swore to myself, as one ball succeeded another until there were three or four a week and the faces of the revolving guardsmen seemed as silly as their vapid conversation among the hydrangeas at supper." This was the last season before the war, and the summer of 1914 was "the most idyllic in years," sunny, warm, and "eminently pastoral." "For the modern imagination," writes Paul Fussell, "that last summer . . . assumed the status of a permanent symbol for anything innocently but irrevocably lost." It was an indelible reminder of "the change from felicity to despair, pastoral to anti-pastoral,"[12] an emblem of the last blush of innocence that transformed a hopeful and optimistic era into what Gertrude Stein would call the lost generation. For the scarred, postwar survivors, all pre-summer 1914 romantic and altruistic values would be viewed with a cynical eye, and all things scientific and technological would bear the potential of enhancing the deadly machines of war.

London in 1915 was transformed. Most of the young men had disappeared, except for the pacifist intellectuals, the elderly, and the sick. D. H. Lawrence wrote of that winter: "The spirit of old London collapsed. The city, in some way, perished, perished from being the heart of the world, and became a vortex of broken passions, lusts, hopes, fears, and horrors." Bertrand Russell went on to say: "[London's] inhabitants began to seem like hallucinations." Virginia Woolf described the cadaverous look of silent people, huddled on the streets and buses. These descriptions would reverberate in T. S. Eliot's postwar epic poem, *The Waste Land*.

Before the war and her coming out (and unknown to her mother), Nancy renewed her acquaintance with the pretty, blue-eyed, and exceptionally bright Iris Tree, which transformed a restless space of time into one of alternating joy and sorrow. For many young people like Nancy, the beginning of the war marked a period of overt defiance of parental and social demands and of artistic and sexual experimentation; as the war continued with no end in sight, it became a time of reckless abandon and growing despair.

Nancy and Iris had met as children at one of her mother's tea parties, and they disliked each other at first. Iris had made fun of one of the other little girls; "Niminy-Piminy little Miss Banana Curls," she called a pale little girl, as Iris later recalled, and the egalitarian Nancy rebuked her sharply: "If you don't like my friends, you ought not to come here." Iris many years later added: "[This was] a snub which shamed me then, but now seems significant of so many loyal defenses and offensives that influenced her life."[13] Iris became Nancy's best female friend.

At seventeen, a year younger than Nancy, Iris was studying painting at the Slade School, and her friends included the exotic artists Wyndham Lewis and Augustus John. She was too young to apply for university studies, even though she took the exam and received the highest score. The daughter of Sir Herbert and Lady Beerbohm Tree (Herbert, the brother of Max), Iris had already rebelled against everything her family represented in order to become a "bohemian." Nancy would soon do the same, but her rejection of social class and family was more complex, as if she were both imitating and rebelling against her mother's conduct: "My mother's having an affair with Thomas Beecham. I can do as I like," she said, a measure of embarrassment accompanying her defiance.[14]

Nancy loved Iris's romantic ways and her love of reading and writing poetry. The two young women read their poems to each other and shared each other's dreams. Iris also enjoyed the outdoors, which was always so important to Nancy, and they hiked in the countryside and ran on the beach. On weekends, Iris joined Nancy on visits to her father, still awaiting Maud's return, first at Nevill Holt and later at his elegant residence at Wansford, a small village east of Holt. Bache was now living there permanently because he could no longer maintain the grand estate in Leicestershire. Iris sensed that the palpable distance between father and daughter was due to the fact that Nancy reminded Bache of his estranged wife. Of the young women's wonderful summers together, Nancy wrote in *Sublunary*:

Do you remember in those summer days
When we were young how often we'd devise
Together of the future? No surprise

Or turn of fate should part us, and our ways
Ran each by each . . .
    . . . while the flowers
About us waved in harvest plumes. . . .

Your scarlet dress grew vivid, and your hands
Evoked with witty gesture, palms of glee,
Things we had laughed at lovingly—for then,
Ah even then we loved our memories. ("Iris of Memories")

Throughout her life, Nancy found spiritual rejuvenation in nature. Even as
a young girl, as she wrote in the poem "Adolescence," she knew that whenever a "sense of wrong" accompanied "tearful introspection," her sorrow would
vanish once the "thronging stars . . . descended to new hands and hurrying
feet." She could "worship" in nature and gain "hold [of] the world's perplexi-
ties" and regain the "stirring of heart's blood."

Iris was aware of their differences. Nancy was not only introspective and
self-critical but also goal-oriented: "Unlike me," she was "devoutly studious";
she "read, spoke, [and] wrote many languages fluently, and published poems
in English, French, Spanish. These poems and critical essays reflected the
side of her nature [that was] pensive, purposeful, [and] gleaning."[15]

For Nancy and Iris, like most of their friends, the eve of the war was also
a time of "romantic discovery in which the strictures and sentimentalities of
Victorian and Edwardian England were rejected. . . . Transition and danger
were in the air." As a result, Iris continues,

> We responded like chameleons to every changing color, turning from Meredith
> to Proust to Dostoevsky, slightly tinged by the *Yellow Book*, an occasional absinthe
> left by Baudelaire and Wilde, flushed by Liberalism, sombered by nihilistic pes-
> simism, challenged by Shaw, inspired by young Rupert Brooke, T. S. Eliot, Yeats,
> D. H. Lawrence; jolted by Wyndham Lewis's *Blast* into cubism and the Modern
> French Masters, Epstein's sculptures, Stravinsky's music (booed and cheered); the
> first Russian ballets and American jazz; nightlong dancing; dawn-long walks; exul-
> tant, longing, laughing loves unspotted by respectable sin.[16]

They rented a modest studio flat on Fitzroy Place, near Bloomsbury and
the Slade, where they were free to dress (in wools and linens woven at the
arty Bloomsbury group's Omega Workshop), drink, smoke, write and read poetry to each other, entertain their admirers, and essentially do anything they
pleased. They formed their own "Corrupt Coterie" of artists and writers, with
Alvaro "Chile" Guevara, Robert Nichols, Evan Morgan, Osbert Sitwell and

his brother Sacheverell, Edward "Bimbo" Wyndham Tennant, and Tommy Earp. Occasionally, Augustus John and Wyndham Lewis joined them. Several of the men, all gifted and hard-working artists, sooner or later became Nancy's lovers. When she first met Guevara, she was "struck by his fine, sensitive hands [and] saw revealed in his pale face an artist suggestive of fine quality." His paintings would later be owned by the Tate Gallery; his full-length portrait of Nancy was bought by the National Gallery of Victoria in Melbourne, Australia.[17]

The Coterie met at the Eiffel Tower on Percy Street, just off Tottenham Court Road, a small French restaurant owned by an Austrian chef, Rudolph Stulik. Many thought a more appropriate name would have been the "Uffizi" or the "Louvre," because its walls were covered with paintings. The restaurant owed its fame to Augustus John, who discovered it and in the 1890s turned it into an artists' rendezvous. Its French menu was designed by Wyndham Lewis, and a note on the cover described its special dining rooms, including the Vorticist Room, with paintings and ornaments by Lewis, and the Vorticist Anti-room, with works by William Roberts. One could still find absinthe there and, if one wanted—like Arthur Symons, still in his 1890s dress, his long Inverness cape and wide-brimmed, high black felt hat—recapture the decadence of Paris in the 1890s and become, as Nancy put it, "la *sorcière aux yeux glauques* [the sorceress with lugubrious eyes] that had been the undoing of so many a soul in France."[18] Stulik had bins of Imperial Tokay from famous Hapsburg vineyards, bottled in quaint old bottles, some with the seal of the last emperor's grandmother, dated 1802. These were not on the ordinary wine list.

Nancy and her friends met frequently and drank wine (as Stulik put it, they could "hear the anchels [*sic*] sing") and discussed literature, painting, music (particularly the new Negro jazz), and politics. The Eiffel Tower was, Nancy wrote in *Sublunary*,

> wherein is found no lack
> of wits and glamour, strong wines, new foods, fine looks,
> Strange-sounding languages of diverse men.

Others who frequented the Tower and became Nancy's friends included Nina Hamnett ("the Sybil of Soho"), Marjorie Craigie, Jacob Epstein, Lytton Strachey, Robert McAlmon, Curtis Moffat, Marie Beerbohm, and Frank Dodson, the nervous one in the crowd. They often met upstairs in an exclusive, avant-garde dining room filled with glowing aspidistras.

Stulik earned "masses of money but . . . lost yet more through being kind." He always made sure that people were served his special chicken livers, followed by strawberries and champagne. However, there were occasions when, for example, he had to ask John Davenport for money to buy eggs for the omelet he had ordered. Otherwise, he generously dispensed rich food, such as canard pressé and sole dieppoise—even to the poor, fragile, and consumptive Ronald Firbank, who was one of Nancy's favorites. Many years later, she wrote an essay about Firbank and called him fabulous, witty, "brave and adroit indeed," because he hid his severe health problems from their company.[19]

Curiously enough, despite Iris and Nancy's "cohabiting without censorship," in Iris's words, and their "drink, cynicism, and unlimited promiscuity," as Richard Aldington phrased it,[20] they were uncomfortable setting the trends that soon became widespread. They felt the need to dress in disguise when they went out, to wear costumes of their own making. Once they were arrested for swimming at dawn in the Serpentine, emerging before the authorities drenched in homemade outfits of velvet, chiffon, ribbons, feathers, spangles, and artificial flowers. They were more insecure in their search for identity and defiance of convention than they knew or could admit. All the same, their flouting of convention, particularly Nancy's capacity for alcohol and affairs, was grist for the gossip columnists, raising questions about decent and indecent behavior for women.[21] In "To the E. T. Restaurant, " Nancy called the Eiffel Tower "our carnal-spiritual home."

The contrast between outings with the Corrupt Coterie and the tedious dinners with Maud was striking, and Nancy enraged her mother by her rebellious behavior. Once she appeared at a dinner party in a black evening waistcoat and white slip, instead of a shirt. Her thick theatrical makeup and association with "dangerous, bohemian types" deeply offended Maud. Iris admitted: "We were bandits, escaping environment by tunneling deceptions to emerge in forbidden artifice, chalk-white face powder, scarlet lip rouge, cigarette smoke, among roisterers of our own choosing: Augustus John and his gypsy models at the Café Royal; . . . and the then young wise owls of the Bloomsbury clique, . . . and the 'coterie' crowned by Diana Manners."[22] After Nancy's and Iris's parents learned of their "forbidden playgrounds"—their indulgences in bacon and eggs at cabmen's shelters and in beer and brandy at public houses—they confiscated their keys; the girls made new ones.

Iris and Nancy dressed up for parties and balls at Albert Hall in fabrics influenced by Bakst and Beardsley, and Iris recalls, "I still see Nancy, crowned with feathers, streaming with ribbons and simmering expectations." Once at their destination, Nancy was more adept than Iris in finding a companion-lover. She had a physical magnetism that attracted men. The writer David Garnett recalled first seeing her the month the war began: "[Nancy] made a great impression on me. She was very slim with a skin as white as bleached almonds, the bluest eyes one has ever seen and very fair hair. She was marvelous." When she spoke to him of G. M., Garnett admitted: "How I wish I had been ten years older or Nancy ten years younger, because then perhaps I might have been an old man whom she could love."[23]

Nancy's choice of partners seemed eccentric to her friends; she never fancied a man with compatible interests, and she romanticized each and was inevitably disappointed: "Her eye was never for the obvious. . . . It may have lighted upon attributes to which we were blind, or provided those enchantments that often were abruptly disenchanted."[24] Nancy confessed in a poem that she never chose a man she could truly care about; this removed the potential element of jealousy, either another man's or her own:

All were there,
This life's alarmers, sowing their future
harvests,
Rife weeds of conflict—
all but one
That I name never, Jealousy.

The coterie continued to meet at the Tower and to scout out all-night jazz parties; drink heavily in pubs, river barges, and Bloomsbury attics; and swim regularly at dawn or at midnight. And always eager to locate new places and pleasures, they discovered the Café Royal on Regent Street, and this became a second, favorite hangout where they consumed beaker after beaker of wine and ale. According to Iris, they especially enjoyed parties given by George Gordon Moore, an American millionaire, because they lasted from dinner to breakfast and were bursting with red and white camellias and "rocketing with champagne and the new sound of Negro Jazz and Hawaiian bands." Nancy loved the jazz. Its rhythms transported her to the kind of paradises she imagined Baudelaire and De Quincey had found through opium. Diana Manners, a frequent guest of honor, gave the feasts a legendary, mythic quality, "of the glory" that was Greece, the "grandeur" that was Rome.[25] Nancy's scrapbooks from this time bulge with photos of her friends—Iris, Diana, "Bimbo" Tennant, Julien Grenfell, Evan Morgan, Curtis Moffat, and Duff Cooper.

In addition to her flamboyant social life and pensive musings on literature with Iris, Nancy spent long afternoons and evenings with people of great reputation, discussing the new art and new ideas. She and the renowned Arthur Symons, for example, as she recalled in a rather quaint phrase, had "known each other lengthily, since 1915," when they had met at the Eiffel Tower. Nancy idolized Symons as the ambassador of contemporary French literature to England, and Symons admired Nancy's intellectual gifts. In the mid-1920s, he asked her to translate a volume of Mallarmé's poems. Through Symons, Nancy was introduced to other intellectual icons of the time, such as Havelock

Ellis, whose work she and Symons read aloud to each other, marveling at his great knowledge and "calm approach to the facts and mysteries in nature."[26]

In 1914, a series of articles in the *Times Literary Supplement* reported on the paucity of recognized new literary talent in England.[27] The most revered novelists remained Arnold Bennett, Joseph Conrad, Compton Mackenzie, H. G. Wells, Hugh Walpole, John Galsworthy, and Gilbert Cannan, most of them over fifty years old and still writing in the conventions of the time and advocating its manners. The most highly respected poets were John Masefield and Georgians like Rupert Brooke, Hilaire Belloc, and Lascelles Abercrombie, with their diluted, inferior imitations of late Romantic poetry.

At the same time, just before and during World War I, a literary revolution was coalescing in England, one as momentous as Romanticism over a century earlier. Its four major innovators were Ezra Pound, T. S. Eliot, James Joyce, and Wyndham Lewis. Although Joyce lived in Trieste and Zurich during this period, he published in London; the others lived, wrote, and published there. Only after the war did Paris become the creative center of the world. (London may have remained behind, particularly in the visual arts, because Roger Fry and Clive Bell, the arbiters of taste, were focused on the "Post-Impressionists.")

Between 1914 and 1915, Nancy met a number of writers and artists, and she was swept up by the energy and personalities of the new creative voices, of the Imagists, Vorticists, and Bloomsbury group. According to Janet Flanner, Nancy would play no small role in the artistic renaissance taking place: she ultimately "became a kind of general Egeria to the postwar London literary generation, knew everybody, was known by everybody."[28]

The Legends, in Art and Life

Ezra Pound

Ezra Pound was already a legend when Nancy first met him at Nevill Holt, where he visited Maud regularly to campaign for the new arts. In 1912, under the influence of T. E. Hulme,[29] he had created Imagism, a literary movement that demanded that poets "Make It New!"—that they revolt against the "blurry, messy," sentimental poetry popular since the turn of the century. Pound eventually introduced Nancy to most of the early Imagists—F. S. Flint, Ford Madox Ford (né Hueffer), William Carlos Williams, Richard Aldington, H. D. (Hilda Doolittle), Amy Lowell, Harriet Monroe, Marianne Moore, and T. S. Eliot—and under his influence she rededicated herself to becoming a poet.

Imagism would change the direction of twentieth-century literature in advocating short free verse composed of vivid and precise ("hard and dry") visual images. Everyday language would reflect the author's *response* to a subject, without cosmic or personal commentary, and like a flower, the poem would evoke in the reader an unfolding of associations and feelings. Rhythms would grow out of and modify previous lines. Pound's "In a Station of the Metro," about the maze of women's beautiful faces suddenly emerging from the Paris Metro, is a famous example:

> The apparition of these faces in the crowd;
> Petals on a wet, black bough.

One envisions unearthly, exquisite, indistinct, and delicate faces juxtaposed against something damp, dark, and weighty. Pound creates an image, a verbal painting, of the impact of technology in the modern world on innocence, human vitality, and nature.

Pound now visited Maud in her new home almost daily to extol James Joyce, in dire need of financial support to complete *Ulysses,* and she gave him money to send Joyce anonymously. Pound later pleaded for Wyndham Lewis at the war front ("far too good an artist . . . to risk being sacrificed"), and Nancy saw him assist Yeats in staging his play *At the Hawk's Well* at Maud's home. Nancy, however, dated their first meaningful encounter in 1916, when they consoled each other over the death of close friends in the war.[30] Later, when she became critically ill, Pound remained at her side, and their long love affair began.

From the beginning, Nancy found Pound physically appealing; she initially compared him to Rodolfo in *La Bohème.* She was attracted to his thick, wavy red hair, pointed beard, and lynx-like green eyes — "so striking behind his pince-nez." She liked his eccentric dress, the black and white checkered trousers he favored, and his sweeping black cape, large black hat, yellow chamois gloves, and cane. She was completely charmed by this man, who would assume three distinctive pseudonyms (William Atheling, the Poet of Titchfield Street, and Alfred Venison), admitting, "There was a good deal of 'panache' to him, a certain flamboyance." His "learned blasts" might "alarm," but he was "vibrating and dynamic [and] he could certainly become ecstatic." Nancy found him a "living classic."[31]

She had good reason for thinking so. In addition to formulating Imagism, by 1912 he had published numerous translations, essays on the Latin poets of the Renaissance and French troubadours, as well as six poetry collections. Nancy reveled in his intellectual prowess and became one of the earliest scholars of his work, tracing the origins of his subject matter "from the classics, Chinese, Japanese, ancient Provencal balladeers, the Troubadours, and Italy." She was even conversant about *Cathay* (1915), his transformation of

Ernest Fenollosa's translations of Chinese poetry into free form, his redesigning of Chinese characters as ideograms or compressed visual metaphors.

Pound would later immortalize Nancy in the *Cantos*, as well as in his casual verse—for example, warning Richard Aldington, another of her admirers, to be wary of her:

> Behold what perils do environ
> The man who meddles with a siren.

Nancy had been unable to return Aldington's ardor. "To me," she confessed, "he looked the typical Englishman, and not the type I find particularly comely. His hair was cider-red, his cheeks rosy, not large," and she found him, at one and the same time, shy, good natured, and arrogant.

In the *Cantos*, Pound assigns Confucius the role of uttering Aldington's, or anyone's, dire fate in loving Nancy. In Canto 80, he writes:

> "And I be damned" said Confucius:
> This affair of a southern Nancy. (80/495)

Elsewhere in the same canto, Pound describes how his feelings for Nancy permeated all of Italy. Punning on "Italian," he says she was "beloved in the eyetalian [Nancy's word] peninsula" (80/510). Her presence also transformed the countryside in the south of France during their drives along narrow curving hills and their stopovers at inns where troubadours once sang to their ladies:

> Nancy where art thou?
> Whither go all the vair [fur] and the cisclatons [silk]
> and the wave pattern runs in the stone
> on the high parapet (Excideuil)
> Mt Segur and the city of Dioce. (80/510)[32]

Nancy was dazzled by Pound's crusading spirit in promoting better literature. He was the first writer of any status to recognize Frost's, Lawrence's, Eliot's, and Joyce's gifts and published some of the earliest work of William Carlos Williams, H. D., and Marianne Moore. He worked tirelessly to promote each one's reputation and thought carefully about the most appropriate venue for each writer.[33] It is remarkable that when he sent Harriet Monroe poems by Yeats, Eliot, and Rabindranath Tagore, he was passing on the early work of three future Nobel Prize laureates.[34] Pound's energy and self-sacrifice for the sake of art were irresistible to Nancy, and her idolization of him in their five-year affair after the war really began when she was in her late teens.

Like Pound, Nancy would come to believe in the sacred mission of art to change history. During both the Spanish Civil War and World War II, she wrote poems and edited anthologies to promote anti-fascist sentiment. By that time, Pound had exchanged his reverence for free thinking for the ideology of fascism, and Nancy's contempt for him was profound and permanent.

Not only did Nancy find Pound's dedication to art and his physical appearance highly appealing, but his background fascinated her as well. An only child, born in Hailey, Idaho (a mining town whose main street accommodated forty-seven bars), he was the grandson of a Wisconsin congressman who had been born in a log cabin. Pound's father was in charge of the Hailey Land Office, and he later worked at the United States Mint. His mother, the genteel Isabel Weston Pound, was brought up in Washington, D.C., and, to her son's chagrin, was a descendant of Henry Wadsworth Longfellow. The family moved to the outskirts of Philadelphia when Pound was four, and the child enjoyed frequent trips to the Liberty Bell and the other American treasures in the city. Pound idolized his parents and extended family. When he was twelve, a favorite aunt took him to Europe, and the boy discovered in Italy a paradisal world he would never forget. (In 1930, his parents accepted his invitation to move to Rapallo so they could live near each other.)

Throughout his childhood, like Nancy, he had loved the outdoors. At fifteen, he entered the University of Pennsylvania and met William Carlos Williams, who became a lifelong friend. He played chess, tennis, and lacrosse and fenced; he read Anglo-Saxon and the Romance languages; he was transfixed by the Provençal troubadours. He met H. D. (Hilda Doolittle), a Bryn Mawr student, at a Halloween party; he was dressed as a Tunisian prince. They had an affair and a short engagement. H. D. later married Nancy's rejected suitor Richard Aldington and also pursued a bisexual lifestyle. Pound, in a typical act of witty braggadoccio, said that one of his greatest life achievements was introducing H. D. to brie cheese. H. D. told Nancy that one of her great life experiences was her analysis by Sigmund Freud.[35]

Nancy loved to hear about Pound's adventures. After his postgraduate work abroad, he had taught Romance languages at Wabash College in Crawfordsville, Indiana. Increasingly disillusioned by the cultural decay in the United States, he proclaimed that he had discovered "the Athens of the West" in Crawfordsville: apparently Lew Wallace, the author of Ben-Hur, had died here. After a few months at Wabash, his landlady, intending to make his bed, discovered a stripper from a local burlesque house in it. Pound had gone off to teach, and she phoned the college president. Pound argued that he had found the young woman penniless in a blizzard and was only offering her shelter. He was immediately dismissed. At the time, he was also engaged to someone else to whom he had given a diamond ring presented to him by yet another woman, a pianist fifteen years his senior who cultivated the music of Scriabin.[36]

Delighting in his every eccentricity, Nancy particularly liked the apocryphal tale of his dinner with Yeats and Ford Madox Ford, when he ate rose petals (or tulips; the legend had become controversial) and wore a sombrero, a coat with blue glass buttons, pants made of green billiard table cloth, and a single turquoise earring. She loved hearing the literary community compare anecdotes about his appearance with this or that fellow writer. She was always amused to see the flashy and flamboyant Pound with Eliot, who, in his conventional stylishness, projected an elegant appearance.

G. M. enjoyed teasing Nancy about Pound and her other new friends when they met for lunch. "Chaos!" he called the labors of Pound, Eliot, Wyndham Lewis, and Joyce, and Nancy "ventured to murmur 'Not chaos to me.'" After these brief interchanges, he turned the subject to Nancy's writing and urged her to work assiduously: "If you go out and amuse yourself when you can't write, your art life will waste into nothingness." Another of their frequent debates involved G. M.'s aversion to homosexuality: "Think of two men calling each other 'darling,' as I am told some of them do! Oh no, my dear Nancy, it does not bear thinking about! . . . It is against nature." Nancy pondered: "I thought I would ask him how it could be against nature, since man is part of nature, and certain men, etc. No matter how one might feel, why not be detached, surely one could not but accept the fact."[37] He frequently reminisced about his enchanted days with Nancy's mother.

T. S. Eliot

Although Nancy's adoration of G. M. never diminished, she was inspired by the younger, more dynamic writers such as T. S. Eliot, and since they had many mutual friends, they invariably attended the same events. According to Pound, in a letter to Harriet Monroe, Eliot's wife, Vivienne, knew of the women "who would gladly have lured her husband away. Nancy Cunard was one such." Indeed, on one evening after the London ballet, Nancy scoured the theater from her mother's box in search of Eliot. She "longed to see [him] again."[38] Although she was unsuccessful on that occasion, Nancy and Eliot subsequently did have a brief affair. Afterward, Eliot wanted to erase the experience, and Nancy kept their secret until his death, despite his earlier malevolent treatment of her.

Nancy was enamored of Eliot even before she met him. He was another member of her pantheon of creative artists who had modernized poetry by using sharp, precise imagery to create subtle, suggestive poetry. Nancy was overwhelmed by Eliot's poetry, for it was responsive to the new psychology she had found so exciting—evoking how, as in "The Love Song of J. Alfred

Prufrock," feelings of insecurity, inferiority, and even sexual inadequacy color one's entire external world. Eliot's inhibited protagonist, whose very name suggests business rather than pleasure (with overtones of the clergy and femininity: J. Alfred Pru-"frock"), dreads vigorous activity in the world, let alone with a woman. An evening in which he tries to imagine romance can only mirror his consuming sense of impotence and increasing paralysis, a life in which inaction has overtaken action. Eliot invents rhymes and jagged lines that evoke the new jazz:

> Let us go then you and I
> When the evening is spread out against the sky
> Like a patient etherized upon a table . . . [39]

Nancy fell in love with Eliot when she first read "Prufrock."

In 1965, after hearing about his death, Nancy wrote his longtime friend John Hayward a long prose poem that recalled their first romantic evening together at one of her mother's balls. She wrote a mixture of details and ambiguous generalizations: she had worn a panniered Poiret dress, "red and gold with cascading white tulle on the hips"; Eliot had arrived in a dinner jacket. Bored once again after dancing with the Prince of Wales, she walked into the supper room: "It was then, Eliot, you came in, alone too, for the first time to my eyes." She felt as though she knew him well: "well raised on you, somewhat versed in you or at least Prufrock"; recalled receiving a copy of "The Lovesong of J. Alfred Prufrock" from an Irish soldier with whom she had made love; and admitted: "From that day on, he . . . and you came together, . . . gratuitous, fortuitous, this linking, one well may say. Such things make a 'complex.' It is magic." Already seduced by his poetry, she now responded to his physical appeal: "Your words," she added, "got into my fibre": "I never told you this, oh never, never. Seized was I by your looks, your way, your eyes, at that ball. 'The solitary eagle,' that is you."

After a dinner of champagne and lobster, she took the initiative: "So entranced was I by you I suggested 'a tryst' for the next night. You certainly came to it." They had both been invited to dinner by their mutual friends Mary and John Hutchinson, but "I begged you not to get us there, and in the end I won." Instead, they went to the Tower, and Nancy led Eliot to a private room upstairs, where they sat on the floor by a gas fire. A waiter soon found them "as close as could be," and they reordered double gins: "Eliot went on talking while I admired his gradual unthawing." His poetry, she told him, had "put its frenzy into me": it "changed my life." At the end of the evening, they spoke intimately, if somewhat formally, about their tryst: "Is it passion and repression,

repression as well as passion? . . . This sort of thing we talked about so close to that good gas fire."

John Hayward's response was intended to quell the fires of Nancy's recollection. Not without a sense of humor, he began: "Thank you very much for your letter of 7 November—and particularly for the curiously appealing and human touch in its top right-hand corner—the cigarette burn, which made you seem near and real." As to the letter's substantive content, he was sober:

> I had known Tom since my undergraduate days exactly forty years ago: we shared this flat together for twelve years (1945–57) until he re-married; and it is difficult to relate the Tom I know so well with the bitter-sweet dandy (am I thinking of Florestan or have I got the wrong name?) of your poem. You have certainly given a fascinating picture of the brightest young things at that critical stage in their emotional development, but I'm not sure that you've quite succeeded in expelling or resolving the "personal" element from the pure poetry of the occasion remembered. O those enchanted evenings—a flood of quotations from Baudelaire and the rest come surging into my mind. . . . "O Saisons, O Châteaux, . . . quelle âme est sans défaut? [Ah seasons, Ah chateaux, . . . what soul is without fault?]"
>
> Of course I don't mind your showing the poem to some choice friends, but I suggest that you should choose none who might conceivably take offense or objection to the intimate nature of the occasion recollected. [The following is handwritten:] You know how awful people can be—how prone to hint at "revelations!"[40]

Three of Nancy's letters of the 1960s allude to the affair. In addition, it is of no small interest that Eliot gave Nancy an extraordinary gift in the early 1920s. She had always been meticulous about her scrapbooks (with clippings and photos) and commonplace books (one of which consisted of poems written by friends in their own hand; if inscribed by someone else, Nancy scrupulously added "in —'s hand"). In the middle of the commonplace book is "Gerontion" in its entirety, inscribed in Eliot's hand.[41]

In the beginning, Nancy found Eliot fascinating. Like Pound, he had an extraordinary breadth of intellectual interests and, as one of his friends described him, was a *profound* man—"profoundly learned, profoundly poetic, profoundly spiritual."[42] Eliot's undergraduate discovery of Symbolism, which extolled art as religion because the poet revealed the Unseen, changed his life. It permitted him to be a poet while fulfilling his mother's expectation that he lead a life of moral rectitude and service.

As in her relationship with Pound and the other great writers she would come to know, Nancy displayed an insatiable interest in her idol's background. The elegant young man from St. Louis was the child of a distinguished British family whose ancestors had moved to Massachusetts in the seventeenth century. Andrew Eliot was a juror at the Salem witch trials (at the same time one of Hawthorne's ancestors was a judge).[43] And although Eliot's paternal great-grandfather had been elected president of Harvard University a century later, he rejected the position in order to remain a Boston minister. His son, William Greenleaf Eliot, yet another distinguished Unitarian minister, founded Washington University in St. Louis. The school would have been called Eliot University had he been less modest.

William's son, Henry, married Charlotte Champe Stearns, and T(homas) S(tearns) Eliot was the youngest of their seven children. Henry gave up his youthful dreams of being a painter for a business career. Eliot's mother, the granddaughter of an original settler of the Massachusetts Bay Colony, was revered by Tom for her intellectual interests. Eliot told Nancy she had given up her aspirations of becoming a poet to become a teacher. She was devoted to him at the same time that she brought him up in her family's tradition of self-denial and public service. (Several of Eliot's biographers indicate she did not like children.) Eliot also recalled his father's emphasis on moral fastidiousness. In fact, he instructed his children that sex was a nasty enticement of the devil, and since he believed that syphilis was God's punishment for this evil, he prayed that a cure never be found.[44]

Virtually all of Eliot's biographers attest to the man's meticulously proper public demeanor and conduct. Although his good friend Herbert Read hints at his affability, one can understand that a member of the Corrupt Coterie might weary of a perpetually righteous Eliot. According to Read, when speaking of Eliot's moral rectitude, "In conversation he would freely express his disapproval of the conduct of his friends. But I do not remember that he ever brought friendship to an end on such grounds. . . . I was reproved only once with something like sternness." Nancy was undoubtedly familiar with the side of Eliot that Read adored, the serious but not solemn man, the kind and sympathetic Eliot.[45]

All the same, Nancy sensed that Eliot's early training had left him believing that humanity's flawed nature must be purified through austerity. As a result, he was incapable of enjoying the most humble pleasures: he considered buying candy, for example, an indulgence. Furthermore, Eliot's social rigidity, Nancy believed, was due to the elitism he assumed as a transplanted descendant of the British upper class. Eliot had apparently never felt at home growing up in America. He said of his youthful alienation: "Some day I want to write an essay about the point of view of an American who wasn't an American because he was born in the South and went to school in New England as a small boy with a nigger drawl, but who wasn't a southerner in the South because his people were northerners in a border state and looked down on all southerners and Virginians."[46] As a result, Eliot was often teased for cultivating a British identity—for example, for speaking with a better English accent than any English person. Virginia Woolf was even known to quip: "Come to dinner. Eliot will be there in a four-piece suit."

Although Nancy told Pound that she loved Eliot when she first knew him, Eliot is the only major writer whom she refers to disparagingly in her memoirs. As she grew to know him, his aristocratic leanings and racist attitudes became increasingly offensive to her. Eliot is conspicuously absent among the well-known poets she invited to contribute to her anthology, *Negro*, and his response, when she asked him to comment on fascism for her publication during the Spanish Civil War, was one of indifference. Once again, Read comes tepidly to Eliot's rescue and argues against charges of his ultraconservativism (and anti-Semitism): "Eliot did not believe in democracy, and who can blame him? He believed in a 'community of Christians,' in 'roots,' and above all, in 'tradition.'"[47] Of course, when Pound later became involved in global politics, he took a stand even more reactionary than Eliot's.

If Eliot's sense of social propriety and his class and racial superiority weren't enough to alienate Nancy, his consuming interest in religion might have sufficed. However, as her letter to Hayward illustrates, Nancy sensed in Eliot the dichotomy between the inner and outer man, the private and public person. That is, despite his Prufrockian puritanical inhibitions, Nancy sensed Eliot's suffering—his guilt over his romantic longings: "Do I dare? Do I dare?" He, too, had "lingered in the chambers of the sea," longing for seagirls to sing to him. Nancy, well versed in the behavior of men, understood that his moral rigor was a manifestation of his religious agony and that the antidote to his problems, like those of the inhabitants of "the waste land," was, as he wrote in that poem,

The awful daring of a moment's surrender.

In addition, Nancy could easily identify with a victim of gnawing guilt, carrying the same burden about her own sexuality, which she would reveal in her poems.

That Eliot turned against Nancy is evident in the ninety-line Fresca passage in "The Fire Sermon" section of *The Waste Land*, which Pound excised during the time he and Nancy were involved. The passage clearly indicates Eliot's preoccupation with Nancy. He characterizes Fresca/Nancy as an immoral, rich, and beautiful siren who has literary aspirations. However, considering that all of Eliot's voices merge in the figure of Tiresias in *The Waste Land* (as the poet informs us in note 218), one might suggest that Maud, as well as Nancy, is also the modern-day Iseult, the girl in the hyacinth garden, the Lady of the Rocks, the deadly-holy Belladonna, Dido, Lil, the woman violated by Tereus, the typist, Mrs. Porter and her daughter, Miranda, and the Rhine Maidens—Eliot's serial images of violated innocence:

> Fresca! in other time or place had been
> A meek and weeping Magdalene;
> More sinned against than sinning, bruised and marred.
> The lazy laughing Jenny of the bard.

Eliot seems to understand Nancy's compulsive but shame-laden need to give herself to soldiers during the war. Yet in the following, he is merciless in judging her:

> (The same eternal and consuming itch
> Can make a martyr or plain simple bitch);
> Or prudent sly domestic puss puss cat,
> Now autumn's favorite in a furnished flat,
> Or strolling slattern in a tawdry gown,
> A doorstep dunged by every dog in town.
> For varying forms, one definition's right:
> Unreal emotions, and real appetite.
> But women intellectual grow dull,
> And lose the mother wit of natural trull.
> Fresca was born upon a soapy sea
> Of Symons—Walter Pater—Vernon Lee.

And citing the two schools of writers Nancy had read as a student, he continues, less convinced of her artistic endeavors than of her sexual feats:

> The Scandinavians bemused her wits,
> The Russians thrilled her to hysteric fits.
> For such chaotic mishmash pourri
> What are we to expect but poetry?
> When restless nights distract her brain from sleep
> She may as well write poetry, as count sheep
> And on those nights when Fresca lies alone,
> She scribbles verses of such a gloomy tone
> That cautious critics say her style is quite her own.
> Not quite an adult, and still less a child,
> By fate misbred, by flattering friends beguiled,

Fresca's arrived (the Muses Nine declare)
To be a sort of can-can salonnière.[48]

Most troubling to Nancy was Eliot's well-known, unkind treatment of his wife and, above all, his hypocrisy: Eliot could be as vulgar as he was meticulous. Setting aside the complexities of his personal life,[49] the fact remains that the creator of J. Alfred Prufrock was not entirely a prude or a prig, whereas Nancy, although sexually liberated, despised obscene language and vulgar jokes. Eliot was a practical joker with a bawdy, sometimes intensely crude sense of humor. He wrote and sent friends pornographic verse about King Bolo (and a hairy "Big Black Kween") and Colombo (Christopher Columbus), a pederast-rapist who has problems with his bowels. His journey to the New World, as Eliot depicts it, is filled with graphic evocations of bodily functions and sex. Although the notoriously uninhibited Wyndham Lewis had published two of Eliot's poems in *Blast*, he rejected "Bullshit" and "Ballad of Big Louise" on the basis of his decision to have no words in his magazine "ending in -uck, -unt, and -ugger." The poems were eventually published in the 1990s, as *Inventions of the March Hare Poems, 1909–1917*.[50]

As late as 1957, Eliot wrote a preface to Charles-Louis Philippe's erotic *Bubu of Montparnasse*, which he had first read in 1910. After mentioning that he had read the complete works of Philippe, he praised *Bubu*'s Dickensian balance of realism and sentimentality; to him it was a work both "compassionate and dispassionate." *Bubu* is filled with such passages as

> Finally, weary of having walked so long, he felt his old desires goading him. For the sake of peace he took the first [prostitute] who come [*sic*] along, and on a sordid hotel bed, for the price of two francs, he poured himself into a dirty girl as into a public sink.[51]

With regard to Nancy and Eliot's brief intimacy, it is probably safe to say that Eliot was too intimidated by Nancy's forthright sexuality to remain her friend. From Nancy's point of view, Eliot's quest for grace, as well as his devotion to the church, hierarchical English society, and the monarchy—and, even more important, their distinctly different political orientations—prevented a lasting relationship.

Wyndham Lewis

A third great legend of the time who befriended Nancy was Wyndham Lewis; like Pound, he would later become her lover. Lewis was a brilliant painter, novelist, and essayist who eventually produced close to 50 books, 100 paintings, and 1,000 drawings. Nancy saw him regularly at the Eiffel Tower, but it was at a tea party that Nancy heard Eliot declare Lewis the best prose stylist alive.[52] Pound, like Eliot, agreed that Lewis was *a*, if not *the*, leading figure of the English avant-garde during the first half of the twentieth century, prescient in his desire to create a new culture after the war. Lewis's new movement, Vorticism, inspired international attention, as well as Nancy's rapt admiration.

When they first met, Nancy found Lewis intellectually dazzling. She shared his interest in contemporary philosophy, in what William James called "the problem of being"—the inability of reason to grasp the ultimate absurdity of life. ("Not only that *anything* should be, but that *this* very thing should be, is mysterious," as Lewis wrote out James's quandary.)[53] She was fascinated by Lewis's mission to portray the machine as the dominant reality of the new century and to capture the *potential* energy in the machine, which he called the "vortex." His goals were straightforward: "We only want the world to live and to feel its [the machine's] crude energy flowing though us." Pound, uttering what Nancy had called one of his "learned blasts," more colorfully compared the vortex "to any kind of geyser, from jetting sperm which would repopulate Britain . . . [to any such force that had swept] out the past century as surely as Attila swept across Europe."[54]

Believing that "if you were a 'movement,' you were expected to shout," Lewis had founded the Rebel Art Center and *Blast* magazine. Published only in 1914 and 1915, *Blast* was oversize and thick; its name was printed in three-inch-high black capital letters that extended diagonally across the length of the twelve-inch violet-red cover. It listed hundreds of things to "blast" and "bless." "Bless" France "(for known and unknown people), castor oil, and the Pope." "Blast" the "post office and James Galsworthy."[55] Lewis designed a provocative cover with barely readable lines by Pound, describing English and French poets "with minds still hovering about their testicles."

When Pound learned that Lewis was going to publish a magazine exalting technology through concrete, impersonal poetry, he concluded that Vorticism was closer to his goals than Imagism. In fact, Pound conceived of the name "Vorticism," understanding that the artist would unemotionally (that is, like a machine) convey the vortex or "point of maximum energy" inherent in the power of a machine or even at the heart of an abstraction or in nature.[56] And because Lewis exalted the artist at war with a rotting and trivial society, he agreed that "all our work [is] the work of outlaws."

As Lewis introduced Nancy to his radical new ideas, she became a contributing member of the *Blast* group and publicly advocated the new aesthetic. She besieged her friends with vivid encomiums of Lewis's ideas and incorporated the language of Vorticism into her daily vocabulary. Writing about

England's prewar problems in a notebook, for example, she addressed "the obscure vortex of England's revolutionary troubles [coal strikes]." She would title her first volume of poems *Outlaws* and design the cover of her anthology *Negro* in a style almost identical to that of *Blast*.

Late in the war, Lewis served as a gunner in the Royal Artillery, but at the behest of Nancy's mother (at Pound's request), he became an official war artist. He altered his style by using naturalistic rather than geometric and abstract forms; he also modified his exaltation of the machine. In his famous painting *A Battery Shelled*, man is portrayed as a machine amid, and as part of, the dehumanization of war. Lewis conveyed the far-reaching implications about human nature—a horrific portrait of man-made violence. At this point, his feelings corresponded with Nancy's revulsion to the horrors of the Great War.

Nancy was enchanted not just by Lewis's extraordinary mind. He was also charming, vivacious, and distinctively good-looking. She was attracted to his very fair skin, dark eyes, and extremely dark hair. (He also favored black clothing.) She even enjoyed what she initially considered were his eccentricities, such as his ordering the same dinner day after day—soup, a mutton chop or two, a trifle or ice cream, and champagne. After they began their affair, she wrote him: "Dear, dear, Lewis. I get warmed when I am with you—you are a sort of black sun, dark earth, rich and full of new things, potential harvests, always dark, plein de seve [full of juice], oil, blood, bread and comfort. . . . I cannot get a nearer word than Rich. I love you very much." Nevertheless, she would soon realize that his appeal arose entirely out of his abundant talent. On a day-to-day basis, he was self-indulgent and manipulative, and she grew to despise his intense jealousy, which he expressed even as he flaunted his own conquests. He was an inveterate womanizer who, at the same time, openly admitted his intellectual contempt of women, as well as his scorn of the rich. The result was that the higher a woman's social class, the more shabbily he treated her. Eventually, he was to have affairs with two of Nancy's closest and wealthiest friends, Iris Tree and Sybil Hart-Davis.[57]

Nancy also had problems with Lewis's language. He had developed a sense of humor that, as their mutual friend Augustus John observed, would have made Rabelais blush. Lewis's vulgar side, like Eliot's, repelled Nancy, who remained puritanical about language and humor. In fact, the more Lewis told her about himself (usually with pride), the less she liked him. He had graduated from the Rugby School twenty-sixth in a class of twenty-six and yet won a scholarship to the Slade, where he was expelled for indolence. To Nancy's horror, she learned that he regularly reported the details of his love affairs to his mother, whom he warned "not to catch Cockney" from her boyfriend.[58]

Perhaps the most positive mementos of his and Nancy's relationship are the sketch he made of her in Venice and several earlier Cubist portraits. After that, Lewis went on to write more fiction and nonfiction, including *Time and Western Man*; his renown as a painter declined when he turned to portraiture and was no longer on the forefront of modernism. Today he may be one of the most neglected of the artists before World War I.

The Bloomsbury Group

Nancy was involved with one of the most important and long lasting of London's artistic circles during the early part of the century, the elegant and intellectually elite Bloomsbury group.[59] Virginia and Leonard Woolf would, in 1925, publish Nancy's *Parallax* at their Hogarth Press, having already hand printed T. S. Eliot's *Poems*, the English edition of *The Waste Land*, Virginia's experimental *Kew Gardens*, and numerous other landmark works by Sigmund Freud, E. M. Forster, Gorky, Dostoevsky, and Tolstoy. To be accepted for publication by the Hogarth Press was a much coveted prize.

Although the "Bloomsberries," as they were affectionately called, included some of the most gifted artists and thinkers in England, Nancy was not a formal member of the group. She sometimes joined "the young wise owls of the Bloomsbury clique," as Iris had described them, and was often seen at their parties, especially during the war period. But throughout her life, Nancy turned away from groups with cult-like tendencies; furthermore, she found the manners of the Bloomsbury people distasteful. They flaunted their superiority and nonconformity, were apolitical, and were boastful about their sexual adventures. In addition, Nancy was skeptical about their emphasis on rebellion and bohemianism. They flirted with the competing social hostesses of the time while remaining highly contemptuous of them: the Ladies Colefax, Oxford, and Ottoline Morrell, and perhaps the most successful one of all, Lady Cunard. Finally, a public rift between Wyndham Lewis and Roger Fry convinced Nancy that the effete Bloomsbury group was arrogant enough to consider art solely the privilege of the socially and financially elite.

It may be equally true that Nancy's detachment from the group was due to Virginia Woolf's rejection of her—specifically, Virginia's jealousy of her. As the Woolf diaries reveal, when Nancy and the Woolfs first met, Nancy visited them frequently at their home in Richmond and then in London. And Virginia, who rarely went out, reciprocated by calling on Nancy at her home.[60] But Virginia grew to fear that Leonard would replace her with Nancy in their complicated relationship. As a result, Virginia admits with a certain degree of guilt, she stopped inviting Nancy to visit and also avoided any party that Nancy might attend. She was then haunted by such remarks as "Raymond

Mortimer gave a fancy dress party [and] said how lovely Nancy had looked, that I had missed the greatest sight of the season." She felt like a failure for rejecting Nancy: "I should hate failure, and not to fail, we must keep pressing forward, thinking, planning, imagining, . . . accepting Nancy Cunard."[61] Before publishing *Parallax* at the Hogarth, Virginia relented and invited her to another party, although her antipathy remained:

We had a party the other night—Siegfried Sassoon, Mortimer, Duncan, Vanessa. Nancy Cunard shouldn't have come—the anxious flibberti-gibbet with the startled honest eyes, and all the green stones [beads] hung about her. We met at Raymond [Mortimer]'s, and she slipped into easy desperate sounding chatter, as if she didn't mind saying everything—everything—had no shadows, no secret places—lived like a lizard in the sun, and yet was by nature for the shade. And I should be re-reading her poems to choose a title.[62]

The moments of "twinging" jealousy over Nancy also continued: "Here I am waiting for L[eonard] to come back from London, and at this hour. . . . he has been seeing Nancy Cunard." It was "during such agony," she wrote, recalling another such evening, "such was the strength of my feeling that I became physically rigid. Reality, so I thought, was unveiled. . . . There was something noble in feeling like this; tragic, not at all petty . . . I felt lonelier. . . . I'm an outcast." Virginia could not forget Leonard's first reaction to Nancy, when he found her both enchanting and vulnerable. Nor did she forget Leonard's reaction after an evening with Nancy and the "armor-plated" intellectual John Strachey, her lover at the time: "[There clearly] was no toughness in Nancy. [She was] sitting on the sofa, gay but vulnerable, unarmored, with her mind not entirely upon 'the reality around her.'"[63]

The Bloomsberries were all, as Leon Edel called them, highbrow bohemians, a "House of Lions": "eccentric, insolent, arrogant, egotistical," and "preoccupied with neurotic personal relations." They revered G. E. Moore's thoughts in *Principia Ethica* (except for his sexual puritanism)[64] and were totally committed to Art for Art's Sake. Virtually all the men had been educated at Cambridge, and generally, the group turned away from the traditional values of the haute bourgeoise to their religion of art. They held weekly meetings at Gordon Square and Fitzroy Square to discuss "the good," "the true," and "the beautiful" and to affirm their commitment to cultivate the beautiful as the good. As aesthetes, nothing mattered but high states of mind—their communion with love, beauty and truth.

To Nancy, their manners, exalting high-mindedness and ostensibly rebelling against class, were hypocritical. They continued to enjoy the world of high society and the things it could afford. Lytton Strachey was delighted to meet the Duchess of Marborough in the Cunard box at the opera and subsequently be invited for the weekend. Even Virginia Woolf was flattered, if cutting, after Lady Cunard invited her to her house: "I think I may say I am now among the well known writers. I had tea with Lady Cunard—might have lunched or dined any day. . . . Ridiculous little parrokeet faced woman. . . . Flunkeys, yes; but a little drab and friendly. . . . Coarse and usual and dull these Cunards and Colefaxes—for all their astonishing competence in the commerce of life."[65]

Despite her contempt for the Cunards and Colfaxes, Virginia involved herself in their petty rivalries. In the essay "Am I a Snob?" she recalled her first meeting with Nancy's mother:

> Lady Cunard's butler asked me to dine with her ladyship—whom I had never met. Sibyl [Colefax], when I explained the situation, was furious. "I've never heard of such insolence [of inviting someone to dinner one had not met]." She abused Lady Cunard [and] strongly advised me to have nothing to do either with Lady Cunard or Lady Cholmondely. . . . Once I played the same trick on her. Throwing over an engagement, she imputed to me the vilest motives—I had been seduced by a better engagement—I had been dining, she was sure, with Lady Cunard or Lady Cholmondely.[66]

Nancy's pranks and romances within the Corrupt Coterie were like child's play in comparison with the Bloomsbury group's complex and unconventional lifestyles. Vanessa Bell, married to Clive, had a three-year affair with Fry and an even longer one with Duncan Grant, who was bisexual; she accepted the triangular relationship with Grant, and many of his male lovers became her lasting friends. For a time, Virginia Woolf was also in love with Grant; she later turned to Vita Sackville-West, who had been married to Harold Nicolson. Grant was also the lover of his cousin Lytton Strachey (who lived with the painter Dora Carrington and her husband, Ralph Partridge, whom Strachey loved). In addition, Grant was the lover of Maynard Keynes, Virginia's younger brother Adrian, and David "Bunny" Garnett. Keynes, the lover of both Duncan and Lytton, threatened the precarious balance of the group when he introduced his wife, Lydia Lopokova, a Russian dancer, into the group. At some point, it became known that Grant, not Clive Bell (Vanessa's husband), was Angelica's father. On the day she was born, Garnett, who was married and had children, announced that he would marry Angelica. After his wife died, when he was fifty and Angelica was twenty-four, they married. The ménages à trois and à quatre are too numerous to cite.[67]

Nancy formed a lifelong friendship with David "Bunny" Garnett. The handsome, fair, blue-eyed Garnett probably interested Nancy because he was the outsider in the group, looked down on by some because he lacked their education, social background, and wardrobe. He had been educated by his famous literary family before attending the Royal College of Science, where he majored in biology and discovered a new species of fungus. At twelve, he traveled to Russia and lived with shepherd boys on the steppes; he later rescued Indians from prison and then flew an airplane solo in 1913. He also became a friend of T. E. Hulme, D. H. Lawrence, and H. G. Wells and wrote several novels and a three-volume autobiography; his hobby was beekeeping. He always felt like an outsider, was indifferent to luxury, and rarely had any money.

Garnett wrote about the Bloomsbury parties that Nancy attended. They were open to all, so one might run into the likes of Picasso or Douglas Fairbanks on any given night. At one, Nancy and Garnett noticed the servants peeking into one of the rooms as their beloved Mistress Vanessa Bell sang the risqué "Never Trust a Sailor an Inch Above Your Knee." The housemaid, weeping uncontrollably, had to be led to her room by the cook: how unrefined was milady! At another party, a costume revelry, Duncan arrived as a pregnant prostitute with a friend who came as a eunuch; at another, guests undressed; at yet another, Duncan, Clive, Vanessa, and Marjorie Strachey presented a farce and acted out complex love relationships of men disguised as women, and vice versa. Once, Vanessa performed a striptease and later made love with Maynard Keynes on a sofa. The group's relaxed behavior extended to their language, and their use of vulgarities also offended Nancy. According to Edel, Virginia was fond of four-letter words and in her milder moments made remarks such as "I knew there were buggers in Plato's Greece [and now] in the sitting room [here]. . . . Sex permeated our conversation. The word 'bugger' was never far from our lips. We discussed [it] with the same excitement and openness that we discussed the nature of the Good."[68]

Nancy endeared herself to Garnett because of her devotion to G. M.; Garnett had become his trusted friend. She once wrote him: "You know G. M. is really very ill. . . . Now, in vain, I ring up. Where are you while being 'out'? Do communicate with me before Sunday. . . . Or if we miss, don't fail to go and see G. M. Did you know he was as ill as he is? I am very upset. Affectionately, Nancy."[69] G. M., too genteel to tell Nancy about his prostate problems, was up and about when they next visited him.

Nancy's Early Poetry

Nancy's first published poem, "Soldiers Fallen in Battle," appeared in the June 1916 issue of the *Eton College Chronicle*, a year before Wilfred Owen wrote "Anthem for Doomed Youth"; both are similar in subject and imagery. Nancy begins:

> These die obscure and leave no heritage,
> For them no lamps are lit, no prayers said,
> And all men soon forget that they are dead,
> And their dumb names unwrit on memory's page.

After this, she published seven poems in the first of Edith Sitwell's six-volume *Wheels*; Nancy wrote the title poem, and George Moore praised her "exquisite ear for music" and said that the poems were "much better than I had thought."[70]

The poems are the work of a young writer experimenting with forms, especially the sonnet. They reflect an unpolished but talented young mind influenced by Matthew Arnold, Donne, Shakespeare, and Yeats. "Sonnet" antedates Yeats's "Sailing to Byzantium" ("That is no country for old men"), but rather than seek creative refuge in the world of timeless art, the poet laments her inescapable participation in a world of suffering and spiritual emptiness. With overtones of war in the opening lines, the poem focuses on how fate designs and dissects our souls. In a universe without mercy or God, a random force drives the world, and death, sin, and folly mock human endeavor. In "Wheels," there is a sense of futility, almost of hubris, in anticipating survival:

> This is no time for prayers or words or song.
> With folded hands we sit and slowly stare.
> The world's old wheels go round, and like a fair
> The clowns and peepshows ever pass along.
> Our brains are dumb with cold, and worn with strife,
> And every day has lingered on our faces
> Marking its usual course and weary paces
> With cruel cunning care and sober knife.
> Fate, like a sculptor, working with great tools,
> Now moulds his genius into clever ways;
> Our souls are cut and torn all for his praise
> When his great masterpiece is praised by fools;
> Yet winter comes like death, and takes the pride
> From his strong hands that held us till we died.

Images of a caravan, wheels and spokes, the circus, and cunning clowns merge in a Bosch-like image in the brooding title poem. Nancy seems to be saying that any attempt to make sense of human experience falters in a random "painted world" around which our lives and thoughts "form a jangling chain." We are driven in caravans by "the cunning of a thousand clowns" in a universe where innocence is overwhelmed and disorder reigns. At the head of our caravan is "Folly" (interestingly, the word Samuel Beckett uses in his last poetry to describe the madness of the human condition). Folly assumes the trappings of a satanic pied piper, scoffing at our attempts to find a home in the circus of the world and mocking our deepest emotions that might imply some hope of repair:

> Folly beats a drum with golden pegs,
> And mocks that shrouded Jester called Despair.

In "Remorse," a Shakespearean sonnet, Nancy confesses the indiscretions of her present life and imagines their consequences when she ages. One feels her guilt and need to accept the punishments she will endure. The poem suggests the empty passion Eliot will later depict between his carbuncular young man and typist in *The Waste Land*. She writes:

> I have been wasteful, wanton, foolish, bold,
> And loved with grasping hands and lustful eyes
> All through the hectic days and summer skies,
> And through the endless streets; but now am old
> And ill and bad—content with discontent,—
> Enduring the discomfort and the blows
> With sunken head and heart that shaking goes.
> Resigned to sit and wait in punishment,
> A martyr without claim, a parody
> Of classic crowned apostles and sweet saints
> Now praised in marble and in gorgeous paints
> Or singing in loud scores of harmony. . . .
> I sit ashamed and silent in this room
> While the wet streets go gathering in their gloom.

"Uneasiness" portrays a woman obsessed with lurking terror: "Tonight I hear a thousand evil things," during a "night [that] is young." The external "small bitter things" become indistinguishable from the inner self "with hearts, and maybe wings, / . . . That creep and grind and tear each other's souls." "From the Train" is a short image of the world of commerce and industry to which she cannot relate. After two parallel stanzas, the first cited below, she asks: "What can these ever mean to me?":

Smoke-stacks, coal stacks, hay stacks, slack,
Colorless, scentless, pointless, dull;
Highways, highways, roadways, black,
Grantham, Birmingham, Leeds and Hull.

Again, she anticipates Eliot's images of the modern urban city in "The Fire Sermon" section of *The Waste Land,* as well as his cadences in "Coriolanus."

● ● ●

As the decade came to a close, Pound disappeared from London, although his seminal role in the postwar London literary scene was soon more than amply filled. Eliot, largely through his magazine the *Criterion,* became the most important voice of the avant-garde and by 1920 was England's, if not the Western world's, most important critical voice. With the publication of *The Waste Land* in 1922, Eliot became a literary giant. The new forms designed by Pound and Eliot were as revolutionary and stimulating to the writers after them as Wordsworth's and Coleridge's had been to their successors after the *Lyrical Ballads.* Another artistic renaissance would follow in Paris, where Pound had moved and Nancy would relocate. But before then, she would suffer the effects of the war in London.

3

Counterpoint of War in London

There had been no war between the Great Powers since 1891.
No man in the prime of life knew what war was like. All imagined
that it would be an affair of great marches quickly ended.

—A. J. P. TAYLOR

The sheltered country girl reached adulthood during her brief stay in Munich and plunged into the bohemian life of London when Imagism, *Blast*, and the Bloomsberries were in the ascendancy. Intellectually and creatively nurtured by the distinguished artists she met, she was also bolstered by her friends in the Corrupt Coterie to rebel against convention and authority. She seemed to have found satisfaction in her new independence. However, from the mid-1910s until the end of the decade, Nancy faced serious moral and psychological challenges, and the Great War was critical in shaping her worldview. The Cunard family friend Prime Minister Herbert Asquith had been one of the architects of the war, and the government's optimism, alongside the grave reality of the war, gave Nancy an indelible lesson regarding the appalling disjuncture between diplomatic posturing and military reality. In 1916, she fell in love with a soldier who, after their very brief affair, died on the front. According to many who knew her, she never recovered from his death.[1]

The international situation and its impress on the home front created the counterpoint of war that played out alongside Nancy's daily activities. As early as 1915, at the same time that Nancy was interacting with the artists revolutionizing the literary world, she also suffered the war deaths of her friends Julian and "Billy" Grenfell, Raymond Asquith, Edward Horner, Cecil Macmillan, Charles Lister, and Patrick Shaw-Stewart; many more of her friends and acquaintances would subsequently fall in battle. Nancy, acutely aware of the events of her time, found her own way of responding to the unimagined destruction of the Great War. Casual sex became her means of comforting soldiers who were soon to face death or maiming. Although William Carlos Williams believed that her profligacy was redemptive, a pure act of "purgation," and Harold Acton referred to her as an "ascetic voluptuary" (her "liaisons were cerebral"),[2] both failed to understand the profound remorse that followed each encounter. Nancy's guilt as a "survivor" overwhelmed any satisfaction she might have felt in providing a distraction or pleasure to those going off to war, let alone any personal satisfaction. As her poetry reveals, she suffered shame, fear, and loneliness at the same time that she continued these "rituals"—feelings she confided only to Iris. By 1919, her intense awareness of the war and its costs in human lives, as well as her efforts to define herself personally and professionally, led to a nervous breakdown.

The Great War

William Manchester tries to make sense of what he calls the inane crimes that incited the Great War: "The explanation was not only complicated; it didn't even make sense." In effect, the Austrian archduke Ferdinand's assassination was just an excuse—an "insult"—around which Germany and the other nations waged battle.[3] The industrialization of Europe until this time had provided prosperity and social improvements, but it had also sparked a widespread nationalistic fervor that led to rampant jingoism and militarism. As popular fiction, newspapers, and magazines recounted each nation's martial history and revived local mythologies, they conjured up old enmities (for example, between Germany and Russia) and invited invidious comparisons with other nations. The modern Olympic Games, not yet twenty years old, set the tone for the heightened physical preparedness of the soon-vying warriors.

A spirit of competitive expansionism increased as nations formed alliances—each, honor bound to fight for the other. It was within this context that the Serbian insult to the Austro-Hungarians—in the murder of the archduke—had to be punished. Austria responded for the sake of its honor (and to forestall Russian hegemony in the Balkans). And Austria's ally, Germany, targeted nations linked with Serbia: Russia, France, and Britain. Many thought the conflict would end by Christmas.

Britain, true to its entente with France, entered the fray when Germany attacked the tiny, neutral country of Belgium. Unlike the other European nations, Britain lacked new territorial ambitions, although it clearly wanted to maintain the endless day of its colonial empire. But World War I was, if such a term may be applied, a schizoid period, both for those on the front and for those at home. There was an absurd disparity between the high-minded, ideal-istic men who fought in the war and the inadequate, anachronistic war plans that materialized. The war makers were under the illusion that "war [was] merely . . . one of the tools of statecraft. . . . They almost all believed that wars could be limited in scope and effect, and that modern industrial economics had rendered large, prolonged war impossible. They were, of course, com-pletely and disastrously wrong."[4]

When Britain declared war, an army arose that consisted entirely of vol-unteers—men fighting out of choice, rather than coercion. The pride of the most powerful nation in the world was reflected magnificently in the en-thusiastic volunteerism of its citizens. When Lord Kitchener posted "Your Country Needs YOU" and warned that it might be a long war, civilians spilled into the streets around each recruiting center. Kitchener called for 100,000 initially; by the end of the first week, 175,000 had volunteered; by the end of the month, 750,000. By the end of 1915, about 2.6 million had enlisted in Kitchener's Armies.[5] This ardent allegiance to nation was echoed by a sense of brotherhood in the battalions that subsequently formed. Single units called "Pals" collected men with common interests. They might have come from the same town, school, or university; they might have worked at a simi-lar job; one group, the "Bantams," consisted of men under 5 feet, 3 inches. Pride of country and cause was so intense in London that able-bodied men not in uniform risked having the humiliating white feather hurled at them, the emblem of cowardice. Factory workers wore badges that justified their presence in the city.[6]

The military was ill equipped for the extraordinary number of recruits and for the kind of battle that followed. British war plans, designed by the Regu-lar Army, relied on old-fashioned tactics—memories of Napoleonic victories sealed in a decisive clash of armor, of walking and running in battle, of rally-ing the cavalry. Diplomats and top military personnel were unprepared for a war that combined old strategies and new technologies—of cavalrymen, horse artillery brigades, flame throwers, heavy steel artillery; of automatic weapons, long-range rapid-firing artillery, barbed wire, and aircraft. The uselessness of the cavalry was not acknowledged until the Battle of the Somme in 1916:

Each year the industrial revolution had been clanking out new engines of death, but the graduates of Sandhurst . . . accepted them grudgingly if at all. Lord Kitch-ener dismissed the tank as a "toy." . . . Sir Douglas Haig . . . called the machine gun "a much overrated weapon." . . . The Stokes trench mortar was rejected twice. [It was] finally introduced by Prime Minister Lloyd George, who [was] branded "ungentlemanly." . . . The general staffs . . . insisted that no one should have a voice in prosecuting the war unless he had spent forty years in uniform. As Basil

Liddell Hart acidly noted, "this would have eliminated Alexander, Caesar, Cromwell, Marlborough, and Napoleon."[7]

Nothing deterred the rush of enlistees. Supplies and uniforms vanished almost immediately, and many young men drilled in civilian clothing. (There was no problem regarding steel helmets, since they wore none at the beginning of the war.) With a shortage of barracks, training areas, and rifles, many soldiers lived in tents or at home during the winter and practiced with sticks. For some, training consisted of marching to and fro and of practicing the fastest ways to enter and exit a train. Due to an insufficient supply of experienced instructors, elderly officers retired before Queen Victoria's death were called up. With munitions in short supply, 5 to 10 percent of the newly manufactured shells were "duds" (the word coined at the time).

London could boast that it was the most cultured city in the world, with a population of 7 million that dwarfed those of the other major cities of the world. Its slums had been nearly eliminated; crime and serious illness had been reduced. In effect, the greatest power in the world had been challenged by the strongest army in the world, but there was no doubt in any British mind that this highly industrialized, financial capital of the world—a Britannia that unequivocally ruled the waves—would be triumphant.

In meeting that challenge, a generation brought up on personal control and fierce patriotism and educated by the words of Tennyson, Robert Bridges, and Rupert Brooke would sacrifice itself for God and country. Brooke, Nancy's friend and the author of virtual wartime scripture, intoned:

If I should die, think only this of me:
That there's some corner of a foreign field
That is forever England. ("The Soldier")

A Cambridge graduate and president of the Fabian Society, Brooke had written: "There are only three things in the world—one is to read poetry, another is to write poetry, and the best of all is to live poetry." He died on the way to Gallipoli.

Nancy grew to despise the idea that to die for one's country was only proper and patriotic. But this sensibility was reflected throughout popular culture, and the idyllic English countryside, the subject of Georgian poetry, was transplanted to the war front in songs and poetry that created nostalgic equations of love and war. The soldiers in Picardy and on the Somme, like every London citizen, knew the popular song "The Roses of Picardy," in which England's beautiful roses filled the landscape of the battlefield.

People bought records of soldiers marching to drill sergeants' commands. David Jones's *In Parenthesis* became a best-seller; it rationalized war as the recovery of medieval chivalric values. Extremely popular thrillers like the Yellow Jacket series were set in wartime—formulaic mysteries and tales of espionage—and they always delivered a happy ending. Music halls and theaters sponsored shows about inevitable triumph; the renowned Harry Lauder, who traveled to the front, avowed the same in his performances. A study of the trench newspapers revealed that the word "defeat" was never used in the press, with the exception of one U-boat incident in 1917.[8]

In the beginning, Nancy took part in keeping public morale high. She danced in the "Omar Khayyám" charity matinees. When she performed "The Persian Garden Suite" wearing a toga and slippers, her image, in a particularly graceful pose, appeared in numerous newspapers. After she and Diana Manners sold programs for charity concerts, one photo caption described "Some Kindly 'Souls' Who Are Enabling . . . a Patriotic and Splendid Future."[9] Meanwhile, life on the warfront grew increasingly dismal, and Nancy avidly followed the news reports so she could track the events of the war. During the Ethiopian crisis and Spanish Civil War, she would distinguish herself as a war reporter. She would also write poems excoriating the desecrations of war.

Most of Europe's manpower was concentrated in a race extending from the Alps to the North Sea, as lines of opposing armies moved west and north seeking to outflank one another. By the end of 1914, the French and British were defending a network of trenches almost 475 miles long, with one soldier situated every four inches. By the end of the war, the British had dug 15,000 miles of trenches on the Western Front, which, combined with those of the Central Powers, were enough to circle the earth. Nancy was not amused by those who believed that the war had become an experiment in new social relationships: "It was almost embarrassing that an almost feudal cavalry class had to get off their horses and lie in the mud while industrious mechanics protected them with machine gun fire. . . . Ajax and Hercules were level with . . . the industrious mechanic."[10]

The 1913 entering class at Oxford lost 31 percent of its members, many of them acquaintances of Nancy and Iris. Those who returned on leave described the battles. The generals often remained behind the lines, seemingly blind to the realities in front of them. Committed to their old-fashioned rules of combat, most of their directives faltered against the kaiser's defenses. Some in the high command regarded trench mortar as "ungentlemanly"; they preferred the cavalry and continued to stride "about in gleaming field boots and jingling spurs or tour the lines in Rolls Royces, cursing slack discipline. . . . [Others] cherished their monocles, spotless white gloves, and black-and-silver saber knots." If a soldier looked even remotely disrespectful, he was punished. As one observer put it: "The minds and limbs of war were almost fatally divorced." The intense need to win was paramount, and trench briefings were "primitive," as "armies clawed at one another like dinosaurs whose brains had imperfect communication with their bloody claws and limbs."[11] Often at dawn,

> Tommies would crawl over their parapets, lie down in front of jump-off tapes and wait for their officers' zero-hour whistles. Then they would rise and hurtle forward toward as many as ten aprons of barbed wire with barbs as thick as a man's finger, backed by the pulsating Boche machine guns. A few trenches would be taken at a shocking cost—the price of 700 mutilated yards in one attack was 26,000 men and the beleaguerment would start again.[12]

The "successes" of the new war technology were apocalyptic: previously unimaginable slaughter that was the product of human inventiveness—machine-gun bullets and artillery bomb shells, Zeppelin bombings, and a variety of lethal gases that killed by slow asphyxiation (each marked by a unique scent: perfumed mustard gas; peppery pineapple chlorine gas; and phosgene, reeking of rotten fish). The suffering caused by each was indescribable. By the end of the war, 5.7 million British men had fought; 908,371 had been killed; more than 2 million (over one-third) had been wounded; 240,000 suffered full or partial amputations; and civilian casualties mounted to 30,633. During an average day on the Western Front, 2,533 men died; 9,121 were wounded; and 1,164 were blown up and therefore unidentified.[13]

Life in London had changed profoundly. Before the war, Nancy, like any English citizen, could live her life barely aware of the state, except for the sight of an occasional policeman or post office. With Asquith and the Liberals in power, the state helped only those who were unable to help themselves.[14] Now, ordinary, everyday activities had changed: paper banknotes had replaced gold coins; flower gardens had been transformed into vegetable gardens; women worked as ambulance drivers, farm laborers, blacksmiths, munitions makers, and gravediggers; the "God Save the King" tradition was initiated. "In Memoriam" notices in the press seemed to grow longer each day.

Personal restrictions were enforced. Homes had to remain in darkness at night due to air raids and to conserve coal; the government began to control prices; restrictions were placed on restaurants, theaters, train travel, and alcohol and clothing sales; even foxhunting was prohibited. British summer time (equivalent to daylight savings time in the United States) was implemented by an act of Parliament. Eventually, a new army had to be formed, because the soldiers in the old army had been injured or killed. Men up to fifty years old were "combed out." (Even when conscription began in 1916, many continued to volunteer, although they were once again rejected primarily for health reasons.) The entire generation that had been wiped out was replaced by older men. As one reporter put it, the new enlistments were "robbing the cradle and the grave to feed the holocaust."[15]

Paul Fussell reports that, except for sex and drinking, the greatest amusement for soldiers on leave was "in language"—the simple act of speaking to people, reading books and papers aloud, and listening to poetry. Nancy and Iris were hospitable in fulfilling all the soldiers' needs. Iris comments that these "youthful men" were restless and intense, and it was difficult "to augment their thirst for exploration through all the realms of being, released as they were on the wave of a new epoch." She recalls early rendezvous with the soldiers, when she and Nancy were prodigious in their generosity, "when desires were heightened to a brief fulfillment before sacrifice and the last prodigalities were showered upon our youthful intemperate young men."[16]

Many of the soldiers knew that their generation was bleeding to death, and their patriotism turned to cynicism and hopelessness. Siegfried Sassoon hurled his military cross into the sea and prayed "that you may never know / The hell where youth and laughter go" ("Suicide in the Trenches"). Nancy and Iris learned a great deal about the war from the soldiers, particularly on their dates and when they worked in the canteens. They heard about the mass graves in France and Belgium where many bodies were buried together under a single headstone. Eventually, there were 2,500 British war cemeteries in the two countries.

The young women listened to and consoled their guests. The soldiers spoke of the three B's—barbed wire, bullets, and bayonets—as well as of starvation and, if they were lucky, the stretchers that would carry them to a casualty clearing station. They felt guilty in wishing for a "blighty" or "jammy" wound, one that was not disabling but serious enough to remove them from battle. The alternative was unthinkable: to be half-buried in the trenches. For most, the "trench" would become their universe: "You had a trench knife, a trench cane, a . . . trench periscope, and if you were unlucky, trench foot, trench mouth, or trench fever."[17] To live in the trenches was to abide the unabating stench of urine, excrement, and rotting flesh. It was to live with large black rats that fed on the dead around them, and the rats were the size of cats. The filth of the trenches was a breeding ground for diseases like Weil's syndrome, a jaundice spread by rats; gangrene from the manure in the soil; skin blisters, vomiting, and eye pain from residual poison gas; unending itching and sores from lice, which also carried typhus and the new disease, trench fever; and shell shock, the sudden rush of air that entered the spinal fluid. There would be 80,000 cases of shell shock on the Western Front.[18] The psychological damage from everyday occurrences—finding a decomposed body on barbed wire, walking in the soil and stepping on the leg of a man or horse—would be inestimable.

Only seventy miles from the front—the "stinking world of sticky and trickling earth"—was the rich velvet of London theater seats and the perfume, alcohol, and cigarettes of the Café Royal. It is therefore not entirely surprising that many soldiers, a short distance from home, received regular mail deliveries—packaged sweets from Harrods or Fortnum and Mason, footballs, books, cigarettes, wristwatches (a trench fad), and everything from gramophones and binoculars to anti-lice medications. With their brand-new footballs and other equipment, some soldiers stood far behind the lines and played sports; others read aloud or performed plays. Shortly before the Somme, ceremonial horse shows were held.[19] At night, the full war resumed, and for those in the ditches and not at artillery, it was necessary to contract their bodies into as small a space as possible. They lay in a fetal-like position with virtually no mobility.

The British remained at war for 1,500 days—four years and three months—and back in London, as in any British town or village, the staggering death tolls, as well as every citizen's daily encounters with the war-wounded, eradicated earlier notions of honor and glory and exposed the gruesome truths of war. T. S. Eliot, later in *The Waste Land* (1922), transfigured the Georgian paradisal English countryside into a more realistic image of the moral and spiritual drought of both the country and city:

> I think we are in rats' alley
> Where the dead men lost their bones.
>
> What branches grow
> Out of this stony rubbish?

From the start, Nancy followed the radio and press coverage of both major and minor events.[20] Queen Mary expressed her despair that the war would never end: "The length of this horrible war is most depressing. I really think it gets worse the longer it lasts." Nancy was similarly demoralized and, like so many others, wrote to the soldiers and mailed gifts to the front. She later wrote a poem that echoed the queen's sentiments:

> No god is yet arisen, who with fair
> Firm judgment should arrest this course of war
> And make destruction cease; say: "Nature's law
> Too long hath broken been." None yet may dare

Hold out a mighty hand, bid Death withdraw,
Or break the current of this world-despair. ("War")

Iris speaks with great frankness about her own and Nancy's experiences. What "bound us," she explains, was a sense of "loneliness and death," followed by a cycle of hedonism and guilt—guilt that they were still alive as others were dying:

> Together we had braved the panic of first bombings over London, and watched their fires redden on sky and river, ourselves burnt out by the terrible gaieties of last encounters, now made unreal by the realities of war—all the metal and struggle, trains, ships, mourning, noise of unknown distances from which we were excluded as figures of illusion—a theme that left its shadow on us both in different ways.[21]

During the air raids, bombs pounded London as though the city were a battle-field. Since the raids usually occurred after midnight, buses, taxis, and cars, along with many citizens, disappeared from the streets by 11:00 P.M. Telephone and telegraph service ceased. The skies were emblazoned with great pencils of light streaming upward from the city's numerous searchlights crisscrossing the heavens in hunt for the elusive Germans.

There had been two responses to the blasting sirens. Many people left their homes only when it was imperative and immediately rushed for cover when the sirens began. Most ran to the nearest tube station, but some fled into the closest shelter, often a flimsy wooden building that shook from side to side. Others raced into hotels and joined the guests on their nightly (or twice night-ly) pilgrimage to the basement. The population grew expert in the sounds in the air: the dull booms from an explosion, the whistling or shriek of shells, the rattle of shrapnel fragments on the roofs and streets. The first American killed during the London air raids had been staying in a hotel—Lena Gilbert Ford, the one-time beauty from Elmira, New York, who wrote "Keep the Home Fires Burning."

Many Londoners defied the enemy by seeking out theaters or restaurants that had remained open. Their attitude was not one of careless indifference but of intentional defiance of the Huns' efforts to terrorize them. But when the sirens began, they, too, ran to the closest tube and felt "the sensation of being a helpless part of an evil-smelling mass that slowly coiled its way up what seemed hundreds of steps"—all of this in almost total darkness. After-ward, they also shared the relief of being "vomited out of the black-hole into the fresh air!"[22] On occasion, a defiant child raced his bike through the streets while bombs and antiaircraft guns spit their shells into the street.

Nancy, Iris, and their friend Diana Manners were part of the defiant citizenry. They disguised their sense of imminent danger by dressing up in elaborate gowns and going out to meet friends—to converse, drink, dance, and flirt. One journalist described them as an "inseparable trio of beauties—a kind of Mayfair troika of friendship, elegance, intelligence and daring . . . leaders of the new generation of debutantes, in evening clothes, [who also] watched the Zeppelins." Yet when the sirens roared, they also ran for cover in the tubes and became a part of the foul-smelling, frightened fugitives wondering how they would get home—and, indeed, if their home would still be standing. That they remained safe increased their survival guilt. Iris repeats that after they returned home "by ourselves then, we tasted the guilt of our immunity, reproachful pain accusing those it spares. And the grave evenings [following a spree of parties] seeped through us with their chill of loneliness and death."[23]

As the war continued, losses mounted in staggering proportions; the enemy was "bleeding the Allies white." Of the 70 million mobilized, over one in eight was killed or died in active service.[24] Throughout, Nancy and Iris pursued the same lifestyle: mixing with writers and painters, raising money and volunteering for other wartime charitable work, taking country walks together and reading aloud or writing poetry, participating in the colorful adventures of the Corrupt Coterie, and attending to their sexual ministrations before soldiers departed for battle, followed by a sense of despair and loneliness. Even when they escaped to the countryside, they allotted time for the soldiers. If they traveled to Kent to Iris's mother's house, as Nancy wrote in a poem, after they "walked through rusty autumn woods or across hop fields," they made their way to the village station, where young admirers arrived on farewell leave before departing to the bloody fields of battle. The young men, eager for amorous adventure and war, were loaded down with weapons, gas masks, food tins, and entrenching tools—all buried in their coats and caps. They also carried one or two talismen that they stroked in magical rituals that might keep them alive. This reinforced the sense of mission in which Nancy and Iris made their romantic liaisons.

Several times during the war, G. M. insistently asked Nancy to "tell me about your lovers." She concluded that it would be impossible to tell him about her experiences, "disjointed accounts of late hours at wild parties, . . . of drinking in the Café Royal Brasserie with tipsy poets and 'chaps' on leave, of poker-playing, war-work in canteens—even of the dread, more and more justified, that every young man one liked was going to be killed at the front. All of it would have had to be told in slow detail. No, no; unthinkable."[25]

As Nancy followed the news, she read about the Marne, where the British fought the largest battle since Waterloo; the devastation at Gallipoli, site of the Homeric tragedy of the Anzacs (Australians and New Zealanders); Ypres, where the Germans released 168 tons of poison gas. The slaughterhouses of Verdun, the Somme, and Passchendale were to follow. In one poem, Nancy described all of humanity as "weary armies on a solemn march," pursuing the charade of peace. In their glorified rationalizations of war, she wrote, they denied the grotesqueries of battle and blindly embraced a vision of "their own decease," in what were, in fact, glorified "dreams of death." If she had "a firmer heart," she continued, "devoid of hesitation" during these "barren times," perhaps she could understand their professed noble aims and find a meaningful justification for the slaughter of war. Then she could get beyond their foolish dreams and "write a song to conquer all our tears" that would last "forever through the folding years" ("The Carnivals of Peace").

Military and administrative failures had forced Asquith's resignation in 1916 and his replacement by Lloyd George and the new coalition. The nation, deeply affected by Britain's losses, was periodically buoyed by patriotic statements issued by the new prime minister and others: "Every position must be held to the last man; there will be no retirement, with our backs to the wall, and believing in the justice of our cause each of us must fight to the end."[26] There were other resignations by friends of the Cunards, such as Lord Haldane, because of his German education.

The British had passed the Aliens Restriction Act in 1914, limiting jobs and areas of residence for those of German and Austrian heritage. Males of military age had been interned; mothers and their children were urged to return home. After the sinking of the *Lusitania*, all alien males were interned; women and children were deported. (By 1916, at least 32,000 had been interned and 10,000 deported.) The enemy's chemical warfare, its zeppelin raids, and the sinking of the *Lusitania* led to enormous anti-German sentiment, and this was reflected in every area of life: Thomas Beecham refused to play German music; the Lindenhof became the Hotel Westminster; editors of the *Cambridge Medieval History* rejected previously accepted papers from German scholars; King George changed his family name from Saxe-Coburg-Gotha to Windsor; sauerkraut was no longer served in restaurants.[27]

Nancy and Iris continued to do their part in the war effort, after which they resumed their more ordinary activities, but these were always profoundly altered by their encounters with soldiers. They spoke about their experiences together; Nancy tried to express her feelings in writing, reflecting in an early poem the understated: "There were wandering journeys . . . in dusty trains," after which "we [told] our dreams more slowly" ("Iris of Memories"). Later, she was more specific in referring to the young men she had met. Many of them, for example, had confessed their fears that an order to France or Flanders was virtually a death sentence. (For every nine ordered to either location, five were killed, wounded, or missing in action.) Nancy and Iris knew young men from Oxford and Cambridge who called themselves the "Suicide Club." They were so named because they boasted of looking death straight in the face and laughing, but it was clear that they were also frightened. Nancy refers to them in her poem "Destruction," in which a personified death figure follows men sacrificing themselves to the inferno of their own dreams:

> I saw the people climbing up the street
> Maddened with war and strength and thought to kill.
> And after followed Death, who held with skill
> His torn tags, royally, and stamped his feet.

Although Death follows and is the conqueror, his victory, unlike Donne's in "Death Be Not Proud," is real, not pyrrhic:

> Death followed with proud feet and smiling stare,
> And the mad crowds ran madly up and down.

Death, "laughing at their bitter pain," knows that men "will forever take up their guns."

Many of the soldiers left Nancy's bed for the bottomless mud of Flanders Field, where long poppies eventually grew between the crosses to mark 150,000 new graves. Nancy knew, as everyone knew, about the grisly occasions when mass graves were opened to identify remains: bodies blown to bits; identity discs discovered on shattered corpses. Most terrifying for the soldiers, and difficult to listen to, was the young men's uncertainty of any kind of burial — so many bodies had been ripped apart and sunk into the mud on which their replacements would sleep.

Wartime Affection and Disaffection

In 1916 Nancy met a Grenadier Guards officer, Peter Broughton Adderly. A bright, handsome, and friendly man, Peter loved children, and he won their hearts through his sincerity, charm, and kindness, just as he won Nancy's. She recalls their five-day romance, after which he was killed: "My love and I sitting in a tree, and under a tree, read aloud to each other several days running from *The Story Teller's Holiday*, the beauty of the writing, the mood of the book and our own and everything about those hours being unaccountably moving. They were hours put away for ever soon after under the seal of death."[28] If Nancy never recovered from this loss, it may be that Peter's death immortalized the idealization of early romance that life inevitably undermines.

If Daphne Fielding is correct in placing this relationship in 1916, rather than 1917 or 1918,[29] it is not surprising that everyone was shocked when Nancy announced later in the year that she was going to marry Sydney Fairbairn, also an officer in the Guards, a tall, dark-haired, and handsome Australian who had been injured at Gallipoli. As the London press reported Nancy's engagement, "A halo of mystery was made to shroud the event for the world at large. Perhaps it was out of deference to broken hearts." In the midst of the terrible war, the social columnists had at last something to write about. In September, one desperate reporter had written: "There has been a revolution in journalism so far as the dailies are concerned of late. Have you noticed that we have hardly any mention of Lady Diana Manners, Miss Nancy Cunard and their friends? This will never do. We cannot allow our fashionable beauties to retire as easily as cabinet ministers."[30]

While well educated and the son of a socially respectable family, Sydney was culturally and intellectually unsophisticated, as different from Nancy as Bache had been from Maud. He was certainly unlike Peter Broughton Adderly. When Maud asked, "Are you sure you want to go through with it?" Nancy replied, "I gave my word and I must." Nancy's sense of honor triumphed over one of Maud's rare insightful moments.

No fewer than twenty-seven items about the engagement appeared: "The only child of two tremendously rich people, Miss Cunard is one of the catches of the season. . . . He is one of the best looking in his regiment. . . . It is a case of the brave deserving the fair all over again"; "Miss Nancy Cunard is having a splendid trousseau made. She and her mother have most original ideas. They give many hints to those who design their own gowns."[31] There was even greater coverage of the wedding. Many articles described Bache in connection with the Cunard Line; Maud, in terms of her "huge fortune." One reporter spoke of "Nancy who seems such a baby." Another wrote: "Miss Cunard is 'an exquisite specimen of English girlhood.' . . . Her hobby in life will probably be dogs."[32]

Nancy married Sydney in the afternoon of November 15, 1916, at the Grenadier Guards' Chapel. She wore a long gold dress, a turban-shaped toque of orange blossoms, and a net veil that covered each shoulder and was the length of her dress. She omitted most of the traditional accoutrements—gloves, a bouquet, and bridesmaids. Maud wore rose velvet and sable. The guests included the French, Italian, and Spanish ambassadors and an assortment of dukes, duchesses, lords, and ladies. The ceremony was followed by Maud's curious ritual in which the still-estranged and now embarrassed Bache showered silver coins on the guests, rather than rice on the bride and groom. The newlyweds went to Devon and Cornwall for their honeymoon. When they returned, they moved into a house on Montague Street, a wedding gift from Maud. Shortly after the wedding, the press renewed its vigorous coverage: "I am sorry I re-ferred to Mrs. Sydney Fairbairn by her maiden name, Miss Nancy Cunard, the other week. But some of these maiden names, when they belong to highly pop-ular people, have a habit of sticking in the mind." When "the highly popular people" married, another reporter queried (still using their previous names), "I wonder if I shall live to see a queue outside the butcher's with Lady Diana [Manners], Nancy Cunard, Elizabeth Asquith, and all the rest of the most pho-tographed young women waiting bags in hand . . . at the fishmonger's."[33]

Nancy referred to the twenty months she spent with Sydney as one of the most unhappy periods of her life. Photos in her scrapbook reveal a cheerful husband and a somber wife. It was one thing to spend an evening with a wounded soldier; another, to marry him. Although there is no evidence to support this, Anne Chisholm suggests that Nancy "may have found the sexual side of her marriage difficult"; perhaps, she also suggests, she felt as trapped in marriage as in living with her mother. But given the brevity of Nancy and Sydney's courtship and, more important, its rebound nature when Nancy was mourning Peter's death, it seems inevitable that the marriage fail. Even re-porters at the time observed that Nancy was not thriving: "I am sorry to hear that Mrs. Sidney [sic] Fairbairn, better remembered perhaps as pretty Miss Nancy Cunard, is suffering from a horrid attack of bronchitis."[34]

After separating from Sydney (they were not officially divorced until 1925), Nancy refused to move into her mother's home, and this became one of her darkest periods. "The many young men I loved were all dead," she wrote. She decided to return to the bohemian life; this was the same time when, perhaps not coincidentally, Sydney had been recalled to the front.

Nancy remained as striking in appearance as ever—elegant, extremely thin, smoking, drinking, and "very 'bohemian' in her habits." She developed her friendship with Sybil Hart-Davis, who was part of the Wyndham Lewis–Augustus John group, which aroused Iris's jealousy. Nancy's relationship with Iris had been the first of her passionate, nonsexual alliances with women; Sybil would be the second. Nancy found a combination of affection and se-curity with women that she rarely found with men. Iris, now married, told her husband: "I was at first jealous [of Sybil], then pained, but in [a] saner mood I realized that there was no cause for envy or distress." No one could love Nancy, she continued, "more than me. . . . One loves [Nancy's] abandon-ment to pleasure, her priesthood to it." She avowed her abiding love.[35]

Sybil was eleven years older than Nancy, the mother of two children and a sister of Duff Cooper, and during one summer, Sybil, Nancy, and the chil-dren shared a country house in Oxfordshire. Both of their husbands were on the front (although Nancy had no intention of returning to Sydney, she still wrote him regularly and sent him sweets), and Nancy found another role model in her older friend. The pretty and unconventionally chic Sybil was well educated, witty, and charming. Nancy thought that Sybil was the most liberated woman she had ever met.

During that summer, Nancy read a great deal and discovered the work of the provocative Norman Douglas. The successful, critically acclaimed, and uncloseted gay author of *South Wind* would become one of Nancy's beloved older friends, as G. M. continued to be. Nancy and Sybil also spent a great deal of time with Mary and John Hutchinson, who became Nancy's loyal friends. Nancy discussed with Sybil, as she had with Iris, the old and new literature and the latest psychological theories, including the work of her friend Havelock Ellis and his *Psychology of Sex*. For a good part of their time, however, the two women held wild parties with their London artist-friends and military officers, and everyone drank heavily.

They were keenly aware of the daily postings of the war dead, and Nancy now had "sometimes two or three [officers] at the same time." She told Sybil she had been "lost" after Peter died. Sybil's son, Rupert Hart-Davis (later the esteemed publisher), recalled their day parties:

> My sister and I spent the long daylight hours playing outside, while inside the house [it seemed] a perpetual party—young officers, wounded and whole, artists and writers, Augustus John in the uniform of a War Artist, "Chile" Guevara, . . . the Sitwell brothers, over from some camp or barracks, and a forgotten crowd of others. Drink (I suppose some form of fairly potent cup) was dispensed from huge glass jugs, and there always seemed to be plenty.

He also reported an event reminiscent of Bache's return to Holt when his wife's guests were exchanging cries from the "Ride of the Valkyries": "Once my father came home on leave from France, suspected that some guest was my mother's lover and threatened a fist-fight. Nancy, my mother, my sister and I locked ourselves in the bathroom till the din subsided."

Nancy returned to London at the end of the summer. As she walked through the city, the reality of the war dead was omnipresent. Hourly memorials for the deceased, recited to the music of Chopin or Mendelssohn, frequently included prayers with "always in our heart," "never forgotten," and "in our thoughts always"—words also carved on the headstones.[36] Lines from war poems were also recited:

> They shall grow not old, as we that are left grow old:
> Age shall not weary them, nor the years condemn,
> At the going down of the sun and in the morning
> We will remember them. (Laurence Binyon, "For the Fallen")

Nancy evoked the mood of the times in a later poem, of the horror of war for both the soldiers and those left mourning them:

And yet we live while others die for us;
Live in the glory of sweet summer, still
Knowing not death, but knowing that life will
Be merciless to them—and so to us.
Blood lies too rich on many battlefields,
Too many crowns are made for solemn sorrow;
We rise from weeping, and the cruel morrow
Has nought, but to a further sorrow yields. ("War")

The many people dressed in black on the city streets had received news of their sons and husbands by a letter returned from the front with the word "KILLED" stamped on it. A telegraph boy later carried the dreaded news on a red bicycle.

Makeshift street and church shrines appeared daily—places for grieving and praying. Some parishes put up as many as ten shrines. In 1918, the Hyde Park memorial became a site for as many as 60,000 people at one time. Cemeteries were built near medical centers; a bugle sounded at least twenty times a day, announcing funerals. There were always new advertisements for "dealing with the war"—séances, palm readings, spirit photography, and other magical rituals. The YMCA offered sober entertainment; there were concerts for and by the wounded soldiers: up to hundreds at one time, in their blue or gray hospital uniforms, participated. Most had lost an arm or leg, or more. They sang in chorus like schoolboys; they were cheerful, not downhearted.

Every evening at Charing Cross station, trains arrived from Dover, carrying the wounded, who were then transferred to waiting ambulances. Many of the soldiers smiled beneath or above their red bandages. So many—almost an entire generation—had been destroyed. Those who returned, wearing a stripe on their sleeves for each wound or silver badges that marked their discharge due to disability, were forever changed, with severed limbs, rheumatism, pleurisy, ulcers, chlorine gas poisoning, malaria, shell shock, or another mental illness. Of those who had stayed at home, particularly women, thousands suffered the effects of anxiety, aggression, and grief. Because so many of the 36,000 hospital beds set aside for the military were occupied, emergency units opened throughout London. At the end of the war, another terror struck: sixty people a day died from the flu and pneumonia epidemics.[37]

As so many war writers have said, the loss of innocence was incalculable. Perhaps Hemingway said it best in A Farewell to Arms: "Abstract words such as glory, honor, courage, or hallow were obscene beside the concrete names of villages, the numbers of roads, the names of rivers, the numbers of regiments and the dates." Charles S. Sorley, killed when he was twenty, had begun a sonnet:

> Such, such is death: no triumph: no defeat:
> Only an empty pail, a slate rubbed clean,
> A merciful putting away of what has been.

The *Oxford Book of English Verse* had an abundance of poems on loss.

Nancy, always a voracious reader, knew these poems, as she knew the popular tunes and cynical parodies they inspired. "If You Were the Only Girl in the World" (1916) had been answered by Sassoon's sharp rejoinder that such songs "mocked the corpses round Bapaume." The talented Edgell Rickwood, who would share many of Nancy's social causes and later become her lover, wrote poems that reiterated Hemingway's unromanticized vision of war and sacrifice, expressing his disdain for England's patriotic poets. "Under the Sign of Donne" begins: "I knew a man, he was my chum," yet "he grew blacker every day" and could "not brush the flies away." And in a bitter letter to Nancy's friend Osbert Sitwell, Wildred Owen, the greatest of the war poets, rendered his training of new British troops:

> For fourteen hours yesterday I was at work—teaching Christ to lift his cross by numbers, and how to adjust his crown; and not to imagine his thirst until after the last halt. I attended his Supper to see that there were no complaints; and inspected his feet that they were worthy of the nails.[38]

In many poems in *Outlaws*, not published until 1921, Nancy confesses that her sexual promiscuity emanated from her despair toward the war. In "What Is This Cry for Toys," she is both maternal and childlike, giving herself to what Wilfred Owen called "the pity of war." She reveals her compassion and sense of self-sacrifice; she views both the soldiers and herself as victims of war with silenced voices and mechanical behavior. She is filled with tenderness for the soldiers entering battle and fully aware that her liaisons are solely gestures of sympathy:

> What is this cry for toys? you've had them all;
> This clamoring for lovers? take your choice:
> Outgrown and senseless dolls with timid voice,
> Like marionettes unstrung they can but fall
> Into your merciful hands, your tender grasp

That pities them and tidies up their tears;
The while you wince, yet put away their fears.

"Yet When the Night Draws On" is about her indiscriminate selection of lovers. She would offer any soldier a different kind of "rest" than his certain fate of ultimate sleep. She anticipates Hemingway's ironic play on the word "arms" in A *Farewell to Arms*:

> Yet when the night draws on, you long for arms,
> Arms to unfold, becalm your soul away,
> Gestures to quell, a voice that says: "To-day
> Is a spent nightmare, rest you from alarms
> And be unharassed; you have done with fear
> For a short season and shall claim reward,
> That share of victory that has been stored
> For you in well-kept sequence, costing dear."
> And in the sunset stillness of that hour
> Maybe you'll dream of lying down with Death,
> Your ultimate lover; but your soul and breath
> Must first be parted by that unknown power
> Of time or fate, whatever name is given
> To that strange path that's said to lead to heaven.

Nancy recalls the variety of her young soldiers, all of whom she found equally beautiful. Even those who "stole and swore" were more innocent than the engineers of the war. The elegiac mood of "The Lovers," as well as its gentle tone, rhymes, and rhythms, remind one of Shakespeare's "golden lads" and A. E. Housman's "rose-lipt maidens":

> Hundreds of lovers there have been,
>   Princes and clowns and fools;
> Mighty, timid, low, obscene,
> And some whose hearts were never clean
>   Who set aside all rules.
>
> Dark lovers from the burning lands,
>   And giants from the plain,
> And some with wicked cruel hands
> And some God made and understands,
>   And more than Death has slain.

Pale boys too beautiful to live,
    Too wild and proud and young,
With eager eyes and hearts that give
A love this life cannot forgive.

. . . .

Now Death has stolen all away
    And bade them love and kiss
Pale shadows of a yesterday,
With empty hands and hearts that sway
In darker worlds than this.

In "1917," nature goes awry because of humanity's activities. The sun responds to the hatred that motivates human war-making:

The curtains of the sky are tightly drawn;
As in a horrid sunken maze the sun
Is veiled with wickedness, and all the streets
Shine horribly and wanly at noontide.

. . . .

And in the silence of the winter night
There are as yet no signs of moon or dawn.

This unending war has bred vacancy in nature, and hopelessness, fear, and weariness in the human realm:

In the minds of men there is no hope,
No spark of courage to foresee the end
Of the long-reigning period of this war.
While like the murmur of a thousand clocks
Wild apprehensions crowd into the days,
And force their weary fingers at our throats.

Again borrowing an image from Eliot, she comments on the fruitlessness of even pretending to accept the war:

There is no use in putting on a mask
. . . to death and strife.

Ultimately, war must end but so, too, will the ideals for which it has been fought:

And when the war is ended, glorious dreams
. . . planned and nurtured with our blood . . .
Will float unseizable from our weak hands;
And there will be no joy of road or sea,
No freedom of fresh countries and rich towns,
No glory in a peace that comes too late.

The Great War—so named "to prevent [people] from forgetting that the history of the world is the history of war"[39]—was unprecedented in its carnage. At Verdun, 750,000 died, and at the Somme, 30,000 were killed in the first half hour.

● ● ●

In 1917, the American Expeditionary Force entered the war, and gradually the tide of battle turned decisively. At 11:00 A.M., on November 11, 1918, all of London rejoiced when the armistice went into effect. People celebrated for three days, cheering, crying, climbing on top of cars, throwing paper from buildings, racing in and out of pubs. One rainy day, they climbed Nelson's Column in Trafalgar Square. Tommies walked the street with two, three, or four girls flanking them. The "Yanks," the name that replaced "Sammies," had been treated as saviors from the day the million doughboys had arrived, with parades and chants of "Give 'em Hell!" in front of Buckingham Palace. American flags decorated Trafalgar Square, and large and small celebrations took place everywhere. During the demonstrations, Nancy wept: "Oh Peter, it's too cruel, all the associations of this place and the waves of thought . . ."

1. Nancy, holding Buster

2. Nevill Holt

3. Irish patriot Robert Emmet, Nancy's "great-granduncle"

4. Maud and Bache Cunard

5. Nancy, at school

6. Iris Tree

7. The menu of the Eiffel Tower

8. Augustus John, self-portrait

9. Wyndham Lewis

10. *Blast*, the voice of Vorticism

11. Edward, Prince of Wales

12. Ezra Pound

13. T. S. Eliot

14. Virginia Woolf

15. Nancy (*second from left*) and her friends volunteer for war charity

16. Nancy (*right*) in a tableau vivant at a war-bond event

E. O. Hoppe

MISS NANCY CUNARD

The engagement of Miss Nancy Cunard to Lieutenant Sidney Fairbairn was announced some little time ago, and the date of the
marriage will, we understand, be shortly fixed. Miss Nancy Cunard
is the only daughter of Sir Bache and Lady Cunard, and Lieutenant
Fairbairn is in the Grenadier Guards

17. The announcement of Nancy's engagement

18. Sydney Fairbairn, Nancy's husband

**THE AUTHOR OF " OUTLAWS " : MRS. SYDNEY FAIRBAIRN,
FORMERLY MISS NANCY CUNARD.**

Mrs. Sydney Fairbairn, the daughter of Sir Bache and Lady
Cunard, is well known as a poet, and used to contribute to
" Wheels," the yearly production of the smart intellectual set,
which contains the work of such authors as the Sitwells, Aldous
Huxley, etc. She has recently published a new book of poems
entitled " Outlaws."—[*Portrait-Study by Bertram Park.*]

19. *Outlaws* is published

4

Postwar Breakdown

Who has ever explained away the sudden invasion of despair?

—NANCY CUNARD

In January 1919, Nancy, not quite twenty-three, contracted a severe case of the life-threatening influenza that was stalking the world; pneumonia followed. She also experienced a "serious case of nerves" and "uncertainty about self nearly all the time." As the year drew to an end and at the urging of her physician, she spent a month at a rest home in Surrey.

Always impatient when she was incapacitated, Nancy's attitude toward the flu, despite its severity, was anger and frustration. She convalesced at her mother's house on Grosvenor Square and after three months, still exhausted physically and mentally, went to the south of France to complete her recuperation. Her school friend Marie Ozanne became her traveling companion. Nancy was comfortable talking to Marie ("Am I really an iconoclast of people's ideals?"), flattered when Marie said that she "should, she must" become a writer, and relieved to forgo the company of her mother and Thomas Beecham. The two women traveled widely during April and May—to Eze, Beaulieu, Antibes, Cagnes, Cannes, Frejus, Grasse, Gourdon, Avignon, Vaucluse, Les Baux; they returned in June.

From April until December 1919—the trip to France and first six months back in London—Nancy kept a locked diary, a chronicle of her experiences and meditations so detailed that they filled three volumes.[1] Within them she included memorabilia—photos of ruins, bridges, churches, rivers, flowers, sunsets, and mountains, as well as dinner invitations, menus, notes from admirers, clipped magazine images, and poems as she was composing them. Her entries include the usual details—of scenery, the men she met, "dry meals worthy of a tramp's indigestion and indignation," the books she was reading (by G. M., Swinburne, Kate Chopin, Maupassant, Tolstoy, Dostoevsky, and "the vulgarian Compton MacKenzie"), and witty anecdotes. In the mid-1950s, Nancy asked a locksmith to open the diaries, and she added retrospective comments.

The three volumes offer a unique vantage point from which to gain a glimpse of the authentic Nancy—a Romantic in the literary sense of the term, gifted with an astonishing intelligence, facility with language, and sense of humor. In their candor, they also offer an opportunity to learn about her wild escapades, as well as her dreams and deepest fears as she contemplates her life, especially her future. Reading the diary is like listening to an inner monologue. In the first section we discover a highly nervous, insecure, childlike Nancy, frightened to be alone and to meet people. She feels compelled to assume different roles to be successful and frequently tells herself, for example, to laugh a great deal or to dress in a specific way. In the London section, we meet the same insecure celebrity socialite. Now back in the world of her friends, she mourns Peter, reexperiences her former survivor guilt, and indulges in a great amount of both alcohol and sex. Her usual escape mechanisms, however, grow increasingly unsuccessful, and she is overwhelmed by her inability to fulfill her present needs: to be free of her mother in a home of her own and to do something significant with her life. She still bears the public image of a rich, beautiful, and self-indulgent daughter of the aristocracy.

In Her Own Words

The diary is filled with arresting observations. Negotiating a train station in the south of France "is like going to one's execution, feeling both will be delayed and disordered, untidy, ghastly with crowds." In Nice, "the cocottes walk in a peculiar way as pleasing . . . as the meringues and fantastic cakes in one of their superpatisseries." Nancy recounts several heated debates about French and English men "and the way love is conducted in the two countries—lack of enterprise in . . . the latter and lack of imagination and originality in the former." Her experiences vary in seriousness. At one point she jests, "We turn from the sublime and wallow in the ridiculous, that net of irresponsible laughter and jokes that passes for wit." At times she is optimistic: "It is good to think one *could* do *anything* one wanted—a doctrine of liberty [with] money and health for foundation, and then as many temples and palaces built by imagination as you please."

Large sections of the diary record Nancy's oppressive associations with the war, including her first and last entries. Departing on a rainy day, April 9, 1919, she notices that the train is filled with nannies and

German carriages of red, hard plush (a curious spoil of War). Amiens and the surrounding houses [are] all battered and broken with shells and air-raids; on the left, trenches, and the frightful melancholy of northern France heavy over everything.

Returning to London on June 6:

Here is all the green gloom of England rising up around me, the depressing . . . long, damp fields. . . . My first impression of return—everyone dead, Denny, Edward, Patrick, Raymond, George, Billy.

Mainly, she writes about two or three interrelated subjects: her intense longing for direction in life, and the depression, if not despair, imposed by her sense of aimlessness. Unable to tolerate loneliness, she describes the panic she feels when she is not actively engaged in activities. Most striking—because she believes it will lead to her salvation—is her quest for a transcendent ideal, either in romantic love or in nature. Either, she hopes, will end her loneliness and provide lasting happiness. This quest is not simply the product of the young woman's fancy; it will become an abiding passion for the rest of her life and later manifest itself as well in the pursuit of social causes. I quote at some length from the diary because it affords an extraordinary window into a brilliant and troubled mind.

Nancy was always optimistic at the beginning of an experience, and it was in this mood that she described the allure of travel: "I started this voyage with the presentiment that everything would change henceforth and for the good." But her enthusiasm soon waned: "There's a vague promise of excitement in the air and nothing ever happens"—a statement of disappointment that would often occur after her initial optimism. Such lines recur as "Oh God shall I ever get into any *mood* here, and not be finding it forever incomplete?" She makes the unexpected admission that, had she the choice, she would pursue a life of leisure: "I'm more than ever convinced that a life of leisure can be made flawlessly perfect and scientifically right (with never a moment wrong or incomplete) but that [one] who [accomplishes] this (and after how much labor) is a genius," perhaps revealing her fear of failure in the present world she inhabits.

All the same, she is overwhelmed by leisure time because it brings forth unwanted introspection and anxiety, "the surging up of old discontents. . . . I suffer from it too often here, have too long a leisure to worry about nerves."

Sometimes she is soothed by a "long solitary unspoiled walk": she sees "a hurricane along the coast" and feels a kinship with the fluctuating waters, "the little black waves tumbling on like a helpless baby and sudden patches of transparent stillness." Yet when the doctor says, "*Vous avez l'air vannée* [You look weary]," she spends "days and hours wondering when the nerves of the mind will be cured. I keep them darkly to myself but shudder—too often. Down to the sea this morning—it's in a fine restless thundering agitation of blue and white." The sun, heat, evening chill and breezes are alternately "oppressive" or "luxurious," depending on her mood.

Nancy is gifted in the genre of travel literature. Her descriptions are vivid and historically informative; she often paints verbal portraits as though she were observing through the eyes of a painter and then exposes the Romantic's passionate search for a transcendent harmony in nature to obliterate the pain and disarray of ordinary experience. She feels at peace after climbing the heights of La Turbie,

> another high-built town, with a fine fragment of a Roman column [and] a ledge where you stand much as when Christ was devil-tempted, and all the country round is entirely in accordance with Piero della Francesca, some of the mountains waiting for one of Tura's hermits and the sea feathery and rippling. Here you cannot but linger on evocations of medieval Christianity, early Catholicism, martyrs, prophets and miracles. . . . They appear slowly in the exaltation of pure pale air. They stay with you till you think their meanings are unwound and digested and . . . fade on the descent. There remains the remembrance and knowledge of a certain hill of stones, a certain tree, a primitive persistent etherealized blue.

To the Romantic, departing from the mountaintop with its inspiring imprints means reentry into the "vulgarity" of the real world. Nature has illuminated "the secret of the incompleteness of self." Nancy has come to better understand "the strange contrasts of life—an unending theme"—specifically, the sacred and the profane: the "timeless wonder on the mountain top" and the reality of "Monte Carlo [and] vulgarity." At the end of the day, she sits "on the pavement of the Café de Paris drinking hot bad cocktails, exhausted and deplorably impressed by the monstrous façade of the Casino . . . ; my heart and senses screamed."

Because Nancy loathed the idea of wasting time, she despised sleep, yet in her present condition she was often overwhelmed by it: sleep revealed "the uprising of the animal and the overthrow of mind. Deplorable." Another life-long problem mentioned early in the diary is her inability to find perpetual exaltation in nature—another reason for her later frenetic travels: "In the olive trees on a little hill over the bay, [I am] empty of thought, desire and imagination."

The diary also reveals how easily Nancy could meet men—flirt, drink with, and romance them and also discard them; at the same time, we see how she idolized men, provoked them, and then became distraught if they questioned her devotion or abandoned her. One cannot help but note her mortifying self-consciousness in social interactions, particularly her frequent sense of worthlessness when she is introduced to men. Her entries about her social insecurities are interspersed with recollections of Maud's harangues regarding her worthless life and sickly appearance. One has no doubt as to the origin of this highly desired woman's insecurity.

Nancy finds one new boyfriend on the trip; she writes to four at home: the American Jim McVickar, George Moore, Harry Melville, and Zigomar, for whom she cared most (and to whom she gives no first name). John Hutchinson, enamored of Nancy in London, joins her and Marie occasionally. Nancy is fond of Hutchy but not in love with him. She relates an incident when they are in bed and a visitor arrives with a "frantic knocking and shout of 'Nancy.' My God it was Mrs. Hiofa Williams—so I flung myself out of bed and shot the bolt, Hutch looking to see if he should hide under the bed . . . or get out of the window."

The promise of new romantic euphoria arises one night in Eze when Nancy becomes smitten by a "buffy [inebriated] tenor." He sings "all through dinner only top notes and in the most natural way [and is] unforgettable." She finds him enormously appealing:

I'm in an immense jolly Rabelaisian mood, strung up to any vulgarity to outdo them all—wild gestures and excited words, singing too even.

However, "in despair" because her doctor has warned her "of people who dance too wildly dropping dead," she tears up her blue feathers and flowers. Then, remembering the many inept physicians who had prescribed massages for her (one doctor "with erotic persistent eyes" "kneeded and tore at [her] muscles"), she saves the evening: she defies the medical establishment as an

Apache dancer suddenly appears and the crowd clusters in mock terror. It's my cue to snatch him, somewhat surprised for a dance. They love that, laugh and applaud. . . . The Apache warms to it. We whirl into the arms of the sergeant de ville who comes on a mock arrest and later apologizes to me! The tenor reappears and sings.

Before everyone in the room, Paul, the tenor, invites Nancy into his Rolls Royce for a drive to Nice: "All are really rather shocked and I'm enchanted with this smack of Riviera . . . wondering how many would have laughed with me."

Sober and self-conscious the next day, Nancy worries that her behavior may have offended the other guests: "Oh these reactions and aftereffects when the mind is so clear and yet so agitated, flimsy and unstable." Perhaps nature will subdue "her nerves which terrorize and dismay." Nature and poetry console her,

> a thunderstorm . . . a wonderful transfusion of pale persistent cloud wraiths slowly creeping over the mountains, touching Eze like the soft blue of a brush dipped in water. . . . I read Swinburne indefatigably and marvel still at the old beauty of his alliteration, rhythms and development of ideas.

She thinks about memory and how words revive emotions associated with past experience. In true Romantic fashion, she recollects in tranquility the tenor and glamour "of one southern night. . . . The last of the blue feathers." She hears Paul sing; it might be the song of the nightingale:

> Echoes [and] . . . refrains. Hasn't one always realized music was of closer kin to wine than every other thing, a more potent factor even to ecstatic happiness? . . . Love, exaltation, art, speed, rhythm, all the same one thing.

Recollections make one alive again, even if despair inevitably returns:

> They haunt one, words and melodies, the expression of an eye, the curve and bend of a forehead. . . . Words, are you transplanted into the dead world of past impressions? Such stuff as dreams are made of indeed. . . . And imagination, as dangerous as the fire that annihilates and yet falls back on itself, self-conqueror—what a paradox, and how wishes spring to one—a scented dimness of the room, some talk of balalaikas and other stringed exotics, the little tenor entering with a sentimental French song. . . . Much good it does one to wish that, lying here in a litter of old letters from Hutchinson and cigarette ash at 5 of an afternoon with racing pulses in an attitude of waiting. . . . Who has ever explained away the sudden invasion of despair?

Incapable of relaxing or being alone, Nancy drinks "a solitary beer, morosely." She finds "the moon is wasted." Uninspired and unable to locate meaning in her life, she feels "like a child . . . without any possibility for thought, writing or reading." All the same, she is fluent in metaphoric thought:

> I am full of discontents tonight; my mind is like a disordered room, littered and scattered with useless furniture; the clumsy ungainliness of words. . . . Effort or no

effort, like travelers wondering how to unpack and sort all this baggage, . . . half-minded to leave it to some desultory professionals for arrangement. . . . My project-ed return, not that of a disillusioned world-battered Tannhäuser, with clamorous hands . . . but as a rollicking thought-monger who found no market for his goods.

She projects her mental state onto the Riviera and asks some dazzling questions about Monte Carlo:

Where are the foreign princes, doubtful diplomats, sly orientals, nimble fat Greeks, neurasthenic Russians and busy cosmopolitans? Paris, London, New York. The fantastic women, the pearls waiting to be bought, the jewels that are, the trembling hands of losers, the hidden revolvers, pink champagnes, galaxies of glass motors, arrivals, departures, banquets, balls, batailles de fleurs, romances, rastaquouères [foreigners of suspicious rank or wealth] and royal liveries? Paris, London, New York . . . the magnificence of head-waiters almost offering their souls as a new dish for a potentate, the quarrels, scandals and curiosities, the immense fortunes made, doubled and lost.

She looks for a new experience, aware that events and people cannot provide infinite variety: "Oh the fatality of things twice done in the same way." Unsure of her identity, she will take the role of a gay sophisticate with new acquaintances: "the best attitude for their reception being light-hearted laughter and lack of surprise." Yet this stratagem embarrasses her: "Talk, Talk, working oneself up to any eventuality, laughing at nothing, becoming semi-intoxicated by one's own unending silliness."

Despite her self-consciousness and discomfort in such role-play, when she sees the tenor and *he* acts differently, she feels paralyzed and is utterly confused about how to respond:

A change comes over him and everything gets hopeless and half-hysterical. I have not an atom of impulse and can't move from the table. It's the moment of lost opportunity. We sit there in a torment for an hour or more. I'm dumb and in despair, ill, shaking.

Aware that she might have missed the chance to feel alive again, she is overjoyed when he provides her another opportunity:

Outside the tenor follows, . . . seizes the hand, urges a drive to Nice, . . . becomes most ardent. It's a dream that paralyzes every word one should have said. The whole night surges up, mysterious, phantasmagoric, ending like this.

She is torn between the wish for adventure ("serenades, avowals, adventures, trembling in the midnight air") and a sense of decorum ("and embarrassment"). She is also frightened of going with him "in a little southern street at 2 A.M. with an unknown charming(?) character, sprung into one's life God knows where from or why. Is he adventurer, viveur, thief?" Once again, she hesitates between desire for adventure and embarrassment over unconventional behavior. When Paul openly expresses his love for her, she is skeptical:

> Lord, how quickly they fall in love here. How utterly—with all the hot-headed impulse of a Southern opera, if one is to believe such phrases . . . —erotic, dramatic, and funny. Thank God one has got one's sense of humor still. . . . Is one to believe words?

Nancy gives in to her impulses, rationalizing her distrust as a matter of cultural differences:

> So swept up is one by the difference of ideas and life here, we [drive] to Nice. . . . [I] jump into bed and refuse to think. . . . [A friend] was amazingly right about the Frenchman's point of view, that everyone of them treats love as a religion and goes through the same routine and technique. I'm learning things these days . . . ! But one must assimilate without indigestion or shock, and it's depressing inevitably.

Her need to find the ideal man is fulfilled when she sees a Belgian soldier with numerous ribbons. Her idealization of him is telling. She finds him

> without a trace of vainglory, exaggeration or pretense, modest, quiet, using every word with beautiful phraseology, in a fine voice, less affected by anything in life than anyone I've seen ever—solitary and contented, full of the most complete calm, with a beautiful expression and yet full of heart and feeling, a Christ-like character, walking the world without any fear, and a knight of justice, and all that he said—was so right and true one was touched, stirred to the innermost.

She invents a fairy tale about his past: "It struck one he must be the natural child of some unknown love, brought up by an old woman that he goes to see every Sunday, careless of what might happen to him in life, intolerant only of injustice." By contrast, the French are materialistic and ostentatiously earthy: "God what a cultivation of sexuality. . . . Everything is conducted, like so much marketing and bargaining."

Despite her protestations, when Paul returns she joins him in another night of lovemaking. She play acts until she reaches the moment of "abandon," "intoxication," and "love" but afterward feels no warmth toward him. She would escape into the night if she could. Having returned to reality, as having descended from the mountaintop, she wants to be by herself. The idea that Paul might want a commitment is unacceptable: she wants her freedom and will come to him only on her terms:

> We return to Beaulieu in the tenor's car, driven at a stupendous speed, drink cocktails, dine on the balcony. He talks well, but always returns to the childish. I am again under the impression of having the difficult task of inventing a part while acting it. . . . One slinks away in the opposite direction too surprised for fear. . . . Oh contrasts, up into the high arms of love, and down to the unfathomed strange depths of dissatisfaction: the play is over and the curtain fallen on you—and on them—dual actor-and-audience. . . . God, I wish I were alone. . . . Leave me to come back to you of my own free will.

The next day, she responds to "gales of wind, purity of day, alone, . . . songs and poetry racing in the mind. Walk, think, dream, write, try not to analyze, be content with the constant flow and motion of the sea." She writes a lovely poem that ends,

> I will go back to the harsh and the bitter
> Conclave of waters, the masterful sea,
> That sorrow my shadow, my sister, my chosen
> Eternal companion may purify me.

Having had the tenor, she is bored when she next sees him, with his blue-belted overcoat lined with fur, sporting cap, and chauffeur-driven white car. Since it is extremely difficult "to have any consecutive conversation" with him, she plays with his black dog. The following day she writes to her London boyfriend, Zigomar, and idealizes him in a poem, "Praise":

> You are priest of Possibility
> Hero of new-discovered continents
> Pure as the endless sea, spirit of love
> Created from the essences of stars . . .

There is an epilogue to Paul and Nancy's drama. Even though she has rejected him, she becomes troubled by his retaliatory indifference: "So ardent at first, and now the best exponent of the disappearing trick—but why, why, why . . . and nobody ever answers. . . . *Ce mystère de Paul.*" In search of consolation, she goes to Castillon and climbs to the top of the mountain, listens to the birds, gazes at the solitary tree at the peak of the ruin, and vows, "I *shall* one day stay" forever "on the altitudes."

Having created her own crisis, she returns to Zigomar: "I long for you. . . . One has not the least vestige of ties or attachment here." In the meantime, her poem to him, "Praise," has overwhelmed him. Nancy begs him not to be frightened by her words and to understand that she loves the feeling of rapture that love arouses in her. She also wants him to view her as a person, not as an ideal:

> Why indeed should I not put you where I will in my heart? Ah yes you were troubled slightly by that poem. . . . The mistake lay not in my mood . . . but in my sending it. . . . You seem to think of me as the very . . . essence of—is it fantasy? You are a spectator full of praise, but will you enter into a more dual state of comprehension, see me as any one of your friends, . . . not the solitary priestess of dreams.

Her following comments, on her poem to him and on how poetry takes on a life of its own, repeat this:

> In a poem there's nothing one won't say. It's the sensuality of art. [You should just] see that mood—Am I clear? Not as lucid alas as the results of a long conversation. . . . Leave my unsettled poetry alone, and be reasonable enough to think of me as reasonable. Difficult things indeed.

In directing her thoughts to life, not poetry, she admits a great deal about herself in the following: her desire for happiness, her pain in his distrust and unwillingness to commit himself to her, and her many unrequited love affairs. She tells Zigomar not to worry if he decides to leave her, although she cannot deny her need for the purity, perfection, and contact with the ideal provided by romantic love. Her confusion about love seems clear. Although Nancy wants every man to want her, once she is desired, she becomes fearful, distrusting, and oppressed. She is torn between her quest to find the idealized man who will make her feel whole and the alienation she experiences in the aftermath of her union with the ideal. But she fails to understand this:

> Perhaps you think I'm mad, do you? It's opinions of that kind that drive one into the whirl of one of the greater debauches of mind, thereby revealing, confessing much weakness and instability. . . . And when all is said and done, one is so tired, either with the eternal conflict between two egos, or with the relaxation of some final understanding, rare fruit that one craves. . . . I don't idealize, but I love traveling through every phase of imagination, the impossible and the possible. . . . And above all remember I shall not be hurt. One has been through so much of that (Oh youth, say you). I *am* bitter but I can master it.

Despite her last disappointment, the trip ends with an affirmation of nature and the human imagination. Arles Cathedral is dazzling with its richly carved cloisters. The Roman theater and its bullfights exalt life, forbidding "swords or blood drawn by either bull or man." When the "man strikes, out of the wooden knife comes a flag to signify the death blow!—amazing and simple ingenuity on the same principle of surprises." She has felt ecstatic escape and exaltation in nature: the "pure enchantment of Avignon—the sky, the mountains, the rush of great streams and crops of brown, green, red, ochre, yellow, the blood of poppies, and fabulous cypresses." She has been most "enchanted by the country between Avignon and Pont du Gard—that large white plain with its cultivations and its barrenness—its most sudden change of earth from pale yellow to an almost blood red, . . the delight of passing villagers with old gray churches, the wind and the color of the dust-clouds, . . . the pale young harvests turned into slender waves by a breeze . . . and the large murmur of progressing waters under the aqueduct."

London

The remainder of the diary is filled with Nancy's pledges to finalize her separation from Sydney Fairbairn, find purpose in her life, and locate her own house, although Maud, of all people, chides her: "Only the *banal* need a home." As soon as Nancy begins the return trip to her mother's house, her behavior belies her anxiety and she becomes unusually flamboyant. She announces to Marie at the station: "Champagne is champagne in a train more than anywhere, and I shall certainly always drink with anyone as indeed will I, do I, talk with any stranger."

Her first activity in London is a walk through the Ritz, where she does not recognize anyone. Still "quite exhausted and trembling at heart," she thinks of the prewar days of 1913 and a melody comes to mind, with "tangos and dancers, grand-dukes and soupirants [admirers]." Trying to be positive, she proclaims this "a new epoch" and goes shopping: "I fancy I had a very good figure . . . and was much seen!" She stops at galleries to see the Matisses and de Chiricos, admiring the latter's "hard-straight colors, great sense of architecture, and the striking quality of his logic" from "that indescribable class of psychology, the psychology of instinct."

On the one hand, she tries to engage in activities in order to feel better; on the other, she is preoccupied with the devastation of the war. The

lamentation of England ris[es] up around me, . . . damp fields, tunnels, . . . my first impression of return—everyone dead, . . . personal and acute people, the lovers of last year—this monstrous land much more ravaged by war (to us and naturally) than the great . . . continent.

One of her friends has committed suicide:

And now André is dead too—dead of a sudden suicide in Rome. This is the eternal shock and sorrow to one's daily life. André of the Pagliacci face and moods—dying so, indeed.

Her enthusiasm for "the new epoch" begins to diminish. What "of tomorrow and the new era now?" she asks. The Whitsuntide holiday is coming, which means "the horrors of . . . closed shops." Once again, she dreads the

terrible cry of idleness. What *shall* I do? Enter Mother in shining yellow satin and Thomas Beecham [and] many battles over going or *not* going to the opera.

The holiday becomes "an episode in boredom." After meeting a number of old friends, she ends up at the Eiffel Tower, where

we . . . drink vile and ever sweeter champagne—slight buffiness and I getting more and more amorous, infatuated now, a great kissing of hands and feet, and very curious phrases about "when a woman gives me her lips." Why must the first days of London be like this, and I fresh and hopeful?

A change in geography has not altered Nancy's state of mind.

Nancy began seeing several men at the same time in a frenzy of activities: she had one escort to the Ascot races, another for cocktails at the Tower and dinner at the Ritz or Savoy Grill, yet another for the theater or opera, and still another for dancing and more drinking at a nightclub before a final sojourn to a brothel still open at 4:00 or 5:00 A.M., serving both customers and fried eggs. Nancy was a gifted flirt. On more than one occasion, she passed suggestive notes to men who interested her: "How do you like my dancing and my appearance? Shall we sing? Yes!" and received such replies as "Yes quite quite."

As Nancy chronicles these days of "hysterical laughter," she and her friends appear to be constantly drunk—"buffy" or "blind"—most of the time, talking of "the psychology and philosophy of drink and its mental aftermath." She describes dinner with Lady, Prince, or Count So-and-So, and her lists of engagements are lengthy. She dines with the Aga Khan ("So *this* is the return to civilization . . . !"); another night she sits between Maynard Keynes and Lytton Strachey, adding that she "loved both." Her other boyfriends, and most are mentioned by one name only, include Eddie, Jim, Bruce, Alexander, Beale, Basil ("I love him and have a great flame of the old passion. We go to Queen Street—nice rooms. . . . So his wife has gone to America and left him too"), the Russian Soldatenkoff (after their rendezvous, she says, "then this dreary useless talk and questioning begins. . . . Like two beggared idiots waiting for the end of the world and not understanding each other in the least—all these mistakes [no matter how small] come from the excess of one's heart's kindness—intolerable mistakes"), Kirkwood ("took me home and became rather soppy—this at 4 A.M. and almost sober"), Shearman ("in love with me," but "he seems a little shy . . . as yet"), Stewart (never "without a huge thermos of champagne"), Stuart (who told her she "looked like Mrs. Vernon Castle, which pleased"), Collins ("touch of the writer, was very funny tho' saying I was like Mary Queen of Scots, same brow and neck and that I behaved like her—well, well, well"), Bosio ("[whose] passionate love for me was a little mystifying"), and Ralphie ("I thought how divine [he] was, and that *someone* could have had a delightful, enchanting life married to Ralphie").

One evening she went out with both Bruce and Eddie. They danced, "sang *all* the buffy Oxford songs we could remember and were answered by a buffy group of men on the road." She adds: "I sang very loud and very well one or two serious songs." "Finally Bruce gave out and went to bed." Then, in a sexually explicit admission, she writes:

> Eddie and I did some more talking and thought the moonlight looked good enough to go out in, so got undressed and wandered like the Babes in the Wood into the big field, lay under an oak and — [*sic*], went on talking, perhaps a trifle more dreamingly now. We were hungry after this.

To her distress, Eddie espouses "a somewhat cruel theory that 'the lover' can never be 'the friend,' that [when] a friendship becomes sensual it's ruined." He suggests that she become the mistress of a millionaire rajah.

It comes as no surprise that Nancy's depression returned: "These parties kill me, in bed all day with one's thoughts whirling and each time more and more so. Wished very much I was stronger." Although, she writes, she would prefer "a *water* dinner at the Ritz," she still pursued her frenetic life, drinking a great deal to feel less depressed and to disguise her terrible shyness. After Eddie, she "sank into a coma of great weariness and dumb depression. . . . [Drinking] makes things better, smoothes down the bitter silences and comforts the nerves, *dissipates my shyness*." And since clothes, like alcohol, seem to allay her shyness, she decides to follow the example of some friends by taking a dozen fittings for a dress: "My God, what a help and moral support clothes are." Still, meeting new people remains stressful: "Another thing I noticed was the way one got *terribly* depressed and hating everything, say while dressing, . . . and then went down and saw . . . new people and places."

Her self-recriminations are more severe than in France. She knows she is excessive in everything she does. Once, after drinking too much and waking with a fever, she writes:

> I find life quite impossible, as I cannot enjoy a thing without carrying it to all extremes and then nearly dying of the reaction—it is weak-minded, certainly it is.

Preoccupied with her self-worth, she worries if others will like her. Writing about her "shocking super-sensitiveness," she excoriates her

> gnawing and probing and exaggerating and lacerating state of mind. I seem to want too much, hence a mountain of unhappiness. . . . Idiotic over-developed introspection.

She expresses her deepest concern and melancholy: "You cannot constrain love, nor make it. . . . So I shall be alone . . ."

Many years later, Nancy said that the only men she loved during this time were the American Jim McVickar and Ted Ralli. Nancy and Ted were graceful dancers, who always attracted an audience. At one point, they considered dancing professionally. Nancy never pushed Ted away, as she had her tenor friend; she thought her experiences with him "very happy days, these," but she was always frightened that he would leave her: "There is always . . . the longing for happiness to be ratified and enduring." And she had every reason to fear losing him. When they discussed infallibility, she was deeply hurt when he said that he "knew no one who could quite fill this word, [and] I said *yes* and thought of Marie, [and] tried also to make him believe that *I* was or *could* be so, but failed!"—a revelation of a major source of her despair: her need to be perfect.

Within the diary, Nancy tells of a weekend in Paris, when she was introduced to the "odious Elsa Maxwell" and attended a Poiret ball, where the designer and his staff wore huge scarlet coats. ("Poiret . . . has seen so much blood in the trenches he can think of no other color!") Although Nancy kept a busy schedule of parties and luncheons, she felt isolated by her shyness, vowing "never to go to Paris again without a chap or even several." The diary also records Nancy's less piquant activities back in London—her flair for dominoes and card games, particularly bridge and poker, and the evenings she and her friends revived the Coterie's gag of painting their faces and giggling as they walked around Piccadilly.

Nancy was happiest when she saw her closest friends—Sybil, Iris, Diana and Duff Cooper, Hutch, Marie, Chile (in love with her), and her cousin Edward. Once she traveled to Cambridge with Edward and spent an exhilarating day talking about Freud and his dream theories. She returned home, studied Freud's theories about obsessions and dreams, and began contemplating her own: "I had the old dream myself of being stifled by an unknown man." Nancy and Edward also dined with Harold Nicolson in Paris, but it "made my heart sink" when "he insisted on going to Montmartre's filthy little restaurants." When they reached the Apollo, Nicolson fell on the floor "to amuse the tarts." It had remained stylish for the rich and famous to end the evening with "tarts and toughs." Nancy also spent a weekend in Brighton, where she turned the conversation with Hutchy to the "same old subject, whether it is possible to combine love and friendship." She felt so isolated during the weekend that when she returned home she confided to her mother how unpopular she felt: "[I] cried for an hour . . . *got that awful feeling . . . that nobody likes one really*." Nancy found Maud's indifference "very wicked."

She also spent weekends with other public figures—one in Oxford with former prime minister Herbert Asquith and his wife, Margot. But in spite of the Asquiths' celebrity guests, Nancy found no one to talk to, and she lamented the paucity of available drink. At the home of the American society hostess Mabel Corey, she found the opulence of the surroundings "revolting" and the ingenuous behavior of the guests "bewildering": "'Mabel Gilman,' the light opera star, married to an impotent steel king—a curious world this." She lunched with Nellie Melba, Lady Randolph Churchill, and "her awful husband Porch" but spent most of the time in her room: "I loathed Mrs. Corey . . . and everyone here. It's the last time, said I."

At one point, Marie Ozanne told Nancy that people were gossiping about her, that "my name and reputation were so bad that I should never go to Court again, but that the King was going to send for me to have a talk." Nancy turned to Housman's "lovely" *Shropshire Lad* and became very sad.

After the peace treaty was signed, on June 28, 1919, "news of it came out on the screen of the Pavillion Marble Arch where I was at the moment." She felt the continuing desolation of Peter's death and "*hated* the demonstrations of collecting crowds." She found it difficult to go to the Ritz, decorated with the flags and flowers she called "peace-atrocities." Although she continued the cycle of dinner-opera-Ritz-champagne-and-dancing, her mind was fixed on leaving London.

Respite in Surrey

Nancy grew obsessed with the question of what to do with her life. One friend suggested that she and his wife open a hat shop and have children: "(God!) I laughed, there being no answer." Instead, she joined Marjorie Trefusis in looking for a country house. Marjorie had also been living at home with an overbearing mother and "loathing it." On July 10, they moved to Turks Croft, in Surrey, for the rest of the summer. Maud provided Nancy with an allowance.

Nancy arrived with the only material possessions that mattered to her: a typewriter, a few photos, and the ebony and ivory bracelets she had been collecting. She now had a tranquil environment in which to reflect and write; she and Marjorie discussed poetry, and Nancy worked on her lyrics. She was happy lying on the lawn near the garden reading and writing. George Sand made her realize "how much more of a *romantic* I am." The summer would be recuperative: "I think there will be no stress or too wild a collection of adventures." She and Marjorie even had a brown dachshund named Beaver.

Nancy loved Marjorie's natural sympathy. They spoke of "one's sensitiveness," of past lovers, and of the way men think. Nancy came to believe that the casual affairs she was still juggling were far less important than this summer of poetry and friendship. Once again, she had found the maternal support that calmed her, as the frenzied love affairs and social rituals had not.

Nancy had been publishing in a number of literary reviews and newspapers. When she sent "In Answer to a Reproof "to the *English Review*, she received the response: "Dear Mrs. Fairbairn, I like your poem for its intellectual sense of freedom, and am publishing it next month. Austin Harrison, Editor." He soon wrote: "I enclose a guinea, which is unfortunately all we can afford to pay at this juncture, when people seem more anxious to jazz into bankruptcy than to create wealth."[2] She had even been encouraged to compile a volume of verse. The publisher William Heinema......tified her that he wanted immediate publication, not "verses spread over magazines and newspapers."[3] It was an exhilarating time, the dawning of a sense of purpose, encouraged by a recognition of her gifts.

Nancy and Marjorie entertained old friends, and Nancy added photos of them, as well as of the house ("The Best Bedroom"), to her scrapbook. Guests at their more formal dinners included the Granville Barkers and the Bertrand Russells. On one occasion, G. M. and Maud arrived, and an embarrassing scene ensued. "In a veritable outburst," Maud said to Nancy: "'You have no sense, knowledge or experience and no plan of life'—which subject she enlarged upon" (Nancy graciously attributed her mother's rage to frustration about "something prior to arrival"). She and Marjorie subsequently stomped around the fields at a fast pace, renouncing mothers, irritated but laughing. Nancy again called Maud "a polished termagent."

Another time, when Nancy was with Hutchinson and they were reading aloud some work by G. M., she blurted out the idea that had been continually on her mind: "[G. M.] *must* be my father." They wondered: "But what of my long limbs and general shape of body? Shall we ever know?" If it were true, she repeated softly, she would surely have been a much different and happier person.

As the summer and her time with Marjorie drew to an end, Nancy reexperienced moments of loneliness and desperation. She wrote: "August 29 began my long mood of depression, hardly noticed at first. . . . It grew on me subconsciously." The lease in Surrey would soon expire, and the idea of returning to her mother's house was intolerable. "[I was] more wretched than ever before at not having a home of my own. I must, I *must* and sacrifice everything else to it." She returned to London, alone, "depressed by the thought of 'no one to go about with now.'"

In October, unable to deal with her depression, Nancy went to a rest home at Hindhead, Surrey; she stayed until mid-November. She had massages regularly; she also stopped drinking. She remained in bed during the first two weeks and was then visited by the princess of Monaco and a few close friends. She read all of Hardy's novels, Gauguin's letters, G. M., and Dostoevsky. She felt relieved to be free of any rendezvous at the Ritz or Tower.

Yet when she returned to London, she "found the usual adventure, a stranger who thought me flippant! He was a good dancer," adding, "but I lost him, am so alone again, climbing the stairs wearily—ALL THIS TIME WITHOUT ANY DRINK." At the end of November, she visited her father at Haycock. Bache, who "read the paper, ceaselessly, roll[ed] cigarettes, then read a magazine," seemed lifeless. Nancy's love for her father was unwavering, but she found no sense of emotional connection: "One feels more and more remote after an hour or two with Sir Bache, as if no kind of existence were left one at all. . . . I believe no one would come to look for one here no matter how long one disappeared; . . . Sir Bache with his eternal patiences and small-talk (when any) sap one's energy and patience a good deal."

When Marjorie became engaged to be married, Nancy took a room above the Eiffel Tower. Although she had been to Paris and was very happy when one of her poems was accepted by the *Week-End Review*, she said of her psychological state, with her emotional mainstay to be married: "My capacity for happiness is starved." She took on both old and new lovers. A new one, mentioned in one of the last entries of her diary, was the up-and-coming poet Robert Nichols, who published a sonnet sequence to Nancy, with her "sunflower hair." *Sonnets to Aurelia* was published with a crimson cover and an "N" planted over a wreath of bay leaves that circled his name. He admitted in one poem "knowing, alas, too well / That outward heaven hides an inward hell," but others, as Nancy said, "tell of every kind of lurid occasion that never arose at all between us—poetic licence if ever there was." Nancy's rejection of Nichols drove him to hold a Colt revolver to his head and beg her to stop him from blowing out his brains. She calmly picked up the gun and put it out of sight.

In 1920, Maud moved from 9 Grosvenor Square, a house originally owned by the first Earl Farquhar, a close friend of George V, to London's most expensive and fashionable area at Carlton House Terrace. She was now acclaimed as a generous patron of musicians, writers, and the theater. Through her influence, the Old Vic had been saved, and she made enormous contributions to the production of opera; she also continued to collect money from her friends for James Joyce so he could live and write without financial worries.

A curious incident occurred shortly after her move that was reminiscent of Nancy's with Nichols. On the afternoon that Maud was to introduce the Prince of Wales to another of Nancy's friends, Wyndham Lewis, the latter arrived, taciturn, pensive, and self-absorbed. As soon as they sat down to luncheon, Lewis placed a pearl-handled pistol on the table. "Did he intend to assassinate the Prince? Was he going to commit suicide?" Recalling a line from *The Duchess of Malfi*, Maud remarked "Oh! What an elegant object, is it loaded with black pearls?" whereupon she dropped it in her purse.[4]

In the same year that her mother moved to her new home, Nancy left England for Paris.

• • •

In 1955, when Nancy, now fifty-nine, was preparing her memoir of George Moore, she had a locksmith open the diary: she was looking for references to G. M. Reading about her return to London in 1919 reopened deep wounds, and she inserted an addendum to the diary. From her comments, one would think that Maud were still alive and Nancy a captive in her house: "Her Ladyship . . . telling me constantly 'Do something. Make good! You're wasting your life.' What were the facts? . . . I had married a foul man. . . . I loathed him, knew it was an idiotic thing to do, but did it, went through with it so *as to get away from Her Ladyship and have a home of my own.* It was war-time. The many young men I loved were all dead. I was *always* in love."

In the addendum, Nancy comments on her major problems in 1919: her unresolved separation from Sydney; her continuing devastation over the death of Peter ("whom I loved entirely and wanted to live with. . . . *That* changed me. . . . And so it was. The despair his death caused me . . .”); her physical weakness from the flu and pneumonia (“hence all the references to feeling like hell—all of which was made worse by incessant drink, drink, drink, drink . . . —God!”); and her desperate need for her own house or flat. In addition, “At this time I had not one penny of my own; Her Ladyship gave me, voluntarily, what she might have settled on me; I felt I could not count on it and how rightly felt that—she could and would have cut it off had she so wished.”

Her final comments are moving: “Damn . . . Her Ladyship most for the total lack of sympathy about her! I wish there had been ME now with ME then—we should have gotten on very well. . . . The ME of now and the ME of then. But when did the ME of now begin? Begin is not the word—but when was there a leap out of the uncertainty about self nearly all the time?”

The regeneration that she writes about in the last sentence would take place in Paris.

5

Return to the World in Paris

Nancy was a great woman and the best mind of
any Anglo-Saxon woman in Europe.

—JANET FLANNER

When Nancy moved to Paris in 1920, she felt reborn: at last she had found a
home. "I have come to France forever," she said, with relief and exuberance.
She was overcome by the city's beauty: every view approximated art, and her
eyes became the eyes of a painter. She was also infected by Paris's "extraordinary [and] permanent state of avant gardism."[1] The city was encouraging new
social, artistic, and moral freedoms, and Nancy joined artistic circles that were
as gifted and revolutionary as those she had belonged to in London. During
the first of her eight years in Paris, the city not only nurtured her intellectually and creatively; it also galvanized her emotionally. She published three
volumes of poetry and pursued new and serious romances. Her social and political concerns intensified. The highly diverse population of Paris heightened
her awareness of the inequities of the British class system; later in the decade,
she became troubled over the fascist state enveloping Italy. The latter, along
with what became her permanent sadness regarding World War I, gave her
grave fears of a second cataclysmic war.

Her response was not unique. Paris, during the decade, was a dazzling center of frenetic energy and prodigious creativity, and yet, for all its gaiety and
sophistication, an underlying cynicism and sadness enveloped the city. Maurice Nadeau attributed its mercurial moods—its postwar "madness"—to the
spiritual and emotional devastation of World War I. The grandest of human
talents had been subverted to the meanest of human purposes:

Science['s] noblest efforts . . . perfected only another extermination weapon. . . . Philosophies . . . fabricat[ed] excuses to keep [man] in ignorance of the shameful [war] trade he was being made to ply. . . . Literature [was] merely an appendage to the military communiqué. [All of these] universally bankrupt the civilization turning against itself, devouring itself.[2]

After the war, the French, like people everywhere, searched for solutions to fill the void left by shattered prewar ideals. Older but still lively radical political communities appealed to many: Communism, socialism, and anarchism. Also appealing were the philosophical ideologies systematized by Nietzsche, Freud, and the phenomenologists. A number of relatively new aesthetic ideologies were also attractive—vertiginous mixtures of the "left" and "right"— Futurism, Dadaism, the soon-fashionable Surrealism, and even the less political, residual Cubism and early works of Abstract Expressionism. Voices from abroad, of the Vorticists, Suprematists, Die Brücke, and Der Blaue Reiter, also gained a following. A revolution in the arts, with entirely new uses of color, perspective, and linearity, might counter the decadence, waste, and distortions of reality—the "lies," as Hemingway had called them—of earlier works and times.

The New Culture and New Romances

The combination of the current artistic, moral, and social freedoms and the rebellion against prewar values of ambition, industry, and materialism made for a unique kind of bohemianism. One thing was clear: the immorality of the war excused any and all current renegade behavior. The most outrageous acts or artistic or political statements were tame in comparison with the hypocritical (and lethal) manners of the older generation. The "lost generation" was lost only to the extent that it separated itself from the values of the recent past.

Women and fashion, like the new morality, seemed to be making up for lost time. The French suffragettes, wearing the designs of the great couturiers, such as Poiret, Worth, Molyneaux, and later Chanel, proclaimed the new freedoms. Heavy corsets, long hobble skirts, and the well-rounded bosom and hips, separated by the smallest waist one could manage for the stylish "S" shape, were discarded for artificially flattened chests and straight hips, short skirts, silk or nylon stockings (rolled around garters at rouged knees), and mask-like makeup covered with layers of powder, a "bee-stung mouth" of orange or red, and cream rouges and eye shadows. Skin creams of crushed almonds and moisturizers, as well as depilatories, brightly colored (red, gold) lacquered nail polishes, and the multitude of new cosmetics, were hard for shopkeepers to keep in stock, along with the recently marketed Trojan condoms. William Wiser observed that Nancy Cunard "was the archetypal Twenties woman." She styled her hair and "wore the short skirts and boyish fashions as if she were the principal model for the new mode." He continues: "Nancy Cunard was a beauty in the jazz age mold, extremely slim as the fashion decreed, elegant, and to all appearances, reserved."[3]

Whatever Nancy wore was imitated by stylish women: the new seamless stockings, which made the leg look naked; African earrings, bracelets, and pendants; long amber or pearl necklaces; jeweled or fabric bandeaux; leopard coats; and slim, long cloche hats or turbans. Women also copied Nancy's hair style—short and shingled or bobbed (and many tinted theirs gold)—and arranged it with what Nancy called "beavers," two strands of hair that curved across the cheekbone. The foreign press followed her whenever she traveled, noting the geometrically patterned designs that Sonia Delaunay had created for her or, as the *Daily Express* observed in Monte Carlo, how "Miss Nancy Cunard . . . who admires eccentricities in dress and appearance . . . carries out her ideas with courage and success. She was one of the first to adopt the Eton crop, which is becoming more and more popular. The latest woman to follow her example is Lady Wimborne." The next day, reporters noted: "Nancy Cunard wore a mauve tulle scarf tied across her eyebrows, with floating ends, under a big gray felt hat, which looked, oh, so Spanish. . . . Her fashion of wearing a black ring round the eyes seems to be growing."[4] Women imitated Nancy's social behavior as well—smoking cigarettes in long ivory holders, drinking, and flouting their independence and rebellion in free love and free talk. "The new heroines were social outlaws," writes Wiser, about Lady Duff Twysden and Nancy Cunard, with their "lean and hungry look," and Zelda Fitzgerald, the "I-don't-care girl" of the Jazz Age.[5] These were the sirens everyone wanted to become—chic, emaciated, and emancipated.

In 1922, there were eighty French feminist societies, and their membership reached 60,000. The best-selling novel of the new decade was *La Garçonne*, about a nineteen-year-old woman who bears and brings up an illegitimate child. Although the book caused a scandal and President Poincaré considered banning it (but finally did not), everyone read it, particularly when its author, Victor Margueritte, was forced to resign from the Légion d'Honneur.

Paris became an oasis for talented women, offering both artistic and sexual freedom. Most who had married were now divorced or widowed; those who became pregnant, including Janet Flanner and Djuna Barnes, had abortions or miscarriages. Women were free from the heterosexual imperative,[6] and even those like Nancy, who were not lesbian or bisexual, cultivated strong emotional relationships with other women, supporting and inspiring one another in their work. Sylvia Beach, the Presbyterian minister's daughter from

New Jersey, opened the legendary bookstore Shakespeare and Company across the street from the native Parisienne Adrienne Monnier's equally famous La Maison des Amis des Livres. Sylvia and Adrienne were companions who encouraged each other in providing a gathering place for local artists to exchange ideas. Nancy saw both women frequently at their shops, for it was here that people discussed the host of radically new perceptions of reality and self in the areas of science, philosophy, psychology, linguistics, and art. Bertrand Russell and Alfred North Whitehead, for example, sought to establish, in a single system, all the valid principles of mathematical reasoning—a set of axioms upon which all rules would follow. But others, like Werner Heisenberg and Kurt Gödel, claimed that the observer influences the observed and that any axiomatic system has undecidable propositions (for example, although we ought to be able to see ourselves in a mirror, we cannot see ourselves with closed eyes). Nancy enjoyed listening to the conversations about the most-talked-about authors, including Martin Heidegger, Ludwig Wittgenstein, Ferdinand de Saussure, Ernst Cassirer, Arthur Eddington, Carl Jung, Freud, Joyce, and Yeats.

Gertrude Stein was the best known of the wealthy lesbian celebrities. Coiffed as a Roman emperor, she and her partner, Alice B. Toklas, hosted the most fabulous of the salons—some for men and women, others only for women. Gertrude, rejecting traditional literary forms, had been experimenting with language. In "A rose is a rose is a rose," she captured the authenticity of her experience; as she put it, she "addressed, caressed, possessed, and expressed" the flower as it unfolded before her. She also created erotic literature, using, for example, the word "cow" as a code for orgasm; hence, her love story to Alice: "A Wife Has a Cow, a Love Story."

Natalie Clifford Barney, the other wealthy lesbian hostess, dedicated her life to celebrating sensuality, beauty, and free love. A collector of beautiful women, she held events to demonstrate the solidarity of lesbianism, such as pagan dance rituals in homage to Sappho. Among Natalie's many lovers were the heiress Romaine Brooks, the French painters Marie Laurencin and Renée Vivien, and the beautiful Dolly Wilde, the niece of Oscar Wilde. Regulars at her teas included the heiress Bryher (Winifred) Ellerman, H. D. (Hilda Doolittle), and Greta Garbo and her lover Mercedes De Acosta. Others, like the journalist Janet Flanner, the German-Jewish photographer Gisèle Freund, and the novelist Djuna Barnes, were more circumspect in attending Natalie's salon. Whenever Janet visited, she acquired piquant details for her New Yorker articles: Mata Hari did not stand before a firing squad naked beneath a mink coat, as many thought, but wore a suit tailored for the occasion (and white gloves).[7]

One of the most talented, good-looking, and tortured women of the era was Djuna Barnes. The one-time lover of the homosexual painter Marsden

Hartley, she had a long affair with Natalie Barney and both wrote the satiric *Ladies Almanack* and drew its bawdy illustrations—a "Who's Who" of contemporary lesbianism. Djuna later fell madly in love with the artist Thelma Wood (also Edna St. Vincent Millay's lover) and wrote *Nightwood* about their breakup. She later reworked the novel into a stream-of-conscious evocation of erotically obsessive relationships set against the backdrop of a politically menacing era.

According to Andrea Weiss, the extraordinarily beautiful Nancy Cunard, like Kay Boyle and Mina Loy, befriended many of these women: "Nancy was one of the few heterosexual women in [Bryher Ellerman's] group of female friends in Paris." Bryher recalled that she was so stunning that all heads turned when she walked into a room, and even the *Paris Tribune* reported that "the pulse of the Inner Circle of Montparnasse is beating much faster [since] Nancy returned to Paris."[8]

She went everywhere, attending parties and cultural events with people of every sexual, political, and aesthetic inclination. Among her artist friends was Man Ray (born Emmanuel Radnitzky) from Philadelphia. Cofounder with the French artist Marcel Duchamp of the New York Dada group, he was creating his "Rayographs" when he met Nancy—photographic images of miscellaneous objects on paper directly exposed to light. Soon the face of his lean, sensuous, and uninhibited model-lover, Kiki, with her dark bobbed hair and bangs, heavily rouged cheeks, and remarkably large green eyes, was on display everywhere. Nancy socialized frequently with Kiki and Ray, and he often photographed her.

Another of her good friends was the poet Robert McAlmon, whom she had known in London. Even then, McAlmon had an astounding capacity for alcohol. He could drink six double-whiskies in half an hour and remain sober. McAlmon seemed to know everyone and to "almost compulsively . . . consume people." He danced with all the elegant, witty, and beautiful women of Paris and was frequently seen with Joyce, Hemingway, George Antheil, Louis Aragon, Gertrude Stein, Malcolm Cowley, Fernand Léger, Francis Picabia, Duchamp, Pound, Dos Passos, Stevens, Yeats, and Williams, to name a few of his "closest friends." A minister's son from Kansas, he was generally considered wild and daring, a handsome, slim, muscular, and charming bisexual, and he was famous for saying "I guess most of us can't be rated he-he-masculine, but we are not fairies. There are no real homos, male or female, but there is the bi-sex, and in more people than know it about themselves. Personally the types I object to are the female who droops female sex appeal or the male who swaggers with virility. They are the real abnorms."[9]

In a demonstration of his dashing and often erratic style, McAlmon ardently pursued two of the most desirable women in Paris, Kay Boyle and Nancy:

when he went out with one, he spent the evening looking for the other. San-ford J. Smoller describes McAlmon and Nancy's affair as a shared rebellion against conventional relationships: they were emotionally "like two ships pass-ing in the night."[10] McAlmon recounts a famous party given by Hilaire Hiler (né Harzberg). Hiler was a post-Cubist painter, costume designer, and former itinerant jazz saxophonist ("I've been running away from myself so much that most of my possessions have been lost"). McAlmon recited his poem about the "straw-haired" Nancy, as Kiki sat on the piano and wailed, in her tough coarse voice, about longing and passion. McAlmon then impulsively trans-formed himself into a would-be Nijinsky and leaped around the room in spec-tacularly high entrechats. At the same time, the poet Robert Desnos grabbed an imaginary partner and performed an apache tango. Hiler, at the piano, suddenly began to weep for a girl who had left him, imagining her dead. Nancy put her ivory braceleted arms around him and comforted him, "her eyes like sapphires, but bluer than any sapphires, even her warm laughter say-ing 'Nobody is ever betrayed, darling, nobody ever dies.'"[11]

Nancy had love affairs with highly gifted men during her Paris years, includ-ing Pound, Tristan Tzara, and Louis Aragon, and once again, she joined their famous artistic circles. She commented on the revolution occurring in the arts, especially by the Surrealists, adopting some of their flair in her rhetoric:

> Dada, although Done by its creator Tristan Tzara, had spawned some descendants who lacked the pyrotechnical brilliance of his intellect, yet banged the same drum. Surrealism was triumphant at that very moment. Its wordy battles and battling poets were constantly to the fore and Aragon was one of its two founder-leaders. . . . In films and photography there was a new vision and a new technique. . . . Writ-ing [was] bent on lassooing dreams and coralling the subconscious into strangely evolved sentences. As for painting! Painting was as it had never been before in the whole history of art.[12]

Nancy was overwhelmed by the abundance of magnificent art in Paris. An avid walker and gallery goer, she could see the extremes of the prewar and postwar imagination on display everywhere. The by now familiar Post-Impres-sionists were in the shops along the streets bordering the Luxembourg Gar-dens, along with their Cubist and Fauve successors. Galleries like Georges Bernheim and Galerie Surrealiste were showing the biomorphic and geomet-ric abstractions of Arp, Miró, and Mondrian. Picasso was exhibiting guitars constructed of painted metal rather than paper. Among the most startling in-ventions, even in their many reproductions, were Duchamp's "readymades"—a signed urinal—and his goateed Mona Lisa with its brash title, L.H.O.O.Q. (L'Elle a chaud au cul [She Has a Hot Behind]). Nancy was excited when she saw on display her friend Constantin Brancusi's highly polished, elegant *Bird in Space*, at one and the same time abstract and representational. She began to collect Dadaist and Surrealist art.

She made new friendships and renewed old ones with some of the American expatriates, including William Carlos Williams, Hemingway, Antheil, Pound, and Virgil Thomson. Throughout the decade, Paris was like a magnet to people everywhere—the home of Joyce, Picasso, Mondrian, Beckett, Dos Passos, Fitzgerald, Magritte, Miró, Giacometti, Chagall, Diaghilev, Gershwin, and Copland—not to mention many talented others who frequented the homes or workplaces of Gertrude Stein, Sylvia Beach, Stella Bowen, Adrienne Monnier, and Natalie Clifford Barney. Many of Nancy's friends settled near the abbey of Saint-Germain-des-Prés, the oldest church in Paris, and the café Les Deux Magots, once a wholesale textile depot and now a meeting place for local and expatriate artists and intellectuals. Deux Magots's two rival establishments, Brasserie Lipp and Café de Flore, were nearby.

She also met writers and painters who were publishing in the countless little magazines that prospered during the 1920s. Most prestigious was Maria and Eugène Jolas's *transition*; most of its eclectic contributors shared similar attitudes born of the Great War. They declared in two famous issues their rebellion against reason, science, and materialism for the exaltation of the imagination and its metaphysical potentialities. They demanded cultural transformation through the "Revolution of the Word" and rebellion against "all rationalist dogmas." To Jolas, a former reporter for the *Chicago Tribune*, theirs was a common "Revolt against the Philistine," against "plutocratic materialism"—in short, against "the ideology of a rotting civilization."[13] Their focus was not unlike Lewis's and Pound's, earlier in London (who saw civilization as "a bitch gone rotten in the teeth").

Transition, chiefly associated with James Joyce and Gertrude Stein, published an extraordinary group of artists. It remains most famous for its seventeen installments of the later- titled *Finnegans Wake*—the stunning showpiece of the "Revolution of the Word." Joyce's *Ulysses* (1922) had had an electrifying effect on the Paris intelligentsia. According to Janet Flanner, it was the single most exciting and defining event for the Paris expatriates: "It burst over us . . . like a gift of tongues. . . . It [was] the library of our minds." Nancy mentions "plung[ing] into a total reading of *Ulysses* in the winter of 1925." Here and later in *Finnegans Wake*, she marveled at Joyce's extraordinary exploration of the inner world—of the nondidactic and universal, the "unequivocal dream."[14]

The implications and manifestations of the postwar mentality touched every aspect of life—from fashion, dining, and drinking styles (with the liberated flapper ordering the new cocktail "Between the Sheets") to popular culture, especially the increasingly stylish American jazz, which celebrated blacks as primitive and pristine, reminders of preindustrial and prewar inno-cence. Hence, the enormous allure of entertainers like Josephine Baker ("La Bakaire," née Freda Josephine Carson) and Sidney Bechet (who sailed to Paris on a cattle boat); both became culture heroes. Jazz became the rage, a release of basic emotions in new and complex improvisational forms. Nancy followed Bechet wherever he played. His "shimmy" pop was à la mode, much like the "char-less-ton," which brought huge crowds to the burgeoning new clubs and bars. Nancy, like other Parisians, wanted to learn all the new dances, and one black dancer started a Black Bottom industry: he taught the dance to sixty dance masters, who then opened their own studios. Dancing became almost as popular as drinking. Robert McAlmon reports that as "Kiki sang vulgar French songs, Pascin, Kisling, Desnos, Nancy Cunard, Mary Reynolds, Mar-cel Duchamp, Brancusi, Kay Boyle, . . . and whoever, sampled the drinks" and danced alone as they "interpret[ed] their own moods and the spirit of the beer or punch."[15]

Nancy loved to dance, and she frequented all the night spots—the black cabaret Le Bal Nègre, Le Grand Duc, Chez Florence, Chez Josephine, Boule Noir, and Plantation, famous for its mural of a Mississippi steamboat and chalk drawings of blacks on a blackboard. Nancy's rejected former lover Richard Aldington criticized her for going to "nigger cabarets."[16] Both con-temptuous of and undeterred by his racial bigotry, Nancy called the Planta-tion one of her favorite places, along with La Perle, where the working girls dined. Like Apollinaire and the art dealer Paul Guillaume, Nancy came to be known as a "negrophile," an addict of black culture, as well as an avid col-lector of African sculpture and painting. Aldington's disapproval of Nancy's activities was an early example of the animosity her friends and family would express in response to her high regard for blacks and black culture.

Also among her favorite clubs were Zelli's, Café d'Harcombe, Cyrano's (the Surrealists' hangout), Le Grand Duc (where Langston Hughes worked as a dishwasher and waiter), and Dingo's. Bricktop's was owned by Ada "Brick-top" Smith, a black, red-haired woman from Chicago who sang Cole Porter songs and who taught the Charleston to Nancy, Zelda and F. Scott Fitzgerald, Hemingway, and the Prince of Wales. Bricktop's was also a hangout for a cast of Montmartre characters, many of whom became Nancy's friends—Flossie Martin, a fleshy, orange-haired chorus girl acclaimed for her drinking forti-tude; Sylvia Gough, a world-weary and slim beauty who challenged Flossie in beverage consumption; and the English painter Nina Hamnett, who sang bawdy ballads like "She Was Poor but She Was Honest," as well as Kay Boyle, McAlmon, Man Ray, and Kiki. Nancy very much liked the Jockey (Pound's hangout), where, as McAlmon put it, "almost anyone of the writing, painting, gigoloing, whoring, pimping, or drinking world was apt to show up."[17] She especially favored Louis Moyses's Le Boeuf sur le Toit, which she and Tristan Tzara visited regularly.

Nancy joined the electrified crowds that raced to see black American entertainers at the Théâtre des Champs Elysées—"La Revue Nègre"—with its newly arrived Josephine Baker, eighteen, who appeared totally nude except for a pink flamingo feather between her legs (and gold-painted fingernails). She was carried on stage upside down with her legs in a split on the shoulders of a tall black man. She was an unforgettable "Ebony Venus," and audiences screamed in delight. Among those who saw her later at the Folies-Bergère, adorned with only a belt of uptilted bananas around her hips in an astounding display of the phallic, were Picasso, Picabia, Rouault, Alexander Calder, Le Corbusier, and Aragon. Few suspected that she would receive the Légion d'Honneur and Croix de Guerre for her work in the Resistance during World War II.[18] Little did Nancy know that she would become Josephine's neighbor in Lot, France, during the 1950s.

Baker's hair, slicked down with a spit curl like an upside-down question mark on her forehead ("a Bakerfixer") became stylish; so did Poiret's gown "la robe Josephine," which made the color pink fashionable. Miss Baker's caramel coloring caused a suntanning craze, and even her Americanized way of speaking French became popular. As one journalist vividly explained: "The French proved for the first time that black was beautiful." Cecil Beaton photographed a series of images in which Nancy wore a sparkling skullcap, her way of approximating Baker's brilliantined hair. This adulation of blacks was "the acute response of the white masculine public in the capital of hedonism, . . . Paris." Everywhere in Paris, blacks and whites mixed "as casually as bohemian and aristocrat."[19] Black performers such as Adelaide Hall and Florence Mills were courted as guests for Paris's most fashionable parties.

As Henry Louis Gates Jr. points out, the striking vitality of the blacks in Paris demonstrated a new model of physical beauty, and African art became the model on which new art forms were created. As Picasso and others had demonstrated, modernism was a "Cubist mask [covering] a black Bantu face."[20] The glorification of the primitive, the exaltation of the black's innocent sensuousness, revived the celebration of Gauguin's and Rousseau's "noble savage." When Antheil returned from Africa and premiered his *Jazz Sonata* and *Sonata Sauvage* in Paris (1923), Pound, Joyce, Léger, Darius Milhaud, and Erik Satie were in the audience.

Nancy, still collecting African statuary and wearing more and more ivory bracelets, would embark on *Negro*, her ethnographic history of black culture, in the early 1930s, but it was in 1920s Paris that she defined her earliest interest in "ethnography, the study of sculpture, carving, and other handmade objects once thought of as the work of mere 'savages' from ancient Africa, Oceania, and of the Indians of both the Americas." She recognized the impact of African and Oceanic art on the avant-garde, on Picasso and Matisse, who, she said, "had first bought, for almost nothing, a great painted Congo mask . . . and this event has been quoted many a time as the entry of primitive art into the realm of advanced modern painting." She praised the Surrealists for being "the first to create the juxtaposition between abstract painting and the often equally abstract or geometric designs which sprang from the minds of the pre-Columbian and other tribal artificers."[21]

In Love with the Artist-God

Although Nancy had frequently seen Ezra Pound in London—and idolized him since—they did not become lovers until early 1921, after her near-fatal hysterectomy, a subject of considerable commentary. Anne Chisholm suggests that perhaps Nancy chose to remove her womb because she wanted complete sexual freedom without fear of pregnancy. Perhaps, she also suggests, she had "doubts about [her] femininity and capacity for . . . deep feeling."[22] Her awareness of Mussolini's increasing power and fear of another war may have convinced her of the immorality of bringing children into such a world.

While these psychological explanations may be plausible, it is also possible, as some thought at the time, that Nancy had an abortion.[23] In 1921, such procedures were often hazardous and could lead to uterine infection and perforation, necessitating hysterectomy as a life-saving operation. Nancy lived in the pre-antibiotic era, when hysterectomies for severe infection were not uncommon, and the gynecological surgical procedures that preceded the hysterectomy and the peritonitis and gangrene that followed are in keeping with the last explanation. Medical details regarding her ailment can be found among her papers, as well as her notation of the 100,000 franc surgical bill. Her parents, during her three-month stay in the hospital, were told that she had only a 2 percent chance of survival. This item, irresistible to the London press, generated many articles that fortunately omitted the details: "By the way, Nancy Cunard is much better now. She has, of course, been terribly ill in Paris, and underwent an operation from which a recovery is almost unprecedented." A later report stated that "she is progressing as well as can be expected after a long and serious illness. Mrs. Fairbairn . . . was a war bride and as Miss Nancy Cunard was a most popular girl, and always extremely well dressed." It concluded with the odd (now ironic) detail: "She disliked jewelry, and seldom wore any."[24]

Pound visited Nancy during her hospitalization, and for five or six years after her illness, Nancy was deeply in love with him. As James Wilhelm's fascinating paper reveals, their long correspondence exposes a woman who "wanted him passionately and, when rejected, stood by him, as so many of the women who loved him did."[25] Pound had come to Paris because he thought London had become "waterlogged" and "moribund," afraid he would "wake up one morning with webbed feet," as he had said before leaving the United States. Cocteau and Picabia had told him that Paris was entering a golden age.[26] Not only had most of London's artistic innovators moved here, but Paris offered an ideal retreat from the three American P's: puritanism, philistinism, and prohibition. In addition and of no small significance, living in Paris was very inexpensive—hence, the extraordinary number of American artists there. Pound and his wife, Dorothy, took a studio flat that, as Hemingway described it, was as poor as Gertrude Stein's was rich.

Once he arrived, and having perfected the look of one of Whistler's Latin Quarter figures, Pound sought out old friends—Ford Madox Ford, Wyndham Lewis, Yeats, and Nancy—and made new ones: Brancusi, Cocteau, and Gertrude Stein (who soon severed their acquaintance after he fell out of and broke one of her favorite chairs). He spent a great deal of time with George Antheil, the composer of the revolutionary *Ballet mécanique*, and his friend Olga Rudge, a young violinist with whom Pound later had a daughter (whom they gave up for adoption) and who, much later, in 1943 and until the end of the war, joined Pound in a ménage à trois that included his wife.[27] He continued to champion fellow writers and told any potential patron "You must help Joyce," whom he introduced to virtually everyone he knew.

Pound encouraged Nancy to write. In 1921, she sent him a poem, and he encouraged her to be more experimental. He also encouraged their romance. In the same letter, he said: "Lovely Nancy: . . . I wish you would . . . deliver me from the ferocious mercies of wandering American females." In 1922, when Dorothy Pound was visiting her parents in London, Nancy and Pound took the first of their walking tours, in southern France. Pound's knowledge of the region was "astonishing": Nancy was stunned at his "enjoyment in how many places, gathering knowledge from how many things. He was . . . a man of great appetite intellectually, of driving energy."[28] Nancy would always attribute her love of the French countryside to Pound. At about this time, she also rented an apartment on the Quai d'Orsay, where they could meet.

Later that year, when she was en route to Venice on the Orient Express, she wrote him a puzzling but erotic note, which may make better sense if (1) the second line is read first and (2) it is read as though Pound were speaking:

Beneath me *not* H. D. [Pound's former lover], but her remplaçant
I wish I had the corollary to my last night with me now—You.

They exchanged love letters when Nancy arrived in Venice. "If I should find a place and October (or even sooner) would be fine, could you come? and stay in it?" she asked, ending the letter, "I love your letters, and yourself." She signed many of her letters "Avril." Almost all of Pound's letters, which Nancy kept, were destroyed at her house in Réanville during World War II, so one has to imagine the words she was responding to. Again she writes from Venice and envisions his visit with her:

> Tennis is going on at the Lido. I will watch you after we have bathed together. Do come. Do come. I can see us at breakfast splitting a fig, muttering over the foulness of the tea. . . . Now and then a scandal will raise our laughter; there will be hours devoted to the two typewriters. Do come . . .

Although Nancy rented a flat with two terraces, Pound could not meet her. Unable to hide her enormous disappointment, she responded:

> I wish I could send them [the terraces] to you—I wish you could be here, and I understand that you can't, alas. But that means NEXT YEAR doesn't it? Shall I not look for a place with one long room, . . . empty and waiting to be "done up" by me? Yes indeed—I will look now, this month—and next year, perhaps we shall be Les Aimants de Venise [the Lovers of Venice]—beginning with the spring.

When she received his "first letter *here*," she was "very much thrilled," although he had been thinking about their romance in Paris. She replied: "Darling, you welcome me—for I have had sourish days in Venice and wished myself elsewhere, in Paris I think, for all the sun and the glamour, [although it is said]: 'il faut être à Venise avec l'amoureuse [one must be in Venice with a lover].'"

She wrote that she had found a scorpion, which reminded her of his astrological sign, a good omen, but she feared that she would never find another one. Once more, her solitude and longing are evident: "*Promise me* that you will come here next year, write it to me. . . . When shall I see you again? . . . I wish I didn't wish for you so much. God the roofs and the cupolas and the sunset. Who will come to this house to live?" Pound replied that he was working on Eliot's *Waste Land* and the *Dial* magazine. Nancy's responses fully admit her loneliness and dependence on alcohol: "I am dull without you, and do not seem to be able to settle to anything. I have no application"; "I am getting so drunk on this Bianco Vermouth, alone, surrounded by the Paris nostalgias. . . . Where *are* you, where were you?" In some letters, Pound included his most recent poetry and suggested that she visit specific churches and paintings. She then researched the Malatesta for him, like the Gemisthus Plethon, which he referred to in the *Cantos*.

Early in 1923, Pound planned a trip for himself with Nancy and Hemingway. Nancy and "Hem," who had first met in Paris, got along well; he had even more serious problems with his mother than Nancy had with hers. Grace Hemingway would shortly condemn *The Sun Also Rises* as "one of the filthiest books" she had ever read; since his childhood, she had urged her son to call on God to reform his ways. Nancy understood that Hemingway's private unhappiness was covered up by drinking and rudeness—hence his pretense that he was beyond pain and his bragging that "he'd beat up any guy he didn't like."[29]

Nancy changed her plans once she arrived in Rapallo: Dorothy was there, apparently unthreatened by this infamous "vamp." Nancy decided to go instead to Florence, where she found McAlmon and the Sitwells. She was finally introduced to the multitalented writer Norman Douglas, whose work she had liked so well in London and who, like G. M., would become a beloved mentor. She was twenty-seven; Douglas, fifty-three. She continued writing Pound that she missed him. During the summer of 1923, she took a walking tour of Provence with John Rodker, who had published Pound's "Hugh Selwyn Mauberly"; they subsequently went to the Dordogne Valley; on both trips, they took Pound's "prescribed tour." Pound moved to Rapallo in 1924 (with the intention of educating Mussolini, as Confucius had educated the Chinese rulers). Until 1924, Nancy had been writing "*Dear* Ezra, I love you as ever"; "How sad not to see you"; "[I am] devoted to you Ezra." In 1925, she wrote "Ezra, Ezra—I hope there will be *no one* at Rapallo but our good selves." But when, in 1926, she learned that Pound and his wife were to have a child, she stopped writing. In one of her last letters she said, "I kiss your red hair and general lion-like aspect." It may be of some significance in understanding Nancy's moral values, as well as the influence of her childhood on her adult behavior, that she terminated her pursuit of Pound when he became a parent.

Wilhelm writes that Pound's passion for Nancy waned after he met the more submissive Olga Rudge, long before the birth of his son, Homer Shakespear Pound. Furthermore, "[as] much as Pound was fascinated by Nancy (and who wasn't?), there was still the suspicion that no man could ever tame her."[30] Yet, as Nancy's papers reveal, Pound remained attracted to Nancy, at least until 1932. After Franklin Delano Roosevelt's presidential election, he wrote and asked her, somewhat incoherently, to see him:

> If you WONT come to Paris in Maggio the best I can suggest wuld be Merano. . . . That wdnt be very far into the countries you object to. . . . After the four shits Frankie begins to look like a decent president. Some surprise as there hasn't been one for so long one had forgotten the possibility. . . . Sprry you gtter be in THAT

damn city instead of the other more damned city (or less . . . on the whole less . . .)
ma che! Hem has caught 32 sword fish. how's that for bein american.[31]

Nancy eventually limited her dealings with Pound to professional matters.
She was the first to publish *A Draft of XXX Cantos* (1930), when she ran the
Hours Press; she also invited him to contribute to her anthology, *Negro*. But
by the time of the Abyssinian crisis in 1935, when Nancy represented the Associated Negro Press in Geneva, a staunch advocate of Haile Selassie against
Mussolini, Pound's contemptuous remarks about Abyssinians and Jews destroyed any affection she still had for him. And when she collected poems for
the Republican cause during the Spanish Civil War, he called her contributors (Auden, Neruda, Tzara, Spender, Aragon) "all diarohea" and said, "Kikes
[are] financing both sides. All France is KIKED." Hemingway later explained
to Nancy that the reason Pound had become a fascist was because "one goes
where one is appreciated," and Pound was respected in Italy, unlike in London, the United States, or France.[32]

While Hemingway's explanation seems inadequate, there may be some
truth in it: after Pound traveled to the United States and failed to gain an appointment with Roosevelt (Henry Wallace spoke to Pound for ten minutes),
he returned to Italy and changed the focus of his radio broadcasts from matters of culture to obscene and incoherent attacks on FDR, Eleanor Roosevelt,
Jews, and blacks: "New York meat is slaughtered by Jews. Maybe there is less
of it now." Pound was furious that no one took him seriously as an economist
and a politician, as incoherent and bigoted as his ideas were. Since life *is* often
stranger than fiction, it is ironic that during the war it was Nancy who, as a
translator of Italian radio reports into French, translated Pound's speeches for
the Allies. Even then, she was tormented by her inability to reconcile Pound's
poetry and politics:

> I do not know. They simply cannot be, and yet both are there in one living man.
> One would have thought that, to someone so hypersensitive, the very vulgarity of
> fascism would have been repugnant, even leaving out entirely its fundamental prin-
> ciples. I have known Ezra Pound to be a very human kind of person, for example
> when he replied to an appeal I circulated in the early thirties asking for funds to aid
> the defense council of the Scottsboro boys.

She continues, "Some years later, after we had had our dealings over the volume of *Cantos*, he became very antisemitic, and I received a letter from him
in the middle of the Ethiopian War telling me he hoped I realized that 'the
Abyssinians are BLACK JEWS.'"[33] After the war, when Pound was arrested

and charged with treason but found mentally unfit to stand trial, Nancy wrote him a scathing letter, which began:

> I have been wanting to write you this for some time—for some years—but I could not do so because you were with the enemy in Rome. You were the enemy. . . . [William Carlos] Williams has called you "*misguided.*" I do not agree. The correct word for a fascist is "scoundrel." I am aware of the symposium of six American writers who have tried to whitewash you, in which the word "misguided" was applied. I cannot see what possible defense, excuse or mitigation exists for you. . . . Nor do I believe anything concerning the "advanced state of schizophrenia," "madness," etc. that was used as a means to secure your non-execution. I do not believe you are insane or half-crazy. . . .
>
> Having heard you on the air speaking from Rome, there might be some excuse for calling your talks those of a man insane. It was all idiotic, the more so in view of the facts that already belonged to history. But then, by that count, Goering, Goebbels, Hitler . . . —the whole gang of criminals—were just merely insane.
>
> Fascism uses the same hatreds and the same lies the world over. Fascism is not insanity, unless evil itself, all evil, be insanity (a point that can certainly be argued, psychologically and philosophically, *in the abstract*. War is not abstract).[34]

She protested that friends, like William Carlos Williams, visited Pound at St. Elizabeth's and then successfully petitioned for his release. She broke her silence toward him only once. After receiving her copy of the *Pisan Cantos*, she wrote him the brief "Perfectly BEAUTIFUL the Cantos." Ironically, Nancy's love affair with Pound in the 1920s not only had inspired her to write three books of poetry, but also had activated her anti-fascist inclinations. Aware of Mussolini's growing power on one of her trips to Rapallo, she took up the first of her political causes on her next trip to Venice by agitating for higher wages for gondoliers and hotel workers.

All the same, many of the poems in her second volume, *Sublunary*, are about Pound and about how passionate sensuality penetrates the mysteries of a higher spiritual order and bestows an understanding of the cycles of life, suffering, and death. Romance and sexuality lead to rapture and revelation. Although Nancy expresses a range of feelings toward Pound in the volume, in "I Think of You" she uses natural and sexual images to revel in his godlike power:

In the fields
When the first fires of the nightly diamonds are lit,
When the stir of the green corn is smoothed and silent,
And the plover circling at peace like a thought in a dream,

I think of you,
Finger the last words you have added to my rosary.
On a white road
High-noon and midsummer witness my love of you
Grown as a firm tree,
Rich, upright, full-hearted, generously spreading
Long shadows on the resting-place of our future days.
In a town
I meet many with the thought of you in my heart,
Your smile on my lips,
I greet many
With the love that I have gathered at your fountains,
. . . .
I go to the feasts adorned
In a scarlet vestment,
Bejeweled and hung with many trappings—
Under these
Burns the still flame that your hands alone may touch.

The extremes of anguish and exaltation that she feels with Pound often take on religious dimensions. She laments her inability to comfort him on a particular day and offers herself in surrogate sacrifice, "So You May Nail Your Sorrow to My Name's Cross," as she titles the poem. In another, "You Have Lit the Only Candle" ("in my heart that I am bound to worship"), she pays renewed religious homage to Pound. In their sexuality, Nancy feels pure and blessed. She is uplifted and innocent in her desire, "absolved" of sin and "barren" of shame.

The "sharp / Straight flame" of Pound's love "is silent," although, "like a saint" it performs its ministrations and lends her a "steadfast radiance." It is "the only candle that shall illumine my wayward paths," she writes. She will remain in a state of grace until death, when she may face other forces of the universe,

the time . . . when its flame must
tremble and start,
Facing some great wind of eternity that rends and masters it.

"The Spiders Weave" conveys an entirely different mood: Nancy's fear that physical desire will overwhelm her. With an extended image of spiders (which she calls Pound's astrological sign) as emblems of human passion, she describes how their invasion into our living space overwhelms us. Set against the fallen apple and other post-Edenic images, she says of passion:

The summer days were harsh with drought;
On earth there was no movement left
Beyond the apple's fall, when out
Of those dry husks the spiders crept.

Lust, our legacy after the fall, is both conscious and unconscious: "In my mind," she writes, "other spiders ranged / . . . laced with desires," and they mixed with the dreams of "the waking hours." A prophet warns her of the cunning nature of passion and that the heart "must be aware." Her hope lies in some unforeseen salvation. But in the end,

The spiders wove again their keen
Dry webs, and stalked the earth unkempt.

In a more secure mood, she reflects on the way Pound consumes her every activity. She is aware of him in her travels, for example:

Green runs the grass there,
In a great wind under the Downs after sunset;
Our feet trod the plain.

Even nature is transformed by her recollection of their earlier passion. Although five tall trees initially "austerely" watched her "return alone," they begin to

Watch our ghosts move together again,
They wait as beacons—
Five trees burning,
Dark intensities in a silent land. ("Pays Hanté")

Tristan Tzara and Louis Aragon

After her complicated affair with Pound, Nancy became involved with Tristan Tzara in a relationship that, for Nancy, was atypically relaxed and free of contention. Like Nancy, Tzara believed in the sacred mission of art and, fortunately, in person, was not the nihilistic eccentric he was rumored to be since founding Dadaism in 1916.

Motivated by the horrific human cost of the Great War, Dada was a pacifist movement that expressed itself in a nihilistic rejection of traditional values. "To us," said Tzara, "it was a war of false emotions and feeble justifications. . . . Honor, Country, Morality, Family." His goal was to create an art free of logic in order to evoke free associations that would expose the absurdity of "knowledge" and language—specifically, those concepts that had led to the Great War. "[Any] philosophy is the question," he argued. "Everything we look at is false. I do not consider the relative result more important than the choice between cake and cherries after dinner. . . . If I cry out: "*Ideal, ideal, ideal, Knowledge, knowledge, knowledge, Boomboom, boomboom, boomboom,*" I have given a pretty faithful version of progress, law, and morality, [etc.], only to conclude that everyone dances to his own personal boomboom."[35]

Tzara, born Samuel Rosenstock, had taken for his name two words that conveyed the nonsensical, aggressive nature of contemporary culture. He had made his first proclamations in Zurich, where many of Europe's most distinguished people lived—Joyce, Jean Arp, Stefan Zweig, and Franz Werfel, as well as Einstein, Lenin, and Jung. Tzara began his artistic mission with five other men at a cabaret. They looked like a six-piece band, but each one "played himself" as if he were a solo instrument.[36] They shredded news articles and read isolated words—"a sound poem"; they performed "simultaneous poems," with different voices reading a random piece in different languages simultaneously. Painter friends arrived and randomly mixed garbage and paint; people danced in Cubist designs (as best they could), often accompanied by African drumbeats, sometimes with screams. Their intent was to reflect the meaninglessness of everything.

It amused Nancy to learn how carefully Tzara, Picabia, Arp, and Duchamp planned their shocking antics. When Tzara delivered the first Dada manifesto, he did so with a brioche dangling from his left nostril; at the first Dada "event" in Paris, he read a poem—an arbitrarily selected minor newspaper item—accompanied by cowbells, castanets, and rattles. He and his cohorts received the responses they sought—hissing and insults, with vegetables and fruits, and on one occasion, a veal cutlet, hurled at them. By the time Tzara performed his *Vasoline Symphony*, the gendarmes were stationed in assigned places.

Nancy and her friends Eugene McCown and René Crevel performed in Tzara's play *LECMOM 3rd Diens*, which had seventeen roles (most played by a few people). The author's only prerequisite was that the actors dance on stage when they changed and made themselves up. Tzara defined Nancy's character as "pretty, full with spirit and joy in life." Since there were usually riots when any of Tzara's plays were performed, Man Ray, Milhaud, Satie, and other friends participated in both the plays and the police skirmishes that followed.

When Nancy's friend Norman Douglas met Tzara, he expected him to be near psychotic. Instead, Douglas discovered that "the mystery man of ethical and artistic revolution, [whom I] pictured . . . as a thunderous *ex-cathedra* giant, ominous, black-bearded, [and] full of blast," was reserved and polite.

In fact, Tzara was conspicuous for his cogent intelligence (which Nancy had called his "pyrotechnical brilliance"), charm, and wit. He was pale and very slender, and his dark, large eyes had an unusual intensity; he wore a monocle.

Nancy always said of their relationship, "Lord, how we laughed," forever astonished at their uniquely similar sense of humor and comforted by their unwavering and gentle affection for each other. One night in a café, Tzara impulsively devoured the entire contents of a mustard pot. After fits of laughter and confused sounds of "handkerchief" and "cloud," he conceived of a play, *Mouchoir de nuage*, which he dedicated to her.

Nancy became closely involved with the Dadaists, fascinated by the similarities of their broken syntax and the general dynamics of other avant-garde artists: Cocteau, Antheil, Man Ray, Dalí, Picasso, Braque, Gris, Ernst, "and how many more." Sometimes she and Tzara spent the day discussing art, or they worked on separate or joint projects. Nancy translated Marlowe's *Faust* for him for a French production. They spent their evenings with the Dadaists or other highly talented people: Brancusi, Man Ray, his model Kiki, Iris Tree, and McCown. They often dressed in artists' colors, as Nancy had been dressed as a child: like a Manet in black and white or a Renoir in pastels. They also dressed exquisitely for Paris's most sumptuous costume balls. One photograph of Nancy and Tzara at the elegant Beaumont ball in Paris was widely published: she is standing in profile in a silver pantsuit and wearing a mask over her eyes and a top hat; he is kneeling and kissing her hand.

Most frequently, they met at the elegant Le Boeuf sur le Toit, which catered to both Parisian society and the intellectual avant-garde. It had been named after Cocteau and Milhaud's Dadaist opéra bouffe. The Dadaists scribbled sketches and posted them on the café's walls, but Nancy and Tzara's favorite table was under Picabia's painting *L'Oeil cacodylate* (the salt used in treating venereal disease), with the artist's trademark multiple eyes and dotted torso. Cocteau was a regular there—at the drums, in his signature opera hat and red tie, and he often sat beside eighteen-year-old Raymond Radiguet. The hired pianist read Rimbaud to himself (with the poems propped on the music rack), as he played jazzed-up variations of Bach fugues. Georges Auric or Milhaud played the piano when he stepped down. Other musical regulars included Erik Satie, Arthur Honneger, and Francis Poulenc. After a time, people like King Ferdinand of Romania, Grand Duke Dimitri Pavlovich, and Dayang Muda with Coco Chanel became patrons. Proust presumably said, as he was dying in 1922, "If I could only be well enough to go once to the cinema and to Le Boeuf sur le Toit."[37]

As much as Nancy cared for Tzara, she ended their affair (1924), because she was still emotionally involved with Pound. But she remained in touch with him for many years; he fought in Spain during the Spanish Civil War and during World War II was her contact with the maquis when he was direc-tor of Resistance broadcasts in the south of France.

Although the Dadaists were not programmatically political, they had a great deal in common with the Surrealists. In words Tzara might have used, Aragon called for

> no more painters, no more writers, no more sculptors, no more religions, no more republicans, no more royalists, no more imperialists, no more anarchists, no more socialists, no more Bolshevists, no more aristocrats, no more armaments, no more police, no more countries, enough of all these imbecilities, no more, no more, no more, no more, no more.[38]

The Surrealists would turn the Dadaists' negativity into an affirmation of the irrational, dreams, and chance, and these, they hoped, would become path-ways to a new society.

Louis Aragon made Nancy forget Pound, and they had a long and intense affair. When they were first seen together in 1926, both men and women were dazzled by the couple. His good looks were legendary. He was tall, thin, and dark—a man of charm, good manners, and remarkably beautiful blue eyes. Buñuel said he was "so handsome, you can't believe [it]." Others found him as "beautiful as a young god but terribly shy."[39] Nancy's beauty, too, was often described as "incandescent" or "stunning" in the fashion and society news. Tall and slender, she "carried herself with an erect military bearing, walking quickly . . . with an unusual scissorslike movement of her long legs, . . . lead-ing others, always out in front a step or two. [Her] head had a sculptured look, and her features, sharply defined, . . . were accented by a pair of light blue eyes. . . . No one ever forgot Nancy's eyes," "large and lustrous and more star-tlingly turquoise blue than any ever seen. They gleamed from the von Don-gen eye shading around them—a new fashion [created by Nancy]. . . . Her exquisite . . . head was usually tightly turbaned, holding a regular life fountain of light hair—near blonde but untinted and with a natural slight wave." Her arms were "elbow deep in African ivory bracelets."[40]

From the beginning, Nancy saw Aragon as a person of extremes—intense and at times violent; at other times, very charming. She admired his "innate competence" in all his endeavors, as well as his total absorption in whatever he was doing—"a demon for work" who seldom tired: "He once wrote in front of me . . . a long analytical essay, *Philosophie des Paratonerrés*, which he began one evening before dinner and finished some thirty-six hours later, with hardly any time off for sleep or meals. The subject of this 10,000 word criti-cism was philosophy, stretching from Heraclitis to Spengler, through Marx, Engels and Dühring."[41]

They had a great deal in common, from a deep commitment to human rights and belief in the social function of art to an antagonism toward the society that had produced the Great War. Nancy was also fascinated by his and Breton's goals, which became the mantra of the Surrealists—their commitment to unifying the inner (dream) and outer mental worlds. Aragon invited Nancy to meet with the Surrealists at Cyrano's,[42] and she often joined in their conversations regarding how unconscious thought is purposive in the most unexpected aspects of everyday behavior. Nancy had been studying Freud since 1919; in 1930 she would publish Samuel Beckett's *Whoroscope*, a poem that relied on the interweaving of conscious and unconscious thought processes.

The Surrealists had found a broad and encompassing salvation in psychoanalysis that served several postwar needs. Freud had explained civilization and its discontents and at the same time provided a kind of metaphysics for the exile, adrift amid the recent loss of religious, social, and family values. Psychoanalysis also promised an inner coherence to fill the personal or cosmic loneliness of the times, the malaise of the postwar world. It provided validity for the irrational life and for the "automatic" formulas of the Surrealists' spontaneous, dreamlike, "pure" art forms. In order to fulfill these needs, groups of thirty or so young people met religiously at least once and often twice a day. Nancy notes of one such meeting:

> There was *la période des sommeils* [sleep], during which several surrealists . . . went into a sort of trance and spoke aloud the thoughts of images that came through their subconsciousness, which were taken down, and occasionally published. . . . There was also a game they often played . . . which can be compared, on a high intellectual level, to the game called "Consequences." One person writes a sentence, which is then covered save the last word, and the next person writes a sentence onto it. All at random, until a complete text has been completed.[43]

But it was the Surrealists' bitterness toward World War I and their commitment to exposing the false dreams and hollow values that produced it that were again particularly meaningful to Nancy. As she put it: "All the jingo values of *La Patrie* and *La Gloire*, the militarism so real to France, were anathematized, and colonialism was consistently denounced."[44] The Great War remained an abiding topic of conversation between Nancy and Aragon.

Aragon adored Nancy for her intense curiosity about his work and her unfeigned fascination with Surrealism. In return, he encouraged her to write and shared her interest in avant-garde and primitive art. He was so supportive of her desire to collect African and Oceanic art that he took her to English and French ports in search of the ivories that returning sailors had sold to curio shops and junk dealers. (Afterward, they would stop on the road for huge dandelion salads with omelets and wine, which they shared with equal relish.) Aragon later collected paintings by artists whom Nancy already favored—Picabia, Tanguy, Dalí, and Duchamp. Now, and for many years to come, he worshipped Nancy and wrote poems to her, as well as the novel *Blanche, ou l'oubli*.

Not all of Aragon's artistic and political interests were congenial to Nancy. "The ephemeral is a divinity as polymorpous as its name," he wrote in *Paris Peasant* (1926), where he tried to construct a new mythology of modern life. Gas pumps, he believed, with their strange dials, bright colors, and words in a foreign language, have an allure akin to primitive deities: "O Texaco motor oil, Eco, Shell, great inscriptions of human potential."[45] In addition, Aragon was fervently drawn to Communism and had joined the party in the late 1920s. But his long disputations on the subject had a limited appeal to Nancy. Regarding herself as an anarchist, she wanted immediate action, not theory. "Up and at 'em!" remained her battle cry.

As Nancy came to know the Surrealists, she questioned some of their values: "There was *le côté noir* [a dark side] to it," she wrote, adding: "The suicide of young men, either from postwar despair, the despair of an artist or of a man who could not bear his inability to express himself fully, was in a sense honored." Nancy, always well mannered and polite in public, also disliked the Surrealists' bizarre public antics, their "waves of *le scandale pour le scandale*,"[46] which included a notorious demonstration at Anatol France's funeral with their manifesto "A Corpse (Have You Ever Slapped a Dead Man)" and their "Hands off Love" essay, defending Charlie Chaplin for his "inherent right" to ask his aggrieved and divorcing wife to perform "unnatural acts."

Nancy was deeply moved when Aragon shared his background with her. The illegitimate son of a well-to-do right-wing politician, he was named Aragon in honor of his father's former Spanish mistress. He was brought up in an all-female household, and his grandmother told him that his young mother was his sister. On the occasions he visited his father, he addressed him as *parrain* (godfather). When Aragon was twenty, his mother told him the truth of his birth but bound him to secrecy, which he respected until she died twenty-five years later. Like Nancy, he had turned to reading and writing at a very early age; he studied medicine for five years before deciding to write and serve humanity.[47] Nancy thought his early life might explain his flamboyant and erratic behavior. For example, after spending four years writing the novel *La Défense de l'infini*, in November 1927, with Nancy at his side in a Madrid hotel, he ripped up the 1,500-page manuscript and hurled it into the fireplace. He was performing a religious ceremony to appease his Surrealist friends who regarded the novel as a decadent, bourgeois genre. Nancy saved as many pages as she could from the flames.[48]

When Nancy arranged for G. M. to meet Aragon, G. M. ranted on about "iconoclasm gone crazy" and the "insane technique" of the new generation. Aragon smiled gently and answered him with due deference. G. M., usually critical of Nancy's admirers, liked Aragon immediately and was impressed by his intellect, beautiful diction, and humanistic vision of life. He found Aragon's commitment to art irresistible: "That young man . . . would probably go far." He even acknowledged that he was good looking.[49]

Despite their common interests, Nancy and Aragon had a very stormy relationship. In Spain, Italy, Holland, and Germany, they had violent, drunken arguments. When Nancy was sober she was charming and reasonable, but when she drank too much she could become abusive and break anything within hand range. Her bracelets often left their mark on her lover's face. In addition, both Nancy and Aragon were easily angered, and each complained that the other was too demanding sexually. Aragon agonized over Nancy's infidelities; her penchant for running off with another man for a few hours nearly drove him mad, and he was always suspicious of her. On one occasion, while Aragon was writing *Traité du style* in Normandy, with Breton in the vicinity writing his famous *Nadja*, their friendship nearly ended. After reading their work aloud, as they often did in Nancy's presence, Breton became intimidated by Aragon's fluency and brilliance, and Aragon worried that Breton was both mocking his writing and planning to take Nancy away from him: "I suddenly discovered jealousy [and] I can still hear André laughing at the pages of the *Traité*."[50]

Observing their frequent battles, breakups, and reconciliations, a friend commented: "Louis always seems to be packing or unpacking."[51] Regardless of this, in January 1927, the British press contained this news:

From Paris comes the news that Miss Nancy Cunard . . . is soon to marry again. The gentleman in the case is Mr. Louis Aragon, who is described as very clever, very modern, very realistic, and in a way, highbrow. He would have to be in the forefront of the newest intellectual movement to please Miss Cunard, who is one of the three or four English girls who find Montparnasse more to their taste than Mayfair, and to whom none would deny cleverness. . . . Her verse [has] gained many admirers.

Less than two weeks later, the papers printed: "Miss Cunard asks us to state that the rumor that she is engaged to Mr. Louis Aragon is entirely without foundation."[52]

The dramatic end of their affair occurred in Venice in 1928. Aragon attempted suicide with sleeping pills and was discovered by an English friend. As more than one person has observed, it is curious that he, trained in medicine, underestimated the lethal dosage. Shortly after their breakup, Aragon characterized Nancy as

aristocratic and British, like a character from a novel, with the assured demeanor of women accustomed to being entertained, and entertaining. She dressed very well, with a touch of eccentricity, . . . spoke polished French, with no accent, [and] sometimes us[ed] amusing or picturesque Anglicized turns of phrase, in a melodious, siren's voice. . . . Nancy drank and became drunk often. Then she would become unpleasant, slapping her companion's face with the ivory or metal which clasped her from wrist to elbow. Sometimes she too bore traces of one of these violent scenes, which she disguised with thick purple veils attached to one of the small extravagant hats then in fashion. She was also a traveler by nature, crossing the seas on an impulse, . . . suddenly sending impenetrable telegrams, written while drunk, arranging a rendezvous in Bermuda or Naples as other people would issue invitations for a weekend in the country.[53]

Still, Aragon remained in love with Nancy. He hung a life-size reproduction of a Man Ray photo of her in his apartment. For many years after he married, he met with her from time to time in a friend's office. (His wife, who "felt that she was still fighting for Aragon's heart," would not allow Nancy into their home and even forbade the mention of her name.)[54]

Aragon had met his wife in 1928; the petite, red-haired Elsa Triolet was a prolific author and a recipient of the Prix Goncourt. He said that Elsa had strongly influenced his writing and added the curious comment: "I was her dog. It's my fashion." Similarly, Aragon, nicknamed "the wild duck" before he met Nancy, came to be known as "le Cunard sauvage," since most people thought that she was clearly the more dominant of the two.[55] All the same, Nancy would come to state many times during the last years of her life that Aragon was the only man who ever truly loved her, and he remained devoted to her.

Even Elsa admitted that her husband's most beautiful love poetry had been written for Nancy, and most of the poems in his ironically titled *La Grande Gaîté* are about his unhappiness with her. "Poem to Shout Among the Ruins" begins:

Let us spit if you want
On what we have loved together
Let us spit on love
On our unmade beds
On our silence and on the stammered words
On the stars even if they were

Your eyes
On the sun even if it were
Your teeth
On eternity even if it were
Your mouth
And on our love
Even if it were
Your love
Let us spit if you want.

Some of his war poems, about the altered political and emotional world, also invoke his passion for Nancy. Virtually every collection of Aragon's poetry in print contains Nancy's English translations. Her rendering of "Tcheliab-traktrostroi Waltz" begins:

This is an ancient waltz
That the idle danced amid sighs,
It would bring a catch in the breath
When they gazed in each other's eyes.
Today a peculiar baton
Whirls to the stale elixir
For what spins without losing breath
Is the mortar and concrete mixer.

Although Aragon suffered Nancy's rejection for many years, their common interests brought them together in later common causes. Both fought against the fascists during the Spanish Civil War and World War II. In the latter, after being taken prisoner by the Germans and escaping to the unoccupied area, Aragon became one of the heroes of the Resistance for his bravery and contributions to Resistance journals. To this day, many of his poems chronicling the Nazi occupation of France remain legendary. During the most difficult time of her life in 1960, Nancy called on Aragon to defend her sanity to a world that seemed to have abandoned her. This was not the last time he came to her rescue.

Beginning Lifelong Friendships

Nancy lived in several apartments in Paris, including the one Modigliani had occupied until his death in 1920. She spent most of her Paris years at a first-floor apartment on the Ile Saint-Louis, on the corner of rue Le Regrattier.

It was near the home of her childhood friend Iris Tree and overlooked Notre Dame and the Seine. Raymond Mortimer recalls how she would laughingly apply an early T. S. Eliot line to one of its blood-red painted rooms: "[It has] an atmosphere of Juliet's tomb."[56] She also had green-paneled walls and a low-ceilinged sitting room with a comfortable plum-colored velvet settee. All the rooms were filled with African carvings, some erotic in nature, and with what her less stylish friends called "outrageous paintings": two de Chiricos; two Tanguys; a large Picabia gouche of a man with four pairs of eyes, a vermillion-dotted body, and one arm sheathed in black, as well as several McCowns; sketches by Wyndham Lewis; and *Faun*, a painting by Pound's great friend, the Vorticist Henri Gaudier-Brzeska, whose war death had brought them together.

Always restless, Nancy often traveled and frequently visited friends for a few days; she perpetually worried about overstaying her welcome, even though she invited the same friends to stay for weeks and months when she rented a house. In February 1922, she visited Curtis Moffat and Iris Tree near Menton; in March, she went to Monte Carlo; in April, Fontainebleau; during the summer, she went to Eddington, England, with Iris, Diana Cooper, Prince Faid, and Aldous Huxley and then joined friends on a yacht in Deauville; in September, she went to Spain; in October, to Venice with Eugene McCown, Robert McAlmon, Wyndham Lewis, and Osbert and Sachie Sitwell. In the mid-1920s, she began spending long periods away on walking tours in France, Spain, and England. Her scrapbooks are filled with photos of her friends, often in silly poses.

She maintained her scrapbooks throughout the Paris years, adding clippings from British, French, American, and German sources about cultural events and about her friends ("Mr. Alvaro Guevara is the Latest Lion of the Brush"). The 1924–1925 scrapbook, for example, is filled with news columns about the most recent work of Eliot, Pound, Wyndham Lewis, and the Dadaists (especially Tzara) and Surrealists. She saved, as she would throughout her life, every poem by Aragon that was published in the press. She also saved poems written by some of her admirers. One, verging on Petrarchan lovesickness, wrote:

Nancy, Nancy
Caught my fancy,
Caught my fancy in a thrice.
First, I thought her very nice,
Very elegant and pretty,
Very charming, very witty;
Then I lost my heart completely,
Could no longer think discretely;

Suddenly became much thinner,
Lost my sleep, forgot my dinner;
Slowly pined and sadly languished
Till I asked myself in anguished,
Anguished voice, with face aghast:
Have I met my fate at last?
Is this real or is it fancy,
Is she here and is she Nancy?

She collected items on blacks in Paris, jazz, Diaghilev, Antheil, Stravinsky, Berenice Abbott, modern music (Futurist, Danish, British) and theater, and an unusual one about an "Amazing Scene" in Paris that described how "Youths with Howls and Whistles Hold up Russian Ballet Performance" and "Bills Printed in Blood-Red Rained on Head of Audience." She also saved an essay she wrote, "House Hunting in the Dordogne." She clipped some striking images of herself: Wyndham Lewis's Venice drawing, commissioned for *Sketch*; the costume ball photo with Tzara, also for *Sketch*; Manuel Ortiz de Zárate's painting of her as a madonna; and Curtis Moffat's photo of her before a mirror, taken for the *Frankfurter Zeitung*.[57] She kept articles of the mid-1920s that she had been asked to write for *Vogue*, such as "Paris Today as I See It: A Record of Recent Events—Theatrical, Literary, Artistic." In the July 1926 issue, she highlighted Dada, Surrealism, and Josephine Baker.

She visited her mother in London regularly. Her father had become ill in 1925, and Nancy visited him frequently at Haycock and nursed him in his illness. After he died in November 1925, she told friends how difficult it was to see him dying before her eyes. In his will, he wrote: "I beg that my funeral may be of the most simple kind and that black horses be employed. I would prefer to go to my grave in a farm wagon to a hearse if convenient to my relatives and I ask that there be no flowers."[58] He left Nancy the sum of £14,418 13s 2d, in addition to a family heirloom and gift given to him by his hunting friends. He did not mention Maud in his will.

Although Nancy and her mother were always impatient with each other, they shared an ardent commitment to the arts, and Maud encouraged Nancy to write. She even acted like Nancy's agent, entertaining editors at every opportunity and defending her daughter's poetry against criticism from friends, regardless of their social or political standing; ever since her move to Grosvenor Square—and now at London's prestigious Carlton House Terrace—she had been hosting the most important emissaries of government and the arts. By 1926, she had changed her name to Emerald, which a numerologist had advised. As she explained to G. M., who was close to cardiac arrest when he thought she had remarried: "Emerald is not a surname but the jewels I wear are emeralds and since I am nicknamed The Emerald Queen I have adopted it as my Christian name."[59]

Also encouraging Nancy to write were three American women who would become her closest lifelong friends. Kay Boyle recalls first meeting Nancy in Paris, "when all of us danced on a summer night in a square where an accordion and a violin and an old piano were being played. . . . Nobody marveled at the sight of a piano set out in the public street, because that was the 'twenties, and anything was possible."[60] Kay, from Cincinnati, Ohio, and former editor of the prestigious experimental magazine *Broom*, had moved with her French husband to France in 1923. They divorced shortly afterward, and Kay became so fascinated with the "Revolution of the Word" contributors to *transition* magazine that she joined the editorial staff . She eventually wrote more than fifty books—including novels, short stories, poetry, and essays—and was a journalist as well. The recipient of many literary awards, her moral imperative, in life and in literature, was to actively engage in social and political causes.

Solita Solano and Janet Flanner, two aspiring American journalists, had arrived in Paris in 1922. Outspoken suffragettes, they would be immortalized as Nip and Tuck in Djuna Barnes's *Ladies Almanack*. When Eugene McCown introduced Nancy to them, the three women became instant soul mates. Janet recalled Solita's first impression of the gold-haired Nancy: she was "riveting, with eyes as blue as sapphires, a cause of wonder anywhere." Of all the women Janet and Solita were to meet during their first years in Europe, they felt closest to Nancy. As Nancy's enormous correspondence indicates, she would confide her most private thoughts to them for the rest of her life.[61]

Solita was a highly talented Boston beauty—an actress, novelist, poet, art and drama critic, editor, and journalist. Her lovely, sensitive face, short dark hair, and soft blue eyes inspired even the discriminating connoisseur of women, G. M., to nostrums of high praise. Janet, the handsome daughter of Quakers who had founded a settlement for African Americans, had left the University of Chicago to work at a girls' reformatory and married a man named Lane Rehm so she could get to New York. Once she arrived there, she became part of the Dorothy Parker Round Table at the Algonquin Hotel. When she and Solita met, they became inseparable. Solita, a drama critic for the *New York Herald Tribune,* was offered a job abroad, and the two women settled in Paris until World War II. They left for the United States shortly before the occupation and returned to France after the Liberation. Janet was the *New Yorker*'s famed "Genêt" (the French pronunciation of "Janet") for fifty years. Before the war, she wrote about art and literature; after it, about politics. Her focus was the French response to what was occurring in Paris, rather than her own.

Nancy was flattered on the occasions Janet wrote about her for her American readers: "Nancy Cunard is an extraordinary looking, eccentric, gifted — one of the best modern — English poets." Earlier, she had written: "Miss Cunard is one of England's best, if most infrequent poets. . . . With Wyndham Lewis of *Blast* fame and others of the early *Wheel* group, Miss Cunard has long been an intransigent hub of modern literary interests, has a small and severe collection of great modern paintings and an enormous collection of African art, is still beautiful, a tireless traveler, and a remarkable letter writer."[62]

The close kinship of the three women gave each a sense of family that functioned as a "surrogate blood-tie" for the rest of their lives. Here were three independent married women estranged from their husbands. Janet called them "a fixed triangle" and later boasted: "We survived all the spring quarrels and the sea changes of forty-two years of modern female fidelity." When one wrote another in the trio, she signed her letter with a tripod or the fraction ⅓; when Nancy wrote to both Janet and Solita, she began with the singular "Darling." Shortly after meeting, they had begun to share a recipe for staying thin: "work, worry, and sex." Most important, they shared a disdain for pretension and pomposity and a deep interest in one another's work. Janet admired Nancy's *Outlaws* (1921) and believed that her long poem *Parallax* (1925) was superior to *The Waste Land*.[63]

The great photographer Berenice Abbott frequently remarked on their striking appearance and how "smart and elegant" they were. Contributing to their glamour were Maud's unwanted Poirot and Vionnet gowns, which she sent Nancy, who shared her splendid gifts with her friends. It was thus in great style that the fashionable trio frequented Paris's most stylish restaurants and pursued conversations late into the night. Solita acknowledged that they must have been striking in appearance because "painters begged them to sit for them." They were captivated by "Nancy's Egyptian head with Nefertiti's proud eyes and fine taut mouth painted scarlet" and Janet's "magnetically handsome" face.[64] The threesome wore less fashionable garb when they danced in Montmartre cafés and with crowds in the streets and when they socialized with blacks, gays, and lesbians.

Janet and Solita spent a great deal of time at Nancy's ill-heated apartment, which they called "the Grattery," on rue Le Regrattier. Nancy, almost a chain-smoker, had already developed a chronic cough and, as her letters of 1926 suggest, the early signs of rheumatism. But she entertained regularly, and Janet and Solita were among her favorite guests. Some of her parties were informal, like her gatherings with G. M., Duchamp and his beautiful friend Mary Reynolds, Havelock Ellis, and René Crevel. Others resembled Maud's grand soirées. One Christmas, when she was living with Tzara, Nancy devised a party at La Rotonde in honor of G. M.: she invited only young people, with the exception of Brancusi ("a fine bearded-old-shepherd of a face and to my mind one of the greatest sculptors of all time") and beautiful women.[65]

Although Nancy had come to know a great number of people in Paris, she was often lonely. Janet Flanner suggests that Nancy's emotional isolation was due, in part, to the fact that she was British, while she herself had a "double . . . satisfaction in living there," meeting the French while surrounded by American friends and acquaintances. Nancy knew the same Americans but, as Janet explains, was treated like a foreigner by people like Edith Wharton, Archibald MacLeish, John Dos Passos, e. e. cummings, Hart Crane, and Djuana Barnes. And, she adds, Nancy lacked a stabilizing significant other or the inner resources that allowed people like Scott and Zelda Fitzgerald to set themselves apart without additional emotional support.

Solita attributed Nancy's isolation to her strong social conscience. Often depressed or outraged "by social injustice," Solita writes, Nancy's anger was unique. Any "infringement of justice" provoked such passion that she would become visibly shaken and start an all-night debate: "She cared all too much."[66] Another factor that set Nancy apart was the continual intrusion of the press. Throughout the years in Paris, she was the object of scrutiny on every subject from her clothing to her health; she was always in the news when she visited her mother and was at times subtly and facetiously described as a dilettante "poetess":

> When a year or two ago, Mrs. Fairbairn, Lady Cunard's poetess daughter, took a flat in Paris, most members of the artistic and intellectual circles in London of which she had been such a well-known member, were afraid that she was lost to them forever. . . . Now however, she is back in England for a few months.
>
> Lady Cunard so adores London that she will hardly ever leave it, and her daughter, the poetess Nancy Fairbairn, tries her hardest to lure her over to Paris, where Nancy now passes most of her time.

One of the more humorous variations was in the *London Mail*: "Nancy vows she won't stand us anymore. Whenever she can she leaves us for Paris. . . . As a rule, Nancy affects the Society of Futurist Artists and Highbrows, whereas the friends of Lady Cunard are either statesmen, brilliant Society beauties, or operatic celebrities who don't bother their heads about books and things."[67]

However, when Nancy published *Outlaws*, *Sublunary*, and *Parallax*, she was overcome by the popular press's indifference to her poetry and its obstinate focus on her clothing or bohemian life in Paris. Serious critics wrote laudatory reviews, and she had already received flattering notes such as the one from the *Saturday Review*'s editor in London: "Rereading your verses has given me a real thrill today. I like them better than any of the very modern stuff that has come my way; they are so free in form and yet so severe in expression." But when her most important critic, G. M., reviewed her work with only qualified praise, stating that her poetry "revealed more genius than in the great mass of her contemporaries but less talent. . . . Genius cannot be acquired . . . but talent can be,"[68] she was devastated. The well-respected Janet Flanner may have publicly called *Parallax* "superior" to *The Waste Land*, but Nancy's underlying insecurity did not allow her to embrace the positive reviews.

The *Daily Chronicle*'s report, following the release of *Parallax*, began, "A striking young woman . . . is Miss Cunard, : . . much happier and more at home in Paris . . . the Paris of Montparnasse—than in London, where she might have been a social-light [*sic*] if she had wished." One writer questioned what Tennyson would have thought of ladies who wrote poems containing such lines as "I hear life's maggot gnawing its last shred"; another included the dubious compliment: "[Her poetry] has a complexity and grasp of reality which is frequently lacking in women's poetry." Under Nancy's photo in the *London Mail* with a caption announcing the publication of *Outlaws*, the columnist wrote: "She writes poetry that we can't for the life of us understand, even when we try ever so hard." The remainder of the article focused on her stylish hat.[69]

Many journalists seemed obsessed with Nancy's "defiance" in publishing under her maiden name: "Perhaps because she is a poetess and very modern in her ideas, she is known as Nancy Cunard always, [ignoring] that some nine years ago she was married." Others ignored the name she had used on her books: "Mrs. Sydney Fairbairn has long given up mere society for the more stimulating company of artists. Mrs. Fairbairn is a pattern of independence and has written poetry. She spends much time in France." This curious focus on Nancy's surname ended when Sydney remarried in August 1926, although coverage of the marriage, even the brief item in the *New York Herald*, contained more information about Nancy than the bride and groom, ending: "Miss Cunard is very much of the artists' set in Paris, and happiest in that environment."[70] Feminist critics studying women in 1920s Paris may be tempted to view Nancy's use of "Cunard" rather than "Fairbairn" as a gesture of her defiance of repressive, patriarchal power, but I would argue that, despite Nancy's commitment to liberal political and social causes and despite her own life experiences, she was not involved in classic feminist issues. Interestingly enough, she never removed her wedding ring.

Although she was to put her career as a poet on hold as she took on the role of publisher and social activist, she clipped every review she could find for her scrapbooks, including the positive ones, which deserve mention. Some, regarding her first volume, *Outlaws* (1921), included the following:

Nancy Cunard has an unquestionable gift of language, even of eloquence, . . strong and skillfully fashioned. (*Times Literary Supplement*, 24 February 1921)

A Poet Worth Watching, . . . a first book, . . . but it is something more; it is the work of a young poet of considerable quality. . . . The language has almost an Elizabethan flourish, something of the old confidence and genius that have so largely given way to cheek and cleverness in the poetry cliques to-day. (*Evening Standard*, 6 April 1921)

[They are] entirely genuine and strangely individual poems [with] an independent poise, movement, and even tranquility. (*Nation and Atheneum*, 7 May 1921)

[With] energy and economy [and] by sheer intrepidity, she lifts herself above the throng of poets of our time. (*New Age*, 26 May 1921)

Reviews of the second, *Sublunary* (1923), included these:

It is poetry with a sense of dignity and of responsibility to the high standards of its art. [With] vision, melody and form, . . . Miss Cunard has a swift eye for the details of a scene and a delicate sense of atmosphere. She can sketch a landscape and evoke its sentiment in a very few telling strokes. (*Daily Telegraph*, 15 June 1923)

In the descriptive passages is always emotional meaning. . . . Sincerity ranks, among the intellectual virtues, far above agility. This poet has both. (*Saturday Review*, 28 July 1923)

Most noteworthy for a certain dignified intellectual quality and a determined shapeliness, a gracefulness of form. (*Evening Standard*, 29 July 1923)

Nancy's first two volumes were written in what came to be known nearly four decades later as "confessional poetry," associated with Sylvia Plath and Anne Sexton.

The remarkable *Parallax* (1925), about twice the length of *The Waste Land*, addressed the same subject as Eliot's: the disintegration of values in the modern world. Unlike Eliot's personae, however, Nancy's figures illustrated the inability to maintain a moral and spiritual value system due to the relative nature of individual perception and reality itself. In this, Nancy anticipated the metaphysical-ontological relativism that marked much of the twentieth century's turn from traditional values to a plural secularism. Her intellectual clarity, unique concrete images, and occasionally passionate confessions distinguish *Parallax* as her greatest poem. Some of its reviews applauded Nancy:

[One of the few new poets who] rejects the older forms of poetry, . . . [to] give the work a passionate, an almost tragic quality of expressing themselves in a way that has never been tried before. T. S. Eliot is the first who heard the new music in its full harmony. Miss Cunard has caught strains of it too. She is not piping over again Mr. Eliot's tune [but] adding her own motifs and orchestration to the general theme. Their resemblance to Eliot are at once as obvious and as specious as the resemblance between Keats and Shelley. [Miss Cunard] has an understanding of the zeitgeist, which distinguishes the true poet. (*Outlook*, 4 July 1925)

Miss Cunard has a very considerable expressive power. Her language is alive and free from the poetaster's time-worn turns of speech. (*Guardian*, 6 July 1925)

Miss Cunard's poem would never have been conceived without the example of Mr. Eliot. But even when this is recognized, Miss Cunard's poem shows the individuality of its author; she transcribes emotions . . . with remarkable subtlety. It seems to be the creation of a resilient mind. (*Nation*, 2 May 1925)[71]

Nancy retained a residence in Paris until 1928, and as the years passed she traveled more frequently but with increasing dissatisfaction. Despite the glamour of her itineraries and the celebrity of her companions, she was bored and isolated. In "Voyages North" she explains her earliest reasons for traveling, her need for an escape from the "hours interminable" in the city. Since "the first breath of country" invariably offered inner calm, she would travel the world and observe different landscapes and cultures:

—But if I were free
I would go on, see all the northern continents
Stretch out before me under winter sunsets;
Look into the psychology
Of Iceland, and plumb the imaginations
of strange people in faraway lands
walk through the days
Enjoying the remoteness,
and laughter in foreign places.

If she could "learn / More than one could remember," she might be released of her memories of wasted time, as well as the guilt of sexual dissipation:

I should cure my heart of longing and impatience
And all the penalties of thought-out pleasure,

Those aftermaths of degradation
That come when silly feasts are done.

"Wise and prodigal," connecting with nature, she would be "made human by imagination," free to say farewell "to memories" and "analytical introspection." She could then recover the elation of spiritual transcendence through nature, become one with the universe again, and "stand on a northern hill-top / shouting at the sun!"

From the 1920s until her last, pain-filled years, Nancy pursued her restless travels. When she was in a large city, she yearned for the countryside; when she bought a house in the country, she traveled to seasides or lively cities. As one reads her letters from these Paris years—including walking trips in Provence, the Dordogne, and Dieppe, and visits to London, Venice, and Rome—it is clear that she traveled for the excitement of new environs as an antidote to loneliness. One is also astonished at the unusual number of locations from which she writes, with return addresses at countless hotels, at Cook's, and at various banks. Leonard Woolf had been astute in observing that life had hurt her and that beneath her laughter and gaiety was an air of sadness.[72]

In all her letters, Nancy writes of beautiful places, asks her friends specific questions, and answers others. In a letter from Switzerland, she ponders the requirements of a good day's work: "Is it true that 600 words is a fair, even a good amount per day? So says Virginia Woolf." Her postscript is: "How transplanted I feel and must seem—and yet, doesn't one take root almost anywhere?" When she is aware that she is confessing her loneliness, she rejects self-pity and interrupts herself to say, for instance: "I am alone. . . . Let us leave the emotional well [or] the 'inner violence' in the background."[73]

After a trip with Aragon, Nancy is unusually candid in confiding to Janet/ Solita that she is lonely, yearning to write, and drinking to distract herself from boredom. She begins: "Well back in the Grattery . . . but for what purpose? Oh, were it a poem. . . . So I take up the leak (for I cannot call it a pen) to tell you that our tripod, triumverate, and triplicity standeth firm, though its three legs be now straddled over the very world. *How I know* the[se] engulfing moods, . . . the insurmountable mood, like a wall rising between . . . the rest of nature." She is lethargic: "Alas, alas, more days than not it seems too far to reach for the last French book or to reread a letter." Life seems to have come to a standstill: "In such circumstances one notices mainly just how the wind blows the dust and that last week's flypaper was then in about the same condition as today. And alas, boiled beef and the changeless carrot of one's own trimming." She then specifies the remedy for her problems: "Only *at night*— after a nip out of a tooth glass maybe, one's self returns to one's self."

Another trip with Aragon is boring until she feels inspired to write: "A certain amount of petty annoyance came to me for not knowing how to dispose of the days. Essentially a place for work, from dusty dawn to dewless dark, very little work got done. — An *idea* came however — a long one — for a poem." Nancy does not delude herself about the problems she creates with the men who love her. Of Aragon, whom she respected for the rest of her life, she writes: "He is delicious — in perfect training, *always* to write at will, any place, of anything. And he is a very sweet person. Were I not myself so irreducibly myself I should be very happy. I am, as far as can be." Sometimes she has moments of elation, but they are short-lived. She writes her darlings from the beautiful Dordogne: "I was much moved [by] a wild and awakened landscape, cut, bound corn, steeping in damp. Joy and heart's ease at being again in the country (after Paris) — that was ghastly — so tarnished and hostile," and she concludes: "I laugh — laugh — but I have been desperately glum."

Similarly, from Switzerland, she writes: "You will have realized that I am now alone . . . and slightly drunk, so that Eliot's 'Whispers of Immortality' suddenly appears very significant. *Why* would take too long to explain." In another letter from Venice, she admits: "You had guessed I will be longing to leave whatever place I would be. . . . And let us go to that bar together, get drunk, and weep, palm-clasped or hand-clapping if need be on the way back — yes, but back where?" She also writes: "I am alone, but there is no wine."

Nancy had begun to feel ill. When she was only thirty, she described in a diary the neuritis in her right arm, "a shocking, startling pain": "Imagine the nerve — it's a long, thin plant encased in a bone. Then suddenly it becomes thinner, twists about as if to be off on a journey, turns and grinds on itself." But she kept her physical complaints to herself. She ignored them, mocked them, and defied them for at least the next twenty-five years.

• • •

Nancy would leave Paris in 1928, having idealized the city just as she had idealized Pound. She had overestimated the pleasures of entertaining and traveling; she had found the excitement of participating in the avant-garde insufficiently fulfilling. She was deeply discouraged about her poetry, despite each volume's positive reviews. Nancy may have become one of the great celebrities and symbols of the creative vitality of the era, but she still felt she lacked a defining sense of purpose.

20. Nancy and Tristan Tzara at a ball in Paris, as photographed by Man Ray

21. Louis Aragon

22. Janet Flanner

23. Solita Solano

24. Kay Boyle

25. Aldous Huxley

26. William Carlos Williams

27. Constantin Brancusi

28. Nancy models a coat designed by Sonia Delauney, as photographed by Curtis Moffat

29. Nancy, a fashion icon of the 1920s, as photographed by Barbara Ker-Seymer

30. Nancy, as photographed
by Man Ray

31. Nancy, as photographed by Cecil Beaton

32. John Banting, portrait of Nancy

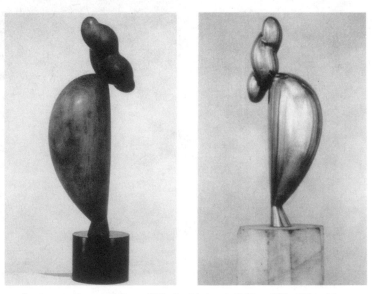

33. Constantin Brancusi, *Jeune Fille Sophistiquée* (*left*) and *The White Negress*

34. Oskar Kokoschka, *Painting of Nancy Cunard*

A WELL-KNOWN FIGURE IN LITERARY AND ARTISTIC CIRCLES
AS A SPANISH ARTIST SEES HER : NANCY CUNARD ; BY ORTIZ
DE ZARATE.

35. Manuel Ortiz de Zárate, Nancy as a madonna

36. Eugene McCown, *Portrait of Nancy Cunard*

37. Alvaro Guevara, portrait of Nancy

38. Wyndham Lewis, drawing of Nancy

39. Nancy, as photographed by Curtis Moffat

6

Reluctant Icon

Nancy Cunard . . . inspired half the poets and novelists of the 'twenties.
They saw her as the Gioconda of the Age.

—HAROLD ACTON

When Nancy lived in Paris, she was as much an icon of the Roaring Twenties as Zelda and F. Scott Fitzgerald. She was astonishingly beautiful and a fashion trendsetter, and her photos, along with details about her life, appeared in magazines and newspapers on both sides of the Atlantic.[1] Close friends described Nancy as "talented, rich, [and] energetic" but at the same time as "relentless, melancholy, driven, [and] wasted." They thought the combination of her creative talent, along with the prevalent social and moral freedoms of the era, led her, like many others, to "alcoholism, madness, and despair." Mary Hutchinson called attention to what would be Nancy's lifelong restlessness, solitary nature, and inner sadness: "She seemed always on the move, . . . dissatisfied—unsatisfied. . . . What was she seeking? . . . She kept up perfectly her facade, behind which one [saw] something moving—an independent, romantic and melancholy shadow which one [could] never approach. The facade was exquisite, made of gold leaf, lacquer, verdigris and ivory."[2]

If Nancy was lonely and misunderstood as a child and treated as a social oddity when she left her aristocratic home for bohemian Paris, the public adulation she received as a gay, liberated flapper was entirely misdirected. Nancy stubbornly insisted that the "'Jazz Age' (or whatever epithet was used to lend that decade a special aura) hardly added up to what it was often proclaimed to be." She abhorred the inaccuracy of the phrase "the wonderful twenties." More than once she exclaimed: "To hell with those days! They weren't so super-magnificent after all!" Janet Flanner knew that the 1920s were a painful time for her because she was idealistic and therefore vulnerable and melancholic, as her poetry reveals. All the same, as the popular press and most observers viewed her, she "had it all"; even to casual acquaintances, she was unique and unforgettable. As one put it: "Everybody old, it is hoped, can look back on one person who was incomparably bewitching," adding "and I have never met anyone comparable to Nancy Cunard."[3]

The beautiful, elegant, intelligent, sexually liberated, and charismatic Nancy Cunard became the stuff of literary myth and was immortalized by writers and artists in Europe and America. Despite her many protestations, she became a legend. Hemingway, some believe, fashioned Lady Brett in *The Sun Also Rises* on her (rather than Duff Twysden),[4] and she is the indisputable heroine of novels by Aldous Huxley (*Antic Hay*, *Those Barren Leaves*, and *Point Counter Point*), Michael Arlen (*The Green Hat*, *Piracy*, and *Lily Christine*, among others), Wyndham Lewis (*The Roaring Queen*), Louis Aragon (*Blanche, ou l'oubli*, and *Le Con d'Irène*), and Evelyn Waugh (*Unconditional Surrender*), and of plays by Tristan Tzara (*Mouchoir de nuage*) and Huxley (*The Gioconda Smile*). Even her beloved mentor G. M. had her in mind when he disrobed a beautiful woman in *Ulick and Soracha*.[5] She was the subject of a section of T. S. Eliot's original draft of *The Waste Land* and a figure in Ezra Pound's *Cantos*, Pablo Neruda's Spanish Civil War poems ("Waltz"), and numerous memoirs and poems by Kay Boyle and William Carlos Williams, as well as the focus of many respected writers who are lesser known today, such as Robert Nichols, Robert McAlmon, Hilaire Hiler, and Bob Brown. The following, from Richard Aldington's short story "Now Lies She There: An Elegy," typifies the way most writers introduced her persona:

> Constance is . . . the wreck of a noble woman. . . . In destroying herself she destroyed plenty of others. . . . She was lovely enough to seduce a saint.[6]

Nancy was also painted by Oskar Kokoschka, Manuel Ortiz de Zárate, Alvaro "Chile" Guevara, and Eugene McCown; photographed by Man Ray, Cecil Beaton, and Curtis Moffat; and drawn by Wyndham Lewis. She was sculpted numerous times by Brancusi (Nancy was unaware of two until photographs arrived from the Guggenheim Museum: "[There was] one in wood [*Jeune Fille sophistiquée*], the other in bronze [*The White Negress*]," she said, "both utterly unlike what I take to be my 'line,' but exquisite things").[7]

One can easily visualize Nancy in the 1920s, her head "so gracefully poised [that] it might have been carved in crystal with green jade for eyes."[8] She was "a tall wraith of a woman looking as though any wind might blow her away," visiting friends and artists, often exposing what Leonard Woolf had called her terrible vulnerability; at other times, appearing more confident and ca[...] free. The shy Samuel Beckett, hardly a womanizer like so many of her artis[...] friends, was fascinated by Nancy's "good mind" and talent, and he praised her long poem *Parallax*. But he was also very much "taken with Nancy, . . . [for] her striking looks [and] remarkable energy." He found her an excellent talker, and they met for cocktails at the Café d'Harcourt on "long summer evenings" or for concerts or dinner in Montmartre, followed by conversation.[9] He, too, over twenty years later, included her in his work, using the name Cunard six times in Lucky's famous soliloquy in *Waiting for Godot*. As Nancy's correspondence until the end of her life reveals, Beckett, Aragon, and Neruda—among all the artists she knew—lingered most in her thoughts; she would call for them before her death.

One can imagine Nancy with some of her male friends—some lovers; others not, like the good-looking William Carlos Williams, who idealized Nancy as his poetic and sexual muse. On the day she visited the poet and his wife, Flossie, at Villefranche, he thought that she was

> surely one of the major phenomena of that world. . . . If there was anything that was not on that courteous, cultured, and fearless mind, I have yet to discover it. Nancy was to me as constant as the heavens in her complete and passionate inconstancy. Out of passion, to defeat its domination, that tall, blond spike of a woman whose mind never, that I knew, was clouded by drink, kept herself burned to the bone. What else have martyrs done?[10]

They had first met when Williams copublished *Contact* with Robert McAlmon, and they liked each other immediately. In their earliest conversations, they discussed the immorality of pre–World War I values. When Williams subsequently coedited, again with McAlmon, *Pagany* magazine, Nancy contributed an essay, along with Nathanael West (who submitted a section of *Miss Lonelyhearts*), Marsden Hartley, Erskine Caldwell, and Williams. Williams always charmed Nancy with what she called "amazing stories" about his doctoring experiences in his native New Jersey, with its 200-year-old Italian communities. She admired him for his kind-heartedness and generosity, for sharing his skills and spirit with the less fortunate.

In his autobiography, the poet Williams describes Nancy as virtually saint-like in the purity of her acts. At the same time, the physician observes her penchant for drinking and aversion to food: she was

> straight as any stick, emaciated, holding her head erect, not particularly animated, her blue eyes completely untroubled; inviolable in her virginity of pure act. I never saw her drunk; I can imagine that she was never quite sober.

e understood the effect of the war on Nancy and her friend Iris:

> There was nothing left in either of them . . . , and yet they were young, appealing and assailable. . . . They were . . . quiet in their moods and . . . profligate in their actions.

Comparing each to a piece of beautiful sculpture, to a Galatea coming to life, he writes: "By their profligacy they were asserting a veritable chastity of mind which no one could disturb."[11]

Williams makes clear in the autobiography that he felt no sexual desire for Nancy or Iris, because of the purity in their pain: "Their 'suffering' came through with a depraved saintliness. Depravity was their prayer, their ritual, their rhythmic exercises. They denied sin by making it hackneyed in their own bodies, shucking it away to come out not dirtied but pure."[12] He focuses on Nancy's chastity of mind, on how her profligacy, taken to the extreme, had become her salvation: her innocence of mind and open sexuality created the white flame of her existence. Interestingly, one of Williams's literary critics, Harry Ahern, addresses the professional and personal Williams as a divided personality, which he describes in Dr. Williams and Mr. Hyde terms: as a physician, Williams was detached, objective, unemotional, and dispassionate; as a poet, he was intense, irrational, and erotic.[13]

He is candid about the tension in his life between lust and asceticism: "I am extremely sexual in my desires: I carry them everywhere and at all times I think that from that rises the drive which empowers us all. . . . A man does with it what his mind directs." And his mind directed his sexual abstinence before writing. One of his biographers connects Williams's purity in his "working abstinence" with the purity of Nancy's promiscuousness. According to more than one of his biographers, Nancy was his poetic muse.[14]

She fascinated him; he arranged private visits with her and then wrote about her in his journal; when he wrote poetry, he worked in his attic study, where he had posted a photo of her. Nancy also became the spur for his more uninhibited sexual activity with his wife. He describes in graphic detail their bubble baths in Rome and focuses on his wife's vigorous sexual needs: "What was this Parisian thing, this virus, that could so transform American women? . . . What was it about the intensity of this world [that] blew women into Amazons?" His biographer, Ahearn, explains: "Even Flossie, whom Williams had come to rely on as the stable, staid, and dependable housewife, revealed unexpected tendencies toward depravity during their sojourn in Paris." But Paul Mariani concludes: "In fact Nancy Cunard seems to have been the direct inspiration for *his* newly found freedom of sexual expression."[15]

Nancy and Williams introduced each other to prodigiously talented people. Nancy arranged for him to meet Tzara and many of the Dadaists and Surrealists. Williams brought Nancy closer into the company of Sylvia Beach, Adrienne Monnier, Peggy Guggenheim, and James and Nora Joyce. Williams recalls many unusual occasions with Nancy: her luncheons, followed by at least four sets of tennis with Hemingway and Harold Loeb, and her dinners that lasted from 10:00 P.M. until 5:00 A.M. with Iris, Clive Bell, McAlmon, and Bryher. At many of their soirées, they spoke of the terrors of the Great War, especially the zeppelin raids. Nancy's parties were always gala drinking events, and Williams vaguely recalls Jean Cocteau, John Rodker, and the Prince of Dahomey (a king's son from equatorial Africa)—within a dense crowd dancing in "drunken hilarity"; it was one of the most alcoholic evenings of his life.[16] In a more lucid, less dramatic recollection, he is taken with how Nancy wrapped a checkered handkerchief around her neck to hide fresh scratches after climbing a tree.

Williams visited his "exceptional" friend whenever he was abroad and before returning home always sent her flowers. They corresponded for many years; in 1931, he invited Nancy and her lover Henry Crowder to visit his New Jersey home, which they did. Williams later contributed to Negro and became chairman of a committee for medical aid to the Loyalists in Spain. He visited Nancy after World War II, and their long discussions now turned to France during the occupation and Ezra Pound's institutionalization at St. Elizabeth's.

Nancy was the stuff of fiction making, but she became increasingly depressed by what was published about her. She was initially forgiving to Michael Arlen, almost forgotten today but then the author of unprecedented, best-selling popular fiction. "Never mind," she remarked about Arlen, the first of the novelists to fictionalize her, "[he] made some money."[17] During their affair, she begged him to write better prose, but his regard for profit remained foremost, even if he portrayed the woman he adored as a reckless goddess-siren. After reading his fiction, one suspects that Nancy was more disturbed by his awkward, sentimental prose than by his portrait of her.

Although Arlen and Nancy did not become lovers until they met again in Paris in 1920, Nancy had first been introduced to Michael Arlen (born Dikran Kouyoumdjian) in London during the Corrupt Coterie days. The exotically handsome, dark-eyed, and intense young man had moved to London after briefly studying medicine at the University of Edinburgh; he wanted to become a writer. As soon as Nancy met him, she became interested in his Armenian background. His parents, persecuted by the Turks, had moved to Bulgaria before settling in England. Arlen had a passionate interest in the ethnically oppressed, and he and Nancy talked at length about the brutality of the

Turks during the Great War, an incident in recent history that stirred Nancy's interest in ethnic prejudice. An advocate of national pride and courage, Arlen published in magazines that encouraged his countrymen to pursue the fight for human justice, to become the "guerrilla fighter, bandit, and rebel."[18] This resonated with Nancy.

When Nancy saw Arlen later in Paris, she realized at once that he felt like an outsider in fashionable society. He had begun to pay particular attention to his dress, and she playfully dubbed him "The Baron." The now-elegant young man, twenty-three (Nancy was twenty-four), was smitten with her for two years. Nancy writes in one of her *Memoirs* that they spent most of their evenings in restaurants that catered to tarts (probably her choice), and "it was always champagne, and our heads were often swimming." Her other admirers must have followed them around Paris because, as she writes in her brief account of Arlen, other men and Arlen often glared at each other. Arlen wanted to marry her, but, as one of his male characters admits, he felt inadequate: he was merely "a man of my time . . . [who] may never rise above himself." By contrast, Nancy was, as he describes her persona in *The Green Hat*, a woman "of all time. She was, when the first woman crawled out of the mud of the primeval world. She would be, when the last woman walks towards the unmentionable end."[19]

Arlen had first portrayed Nancy as Virginia Tracy in *Piracy* (1922). The novel begins in May 1921 but is a retrospective of events since 1916, when Ivor, the writer-hero, meets Virginia. Shortly after it begins, the narrator describes the postwar atmosphere: "Death had lost some of its terror, and life had gained it. Life had lost something of its value but death had not gained it—despite all the pomps of honor and medalry with which the survivors had belauded it." Immediately recognizable are the Café Royal; the Eiffel Tower Restaurant (Arlen's "Mont Agel") and its Viennese owner, Stutz (Stulik); the bearded, "epic" Augustus John; and Nancy's parents, Lady and Lord Carnal. The Nancy femme fatale, Virginia Tracy, overwhelms the handsome, wealthy, dark-complexioned, brooding Ivor Pelham Marlay, who "had always indulged in a very high level of thinking." Nancy and her friend (Iris Tree is called "Lois Lamprey") "intoxicate each other into brilliance and often into truth."[20]

Nancy was gracious after she read the book; after all, Arlen needed the money. But she was not happy with his deification of her promiscuity:

> Wanton and faithless, she was given over to regrettable pleasures with post-Impressionist poets, Bloomsbury intellectuals and athletic Americans. . . . I could see the "unbalanced girl" taking lovers as she had eaten strawberries, with the absorbed ecstasy of an early Christian giving herself up to the pleasures of martyrdom.

The prose could only exasperate her:

> Most of all, you would admire the golden curls which tumbled, not wildly, down each side of her face while the golden hair from which they tumbled was drawn tightly back from her forehead as though grudging itself the waves that insisted on waving.

As Ivor returns to the year 1916, he describes his first significant meeting with the married Virginia, who tries to stop him from pursuing her: "But suddenly his one arm took Virginia bodily and pressed her to him and her face up to him. He kissed her lips." Despite her self-recriminations ("I misbehave frightfully"), she later telegrams Ivor and asks him to meet her and choreographs the seduction scene. Ivor realizes: "She wasn't real, of course! She was only a legend, a legend of a night in Avignon." When he proposes that they become lovers, she suffers excruciating pangs of conscience: "I've been such a beastly person. . . . I was so easy, Ivor. . . . I don't deserve [you]." After a mysterious operation, during which "steely things" are left in her body, Ivor wants to marry Virginia, but she writes him: "I am your mistress, and you are my lover. I am your woman and you are my man. Oh, Ivor, let's go on like that." During her recuperative period, she gets a chill and dies.

In her diary of 1920, Nancy discusses both the excitement and the boredom she felt with Arlen. She invited several friends to her rented summer house near Boulogne, including her cousin Victor, Marjorie Trefusis, and "Chile" Guevara, who idolized her. Nancy was accustomed to socializing with past and future admirers—in this case, Guevara. However, when Arlen, Guevara, and Nancy were left together in a room, as she writes: "The Baron . . . could be as sullen as distant thunder, . . . brooding and brewing. I admit that some of this . . . was my fault. God, how I loathed him." Back with him in Paris, however, her anger over his jealousy "would pass. . . . Our Montmartre nights were a delight. . . . We would go and dance, . . . always [with] champagne." The turning point occurred when Arlen quasi-proposed, in a manner that reminded her of their first days in London, when money and class stirred his feelings of inferiority: "If I were rich, I should ask you to marry me. . . . But as I'm not, there seems no point in doing so, d'you see?" "Marry the Baron indeed!" she concluded the entry and affair.[21]

In 1924, Arlen published *The Green Hat*, the sentimental novel now out of print that was one of the first million-copy best-sellers. Arlen, publishing the book at the same time the press was photographing and chronicling Nancy's activities, undoubtedly helped create her reputation as a woman who turned men into swine. The *New York Times* book reviewer called the novel a brilliant portrait of a passionate, intelligent, suffering woman." Others said that Arlen "tells you confidently things that wouldn't take in a goose," at the same time that the book is "on everyone's night table."[22]

Arlen had mastered a new genre: escapist melodrama with simple plots about the rich and their sexual indulgences. Neither the old guard (Bennett, Galsworthy, Shaw, and Wells) nor the avant-garde (Proust, Joyce, Lawrence, and Woolf) allowed for light reading, and Arlen more than amply provided this. After being welcomed by Nancy and her friends at the Café Royal, he had made profitable use of what he saw beyond Nancy: the wily ways of sophisticated women and the nonchalance of the wealthy.

After *The Green Hat*'s unparalleled success, many people knew that his promiscuous beauty—the divine hedonist-martyr—was Nancy Cunard. Again, his heroine transcended ordinary morality at the same time that she suffered for it: "It is not good to have a pagan body and a [pure] mind as I have. It is hell for the body and terror for the mind."[23] Perhaps the great success of *The Green Hat* was due to Arlen's ability to convey the unique qualities of a woman who could inspire idolatry. In many ways, Arlen's portrayal of the Nancy figure as saint and siren is similar to William Carlos Williams's description of Nancy.

Arlen had named his new heroine Iris (the name of Nancy's best friend, Iris Tree), and Nancy had every reason to be unenthusiastic about the book—not only because it portrayed her again as the seductive innocent but also because Arlen's prose was even more puerile and mawkish than before. He had tried, for example, to describe Iris's graceful manner of walking, with this alliterative result: the "very gallant lady glided rapidly through the midnight mews of old Mayfair."

Repeating that she is indescribable and mysterious, he borrows (twice) the title of Nancy's poems, *Outlaws*. She is larger than life and country: "You felt she had outlawed herself from somewhere, but where was that somewhere? You felt she was tremendously indifferent as to whether she was outlawed or not." He, a trifling man, finds it perplexing to understand her. Yet as mysterious as she is, he idealizes her as a goddess, body and soul, much as G. M. had idealized Maud:

[She was] as some one who had by a mistake of the higher authorities strayed into our world from a land unknown to us, a land where lived a race of men and women who, the perfection of our imperfections, were awaiting their inheritance of this world of ours.

On occasion, he seems to understand the Nancy figure:

[She] is a much misunderstood woman, who for gallant and quixotic motives allows her reputation to be far worse than her conduct deserves. . . . Beneath her dashing, modern exterior and her bold disregard for conventions like chastity, she is a romantic idealist.

But then, typical of his romantic excess, he writes, in Iris's virginal voice:

I am a house of men, . . . of their desires and defeats and deaths. . . . Ah me, ah me. Oh, dear.

But she is indescribably "lovely" and "greater than religion": "Her lips were silken red, and I thought just then that to kiss them would be to kiss the infinite."

When *The Green Hat* was filmed in 1929, with Greta Garbo playing the Nancy figure, the legend of "the gallant lady who was perhaps foolish"—the benign first caption of the silent film—became even more widespread. The film board of censors insisted on a laundered version of the novel—and the title was changed to *A Woman of Affairs*, along with all the characters' names—but the film was advertised "for adults only," and everyone knew it was a story of passion, suicide, and venereal disease, now altered in the film to embezzlement. In the novel, Iris's "beloved" commits suicide rather than infect her with syphilis.[24] Successful around the world and recipient of the Academy Award for best "adapted screenplay" (1928–1929), the film followed two stage versions of the novel, in which Tallulah Bankhead and Katharine Cornell played the Nancy character, in London and New York. The Nancy Cunard legend continued into the next decade, and a second film called *Outcast Lady* was produced in 1934, with Constance Bennett in the lead role.

After *The Green Hat*, according to most reviewers, Arlen's work became "old hat." In 1925, he published a collection of vignettes with the extravagant title *May Fair: Being an Entertainment Purporting to Reveal to Gentlefolk the Real State of Affairs Existing in the Very Heart of London During the Fifteenth and Sixteenth Years of the Reign of His Majesty King George the Fifth: Together with . . .* and, two years later, *Young Men in Love*. The latter had some new material, including the Nancy figure's lack of awareness "that her childhood was lonely, unhappy, and neglected: that she was, in short, the poor little girl of the story books."[25]

In 1928, Arlen married the beautiful Atalanta Mercati, the daughter of a Greek count, and moved to Cannes, but he still modeled his heroine in *Lily Christine* on Nancy as he portrayed married love as unattainable. His heroine has "long slender legs" and is "a swift, moving, reckless, white-faced young woman, the very incarnation of youth, fearless and intent, charged with purpose. . . . He would die for her. Yes, he would."[26] Like her predecessor in *The Green Hat*, Lily dies in a car accident. By this time, Nancy's initial tolerance for The Baron's early literary endeavors had turned to despair.

Aldous Huxley, the handsome grandson of Darwin's great proponent, the biologist T. H. Huxley, and brother of the biologist Julian, was unable to pursue the scientific career he desired because of a serious eye condition contracted when he was at Eton. Barely able to read, he nevertheless was graduated from Oxford, was rejected from serving in the war, and returned to Eton to teach. (One of his students was Eric Blair, who adopted the pen name George Orwell.) Having already published the first of his forty-seven books (he later wrote screenplays, including *Pride and Prejudice*, which starred Laurence Olivier, and *Jane Eyre* with Orson Welles), he turned his talents, most notably his acerbic wit, to the novel of manners. His target was the postwar generation, particularly the young and wealthy. Huxley had a gift for creating figures one could laugh at or pity, but with whom one could never identify. His brilliant reconstructions of their conversations were controlled by a highly sophisticated and subtle irony. Huxley would become a critically acclaimed and best-selling author in both the United States and Britain; he is now best known for his futuristic fantasy, *Brave New World*.

When Huxley met Nancy, like Arlen, he gained some hefty grist for the mills of his imagination, and after she rejected him, she became the target of his jaundiced wit. They had also met in London in 1917 during the war and frequented the Eiffel Tower and Café Royal. Their mutual friends included some from the Bloomsbury group and others from the Corrupt Coterie. Both Nancy and Huxley had also published in Edith Sitwell's *Wheels* collections. When they met again in Paris, Huxley had left Eton to join the editorial staff of the *Athenaeum*; he had also been married for three years. In January 1923, he signed a contact with Chatto & Windus to write two books a year for the next three years, one in January and the other in July. But he failed to deliver his second book, because he had fallen passionately in love with Nancy. It was, as he expressed it, "against reason, against all his ideals and principles, madly, against his own wishes, even against his own feelings."[27]

Nancy could not return Huxley's strong feelings. She refused to allow him to live with her because he was married, and after about a year, his wife gave him an ultimatum to return home for good. And return home he did—at dawn to find his wife, Marie, awake and desperate. She had packed through the night, and they left London the next morning. During the next two months, Huxley wrote the acclaimed cynical postwar novel *Antic Hay* (1923), in great part, about Nancy, here called Myra Viveash. One of Nancy's diaries indicates that she and Huxley saw each other secretly over the following years, when he again begged her to live with him. But after he had a child, she told him, as she had told Pound, that she had to end their relationship.

One of Huxley's critics asserts that Huxley's fictional characters were his spiteful revenge for unrequited love. Whether or not this is true in *Antic Hay*, the male hero is obsessed with Myra, who is portrayed as a disintegrated woman, a dangerous aristocrat who plays "for a bit with the clever mouse and sends him away without eating him because she doesn't find him tasty."[28]

Although distinctly more inspired in characterization and polished in style than Arlen's novels, *Antic Hay* presents a heroine and "lost generation" that both recall Arlen's moral landscapes and anticipate Hemingway's in *The Sun Also Rises* (1925). Huxley creates a group portrait in London, rather than Hemingway's linear plot with individualized characters in Paris and Spain. But Huxley's attention is also on a lost generation in search of values while in the frantic pursuit of pleasure. It is Huxley's tone that is unique among his contemporaries. Hemingway is sympathetic to the physically and spiritually wounded survivors of the Great War; Arlen's attitude is confused; Huxley is cynical and satiric.

His hero is a gentle young Oxford tutor named Theodore Gumbril Jr., who is tired of the stale world in which he lives and the unconvincing theologians, mediocre artists, critics, scientists, and incurable romantics who inhabit the world of academe. In rebellion against traditional morality, the young man becomes, in Huxley's words, a "massive Rabelaisian man [of] exuberant vitality, [a] great eater, deep drinker, stout fighter, [and] prodigious lover." He becomes obsessed with the willful, alluring, and dangerous Myra Viveash (Nancy), who shares in some of his pleasures but then rejects him; he responds with fits of jealousy and self-hatred.

In Huxley's portrayal of Myra (frequently called "Mrs. Viveash"), he neither idolizes, rationalizes, nor condemns her sexual prowess. She is "exquisite" and "marvelous," a formidably intelligent and liberated woman. Although she tortures and humiliates her lovers, she is at the same time incapable of love, and it is unclear whether Huxley's portrait of her self-destructive nature is intended to evoke sympathy or distaste; at moments, she is deeply moving in her loneliness.

Huxley draws on Nancy's most defining physical characteristics to fashion his heroine: her delicate walk, unforgettable voice, and magnificent eyes. For example, "He watched her as she crossed the dirty street, placing her feet with meticulous precision one after the other in the same straight line, as though she were treading a knife edge between goodness only knew what invisible gulfs. Floating she seemed to go, with a little spring at every step." One notes the religious overtones, however ironic, that Nancy inspires in Huxley, as she had in Arlen: "Her voice, as she spoke, seemed always on the point of expiring, as though each word were the last, uttered faintly and breakingly from a death bed—the last, with all the profound and nameless significance of the ultimate word."[29]

Huxley's descriptions of Mrs. Viveash are also highly detailed and sensuous. Standing in a room of people, "she threw back her cloak, revealing . . . a bare shoulder, a slant of pectoral muscle. She was wearing a white dress that, leaving her back and shoulders bare, came up under either arm to a point in front and was held there by a golden thread about the neck." Huxley draws on his own experience and knowledge of other men who succumbed to his heroine's overwhelming allure. One of the characters, Shearwater, admits: "'There was a time . . . years ago, when I totally lost my head about her. Totally. . . . Towards the end of the war it was. I remember walking up this street . . . in the pitch darkness, writhing with jealousy.' He was silent. Spectrally, like a dim, haunting ghost he had hung about her; dumbly, dumbly imploring, appealing."[30]

Huxley incorporates events from Nancy's life to explain Myra's behavior. The only man Myra/Nancy ever loved was killed in the war:

> "Did you ever know Tony Lamb?" she asked.
>
> "No," Gumbril answered. "What about him?"
>
> Mrs. Viveash did not answer. What indeed about him? She thought of his very clear blue eyes and the fair bright hair, . . . and all the rest of his skin was as white as milk. "I was very fond of him," she said at last. "That's all. He was killed in 1917, just about this time of year. It seems a very long time ago, don't you think?"

In the novel, Peter Broughton has become the symbolically named Tony Lamb. Myra later reflects: "It revolted her . . . to think how often she had tried [to care about other men]; she had tried to like someone, anyone, as much as Tony. She had tried to recapture, to re-evoke, to revivify. And there had never been anything, really, but a disgust. . . . Nothing's the same now. I feel it never will be." Huxley reveals a genuine sensitivity to Nancy's loss:

> She remembered suddenly one shining day like this in the summer of 1917, when she had walked along this same street, slowly, like this, on the sunny side, with Tony Lamb. All that day, that night, it had been one long good-bye. He was going back the next morning. Less than a week later, he was dead. Never again, never again: there had been a time when she could make herself cry, simply by saying those two words once or twice, under her breath. Never again, never again. She repeated them softly. But she felt no tears behind her eyes. Grief doesn't kill, love doesn't kill; but time kills everything, kills desire, kills sorrow, kills in the end the

mind that feels them; wrinkles and softens the body while it still lives, rots it like a medlar, kills it too at last. Never again, never again. Instead of crying, she laughed, laughed aloud. . . . "Never again," murmured Mrs. Viveash.

Huxley and Nancy return as characters in *Those Barren Leaves* (1925), a novel that strips the pretensions of the guests at an Italian palace party hosted by a Mrs. Aldwinkle. One of the guests, the poet Francis Chelifer, falls hopelessly in love with the Nancy/Barbara figure. Francis rationalizes her rejection by childishly discrediting every illusion he has had about her. And although he knows "she was flattered to have me abjectly gamboling around her," he continues to abase himself for her pleasure. In one sequence, Huxley draws on an actual event during which he, like his character, paced in front of Nancy's house all night. He substitutes (and satirizes) as his rival a character modeled on Michael Arlen, "the swarthy Syrian . . . [who] never lost an opportunity of telling people he was a poet [with] an artistic temperament."[31]

The critical and commercial success *Point Counter Point* (1928), also about the postwar period, barely disguises Nancy as Lucy Tantamount. In part, the novel is an attack on the effects of science in the modern world; more generally, it is a complex and bitter satire of contemporary life and manners through the simultaneous observations of various characters who function like themes or instruments in a musical composition. Once again, the heroine's physical characteristics are Nancy's: she has blonde hair, blue eyes, and, beginning with the same dozen or so words as in *Antic Hay*, the same manner of walking ("placing her feet with meticulous precision one after the other in the same straight line, . . . with a little spring at every step").[32]

The novel is another roman à clef, about several celebrities of the time: Aldous and Marie Huxley, D. H. Lawrence, Katherine Mansfield, John Middleton Murray, Oswald Mosley, Nancy, and even Lady Cunard. Shortly after the book begins, Walter Carling, the married speaker (Huxley), says, "What he wanted was Lucy Tantamount. And he wanted her against reason, against all his ideals and principles, madly, against his own wishes, even against his own feelings—for he didn't like Lucy; he really hated her. . . . It was for Lucy that he was making [his wife] Marjorie suffer." He describes his wretched condition as her rejected lover:

His caresses were like a drug, at once intoxicant and opiate. . . . She would cease to be herself, she would become nothing but a skin of fluttering pleasure enclosing a void, a warm, abysmal darkness.

"Lucy!" Her eyelids fluttered and shuddered under his lips. His hand was on her breast. "My sweetheart." She lay quite still, her eyes still closed. A sudden and piercing [parrot's] shriek made both of them start. . . .

7

Nancy as Publisher

Her many friends in London and Paris will be sorry to hear that
Nancy Cunard, Lady Cunard's poetess daughter, is deserting them
all for . . . a little French village.

—DAILY CHRONICLE, 14 JULY 1927

Nancy was weary of hearing her mother say that her life would amount to nothing, and she was depressed by her public image as an irresistible, irresponsible
siren. In late 1927, she used the money her father had left her to buy an old
peasant house in the small village of La Chapelle–Réanville in Normandy,
sixty miles from Paris. She rallied all her energy and renewed her optimism
("Up and at 'em!") and started a small publishing house, hoping that she, too,
like those who had opened small firms in England, France, and the United
States, could introduce new and experimental work in handsome, hand-printed, limited editions. The Woolfs had begun the Hogarth Press nearly ten years
before, and J. P. Morgan's nephew Harry Crosby was expanding the Black
Sun Press. Robert McAlmon's Contact Press, Edward Titus's Black Maniken
Press, David Garnett and Francis Meynell's Nonesuch Press, and Gertrude
Stein's Plain Editions, among many others, were similarly dedicated to quality
rather than profit. Included in the extraordinary range of writers published by
these houses were D. H. Lawrence, André Gide, Paul Valéry, Jules Romains,
Hart Crane, Katherine Anne Porter, Thomas Wolfe, John Dos Passos, Thorn-
ton Wilder, Gertrude Stein, Jean Cocteau, Countee Cullen, Henry Miller, F.
Scott Fitzgerald, Proust, Pound, Hemingway, Eliot, and Joyce.

"The thought of printing had long attracted me," Nancy wrote, "not so
much from the purely aesthetic point of view as from the sense of independent creativeness it might give one."[1] In 1928, she paid the American journalist

Bill Bird £300 for his Three Mountains Press and renamed it the Hours Press, a reminder of the arduous work required in authoring a book. She installed Bird's "beautiful" 200-year-old Belgian Mathieu hand press at Réanville and later at 15 rue Guenégaud in Paris when the problems of acquiring supplies and maintaining heat and electricity became insurmountable. Even then, Nancy's activities were pursued by the news media: "The pulse of the Inner Circle of Montparnasse is beating much faster now that Nancy Cunard has decided to pack up and come back after a year and a half . . . down in the country. She returned after Christmas to arrange for space to set up her printing press."[2]

The Hours Press

When Nancy started the press, Bird delivered the machinery and supervised its reassemblage (in a stable). He also provided the new publisher with an experienced typesetter named Lévy, a self-proclaimed former anarchist and outspoken skeptic about his employer's future competence in the difficult task of hand printing. Nancy was remarkably adept in her new profession, and she worked continually during every waking moment. She quickly mastered and even invented shortcuts for the work at hand, and the disgruntled Lévy railed at so capable a novice: "Beginners should not behave this way!" They should take at least seven years to acquire printing skills.

Her goal was to publish both experimental writers and the best writing she could find. Unlike other small presses, the Hours did not reprint classics; it published original work with covers in experimental designs. Nancy enlisted old and present friends (Robert Graves, Louis Aragon, John Banting, Richard Aldington, Pound, Havelock Ellis, G. M., Arthur Symons) and sought out lesser known or totally unknown writers (Walter Lowenfels, John Rodker, Harold Acton, Bob Brown, Brian Howard, Laura Riding, Samuel Beckett); she published no poetry of her own. Her goal was to encourage and reward her writers with singularly beautiful editions of their work. When James Joyce offered her the opportunity to publish a major work, she had already closed the press.[3]

The Hours Press was a unique collaborative effort between Nancy and her authors, and she strengthened old friendships and made lasting new ones. She became the most successful of the small publishers, producing twenty-four books from 1928 to 1931 and tripling her investment. She enlisted photomontages, drawings, and typographical art for her covers from Yves Tanguy, Louis Aragon, Man Ray, Marcel Duchamp, and others. She published an elegant collection of Eugene McCown's paintings, drawings, and gouaches.

Henry Crowder's *Henry-Music* may have been the first instance in which poetry was set to jazz and published. Most of Nancy's books were between ten and sixty pages long; few exceeded a print run of 300 copies. After only eight months, the Hours Press was well known in England, the United States, and France. Reviews were, typically: "[The Hours Press is] one of the most interesting of the newer small presses . . . issuing exquisite limited editions." Many years later, Nancy was told that her books were an inspiration to other printers and that her style of printing had become the norm.[4] She was proud, decades later, to find her books on display with other fine books at the Victoria and Albert Museum, selected for their handsome design, binding, "general taste," and individuality.

Her success was due to the skill and dedication with which she worked. As she modestly explained: "The ways of type were friendly to me." Before she began, Virginia and Leonard Woolf had advised her against the onerous task of hand printing: "Your hands will always be covered with printing ink." But unconvinced by the Woolfs or by her assistant, Lévy (who, as she put it, enjoyed watching her make mistakes), she grew accustomed to working up to sixteen hours a day.

She mastered the difficulties of publishing: she accommodated herself to the short days and "horrible cold" of winter when the electrical system failed; she struggled in the summer heat to keep drying paper damp. She looked for ways to keep ink from evaporating. She discovered the subtleties of using different size type and paper: 11-, 16-, or 17-point Caslon Old Face on Velin de Rives, Haut-Vidalon, or Canson-Montgolfier paper. She met the challenge of using two or more sizes of type: "It is then that *les blancs*, the spaces, must be so carefully thought out and fitted" and then "balanced by the fitting of ornaments." With the eye of an artist, she chose the color and texture of each wrapper, the leather spine, and the appropriate cover design and lettering. Her books ranged from scarlet, vermilion, and puce to pale blue and daffodil. She ascertained the most effective way to remove ink from her hands and when and when not to wash them: "After a rinse in petrol and a good scrub with soap and hot water, my fingers again began to acquire a slight ingrain of gray, due to the leaden composition. I soon learned that greasy black hands do not matter when one is at the proofing stage, but an immaculate touch is most important in handling the fair sheet when one has achieved the pulling stage."[5]

She also devised a method of dealing with royalties in a meticulously organized ledger. On one side of it, she recorded the printer's time and cost of light, heat, paper, binding, postage, and circulars; on the other, she listed orders and payments. After deducting the costs of production, she sent authors one-third of the proceeds. Books could be purchased in London, New York, Paris, and

Florence or directly from Reánville. Pleased with her organizational skills, she wrote: "There is a great deal to be said about doing things oneself, by one's own system." And to avoid permanent fatigue from this back- and wrist-breaking work, she discovered that sitting on a bar stool gave her maximum ease in typesetting. Regardless of where she was, she carried a homemade clipboard, crammed with notes on numerous subjects, her many papers held together by a strong elastic band.

Nancy was aesthetically moved by her tasks: "The smell of printer's ink pleased me greatly, as did the beautiful freshness of the glistening pigment. There is no other black or red like it." She was in love with the process: "For such is one's absorption—at first especially—that it matters little to the appraising part of one's mind what one is transferring, from written or typed pages to what will become the printed page. . . . The experience itself! and minding one's p's and q's, d's and b's, in all this upside-down-inside-out world of printing." She felt a special pleasure in publishing a long poem. She said of one by Aldington: "An intimate communion with a long intense poem is already there, if one reads it as often as one does, say, *The Waste Land.* . . . Letter by letter and line by line, it rises from your fingers around the type." Many said of Nancy, "One would have thought that [she] had grown up a printer." The *Paris Tribune* wrote of her venture: "Miss Cunard . . . has ideas about printing, in regard to type, size and form which no one seems to know where she learned. No doubt, they just came to her, as she herself did to the print shop."[6] Nancy herself thought that she had inherited a specific gift for handicrafts from her father.

Her memoir *These Were the Hours* (1969) is an inspiring record of the excitement of publishing, of touching print, of holding a new book in one's hands. It is a modest and loving account of the genesis of a published book, filled with remarks like "the simple sewing of the pages was a pleasure to me." *Hours* contains no mention of her family, and it alludes only in professional terms to her two lovers during this time: Louis Aragon, through the spring of 1928, and Henry Crowder ("an enchanting aide and companion"), whom she met in Venice that summer. When she discusses authors who were past lovers—Pound, Aldington, Guevara—she speaks of them as colleagues.

Nancy's house, which she called Le Puits Carré (Square Well), after the beautiful old stone well in front, was constructed of honey-colored stone, and its walls were three feet thick. She paid little for the house, since it not only was in need of major restoration but also presented seemingly irreparable water, heating, and electricity problems. It stood in the middle of a neglected orchard and was surrounded by fruit trees and wildflowers. Two outhouses occupied the slope of a hillside. Nancy redecorated the house with her father's elegant furniture, but the rooms had an odd configuration since each opened nto another instead of a corridor, and it was necessary to pass through the kitchen to reach the bedrooms. She again distributed her few photos from Nevill Holt, including the early Victorian portrait of her grandmother; painted the walls green; and hung her de Chirico, Picabia, Malkine, and Tanguy paintings. Her numerous African and Oceanic figures, perhaps a thousand African ivory bracelets, and Pre-Columbian and other tribal artworks were displayed on shelves and tables. Since she had long believed that such iconic figures had had a great influence on contemporary art, she wanted to create a sense of unity in her work and home environment.

A young woman from the village helped out a few mornings each week, but Nancy cleaned and dusted the house regularly; she was very tidy. Since she had always considered food an unpleasant requirement of survival, she cooked only as necessary on her old wood stove with the herbs she cultivated outside the kitchen. She often repeated an old Leicestershire adage to her friends, whom she delighted serving: "A yegg or nuthin' for thee and me." With her predilection toward vegetarianism, she gathered the fruits of the field, including dandelions and mushrooms, which were near the house. As she picked her fruits and vegetables, she also collected various kinds of stones and insects, particularly beetles and moths, along with other unusual native flora and fauna—all of which she added to her house displays. She relished objects, as Harold Acton said, that were "indigenous, natural, [and] primitive."

The well was located in a beautiful area with lime trees whose branches trailed the ground. Not only did they provide shade, but, in the springtime, their golden tasseled blossoms perfumed the air. Nancy placed a table and benches under the trees, as well as an electric lamp that she hid in the branches, and created a bucolic dining area in which to entertain her guests. She left wine in the well to cool. Acton remarked of her tastes: "The furniture, a mixture of solid English and African, had counterparts among her friends,"[7] whom she enjoyed entertaining—which she did with natural ease. Friends from London, such as Kay Boyle, John Banting, Bridget Patmore, Aldington, and Acton, were often invited. Janet and Solita frequently visited from Paris, as did Aragon and his Surrealist compatriots, particularly Georges Sadoul and René Crevel. Sometimes incompatible collections of people arrived in Réanville without notice, and the civility and tranquility of their day in the country evaporated. Most of the Surrealists, for example, not only enjoyed and discussed pornography but also were misogynists. If they visited during the same time as Solita and Janet, this hybrid of highly contentious and outspoken visitors posed a robust challenge to their hostess.

Nancy was very happy during this period. She said good-bye to everything but hard work, the production of beautiful books, and the pleasure of enjoying the countryside and entertaining her friends. Maud had been incorrect in telling her that her life would amount to nothing.

These Were the Hours describes all of this in detail and is also an interesting profile of her authors, both famous and unknown, in their various stages of modesty, insecurity, or arrogance as they parted from their most precious possession—for delivery to the reading public. Nancy also describes in masterful, brief strokes little-known physical or personality traits of her authors. Working with such a heterogeneous group, she gained insights into human nature, some less welcome than others, and she shares these as well.

G. M., who said he wanted to start her press off "with a good *bang!*" (how unlike Moore's generally impeccable diction was that very peculiar word "bang," she thought), was willing to give her his revised edition of *Peronik the Fool*, but he wanted something in return. He asked that she write an introduction, a recollection, of his visits with Maud at Nevill Holt, "an idea," she said, that "made me quail."[8]

Not only did some of her friends arrive unannounced, but some of the world's most famous authors did as well. As she reports, "I suppose James Joyce was my most famous visitor, . . . and maybe if the press had gone on longer it would have been my honor to publish a work by him." Joyce appeared at her door several times, spontaneously. He wanted her to prod Maud into financially aiding his friend, the tenor John Sullivan. But even more important, he wanted Maud to entice Thomas Beecham into listening to Sullivan. Joyce was publicizing Sullivan's talent with the same passion as Pound had publicized his. Nancy recalled: "The knock on the door revealed a tall, austere figure whose hands went faltering after some piece of furniture, for he was nearly blind already." He said, "I am James Joyce, and I have come to talk to you about something it seems to me it is your duty to accomplish." She continues, "He appeared so nearly blind that I wondered in consternation how he came to be out alone like this, and helped him to a chair. It made one shudder to think of him alone with his stick in the crowded streets of Paris." Nancy tried to convince him that he would have a much greater influence on Maud: "It was he, great and esteemed, who would be so much more likely to be listened to," she repeated. Joyce insisted several times that it was her "duty" to help the tenor gain proper recognition. Nancy subsequently did speak to her mother, but no assistance was forthcoming. Joyce visited Nancy on two other occasions with the same urgent request.[9]

One of Nancy's anecdotes reveals her naïveté and prudishness. She had always disliked pornography and cited this as the reason for not publishing *Lady Chatterley's Lover*. She also kept in her possession and never showed anyone Aragon's handwritten and pornographic *Le Con d'Irène*, published in a

Nancy's faith in Beckett's genius was unfaltering, and she worked tirelessly to help him gain a literary reputation. She insisted that the personable but shy writer accompany her to various Paris literary hangouts, and she introduced him to her artist friends. Although Deirdre Bair believes that Nancy and Beckett remained just friends, she admits that many people at the time believed that Nancy was the assertive wooer in their eventual affair. Regardless of the precise nature of their relationship, this was the beginning of a lifelong friendship. Beckett always "loved her spunk and verve, her decisiveness, originality and outspokenness." Furthermore, since Nancy had been generous to him when others were indifferent, he felt that "nothing she would ever do would sway him from absolute loyalty to her."[15] Until near the end of her life, the tall, lean, and blue-eyed couple corresponded and could be seen from time to time at popular bistros in Montparnasse.

Nancy recognized the talent of other young writers at her Hours Press. She said of the hermetic quality of Laura Riding's poetry that, as enclosed as it was in the poet's private images, its new techniques would be a forerunner of a new poetic movement. She recognized in Riding, perhaps because of her own poetic style in *Parallax*, a reconciliation of seeming irreconcilables—the concrete images that Pound and Lewis demanded, combined with the emotional sensibility of the poet. Nancy also noted Riding's debt to Gertrude Stein in her repetition of words and simplification of statements. In contrast, she published Robert Graves, whose poetry appealed to her because of its directness of impact. Nancy writes as a New Critic when she discusses his "Oak, Poplar, Pine" and "Act V, Scene V."

Nancy was honored that Arthur Symons wrote essays expressly for her press: *Mes Souvenirs*, on Verlaine; "Bohemian Chelsea"; and one on the Indian poet Sarojini Chattopadhya. Her commentary on Chile Guevara's poem-fresco *St. George at Silene* reveals an extensive knowledge of art history. In her chapter on Norman Douglas, she speaks less of Douglas's work, *Report on the Pumice-Stone Industry of the Lipari Islands*, than of her adoration of the man, which prompted her memoir *Grand Man* (1954). Douglas had been the author of several novels and novelettes, travel books, an autobiography, essays, games, limericks, and scientific and anthropological treatises. "To me," she writes, he is "the complete meaning of 'a grand man'—strong in character, lively, generous, creative, witty, honest, a forceful personality as much objective and subjective, an enchanting companion—and a magnificent writer."[16] Despite his dubious personal reputation, he had been a good friend to a group of distinctly talented people, including Artur Rubinstein, Rupert Brooke, and Frank Harris.

These Were the Hours, along with its fascinating description of the art of printing, is a remarkable series of critical essays on the avant-garde. As she approached her mid-thirties, Nancy had demonstrated a talent for poetry, hand publishing, and literary criticism. What she considered to be her greatest achievements lay ahead.

Henry Crowder

A narrative of Nancy's life during this time must include an introduction to Henry Crowder, the black American jazz pianist who took Aragon's place, as both her lover and her assistant in running the Hours Press. Nancy met Henry in the summer of 1928 when she traveled to Venice with her cousins, Edward and Victor Cunard—a trip that transformed her life. Already observing fascism's rising power in Italy during her visits to Pound in Rapallo, her Venice trip intensified her consciousness of the political oppression overtaking the country. Meeting and falling in love with Henry provided a reason to close the Hours Press and begin what would be a lifelong and worldwide crusade for human equality.

Venice was hardly new to Nancy. As a teenager, she had spent summers there with her mother; in the early 1920s, she had rented summer houses on the canals with or for her friends. Nancy found Venice utterly beautiful, a living work of art of dazzling and shimmering pastels. Its evening pageants—of carnivals, masked balls, and yacht parties, preceded or followed by exotic dancing and drinking in gala bars and restaurants—excited her. Through the 1950s, with the exception of World War II, Nancy traveled there frequently to vacation or to visit Norman Douglas.

Even before meeting Henry, Nancy was a celebrity in Venice. The Lido was a gathering place for the rich and famous, notorious for its spontaneous "dawn-revels," which Nancy and her friends attended after carousing in the "sinister new night-bars" that collected a spirited assortment of people. These were the "gala" days of "passion and love, and intoxication."[17] As early as 1922, at the time of her affair with Wyndham Lewis, Nancy had organized ambitious day and evening plans for her house guests. During the day, they toured the galleries and cathedrals, with Lewis lecturing, for example, on the superiority of Tiepolo to Carpaccio. In the evening, she occasionally hosted masked balls for the luminaries of Venice, London, and Paris, further enhancing her status as an international celebrity. At her less formal dinner parties, her guests were joined by "regulars" like the Sitwell brothers, "Willie" Walton, Eugene McCown, Robert McAlmon, and Douglas. At one party, McAlmon, always eager to demonstrate his physical agility and display his lithe, slim figure, entertained Nancy's guests by performing perfect handsprings. When he repeated the stunt, he made fun of the stout Gertrude Stein, "asking rhetorically if she would try some handsprings" and jesting that "she was the one and only of her generation, lost or wandering."[18]

If the liquid supplies became depleted, Nancy and her friends raced over to the majestic Hotel Danieli, where Douglas might dash off the history of Rome. At the same time, it was becoming increasingly clear to everyone but Douglas that Mussolini was transforming Italy into a brutal dictatorship. One afternoon, in fact, a young Fascist had ordered one of Nancy's friends to remove his hat while the nationalistic "Giovanezza" was being sung. Nancy respected Douglas's expertise on the historical fall of the Roman Empire, but she despaired over his blatant indifference or blindness to the spiraling and sinister changes occurring in his beloved Venice. It would be Nancy's misfortune to realize that two of the people she most loved had grown indifferent to world politics. G. M. had said, as Douglas might well have agreed, "Politics bores me," insisting that food was a far more interesting subject.[19]

All the same, at least for the time being, as the brilliant Turneresque light reflecting from the Venetian waterways remained vivid and pure, Nancy enjoyed both her political and apolitical friends. McAlmon recalls one lazy afternoon when he and Nancy relaxed with other vacationers. He sounds like Hemingway's Jake Barnes in *The Sun Also Rises* as he recalls

> sitting one day with a Lady Colebrook, Nancy Cunard, and the better-looking of the Di Robilant boys of Conte Mundano. Next to us was an obviously American woman, certainly an ex-actress Nancy believed. I glanced at her and listened to her . . . being bravely witty, . . . an aging woman who'd been about a bit and knew it wouldn't get her anywhere to sit down. A darn fine type. It was Marie Dressler [the silent movie star].[20]

Nancy became one of Venice's most glamorous celebrities. As Henry Crowder recalled many years later:

> The girl proved to be a positive sensation in Venice. Everywhere she went on the streets she was followed by curious crowds. If she stopped to look into a shop window she was immediately surrounded by gaping people. . . . At St. Mark's Piazza . . . [she would] feed the pigeons [and] immediately become the chief attraction there. The painters of the place clamored for her to pose.[21]

Pound had left Paris in 1924 for Rapallo, attracted not only to the country of his beloved Dante but also to Mussolini's promise of a new Italy. Pound's latter enthusiasm, in matters of culture and politics, was not unique. It had been shared early in the decade by voices as disparate as George Bernard Shaw and writers in the *New Republic*.[22] Mussolini would, of course, lose any credibility in the years to come, but in the 1920s, despite his murder in 1924 of the socialist leader Giacomo Matteoti, who had spoken out against fascism, he was enormously popular on the home front: Italy seemed to have become more nationally productive and powerful.

If one can rely on Thomas Mann's authority in tracing the irrational nationalism that characterized Italy and its fall from elegance to decadence in "Death in Venice" and "Mario and the Magician," one can well imagine the Venice that Nancy was visiting during the 1920s. Mussolini's goals were apparent: "Everything for the state, nothing outside the state, nothing above the state." The former socialist, now bearing a nationalist banner, had promised to restore Italy to its supremacy and glory during the Roman Empire. Mussolini organized armed thugs in black shirts to deal with dissidents (like the "criminals" who encouraged labor strikes) and controlled the press with his newspaper, *Il Popolo d'Italia*. A society without racism reaching across all classes might have been desirable to Nancy, but Mussolini's brand of nationalism, his irrational sacred sense of heroism and glorification of war, seemed like a reiteration of the Great War's motto of how sweet it is to die for one's country and was anathema to Nancy. She was well read in Nietzsche and well aware now, as she would be during the Spanish Civil War and World War II, of the potential misuses of the exaltation of human power. She was also suspicious of mass politics and the concept of a perfect society that worshipped itself in public festivals. And while she despised Mussolini's regimentation of children in the Balilla Fascist youth groups and his insistence that women limit themselves to childbearing, most alarming were the Organization for Vigilance Against Anti-Fascism (OVRA), his secret police force, and the concentration camps he was openly building in the Lipari Islands for dissidents, another phenomenon she would encounter during the Spanish Civil War.

Mussolini's growing power had troubled Nancy as early as 1922, when she rented a house for the month of October. The Fascists' swift takeover throughout the country was alarming: Bologna in May, Milan in August, and at the time of her vacation, "Mussolini, only twelve days from Rome." She was also shocked by the irrationality of the pro-Mussolini population in two incidents that might have been taken out of "Mario and the Magician." In both, a group of Venetians linked her to Mussolini's enemy, Communism. One occurred when she was caught in a rainstorm and her rust-colored macintosh turned red. This caused "fury among the black-shirted rowdies in the street." Another day, the scarlet trim on her navy-blue jacket attracted equally hostile attention from onlookers. These small events marked the acceleration of her social activism, albeit on a very minor scale. Her first cause involved agitating for higher wages and better living conditions for gondoliers. Nancy befriended several and even learned to maneuver a gondola; she used to row with a man she called "my philosophical gondolier, Angelo Trevisan." The second cause involved aiding a hotel maid, "an endearing, love-crossed maid," in leaving the country. "One day," Nancy recalls, the woman "fell on her knees embracing mine, begging me, weeping, to take her out of her unhappiness in Italy," which Nancy tried to do.[23]

During the summer of 1928, on another visit to Venice, Nancy met Henry Crowder, probably the love of her life. Knowing how captivated Nancy was by jazz and jazz dancing, her cousin Edward had taken her to the Luna Hotel, where Eddie South's Alabamians were playing. Nancy was overwhelmed: "Here we met some people to me as being from another planet. They were colored musicians"—"Afro-Americans," as she referred to them, a unique term at the time—who "played in that 'out of this world' manner which, in ordinary English, would have to be translated, I suppose, as 'ineffable.'"[24] She was dazzled by the "jazz, swing, and improvisations." She and her cousin stayed until the band's last number at dawn and then invited the group to join them. "I had never met such enchanting people," Nancy said, in terms of their "charm, elegance, beauty—their art, manners, the way they talked with us. *Enchanting* people." But it was the African American pianist, Henry Crowder, whom she most liked: "Like so many colored American musicians, he had achieved his high level of execution as a pianist through his own innate musicianship rather than by academic study. . . . But he could also read the most difficult scores, extraordinary for people who play by ear and instinct." This man, a year older and of "great good looks," was, as she later wrote, "the first Negro I had ever known."[25] He would become her lover for the better part of seven years, "teach" her (Nancy's word) about American racism, and radically alter her life.

If Nancy had found Louis Aragon, Wyndham Lewis, Michael Arlen, and countless others interesting because of their personal histories, Henry Crowder's life was, to her, utterly unique. As he relates in his memoir *As Wonderful As All That?*, he had been one of twelve children born in the foothills of the Appalachian Mountains; his father was a church deacon in Gainesville, Georgia, and his mother, more than half "Red-Indian," washed the clothing of white families. After his father grew hopelessly in debt, he moved the family to Atlanta, but they remained in squalor and poverty. Crowder's first trip north, when he sang in a quartet touring New England, was a revelation: "The color of my skin seemed to make little difference. . . . Everywhere we went we were received cordially as though we were human beings with hearts, souls, likes and dislikes very similar to everyone else."[26]

Returning to Atlanta brought back his fears of racial discrimination. The city had just emerged from a bloody riot, and Crowder lived with a renewed sense of racial oppression, saying "I learned to hate white people." At the same time, he said, "I have always thought I was as good as anyone and better than a great many. I have never desired to be on a plane of social equality with anyone who does not want me there. . . . But the right to enjoy the privileges accorded to every other person whatever his color, I consider no more than my just due. . . . For myself, the idea of social equality with white people meant nothing to me."

The youngest in the family and an emotional child, he tried "to be goodness itself" in the midst of his religious surroundings. Admittedly fanatical, he had trouble "with the devil" when he became an adolescent. He then attended Atlanta University but had to drop out after a year to earn money; he took a full-time job as a letter carrier. After his love affair with a local girl who became pregnant—Crowder was certain he was not the father—he resolved never again to "blindly trust another woman." He moved to Washington, D.C., where he had a number of jobs and an affair with a hotel housekeeper. For the next four years, "the devil and I continued riding together": he worked in an area known as the "Division," the Washington brothel area, where he played the piano; at another brothel that catered to wealthy white men, he played the piano again and earned $80 to $90 a night. He left his mistress when he met the daughter of one of Atlanta's leading black families and they married. Crowder was now playing with a dance orchestra at one of the city's finest restaurants. He also took on a political role when he united and became head of an organization of black jazz musicians: "I became a central figure in the jazz musical field in Washington. I was proud of my accomplishment."

Crowder did not volunteer for the war because he was married, but he briefly worked at war-related jobs, like chauffeuring generals around the city. After he opened a barber shop, he tried to renew his musical career. Unable to find work, he went to Chicago. "Luck was with me," he said when he met Eddie South, a well-known jazz violinist who was looking for a pianist for his four-person band. The band was so successful that it made a disk for Victor records, and Crowder earned $250 a week. After Eddie's unpleasant affair with a white woman from the Ziegfeld Follies, they all lost their jobs and went to New York for a stint at $30 a week. One night, the famous singer Marion Harris heard them play, and her escort offered the band an all-expenses paid trip to Europe, with engagements in England, France, Germany, and Italy. Remembering how his recent change in fortune was due to Eddie's affair, Crowder firmly resolved that he would have nothing to do with white women in Europe. Still at war with his inner devil, he had a few casual affairs with both black and white women.

When the band went to Venice, he and Nancy became close friends. After the Alabamians moved to Paris, Nancy introduced him to her friends at the Plantation and the Boeuf sur le Toit, and Crowder worked at both. She invited him to join her in Réanville to work on the press and bought him a piano. "At night, when time could be spared," Henry played Grieg and complex contemporary American music; he also started composing. His greatest ambition was to be a jazz composer, and he devoted every spare minute to his music. In 1930, Nancy published his *Henry-Music*. Man Ray designed the cover, with Crowder wearing a hat and coat and with Nancy's braceleted arms resting on his shoulders. The music was dedicated to Sacco and Vanzetti, whose trial had troubled both of them. Several of the Hours' writers, including Beckett, Aldington, Walter Lowenfels, and Harold Acton, wrote the poems that Crowder set to jazz. Nancy contributed "Blues," inspired by the Boeuf sur le Toit, and "Equatorial Way," which she called "a sort of battle hymn" in which a black man says farewell to the United States and, as she describes it, moves to an Africa that should be his. Nancy makes clear that the poem was "dictated by the romantic notion of the black man's return to the Dark Continent"[27] rather than Marcus Garvey's call for such action.

Crowder was a born teacher, and he introduced Nancy to the complex and agonizing situation of blacks in the United States. She listened with growing indignation to accounts of race riots, lynchings, and widespread segregation. He was eloquent and buoyant, but he was no activist. He tried to shrug off the problem, believing it would not be "mended for a long time." Nancy's answer was that everyone is "born to enjoy a happy rather than an unhappy nature."[28] She began writing to all her friends about blacks, encouraging them to visit her and expand their social circles. She wrote David Garnett in England, her friend since the Bloomsbury days, and asked him to call her when he was in Paris so she could introduce him to the world of black people. She was impatient and impassioned:

> I know some colored people, and very wonderful they are, and you will know them at once (and very much appreciate them) if you come to Paris. . . . Henry . . . is a beautiful musician and a very wonderful person whom you would appreciate. . . . I say appreciate so often because it is their own colored world and exactly names the emotion. Please please do this quickly.

Among her friends, she told him, was a friend of Prince Tovalou, the "rightful king of Dahomey," who had had a terrible time and now lived in Paris. She also frequently wrote: "I seem to be thinking of Africa all the time."

Nancy was successful in introducing many, but certainly not all, of her old friends to her new black friends. Many years later, after Crowder died, she recalled in a letter to Garnett a specific luncheon: "Do you remember Henry, my Afro-American musician? . . . That day, I remember . . . feeling in my element with you, the perfect Englishman, of brain, of charm, of breeding, and Henry, who was becoming my introduction to a whole race and continent—as well as being my love. It was very fine. (I am in suppressed tears of emotion.)"[29]

Both Nancy and Crowder thought they would be free of racial bias throughout France, not just in Paris but certainly in Réanville. Shortly after they arrived at Puits Carré, however, Nancy experienced discrimination firsthand. She had bought Crowder a little blue sports car with a scarlet lining, his "Bullet," and on one occasion, when they were about to travel to the southwest, someone cried out: "*Té! Ils ne sont pas de la même colour* [They are not the same color]." On another outing, they were hit head-on by another car whose driver was clearly at fault. However, in the court at Evereux, Crowder was found guilty and ordered to serve a month in prison and pay a 1,000-franc fine. Since it was a first offense, he was released after paying the fine. Nancy responded: "Henry and I were aroused to hatred for the type of Frenchmen who seize the opportunity of coming down hard on a foreigner."[30]

They had already encountered racism in Venice, where "the fascist-minded . . . stared, [and] the children capered and shouted: '*Ché bel Mero* [What a beautiful Moor].'" When they left the city, a Fascist officer on the train had openly expressed his disgust at seeing a white and black couple traveling, and he created a scene over their tickets. During their visit to London, they were refused lodging at hotel after hotel. Crowder observed: "London and England are infinitely worse for colored people than New York or other cities in the United States." He explained: "It is the shock of the terrible humiliation from being refused so unexpectedly that cuts."[31]

• • •

This was just the beginning of Nancy's encounters with racism: the most painful experiences would come from those closest to her.

8

Prelude to *Negro*

You ask: "Why love the slave,
The 'noble savage' in the planter's grave,
And us, descendants in a hostile clime?"
Cell of the conscious sphere, I, nature and men,
Answer you: "Brother . . . instinct, knowledge . . . and then,
Maybe I was an African one time."

—NANCY CUNARD

Nancy embarked on *Negro* (or *Colour*, as it was first called) in response to Henry Crowder's vivid accounts of "the astonishing complexities and ago-nies of Negroes in the United States." The project was a personal gesture to the man she "closely and violently loved"—and she dedicated it "to Henry Crowder, my first Negro friend."[1] It was also a major effort to fight racial in-justice throughout the world, and in its time was an original and monumental document. In the tradition of her great-granduncle Robert Emmet and those in the Irish Revival, like W. B. Yeats and George Moore, Nancy hoped to restore a sense of cultural identity and pride to a subjugated people: "To what better purpose can [one's] energy be devoted" than the "resurrection of his country's culture?"[2] Her ultimate goal was to undermine any rationalization for racial injustice based on notions of white cultural superiority.

Nancy knew that preparing *Negro* would be a learning experience: "Could I not learn a good deal in Africa, of the Africans themselves, they in their end-less diversity?"[3] But her education exceeded her expectations. A white woman with a black lover, she would leave France, where racial discrimination had been minimal, travel widely, and experience firsthand the vicious racial big-otry she had only heard about. In addition, when her mother learned about her project and two-year affair with Crowder, she initiated a series of events that estranged her from Nancy for the rest of her life and caused Nancy to feel she could never again live in England.

Chaos: *Black Man and White Ladyship*

One day in late 1930, Margot Asquith, Maud's rival as London's most prominent hostess, arrived for a luncheon and asked about Nancy: "What is it now—drink, drugs or niggers?"[4] Although Maud had heard that Nancy was encouraging a black musician friend to study in New York, she found it unthinkable that her daughter might be living with a black man. After all, Nancy had visited her from time to time in London. Obviously, her two-year secret had been very well guarded.

Not only did Margot's remark become the subject of gossip within Maud's genteel circles, but Maud's behavior was so odious that it provoked Nancy to retaliate in a severe, unforgiving manner. First, Maud phoned everyone she knew to ask if Margot's report was true; then she confronted Nancy. Mother and daughter exchanged cruel insults; Maud threatened to have Crowder deported, and Nancy stormed out of the house vowing never to speak to her again. The London press leaped on Margot's remark and fueled the rumor mills throughout Britain.

One reporter asked Lady Cunard, "Have you met Miss Cunard's friend, the Negro musician, Henry Crowder?" and she replied: "Do you mean to say my daughter actually *knows* a Negro?" One by one, Nancy's real and surrogate parents insulted or abandoned her. George Moore, her beloved ally since childhood and a proud, self-proclaimed free thinker, facetiously answered her question "Do you have friends of color?" by saying, "No, I think none, but the subject has never come my way. You see, I've never known anyone of color, not even an Indian. I have met neither a brown man, nor yet a black man. I do not believe I could get on well with a black man, my dear. I think the best I could manage would perhaps be a yellow man." Thomas Beecham, still her mother's paramour, declared that Nancy should be "tarred and feathered" and warned her in a letter to remain in France, "as white friendships between races were viewed with tolerance on the continent, by some, [but] it was a very different pair of shoes in England."[5]

Nancy had no intention of canceling her trip to London. She planned to spend most of her time studying black culture at the British Museum; in addition, she was organizing a screening of the Surrealist film *L'Age d'or* by Salvador Dalí and Luis Buñuel, already banned in Paris, about the hypocrisy of the church.

When Nancy and Crowder arrived in London, she was informed that "steps had been taken" to separate them. Recently unsuccessful in challenging the copyright laws governing *Henry-Music*, Maud embarked on a ruthless campaign to force Henry to return to the United States. ("My solicitor in London," wrote Nancy, "informed me that no bar exists against the entry into England of any person of whatever nationality who is not guilty of offense against the State.")[6] Maud hired detectives to prowl around their rooms above the Eiffel Tower, where they had already stayed several times, and to follow them whenever they went out. Not only did Nancy and Crowder receive profane and frightening phone calls and letters, but strangers threatened poor old Rudolph Stulik, the Tower's proprietor, with imprisonment or death. When the depressed but furious Nancy checked out, a petrified Stulik told her that the harassment had been targeted solely toward expelling Crowder from London, which only enraged her further. They checked into another hotel and remained there for a month.

Nancy became ill with the kind of bronchial infection that plagued her throughout her life. She also began muttering "Enemies, enemies, nothing but enemies everywhere"—true enough now, and, interestingly, the same language she would use during her breakdown in 1960. With the hope of restoring her physically and mentally, Crowder planned a brief holiday in the village of Obergürgl in the Austrian Alps. They would join their friend the talented, gay poet Brian Howard, whose work Nancy had published at the Hours Press. Still enraged over her mother's behavior, Nancy disappeared the night before they were to leave, and when she finally met Crowder at the train station, she was so drunk she lapsed into unconsciousness for several hours. Once sober, she joined a stranger, an English journalist living in Vienna named Roy Randall, and spent the rest of the trip with him.

Howard went to the station to meet his friends, and they began their long journey to his hotel by bus and sleigh. Nancy found the cold intolerable: she thought she would freeze to death. She later told Crowder that she had contemplated suicide during the journey.[7] To make matters worse, because Howard's hotel was fully booked, they were forced to stay in its annex, in a room adjacent to the local priest's.

To the villagers in this provincial Austrian town, the black man and white woman seemed like visitors from an unknown world. Wherever Crowder went, children asked if he would put snow on his face so the color would come off. Nancy remained in a rage. With her mother's words reverberating in her mind and with little heat in her room, both her bronchitis and anxiety grew worse. One night she got drunk and broke every pane of glass in the room with a shoe; she threw oranges and soap at the mirrors; she beat her head against the wall. The entire village became aware of her behavior: the priest sermonized on and off the pulpit about the drunk and noisy couple living next to him.

Brian Howard, who worshipped Nancy's idealism and admired her beauty, was troubled by her constant chatter and drinking:

She talked so much [in] a kind of sober drunkenness. Drinking is now fatal to her, particularly cognac. She has the most marvelous face. The best . . . of our time . . . [and] that extraordinary, wavering, perched walk. . . . She is the only woman I know who can be *really* impassioned about ideas almost continuously. . . . And her bickering with impassive, infinitely patient Henry is very rasping to me. She is in an extremely nervous condition now.

Nancy was behaving so irrationally that at one point she made declarations of passionate love to the exceptionally good-looking Howard, but nothing diminished his regard for her: "I adore and admire Nancy and always will"; "if she attracted me, I'd marry her, I almost believe."[8]

Crowder and Nancy left for Vienna, where they stayed with Roy Randall, the journalist Nancy had met on the train.[9] The two men became, in sequence, the subject of Nancy's amorous attentions. Crowder was so disgusted by Nancy's behavior that he decided to go back to Washington to see his wife. Nancy bought him a round-trip ticket, pleading with him to return to her, which he did after two and a half months.

Even before the trip to Austria, Nancy had heard that her mother was planning to punish her financially. Beecham told her that Maud had disinherited her and cut her allowance: the former was untrue (although Nancy received very little); the latter, correct, although a matter of debate among Maud's and Nancy's friends. All the same, Maud still wanted her daughter to look well, and she continued to send her elegant clothing, which Nancy never wore but gave to her black friends: "Smart young Negresses in Maida Vale, Edgware Road and Nottinghill were thus attired in Her Ladyship's pastel-colored dresses."[10]

Soon after the trip to Austria and in a highly agitated state, Nancy "dashed off" two virulent attacks against her mother. These were probably Nancy's most self-destructive public events, but one can sense the hurt, as well as the rage, that motivated the essays. Unable to forget her mother's remark "Does anyone *know* any Negroes?" she chose to use it as the title of an article for *Crisis* magazine in which she mocked her mother's prejudices: "Does anyone *know* any Negroes? I never heard of that. You mean in Paris then? No, but who receives them? . . . What sort of Negroes, what do they *do*? You mean to say they go into people's houses?" Her second essay, *Black Man and White Ladyship*, was a scathing attack on Maud. To many it appeared impulsive and ill conceived, although to others, like Howard, her mother had behaved with the utmost folly and brought it on herself.[11] The "White Ladyship" section attacked Maud's value system and racism; "Black Man" was a commentary on the slave trade and the history of blacks in British countries. The piece as a whole was an indictment of British upper-class racial prejudice.

Nancy had, as she put it "washed her hands" of her mother, but, in fact, she had washed the dirty linen of her class in public and stirred a depth of public outrage that she never anticipated. Although her essay has been praised subsequently for its vicious wit and brutal honesty regarding racism, for raising the same challenge as Lillian Smith in *Strange Fruit* a decade later, Nancy had been remarkably harsh.

Nancy begins *Black Man* by saying that the events following Margot's remarks prompted her to write. She addresses her mother:

> But your Ladyship, you cannot kill or deport a person from England for being a Negro and mixing with white people. You may take a ticket to the cracker southern states of U.S.A. and assist at some of the choicer lynchings. . . . You may add your purified-of-that-horrible-American-twang voice to the yankee outbursts: America for white folks—segregation for the 12 million blacks we can't put up with—or do without.

She continues:

> Negroes, besides being black (that is, from jet to as white as yourself but not so pink), have not yet penetrated into London Society's "consciousness." You explain: they are not "received!" (You would be surprised to know just how much they are "received.") They are not found in the Royal Red Book. Some big hostesses give a lead and the trick is done!

Buried in this expansive vituperation was the true focus of her attack: "No, with you it is the other old trouble—class."

Then, responding to the rampant gossip that Maud had sworn that if the story about Nancy and Crowder were true "I should never speak to her again," Nancy replied to her threat: "I trust we shall never meet again." She then enumerated Maud's personal flaws, from her extravagant purchases of clothing she never wore to her empty life of insipid social events ("She is so alone—between the little lunches of sixteen, a few callers at tea, and two or three invitations per night") and her need to control others. She called Maud the dupe of jewelers and art dealers and attacked her moral and social hypocrisy.

Nancy mailed out hundreds of copies, meticulously addressing them to her mother's every friend and enemy. Maud remarked: "One can always forgive anyone who is ill." Still, because of her high income taxes, so she said, she did reduce Nancy's allowance by at least one-quarter and later by half, if not entirely. Most people ultimately believed the latter. Nancy wrote her mother about the acrimonious situation between them, as a last-minute gesture to avert their total estrangement, but Crowder, who was supposed to mail the letter, destroyed it and "Nancy never knew."[12] G. M. also threatened to disinherit Nancy from the Manet painting she had loved since childhood, but he later changed his mind.

When Crowder returned to the United States, Nancy returned to Paris and pursued an affair with Raymond Michelet, a young French student who had run away from his conservative, overbearing father, a former police official. At Aragon's urging, Nancy had allowed Michelet, sixteen years her junior, to stay at Réanville while she was in London. Michelet later became a major contributor to *Negro*. When Crowder returned to France in the spring of 1931 and for the next two years, Nancy managed simultaneous affairs with Michelet and Crowder (who took an apartment nearby). She spent three or four days a week with each of them. Many years later, Michelet made the following remarks, which are of great interest because they are the only intimate comments on record from one of her lovers. They also shed light on Nancy's polygamous leanings:

Nancy led three or four parallel lives, which sometimes connected, sometimes contradicted, sometimes remained independent of each other. . . . That was why her personality could be so fascinating.

For it was not just a question of changing moods. Nancy had terrifying rages, often unfair in their excess, for she pushed each feeling to the extreme. . . . But there was something more. . . . Nancy forged ahead, . . . never stopping [or] turning back, burning everything behind her, the things she had loved, the people she might have loved. What was she running away from? . . . She was an enigma.

She [told me once] she needed a day of absolute solitude. [But] she could not tolerate prolonged solitude. She feared it. Even being alone with one person was only tolerable to her in rare moments when she felt in perfect harmony with nature, with external things, with the landscape. . . . At such perfect moments, she was romantic in a way no one would have imagined. In these perfect moments she would show a desperate lyricism that she would later regret, as though she had shown herself naked.Solitude terrified her. When one companion left her side, she had to have another at once. That is why she would pick up along the way the first person who came to her, even if he was the least likely to share her life. . . .

Nancy could weep with emotion, at thirty-five, like a young woman surprised by new love. . . . She could be a woman totally in love, . . . and on the next day, incapable of choosing between two men she loved. . . . She could construct an absurd life in which she lunched with one, passed the afternoon with the other, dined with the first, and spent the night with the second. In each, she went to the limit, whether it was simple [or] complicated, logical or absurd, dangerous or not. She had to seize from each moment everything it had to give. Nancy burned like a flame.[13]

When the time came to go to America to research *Negro*, Nancy turned to Crowder.

Preparations for *Negro*

The First Trip to New York

Nancy's interest in black culture had long preceded her relationship with Crowder; she had been collecting African sculpture, fetish figures, and ivory bracelets since her London days; her love of black jazz had led her to meeting Crowder in the first place. In fact, Nancy had been fascinated with Africa since she was a child. Even if unconsciously, she must have believed that this project would give her some insight into the childhood dreams that still remained with her. *Negro* might be a journey of self-discovery, where she could finally experience the rootedness of a welcoming home embracing her for her differences, one in which she could identify with the persecuted and outcast peoples of the earth. She recalled that at

> about six years old, my thoughts began to be drawn toward Africa, and particularly towards the Sahara. Surely I was being taught as much about El Dorado and the North Pole? But there it was: the Desert. The sand, the dunes, the huge spaces, mirages, heat and parchedness—I seemed able to visualize all of this. Of such were filled several dreams, culminating in the great nightmare in which I wandered, repeatedly, the whole of one agonizing night, escaping through a series of tents somewhere in the Sahara. Later came extraordinary dreams about black Africa—"The Dark Continent"—with Africans dancing and drumming around me, and I one of them, though still white, knowing, mysteriously enough, how to dance in their own manner. Everything was full of movement in these dreams; it was that which enabled me to escape in the end, going further, even further! And all of it was a mixture of apprehension that sometimes turned into joy, and even rapture.[14]

It was clear that she had to close the Hours Press: she could barely concentrate on anything but this "entirely absorbing" project. She hired a manager, Wyn Henderson, to complete her last projects.

Nancy's devotion to *Negro* was one of "utter impassionment," characterized by a "tenacity, as though [she were] a crusader in battle." In less than three years, she planned, organized, and published the book. She lamented not being able to claim any black blood in her veins but was proud "of the AFRICAN part, ah, that is my ego, my soul." She had at last found her calling: "[It] was made for me to do!"[15] One might say that *Negro* was the child she would never have.

She studied at the British Museum, first immersing herself in African American literature; she was deeply moved by its beauty. Crowder continued his tutorials on black racism, using a vocabulary new to her, with words such as "redneck," "Jim Crow," and "crackers." She planned trips to one continent after another where she could live with large black populations. She ran into problems negotiating some, particularly to those regions controlled by the British, because her mother—calling her "nigger lover"—had enough influence to keep her out of certain countries. When Nancy tried to obtain a visa to visit Africa, the British Foreign Office replied that it could not be responsible for her safety if she was traveling with Henry Crowder. Unable to dissuade her, the office finally refused, pointblank, to give her the necessary papers.[16]

From the book's inception, Nancy took control of every detail. *Negro* would have to be printed exactly as she wished, bound in sepia-brown cloth with paper of a specific texture and color (which had to be custom made), and its title, in red letters, would scroll diagonally from top left to bottom right. She would control every phase of its gestation and correct all final proofs. Although Crowder, at the beginning, thought her plan confused and disorganized, the detailed April 1931 circular distributed to potential contributors is remarkably close to the book she produced.[17] As she correctly announced, this would be the first time such a book was compiled.

In July 1931, Crowder booked the first of her two visits to America. They stayed in Harlem, "the so-called capital of the Negro world"—a joint decision, since Crowder knew he would not be accepted at a white hotel, and Nancy wanted to stay with the people she was writing about. After two uncomfortable nights at the Dumas on 135th Street, they moved to the Grampion; Nancy was the first white woman to stay in either hotel.

The Harlem Renaissance of the 1920s had been marked by an outburst of creativity and hope for betterment. The movement had grown out of the need to define, politically and culturally, what it meant to be black. But while successful in the arts, the movement had accomplished little in the way of social change. In addition, by late 1931, with Depression unemployment nearing 25 percent overall, the rate in Harlem was close to 50 percent.

The heroes of the Harlem Renaissance welcomed Nancy—W. E. B. Du Bois, Walter White, Countee Cullen, Langston Hughes, and William

Pickens; they would contribute to her volume. Hughes, like others, initiated a long friendship with Nancy and suggested potentially useful contacts to her, including a man he recommended as the best photographer of blacks in the world. Claude McKay, associated with *Liberator* and the first black to write a best-seller, *Home to Harlem*, was also very excited about Nancy's book:

> We poor Negroes, it seems to me, are literally smothered under reams of stale, hackneyed, repetitious stuff done by our friends, moral champions and ourselves that never strikes people grieving anywhere. We most of us live in fear of the fact of ourselves. And can hardly afford to render even the artistic truth of our own lives as we know and feel it; but it is unimaginable that you could be handicapped or allow yourself to be by the social-racial reactions that hamper us sometimes unconsciously even. And so I hope the stuff you are going to put out will be a revelation and inspiration to us.[18]

Alain Locke, who would write an essay for *Negro* on Sterling Brown's detachment from dialect and gift for capturing the deepest idioms of feeling, was one of the most revered members of the Harlem Renaissance. A Phi Beta Kappa at Harvard and the first black American Rhodes Scholar, he had edited *The New Negro*. He would become another of Nancy's friends.

Nancy spent her days walking and studying what she called the "ghetto-like slums of the Afro-Americans," including the area bordering Fifth Avenue at the curve of the Harlem River. She walked amid "the dead junk and the refuse" and visited the white-owned stores and cafeterias and innumerable "'skin-whitening' and 'anti-kink' beauty parlors." She spoke with anyone who would talk with her. She loved the diversity of Harlem and the physical appearance of its residents; she loved the music of their speech and the pleasure they seemed to get out of life. The joy and sacredness of their prayer deeply moved her. When she went to the dance halls and jazz clubs at night, she distanced herself from the "slumming" American whites, to whom she expressed overt disdain. Being English, she at first believed, was a kind of passport that separated her from the Americans. She preferred the clubs that blacks frequented, like Yeah Man and Striver's Row. She especially loved the children:

> The best thing that remains of Harlem [is] the magnificent strength and lustiness of the Harlem children. As I walked from end to end of it, down the length of 7th Avenue, the schools were just out. The children rushed by in rough leather jackets in the cold wind, some of them playing ball on roller skates, shouting and free. May these gorgeous children in their leathers be the living symbols of the finally liberated Negro people.[19]

She was troubled that American blacks seemed uninterested in their roots. No one, she strongly believed, should "separate Africa from the living Negro." As if echoing Robert Emmet, as restated by W. B. Yeats, she would want blacks to exchange their historical indifference for an awareness of their culture's "terrible beauty" born of pride and sacrifice.

The "Africa" section in *Negro* was essential to rectify a common assumption used to rationalize black prejudice. The continent's lack of either a body of historical literature or a daily press did not mean, she was intent on showing, that its inhabitants were "savage." She and her contributors would produce the first omnibus history of Africa to provide blacks with a sense of their cultural lineage, a starting point from which they could take pride in their noble identity:

> There are no tribal Presses emitting the day's lies and millions of useless volumes. There remain no written records; the wars, the kingdoms and the changes have sufficed unto themselves. It is not one country but many; well over 400 separate languages and their dialects are known to exist. Who tell you [that] you are the better off for being "civilized" when you live in the shadow of the next war or revolution in constant terror of being ruined. Things in Africa are on a different scale—but the European empire builders have seen, are seeing to this hand over fist. And what, against this triumph of organized villany had the black man to show? His own example of Homo Sapiens in better terms with life than are the conquering whites. Anthropology gives him priority in human descent. He had his life, highly organized, his logic, his customs, his laws rightly adhered to. He made music and unparalleled rhythms and some of the finest sculpture in the world. . . . How come, white man, is the rest of the world to be re-formed in your dreary and decadent image?[20]

Because the idealistic Nancy assumed that most of her friends shared her convictions, she was disappointed when many refused to contribute or when they submitted inferior pieces that she was too loyal to omit: Pound gave her a rambling two-paragraph essay on the German anthropologist Leo Frobenius, about black university studies. William Carlos Williams recalled his youthful sexual arousal in the presence of his family's black housekeeper.

During the trip, Nancy's relationship with Crowder became seriously strained. Over the past six months their arguments had grown increasingly acrimonious, and they had spent long periods of time apart from each other. Crowder now candidly expressed his lack of interest in the book and told her it was consuming too much of her time. He seemed to "shrug off" her goals and told her repeatedly that he was no activist and that she should not be attempting a book on this subject. The trip was filled with excessive drinking, feuding, and bad decisions. On one occasion, "when we were liquored up on moonshine," they flew to Washington, D.C., a nerve-wracking expedition for both, since Crowder's wife was there. In New York, Nancy asked him to take her to those parts of town in which he knew he would be unwelcome: "Me, of all people, a great big black man, running around New York with a white woman! I must have been crazy." He constantly worried that his wife would learn his whereabouts.[21]

Crowder had come to believe that there was no color bar in France, that he had felt "as free as a black man could be." In returning to the United States, he felt totally displaced: "Had all of this changed me to such an extent I could never live happily in my own country?" he asked himself; "I had to continually keep telling her that we could not do things in America as we had done them in France." Once, walking down Riverside Drive near 155th Street, a car with two men passed and one yelled out at Nancy: "Why don't you take a white man?"[22] Finally, they left New York on a German steamer and headed back for Europe. They agreed to separate, even though they did not cancel their plans for a future trip together. Crowder returned to his wife. Crowder and Nancy's affair, in its various degrees of passion and disappointment, commitment and distrust, continued until 1935.

The Second Trip to New York

When Nancy returned to New York in April 1932, she was maliciously attacked in the media and barraged by threatening letters because of the break with her family, class, and race:

[There were] many surprises and this time there had been enormous publicity, blather and ballyhoo about me in the American press (*all* of it, not only Hearst's). There were some outrageous lies, fantastic inventions and gross libels. . . . The race-hysteria exploded and surely its most rococo outbursts were embodied in the spate of frantic, unsigned and threatening letters.[23]

She arrived in New York with her artist friend John Banting, and they checked into the Grampion, along with the black novelist Taylor Gordon. Almost immediately, Nancy was bombarded with up to ten interviewers at a time, followed by rancorous and erroneous reports. The press had a heyday over her stay at a black hotel; reporters spied on her and described her socializing with blacks. She was portrayed as either a sexual predator or an easy target for a string of black men. The prurience of the reportage was astounding. Then the press ran numerous stories in which they quoted her two essays about her mother.

Nancy was headlined for a week; her activities became segments in Movietone News. For virtually the duration of her trip, she made headline news.

First, the *Daily News*, like the *Daily Mirror*, erroneously reported that "the Honorable" or "Her Ladyship" Nancy Cunard had been involved with Paul Robeson. The *News*'s lengthy article began:

> The Hon. Nancy Cunard, . . . whose spirited defense of her colored friend Paul Robeson caused an upheaval in London society recently, has been living in a colored hotel in Harlem for the last two weeks, the Grampion Hotel, 128 St. Nicholas Ave., where she has taken a suite. . . . She [made] numerous nightly trips from the hotel with colored men as escorts. Thus far, she has studiously avoided her socially prominent friends in this city although on previous visits she had been entertained in the foremost homes of Park Avenue and Westchester.[24]

Nancy wrote to all the papers and demanded a retraction: "Press Gentlemen: How do you get this way? I am astounded at your story of myself and Paul Robeson. You must correct this immediately. I met him once in Paris, in 1926. . . . He has said so himself. . . . My name is NOT 'the Hon Nancy'; it is Nancy Cunard." She addressed her alleged "rebellion against tradition":

> Here is the true story. Lady Cunard objected to one of my friends being a gentleman of color. I, however, admire everything that has come out of Africa. So would a great many other Nordics if they knew anything about it.
>
> Lady Cunard is American, of a certain type. Enough said. She put the police and the detectives on me in London because I knew a brown-skin. Pure waste of time and money for her; it is not illegal to know a brown-skin.
>
> Of course she has cut me off entirely and disinherited me. But she never had the courage to say so. I found it out all by myself with the bank's aid.[25]

Nancy received one response from an editor at the *New York American*: "We are aware of no misrepresentations. If you would see me for a few minutes the entire matter could be cleared up." The following day, the *Daily News* ratcheted up its rhetoric and published "Nancy Cunard Disinherited for Colored Man, She Tells." The article began:

> Nancy Cunard, descendant of the rich and famous Cunard steamship family, sat yesterday in her Harlem hotel home and told how she broke with her aristocratic mother because of her fondness for colored friends. . . .
>
> "I am astounded at the story," the exotic young woman exclaimed. "Paul Robeson! You must correct this immediately. I met him once in Paris, in 1926 at the Boeuf-sur-le-Toit cabaret."[26]

Robeson had also contacted the press for a retraction. The following month, his wife's divorce proceedings were reported in the *Sunday News*: "Colored Wife Suing Robeson; English Girl in Society Is Rival." The item was accompanied by a photo of Nancy and Robeson, who again replied: "No, . . . it's not the Hon. Nancy Cunard. I know her only slightly." When the *New York Herald Tribune* elaborated on the story, it underscored its own racial bigotry by mentioning Nancy's pride in her American ancestors for signing an antislavery proclamation:

In the gaudy dining room of the Harlem hostelry [the Grampion], which caters chiefly to colored guests, Miss Cunard—tall, slim, vibrant and thirty-six—exclaimed: "If you delve into 'Atavism Spanning the Atlantic' by Babcock, you will see . . . that one of my ancesters, toward 1680, signed the anti-slavery protest in Pennsylvania."[27]

Although angered by the continuing press coverage, Nancy took this as an opportunity to publicize her new project, the "abomination of racial justice" and "monstrous frame-up" of the Scottsboro boys, the nine young blacks from Alabama accused of sexually assaulting two white prostitutes:

And after my private affairs I want something in return: I want money for the defense of the nine Negro framed-up boys held under death sentence to be sent immediately for the *Scottsboro Defense*. [She included a New York City address.] . . .

Why are you Americans so uneasy of the Negro Race?

This question is the epitome of the whole color question as it strikes a plain English person such as myself.

Who'll write me the best answer to this?

I'll print it in my book on Color."

The following day, the coverage was more positive: "Miss Cunard Asks Aid for 9 Doomed Negroes." Again, putting her cause before her own needs—obviously, the press would never apologize—she stated: "I am delighted that the stir I seem to have created may result in some widespread publicity for the opinions about my friends, the Negroes, I am so anxious to spread."[28]

The press was not about to capitulate, and the personal attacks escalated. The *Mirror* and the *New York American* serialized lengthy excerpts from both *Black Man and Her Ladyship* and "Does Anyone *Know* Any Negroes?" They published photos of Nancy with Gordon and cropped out Banting because he was white. Newsreels of "Lady Cunard Going into a Harlem Hotel" were screened everywhere. Nancy received hundreds of hate letters. When one of her friends tried to hide a particularly vicious one, she said: "I'm used to it from home. We have suffered from it too in Merry England . . . subtle but just as vicious." She received, for example:

> Miss cunard, you are making a lousy hoor of yourself asociating with niggers can't you get a white man to satisfy you I have always heard that a negro has a large prick so I suppose you like large ones. . . .
>
> I don't know what they call your kind in England but here in America they call them plain nigger fuckers or prostitutes of the lowest kind that what you are drifting to and that what the people think of you.[29]

The press reprinted Nancy's *Black Man and White Ladyship*. The *Mirror's* prefatory remarks began: "Heiress to a great fortune bearing a proud name, and with socially-prominent relatives on both sides of the Atlantic, Nancy Cunard has chosen to throw her lot with Negroes, fighting for recognition of their race." The *Mirror's* next installment was clearly intended to uproot Nancy: "Miss Cunard, incidentally, has moved to an all-Negro rooming house at No. 203 W. 123rd St."[30] Needless to say, Nancy was unable to remain there. She had already left the Grampion after learning that a hotel employee had been bribed by newspapermen to alert them when she went out. When she realized that her large-brimmed hats were inadequate as a disguise, she had moved to the rooming house.

Lawrence Gellert rescued her temporarily by taking her to a friend's farm in Dutchess County, in New York State, where for a few weeks they worked steadily on *Negro*. The lilacs were in bloom, as Gellert later wrote, "and you became even as a child again, with the long arm of hatred and persecution that reached beyond the sea after you forgotten." He recalled other relaxed moments, such as their walk into a country store where the proprietor neglected to help them because he was immersed in reading a newspaper with the front page headline, "Nancy Cunard Disappears from Harlem." Gellert recollects: "We fled for safety before he even looked up. How you laughed!" Another day, as they rode the Fall River Line boat and watched the stars all night, Nancy told Gellert her greatest dream: that the book would "contribute to that distant day of Negro liberation."[31]

The next month, Gellert accompanied Nancy to Boston to collect essays from various contributors. After meeting the poet Sterling Brown, the three walked down Boston Common, and Brown composed a poem celebrating "an English lady, a Hungarian immigrant, and a descendant of slavery" in the cradle of American independence. Nancy's subsequent visit to the journalist Eugene Gordon surprised him. He had just seen a newsreel about "Lady Cunard Entering a Harlem Hotel." Since Nancy had been described as the leading character in Huxley's *Point Counter Point* and Arlen's *The Green*

Hat, Gordon began reading the novels. When Gellert and Nancy arrived, he opened the door to find the heroine of Arlen's book actually wearing a green hat.[32] Nancy took only one detour on the trip. She missed Crowder so much that she flew to Washington to see him. But for reasons that are unclear, they were unable to meet.

Reporters followed Nancy during the rest of her American trip, and when there was nothing new to write about, they juxtaposed photos of her mother and fashionable friends with those of her daughter and black friends, as though illustrating good and evil. Before leaving America, Nancy considered traveling to the South, but her friends dissuaded her: "[She] would have created a rumpus," said one; another later commented: "If she had gone she would have suffered a more horrible death than Mrs. Viola Liuzzo in Alabama thirty-three years later." Even in Philadelphia, in the most ordinary of situations, she was treated as an interloper. She had her hair done by a black hairdresser, and afterward she "could not think why all the attendants seemed so odd in behavior, as if flustered. At the end they confided . . . that she was the first white woman ever to enter that shop." Naïve, to say the least, she replied, "And my being English did not appear to explain it all away."

Although Nancy and Crowder had planned a trip to Jamaica and Cuba, when Crowder refused to go, she invited a black Bostonian, A. A. Colebrooke, originally from Jamaica and later a literary agent for *Negro*. The *Daily News*'s story, "Nancy Cunard Sails Escorted by Colored Man," began:

> Nancy Cunard, who caused a sensation recently by taking quarters at a Harlem hotel, sailed for Havana yesterday accompanied by a colored man, . . . an Anselm Colebrooke. . . . Confronted by photographers, he threw a protecting arm about the slender young woman and held a newspaper over her face. Miss Cunard occupied Cabin No. 80 and her companion had No. 81.

The *Boston Post* picked up the story and identified Nancy's traveling companion as "one Ansel Colebrooke, colored," alleging that he had deserted his white wife and six children for Nancy. Other papers also printed "fabricated innuendo-allegations" of a police search for Colebrooke. A Baltimore paper reported that the Boston police were looking for Colebrooke regarding a missing car. The *Inter-State Tatler* published "Nancy Cunard and Sepia Gent Sail Away: Romance?" and referred to Colebrooke as "a convicted criminal, wife deserter, and fugitive from justice [and] also a heartbreaker of much ability in Harlem where sepia gigolos are more than numerous." The story became a matter of controversy between the black and the white press. The *Baltimore Afro-America* stated: "Mrs. Colebrook [said] her husband has gone to Havana on business. The condition of the family has improved since Colebrooke, a man of education and a former Elk exalted ruler, secured employment with Miss Cunard." The racial politicization became increasingly curious: "The fact of Colebrook's employment and of his care for his family is supported by the white newspapers because of the desire to use him to humiliate the white Englishwoman."[33] It was later clarified that the press had referred to three different men with the same name and same spelling.

During her three weeks in Jamaica, as in each country she visited, Nancy tried to re-create her Harlem experience—by staying in inexpensive quarters, walking extensively, speaking to the people, and trying to understand each area in terms of its history. She began her essay on Jamaica, in *Negro*:

> It was in 1494 that Columbus first saw the lofty outline of a new land and set foot on it in the name of Spain. . . . The native fisherman with him said they called it "Xaymaca," in their language, a word signifying "a land of springs." . . .
>
> Jamaica was in need of colonists. The mortality amongst English laborers was high, and small increases of souls, such as 1,600 men, women, children and Negro slaves that arrived from the small island of Nevis in 1656, could not suffice. Permission to import Africans was granted by Cromwell.[34]

She met Marcus Garvey, and while she agreed that blacks should try to return to Africa, she, like others at the time, considered him as well as Du Bois, reactionary: neither was sufficiently active in fighting racial prejudice against American blacks and, more specifically, in supporting the Scottsboro boys.

Nancy refused to succumb to the press's harassment in New York; she endured it for the sake of her work. But when she returned to England, the reporters went too far. Numerous stories appeared similar to the one in the *Empire News* of Manchester: "Auntie Nancy's Cabin—Down Among the Black Gentlemen of Harlem." They had all responded to Nancy's statement "I intend to devote the rest of my life to work on behalf of the colored race." The columns were written with the same condescending sarcasm as the *Empire News*'s "I give her less than 12 months in which to change the color of her opinions." For this most unkind remark, Nancy initiated a libel suit against British Allied Newspapers and the *Empire News, Daily Dispatch*, and *Sunday Chronicle*. The King's Bench Division of the High Courts of Justice, on July 14, 1934, settled the case in her favor. Nancy was able to put the £1,500 settlement fee toward the publication of *Negro*, which otherwise would not have been published; she had saved only £350 for this contingency, assuming that no publisher would sponsor such a radical book.[35]

That the bigoted press was paying for a book that argued against bigotry was, she thought, "poetic justice." She later remarked about the settlement: "I have never ceased admiring and marveling at that—as final as a tombstone."[36]

Nancy had briefly considered suing the New York press, but when she learned that she would have to remain in New York for the trial she decided against it.

In August, when she returned to France, she rejoined Raymond Michelet, and they worked on *Negro* continually, translating the last of the French contributions and writing essays that a few contributors had failed to submit, including Nancy's on Harlem and Jamaica. They also spent two weeks at the Tervueren Museum in Brussels, collecting photos and making sketches of African art. Michelet was in love with Nancy, and by the following spring, in 1933, when she went to London to arrange for the publication of *Negro*, she ended their affair. She could not commit herself to the permanent relationship he wanted.

Negro was finally published by Wishart at Nancy's expense. She had been correct in predicting that the book would be rejected by numerous presses, although Jonathan Cape was willing to take it on if Nancy would reduce it in size and change its format. She later said that trying to place *Negro* was like "selling oriental rugs to manure merchants."[37]

Even though Crowder had not kept his appointment with Nancy in Washington the previous year, she had continued to write him and to implore him to return. Then for seven or eight months, she stopped writing. Unemployed and in bad health, he fell into a depression and alcoholism; he was finally hospitalized. After he recovered, "out of a clear sky" he received a cable from Nancy. They resumed their correspondence, and he agreed to return on the condition that he be financially independent. She suggested a job connected to the Negro Welfare League of London, but when he arrived in the spring of 1933 and the job did not materialize, he was enraged. To make matters worse, Nancy was preparing the final manuscript of *Negro*, "up to her ears" in work, with the yeoman help of the poet Edgell Rickwood, who, Crowder believed, had become Nancy's most recent admirer. Rickwood, who helped her design *Negro* and correct proofs, had also contributed to the volume an annotated account of eighteenth-century slavery documents in Europe. Now, according to Crowder, she wanted him, newly returned to Réanville, to also "be one of her lovers in the intimate sense of the word and I absolutely refused." In the meantime, Nancy helped Crowder get a job at a Montmartre café, but in early 1934, he left for London to take another job, and they did not see each other for about eight months.

In late 1934, when Nancy wrote him that she was in poor health, he visited her. She was so ill that she had to be placed in a nursing home, and for several weeks she remained in critical condition. Crowder remained at her side, and after her recovery they went to the south of France, where once again they argued, primarily over money. Crowder still resented his financial dependence on Nancy, but her response was, "The old girl is broke now. Got no money. You're like all the other rats, leaving a sinking ship." One day she said, as Crowder recalls the incident, "We don't like each other any more, so we might as well call it quits."[38] With the exception of a few unsatisfactory meetings and some brief correspondence, the relationship was over. Crowder remained in Europe for a few years, taking on odd jobs before returning to the United States. When a friend wrote to Nancy of his death twenty years later, she replied,

> And so Henry is dead—
>
> How extraordinary it is to me to think of the way this news comes to me. . . . Do you know that otherwise I should *never* have known? Is this what happens when one asks a friend to look for the long-dead past? Pretty obviously, I should never have seen him again. He might have been dead from 1937 to 1947, for all I knew.
>
> Henry made me—and so be it. . . . Others have loved me more (?), and I, perhaps others. No probably not, for me, has this been true. In any case Henry made me. I thank him.[39]

The Birth of *Negro*

Wishart published 1,000 copies of *Negro*, at £2.2 each. Nancy sent copies, at her own expense, to the press and to numerous American and English libraries. But because of the nature and breadth of its subject matter, as well as its size, the book received few reviews. The *New York Times* announced its publication and described but did not review it. Under the caption "Cunard Anthology Is Issued," it began "Nancy Cunard, daughter of a noted London hostess, who has forsworn Mayfair life to devote herself to the cause of the Negro, has just published *The Negro* [*sic*]. . . . She 'denounces' the 'oppression' of '14,000,000 Negroes in America' and summarizes 'the upsurge of their demands for mere justice, that is to say, full and equal rights, alongside their white-fellow citizens.'" The article described the vastness of Nancy's subject matter. The *New York Amsterdam News* called it "distinguished"; the *New Republic* applauded her "singularly rare insight" into race. A few additional, brief reviews appeared eight and nine months later, including one in the *New Statesman*, beginning, "No review can do justice to such a volume." Janet Flanner praised "the first book of such scope"—in essence, for giving unlimited immediate hope to blacks.[40]

Most of the highly positive comments arrived in letters from black friends. Langston Hughes telegrammed: "Your book is marvelous"; Alain Locke, "I congratulate you, almost enviously, on the finest anthology in every sense of the word ever compiled on the Negro." William Pickens, Arthur A. Schomburg, Claude Barnet, and Taylor Gordon sent similar congratulations. Among the few whites who wrote to Nancy, Theodore Dreiser said, "I see that you will probably have an American edition, and I hope it is very successful. If your negotiations happen not to go through, I would not mind suggesting an American edition to a publisher I have in mind, although, of course, I cannot predict his answer." William Carlos Williams called *Negro* "a monumental accomplishment by which further studies relative to the Negro will be measured." Hugh Ford best summed up Nancy's achievement: "Had it not been for her compelling energy—and fearlessness— . . . the scores of contributors inspired by her presence would have . . . postponed investigating their heritage and analyzing their common problems, which, in time, moved them closer to the freedom for which she fought." David Levering Lewis more recently stated that as the Harlem Renaissance "ran down, . . . *Negro*, far more massive in scope [than Locke's momentous *New Negro*], recharged the Renaissance."[41]

At the time, however, the lack of reviews, particularly in the left-wing press, surprised and depressed Nancy. The book was not mentioned in the London *Times*, although Lady Cunard's luncheons, dinners, and teas continued to receive regular coverage; at the same time that Nancy's book was published, one article covered Maud's loss of a bracelet; another, the merger of the Cunard and White Star shipping lines and the launching of the *Queen Mary* steamship.[42] The several hundred copies of *Negro* that languished at Wishart were destroyed during the Blitz.

Nancy and Henry Crowder: Afterthoughts

Nancy's relationship with Crowder, however tumultuous, was her longest love affair, and it radically altered her life. Many details in the last two chapters, drawn from Nancy's and her friends' recollections, make clear that Nancy never wrote an ill word about him; in fact, she rarely alluded to their romance. In *These Were the Hours* especially, Crowder is portrayed as a talented musician, resourceful assistant at the press, and dependable companion on various trips; she discloses in detail the bigotry they encountered and how it affected each of them. Crowder was the "first cause" not only of her project *Negro* but, one can assume by extension, of all the human rights causes that consumed her for the rest of her life.

After they separated, Crowder wrote *As Wonderful As All That?*, a scathing attack on Nancy, as "typical" of the white woman who becomes involved with a black man. He is bitter about how she took advantage of him, her temper and alcoholic fits, her infidelities, and, mostly, his financial dependence on this wealthy white woman. He attributes her ill treatment of him to his relentless skepticism about her goals, to what he calls her arrogant naïveté in thinking that she, a child of the aristocracy, could do anything to change the reality of black inequality.

It is fascinating to read about the affair through Crowder's eyes. He begins by recalling his firm resolution that he would have nothing to do with white women in Europe.[43] Then he makes clear that Nancy initiated their meeting by returning to the Lido nightclub with her cousin several nights in a row before asking, "Won't you sit down and have a drink?"

> With that introduction began my association with Nancy Cunard, . . . an internationally known white woman with a very brilliant mind who speaks four languages fluently and who is a writer and poetess of note. She is also widely traveled and is well versed in the history of art and painting. . . . She was no ordinary person. Everything about her even down to small mannerisms demonstrated high breeding and graciousness.

Then, typical of his retrospective reassessment, he adds: "Had I known then what that introduction would bring I would never have stopped."

A few days later, Nancy invited him to dinner. Again, perhaps only in hindsight, he writes: "I actually began to wonder, if I had not been a fool to have come." Afterward, Nancy took him on a tour of her rooms and introduced him to her art collection. They embraced and said goodnight. A friendship developed; Nancy went to Florence, and they corresponded by telegraph. Once back in Venice, Nancy began socializing with the other band members and their girlfriends. Crowder became "infatuated beyond all reason," flattered to be with a celebrity, a stunningly beautiful, well-dressed woman around whom everyone stopped and stared.[44] He eventually accompanied her everywhere—to barge parties in Venice, premieres of major new music (George Antheil's *Transatlantic*) and films (*L'Age d'or*), and elite gala parties, fashionable nightclubs, and gambling rooms in France, England, Belgium, Italy, Germany, Spain, Switzerland, and Austria. He met her talented friends (Ezra Pound, James Joyce, Wyndham Lewis, Augustus John, Richard Aldington, Louis Aragon, Antheil, among others) and socially prominent hostesses (Elsa Maxwell). Amid such an array of personalities, he grew to feel "what it meant to be on intimate terms with prominent white people and considered an equal in every way."

Despite this, and throughout the book, his frustration at the emotional cost of their relationship is apparent. On his first page, he says, "I owe it to my race to let it be known, [to] disclose all the sordid details of this relationship. . . . It is my hope that the experiences which I have gone through may be of some value to colored men who become enamored of white women." He also makes clear that throughout their affair he was intensely ambivalent toward Nancy. She was irresistible, and he knew he would be hurt: "I reasoned that I was a fool. . . . The affair was too dangerous for me. . . . I was going to get out of the mess." But "I never did. There was the same undefinable attraction, that same something so intriguing and interesting that I could not shake myself loose." As if to protect himself from her power over him, he qualifies his love for her in terms of racial temperamental differences: "Never in my life have I been thoroughly in love with a white woman. Their desires, their likes, their psychology of life are entirely different from that of a colored person."[45]

To the reader's surprise (perhaps a rationalization), he says that early on he stopped loving her, but his mixture of emotions is clearly complex: "Any love I might have had for Nancy had been killed. I saw myself as a pawn upon her chessboard of life," adding, "and even though I was only a player in her game I felt I had been cast for an important part." "Nancy," he goes on to say, "repeatedly told me that I did not care for her which was true. . . . Furthermore I took no pains to hide it."[46]

Crowder writes extensively about Nancy's infidelities and pleasure in hurting men. If one recalls Aragon's suicide attempt and admission that he chose women who degraded him, Robert Nichols's threat to shoot himself, Pound's warning to Aldington to be wary of sirens like Nancy, and the various portraits of her by Michael Arlen, Aldous Huxley, T. S. Eliot, and others, Crowder's comments seem credible. He writes, for example: "I really believe she derived a great deal of personal satisfaction in hearing some man threaten to commit suicide because of her." But he adds: "I always told her I would not prick my finger with a pin over any woman," adding, "She once told me I was the only person who never bored her."[47]

Crowder became aware of Nancy's interest in other men early in their romance, and as Nancy pursued her dalliances, he pursued his own. Nevertheless, except for a few instances, he tolerated her infidelities: with an Italian nobleman and a waiter in Venice; a "blue-black" musician (Crowder's term) called Dan; the black former prizefighter Bob Scanlon; her chauffeur, George; the black dancer Chic Horsey; a petty criminal known as Pollard; Roy Randall, the English journalist en route to Austria; and the banjo player in Crowder's band. Of virtually any of their acquaintances, he said, "All . . . were potential lovers of Nancy's." Even when Crowder returned from Washington to France, Nancy was in the process of moving from one man (Michelet) to another (Rickwood).[48] Crowder portrays his infidelities as a necessary retaliation.

He makes clear that he continually questioned Nancy's motivation and competence in undertaking *Negro*, which she considered her life's greatest work. She began the project, he writes, because "she was bored" and adds:

"To tell the plain truth I did not think she was a person who was capable of doing the work she proposed. . . . Hundreds of dollars [would be] wasted on the compilation of the anthology." Even after she finished the book, he thought that her efforts were a waste of time: "She has tried to break down impregnable barriers with foolish and futile weapons; she has tried to dip an ocean dry with a spoon."[49]

One can understand Crowder's negativism while wondering how much of it was heightened by the frustrations of their relationship. Nonetheless, given the racial situation of the time, it would have been difficult for him to believe that any one person, even the talented Nancy, could change the world. In addition, Crowder could view her only through the lens of his own experience. It must have seemed unfathomable that she could break down the walls that had constrained him.

On a more positive note, he acknowledges that Nancy's commitment to *Negro* "caused her name to go to the four corners of the world. A Negro school in Africa has been named for her." He also concedes that her commitment to the book and to him exacted tremendous social costs, which she readily accepted. He first describes her alienation from friends: "Most of the people that I met through Nancy probably disapproved of her manner in showing her lack of a racial or color feeling. It is significant that as the years passed she saw less and less of the people she saw when I first met her." In addition, he notes that, despite her willingness to relinquish family and social ties, her behavior aroused enormous anger in the black community, as hostile to the sight of a biracial couple as the white community. Once again, Crowder finds her naïve in thinking she could fight racial bigotry: "She was born to the purple but has thrown it all aside. Now she finds herself in a new and hostile environment, among enemies about whom she knows nothing and can never understand."

Throughout their relationship, Nancy gave Crowder money for various reasons: a salary when he worked at the press, which greatly pleased him, and an allowance when he was unemployed, which embarrassed and angered him. He felt humiliated when he had to ask for extra money. At the same time, he believed that a black man was entitled to money from a wealthy white woman: "I tried to explain to her that when a white woman became intimate with a colored man, he usually expected to get money from her." He became infuriated when she was generous and even liberal with strangers: "She rarely passed a poor beggar without giving something." That Nancy socialized extensively with blacks, many of whom Crowder found socially inferior, also irritated him. He believed that "instead of raising the lowest of the black race to her level by associating with them she lowers herself to their level."

As Henry grew more dependent on Nancy and felt no color barrier abroad, he began to forget his black identity: "I had learned what it means to be on intimate terms with prominent white people and considered as an equal in every way. In that respect I think I forgot my color the same as they seemingly did. [At the same time] at night I often wondered why they accepted me on equal terms and yet in my own country I was considered different from others." When he finally returned to Washington, he felt as alienated from black as from white society.

● ● ●

At last, what can one say of Nancy and Crowder? It seems to me that their relationship was grounded in factors that extended beyond race or class. That is to say, they shared needs that had grown out of emotionally similar upbringings and, for a time, were able to ameliorate for the other the wounds of childhood. In so doing, each was enhanced by the other and gained a better sense of self: Crowder composed the music he had always wanted to write; Nancy published it. Crowder introduced Nancy to the black cause; Nancy found a mission in life as a social activist.

Although from vastly different socioeconomic worlds, analogous childhood circumstances underlay the emotional needs that so intensely bound them to each other. At the time they met, they not only were outsiders in the worlds of their birth, but both had also been deprived of the parental nurturing and devotion that makes for self-confident adult independence. Within his family as one of twelve children, Crowder had tried and failed to stand out as the perfect child. Beyond the family, being black and born in Georgia made him a victim of the racial abuses of the time and an outsider in his own country. Crowder found in Nancy, who initiated the relationship, an outsider from her own social class who made him feel not just worthy but special in the light of her culture and intellect.

Nancy also lacked the deeply rooted sense of self-worth and life direction that develop from the care of attentive parents, rather than the cold efficiency of hired governesses. Maud had been an unloving, unempathetic mother to whom childbearing was revolting. Bache was a distant and ineffectual, if pleasant, father. G. M., who was a warm and supportive parental figure and possibly Nancy's father, manifested a barely contained salacious interest in the girl and young woman.

As a result of her childhood, Nancy lacked the inner sense of emotional security and stability that would enable her to feel in control of her destiny, to soothe herself during the normal anxieties of growing up and of adulthood. Specifically, her self-esteem problems burdened her with an insatiable need for both admiration and admired others. At the same time, lacking that sense of wholeness or self-worth that makes for appropriate self-love—and subsequent love of an other—Nancy was incapable of the trust necessary for an enduring intimate relationship with a man. Her beauty and intelligence enabled her to attract a seemingly endless variety of talented men who loved her intensely, yet her emotional insecurity prevented her from believing their expressions of love.

Michelet, like many of Nancy's friends, made an observation that is pertinent here. Although often invited to do so, Nancy would not write her autobiography. She would not, or could not, look back. She always wanted to be somewhere else. As Michelet put it: "What was she running from?" It seems to me that Nancy felt compelled to distance herself from permanent intimacy with Crowder—or any man—by offending him with her provocative behavior and casual sexuality, thus guaranteeing his rejection of her. She ran off with strangers, which infuriated each of her lovers, and this served to confirm her lack of trust in him. Her capriciousness served to protect her against the very rejection it provoked. Her behavior prompted a self-fulfilling prophecy. Every relationship renewed the hope of finding the loving devotion she had been deprived of as a child, and each, in turn, became a repetition of her childhood disappointment. In this sense, her emotional needs were like a bottomless well.

Despite the shortcomings of her upbringing, Nancy did enjoy the sociability and intellectualism of her mother and the people she entertained. She observed that a beautiful, intelligent woman could attract numerous admirers. Like Maud, Nancy grew to enjoy the flattery of men, particularly highly creative men. She could share her good mind with some of the most brilliant of the age—learn from them, and gain their admiration. She was a high-spirited and gifted young woman who naturally attracted friends. From this, one may speculate, she gained the confidence to create the Hours Press. It was clear that she was not going to be another Lady Cunard or, for that matter, follow the traditional role of wife and mother. But it was not until she met Crowder that she discovered for herself the sense of purpose that would define the rest of her life.

For a time, Nancy and Crowder became each other's salvation. Since childhood, Nancy had remembered the dream in which she was welcomed into a group of blacks dancing in Africa. Long before meeting Crowder, she had decorated her Paris and Réanville homes with African art to signal the close relationship between black culture and the modern world. With Crowder, for a time, she found a home not only with a fellow outcast but with a handsome, talented man of African descent—in a sense, a work of art, a dream, an unconscious wish come true.

She discovered the noble savage in Crowder, as well as an artist. She idealized him as the embodiment and spokesman of black culture. Crowder complained that she wanted him to be more African, and when she did so, he would reply sardonically, "I ain't African. I'm American." Although each became the other's victim in their mutual displays of chronic anger originating in early childhood deprivation, in the end, Nancy may have benefited more from their relationship than Crowder. He inspired her toward fulfilling herself as a champion of the underdog, as a moral caretaker of the victimized. This role came as naturally to her as the "good teacher" role had come to Crowder. But hers was a crusade in which he took little interest. As a lifelong victim of a situation that was relatively new to the idealistic Nancy, he was dubious about any possible success in the cause. Unfortunately, after his music was published, Crowder seems to have completed his life's goal as a musician. Only two weeks after his final meeting with Nancy, at the end of May 1935, he signed a contract with Hugo Speck, a white American journalist working in Paris, to collaborate on a book about her: he had "followed the rainbow of a white woman's attractions and found at the end only disillusionment and disappointment." That it was not published at the time was due to the authors' fear that Nancy's mother, still alive, would take legal action. Robert Allen, who provided the book with an introduction and epilogue, learned about the unpublished manuscript in Anne Chisholm's biography of Nancy, published in 1979. Crowder had long before returned to Washington and taken a job at the Customs Bureau. He later became a clerk handling the outgoing mail of the Coast Guard headquarters. He wrote to Nancy after she sent him her book on Norman Douglas: "As for nightclubs—all that is a thing of the past—never cared much for them anyway," and concluded: "I am not happy, and I am not sad."

40. Nancy in Réanville

41. Working the Mathieu press

42. Relaxing with Tristan Tzara

43. African objects displayed in an elegant cabinet

44. A sampling of Nancy's bracelets

45. Henry Crowder

46. *Henry-Music*, published by the Hours Press

47. Press coverage in New York as Nancy prepares *Negro*

48. Front-page coverage continues

49. Langston Hughes

50. An illustration from *Negro*

The nine innocent Scottsboro boys
after their arrest on a false charge of assault on two white prostitutes in Alabama, March 25, 1931

51. The Scottsboro boys, from Nancy's essay in *Negro*

9

Negro

Mumiti wa nhengele a dumba nkolo wa kme.
(He who swallows a large stone has confidence in the size of his throat.)

—BARONGA PROVERB

Negro is a staggering accomplishment—in purpose, breadth of information, and size. Almost 8 pounds, 855 pages (12 inches by 10½ inches), with 200 entries by 150 contributors (the majority, black) and nearly 400 illustrations, it was, and in many ways remains, unique—an encyclopedic introduction to the history, social and political conditions, and cultural achievements of the black population throughout much of the world: the United States, Europe, South and Central America, the West Indies, and Africa. It is one of the earliest examples of African American, cross-cultural, and transnational studies and a call to all civilized people to condemn racial discrimination and appreciate the great social and cultural accomplishments of a long-suffering people.

Scholars today, such as Brent Hayes Edwards, recognize Nancy as the earliest proponent of black transnationalism, of the African diaspora that has challenged colonial attitudes throughout the world. Maureen Moynagh also acknowledges Nancy's seminal role in recognizing the history and accomplishments of Africans, both on their native continent and throughout the world.[1]

Negro's contributors included Theodore Dreiser, Harold Acton, George Antheil, William Carlos Williams, Lewis Zukofsky, Ezra Pound, Josephine Herbst, Arna Bontemps, W. C. Handy, Countee Cullen, Zora Neale Hurston, George Padmore, W. E. B. Du Bois, Langston Hughes, E. Franklin Frazier, Sterling Brown, Walter White, Arthur A. Schomburg, and Alain J. Locke.

Samuel Beckett translated eighteen essays on a broad spectrum of subjects, including a manifesto by the French Surrealists and essays on Louis Armstrong and jazz; the history of Haiti, the Congo, and Madagascar; and commentaries on imperialism. Nancy furnished a poem; an extensive history of Jamaica; an impassioned defense of the Scottsboro boys; and essays on Harlem, color bias, and the "reactionary" W. E. B. Du Bois and NAACP, which, she argued, were pandering to the white ruling class. She also added editorial notes to several essays. Henry Crowder contributed essays on American racism and the absence of a color line in Europe.

The anthology, in seven sections,[2] is extraordinary in its readability—a mixture of scholarship and personal recollection. Documents like Lincoln's "Proclamation of Emancipation of the Slaves" and essays by Booker T. Washington, Nat Turner, Frederick Douglass, and Harriet Tubman, as well as contributions by little-known authors on the pathology of racism and negrophobia of an early nominee for the Supreme Court, are interspersed with newspaper clippings of racially incited events, racist ads, and personal and media accounts of lynchings, chain gangs, body burnings, and activities of the Ku Klux Klan. Some of the vicious and congratulatory letters Nancy received when she stayed in Harlem are also included.

Many of the essays have a matter-of-fact, nonpolemical style, like those on the museum holdings of African art worldwide, explorers' maps of Africa, and economic and demographic statistics. Several deal with black social or work patterns in different countries, the history of black education and the black student, and the future of blacks in business; some address unique characteristics of black speech, music, prayer, and recreation; others are so specialized that they define distinctive black dance movements and the techniques of specific black boxers.

One of the most appealing sections of *Negro* deals with music, especially jazz, that unique black American art form which, according to the composer George Antheil, helped heal the broken spirit and disintegration of moral values following World War I. In another essay, Antheil defines modernism and traces the influence of American jazz and African sculpture on moderns like Picasso, Stravinsky, and Brancusi. Several contributors define the originality, as well as the cultural influence, of performers like Louis Armstrong and Duke Ellington; some address the musicality of black prayer and the musical uniqueness of spirituals and blues. Jazz is at times viewed as the musical equivalent of other remarkable innovations of the era, such as those of Einstein, Freud, and Joyce.

Similarly appealing are the essays on "the black creative genius" (Nancy's term) in classical music. Essayists address little-known composers, conductors, and performers (such as George Augustus Bridgetower, Beethoven's friend who performed the Kreutzer Sonata with him in Vienna in 1805), and the better-known Samuel Coleridge-Taylor.

Nancy further illustrates black creative genius by including musical scores and poetry by people such as Langston Hughes, Countee Cullen, and Arna Bontemps and by whites who write on black themes, including Louis Zukofsky, William Plomer, Florence Ungar, and Nancy herself. Equally compelling are the photos and drawings of nearly 200 African works of art, as well as many full-page photos of black celebrities and smaller images of black essayists and of contemporary life, ranging from Caribbean men at work to a bustling Harlem nightclub. She also includes photos of a 1792 slave ship and of lynchings and burnings.

The preface advances Nancy's plea for racial justice. She intends to record "the persecutions" against "the Negro peoples" and her belief that Communism, "as it wipes out class distinctions," will be the salvation of the black race, an idealization of the party that would be short-lived. She addresses "the spirit and determination in the Negro to beat through the mountain of tyranny heaped on him [as it] is manifested in his rapid evolution, since Emancipation in 1863, of his own cultural organization, as is shown in every sphere of activity—literature, education, business, the law, the press, the theater." She will introduce the reader to "the miraculous theatrical and Musical Negro Firmament" in order to demonstrate a people "so utterly rich in natural grace and beauty" that they have created unique and compelling forms of art that meet the spiritual and moral needs of the modern world. She moves from America across the globe to Africa, "in the iron grip of its several imperialist oppressions":

> Africans are no more than "niggers," black man-power whom it is fit to dispossess of everything. At one time labeled en block "cannibals" and "savages" who have never produced anything, [it is now fashionable] to say that the white man is in Africa for the black man's *good*. . . . The truth is that Africa is a tragedy. The white man is killing Africa.

Although most of the book focuses on America and Africa, Nancy indicates that her work would be incomplete without including the "subtler" forms of prejudice in Europe, the West Indies, and South America. The "Europe" section, for example, protests against the "infamous" and sanctioned treatment of blacks in Britain by the government. Again, the essays vary in theme—from a history of the slave trade to an essay on Pushkin (whose mother was part black). Nancy makes clear throughout that that segment of the "Negro bourgeoisie" that holds "that justice will come . . . from some eventual liberality in the white man" is captive to a foolish dream.

Because *Negro* is little known and long out of print—although Nancy's friend, the scholar Hugh Ford, published a redesigned 460-page version in 1970[3]—it is of interest to review some of the original book's entries, both for their intrinsic merit and to highlight the breadth of Nancy's interests.

The book begins with Langston Hughes's poem "I Too," a Whitmanesque mixture of candor and hope:

I, too, sing America.
I am the darker brother.
They send me to eat in the kitchen
When company comes;
But I laugh,
And eat well,
And grow strong.
Tomorrow
I'll sit at the table
When company comes.
Nobody'll dare
Say to me,
"Eat in the kitchen"
Then.
Besides, they'll see how beautiful I am
And be ashamed—
I, too, am American.

After this, "A Brief Outline of Negro History in the U.S. Until Abolition" by Edward A. Johnson introduces the "America" section.[4] Johnson begins by tracking the first blacks in America, who arrived in Jamestown in 1619 aboard a Dutch trading vessel. Fourteen were exchanged for food and supplies and immediately became slaves, although the Jamestown community would not pass a law institutionalizing slavery until 1662. Blacks performed manual labor and worked the tobacco fields; some were enlisted in the militia, although they could not bear arms unless the colonists were threatened by the Indians. They were not allowed to vote or attend school, but they were taxed.

The condition of the slaves on the New York farms (1664) was better. They could be baptized, for example, and no law prohibited them from attending school. On Wall Street, the center of financial exchange, both Indians and blacks were bought and sold at auction, and "a whipping boss was once a characteristic officer in New York City." An early slave riot occurred in 1712, when blacks, already excluded from schools, were also forbidden to defend themselves when struck by their masters; a militia suppressed the riot. A law was passed about this time in New England to classify slaves as property, "rated as horses and hogs"; and although the Delaware and Pennsylvania Quakers opposed slavery, William Penn permitted it. In South Carolina, Spaniards bribed the slaves who worked the rice fields to join their forces. If they were caught by their masters, they were branded and their hamstrings were cut.

At the beginning of the Revolutionary War, the Virginia governor offered freedom to slaves who would fight for the British. George Washington and the Continental Congress also tried to utilize slaves: masters who gave them to the Revolutionary forces received $1,000; if a black served well until the end of the war, he was emancipated and given $50. About 5,000 blacks fought on the side of the colonies.

"If taught to read, you cannot keep them slaves," begins Wendell P. Dabney, in "Slave Risings and Race Riots,"[5] and he reminds us that blacks in almost all of colonial America not only were prohibited from attending school but also lacked a common language, having arrived from so many different countries. His understanding regarding the "toleration" of black religion, he admits, is unique. He sees it as a product of the white masters' insidiousness, rather than as an example of their concern with spirituality or an emotional outlet. Since "America was a Christian (?) country," he explains, "some semblance of religion was necessary for the benighted heathen from darkest Africa, whose coming [to America] was considered God's method for saving their souls." As a result, while sent to church and allowed to have their own preachers, slaves were completely imbued with doctrines that made them more servile, dutiful, and patient in "bearing the chains that corroded their flesh and brutalized their souls." They were convinced that the greater their trials and tribulations in this world, the more glorious the heavenly home that awaited them. "And so they sang the song that their grandsons still sing: 'You may have all the world, but give me Jesus.'"

Sarah Frances Chenault, at first tentative about the future of her race, concludes with a statement of faith. She begins "The Ku Klux Clan in Indiana"[6] with recollections of how Klans formed when she was a child in the Midwest. David Curtis Stephenson, for example, started his organization "against the Kikes, Koons, and Catholics" by selling memberships for $10 to more than 400 men and women. He pocketed $3 to $4 from each new membership and then built a luxurious mansion and bought expensive cars and airplanes (from which he distributed hate literature).

Chenault is at first ambivalent about the past and future of the black because "those who were not murdered died of broken hearts." Today, however, "the new Negro offsprings of Mammies, Aunt Jemima, Uncle Toms, and slave masters are *not* dead. They sing sad songs and laugh a little." While Sherwood Anderson calls this "Dark Laughter," Chenault knows that "color [is] a nightmare, a mental complex, [and] a chronic disease." All the same, her racial pride and hope for the future is reinforced by her faith rather than by the anticipation of social action: "I am an American Negro woman, . . . grateful to the Creator, since it pleased Him to create me thus, and proudly I join . . . those who, having lost their fear, their color-complex and inferiority-complex, face the future with unbowed heads and uncrushed spirit."

A small part of the "America" section alternates contemporary essays with historical documents. For example, after Lincoln's "Emancipation Proclamation" and essays on Frederick Douglass and Booker T. Washington is the revolting account "The American Congo: Burning of Henry Lowry" by William Pickens.[7] Here and in several essays, the focus is on America in the 1930s, sixty years after Reconstruction, when slavery was replaced by sharecropping, and white supremacy returned under Jim Crow laws; the KKK was in full force, and burnings and lynchings were routine. Pickens's essay is a description of 600 Arkansas sightseers who witnessed a black man being tortured to death for nearly an hour. Henry Lowry, the victim, had approached his master to settle their debit–credit arrangement so he could buy his wife and son a Christmas gift. For his boldness, first his feet were set on fire and the lower part of his body was burned. Then, "to prevent the anti-climax of a slowly-breathed out life, they poured gasoline over the upper part of the body so the victim expired in a great flame."

Two subsequent essays by Pickens, "A Roman Holiday" and "Aftermath of a Lynching,"[8] further describe the mob spirit aroused by burnings and lynchings. On one occasion, before the torch was applied, a member of the mob cut off the victim's ears with a penknife. The spectators always wanted a slow death, so they measured out the gasoline for his body parts and timed the ignition of each part, assuring the audience that his torture would last; they could boast that they had "stretched out his living for at least forty-five more minutes." In another report, after a black man had the temerity to speak with a white woman, he was, "as was tradition," hanged from a tree; his body was also riddled with bullets. Again and again, there are examples of how a white woman's scream or even an accusation of an insult would bring a speedy death to "the Negro victim of her fright or malice." Pickens also tells of a gang of whites in Lake City, Florida, who were searching for entertainment. They met a young black, tied a rope around his neck, shot at his feet to make him dance, and as the rope tightened, reveled in watching him die.

A long subsection is devoted to "Facts from the American Press," and many reports focus on the lynchings and riots that long continued after the Civil War.[9] A clipping from the *Houston Defender* (March 19, 1932), for example, reports how, typically, the promised investigation of a brutal lynching never materialized: three months before, a black, Matthew Williams, had been dragged from his hospital bed and hanged and burned. The eyewitness's account is repeated: "Before they threw the gas over him they cut off his fingers and toes, and threw them on the porches in the yards of the Negro homes, shouting that they could 'make nigger sandwiches out of them.'" Then they threw gas over him, and, while the human torch burned, they passed booze around. A *Pittsburgh Courier* article (June 25, 1932) reports the "Southern justice" administered to a war hero. A girl who "thought" but "never positively identified" him as her attacker joined the crowd of 5,000 that celebrated all night before his execution.

Some of the most interesting readings in *Negro* are anthropological, sociological, or linguistic in focus. In "Harlem Reviewed,"[10] Nancy writes a vivid description of Harlem—from Sugar Hill and Striver's Row to the worst of the ghetto slums ("the Negro population" increases, "but the houses do not expand," nor do the "ghetto walls"; hence the "overcrowding in all but the expensive middle-class lodgings"), and she addresses the history, cultural activities, population diversity, social stratifications, and jargon of the area ("can" and "butt" refer to "posterior"; "daddy" is a "lover" or "protector"). She also describes how the "ofays" (a slang word for "whites") go slumming at black nightclubs, like Connie's Inn, the Cotton Club, and Small's, admittedly searching for good entertainment, which they call "jungle music." Blacks, however, are allowed entrance to these clubs only if they are menials or entertainers.

Nancy's understanding of the social hierarchies in the area are sophisticated. It appears far more common for one group of color to scapegoat another than to confront the white establishment:

Some 350,000 Negroes and colored are living in Harlem and Brooklyn (a second, and quite distinct, area in greater New York), where American Negroes, West Indians, Africans, and Latin Americans have congregated. The latter, Spanish-speaking, have made a center around 112th Street and Lenox Avenue. . . . The tempo of the gestures and gait, the atmosphere, are foreign, [of] the Puerto-Ricans, the Central Americans and the Cubans. Nationalisms exist, more or less fiercely, between them and the American Negro—as [it does] between American Negro and black Jamaican. The latter say they are better at business. . . . The American Negro regards the Jamaican . . . as "less civilized"; jokes about his accent and deportment are constantly made on the Harlem stage. And so they are always [arguing], about empty "superiorities" and "inferiorities," forgetting the white enemy.

Particularly interesting is Nancy's description of a revivalist meeting with the most famous black evangelist in America, Elder Becton. These rituals last from 8:00 P.M. until after midnight on four nights a week, and sometimes the indefatigable participants continue for twenty-four hours. She compares Becton's talent to "Chaliapin's acting of Boris Godunov." The meeting begins as a group of women ("sisters") fan out in the balcony; a small orchestra with an organist plays Bach. A robust chorus and the audience, composed mainly of domestic workers, alternate in singing "long spirituals." All beat time to the music with their feet: "The volume of sound, singing, and beating of feet . . . is soon accompanied by the swaying of bodies—rous[ing] 'the spirit to come.'" The hands clapping in unison carry the soul to even greater heights.

At this point "a forest shoots up—[of] black, brown, ivory, amber hands-spread, stiffened-out fingers, gestures of *mea culpa*, beating of breasts, vibrating ecstasy." People are seized in violent trance, and they leap up and down pounding their chests, as *everything* is performed in rhythm, in half- or double-time. A "girl leaps up and down after the first scream, eyes revulsed, arms outstretched—she is no longer 'there.'" The singing reaches a final climax, and it is "impossible to convey the scale of these immense sound-waves and rhythmical undersurges. One is transported—completely." This has "nothing to do with God," writes Nancy, "but with life—a collective life for which I know no name. The people are entirely outside of themselves—and then, suddenly, the music stops, [and] calm comes immediately." In this prepared atmosphere, Becton strides forward and chastises people for their sins, guiding their ready attention to a specific point of his argument by an adroit word. He is a poet, a dancer, a great actor. To Nancy, these are "concerts"—each one a "gorgeous manifestation of *the emotion* of a race—that part of the Negro people that has been so trammeled with religion that it is still steeped therein."

In an entirely different vein are Zora Neale Hurston's seven essays,[11] most of which have not been reprinted elsewhere. In "Characteristics of Negro Expression," Hurston isolates unique black manners and styles of expression, repeating the term "drama" to characterize speech patterns, body posture, and general behavior. Whatever the mood, she writes, the black innately possesses "sufficient poise for drama," a universal means of communication. Hurston also discusses characteristic folklore that usually involves the dichotomies of God and the Devil, Rockefeller and Ford, the auto and the oxcart. "Jack" is the ultimate folk hero, for Jack can outsmart God. The Devil, in turn, outsmarts all but Jack. Peter, the apostle, is popular because he is hardworking and always active. In animal lore, the rabbit is master, since he is the blood brother to Jack. The bear, lion, buzzard, and fox follow in prowess. In her last three "characterizations," Hurston says that, first, blacks are imitators: "[The black] does it as the mocking-bird," for the sheer love of it, "not because he wishes to be like the one imitated." In dancing, for example, he or she mimics a variety of animals. Second, due to an adaptive mechanism, the black lives without the concept of privacy, because there was no privacy in the African village. Third, because lovemaking is an art, both men and women advertise themselves as skilled craftspeople in the language of their swagger.

Interwoven throughout *Negro* are press reports that validate the claims of Nancy's most shocking essayists. As in the subsection "Facts from the American Press," articles are included from the *New Republic, New York American, Morning Post, Daily Express, Liverpool Daily Post,* and *Daily Herald.* These repeat the atrocities already described by writers like Johnson and Dabney. Press items also report offensive, if less emotionally charged events, like the article in the *Norfolk Journal* (May 9, 1931), relating how the owners of a beach refused Langston Hughes admission and then had him arrested for "disturbing the peace." The title of another, "Color Bar at Albert Hall," is self-descriptive. The *New Republic* (December 16, 1931) bolstered a statistic purporting that, during the 1930s, black men were still sold in the South for $50 to $150 a person, and objections to such sales were silenced by a deadly mob: "Men oppos[ing] the new slave-drivers" are often "murdered outright" to "make a cracker holiday." Josephine Herbst, in "Lynching in the Quiet Manner,"[12] summarizes the portent of many of these widely read articles of the 1930s: "The Negro . . . has never really emerged from slavery. . . . If legality is to be his last appeal, he might as well give up. . . . He can't beat the law game when it is interpreted by white men still dominated by a slave-owner's code."

In "The American Moron and the American of Sense: Letters on the Negro,"[13] Nancy publishes some of the letters she received in Harlem. Two such "moronic" letters follow:

Mrs. Nancy Cunard take this as a solemn warning, your number is up. You're going for a ride shortly. You are a disgrace to the White race. You can't carry on in this country. We will give you until May 15th. Either give up sleeping with a nigger or take the consequences. This is final. X22. P.S.—we will not only take you but we'll take your nigger lover with you.

Miss Nancy Cunard, you are insane or downright degenerate. Why do you come to America to seek cheap publicity? You have not gained any favor but a whole lot of hatred. If I saw one of your publications I would be the first to suppress it. Furthermore I and a committee are appealing to the U.S. department of labor to have you deported as a depraved miserable degenerated insane. . . . You for your nerve should be burned alive to a stake, you dirty low-down betraying piece of mucus. [Here follows a sentence which might be considered obscene and which is not, therefore, printed.]—KKK 58 W. 58

One of the most interesting documents in *Negro* is Antheil's "The Negro on the Spiral, or A Method of Negro Music."[14] The essay relies on two assumptions: that the postwar world demanded (1) an honesty of personal expression and (2) individual cooperation in collaborative or communal events. Meeting the first need resulted in the wholesale rejection of prewar maudlin, artificial belief systems for the innocence, primitivism, and spontaneity of jazz and black art. This impulse toward the instinctual and spontaneous similarly served the Dadaists, just as the quest for unadorned truths embedded in the unconscious served the Surrealists. Antheil's analysis of the relationship between black art and modernism remains one of the best on the subject. It begins:

> Since Wagner, music has had two gigantic blood infusions, . . . the Slavic and, in recent times, the Negroid. . . . The Negro music, like the Negro, has been living for a number of million years under terrible heat; Negro music has, in consequence, been baked as hard and as beautiful as a diamond; it was the only thinkable influence after the *Sacre* and *Noces* had exhausted once and for all every last drop that the primitive Slavic music had in it. The first Negro jazz band arriving in Paris during the last year of the great war was as prophetic of the after-period immediately to come as the *Sacre* was prophetic of this self-same war. . . . This was the war which exhausted the world and left it without a grain of its former "spirituality." . . . The famine was here; there was no hope; a cataclysme, . . . a finality. Nothing could survive underneath this dense heat and smoke except Negro music . . . with a whole school of young composers springing up in Paris deeply influenced by American Negro music. . . .
>
> [Negro] music came with . . . a complete collateral aesthetic in the other arts. Modigliani, . . . painting marvelous elliptical heards; Gaudier-Brezka and Brancusi sculpt[ing] them; Chirico, full of Roman ruins with egg-heads; the Dadaists collect[ing] every bit of Negro sculpture; . . . the Surrealists in 1924 exhibit[ing] it with their own painters. . . . We found ourselves in the Parisian veldt: Chirico, Picasso, Stravinsky, [and] Cocteau were hunters who roamed the wild jungles and trapped every day, every month, without fail, our existence. . . .
>
> We began to realize that home is but a camping ground which we can make simple and beautiful with modern engineering and glass and steel. Still all of these houses carry the feeling of clean straw thatch and mud, as if built for torrid climates.

The essays that follow in the "Music" section cover an enormous breadth of styles—American spirituals, neo-spirituals, songs of the cotton fields, plantation singing, blues, lamentation music, and songs of protest—as well as the originality of figures such as Louis Armstrong, Duke Ellington, Josephine Baker, the Mills Brothers, Bill (Bojangles) Robinson, Ethel Waters, William C. Handy, Alberta Hunter, Florence Mills, and the Ink Spots. Many authors consider jazz an art form created by blacks to facilitate the blending of black and white culture. It is the secular equivalent of church spirituals, expressing and exorcising the blacks' responses to cultural and political repression. It is exuberant and holy, providing catharsis and demonstrating the passion of the soul.

Ernest Moerman writes a poem to Louis Armstrong (translated by Samuel Beckett):

When his trumpet bubbles . . .
poppies burn on the black earth,
and when he sings,
his voice gushes into the lake.

. . . .

and

the rain spouts back into heaven . . .

. . . .

and, always,

his she-notes have more tentacles than the sea.
They woo me they close my eyes
They suck me out of the world.

Armstrong's extraordinary new syncopated rhythms and his capacity to achieve new intensities of sound and feeling motivate Robert Goffin's several essays. "Hot Jazz"[15] defines the new art as one in which the performer replaces the written score with his own creation. Until now, he was the faithful representative of the composer, but hot jazz allowed for independence and spontaneity; one could realize the possibilities of syncopation latent in the simple theme of the composer, as in the *commedia dell'arte* tradition. He continues: "What Breton and Aragon did for poetry in 1920, [and] Chirico and Ernst for painting, has been instinctively accomplished . . . by black musicians." Hot jazz, in short, *is* improvisation.

In "The Best Negro Jazz Orchestras,"[16] also translated by Beckett, Goffin focuses on the two "greatest" jazz musicians, Louis Armstrong and Duke Ellington. The mature Armstrong, he writes, was able to merge into a coherent solo all the styles to date, including Creole, rag, pol, slade, and, particularly, blues. He reduced their melodies to their most essential notational base so he could fill the spaces between each note with his own spontaneous variations. Goffin describes Armstrong:

[He] holds his trumpet in a handkerchief, passes into a kind of excruciating catalep-
sy, and emerges Armstrong the sky-scraper, rockets aloft into the stratosphere, and
blows like one possessed and foams at the mouth; the notes rise in a wailing. . . .
Soon he is lost in the rhythm, he is the master of the rhythm, he is the rhythm,
the force and energy of the music, so that the audience rises to its feet, sways and
dances and laughs with Armstrong and tries to embrace him. . . . Armstrong is the
quintessential of "hot," the genius of improvisation.

Goffin finds Duke Ellington similarly remarkable, although it is impossible, he writes, to compare an individual with an orchestra. All the same,
Ellington is another master of hot, improvisational, and personalized expression—a master of "undiluted spirits," which he transforms in a sort of inspired
trance. Ellington builds on the accomplishments of his predecessors (James
P. Johnson, King Oliver, Sidney Bechet, Fletcher Henderson, Armstong) to
place "intuitive music under control." The result is a form with new disso-
nances and tonal patterns: "the [mastery] of combining improvisation with
ensemble." Having exploited the "hot talent" of each person in his orchestra,
every man performs in his own innovative way *within* a group arrangement.
Ellington is the "genius of cohesion."

Goffin briefly discusses Fletcher Henderson, Don Redman, Cab Calloway,
Chick Webb, King Oliver, Bennie Carter, Noble Sissle, Earl Hines, and Bix
Beiderbecke (a white Iowan of Jewish extraction who died in his twenties),
among others. Frequently, his prose (or perhaps Beckett's translation of it)
has the sound of poetry: "Oh you musicians of my life, prophets of my youth,
splendid Negroes informed with fire, how shall I ever express my love for your
saxophones writhing like orchids, your blazing trombones with their hairpin
vents, your voices fragrant with all the breezes of home remembered . . . !" Ultimately, Goffin links jazz and politics: "It is the Negroes, children of the sun,
who have restored to America something of her old radiance . . . and which
has done more to further friendly relations between blacks and whites than all
the laws and edicts ever issued."

Many essays are devoted to black classical musicians. Clarence Cameron
White, in "The Musical Genius of the American Negro,"[17] enumerates the
accomplishments of about twenty-five conductors, performers, and composers. Joseph Boulogne, Le Chevalier Saint-Georges, for example (1745–1799),
composed two violin concertos and a number of quartets; Cambridge-edu-
cated George Augustus Bridgetower (1779–1860)—Beethoven's violinist
friend—performed his work in Vienna; Edmund Dede composed numerous orchestral works and for many years conducted an opera company in
Bordeaux, France; and the violinist and composer Joseph White taught at
the Paris Conservatoire and successfully toured New York and Boston, per-

forming with special success Mendelssohn's violin concerto and Bach's Chaconne. White's survey extends to the twentieth century and the distinguished Anglo-African composer Samuel Coleridge-Taylor, best known for his choral music. Some contributors address other composers, opera singers, or innovators of the art song. Finally, a series of essays discuss music intrinsic to other black cultures: Creole folk music, Jamaican and Puerto Rican music, Tanda and Haitian merengues, and Xangô, Zulu, Bakongo, and Chewa songs.[18]

The subject of black theater becomes controversial. Robert Lewis applauds Rose McClendon, "the first lady of our stage," for her roles in *Justice* (1919), *Roseanne* (1924), and the Pulitzer Prize–winning *In Abraham's Bosom* (1927) and for her greatest performance, *Deep River* (1926).[19] U. S. Thompson extols Florence Mills as one of the stage's greatest artists, for her performances in *Dixie, Blackbirds,* and *From Dover Street to Dixie.*[20] Ralph Matthews, in contrast, in "The Negro Theatre: A Dodo Bird"[21] finds little to praise in black theater. He says that only three "feeble" roles are open to the black: (1) the droll "po' me" type of Bert Williams, which reinforces the stereotype of the irresponsible, happy-go-lucky black; (2) the slick figure who takes advantage of his more ignorant brethren; and (3) the comic character whose humor is built on smut. For this performer, the spoken word is always twisted to vulgar interpretation, as in the song "My Handy Man," which describes its title character as a man who "beats my biscuits and churns my cream." To Matthews, the all-black successful Broadway musical *Shuffle Along* may have been unique, since nothing significant followed.

The "Poetry" section of *Negro* includes the work of the Americans Arna Bontemps, Sterling Brown, Countee Cullen, Carrie Williams Clifford, Langston Hughes, and the lesser-known T. Thomas Fortune Fletcher, Donald Jeffrey Hayes, Walter E. Hawkins, and Jonathan H. Brooks. Nancy's selection of poems is astute, since many have subsequently become classics, including Countee Cullen's "Incident" and Sterling Brown's "Memphis Blues" and "Children of the Mississippi."

Langston Hughes translates West Indian poetry from the Spanish and French, including work by Nicolás Guillén, who combined the dialect of the Cuban Negro with rhythms of Caribbean folk music (as Nancy's editorial note indicates). White poets writing about blacks include William Plomer, Louis Zukofsky, and Nancy, whose "Southern Sheriff" is a dramatic dialogue in which the poet speaks with a sheriff about black "criminals." She protests the false charges imposed on them, their grotesque punishments, and the inadequate lawyers assigned by the courts. The sheriff says, "Say, didn' Governor Sterling of Texas say / Sometimes you gotta burn a house to save a village?"[22] The last line is taken from an article in the *Southern Worker* (January 2, 1932):

"It may be that this Negro is innocent, but sometimes it is necessary to burn a house to save a village."

An ethnographic map of "Negro Africa," attached to the book cover, is a good introduction to the final section of *Negro*, "Africa." (The book also includes a large folded map, "Ancient African Empires of the West Coast." All the maps are drawn by Nancy.) Raymond Michelet, in "African Empires and Civilizations,"[23] presents an extraordinary overview of the colonization of African nations, describing Sudanese civilizations historically: (1) Ghana (fourth to thirteenth centuries) and Sosso (eleventh to thirteenth) empires; (2) Songhai empire of Gao (seventh to sixteenth); (3) Yatenga, Mosi, and Gurmantché (eleventh to twentieth); (4) Mali (eleventh to nineteenth); (5) Fula of Massina and Banmana of Segu (both seventeenth to nineteenth); (6) Timbuktu and Middle Niger (sixteenth to eighteenth); (7) Tukolor of El Hadj Omar and the Mandingo of Samori; (8) Kingdom of the Coast; and (9) Inland Kingdoms—Hausa, Bornu, Kanem, Baghirmi, Wadai. He then comments on numerous other civilizations for which information is scarce, including Loango, Ansika, Monomatapa, and Manyema.

Arthur A. Schomburg, George Padmore, and others base their contributions on the assumption that the explorations of Vasco da Gama, Stanley and Livingston, and Leo Africanus are well known. As a result, they draw attention to the findings, for example, of Ibn Hankal, a geographer in 1067, and the explorations of Tippoo Tib in Central Africa and Mohammed Koti in Mungo Park.

Earlier sections of *Negro* include the history and culture of Jamaica, Grenada, Haiti, Cuba, Barbados, Trinidad, Guadeloupe, the Virgin Islands, British Guiana, Brazil, and Uruguay. The "Africa" section includes Madagascar, Morocco, Dahomey, Liberia, Nigeria, South Africa, Ethiopia, and Kenya. Interspersed throughout this material are samples of the beautiful calligraphy of a Hausa poem and Kroo and Ewe riddles and proverbs (like the Kroo: *Brow tron lo, eta ne a ne won oh gike* [The world is too large; that's why we do not hear everything]). A. V. Lester describes why the Zulu language is one of the most lyrical of the native African languages.[24] He explains its soft and full vowel sounds, which make it "entrancing to the ear when spoken in the deep musical Zulu voice." He also discusses how difficult it is to learn because of the "curious clicking sounds of the C, Q and X," which demand unique movements of the teeth, tongue, and palate.

R. C. Nathaniels reveals the extreme ethic of the Alaga, a secret society of Eweland, characterized by vengeance and savagery, because any quarrel with or insult to its members is forbidden under threat of extreme pain.[25] E. Kohn describes "A Zulu Wedding at a Zulu Kraal near Durban, Natal":[26] "The first two nights the groom must sleep in the same tent, but there are two women keeping watch to teach him abstinence. The third day he receives the key to happiness, and not before then can he open the apron, which is worn by everyone."

The subsection "Negro Sculpture and Ethnology" was motivated by an exhibition of African art held in Paris in 1931, in which only minor modern decorative pieces were on display. Nancy prints thirty-seven plates of West African sculpture, forty-seven plates of Congolese sculpture, and drawings of different types of Congolese masks and fetish figures. Two pages are devoted to a fraction of her ivory bracelets. Essays explicate the styles of statuary in the Congo and ancient bronzes.[27] "The Term 'Negro Art' Is Essentially a Non-African Concept"[28] by Ladislas Szecsi begins with the assumption that before the Europeans penetrated Africa, the African did not intend to create "art"; people made fetish figures to "house" a spirit. The masks, for example, were indispensable to ritual dances. Always, the intention was to cause fear in wandering spirits disposed to evil. Thus, fearing a gorilla, one would fashion a figure with a gorilla's features. Szecsi adds, "The Negroes have been able to create works of art because of their innate purity and primitiveness. They can be as a prism, without any intentional preoccupation, and succeed in rendering their vision with exactitude and without any imposition of exterior motive."

The volume concludes with essays on colonial exploitation, like "King Leopold's Domination," "French Imperialism at Work in Madagascar," "Pass Laws in South Africa," "How Britain Governs the Blacks," "White Man's Justice in Africa," and "Imperialist Terror in South Africa." George Padmore, the author of several, also writes in praise of Haile Selassie in Ethiopia.

The last essay, the longest in the volume, repeats in its title the sentence that concluded the volume's preface: "The White Man Is Killing Africa."[29] Here Raymond Michelet surveys Africa and the African diaspora, caused by the exploitation of Europeans in Africa. He charts a statistical analysis of working and living conditions. There are detailed accounts relating to colonization in specific areas (including South Africa, Tanganyika, Kenya, French Equatorial Africa, Madagascar, Liberia, and the Belgian Congo) and matters of salaries, taxation, forced labor, police measures, and repressions. Data in each category are reported year by year and region by region.

● ● ●

Nancy seemed fulfilled in creating *Negro* in the way a parent bonds forever with a child. As she told a black who wanted to give her something in return for what she had done: "I am your mother. There is no payment due."[30]

10

Nancy as Journalist:
Scottsboro, Ethiopia, Spain

All you colored peoples
Be a man at last
Say to Mussolini
No! You shall not pass.

—LANGSTON HUGHES

As Nancy awaited February 15, 1934, *Negro*'s publication date in London, she buried herself in social causes. She devoted herself to the defense of the Scottsboro boys, saying, "I'm not thinking of anything else but them all the time." Their first trials, between 1931 and 1933, had been the subject of her long essay "Scottsboro and Other Scottsboros" in *Negro*. The early trials would be followed by appeals, reconvictions, and further trials. Scottsboro would remain of immense concern to Nancy for twenty or so years, when the last "boy" was released (1946) and Heywood Patterson, the first to be sentenced, vanished (1948).[1]

Scottsboro

By 1933, the Scottsboro case had gained worldwide attention, with vehement protest from such people as Albert Einstein, Thomas Mann, H. G. Wells, George Bernard Shaw, Theodore Dreiser, Sherwood Anderson, Franz Boas, Heywood Broun, and Maxim Gorky. Petitions were sent to President Herbert Hoover, inspired by the rallying cries "Free the Scottsboro Boys!" and "Will you let them murder the boys?"

Nancy's long essay "Scottsboro and Other Scottsboros" remains an important detailed chronicle of events before and after the early trials. She makes clear that the prosecutors in both Scottsboro and Decatur, Alabama (the boys were moved to Decatur for the second trial), were intent on executing the youths, and after each appeal, as well as the intervention of both the Alabama and the U.S. Supreme Court, as Nancy writes, Southerners viewed the case not just as an attack on southern womanhood but as a repetition of the humiliation the South had suffered at the hands of Northerners during the Civil War and Reconstruction. She presents a well-documented outline of the early defense, prosecution, and appeals of the nine youths arrested and condemned for allegedly having raped at gun- and knifepoint two women on March 25, 1931. The women, Ruby Bates and Victoria Price, were prostitutes riding on a freight train from Chattanooga to Memphis at the same time as the nine young men.

Citing many documents, Nancy describes the details of their arrest. A sheriff, tipped off by a white boy who had just jumped off the train, stopped the train to search for the black "hoboes" "riding the rails." When he discovered two white girls in overalls, he assumed that "it wasn't possible for Negroes and white girls to be on the same train, in the same car maybe, without the question of rape coming in." The boys denied having seen the girls; the girls denied having had any contact with the boys. But the growing crowd at the train station cried out for an immediate lynching. After the boys were taken into custody by 118 armed soldiers, hundreds more rallied around the jail demanding the lynching. By 10:00 A.M. the next day, 10,000 had joined the mob, and the governor called in the National Guard. The trial of what the local papers called "the Negro fiends" began just twelve days later. Minutes before the trial, as the mob circulated such statements as "the black brutes chewed off one of the girl's breasts," an official from the Scottsboro Electric Company appeared. He assured the crowd that his company had enough juice "to burn up the niggers" and that "everything would be all right in a few days."[2] He knew whereof he spoke: the youths were convicted after a three-day trial and condemned to death.

Nancy reviews the ways in which the trial was a travesty of justice. She argues that (1) the women's medical examinations showed no lacerations or other signs of force and revealed no evidence of viable sperm, in itself conclusive proof of the defendants' innocence; (2) the only known eyewitness was prevented from testifying, and no witnesses were called to verify the defendants' claim that they were traveling to Memphis to look for jobs; (3) seven white boys on the train who spoke with the black boys were not called to testify; (4) the defendants were forbidden to call their families or seek their own legal assistance (two defense lawyers were provided: one, a real-estate attorney who was drunk in court; the other, an absent-minded elderly man who had not tried a case in many years); (5) no blacks or working people were allowed on the jury: only businessmen and well-to-do-farmers were selected; and (6) jury members were not questioned about racial prejudice. Some of Nancy's comments are touching in their naïveté about southern justice, but her conclusion is compelling:

> Is it not astounding that there were no signs of struggle, no disarranged clothing, no hysteria on the girls' part, no guns or knives found . . . and that . . . the victims of rape should have been locked up in the same jail as their attackers for ten days pending trial, whereas their homes were only a few miles away? And that if the Negroes had had any reason whatever to fear arrest they should not have jumped off the train? But most significant in this frameup is the fact that . . . both girls brought no charge whatsoever against any Negroes, and indeed refused to agree to the suggestion made to them that they had been attacked. This point, needless to say, was never brought up at the trial.[3]

She notes the irony that the young men, all under twenty (two, thirteen and fourteen), were urged to relinquish their rights by both black and white political organizations, which she views as primarily interested in their own self-aggrandizement. She includes the NAACP in her indictment:

> These "Uncle Tom Negroes," as they are called (the old-style, "white man's nigger" type), continue with monstrous hypocrisy to make assertions as to the probity of Southern courts. . . . [An] innocent victim [who] has received the death penalty is urged to plead *guilty*, . . . pretending that Southern justice may then extend the clemency of a life-term. (This is precisely what the N.A.A.C.P. attorney urged the Scottsboro boys to do at the initial trial, . . . assert[ing] they might have been set free, oh, some time later.)[4]

The boys spent two and a half years in a rat-infested Decatur jail that had been judged unfit for whites. Not only were they placed in a cell where they could hear the screams of an inmate being electrocuted, but one of the boys was always required to remove the deceased from the execution chamber. According to Nancy, while the NAACP was insufficiently aggressive in defending the boys, the legal wing of the Communist Party, the International Labor Defense (ILD), rallied to their cause. The ILD appealed to the Alabama Supreme Court on January 21, 1932, but the court upheld the verdict and death sentence for all but the two juveniles and adjudicated that they receive a new trial, which never materialized. When the case reached the U.S. Supreme Court on October 10, 1932, the justices ruled that the defendants had not been given due process and "had not been properly represented by counsel," and they granted the appeal for retrial.

Nancy believed that the Court had passed the buck. It had failed to note salient facts regarding the miscarriages of justice—that blacks had been barred from the jury; that a lynch mentality had squelched the defense's request of a change of venue to Birmingham; that Victoria Price had coerced Ruby Bates into perjury, which Ruby admitted in a letter to her boyfriend; that Ruby had told the investigating authorities: "The Negroes never touched me, as they never touched Victoria Price." (Ruby, in 1933, led the march in Washington, D.C., to save the boys, at the same time a petition signed by 50,000 was sent to President Roosevelt.)

In the meantime and for years to follow, the youths remained in jail, beaten regularly by wardens and inmates who were encouraged to assist. Increasingly more bizarre and frightening events followed. After the tall, blond Lester Carter, another eyewitness, finally came forward and testified that the boys were innocent, he was discredited and said to have syphilis; the defense was also discredited because it was "supported by New York Jews." In Scottsboro and neighboring towns, the Ku Klux Klan burned crosses, ammunition stores sold out their supplies, and the locals who expressed sympathy with the boys received death threats.

Nancy wanted her readers, if not the justices, to know about nine frightened boys who had been moved from death cell to death cell, as execution dates and stays alternated over two and a half years. After detailing their terrible physical and psychological condition and citing their letters to their parents, she added that at the time of her writing, all the boys had, and all they would continue to have, "down this vista of torment is the threat of one of the most torturing deaths ever devised, . . . a human being boiled in his own blood, burned and scorched until death comes in five to fifteen minutes." She would like to engrave the entire "extended and deplorable matter" in history, to "last as long as humanity."

She cited John Dos Passos's overview of the situation:

> Our legal procedure is a kind of map of our ruling-class mind. In the South, in a case where Negroes are involved, every white man is given the luxury of being part of the ruling class. You have to realize how physically and emotionally undernourished and starved the small tenant farmers, the small store-keepers, the jelly-beans and the drug-store loafers who make up the lynching mobs are, to understand the orgy of righteousness and of unconscious sex and cruelty impulses that a lynching lets loose. The feeling of superiority to the Negro is the only thing the poor whites of the South have got. A lynching is a kind of carnival to them.[5]

Using the Scottsboro case as the first well-publicized example of racist prosecutions, she moved on to address "the absolute fiendishness of the treatment" of blacks throughout the Cotton Belt American South, documenting forty-seven instances over six months of "frame-ups, murders and lynchings." She told of sheriffs regularly transferring unprotected blacks, who were then ambushed by masked men with guns and whisked away, never to be seen again. She reported instances in which police brutality and shooting "replaced" lynching. She noted that "such methods of Negro terrorization do not attract as much attention as formal lynchings." She comments: "Terror thrives best in the dark; it cannot stand mass exposure."[6]

Nancy had become interested in the Scottsboro boys during her trip to the United States in 1931. Her first response was to send money to each boy's family and then to raise cash for the group's defense. She tried unsuccessfully to sell some of her art, and when she returned to the United States in 1932, she and her friend Lawrence Gellert devised a scheme to raise money to inaugurate the Scottsboro fund. They sold, twice, a present Nancy had received from the Prince of Wales—a gold cigarette case with a royal crest. They showed it to a wealthy female friend, who advised them to take it to her husband for all the money they "could shake out of him." Then, as his wife predicted, he gave it to her as a gift, and she returned it to them to sell at auction.[7]

Nancy wrote her essay in 1933, at the same time that she inaugurated the British Scottsboro Defense Fund in London, acting as its honorary treasurer. André Gide, John Strachey, Aldous Huxley, Julian Huxley, Arthur Symons, Augustus John, Rebecca West, Virginia Woolf, J. B. Priestley, David Garnett, C. R. Nevinson, and Bronislaw Malinowski supported the appeal. She organized charity dances and parties in London and held a private-screening benefit of Eisenstein's *Potemkin*; she also helped organize a demonstration in Hyde Park and a meeting at Shoreditch Town Hall and hosted a "Scottsboro Defense Gala" at the Phoenix Theatre. All funds were sent to the Scottsboro defense in America.

Nancy also marched in demonstrations, sponsored petitions, distributed pamphlets and banners, and held fund-raisers in the poorer sections of London. She wrote poems and ads to raise money for all her causes:

> For the Immediate Unconditional Release of Scottsboro boys . . . and All Class War Prisoners!
> Fight against National Oppression of Negro People!
> Fight against Deportation and Persecution of Foreign-born workers!
> Fight against Fascism!

Once again, her activities attracted broad press coverage. In articles, typically captioned "Black and White Dance [or Party]," reporters focused on the racial mix at her gatherings, rather than the purpose of the event, and often specified, by gender, the precise number of black and white guests. Some commented on Nancy's idealism or rehashed her scandalous visits to Harlem; some concentrated on the effect of her activities on her personal life. The *Daily Express*, for example, stated that "Miss Cunard's attitude towards the Negro race has estranged her from her mother, and has robbed her of many friends, while it has gained her new ones. . . . She goes her way convinced of the justice of her cause, and that it is criminal to discriminate between black and white."[8]

This sort of dispatch reached disparate parts of the world, and the racial profile of each paper determined its editorial slant. In "Nancy Cunard's Exotic Party to Champion the 'Martyred Negroes,'" a West Indian newspaper celebrated Nancy and mentioned some of her old friends at her dance:

> Miss Cunard has long devoted herself to the cause of the Negro race. It is her mastering mission in life and [was the subject of] the night's gathering, . . . a charity dance in the basement of a London hotel. . . . It was exotic. Mr. Augustus John leaned against the bar, breathing air that was practically solid with smoke and enthusiasm. . . . Negroes of all shades of color were dancing with white women to the thudding rhythm of a most efficient band. The exquisitely refined accents of Bloomsbury mingled with the resonant speech of colored people. . . .
>
> Miss Cunard surveyed her achievement, well pleased, as she might be. Thin almost to emaciation, dressed in black with an enormous African ivory bracelet on one arm, she stood as a rallying point for the races which danced and chattered in the cause of her Negro martyrs. . . . She would sacrifice and endure anything for the realization of her beliefs.[9]

At the same time that these columns were being widely circulated, Nancy started her career as a journalist with the Associated Negro Press (ANP), and her reports of Scottsboro circulated around the world. Founded by the renowned black journalist Claude Barnett, the ANP was based in Chicago, and it distributed information to 120 black newspapers in every part of the United States and to over 200 newspapers in Africa; Nancy's articles were translated into French, Portuguese, and other non-African languages.[10]

Nancy would report for the ANP for more than twenty years, posting articles about Ethiopia, the Spanish Civil War, and other major international events from the major cities of Europe, Latin America, and Africa. Barnett considered her reports so exceptional that he remarked that she knew "more about Negroes than any of us." Her work, during the Abyssinian crisis, would be exemplary: "The [articles] stood out. [These] dispatches . . . gave ANP's coverage of the major foreign story of the decade, the Italian-Ethiopian conflict, a perspective and completeness the agency had to have to service its membership."[11]

She was particularly interested in African affairs and often wrote about the repressive measures the French Fascist leagues in North Africa had taken against native workers in Tunisia and Algeria. She also wrote frequently about Europeans in East Africa, specifically in Kenya, whose citizens were clamoring for home rule; two of her special concerns were that "the liberty of the press is . . . attacked" in Kenya and "militants of the Star of North Africa [receive] heavy sentences." She reminded her readers that "in 1882 . . . promises were made that the rights and customs of the natives would be respected." She also wrote feature items, in one, for example, paying tribute to the Dutch anthropologist Bernelot Moens for his racial studies.[12]

Hunger Marches and the British Left and Right

Nancy had returned to London in the spring of 1933, one of the most terrible of the "locust years," as the British referred to the blight of the economic depression. London had become a city of poor housing, ill health, and a widely demoralized population. The year 1933 also marked the Nazi party's ascension to power, and the London press was filled with Hitler's aggressive ambitions. Ever since her visits to Italy during the 1920s, Nancy had been keenly aware of the emerging threat of European fascism. In due time, she would go to Geneva and begin writing about Mussolini and the Abyssinian crisis, a prelude to her anti-fascist involvement with the Republicans during the Spanish Civil War.

In the fall and winter of 1933, at the same time that she was raising money for the Scottsboro boys, she protested against the British government's role in the present economic crisis. She was not alone; many of the British were indignant at the government's incompetence and indifference—if not its conspiracy—in the economic debacle. For Neville Chamberlain to boast in his 1934 budget speech that the country "had gone from Bleak House to Great Expectations" was an outrage.[13]

With half the population living at a standard inadequate to maintain healthy life, unemployment was close to 3 million, and overcrowding and unsanitary slums were prevalent everywhere. Most people were undernourished, and ill health was rife among both the young and the old. Among the most striking events of the time were the hunger marches, organized by fishergirls, hop pickers, shipyard and mining workers—by any assemblage of the unemployed or unassisted (including one rally of 250 blind people). Nancy took part in the marches, wearing a man's overcoat and overshoes, an aviator's helmet, and mufflers, scarves, and gloves, both for warmth and for disguise. She even joined a lunchtime march of 100 striking Midlands coal miners on "the very day *Negro* came out." As she later wrote Janet/Solita:

I walked at Wansford, February 16, more than the eight miles [from Haycock, where her father had lived]. It was at Stamford [that] I met them, up that great road. . . . One thought the dog of the Inn had been put in the soup, just as we were all sitting down, in pretty great cold, eating stew on the roadside. . . . Why the hunger march? In protest against the Means Test, 1934.[14]

The Unemployment Act of 1934 had created the Unemployment Assistance Board, where applicants for financial assistance had to undergo the most stringent evaluations ("means") to ensure that they had no assets available anywhere. The same stringency—or humiliation—was applied to those on the dole. A child wearing a new overcoat was asked where it came from, and parents were subjected to a battery of personal questions. George Orwell noted the common fear that one's dole could suddenly be withdrawn: "The [Means] test was an encouragement to the tattle-tale and the informer, the writer of anonymous letters and the local blackmailer."[15]

Many of the marches were brutally handled by the police. During one, when 2,000 people invaded Whitehall with a petition of a million signatures to protest the cut in unemployment benefits, the police charged with batons, injuring and arresting over a dozen. At another, after a two-hour street battle, thirty people were taken to the hospital. Other marches were more subdued. At one, determined, if weary, veterans "darken[ed] the carpets of the Ritz Hotel and sang 'Tipperary,'" before standing "accusingly outside Buckingham Palace." No one would ever forget the famous 1933 Jarrow hunger march, where crusaders walked for more than a month to London and picked up thousands of supporters en route. When they finally arrived at Hyde Park, with banners, songs, and a petition signed by 12,000, Prime Minister Stanley Baldwin refused to meet with them. Instead, someone from the Board of Trade reiterated the government's initial contention that "Jarrow must work out its own salvation."[16]

Maud Cunard's friend Oswald Mosley had another solution to the current problem, one that aroused Nancy's deepest revulsion. He had already switched from the Conservatives to Labour, but in 1932, he formed his own party, the British Union of Fascists. His platform was that people must "collectively [form] their own police force to deal with the enemy and the exploiter" to create a racially pure state. Mosley's indifference to decency and equality extended beyond the poor to people of specific ethnic origin. He lectured regularly on modern decadence (the catch phrase Pétain later used in occupied France), which he attributed to the "softness" of modern civilization. He would return to a warrior, barbaric, atavistic spirit (his hero was Julius Caesar) and change the composition of society. In July 1934, one of his supporters threw a four-year-old Jewish child through a plate-glass window, and the "Blackshirt" was never criminally charged. Dressed in tight black clothes from head to foot, with his face garnished by a Hitler moustache, Mosley continued to debate whether inferior members of society, specifically Jews, should be castrated or banished to Madagascar.[17] Mosley had his moment in England but was finally imprisoned. Nancy was unsuccessful in seeking full justice for him when, in 1943, she failed in her petition to prevent his release from Brixton jail after only three and a half years there.

Numerous other fascist organizations and popular anti-Semitic magazines, operative since the 1920s, included the *Patriot, Jewish Domination*, and *Nameless Beast*. Prominent personalities, like the powerful Lord Rothermere, who owned the *Daily Mail*, openly supported their points of view.[18] Alternatively, many leftist groups formed that attracted artists and writers—such as the Artists' International and the Writers' International, the latter of which Nancy joined, and the socialist Left Book Club, associated with Victor Gollancz, Harold Laski, and Nancy's good friend John Strachey. Several leftist magazines, such as the *Left Review*, an aggressively egalitarian journal, were also published, and Nancy joined writers like Bertrand Russell, Rebecca West, and Kingsley Martin in contributing to them.

People also took courses in the Russian language, and many traveled to the Soviet Union (including George Bernard Shaw, André Gide, and Lady Astor) to "see the future." It is interesting that the Jarrow hunger marchers, with their sashes and lapel badges, were compared to "the proud proletariats of an Eisenstein film." But if Russia and its Communist ideology seemed the solution to the woes of capitalism, the Communist movement in England remained modest, with only 15,000 members at the end of the 1930s. All the same, its goals seemed urgent and relevant, and anthologies like *New Signatures* and *New Count* appeared in 1933. At least one historian observed that the most genuine expression of political equality at the time was in "the sympathy with the Negro cause, as demonstrated by Nancy Cunard's 900-page anthology *Negro*, published in 1934."[19]

Communism had appealed to Nancy, as it had to many in the 1930s, as a solution to social inequality and fascism. Yet despite Nancy's belief that Communism would better the lives of blacks—and despite her interest in Communism as a political theory—she never joined the party. She was, throughout her life, temperamentally unfit to join any organization, and, furthermore, as one party member who knew her well said, the party "would not have accepted her": the mere prospect "of Nancy taking part in organized meetings or being subject to intellectual or organizational discipline was absurd. . . . She had a romantic notion of exploited blacks and workers as people she could help; she could never for an instant have submerged her own identity in a political organization." Nancy always maintained that she was "an anarchist."[20]

Disillusion in Russia

All the same, Nancy traveled to the Soviet Union in the summer of 1935. She took the trip for two reasons. Both Langston Hughes and William Patterson, one of the attorneys of the Scottsboro boys, assured her that *Negro* would be translated into Russian. She was also interested in visiting the country that had supported the Scottsboro boys and that presumably welcomed blacks as equals. Although she asked Henry Crowder, still in London, to travel with her, he refused, and she sailed alone to Leningrad; from there, she went to Moscow, where she remained for a month. The trip, and the months before it, were highly illuminating; Nancy would not have to wait until the Spanish Civil War to witness the hypocrisy of Soviet promises.

She had spent the beginning of the summer at Réanville with George Padmore, a black Communist activist whom she had first met in 1932 and the author of *Pan Africanism or Communism* and *How Britain Ruled Africa*; Nancy typed the manuscript of the former. Padmore would become her coauthor of *The White Man's Duty* in 1942 and a leader in the Pan-African movement in the 1940s and 1950s; today he is regarded as one of the fathers of African liberation.

When they first met, Padmore was an important member of the Communist Party. Born in Trinidad and a student of medicine and law in the United States, he had gone to Moscow in 1929: the Soviet Union seemed to be the hope for blacks all over the world, especially for those in the colonized nations. Padmore became the head of the Negro Bureau of Communist Trade Unions and helped organize the First International Negro Workers Congress; he also founded the periodical *Negro Worker*. Nancy was deeply affected by Padmore's subsequent experiences.

First, Padmore's powerful position in the party had been suddenly obliterated when Stalin repudiated the party's anticolonial position in his effort to gain Western sympathy in the fight against fascism. Then, expelled from the party in 1934, Padmore returned to England and turned his focus to Africa. Although bitter about his own treatment in Russia, he reminded Nancy that the Communists had expressed "natural kindness" toward blacks. Nancy said, "Nothing has so much upset me as this 'case.' . . . On the one hand, Padmore [is] one of the few people I revere for his integrity and very being. . . . On the other hand, that this should come from members of the ideology (Communism) that I admired. . . . It was unacceptable—and yet it had happened." At the end of the year, she published an article challenging Earl Browder, secretary of the U.S. Communist Party, for not having answered Padmore's open letter refuting the charges against him by former fellow Communists. "The only reply I have read," she commented, "is a continuation of lies and calumnies. . . . Does this suggest that . . . the party is incapable of justifying its procedure?"[21]

Nancy saw very few people when she was in Russia, but they included Langston Hughes and Louis Aragon. There is only one mention of the trip in her papers and correspondence; one of her few social events was a reunion with Eugene Gordon, the black journalist she had visited in Boston. Now a reporter for the Moscow *Daily News*, he invited her to meet his colleagues, who greeted Nancy warmly over glasses of tea; they spoke about *Negro*.

Since Nancy spent a good deal of the trip by herself, she dabbled with a play that, fortunately, she left unfinished. It is about a dozen people who travel on a Soviet ship between London and Leningrad. Although Nancy instructs that it "be played in a lighthearted, perhaps exaggerated manner," comedy was not her métier, and with the exception of a few light passages, the play is unappealingly didactic.[22]

The trip must have been disappointing to Nancy. Representing the State Publications Bureau, Patterson had assured her that the Russians "adored" *Negro* and that he was authorized to present her with three wonderful possibilities: a translation of *Negro* into Russian, a contract to write a book on the African colonies, and, finally, the possibility of organizing a traveling exhibit of African-Asian art. But when nothing materialized, Nancy left Moscow. She traveled to the Tervueren Museum, outside Brussels, to pursue research on the history of the Cameroonians who had settled in Belgium. While doing this, Italy invaded Ethiopia. Nancy had a dream in which a voice told her it was imperative that she take action against Mussolini's monstrous intentions, and she returned home.

Ethiopia

Back in London and a staunch advocate of the revered (at the time) African leader Haile Selassie, Nancy attended protest meetings that attracted black, white, and mixed audiences. At one, at London Memorial Hall, Marcus Garvey's wife addressed more than 250 blacks. "Although 250 may seem a small number to America's immense colored population," Nancy clarified in her ANP and *Crisis* reports, "there are relatively very few Negroes in London." This meeting, which attracted a diversity of professionals, workers, students, and clerics, she wrote, indicated "that the Negroes are rising against Mussolini's vicious aggression on Abyssinia [and] causing the birth of a United Front for the defense of the Abyssinians' rights." That England is watching, she added, was apparent by "the presence of England's best-paid journalists." A resolution was unanimously passed "that a legion be formed for active service in Abyssinia, if and when the war breaks out." A second resolution, sent to the British Foreign Office, the Italian ambassador in London, and the League of Nations, stated that "every avenue be explored to give justice to Ethiopia as a member of the League of Nations."[23]

At the time that Garvey was speaking on Abyssinia to large crowds throughout the world, Nancy wrote, "People are rising and will rise against the clutching hands of fascism that are stretching out to destroy the last black nation in Africa." Optimistic about Ethiopia, she concluded: "In England we are saying: if England helps Mussolini there will be risings in the British colonies. For Mussolini is not only fighting Abyssinia but every black man in the world today—YES, and will have to fight some of us whites too." Nancy sought an active role in the fight against Mussolini during this crisis, yet "everything but reporting" seemed "out of the question for me." She fully committed herself to writing for a number of newspapers and magazines, including Sylvia Pankhurst's *New Times and Ethiopian News*,[24] as well as the ANP, where her fellow journalists on Abyssinia included Langston Hughes, Paul Robeson, and Richard Wright.

Despite the Treaty of Friendship signed by Italy and Ethiopia in 1928, the Italian government had been preparing for over a dozen years to conquer Ethiopia and to subject its people to Italian rule. It seized the Ethiopian railway to ship its own supplies, and Ethiopia's appeals for financial assistance (not military personnel) were denied by the nations of the world. On October 2, 1935, Mussolini openly repudiated the treaty and declared war on Ethiopia; the following day, his troops crossed the Mereb River and began the war. A week later, the League of Nations Assembly condemned Italy by a vote of 50 to 4 (Italy, Austria, Hungary, Albania), denouncing terror and assuring Ethiopia that aggression would not be tolerated. Then, in violation of international treaties made at the League, in May 1936, the Italians entered Addis Ababa, slaughtered 275,000 Ethiopians, and threatened to exterminate an entire population. Groups of up to eighteen aircraft flew over the land time and again and drenched it with mustard gas, soaking the earth with deadly rain and subjecting the population to agonizing pain and certain death. On June 30, 1936, the League of Nations gathered to hear what has become Haile Selassie's historic and prophetic appeal. Respected throughout the world for his modernization of Ethiopia, as well as for his great diplomatic skills, Selassie had returned from exile to address the implications of the League's inaction: "It is us today. It will be you tomorrow." Nancy was present when he spoke.

As Selassie himself remarked, this was the first time a head of state had spoken at the assembled League. "But there is also no precedent," he continued, "for a people being victim of such injustice and being at present threatened by abandonment to its aggressor." He stood before the assembly and began:

"I . . . am here today to claim that justice which is due to my people and the assistance promised to it eight months ago, when fifty nations asserted that aggression had been committed in violation of international treaties."

Nancy wrote report after report about his speech.[25] She also covered a number of lesser known events during Selassie's visit to Geneva, like the "scandalous incident" that occurred as he began to speak. Nine Italian Fascist journalists, aided by the Swiss "Facio," interrupted him with whistles and boos, along with shouts of "Nigger," "Assassin," "Slaver," and "Go back to your war." The "hooligans," she clarified, represented the most important newspapers in Italy—of the stature of the *New York Times* and *Manchester Guardian*. "The public opinion here," she wrote, is that the antics were "staged by order of the Italian authorities." Other provocative incidents followed, such as a bogus garden party at which diplomats, League delegates, and Geneva's most prominent citizens arrived at a locked garden gate; iron placards with "Left by the Negus as a souvenir of his passage through Geneva" had been padlocked onto railings. Nancy ended her report of these incidents by stating that they "show to what depths of imbecility the once great and lovely country that was Italy has fallen. . . . Straws perhaps, . . . pointing to the wind of war."[26] Indeed, Selassie's final words would be prophetic:

> In a word, it is international morality that is at stake. . . . Apart from the Kingdom of the Lord there is not on this earth any nation that is superior to any other. Should it happen that a strong government finds it may with impunity destroy a weak people, then the hour strikes for that weak people to appeal to the League of Nations to give its judgment in all freedom. God and history will remember your judgment.

On July 4, 1936, the League voted to call off its sanctions against Italy, accepting Italy as sovereign over Ethiopia. It did indeed turn its back on a small nation of 12 million citizens without arms and resources to silently endorse a country of more than 42 million with unlimited financial, technical, and industrial means and the ability to create unlimited quantities of lethal weaponry. As Nancy later recalled in *Grand Man*, she attended "that Session, which the powers intended should give the quietus to Ethiopia and end the pleadings of Selassie." When the session ended, "with what disgust was one filled on the way 'they' carried on—breaking their own clauses and covenants, with supra-human cynicism. Such was my baptism in matters of this kind."[27]

The month after Selassie's speech, Nancy was visited by two Haitian representatives who were in daily contact with Selassie. They asked for her help in gaining "moral and financial aid" for Ethiopia through her reports to black and white international organizations.[28] Nancy was incapable of moderation in the service of any cause, so after she filed these reports, she traveled to Addis Ababa and wrote about the thousands of barefoot young men who continued to be killed by Mussolini's bombs. To the Fascists, these bombs were glorious flowers "opening like red blossoms" over the landscape. She described the war:

> The clang of steel on steel resounded again in the Wallege Province valley Monday when a courageous band of Ethiopian patriots engaged a detachment of pillaging Italians in a fierce battle at Lekemti. The marauding Black Shirts swept down on the loyal natives in 80 planes, dropped poison gas bombs, landed and then attacked the defenders with machine guns, rifles and hand grenades. The Ethiopians, although greatly outnumbered, made a gallant stand. Heavy casualties on both sides were reported.

As to the diplomatic front, she added: "Ethiopia has again appealed to the League of Nations for aid. . . . The rumor was current here that nothing definite would be done."[29]

In another article, she wrote about the Fascists' suppression of information: "[With] the very strict censorship imposed by the Italian authorities on all news from Ethiopia, . . . very little is known of the ambitious plans which Mussolini has in the background." She drew the following details, therefore, from the *News Chronicle*:

> It is not for nothing that the Ministry of Colonies is now known as the Ministry of Italian Africa, and that many Italians dream of an empire stretching from the Red Sea to the Atlantic and from the Mediterranean to the Congo.
>
> The activities of the Ministry of Press and Propaganda, which has some 300 employees preparing documents in twenty-eight African languages, are of particular interest to the British Empire. Especially since the Duce's visit to Tripoli, where he was given the "sword of Islam," attention has been concentrated on the Mohammedans.

She reports the construction of a Moslem university in Harar and of radio stations designed to reach Moslems in Arabia, as well as in Africa. In "Il Duce Will Take Boys of Eight to Make Fascist Soldiers," she exposes how "at present many young Moslem chiefs, especially from the French African colonies, are being educated in Tripoli and Italy, where they are assured that the Duce will help them to throw off the French yoke." She describes how natives in the Sudan and in British Africa are being promised that the blacks in Italian Africa will fight to liberate them, adding: "As far as propaganda, among the Abyssinians, . . . some fifty cinemas are already showing fascist films and many schools have been opened. Propaganda is having considerable effect among the non-Aramaic majority of the population, but very little among the genuine Ethiopians."[30]

One can understand why Nancy was interested in the Ethiopian crisis. Not only was it a demonstration of the great totalitarian state versus the small independent state, but it also internationalized the problems of blacks. Ethiopia, unlike the rest of the African continent, had maintained its independence and to many had been the cradle and hope of civilization. It was a land with a rich culture, and its rulers were regarded as descendants of Solomon and the Queen of Sheba. It had been one of the first countries to adopt Christianity and was considered by many blacks as the promised land: its manifest destiny lay in redeeming blacks from white oppression—"Ethiopia shall stretch forth her hands unto God" (Psalm 68:31).

In the United States, the Reverend Adam Clayton Powell had sermonized in Harlem's Abyssinian Baptist Church for Ethiopian resistance to Mussolini. The official anthem of the Garvey movement was "Ethiopia, Land of Our Fathers." The African American response to Ethiopia was as intense as the Leftists' response to Franco's later invasion of Spain. In fact, many were eager to join a volunteer army, but an 1818 federal law forbade the enlistment of U.S. citizens in a foreign army. The penalty was enormous: loss of citizenship, incarceration for three years, and a $2,000 fine.

Frustrated by this situation, the readers to whom Nancy and many others had reported—the international black community, including many from the United States—would express their anger and idealism in the Spanish Civil War, which was to follow. Of the 2,800 Americans who would join the Abraham Lincoln Brigade, some were blacks from America who managed to obtain passage and serve in the Abraham Lincoln Battalion, the George Washington Battalion, the John Brown Field Artillery Battery, the Auto Park, and the American Medical Bureau, all of which were associated with the Lincoln Brigade. These were the people Nancy continued to be interested in during her reporting years in Spain.

From 1936 to 1939, Nancy would primarily cover the Spanish Civil War, but since journalists were allowed only three-month visits to the country, during the periods she returned to London or Geneva, she filed reports on Scottsboro and Ethiopia as well. Even after first arriving in Barcelona in August 1936, she wrote:

There are those who say "Ethiopia is a closed book; it is dead news." We know it is not—although the whole ghastly betrayal in Geneva has marked the end of the first terrible chapter.

The bowing down to Mussolini by the world powers will be very largely responsible for the same lurid state of things as is now in force in Spain [and] if such a state of things does come to pass . . . in France. The betrayal of Ethiopia will be one of the first stages in the next World War.[31]

At the same time that Nancy campaigned for the Scottsboro boys, joined the hunger marches, wrote articles on the plight of the poor, and traveled to the League and Addis Ababa, events of no small magnitude were occurring in her mother's house. Maud, too, was playing a major role in history.

Maud and Geopolitics

Nancy had not seen Maud since 1931, but she was generally aware of her activities. She knew that her mother had uniquely redefined and magnified the role of high-society hostess. In so doing, Lady Cunard had become a participant in one of England's most compelling sagas—the romance of Edward, Prince of Wales, and the American divorcée Wallis Simpson and, following his father's death, Edward's abdication of the throne. As one observer put it, for over a year, "the drama of Edward VIII was enacted" at Maud's house and became "the rallying point of most of London society."[32]

Edward had ostensibly overcome the prudishness of his early manhood[33] and had had several affairs before meeting Mrs. Simpson; most serious and devastating was his romance with another married woman, Freda Dudley Ward, whom he wanted to marry but which the king would not permit. Afterward, he sank into a deep depression.[34] Some of his biographers believe Edward turned to Wallis for comfort, given the stern, unloving relationship he had with his parents. At the same time, these biographers find Wallis's domineering demeanor the essence of her charm (at least to him)—the coquettish ways in which she corrected him and even ordered him about publicly. This offended countless people who knew or merely observed their future king, one of whom sat with the couple in Maud's box at the opera and complained privately to Maud: "What an extraordinary hold Mrs. Simpson has over the prince." Some gossiped that Wallis's allure was entirely sexual, and after King George V learned that she had traveled to China to visit women trained in the art of lovemaking, he ordered a dossier on Wallis's "China phase."[35] Nancy wondered whether Wallis's appeal was her active engagement in political activities, about which the prince had thus far expressed only admiration.

In 1935, now in his forties, Edward openly disregarded royal discretion by appearing publicly with the divorcée and freely declaring his interest in National Socialism: "The prince saw the balance of power in Europe as lying between a degenerate and enfeebled France and a virile and resurgent Germany." He admired the achievements of the Germans in power and ignored the brutal authoritarianism of their regime. He was "mildly antisemitic," in "the manner of so many of his class and generation."[36]

In June 1935, before the visit of a German delegation, he made a statement that infuriated Nancy and caused a furor, both within the royal family and among those who read it in the world press: "There could be no more suitable body . . . of men to stretch forth the hand of friendship to the Germans than we ex-service men, who fought them and have now forgotten all about it and the Great War." Following this, there was "much gossip about the Prince of Wales' alleged Nazi leanings." Nancy's rancor toward her mother deepened when she learned that Maud was providing the means for Edward's successful courtship of Wallis and was encouraging his regard for Hitler; Maud's friendship with the Fascist Oswald Mosley was sufficiently abhorrent. But Mosley had been mesmerized by Nancy's mother. In fact, his autobiography is filled with paeans to her. She was "a work of art," "a bird of paradise," compared to all the other "sparrows" of contemporary society.[37]

In January 1935, when Edward decided to launch Wallis socially, he enlisted the help of London's two leading hostesses, his friend Lady "Emerald" Cunard and her rival Lady Sybil Colefax.[38] For more than a year, Maud's social activities revolved almost entirely around Edward and Wallis. Newspaper reports kept Nancy abreast of her mother's intimate involvement with people she had grown to despise. Maud and Wallis had become friends in 1934, when Wallis and her husband lived on Bryanston Square. A friend had invited the two women to a dinner at which the Prince of Wales was the guest of honor, and the female guests—Sybil Colefax, Margot Asquith, Maud, and Wallis—all vied for Edward's attention. Mrs. Simpson prevailed when she elaborated on the principles of a wonderful new diet and won both the prince's and Maud's hearts.

Wallis changed her name to Mrs. Wallis Warfield, her maiden name, to erase any acknowledgment of her former marriage and to deny, as well, the one before that. (One can well appreciate Ernest Simpson's apocryphal witticism: "I regret I have but one wife to lay down for my country.") Maud told friends she was sure that Wallis and the prince had not lived together, that he worshipped her as a "virginal saint." After all, Wallis had said, "I have had two husbands and I never went to bed with either of them." (A great deal of speculation has linked her romantically with another man, Guy Marcus Trundle, at the same time that she was seeing Edward.)[39]

To the king and queen's displeasure, Maud was extraordinarily resourceful in advancing the royal courtship. When the play A Storm in a Teacup opened, with a story parallel to the prince and Wallis's secret lives, the couple was resigned to never seeing it. Maud arranged for a key scene to be performed privately after a dinner party for them at her house. She subsequently spent weekends with them, again encouraging their romance with one imaginative scheme after another. Many publicly blamed her for the match and fancied that when the king died and Wallis married Edward and became queen, she, Maud, would take on the position of Mistress of the Robes (or so she was informed by her friend Chips Channon). She would at last arrive at court, and "in the role of the queen's favorite, she would assure a shining future for English art and music, an English court similar to that of Frederick the great." Edward was pleased when, at one of her parties, Maud proclaimed him "the most modernistic man in England." She then introduced him to Joachim von Ribbentrop, and Edward was forthright in his admiration of Germany's aspirations. Channon observed that the prince was very much "influenced by Emerald, who is rather éprise [smitten] with Herr Ribbentrop." Edward had already admired Mosley and often said that he "would have made a first-rate prime minister."[40]

The Germans courted Edward during the mid-1930s, and whenever he visited Germany, he was treated with great honor. This was reported in the ten major London newspapers, including the only pro-Hitler paper, the *Daily Mail*, which compared Hitler to George Washington. Now, competing with the other papers in reporting the possibility of a "morganatic" marriage — Edward's marriage without Wallis's becoming queen—the *Mail* tried to win public support for the marriage. But its series of chatty interviews with her failed to sway Edward's superiors from any such concession. Edward VIII ascended to the throne in January 1936, after his father died, and then abdicated in December 1936. All the same, he did not depart empty-handed after his abdication: not only did he marry his beloved in 1937, but Lord Beaverbrook, of the gossip and entertainment tabloid the *Daily Express*, paid him a record £200,000 for the serial rights of his story, *A King's Story*, which was published in 1951.[41] After Edward's marriage, the royal family virtually abandoned the couple (now called the Duke and Duchess of Windsor), suspecting their allegiance to Hitler after their visit to Germany in 1937 when they were Hitler's personal guests. In August 1940, Edward became governor of the Bahamas, an assignment that removed him from England and the Continent.

Edward VIII's abdication naturally ended Maud's grandest ambitions. She avoided social functions with the new monarch (Edward's brother Albert, who took the name King George VI), although she was invited to them. The Cunard nephews were, in fact, the true insiders: Nancy's beloved cousin and friend Victor was privy to the abdication speech before Edward delivered it, and he knew the whereabouts of the borrowed French château at which Edward and Wallis were married. Still, Maud retained access to the most important people of contemporary England: "Harold Nicolson recorded how she 'twitted' Anthony Eden over the Abyssinian crisis: 'But Anthony, why should

Italy not have Abyssinia?'" Nancy would not have appreciated her mother's sense of humor, if that is what it was. Investigations continue regarding Edward and Wallis's role in supplying Hitler with key information about the Allies before and after the onset of World War II.[42]

In recent years, many have come to believe that Edward's abdication had nothing to do with Wallis's being a divorcée. Rather, there is evidence, as Prime Minister Baldwin thought at the time, that Edward's remaining on the throne would have been dangerous to Britain's security, although in the 1930s climate of appeasement, Baldwin carefully guarded his fears with respect to the wedding's geopolitical implications. Today, controversies continue regarding whether or not both the Duke and Duchess of Windsor actively supplied the Nazis with information that might have put the war effort into jeopardy. A program aired in June 2003 on British television documenting the close relationship between Edward and Ribbentrop. In addition, Martin Allen, who has written extensively on Rudolf Hess, states: "The sympathies of the Duke of Windsor to Nazi Germany have long been common knowledge but few have suspected that his wartime activities amounted to treason."[43] The investigation goes on.

The Spanish Civil War:
A War of Poets, Intellectuals, and Idealists

The Spanish Civil War was to become Nancy's greatest cause in the fight against fascism. To appreciate the nature of her commitment, it is helpful to review the European, and particularly the Spanish, political situation at the time.[44]

In March 1936, emboldened by the Ethiopian war, Hitler denounced the Locarno treaties and reentered the demilitarized Rhineland without opposition from Britain or France. This was the first of his overt acts of territorial aggression, and his unqualified success undoubtedly bolstered his ambition to dominate Europe. At the time, England's policy was one of appeasement; America's, one of isolationism. The Great War seemed to have left the Western democracies completely demoralized regarding the usefulness of military intervention.

The major political opposition to Hitler came from the Left—from liberals, socialists, and Communists—with Russia the most vocal of the antifascist nations. In 1935, Communists around the world were instructed to join anti-fascists of any persuasion in a "Popular Front" against fascism. Although Stalin was conducting public bloody purges of his old comrades at home, Soviet Russia was still seen by many in a utopian light. In addition, many liberal intellectuals, fearing the growing might of Nazi Germany and Fascist Italy, welcomed the idea of a union of the West and Russia to combat these enemies. They also longed for an opportunity to actively oppose the growing threat of fascism around the world. If they were naïve about the menace of Soviet totalitarianism, this must be understood in the light of the times, in terms of the world's lack of awareness of Stalin's activities: many of his large-scale atrocities and depredations were occurring in the Soviet Union, where they were perpetrated in great secrecy.

This was a generation nurtured by the poems of Wilfred Owen, novels like Hemingway's A *Farewell to Arms*, and films like *All Quiet on the Western Front*, works that portray the pity and terror of war and that question its value under any circumstances. Yet while many in the West remained unconvinced about the usefulness of any war, for others the Spanish Civil War triggered a call for action against fascist aggression. For a number of those who saw fascism as an unequivocal evil, fighting and writing became inseparable. As Upton Sinclair said of the International Brigades, they were "probably the most literary brigade in the history of warfare"; Stanley Weintraub added, "Writers and would-be writers had come to live their books, journalists to make their news."[45]

Beginning only months after Hitler's reentry into the Rhineland and weeks after Selassie's speech at the League of Nations, the Spanish Civil War provided the honest opponents of fascism an opportunity to fight on the side of democracy. Idealistic people could respond to the righteous call of the Republicans: No *pasarán*—"[Fascism] shall not come to pass." The war stirred strong feelings in democratic-minded people from all walks of life who shared the conviction that fascism was a monstrous evil. The fact that many were also Communists or Communist Party sympathizers seems more meaningful today than it did then, when the obvious menace was clearly fascism.

The Spanish Civil War was the culmination of historic tensions between the rich, who were connected to the monarchy, church, and army, and the landless poor and working classes. During the century and a half preceding the Spanish Civil War, Spain had suffered several bloody civil conflicts, as immortalized in Goya's horrific image of warfare. Paul Preston states that the persisting problem was the growth of a capitalist economic infrastructure without concomitant stable political reform. That is, although the middle class, industrialization, and the overall economic well-being of the country had grown, albeit sporadically, stable democratic institutions failed to take hold, as they had elsewhere in western Europe.[46]

Resistance to the status quo rose in the early twentieth century as workers' unions grew larger, the socialist movement became more powerful, and the middle class gradually increased. In 1931, the last of the Spanish Bourbon kings, Alfonso XIII, fled the country, and a republic was proclaimed. A moderate Republican–socialist government was elected that instituted liberal, democratic reforms. But the new republic immediately faced serious problems. Bitter strife ensued, with farmworker unrest, strikes, lockouts, and military takeovers.

In November 1933, a right-wing government won a close election and took action against the new reforms. In October 1934, fearing the imposition of fascism, miners in Asturias rose in protest, which the army brutally suppressed. Fears of Fascism mounted, and the Left gathered strength. This led to a resurgence of the Right and eventually the formation of groups such as the Falange, which resembled Italian and German fascist organizations that stressed nationalism, patriotism, authority, and order. In February 1936, a broad Left Republican coalition won a bitterly polarized election, which the Right found unacceptable, tolling the beginning of the civil war. Representing the Right, monarchist José Calvo Sotelo had said: "Against this sterile State I am proposing the integrated State, which will bring economic justice, and which will say with due authority: 'No more strikes, no more lockouts, . . . no more anarchic liberty, no more criminal conspiracies against full production.'" He went on to declare: "This State many may call fascist; if this indeed is the fascist state, then I, who believe in it, proudly declare myself a fascist!"[47]

People were either elated or revolted by such statements, and it is fair to say that the passion that drove the Spanish Civil War was the bitter polarization between those on the Left, who believed the political changes had not gone far enough, and those on the Right, who believed they had gone too far. For the latter, the forces of the Left had grown out of control. Assaults on clerics had increased, and, beyond that, claims of such assaults increased, such as the apocryphal tale that a one-time Catholic, Dolores Ibárruri (La Pasionaria [the Passion Flower]), who sold sardines from a great tray on her head, had cut the throat of a cleric with her teeth.[48]

Conspiring with Rightists, the army staged a coup d'état, declaring that only a military takeover could combat such an intolerably chaotic situation. In July, after a rebellion by General Emilio Mola in Spain, the rising star Francisco Franco flew from the Canary Islands to Morocco to take command of the well-trained African Army. With the assistance of aircraft supplied by Hitler and Mussolini, he managed to get this army to Spain and rapidly began his invasion of the homeland. In short order, he conquered much of the west and north; elsewhere, larger cities such as Madrid, Valencia, Bilbao, and Barcelona remained in Republican hands. The rank and file of the Falange joined Franco, who declared himself Commander and Head of State on September 29. The Generalissimo swiftly undertook brutal measures against any Republicans who came under his control. Only Russia, among the Western nations, offered military support to the Republicans, which, along with workers' militias and with volunteers from all parts of the world, enabled them to prevent, for the time being, a total Franco victory.

In cities like Barcelona and Madrid, still under Republican control, a new society was emerging. Customs of class distinction were abolished; properties were seized; workers were taking over and running industries; and in many ways, in the eyes of some like George Orwell during his first months in Spain, a truly egalitarian society was in the making. In late November 1936, Franco was formally recognized by Nazi Germany and Fascist Italy, both of which increased their military assistance. Spain became a testing ground for the Nazis' new weapons of war. In an incident that horrified the world, waves of German bombers, including the terrifying dive-bombing Stukas, laid waste the defenseless citizens of Guernica, killing 1,500 people in a scene of carnage immortalized in Picasso's painting.

To those who knew the reality of Nazi Germany during this time, with its brutality and aggression toward segments of its own population, as well as its claims on neighboring nations, Spain was the only place brave people interested in combating the fascist evil might go. Here they could fight for the good cause and write of the horror that was being perpetrated on the democratically elected government of the Republicans. This is the cause Nancy participated in and wrote about.

As she learned with growing anxiety, control over the regions jumped from side to side: one day an area was held by the Republicans; the next, by the Francoists. Kangaroo courts were held by self-appointed judges to determine the loyalty of the citizenry. Indecisiveness or divided loyalties resulted in torture and death sentences reminiscent of the Spanish Inquisition. It soon became clear that atrocities were being committed on both sides, but the Rightists, with the assistance of Germany and Italy, had military superiority. As for the Republicans, the feeble protestations of the noninterventionist Western nations were both devastating and infuriating. Russia continued to send food and weapons and organized the International Brigades, but it also incited infighting among the various parties on the Left.

The short story, between 1937 and 1939, is that Franco—despite the exceptional bravery of his opposition—gradually and with the aid of German arms, especially air support, conquered Spain. Barcelona fell in late January 1939 and Madrid, in late March. Not only were these years marked by discord within the Left, instigated by the Communist Party, but in 1938, Soviet military aid also began to decline. (In 1939, Stalin signed a nonaggression pact with Hitler.)

On March 27, 1939, Franco's forces entered Madrid, and the war was essentially over. Of the Lincoln Brigade and the 2,800 or so Americans who joined it, 800 were killed in the war. Those from France and other countries suffered similar casualties. In addition to the death toll resulting from combat, deaths at Republican hands numbered about 70,000 and the victims of the fascists were about 150,000.[49] Republicans targeted the clerics; fascists attacked workers. Until his death in 1976, the Generalissimo ruled with absolute authority; he was still executing political enemies in 1975. To most people who have ever read of the Spanish Civil War, Franco remains the fascist who got away. He declared neutrality during World War II so that the Allies had no cause of action against him when the war ended. The most that liberal intellectuals could do over the several decades after the war was to refuse to visit Spain as tourists.

Ultimately, one might say there are two Spanish Civil Wars in history: the war as it was reported at the time in Western newspapers, diaries, and interviews, and the war as it has come to be understood by historians reviewing the era with the aid of perspective and documentation unavailable during the Franco era. As a result, perhaps as much as any other event in the twentieth century, the Spanish Civil War has engendered a number of revisionist interpretations, the most recent since the Soviet archives have become accessible.[50]

One might argue that this reevaluation began with Orwell's *Homage to Catalonia*, along with other essays he published at the time. Orwell began his reports by speaking eloquently about the true egalitarian revolution that occurred in Republican Spain. But, as he also noted, this new democratic society was doomed, not only by the onslaught of the fascist army and the absence of Western aid but also by its so-called allies, Stalin and the Communists, whose lies and nefarious behavior sabotaged the cause.[51]

Orwell's condemnation of the Communists did not take hold at the time, and it is understandable that it did not influence America and Britain, both of which were glad to have Stalin as an ally during World War II. A person in September 1937, compared with someone today, would have read Orwell's essay "Spilling the Spanish Beans" through entirely different lenses. It begins: "The left-wing reporters . . . have prevented the British public from grasping the real nature of the struggle" and continues:

> The fact which these papers have so carefully obscured is that the Spanish Government (including the semi-autonomous Catalan Government) is far more afraid of the revolution than of the fascists. . . . For some time past a reign of terror—forcible suppression of political parties, a stifling censorship of the press, ceaseless espionage and mass imprisonment without trial—has been in progress. . . . The people who are in prison now are not fascists but revolutionaries; they are there not because

their opinions are too much to the Right but because they are too much to the Left. And the people responsible for putting them there are . . . —the Communists.[52]

Some scholars, working in the newly opened Soviet archives, claim that Stalin played a duplicitous game—supporting the Republicans with arms while taking over key roles in their army and government—as a prelude to establishing a Soviet-dominated "people's republic." Yet Stanley Payne, while accepting the view that Stalin wanted to make Spain a Soviet puppet state, ultimately blames the weakness of the Republican leaders as much as Stalin for the loss of the war. In contrast, Paul Preston, who questions the meaning of the newly found documents, believes to this day that the noninterventionist policies of the Western democracies ensured Franco's victory.[53] Regardless of one's judgment regarding the ultimate villain in the Republican loss, everyone agrees that the Spanish Civil War was a great tragedy in European history.

● ● ●

Nancy never recovered from the Republicans' defeat and, until the last days of her life, spoke and wrote passionately of their noble cause. And to her great credit, she was able to personally engage, under the most dangerous of circumstances, in the cause in which she so deeply believed.

11

On the Front Lines
in the Spanish Civil War

It is unthinkable for any honest intellectual to be profascist, as it is degenerate to be for Franco, the assassin of the Spanish and Arab people. Spain is not "politics," but life; its immediate future will affect every human who has a sense of what life and its facts mean, who has respect for himself and humanity. Above all others, the writer, the intellectual, must take sides. His place is with the people against fascism; his duty, to protest against the present degeneration of the democracies.

—NANCY CUNARD

It is the first story, the Spanish Civil War as a struggle between good and evil, rather than its revisionist telling, that concerns us most, because this is the one that Nancy and most of the world believed, including Hemingway, Faulkner, Steinbeck, Dos Passos, Dreiser, Picasso, Mondrian, Henry Moore, Miró, Aragon, Auden, Spender, C. Day Lewis, Langston Hughes, Reinhold Niebuhr, André Malraux, Sean O'Casey, Pablo Neruda, Miguel de Unamuno, García Lorca, and Luis Buñuel. And it was for her indefatigable engagement in this righteous cause that Nancy Cunard should be remembered as one of its undisputed heroes.

"The war began in Spain," wrote Nancy, "and I went there as a journalist, arriving on August 11 [1936] in Barcelona.... Spain took hold of me entirely."[1] She reported for a number of newspapers, determined to cover the war firsthand, initially in Barcelona and its neighboring fronts, and then in Madrid and the war zones surrounding it. She left the cities and made her way to the battlegrounds by riding with local truck drivers as far as they would take her. Then she walked long distances, often in heavy rain, snow, or under enemy fire, to reach the fronts. While covering the war, she also engaged in humanitarian activities that similarly exposed her to grave danger. She gave aid to war-ravaged and starving soldiers and civilians by moving them to safety and distributing food and supplies. From the beginning, Nancy thought that if the Western democracies had aided the Spanish

Republic, Hitler and Mussolini might have been stopped and the future world war prevented.

Her most historically significant reporting, addressed in the next chapter, followed Franco's victory in Barcelona in 1939 when very few journalists remained in Spain, and Nancy lingered as the *Manchester Guardian*'s only eyewitness reporter. Despite persistent bombings from overhead, she walked alongside the cold, starving refugees to the French holding centers near Perpignan. She soon exposed in the *Guardian* France's tacit collaboration with Franco in maintaining concentration camps, not "reception centers," for both the Spanish civilian and military population. Again, the world's major powers remained indifferent ("neutral") toward Franco's brutalities, much as it ignored early reports about Hitler's activities and his camps, but Nancy's articles exposed the inhumane conditions at the very internment camps that were later operated by Vichy collaborators, who merely expanded their population.

During her visits to the camps, Nancy bribed guards to give bread to the prisoners, and she worked tirelessly in enlisting sponsors for the release, where it was allowed, of distinguished intellectuals—scientists, men of letters, doctors—also interned in the camps. In addition, she badgered the *Guardian*'s editor into starting a food drive that eventually provided hot meals to thousands of refugees. After the war, she remained a tireless commentator on the continuing plight of the prisoners still in the camps. She made dozens of trips to Spain and saved many by smuggling them into France, often to her house in Réanville, and she carried on her efforts to find them permanent asylum in Central America. Even when she was arrested by Franco or the French authorities, she planned future rescue missions.

For Nancy, this was not just a war of democracy against fascism; it was also a war in which the Spanish fascists had forced a once-grand people, the Moors, to fight in an army led by the very people who had discriminated against and persecuted them. In addition, like Langston Hughes, Nancy was aggrieved that Franco's conscripted Moors were battling the black volunteers who had joined the International Brigades to fight against Franco. As in *Negro*, Nancy remained committed to exposing both the plight and the achievement of blacks worldwide. In her articles for the American Negro Press, her unprecedented subject matter included not only Franco's contemptuous treatment of his black soldiers but also his exploitation of them as cannon fodder. And while publishing articles about the Moors, she also wrote about blacks, particularly from the United States, who had demonstrated great courage and heroism in the brigades.

George Orwell, who has written the classic description of Barcelona at the time, arrived in Spain shortly after Nancy. Although he intended to write newspaper articles, he joined a militia almost immediately because "at that time and in that atmosphere it seemed the only conceivable thing to do." He believed that "when the fighting broke out . . . it is probable that every anti-fascist in Europe felt a thrill of hope. For here, at last, apparently, was democracy standing up to fascism."[2] Orwell fought with the Workers' Party of the Marxist Union (POUM), a Trotskyite faction, until he was almost fatally shot in the throat. He then returned to England and in *Homage to Catalonia* recounted both his early passion for the cause and his later disillusionment with the Communists who, he was among the first to say in print, had exploited the workers to further Stalin's personal agenda. So unpopular was his stance that most of the 900 copies of *Homage* printed in England in 1938 remained unsold at the time of his death (1950). All the same, his description of Barcelona during the early war days remains unchallenged in terms of its veracity and vividness. Robert Capa, who also went to Spain, wanted to visually record the atrocities of the war. An innovator brandishing a 35-mm Leica, his spontaneous and exceptionally graphic closeups, like many memoirs of the time, support most of Orwell's reports.[3]

Always a friend to people of all classes and backgrounds, Nancy shared Orwell's enthusiasm for the new open society. Barcelona was

> startling and overwhelming. . . . The working class was in the saddle. Practically every building . . . had been seized by the workers and was draped with red flags or with the red and black flag of the Anarchists; every wall was scrawled with the hammer and sickle and with the initials of the revolutionary parties; almost every church had been gutted and its images burnt. . . . Even the bootblacks had been collectivized and their boxes painted red and black. . . . Servile and even ceremonial forms of speech had temporarily disappeared. Nobody said "Señor" . . . ; everyone called everyone else "Comrade" or "Thou."[4]

A new democracy had been born. The wealthy classes had virtually ceased to exist:

> Practically everyone wore rough working-class clothes, or blue overalls or some variant of militia uniform. . . . There was no unemployment. . . . Above all, there was . . . a feeling of having suddenly emerged into an era of equality and freedom. . . . In the barbers' shops were Anarchist notices, . . . solemnly explaining that barbers were no longer slaves. In the streets were colored posters appealing to prostitutes to stop being prostitutes. . . . Revolutionary ballads of the naïvest kind, all about the proletarian brotherhood and the wickedness of Mussolini, were being sold on the streets for a few centimes each. . . . Illiterate militia[men would] buy one of these ballads, laboriously spell out the words, and then . . . begin singing.[5]

As a journalist permitted into the country for a limited period, Nancy began reporting immediately: "The whole next three months [were] spent in towns, villages and going to the fronts. . . . I could think of nothing else."[6] She filed three to four articles a week with the ANP, Sylvia Pankhurst's *New Times*, and Charles Duff's *Spain at War*, *Spanish Newsletter*, and *Voice of Spain*. Over the next three years, she also wrote for the *News Chronicle* (London), *Regards* (Paris), and the *Manchester Guardian*, as well as the *New Statesman*, the *Nation*, *Life*, *Letters To-Day*, and *Left Review*. In some of her early reports, she related the Ethiopian crisis to the new war. She warned repeatedly that the events in Spain were a prelude to another world war. Spain today would become France tomorrow:

> The ghastliness, the magnitude and the closeness of the civil war in Spain, and the possibility that civil war may, indeed, [reach] France, engineered by the alliances of the fascist leaders of diverse countries, is foremost in the minds of all. . . . Today's papers contain the most troubling news of violent and large-scale fascist provocations in Austria on the part of German Nazis. If the fascists in France start a civil war it is impossible for them to win without the intervention of other powers such as Germany and Italy—who are only waiting for the chance.

She could foresee the exploitation of blacks in France: they, too, would be forced to fight on Franco's front lines: "In such a war black African troops, the hundreds of thousands of Senegalese, Ivory-Coastians and other French colonials, would play an immense role."[7]

Nancy took detailed notes on everything she saw, incorporating some into her reports and amplifying the rest in a long treatise on Spain twenty years later ("48 hours, flying hours, was the span given to fliers at the start of the war").[8] She spoke fluent Spanish and Catalan and talked to as many people as she could. Some, like Angel Goded, a waiter, remained lifelong friends. As she walked through Barcelona, with its beautiful public squares and magnificent flowers, she noted the gaunt, unsightly elements of the city: filthy barracks, shabby shops, pockmarked sidewalks and buildings scarred by gun shellings, and roads in poor repair. At night, the faintly lit streets were a constant reminder of imminent air raids. The sequelae of war were already apparent: a scarcity of bread, meat, milk, sugar, and gasoline, as well as the fetid smells of combat emanating from decaying flesh and excrement where rodents and insects gathered.[9]

When she traveled outside the city, she not only took copious notes and photos but often became intimately involved in people's lives. She later wrote of one experience:

There was a day (and the date was Aug. 31, 1936, at exact sundown) in a desert in Aragon—and I alone (of course) sitting on the sand, gazing (after "funeral meats" with a young, dark, strong peasant woman whose little dead daughter I had photographed in a coffin two days before), gazing at immensity. It had been a day that got out of hand, somehow. And the "somehow" was because of her gratitude that there had been someone there, even with the smallest camera, to take a picture of her child. She had plied three of us (one Spaniard, one German and self) with the saltiest ham in the mountains of the world; she had—in fact—made all of us somewhat drunk saying, "The time for weeping is now over; partake: I am grateful to you." (What country else do you think this could be in?)

Unable to share the mother's stoicism, Nancy looked to nature for distraction or transcendence:

And then, I . . . set off [to] the unknown, unknowable, 15 or so kilometers . . . and found the desert. (Dalí has painted deserts but certainly not that part, . . . infinitely finer.) I sat myself down on the earthy-sand, utterly at peace. . . . Such is the story of this land. . . . To me it was infinity, and after death and "realization of all one's desires," and any other simile or image or comparison you can think of. It was complete. . . . How it remains, or comes back, does it not? I suppose a composer would put this into music. It wouldn't be I who would understand his meaning—yet we might be talking of the same land .[10]

When Nancy returned to Barcelona, the militias were in plain sight, either in training or returning from the front. The former drilled in the public spaces: squads of unarmed males positioned themselves next to the lush gardens behind the Plaza de España, marched awkwardly back and forth, and then stood tall. They were pretending to be soldiers, like so many young men at the start of the Great War, practicing without guns because of the dire shortage of weapons. One unit would go to the front only after another had returned and handed over its rifles. Those who came back, often barefoot and in ragged clothing, were exhausted, starving, and filthy. They greeted friends and strangers with a clenched fist, slap on the back, embrace, or prayer, and the air was filled with the odor of excrement mixed with the sweet scent of the abundant flowers. They did not look like an army. In their dark shirts and sleeves rolled to the elbow, corduroy knee breeches, and zipper jackets in every conceivable color, they wore makeshift uniforms. Some used puttees (cloth strips wound from ankle to knee); others, corduroy gaiters or leather leggings; some wore high boots. Many had colored headbands, and there were many different cap styles, each displaying a party badge. Almost everyone tied a red or red and black handkerchief around his neck. (The fascist colors were red and yellow.)[11]

Most striking was their age: half were between eleven and sixteen, all passionate about revolution, even if they had no sense of what was in store for them. Not only had this crowd of eager children no idea about how to use a gun or throw a bomb, but they lacked protective tin hats and even rudimentary maps. As Nancy observed, what these youths lacked in weapons they made up for in spirit, and they were heroes in the villages, greeted with bread, fruit, and blessings. When they neared the front, however, chanting, for example, "Visca P.O.U.M.! Fascistas-maricones!" intending to be warlike and menacing, the sounds "from those childish throats sounded as pathetic as the cries of kittens."[12]

Before leaving for the front, with knapsacks on their backs and blankets across their shoulders, they attended torch-lit ceremonies that celebrated their valor, and red flags danced in the evening light. The boys shouted, stamped their feet, and made castanet-like clattering sounds with their tin plates. The uproar transformed into silence as whistles and hushes indicated that someone was about to make a patriotic speech. Farewells followed, with songs, clenched fists, laughter, and tears. After a circuitous three- or four mile march to the station, during which the soldiers displayed themselves to the entire city, their trains appeared. A band played revolutionary music, accompanied by the flapping of more red flags. Crowds cheered, saluted, and touched them. Mothers, waving goodbye, "might have had an intuition—who knows?—that the good-byes *were* good byes."[13]

Madrid resembled Barcelona as a pulsating center of hope and egalitarianism, despite the city's gaping wounds—shell holes that ravaged its buildings and avenues. Familiar as well was the sight of returning soldiers, filthy and half starved, grabbing bread with torn and dirty hands, and, as one of them wrote, blowing "our noses with our fingers" because all cloths had been used for bandages or cleaning guns. They huddled together like cattle, as they had on the fronts, weathering the frigid temperatures and icy rain and snow. One volunteer was certain that the front must have been like "the era of prehistoric man, before fire."[14]

Local militias had defended Madrid during the first weeks of war—in the streets, around the mountain passes, and finally in newly built barricades. The desperately needed additional manpower finally appeared: British volunteers, who joined the British Battalion of the new International Brigades. Others soon arrived from all parts of the globe. Again, many were barely in their teens—peasants from remote parts of the country who had walked here. Some, like the steelworkers from Hungary, had overcome long, near-impossible journeys, reaching Spain by clinging to the bottom of the Orient Express. These child-warriors continued to arouse deep feelings. Nancy's Paris friend Luis Buñuel recalled meeting the art historian Elie Faure in Madrid: "One day we watched a hundred peasants marching by, four abreast, some armed with hunting rifles, some with sickles and pitchforks. . . . In an obvious effort at discipline, they were trying very hard to march in step. Faure and I both wept."[15]

Perhaps most astonishing in both Madrid and Barcelona was the way people performed ordinary tasks at the same time they feared for their lives. John Dos Passos, working in Madrid on the film *The Spanish Earth* with Hemingway and Archibald MacLeish, contemplated the gratuitousness of survival or death: "I . . . stared at the ceiling and thought of the pleasant-faced middle-aged chambermaid. . . . Perhaps tomorrow morning . . . there'd be that hasty loudening shriek and the street full of dust and splintered stone, and instead of coming to work the woman would be just a mashed-out mess of blood and guts to be scooped into a new pine coffin and hurried away."[16]

Madrid was unique, as Nancy's friend Langston Hughes had told her and as she learned for herself. She could walk or take a streetcar to the most extraordinary places. She could stroll to the trenches at Usera or at the Parque del Oeste, or walk or take the trolley to its last stop at the recently built University City—briefly, the most splendid university in Europe but now a huge morgue of unidentified soldiers. The Casa Campo, a public park, was also on the outskirts of town; political executions took place here. It was the site as well of some of Spain's most lush fields, filled with wheat and heavy cannon, along with the scattered remains of demolished homes—broken beds, shards of crockery, children's toys—the fragments of countless nameless lives.

The first major air strikes against Madrid occurred on October 7; by the middle of the month, the city was under the control of the Republicans, while enemy troops occupied the surrounding areas within a fifteen-mile radius. Nancy left the now relatively safe city of Madrid to get close to the fighting in Illescas and Navalcarnero, two villages that would become famous for valiant Republican resistance despite final defeat. Initially, on October 17, the Republicans had gone to the Illescas front in trucks, but when they left their vehicles, they were mowed down by machine guns. This did not deter other forces in Madrid who, told that the Russians were coming to their assistance, made their way there and counterattacked. Although 6,000 Republicans surrounded the town on October 19, they were beaten back when the enemy charged at them through the local cemetery. The next day, October 20, double-decker buses carried 5,000 additional Republican soldiers from Madrid, and there was such an astonishing exchange of fire that the sounds of battle reached back to the city. On October 23, more of the enemy arrived, and they brutalized the Republicans. Those who left their homes became the first refugees of war in dire need of food and water.[17]

Nancy kept notes for her articles as she made her way to the fronts on October 21, 23, and 24:[18] "On the way to the Illescas front . . . talked with the Scotch ambulance men. . . . About 150 [of ours were] wounded since . . . yesterday. The attack by the loyalists is continuing. . . . No aerial gun at this point to attack enemy planes. . . . The ambulance has much to do." On the left side of the road she saw "three or four field radio sets; three tanks; . . . another tank on side road. Just beyond the point which was the line on October 19th a bridge has been blown up, not known whether by us or enemy." She heard "sounds of war, distant, begin" and saw "a large armored car in the hollow [and] two tanks near it." She continues: "We cut across the ploughed field, towards Illescas with sounds of war, heavy; artillery, considerable; distant machine guns. Three planes pass over us, very high. Said to be enemy. . . . A milician [sic] says that it is not possible to know at this moment whether Illescas is ours or theirs. The fighting is going on."

Back in grim Madrid, she observed a procession of about 3,000 women and girls, some of the growing number of refugees "with babies," on the Avenida del Prado; about "1,000, on the Calle de Alcala." She was preoccupied with their fate and the question, "Hadn't our forces pushed on a few kilometres?" She drove to Mostoles, Navalcarnero, and Torrejón in a camouflaged car draped with thistles and leaves and continued chronicling the number of forces, planes, trucks, tanks, and artillery. At Mosteles, she observed "three or four armored machine gun cars. Barbed wire defenses. Some 2,000 or so hereabouts [for] two days. There are no loyalist planes." At Parla, she stopped at a hospital that had handled 900 cases. At Torrejón, she returned to the firing line.

This was at least the second time she had been there: "As this is the place where the front lines were on Oct. 19, last time I came here with Leon Felipe, it seems that we have advanced a few kilometres, perhaps three." Now, a man "named Zisman takes us on to the firing line." She writes: "Ours were firing. Machine guns on left of road. Good 'sandbag' parapetos to left. Armored car just on right side of road. A little rise in the ground on the right; natural protection from enemy fire, increased by dug-out trench at its base; they shoot over top. The enemy is at 700 meters; Illescas is at 1600 metres." "We run across the road," she adds, "ducking, then talking with those in the trenches . . . for about twenty minutes. Bullets pass. NOISE. In the distance more and bigger noise, muted by distance."

Like other reporters, Nancy had to be alert to the subtle timing of falling bullets, because only seconds separated detonation from explosion. Antoine de Saint-Exupéry, also a correspondent at the front, believed that "waiting for an explosion is the longest passage of time I know. What things go on in that interminable moment. An enormous pressure rises. Will that boiler ever make up its mind to burst? At last! For some that meant death. [How many] souls . . . have won a last-minute reprieve?"[19]

In November, Nancy's three-month period in Spain expired. Before returning to Réanville, she traveled briefly to North Africa, to Tangiers and French Morocco, "where much was to be learned about the way the Moors were impressed (mainly) into a war that was no concern of theirs."[20] After she returned to France, she pursued a project encouraged by Pablo Neruda and his friends.

Poets of the World Defend the Spanish People and *Authors Take Sides*

Nancy had met the great Chilean poet and future Nobel laureate Pablo Neruda shortly after she arrived in Madrid. In keeping with the Latin American tradition of honoring poets by giving them diplomatic assignments, he had been appointed Chilean consul in Madrid. His house, La Casa de las Flores, was a gathering place for left-wing intellectuals, and Nancy met a cadre of people there deeply involved in the Republican cause: Luis Enrique Délano, Rafael Alberti, Federico García Lorca, Luis Cernuda, Manuel Altolaguirre, Arturo Serrano Plaja, Miguel Hernández, Delia del Carril, and José Bergamín.[21] She was extremely happy to be back in the company of artists and writers. Sometimes they spoke about their work. Nancy told them she wanted to publish a collection of poems by British writers about the war; she hoped to awaken an indifferent world to the horrors of the time. She felt completely at home with her new friends and was flattered by their admiration of her for acting on her ideals—for having come to Spain to talk to its people, for going to the front to witness the terrifying events of the time.

Neruda, whose inspirational *España en el corazón* (*Spain in the Heart*) was distributed at the front, was often asked to read a poem at Las Floras. His famous "I'm Explaining a Few Things" begins:

You are going to ask: and where are the lilacs?
and the poppy-petalled metaphysics?
. . . .
My house was called
the house of flowers, because in every cranny
geraniums burst. . . .

....
One morning the bonfires
leapt out of the earth
devouring human beings—
. . . and from then on fire,
gunpowder from then on,
and from then on blood.
Bandits with planes and Moors,
bandits with finger-rings and duchesses,
bandits with black friars spattering blessings
came through the sky to kill children
and the blood of children ran through the streets
without fuss, like children's blood.

....

Come and see the blood in the streets.
Come and see
the blood in the streets.
Come and see the blood
in the streets!

Meetings at Las Flores became more focused on the obligation, as Neruda put it, of "the poet [to] become part of the struggle, . . . the sweat, the bread, the wine, the dream." Events that had pushed him—after all, a diplomat—toward a more active role in the war were the political activism of his friends and, even more so, the fascists' sadistic treatment of two great Spanish writers. The philosopher-writer Miguel de Unamuno, rector at the University of Salamanca, had been condemned for castigating Franco's treatment of civilians, and after being driven at gunpoint from the university he suffered a fatal heart attack. Perhaps even more intolerable to Neruda was the hounding and subsequent murder of his friend, the poet-dramatist Federico García Lorca, who was just thirty-eight. A populist writer not particularly active in leftist politics and a man beloved by the people, Lorca was dragged through the streets of Granada before being taken to the mountains and placed before a firing squad. His body was never recovered. In the poem just cited, Neruda had also written:

Federico, do you remember
from under the ground
where the light of June drowned flowers in your mouth?
Brother, my brother!

Nancy understood Lorca's mythic stature alluded to in the poem. After Lorca was arrested, she explained, they "held him for two days, and then took him out and shot him just before dawn, under the moon, in a field, on the edge of Granada. . . . His body was buried in a cornfield. Since then, the peasants, knowing this, have never sowed that patch with wheat. Instead, they have put wild poppy seed on the spot, so that every year a blaze of scarlet shows through the green and gold of the corn. And for this many have been jailed."[22] After Lorca's death, many believe, the war destroyed the renaissance in the Spanish arts then taking place. In fact, most of the writers associated with Las Flores were exiled after the war (Hernández died of starvation in prison), and the literary renaissance moved to Latin America.

When it came time for Nancy to leave Spain, Neruda, who also considered the poet the unacknowledged legislator of the world, encouraged her to continue her anti-fascist activities by publishing the collection she had been thinking about. And so she did. When she returned to France, she restored the Mathieu hand press and launched a new kind of literary genre. She gathered the imprimatur of well-known writers on a subject of international importance, the Spanish Civil War, and printed six pamphlets, or *plaquettes*, called *Les Poètes du monde défendent le peuple espagnol! (The Poets of the World Defend the Spanish People!)*. Each leaflet contained poems in English, French, and Spanish by Nancy's and Neruda's friends, including Tzara, Aragon, Langston Hughes, W. H. Auden, Brian Howard, Nicolás Guillén, Rafael Alberti, Gonzáles Tuñón, Vicente Aleixandre, and García Lorca. The poems were sold in Paris and London, and the funds were sent to Spain.

Auden's "Spain," which Nancy published for the first time, would become the most important poem in English on the Spanish Civil War, a poem so controversial that the author himself later repudiated its political rhetoric and prohibited its reprint for several years. "Spain" represented, at least early on, Auden's vision of the war as a revolutionary situation—in Marxist terms, a manifestation of historical materialism. Stephen Spender's understanding of the poem was that medieval Spain and the European past were equivalent to thesis (yesterday, Franco); the present struggle against them, antithesis (the Spanish Republic); and tomorrow, the revolution and victory of the Republic through Communism, synthesis.[23] Furthermore, the poem illustrated the Marxist notion that freedom is the recognition of necessity (killing):

Today the deliberate increase in the chances of death;
The conscious acceptance of guilt in the necessary murder.

Auden writes:

"What's your proposal? To build the just city? I will.
I agree. Or is it the suicide pact, the romantic
   Death? Very well, I accept, for
I am your choice, your decision. Yes, I am Spain.

He continues:

   To-morrow, perhaps, the future.
   . . . .
   To-morrow the rediscovery of romantic love,
   . . . .
   To-morrow for the young the poets exploding like bombs,
   The walks by the lake, the weeks of perfect communion . . .
   . . . .
   But to-day
   the struggle . . .

Shortly after publishing the *plaquettes*, Nancy launched another project, *Authors Take Sides on the Spanish War*, believing more strongly than ever that, in the least, writers must "take sides." She returned to her methodology in organizing *Negro* by sending out an "Enquête," a questionnaire, asking poets of England, Scotland, Ireland, and Wales their opinions on the war. She handprinted and distributed leaflets to a list of writers in the form of an acrostic:

   Federation
   Assassins of the
   Service of
   Crimes
   International
   Seeking to
   Murder Spanish Operatives.

She received 148 replies to her question: 127 in support of the Republicans; 5, pro-Franco, from Evelyn Waugh ("If I were a Spaniard I should be fighting for General Franco"), Edmund Blunden, Arthur Machen, Geoffrey Moss, and Eleanor Smith; 16, neutral, including those from Aldous Huxley, Norman Douglas, T. S. Eliot ("While I am naturally sympathetic, I still feel convinced that it is best that at least a few men of letters remain isolated and take no part in these collective activities"), Ezra Pound (already involved with the Italian

Fascists: "Spain is an emotional luxury to a gang of sap-headed dilettantes"), H. G. Wells, Vita Sackville-West, and, in a late reply, George Bernard Shaw ("Spain must choose for itself"). Nancy's answer, to repeat, was unequivocal: "It is unthinkable for any honest intellectual to be profascist, as it is degenerate to be for Franco."

Nancy had been innovative, citing well-known writers in an elegant literary form that would reach a wide reading public. Opinions of some non-British artists about the risks of losing the war were already well known, Picasso stressing "the highest values of humanity and civilization at stake," and Thomas Mann, "the salvation of [the artist's] soul." A year after Nancy's questionnaire, Donald Ogden Stewart, president of the League of American Writers, put Nancy's question to American writers and received passionate responses from Faulkner, Steinbeck, Sherwood Anderson, and Robinson Jeffers.[24]

In just two months, Nancy typed and organized her manuscript. Although she had trouble finding a publisher, the *Left Review* published 3,000 copies, which sold out immediately. Again, all funds went to Spain. By the date of its publication, Nancy had already returned to Barcelona.

Nancy's new literary form in which "authors take sides" has continued to this day.[25]

Return to Spain

On this second extended visit to Spain, Nancy was accompanied by her friend John Banting. A special passport was required, detailing a "special mission" for the trip. The French made this difficult to obtain: the Francoists were combing the country for spies, and the most accredited journalists, according to Nancy, had difficulty getting into the country. One had to be *listo*, by which she meant "resourceful," and "I had my ways and means." Before they knew it, Nancy and Banting faced "drawn sabres, bayonets, and angry officials at the frontier. . . . It was touch and go. . . . But enter Spain we did." Banting's explanation was brief: "We went to Spain illegally."[26]

Once again, Nancy chose to travel first to Barcelona, where everyone seemed to be starving and freezing. Theodore Dreiser, who arrived at about the same time, described the city's "sense of impending catastrophe," with everything "infected by fear."[27] Sirens blared, Nancy observed, for five minutes before the anticipated arrival of bombs; on some days, they shrieked all day: although daily bombing did not occur, planes continually crossed the skies to terrify the population. Such was the great gift and advantage given to Franco by Germany and Italy.

Barcelona's five miles of serpentine subways and ample supply of benches and running water had until recently provided temporary shelter for some; now, many spent half the day there. Except for Gaudi's Sagrada Familia, still standing, churches no longer offered relief: fifty-eight had been burned to the ground. Nor did the hotels provide comfort: nerve-wracking sirens pierced the rooms, and the most ordinary amenities were restricted—there were no bed-sheets, since all cloth had been taken for bandages; a vegetable pap fried with sauce was served at each meal because of the lack of meat, milk, sugar, and butter. Inside and outside the hotels, everyone looked frayed: some people had no shoes. It looked as if the population was slowly starving, if not already seriously ill. Every morning, both the old and the young foraged for cabbage and a few sticks of wood. After bombardments, women scavenged the streets for scraps of food. Soap and medication were unavailable.

The only distraction from the despair throughout the city was the music of Pablo Casals, who would become Nancy's friend after the war. "The only weapons I have ever had are my cello and my conductor's baton," he said, and throughout the war he used them to perform countless concerts to raise large sums of money for food, supplies, and medical aid for the Republicans. Nancy and Banting heard him whenever they could, and Casals became a spokesperson for the Republican cause. During the intermission of one wide-ly broadcast concert, he spoke in English, French, and Spanish to the nations of the world: "Do not commit the crime of letting the Spanish Republic be murdered. If you allow Hitler to win in Spain, you will be the next victims of his madness. The war will spread to all Europe, to the whole world. Come to the aid of our people!"[28]

Again, Nancy wanted to get as close to the front as possible, so she and Banting left Barcelona for Madrid via Valencia, where they met with Langston Hughes. They spoke about the war ("Spain survives because it is righteous") and shared their outrage that Moors were battling within a country they had once conquered and ruled. After a ten-hour bus ride from Valencia over the empty countryside of the red mountains, they arrived at what Nancy described as a "freezing and starving Madrid under the December shells." A more elaborate system of trenches, tunnels, and caves had been built during the last year; until then, people remaining in the streets had been routinely lined up against a wall and shot. The ravages of the aerial bombings remained horrifying—demolished streets and streetlights, pitch-black nights, and the combination of endless rubble and perilous paths with mortar holes.

During the day, the city seemed like a battlefield, with continual sounds of machine guns and mortar. Everyone watched the skies for German-built planes; the homeless walked the streets, clutching their most precious belongings. Madrid established a first-aid service for wounded houses (as well as people), run by engineers, architects, bricklayers, and electricians. During the day, they repaired buildings; in their spare time, they planned for a beautiful reconstructed Madrid after the war, a demonstration to Nancy of "that fortitude, that innate faith . . . of the Spanish people."[29]

Nancy and Banting stayed at the Hotel des Anges, and it was so cold that they had to place floor rugs over the bedcovers. Winter this year was particularly icy, rainy, and windy, and there seemed to be a permanent shortage of heat everywhere. Nancy felt cold all the time, and she remained prone to bronchitis. Still, once in Madrid, she immediately resumed her reports. Some of them cited statistics: "Spanish Government military authorities estimated the loss of the dead of the rebels before Santander was taken, mainly by Italians, as follows: Spanish, 57; Moroccans, 1,415; Italians, 2,927; Germans, 1,614; other nationalities, 502." Others described the wholesale destruction of a country just for the sake of destruction: "The army chiefs . . . have massacred their way through two thirds of the country destroying whole towns and villages that have no military importance whatsoever, bombing and shelling particularly the women and children, the old, the sick and the wounded as they fell along the roads."[30] Nancy was again writing "during air raids, in burnt-out towns, . . . in almost pitch darkness." Daphne Fielding writes that by now she had lost whatever religious faith she might have had: "She saw that Franco was supported by the Catholics and that many of the churches were transformed into fascist arsenals," with the high clergy blessing the bombs that would fall on schools and factories.[31]

As in Barcelona, Nancy saw soldiers everywhere, including the Anarchists, distinguished by their berets, the pistols on the hip of their corduroy pants, and the red and black handkerchiefs tied around their necks. There were also posters everywhere and long, colorful streamers hanging from buildings, urging unity. The posters were extraordinary: among the most popular was one with Franco, a German officer, and a cardinal hanging an image of Spain; another reproduced the bombed body of a baby amid enemy aircraft. In the city square, crowds stared at what had become a solemn emblem: a fifteen-foot map in which traditionally advertised vacation sites were symbolically transformed into war images. Badajoz, for example, known for its bullfights, was represented with men and women standing in a bullring before their mass execution by a fascist firing squad. Entertainment was often war-related: cabaret shows with dances that mimicked the sounds of war—tap dancers performing with the rapid clicking sounds of machine-gun rounds. Advertisements touted these shows, as well as the sporting and social activities that were supporting the war effort—for example, "Bullfights for Hospital Aid."

Nancy reported on a number of subjects, from the nature of the fighting in small and large battles to patriotic pieces extolling the Spanish spirit.[32] She reported civil turbulence ("Civilians have risen against the domination of the detested foreigners, the Germans and the Italians")[33] and at times referred to her older causes, reminding her readers about Ethiopia in "Blacks in Spanish Revolution Fighting on Side of Royalists." Sometimes she was cautious about the future; at other times, optimistic.[34]

Her interest in blacks in battle remained ardent—both the Moors conscripted into service by Franco and the volunteers in the Abraham Lincoln and International Brigades. She saw that as the war progressed and casualties in the brigades increased, the "enemy" Moors, like the blacks in the brigades, demonstrated no abatement of courage and competence. Her great fear remained that Franco's and Mussolini's black soldiers, in both Spain and Abyssinia, would be deployed in a world war and propaganda machines would convince blacks at home that the Fascists were fighting in their interest. This sort of sophistry had already begun: "Natives in the Sudan and in British African possessions are being told the black army of Italian Africa will [help] liberate them."[35]

Some of Nancy's articles focused on black volunteers who had come to fight independently of any organized group. "A Negro Girl Is Spain's Hero" profiled a young Cuban woman who had inspired Cubans in Machado's revolution to go to Spain. In "African Negroes Fighting in Spain Against Their Will," she related an interview with Moroccan soldiers. They "were unanimous in their hatred of being driven into Spain to fight in this war; and at no time throughout all these weeks did I hear . . . Spaniards condemn them, for they realized well that these wretched natives could have had no say in the matter." Nancy was particularly interested in the conscripted blacks' exploitation and persecution by the entire spectrum of Loyalists, from Franco and his officers to the rank and file. After all, the Moors had a great history: "It was the Moors who brought culture to Spain as the majority of its beautiful buildings attest. Now, [they] are the unwilling, helpless and miserable tools in the hands of criminals whose aim (which they are attaining) is to destroy."[36]

She reported that North African blacks were used as "shock troops," moved to the front lines and consequently the first to be killed. If they survived, they were ordered to perform "avowedly atrocious terrorizations and massacres" on "Spanish workers almost as miserable and oppressed" as they were themselves. Nancy also wrote about blacks in the International Brigades who rose to higher ranks. Oliver Law, killed in battle, was the first African American to command an integrated troop in combat.[37]

Nancy discussed the contempt in which the racist generals held the blacks. One of Franco's aids, General Gonzalo Queipo de Llano, a revolting and degenerate man, gave frightening and vulgar radio reports about the Moors. He warned his audience that the soldiers would rape all pro-Republican women.[38] She quoted Franco's denigration of his black soldiers as "neither decent nor military, committing reprehensible deeds, often drunk and rowdy, feared and loathed by the population." She cited an official Franco document: "The Moroccans complain without cease. The Spanish people refuse flatly to have anything to do with them or try to understand them. . . . Wounded Moroccans leave hospitals to go straight back to the front in rags. [Some] wander about half naked. . . . The wounded drag about the streets, . . . behaving like beggars." She then commented: "Thus do the imperial fascist 'civilizers' treat their native soldiers, beside using them as human spears in every forefront of destruction, . . . wonderful sho's. It is the eternal case of 'only a black.'"[39] Racism in the ranks also resulted in serious in-fighting, in "violent disputes among Germans and Moors who had to fight alongside each other. . . . The Germans protested against being used in the company with Africans, whom their Nazi racialism had taught them to despise. The disputes ended in many dead."[40]

Nancy wanted her readers to see through Franco's lies, to know that the Spanish citizenry was increasingly sympathetic toward the Moors, which finally encouraged many to abandon their troops. At one point she wrote the best news she could imagine: "[There is] a sensational piece of information. The Moors are deserting Franco, taking their guns, and transferring them to the Republicans":

> The Moorish legionnaires-to-be no longer wait to be conscripted by Franco, but come and volunteer to be taken on as soldiers. . . . When they have become familiar with the rifles and other equipment given them, they desert and manage to slip off into the still savage "unpacified" parts of the Riff mountains [where they give] their guns and ammunition to the fierce Riffan tribesmen.[41]

On occasion, Nancy joined Banting to stop by the International Brigades, see old friends, or visit great art. One day—"we had never seen such big, slow snowflakes"—they were permitted into the basement of the Prado, where they saw what Nancy called "the corpses" of destroyed art. Then they were shown restorations of El Grecos, Bruegels, and Bosches. Nancy was overcome with emotion and gratitude toward those who had worked on these paintings, "using the few candles allotted their frozen, black mittened hands, as famine, bombardment and a cruel winter continued outside."[42] The treasures of Spain had been in grave danger of destruction with the fascists looting and disfiguring the nation's art. Reports of initial fascist desecrations had become so widespread that the outraged Piet Mondrian, Ben Nicholson, and Henry Moore tried to get to Spain, although they were denied entrance. It was imperative that the art be preserved, and Picasso, director of the Prado, assured the world at the American Artists' Congress in 1937 that every measure had been taken: "While the Rebel planes have dropped incendiary bombs on our museums, the people and the militia, at the risk of their lives, have rescued the . . . art." It is estimated that Republicans at great personal risk saved 10,000 great paintings, 100,000 other works of art, and 400,000 important books.[43] Nancy wrote about the brave truck drivers who carried the art to Geneva.

Nancy and Banting often visited old friends at hotels and restaurants, such as the Gran, Chicote, Florida, and Victoria, popular among Red Cross workers, writers, officials, and journalists like Martha Gellhorn, Lillian Hellman, and Herbert Matthews. They saw Hemingway at the Florida; he was a correspondent for the *New York Times* and *Alliance*, a North American newspaper. They spoke of "Hem's" play *War Tourists* and of war in general. Hemingway had not changed his way of thinking since World War I: "They wrote in the old days that it is sweet and fitting to die for one's country. But in modern war there is nothing sweet or fitting in your dying. You will die like a dog for no good reason." He despaired of the oddity of growing accustomed to the sounds and sights of war—to bullets rattling tiles and shattering glass and stone and to puddles of blood in the streets. (Dos Passos, also at the Florida, more matter of factly put it: "A splatter of brains had to be wiped off the glassless revolving doors of the hotel that day.")[44] All the same, the struggle between tyranny and freedom demanded that Hemingway actively participate, so he became a reporter, tackling a variety of subjects. One article in the *Times*, about the heroism of youths, "Brihuega Likened by Hemingway to Victory on World War Scale," recounted a five-day battle when Italian and Moorish forces made their way to Madrid.[45] The same battle formed the basis of "The Peasants" section of André Malraux's great civil war novel, *Man's Hope*.

Nancy's recollection of one meeting with Hemingway is stirring: "I remember him taking off my boots and warming the cold feet. He was enchanting. Such a sympathetic moment—from a non-Spaniard—was never my lot till then, nor yet again."[46] She knew that after the war, Hemingway would publish the very moving "On the American Dead in Spain," a tribute to the Lincoln Battalion two years after the Battle of the Jarama River, which includes the following:

> The dead sleep cold in Spain tonight. Snow blows through the olive groves, sitting against the tree roots. Snow drifts over the mounds . . . and the dead sleep cold in the small hills above the Jarama River. . . .
>
> For our dead are a part of the earth of Spain now and the earth of Spain can never die. Each winter it will seem to die and each spring it will come alive again. Our dead will live with it forever. . . .

Those who have entered it honorably, and no men ever entered earth more honorably than those who died in Spain, already have achieved immortality.[47]

In her articles for the American Negro Press, Nancy often addressed African American interests. For many blacks, the Spanish Civil War was an extension of the Ethiopian crisis, another example of the blacks' centuries-old struggle against oppression. Mussolini's support of right-wing groups in Spain had transformed black Americans' anger at Ethiopia into outrage. Their attitude was, as Danny Duncan Collum and Victor A. Berch subtitle their study of this subject, "This ain't Ethiopia, but it'll do,"[48] and, as such, many adopted the Communists' slogan: "Ethiopia's fate is at stake on the battlefields of Spain." Those who went to fight in Spain, as Nancy wrote frequently, became the pioneers of an integrated military, as yet untried in the United States. The many African Americans who joined the Abraham Lincoln Brigade fought alongside the International Brigades. They were a heterogeneous group from all walks of life. One American volunteer hoped his participation abroad might help in saving the world:

> Since this is a war between whites who for centuries have held us in slavery and have heaped every kind of insult and abuse upon us, [why] am [I] here in Spain today? . . . Because we are no longer an isolated minority. . . . Because if we crush fascism here we'll save our people in America, and in other parts of the world from the vicious persecution, wholesale imprisonment, and slaughter which the Jewish people suffered and are suffering under Hitler's fascist heels.[49]

Paul Robeson and Langston Hughes, also writing for the ANP, frequently discussed the complexity of blacks fighting on opposing sides. Like Nancy, they found no color prejudice or condescension toward blacks among the Spaniards. If anything, they saw them mingling socially and believed the Spaniards resented Franco's conscription of the Moroccans, the very people who had ruled Spain from the eighth to the fifteenth century. Some black volunteers in the International Brigades, however, resented that "their darker brethren, laboring under the yoke of colonial oppression, were fighting on behalf of the fascists." Black novelist Richard Wright tried to explain that the fascists had duped and defrauded a terribly exploited people.[50] Hughes captured the poignancy of the blacks' dilemma in his poem "Letter to Spain":

> We captured a wounded Moor today.
> He was just as dark as me.
> I said, Boy, what you been doin' here
> Fightin' against the free?

Waiting for the End

Nancy and Banting left Madrid at the last minute allowed by their special permit. The trip back to Barcelona via Valencia was unbearably cold as they sat on the floor of an open truck, and they reached Valencia in the midst of an air raid. Another truck driver took them to Barcelona, but he was drunk, which made the ride dangerous and unpleasant. Once they arrived in Barcelona, they were questioned about irregularities in their passports. Banting later remarked that they were lucky not to have been imprisoned and that Nancy had been "much braver than I through the whole complicated" day. When Nancy left Barcelona, she did so in the charitable fashion in which she always left Spain: "There is plenty of evidence that on all her trips to Spain during the war Nancy was as generous as she could possibly be; giving away money, clothes, cigarettes whenever she could, buying food if she could find any and taking it to people she knew were in need."

Shortly after she returned to Paris, Samuel Beckett was hospitalized for a near-fatal chest stabbing. Nancy visited him often, brought him gifts, and tried to cheer him up. After he recovered, they went out frequently. Beckett wrote a friend about how pleased he was to see Nancy, although he thought she had become obsessed with Spain.[51]

Nancy was overwhelmed by the daily reports of Hitler's activities and frustrated by her inability to be on the front lines of any fight: "Back there in the new year of 1938 . . . we were overshadowed by all that was going on; that month it was Austria. . . . One had a premonition of everything going bad. [One thought of] Nazi boots marching through the streets of Vienna." She continued: "I think I have never read so many newspapers as at that time. The effect in English is a sledge-hammer; in French 'un coup de massue,' and I had both. One is worn out, suffocated, emptied of thought. All that remains is a furious sense of indignation. How much I would have preferred to be a regular press-correspondent, to have been right in the vortex at that time."[52]

Since this was not possible, she pursued her study of the living conditions and background of the Moors. She and Norman Douglas traveled to Tunisia in April, and Nancy submitted reports to the ANP, generally on the ills of colonialism and specifically on the terrible poverty and living conditions she witnessed. Three weeks later, she was back in France. She traveled to Geneva and heard the French and British reaffirm their noninterventionist policy in Spain. Once again, she condemned both nations in a series of articles. It was as if the international community wanted to eradicate Spain from the face of the earth:

The nonintervention of France and the other democratic powers was fatal to the Republican cause. Although Roosevelt did declare his support, he ceded to the pressure from his Catholic constituency and did not intervene. Neither did Léon Blum in France. We'd never hoped for direct participation, but we had thought that France, like Germany and Italy, would at least authorize the transport of arms and volunteers.[53]

En route to Réanville, Nancy met a woman named Narcisa, whose husband had disappeared during the massacres of Badajoz. She took Narcisa and her fourteen-year-old son, Gervasito, to Réanville, happy to have them in her home. Within the month, however, when it became clear that Franco would be victorious and that there would be hundreds of thousands of refugees in Barcelona, she became desperate to return to Spain. She left Narcisa and Gervasito in Réanville for Barcelona, where she reported:

> Everything could be summed up . . . by that terrible word "hunger." It was indeed nigh-starvation. . . . With such hunger, how could anyone be surprised at people rushing into the smoking ruins even before the arrival of the rescue-squads? . . . It might shock some to hear of emaciated citizens hunting about for a few dried beans in the shambles among the dead.[54]

After two months, she returned to Paris, "ill, . . . without a penny, and scantily clothed, having felt I must leave everything possible to the bombed-out people in Barcelona." She could not get a hotel room in the city: "Paris seemed rather odd. . . . What was happening? I had seen no papers for forty-eight hours. Presently, it became clear: the first day of 'Munich week.' Soon enough I too felt I had not my head today." She did the only thing she could do: "For me, that last winter of 'Peace-in-our-Time' was spent entirely in writing articles and raising money for Spanish relief. My wish was to get back to Spain." She planned to return in November but was detained by a series of urgent medical treatments for a month.[55]

● ● ●

Nancy asked W. P. Crozier, editor of the *Manchester Guardian*, if she could cover the refugees' exodus from Spain. He agreed to publish her articles with a byline—uncommon in the *Guardian*—but Nancy would have to pay her own expenses. Crozier had two correspondents covering the story from Rome and Paris; Nancy would be his only eyewitness reporter in Spain. Her articles were unique in their depth and candor, compared with the others, whose photos and information were borrowed, for example, from *Le Soir*.[56] Nancy's journalistic style, not uncommon at the time, was colorful and often subjective: she used words like "wretched" and "appalling," and at times began autobiographically: "Today I walked to Le Perthus . . ." Crozier published both her articles and her letters to the editor. Soon after she started, he thanked her for the "extremely useful" and "admirable" articles: "As you will see, we have been giving them prominence."[57]

12

Exposing the Concentration Camps After Franco's Victory

The only thing in view of the circumstances surrounding our epoch that can keep the hope of better times alive within us is the heroic struggle of the Spanish people for freedom and human dignity.

—ALBERT EINSTEIN

The early months of 1939 were marked by a number of whirlwind victories for Franco: Tarragona fell on January 14; Barcelona, January 26; Gerona, February 5; and Catalonia, February 10. On February 27, France and Germany officially recognized Franco's government, and Manuel Azaña resigned as president of Spain. Madrid held out until March 28; shortly thereafter, Valencia capitulated. When the last Republican forces surrendered, on April 1, victory was proclaimed.

After the fall of Barcelona, 500,000 refugees sought safe haven in France, where, in fact, tens of thousands would die in concentration camps at the border near Perpignan. Advertised as "stopping points" or "reception centers," as Pierre Vidal-Naquet has written, many camps, while modest in comparison with Adolf Eichmann's, were grim and barely endurable; many were later operated by Vichy collaborators as transit camps before Auschwitz.[1] The French camps for the Spanish Republicans set up at Gurs, Vernet d'Ariege, and Argèles, among others, merely expanded their population during World War II to include Jews and other "undesirables." Unable to return to Franco's Spain after the civil war, the 7,000 to 8,000 Spanish Republicans finally released from the camps took refuge in France, only to be rearrested and placed in Mauthausen and other camps. With Hitler and Franco in agreement, they were then shot or literally worked to death in stone quarries.[2]

As soon as Nancy received W. C. Crozier's letter of introduction, she headed for the Cordoba area and reached Perpignan on the day Barcelona capitulated, January 26. For this occasion, Franco proclaimed: "The splendid victory of Barcelona is a new chapter in the history of Europe which we are creating. . . . [If] the word of [the established] order . . . was 'They shall not pass,' . . . we have passed, and I say now that we shall pass." Franco's rebels had walked into Barcelona without any resistance.

There were two explanations. The first was that the army was broken after a month of valiant fighting and was badly in need of guns and ammunition. Soldiers were starving, due to the enemy's destruction of their food delivery systems and the food shortage in general. Even the weather seemed to have favored Franco, providing his bombers with sunny skies, whereas the passes through which the Republican army retreated were overcast with heavy snow clouds. The other explanation was that the Republican army decided not to resist, since additional, incessant bombardment would have created an inhuman massacre of the civilian population. All remaining arms could then be withdrawn to the high command and sent to the remaining fronts in Madrid and Valencia.[3]

Reuters reported that after Barcelona fell, Franco was opposed to setting up a neutral zone for refugees on Spanish territory.[4] Before then, the French had vacillated about allowing Spanish Republicans to cross their border. At various times, they had permitted civilians, the wounded, and the ill to enter the country. By January 28, any endeavor to go elsewhere was useless. Trains were stopped in Gerona, and Franco's bombers had destroyed Barcelona's port so escape by sea was impossible. When 15,000 Spanish refugees crossed, they believed they were going to centers organized to care for them, but circumstances had changed radically.

The story of their plight in squalid, often mortal detention, has become a commonplace of the last half of the twentieth century. But at the time Nancy followed the Spanish refugees and described their misery to the world, she was among the first to report on this deathwatch of modern times.

Since the start of the war in 1936, the French, having endorsed a non-intervention policy, had debated the refugee issue. Military personnel were considered particularly undesirable, and every effort was made to immediately repatriate those who had entered the country. At various points, officials argued for the expulsion of distinctive refugee "types," including invalids, the mentally or physically ill, and, most inclusively, anyone in need of material assistance. Those on the Right were vocal about the Spaniards' Communist connections (Would there be a Communist plot against France?) and the expense of housing the refugees. Many also openly expressed concern that France would become "the dung heap of the world," welcoming moral and mental deviants of every sort. Needless to say, the Popular Front, completely at odds with this position, insisted that asylum was a right, not a privilege, and that any other attitude was nothing less than xenophobic.[5]

In 1939, after Barcelona fell, a brief period of hysteria prevailed in the city: book dealers destroyed publications potentially irritating to fascist readers; civilian doctors abandoned a large hospital. The government immediately directed an orderly evacuation of civilians, and the exodus to the borders at Perpignan was swift. Although the French agreed to accept the Spanish refugees, they were totally unprepared for the sheer volume that arrived.

The two coast roads to the border were choked with traffic at the same time that German planes machine-gunning these roads massacred thousands of men, women, and children. Blind soldiers groped their way amid crowds; orphans looked to strangers for protection; women gave birth in open carts; children ran wildly from their families, screaming as they tried to escape the bombs overhead. ("Why have the Reds ordered this lamentable exodus?" asked the rightist press. Others asked, "Why has Franco ordered it?") Those who survived, many of whom had to walk forty miles to a frontier, were exhausted, starving, and frightened; there had been no bread in Barcelona for five days, and electricity and water had been cut by the enemy. The weather was brutally cold; it rained or snowed every day. Hundreds of children contracted pneumonia and died. Many of the aged and ill were left behind.

The very effort to cross the border was onerous. Spanish and French officials on both sides made the exodus and entrance difficult. The Spanish guards were Francoists, and the French soldiers intimidated both the refugees and the local people sympathetic to them. As the refugees entered France, gendarmes pushed them around, and men in white coats asked the women if they were virgins; they asked both men and women if they had venereal disease. One young woman recalled, "My friend Nina, who spoke French, burst into tears as she translated this."[6]

It seems unthinkable that the French agreed to accept 2,000 people a day when during the first two weeks some 350,000 to 500,000 arrived. A nation was sitting, praying, lying, walking, and weeping everywhere in sight. Once the refugees were in Perpignan, it became clear that the local population had been ordered not to assist anyone with food or drink. William Pickens understood the politics of neutrality as the politics of plenty and starvation: "In Southern France are fruits, the best in the world, food in abundance, . . . [and to the Spanish] food, worth its weight in gold. . . . That is 'neutrality.'" To Pickens, the French and their despicable behavior deserved no sympathy: "When there is a human fight going on, other humans cannot be neutral. . . . When a thug attacks the innocent, . . . one certainly then is far from neutral. In an effort to keep the peace with Italy and Germany, is war being avoided or its ultimate horrors lessened or increased by yielding to the bullying type of state heads?"[7]

With everything growing worse hour by hour, as Nancy wrote, Perpignan became, in a day, the "hub," "the center," of the world.[8] Nancy's first two lengthy reports, which she wrote on January 28 and January 31, after waves of refugees had crossed into France ("Today more than ever Franco stands condemned and judged for eternity"),[9] arrived in London within a day of each other, and Crozier published both on February 1. Nancy related the chaos and despair of 300,000 starving people near Le Perthus, Cerbère, and Bourg Madame, when only several thousand had been allowed to cross. Her focus now, as in most of her reports, was twofold: (1) the desperate exodus of the civilian refugees and their arrival at often deplorable destinations and (2) the abominable conditions at the military concentration camps. In the beginning, she was grateful to the French for providing sporadic transport and food. But before long, she saw the spread of typhus, scabies, and rickets among children, as well as the array of diseases suffered by their parents. She was unfortunately correct in predicting the reprisals the Republican Army and particularly the International Brigades would face once they crossed the border. Her earliest report to the *Guardian* from Le Perthus, eighteen miles from Perpignan, began:

> In the cold wind of this narrow mountain village . . . have trudged and waited and stood day-long these broken thousands of refugees. . . . What we have seen today is the first fraction of all that is staggering up painfully on foot. . . . The entire road . . . is filled, blocked, damned with humanity . . . fleeing the advance of the Franco armies. . . .
>
> The tide is made up of women ["80 per cent"] and babies and children and old people and cripples and wounded civilians and a large number of wounded soldiers. All ages, all types—the tradesman, the peasant, the visibly once well-to-do—those . . . who have lost everything in Asturias, Bilboa, Malaga, Madrid, Barcelona. . . .
>
> The scene is on the scale of the whole tragedy of Spain. Almost without exception the refugees are in a frightful condition; they have suffered for so many months now. . . . Families get separated; at moments the men are kept back and the women told to go on; the infants cry; a child comes by bravely carrying a doll as big as herself. . . . The feeling is "Let in all the women, children, old people and wounded [soldiers]. But the fit Spanish soldiers. No." What is to happen to these?

"Yesterday," Nancy continues, she walked with hungry refugees for several miles to La Junquera in the pouring rain and saw that "hundreds are now lying among the rocks between here and Le Perthus. There are no rocks ample enough to shelter them." Wherever she walked, she saw scenes of horror. Villages had been decimated. Houses, once of rock, brick, and earth, were now sprawling ash heaps: "It is impossible to describe the wreckage from these powerful explosives that fell from the sky. Jupiter had no thunderbolt as terrific as these bombs."[10] Humanity was in ruins, the wounded carrying the more severely wounded, mothers embracing children who were already dead.

Nancy pursued a grueling and exhausting routine. As she told Janet Flanner many years later: "I used to consume tea with rum in it and aspirin, which resulted in getting up enough strength to rush out scouring Perpignan" to try to get transportation "that would take me to the army [and] Spanish refugees on the very frontiers." Typical of the modus operandi in all her causes, she spoke to as many people as she could. She found one group during their fifty-eight-hour trek, intoning, "On, on we trudge 'til we are buried alive / Being not men, not anything." Sometimes she walked to the frontiers and forced herself to talk to the arrogant and swaggering Falangists and French officials. Frequently she walked in the rain and sleet to join the refugees. Did they know that before long people from all over Europe would walk the same road? More than once—on the road to Figueras, for example—she, too, had to throw herself to the ground as bombers flew above. Wherever she went, she memorized the words and subjects she would write about.

Early Reports After the Fall

It is clear, early on from her more than thirty articles in the *Guardian*, that Nancy traveled frequently to Le Perthus, Cerbère, Bourg Madame, La Junquera, Gerona, and Figueras. She wrote about husbands and fathers "torn from their families in a fiendish, often violent way." Men were segregated from women, children, and the elderly, and either group was placed in any of several units—in prisons, barracks, factories, convents, barns, or open shacks—all in various stages of dilapidation. As she left the camps, she passed endless streams of starving people on the road unable to find shelter from the bitter cold, often sleeping under trees and on muddy roads or in the open in rain and snow.

"The Exodus from Spain" is one of Nancy's more positive reports about the camps, despite the menacing presence of the French army and hunger and other problems of the refugees. She describes "the French soldiery [with] stacked rifles . . . and squads of men . . . being drilled"; the variety of functioning or abandoned vehicles, particularly wheelbarrows, pervading the landscape; the wretched weather and ceaseless pleas for bread. She writes of "pitiful little groups . . . camp[ing] out, washing their clothes in the streams [with] small camp-fires all along the mountain. There are many babies in arms and infants at the breast." One woman who escaped Gerona with her sick husband tells Nancy that eight planes followed them, machine-gunning them, and when they reached the border they received 20 francs for their life savings of 11,000 pesetas. Filling out the day's events, she mentions ten vans transporting art to Geneva in the midst of continuing "violent bombing." One of the heroic drivers naïvely had asked her, "They attack even the works of art of a country?"[11]

On some days, like the one at Le Perthus, presumably a neutral camp, she forced herself to initiate interviews that disgusted her. The Falangists had been victorious, and "today, at 3:00 in the afternoon, the advance-guard of Franco's troops hoisted their red and yellow flag." At 4:30, Nancy spoke to two of them, in their red, bobbing berets. They boasted of their victories nearby and in Barcelona on January 26: "Between Figueras and Le Perthus there has been no resistance." In the midst of what she called their "insolence" and "overbearing conversation," unidentifiable shots rang out on a nearby mountain. Were they "executions" or the "emptying of civilians' rifles?" There "seemed to be too many for the latter."[12]

She returned to a freezing, dingy hotel room in Perpignan in the middle of the night. Exhausted, shivering, and hungry, and with virtually no light in the room, she wrote three to four pages on the exodus, which she airmailed to the *Guardian*, a combination of fact and impression. She detailed how the Francoists were ignoring basic rules of decency regarding women and children. After a bombing at both Le Perthus and Figueras, it was necessary to evacuate the many wounded women and children to a hospital at La Junquera. One raid had killed 60 and wounded 200. But as Nancy walked to La Junquera, she was horrified to discover that "the Francoists bombed and machine-gunned" everyone on the road so that "all the wounded women and children . . . were victims" before reaching the hospital. Such crimes as this," she concluded, "are beyond comment."[13]

She wanted to publish good pieces, asking Crozier for "some criticism, some suggestions. Are [the articles] too long or too much about refugees?" He immediately replied, "We are printing at present everything you are sending. . . . Your articles are admirable and are just about the right length."[14] After a twenty-hour day and posting her articles, Nancy stopped for her first meal and rest. A dreaded final activity of the day was the hour-long wait at the Prefecture, pleading for another stamp on her permit.

Although undernourished herself, Nancy once again collected food, which she carried by truck to the frontiers. Daphne Fielding describes her distribution of food: "In no time the little she had been able to carry had disappeared into the forest of clawing hands, and even her own hands were scratched and bleeding." On one occasion, a woman cried to her, "Wild beasts—that's what we've become." Nancy also started a food campaign as soon as she arrived in Perpignan, wiring Crozier: "Beseech you open fund immediately in *Guardian* for possibly as much as 500,000 starving Spanish refugees pouring in stop situation catastrophic stop press wire accompanies at my cost wire answer.—Cunard/Hotel Loge/Perpignan." Crozier replied at first with regret, "We cannot open another fund so soon after our last. . . . Every week we print letters about the refugees from one country or another—China, Spain, Czechoslovakia, Germany—and . . . our readers are steadily contributing the whole time."[15] But Nancy was determined. She telegrammed repeatedly: "Up to five hundred thousand starving Spaniards stop eighty per cent women, babies, children stop crippled stop wounded civilians and wounded soldiers pouring into France. . . . This is a frantic S.O.S. for money for food help stop. . . . Rush money to Manchester Guardian Fund.—Nancy Cunard." The *Guardian* opened a fund and collected hundreds of pounds of food, assisted by ads in the *News Chronicle* and *Daily Chronicle*. Nancy herself wrote the advertisements.[16] Then she requested aid for a nonpolitical food-distributing center, the Centro Español food kitchen. Crozier asked her for another ad, and the center received enough money to eventually feed 200 at one time; hot meals were prepared daily for as many as 3,000 to 4,000 people.

Until February 5, the French had rounded up the Spanish soldiers who had slipped through border control and sent them back to Franco's Spain. After that, with no Republican resistance remaining at the frontiers, the French government opened the predominantly military concentration camps at Arlegès-sur-Mer, Saint-Cyprien, Les Haras, Le Boulou, Céret, Fort Bellegarde, Arles-sur-Tech, Amélie-les-Bains, and Prats de Mollo. Nancy walked up to twenty miles each way to visit these camps. Hundreds of exhausted soldiers, she wrote Crozier, marched "to the hell of the internment camp," but there was "no . . . sense of defeat. . . . Another *fait accompli* has been handed to the dictators." Capa photographed soldiers, both as they remained in step on their way to the concentration camps and as they were treated once they arrived, images that support Nancy's contention, among others, that there was a total lack of civility, let alone camaraderie, between the Spanish and French military.

The Spanish soldiers carried their rifles over their shoulders until they reached their last step on Spanish soil. Some stroked their steadfast companions before gently laying them down. Then they surrendered with dignity, in silence. They were searched; their sacks were searched. After this, all their belongings were thrown into a lime ditch. They knew that not all their fellow soldiers had been captured; some had remained in the villages awaiting the Francoists, aware that they faced certain death in challenging the enemy.

Nancy wrote Crozier: "I don't know in what proportions," adding a note of reluctant foreboding: "All I know is that, in a mood very far indeed from looking for symbolism, the last thing I saw yesterday on the roadside in Le Perthus was a broken guitar."[17]

On February 9, Nancy described the French double standard in their treatment of the Falangists and Spanish Republicans in what amounted to French complicity with the fascists:

> French forces fetch away the stacks of war equipment the Republicans have handed over. [Yet] there are numbers of Spanish fascist soldiers, all . . . armed, swaggering up the half-French, half-Spanish hill. They have been allowed a perfectly free entry with their revolvers on them. . . . Today, the royalist fleur-de-lys and the arrows of the Falange can be seen on what is, mainly, French soil; their song breaks out on the mountain, back of here—something like the Italian fascist hymn, "Giovinezza."[18]

She had spent the day watching a scene of military surrender amid what seemed to be the exodus of an entire country: "From 9 until 4:30 I have been watching soldiers pass the frontier-line. They have come by in thousands. . . . Spanish soldiers give up their arms in an orderly way. . . . But all this is only the beginning. . . . On the mountains [on] each side others come, so that the whole land- scape seems to be moving, soldiers on horseback, wounded men, women, children, a whole nation."

With so many crossing, an orderly routine was established for the refugees: "At noon a whistle blows, the frontier is declared shut . . . for twenty minutes or so, [so] that all those trudging up the hill may leave room for the next thousands to enter." A squad of forty in their French blue uniforms "marches smartly" to relieve the frontier guards:

> The refugees arrive with their best possessions, which they surrender—arms, cars, lorries, vans, trucks, petrol tanks, water tanks, and what becomes a herd of horses and small flock of goats and lambs. They repeat, "We have given up everything, so why do they want to fire at us?" Some continue on six miles to Le Boulou, under bomb explosions. Hundreds at Céret walk along dark, damp, and cold mountain paths. Some of the French curse them, while others whisper, "Humanity itself commands us to do all we can for such misery."[19]

In the beginning, Nancy found few differences in the treatment of civilians and the military. On February 10, she visited Le Boulou, which housed men, women, and children. It was not fit to receive human beings. . . . [There are] thousands of men, women and children [in] wire fencing. . . . It is a horrible sight, and all . . . are in the utmost depression. [On] grass trodden down into a sort of grey compost they sleep, in the open.

The lack of medical aid was acute: the wounded lay in ditches; people limped in agony; mothers watched their children die. Many wondered: "Are we worse off here to-day than we might be in Spain?" Some said, "I have heard they want to send us back to Franco." Every comment seemed to end with "I don't know." In the midst of this was an ongoing prostitution industry. As Nancy put it: "Some Marseilles white-slave traffickers have made their appearance. There are many pretty girls in the Spanish migration."[20]

The Military Camps

Nancy typically visited the military camps for a day at a time. They were located in three areas of the Pyrenees—all beautiful farmlands that produced some of the world's finest fruits, vegetables, and grains. Argèles-sur-Mer, where the first army camp opened, had been known for its fine beaches and always attracted a large tourist population. South of Argèles was the area known as Roussillon: the fishing village of Collioure, along with Saint-Cyprien and Barcarès. To the west, near the high peaks of the Pyrenees, were Cerbère, Le Perthus, and Bourg-Madame, where temperatures remained frigid for long stretches of time. Most of the fifteen or so concentration camps were set up in these areas.

Nancy's reports on these camps deserve a place in any historical chronicle of this period: "The conditions in . . . Cerbère, Argèles, Fort Bellegarde, and elsewhere are appalling," she wrote, and the camps are run with "an iron discipline that would be extreme for the worst criminal-convicts in society." Five miles wide, Argèles, for example, faced the sea on one side; on the other, a sandy desert was surrounded by barbed wire and hundreds of armed guards. The soldiers were routinely brutalized—stabbed with a bayonet, hit with the back of a rifle, or kicked in the back—by squads of French soldiers and mobile guards who addressed them with insults and contempt.

Nancy visited Argèles several times, entering through pine glades but finding "not a single tent or shelter of any kind." About 72,000 soldiers lay on the damp, cold ground in subhuman conditions; they slept in the open air. Denied even straw, provided at a few camps, they had dug holes in the filthy sand for their beds. There was no water for washing, no latrines, and barely water for drinking. The stench was overwhelming. The wounded remained untreated for days and weeks; many had to have arms and legs amputated by their comrades. There was nothing to be done if an amputee started bleeding. Less horrific but common was the need of an amputee to ask a friend to cut off a piece of flesh dangling from the remnants of a limb or finger blown off by a grenade.

Once when Nancy visited, she saw three Spanish doctors (no French) and three nurses working "in the wind that blows sand and filth into an open shed." Hundreds in dirty bandages with suppurating wounds remained on the frozen ground; many had high fevers and were suffering from bronchitis and pneumonia. Nancy tried to describe the despondency and anguish among those starving to death, including new prisoners, who had to wait five days for food and were then allotted two ounces of bread and one of rice—for a forty-eight-hour period.

The men tried to help the newcomers by pulling a broken arm or leg into place. Then they cut branches off trees for splints. They bound rope around filthy dressings just to retain a covering for a wound; old dressings were reused; many injuries became gangrenous. Maggots crawling out of casts aroused no concern: this was not injurious, since maggots ate only decayed flesh. On any day, hardly an hour passed without screams filling the air, due to appendicitis, food poisoning, festering wounds, or gangrene. The Right continued to connect the Red Menace with the sick prisoners who might spread epidemics.

There was a clear purpose in establishing such atrocious conditions: to encourage the men to return to Spain, where in all likelihood they would be killed. "Return to [Franco's] Spain," blasted the loudspeakers, and rumbas and tangos blared between announcements. Nancy learned that the 2,000 men who later were willing to return were given every amenity. She grew increasingly worried about the hundreds from the International Brigades at Argèles, since many had been shot at other camps that held brigade prisoners. She wanted to know if those at Argèles might be repatriated to their native countries.[21] She kept up her morale with the extraordinary fantasy that at some future date she would go to Latin America to find a home for these people.

Nancy also visited Saint-Cyprien often; it had opened a week after Argèles. Some 60,000 men struggled here to survive a similar environment devoid of shelters, electricity, toilets, and an infirmary. Its population eventually reached somewhere between 72,000 and 95,000. One day's food rationing included a piece of bread and a tin of two sardines. She entered through a "shambles of broken cars and lorries." It was a special day: "The fields are strewn with dead mules; tonight the 'lucky' ones will eat them in the camp. I saw such a stew being made." As in Argèles, she wrote, "sand and litter of all sorts" blow in the mistral; one could hardly stand up. This was a particularly brutal winter, with "many cases of frostbite and of death from hunger, exhaustion, and exposure." Again, as at Argèles, some of the interned were "bearing up"; others remained "intensely dejected, but none . . . mutinous." They, too, dug little hollows, "as ineffective as a child's sand castles, in which to try to sleep." In many of these camps, a sea of humanity "stretched to the horizon patrolled by Senegalese with bayonets and French Mobile Guards." When new Republican soldiers entered the camps, Spahis from Algeria and French colonial officers pointed "swords and rifles" at their backs and broadcasting vans simultaneously announced: "All facilities will be given men who go back to Spain." Nancy concluded her article: "Such is the military escort of disarmed and exhausted ex-combatants from Spain. Everything [is] done to get them to [go] back to Spain—Franco's Spain." One of the "best" camps was said to be Barcarès, ten miles north of Saint-Cyprian; there were 300 barracks and a paved road—for 13,000 inmates. A military truck arrived once a day with loaves of bread that were hurled into the air, leading to frantic scrambling among the starving.[22]

As Nancy traveled from camp to camp, she saw how Minister of the Interior Albert Sarrault's orders for strict discipline had been meticulously implemented; she observed the lies and insidious methods that achieved his ends. Early on, for example, she reported that French officials, instructed that Sarrault "would be more impressed with security than shelter," shrewdly ordered that barracks be built at Argèles. Naturally, the prisoner-laborers, all ill from exposure or wounds, including the amputees, worked vigorously to build the promised shelters. But once wooden stakes were planted in the ground, the men were ordered to stop working so that barbed wire could be placed around the stakes. Sarrault could now assure his nation that it need not fear "the return of the Spanish hordes." (On a later occasion, when wood was sent into the camp for "barrack construction," the men used it to build a fire, preferring certain warmth to possible deception.)[23] Often the soldiers who started a fire to keep warm were severely beaten.

For more serious offenses, prisoners were placed in the "hippodrome," a hundred-square-foot open-air structure that had a pillar in the middle. The accused, tied to the pillar, spent at least twenty-four hours in the cold, rain, and snow. The most aggressive troublemakers at centers like Le Vernet and Collioure (the site of a thirteenth-century castle) were placed in underground cells and "dealt with" from 6:00 A.M. to 7:00 P.M.—whipped, caned, and tortured in any number of ways. Another prison with no protection against the bitter mountain cold, Le Vernet was renowned for its intimate sleeping quarters: a twenty-one-inch sleeping space on a long wooden plank. If one man turned his body, everyone else was compelled to do the same. More serious violations led to eight days of imprisonment with no food or drink on the first day and bread and water thereafter. Le Vernet challenged its best-behaved prisoners to survive on bread, black coffee, and meatless and fatless soup, to which, on occasion, rotten raw beef was added. Arthur Koestler was imprisoned at Le Vernet.

The camps had many elements in common. In addition to brutality, physical deprivations, and daily humiliations, the prisoners were subject to terrible personal degradation. The food that was distributed, and it was always the same—white navy beans *or* red kidney beans *or* bread and sardines—caused rampant diarrhea. As a result, keeping clean was virtually impossible. With little water and no soap or toilet paper, the men found the smell of their clothing—and of their bodies—disgusting. If this was not sufficiently mortifying, the men were plagued with lice and fleas. Lice sucked more blood, but fleas were more painful. It was impossible to grab the fleas, because they moved so rapidly (and bit continuously). The men learned how to pop lice, squeezing their hard shells between both thumbnails. But even then, the lice left behind eggs, and there was no way to overcome the revolting vermin that filled the seams of their clothing.

For many, their greatest abuse was their treatment as prisoners of war, even though France was not at war with Spain. They felt both enraged and humiliated when they saw a comrade's spirit break and he agreed to be repatriated. It is not surprising that the press corps, physicians, social workers, and aid organizations were restricted from visiting the camps. There is little doubt that the Republican soldiers were treated more harshly than the POWs in German camps in both world wars.

Incarceration of the Intellectuals

In the middle of February, Nancy published several articles that listed a variety of health and mortality statistics, as well as the escalation of suffering from consumption, dysentery, typhus, pneumonia, skin diseases, malaria, and undefined high fevers.[24] She also began a series about the suffering of Spain's *noncombatants* interned at the military concentration camps, a subject that would have international reverberations:

> Practically the whole elite of Spain's intellectuals—scientists, men of letters and of art, musicians, architects, doctors, engineers, journalists—as well as state officials, civil servants and republican military commanders and officers are interned in the infamous concentration camps today at Argèles, St. Cyprien, Les Haras, Le Boulou, and all the others in the department of the Pyrénées Orientales. [Their] only crime was that of defending and remaining loyal to their rightful government. They have been received by France as criminals, and treated far worse than prisoners of

a country that France might be at war with. . . . Every obstacle possible is put in the way of friends or those vouching personally for their removal. . . . Insulted by guards and starving, surrounded by bayonets and sleeping in the icy wind on bare ground are poets of the standing of Auden, of Jean Cocteau [and Nancy provides a list, along with accomplishments].[25]

The international community was shocked and embarrassed by such reports. The renowned journalist Herbert L. Matthews was admonished by the *Times* and the *New York Times*, for which he wrote regularly, not to send "emotional reports" regarding the "inexcusably hardhearted treatment of the refugees by the French officials." But Nancy was undeterred in publicizing the scandal of these camps. Although Crozier was similarly hesitant to print her reports, once again, through her barrage of letters, she convinced him to publish sensitive material—that is, her condemnation of the French authorities. On February 3, she had alerted him of her determination to continue this coverage: "[It] is one of the greatest magnitude. . . . Frontier closed to all cars, vans, etc., which means that the few journalists who do get to Figueras, and back (another problem), do so by luck and chance. I'm going to make my try for it tomorrow. Thirty kilometers I think I *can* walk (I've done it before) if it has to be walking."[26]

Nancy continued her exposé of the military facilities housing thousands of "state officials, intellectuals, and men of science . . . where the French authorities are acting as virtual agents for Franco." She also questioned the Republican government's inefficiency following the collapse of Catalonia: authorities had waited in Perpignan for instructions without the slightest "indication of what [was] expected of them." Crozier accommodated her, if only briefly: "I have included a sentence of this message in the other joint article ["Misery in the French Refugee Camps"[27]] to the effect that the Spanish government was responsible for the lack of organization in the first place, but that the French authorities are responsible for present difficulties."

Two days later, Nancy sharpened her accusations against the French and their alignment with the fascists: "I have tried to keep this indictment of the French authorities as calm as possible [but] must such a scandal be passed over in silence? . . . Orders, obviously, come from Paris." She put the following to Crozier: "How can these things not be printed? They should be. But I know that you have to draw the line: it is very difficult for me to write." Crozier thanked her "very much" for her articles, noting that the *Guardian* had, "I think, been able to use all," except one.[28] When Nancy sent him a list of the artists and intellectuals at Argèles, she identified her source as a "Spanish official, . . . Señor Sanchez Ventura, of the Spanish Embassy in Paris," adding: "I trust there is no doubt as to the authenticity of all this. . . . Indeed, I hope you will not hesitate to publish these facts. If *we* had been Spanish we should most probably be in such camps now . . ."[29] A colleague wrote Crozier: "I do not like Miss Cunard's reference to authenticity. Would you get someone to report whether there is anything in this that we can trust? I do not think that the official whom she mentions is enough." Later, Crozier received notification that "all this is confirmed. . . . It seems certain that there is a great amount of ill-treatment of the Spaniards [by] the French military [and that] the local inhabitants are greatly sympathetic to the Republicans. . . . So probably most of what Miss Cunard says is true, but I do not see . . . the names of individuals in the camps. . . . I have seen them nowhere else." Crozier himself had verified Nancy's story, but since his sources included no names, he printed none.[30] Nancy informed Crozier that any journalist who had exposed these scandals was "now forbidden entry": most press passes to the camps were canceled for a period in both February and March, but Nancy managed to remain in Perpignan longer than most.

Following the Story Outside France

After visiting and reporting about two hospital ships in Port Vendras, Nancy took a boat to Oran. In February 1939, she was one of the first to look into the possibilities of settling the Spanish in this part of Algeria, in French Morocco. Crozier thought she was embarking on a monumental undertaking, but he provided appropriate letters of introduction. When the first British ship carrying refugees finally arrived in Oran, on April 8, the 2,300 aboard were forbidden to debark and were told that "the French are unwilling to shelter this 'extra burden.'" On April 19, nearly half of the 2,300 passengers were still on board, since there were no accommodations for them; they were also given the daily concentration camp food allotment of one piece of bread and a tin of sardines. The French, who also demanded a fee of 300,000 francs for the ship's entrance into French territory, removed "a vital part" of the ship's engine to ensure payment. Nancy later wrote: "From Oran I hear that North Africa is now 'tolerating' [the Spaniards'] presence, putting them in prisons, old jails that have been abandoned as unfit (!). And now the Central zone of Spain is going to come to Oran. And this is only Spain." She thought about the fate of Hitler's victims: "How many are coming out of Czechoslovakia?"[31]

Still writing for the ANP, Nancy sought out news of the International Brigades, particularly the Americans placed in San Pedro prison, near Burgos. She had to rally all her resources and contacts during the periods she left Perpignan to ascertain their travails. The Americans had been imprisoned with the Irish (the most famous being Frank Ryan, of Ryan's Express fame), and most had been captured at Jarama.

The brigadiers, she soon learned, were often treated as brutally as the Spanish soldiers. Guards at San Pedro enjoyed perpetrating sadistic rumors that everyone was going to be shot that night; they later pardoned most men. On the rare occasion doctors appeared, they worked without medication. Patients had to stand at attention and salute even if they were seriously wounded—for example, suffering the pain of a bullet still embedded in their bodies. Once again, screams of pain filled the prison. Soldiers built cemeteries, but it remains difficult to calculate the number who died.

When they tried to take up a collection to pay for a coffin, they were mocked. "The value of the peseta," Nancy explained, "had been obliterated. A thousand peseta note (once worth about 10,000 francs) was sometimes taken 'as a souvenir,' in exchange for one franc."[32]

Mass was compulsory at San Pedro. A photo of Franco was placed above the alter; below was one of the Virgin Mary. To the left and right were photos of Mussolini and Hitler. Machine guns aimed at prisoners were positioned at each corner of the room. Priests often sermonized about the men as rapists and murderers. Following the service, 200 prisoners were arbitrarily selected for solitary confinement and half rations for two months.

Back in the United States, appeals were mounted for the release of the brigade prisoners. Franz Boas, Franchot Tone, Orson Welles, William Zorach, William Rose Benet, and Manhattan Borough President Stanley Isaacs were among the earliest to sign one. The State Department worked diligently to get Americans released. The nation, however, remained divided between the pro-Francoists and pro-Republicans.[33] On February 19, 1938, in New York City, 11,000 pro-Francoists had gathered at the 107th Regiment Armory. The charismatic demagogue and radio priest Father Charles E. Coughlin was one of several speakers. He, like the others, praised Franco, Hitler, and Mussolini for their suppression of Communism. At about the same time, the Grand Exalted Ruler of the Elks presided over his organization's seventy-first anniversary dinner at the Biltmore Hotel, and several speakers denounced fascism before holding an auction of manuscripts and books; they raised $8,000 for exiled anti-fascist writers. Those present included Justice Hugo Black, Raymond Massey, Jean Muir, Rockwell Kent, and Lillian Hellman.

After several hundred members of the International Brigades returned home, the House Un-American Activities Committee set out to establish a relationship between them and the Comintern. Service records of the Lincoln Battalion veterans were marked SOD (Suspected of Disloyalty); veterans of the Abraham Lincoln Brigade, considered a Communist front, were fully investigated, and many suffered the consequences for a lifetime.[34]

In March, with Hitler's occupation of Czechoslovakia and England's concern over his escalating aggression, proliferation of concentration camps, and growing alliance with Mussolini, press coverage of Spain had diminished, with the exception of Franco's rejection of the Republicans' request for either armistice or amnesty. Amnesty would have permitted the previously neutral nations to offer shelter to the defeated Spanish Republicans. It was clear that countless civilians had no home to return to, that the militiamen in Spain would face certain execution, and that a massacre in central Spain was still possible. Nevertheless, the English, at first, could promise only that refugees from Spain, like those from Germany and Czechoslovakia, would be given [its] hospitality "when it was available."[35]

England and the United States sent money and food to private organizations on behalf of the Republicans; the British agreed to allow a certain number into the country if they were reviewed by appropriate committees or were "Spanish personalities"; the United States would accept a few hundred a year; Russia would accept none but contributed $125,000; Mexico was willing to accept a large group but could not pay for its transportation; South America acquiesced in accepting a "certain number" selected individually; Belgium had already taken in 2,000 to 3,000 Spanish children.[36] England considered sending the navy into Spanish ports as an act of mercy to evacuate the Republican government's last supporters, but several arguments undermined the proposal. First, if Franco assured the world there would be no reprisals, the operation would be unnecessary. Second, said Lord Halifax, the maneuver would involve evacuating 5,000 to 10,000 or more people without knowledge of their identity and culpability in regard to war crimes. Finally, the act of employing the navy was technically permissible only for life-threatened individuals, not for a mass evacuation.[37]

The situation for the Spanish and French at the beginning of March was this: Franco refused to repatriate all the refugees; the Catalan side remained closed; 250 returned each day on the Basque side. The French, with 500,000 on the border, requested compensation from Franco for the costs it had thus far incurred, $7.5 million, with an anticipated $5 million more each month, which the general refused. The French Right continued to express contempt toward the Spanish refugees, calling them "scum, thieves, murderers and criminals," and berated them for their ingratitude in regard to their "firm and benevolent care" in the camps ("When one thought of the devotion shown by the French health service, one's eyes filled with tears"). If anything, the Right maintained, the bulk of the Spanish should be repatriated, and this would be "Marshall Pétain's first task at Burgos."[38]

On March 12, Franco reopened all the frontiers in response to France's request, "on conditions which are not yet known," allowing 6,000 to 7,000 a day to return. Although French authorities said that no returnees would be shot, Ce Soir reported that "not much picking and choosing has been done." Two days later, the French minister of the interior officially declared that "if one's future was uncertain, he would not be returned." In short order, however, Franco set up military tribunals in various cities to round up Republicans for everything from military rebellion to knowledge of any offense committed during the war. Nancy wrote about the civilian refugees who had returned to Spain: "Nationalist patrols," she had learned, went "from house to house, searching for those not considered loyal" to Franco. Anyone could be arrested; if a man was not home, his wife or mother was taken.[39]

Louis Stern, in his excellent book *Beyond Death and Exile* (1979), has tried to come to terms with a troubling issue of the postwar period—the French attitude toward the Spaniards—and his remarks frequently echo Nancy's letters and articles. At first, he speculates, the French were torn between expediency and idealism. The opportunistic policies of the government of Edouard Daladier focused on the inevitable war to come, the possibility that the nation might fall prey to the Communists or to the Right, the pragmatic concern that epidemics would spread from the camps, and the concern that the Spanish radicals would upset the precarious equilibrium of the state and furthermore encourage vandalism and pillage. With the breakup of the Popular Front—except for *Le Populaire*—left-wing leaders and the press moved to the right as well. Ultimately, Stern believes, "the main thrust of [government] policy was to come to quick agreement with the new Franco government in Spain. In this light the Republican refugees hung like albatrosses about the neck of the Daladier government." As a result, "all Spaniards were depicted as bloodthirsty revolutionaries who, having been thwarted in their Marxist aims on their own soil, were now determined, in collaboration with the French Communist Party and the Soviet Union, to work their evil designs in France." As Stern explains, to the French mentality, each group—the Spanish Communists, socialists, Anarchists, POUM—was the same as every other one, even though the Communists and socialists disliked each other, and both hated POUM, which reciprocated the antipathy.[40]

French press coverage at the time reflected this position. Typical headlines were "The Army of Crime Is in France" and "Close Our Frontiers to the Armed Bands of the FAI [International Federation of Anarchists] and the POUM." Even *Le Figaro* wrote article after article that France was becoming a depository of undesirables and subversives. Ridiculous rumors were spread: Spanish arms had been stacked away by the International Brigades for the French Communist Party; the Spaniards' crimes ranged from their destruction of French property to their criticism of French food. The Spanish were even condemned for their "arrogance." In a word, it appeared that France would be safe only if the Spanish were incarcerated; the French well understood the public and private proclamations regarding "the perfidy of an entire nation and equated the Spanish republic with Communism."[41]

Finding a Home for the Refugees

After trips to Oran, Paris, and various parts of Spain, Nancy was allowed to return to Perpignan, and she wrote about the heightened misery within the concentration camps, with men still lying in the sand with open wounds oozing out of filthy bandages and with even more aggressively spreading dysentery, typhus, and skin diseases. The prisoners were still wearing the same clothing and underwear they had arrived in; they looked to Nancy as though they had been petrified in the sand. The complete idleness into which they had fallen after two and a half years of fighting, along with the absence of news of their families or of the war, had made them utterly disconsolate. Nancy informed readers that artists and writers could leave these camps if a friend or relative vouched for them in a statement authorized by the prefect of the county or of Perpignan.

She finally decided that if an energized population was not going to liberate anyone from these camps, she would attempt it herself. She had recently received a letter from her Barcelona friend Angel Goded, begging her to help him escape from Argèles: this is, he wrote, "the biggest favor I have ever asked in my life. I am counting on you to get me out of here, and I know you will." Nancy traveled to Argèles immediately and secured not just his release but also the release of four others, all of whom she soon took to Réanville. To assure the authorities of their nonpolitical identity and to enlist the assistance of the Paris organization seeking to rescue Spanish intellectuals, she identified four of the five men as "a famous writer, a well-known cartoonist, an important publisher, and an architect-archaeologist." The writer was the famous poet César Arconada.[42]

They were arrested in Paris. Nancy was informed that smuggling the Spanish into France was a serious offense and that the men would be sent back to Argèles. After two days of furious negotiation, she secured their clearance and whisked them off in a cab to Le Puits Carré, where they remained until early summer. She wrote Crozier, on March 22, "Back home with five refugees. "My 'pensioners' . . . will be going on to South America." They had been "at Argèles, where I went and got them out." With modesty, she said, "What luck to get them out," and explained her need for earlier discretion in writing him: "I will send you a copy of what happened. . . . Purposely I did not write it for the *Guardian*. . . . Anyway, now all have got their 'laisser-passer' from the

Mayor and the Prefect." Fearing that the camps would continue in the event of war and that Franco would conscript the Republican soldiers, as he had the Moors—and having already contacted officials in Mexico to receive the Spanish soldiers—she wrote eight days later:

> Now I am worrying about what will happen if there is war. It is obvious that the French authorities are keeping these hundreds of thousands in the camps to use them in that event. . . . The New World is the answer, and as soon as possible. . . . One thing I do know, and that is that Mexico is going to accept all those who had to leave Spain for political reasons. I had a long talk with a Mexican of the Commercial delegation in Paris the other day and he said that ships will soon be chartered to convey hundreds, and then, thousands.[43]

Persevering in her mission to find the refugees a home, Nancy asked Crozier on June 1 for a letter of introduction to authorities in Mexico, Central and South America, and the West Indies. Also concerned about Hitler's victims and the funds they, like the Spanish, would require, Nancy, a tireless crusader, pursued her editor, "wondering [about] *some* way of helping refugees of all the different nationalities to emigrate to British Honduras. There were two letters on this subject in the 'Times' a month or more ago. What do you think? How should one set about it? A petition to the Colonial Office? I am certain all your generous readers who never cease contributing would endorse one."
On June 6, he replied,

> I doubt whether anything much can be done by private individuals about countries like British Honduras. . . . In the first place a very extensive investigation is required to find out whether conditions are practicable for even a trial settlement. Such an investigation would have to be made, I think, by some such a committee as that which recently went to British Guiana, and I doubt whether inquiries by an individual could be adequate. . . . Very large sums of money would be needed, and I don't think they are likely to be forthcoming."

All the same, he sent her the letters of introduction that she had requested. She did not leave Europe until the end of the year.
On July 6, Nancy returned to Perpignan with David Scott of the *News Chronicle*. Like Scott, she was able to gain "*exceptional* permission to visit the camps which are open to hardly any journalist by a letter to the military and other authorities from the Ministère de l'Intérieur." Crozier immediately printed her appeal for an "Intellectuals' House" for those still in the camps, as well as her reports on camps she had visited for the first time, like Adge.

Nancy also wrote several unusual articles that month, including one about an art exhibit in a concentration camp; another, about Miguel Hernández, the Spanish poet condemned to death. She wrote Crozier that some of the released soldiers had settled in Mexico, Cuba, and the Soviet Union and asked him a favor for an extraordinary reason. She had some idea that *she* might make changes in the camps:

> Several of the camp military commanders have requested that a copy be sent them; they are fair-minded enough to accept such criticism as I have made, and maybe to agree with some. Please, if possible, in view of this, do not have their names cut out!

At the same time that she was writing to Crozier, she was awaiting a "prefect's permission" to take another "friend out of a camp to come and live in my house at Réanville."[44]

A Mythical Apparition

Everyone who knew Nancy has claimed that the major endeavor of her life—and her greatest disillusionment—was the Spanish Civil War. Nancy remained profoundly bitter that the international community had remained persistently indifferent to the war. When she returned to France in the fall of 1939, unable to visit Spain until after the war, she continued her one-person campaign for food. She stood on the streets of Paris with a sheet spread at her feet, asking for contributions "for the starving children in Spain,"[45] and she continued to ask friends for money and clothing. Although she tried to mitigate her anger over Spain's defeat with ongoing anti-Franco activities and publications, including the poems *Nous Gens d'Espagne*, she remained disconsolate about Spain's fate until her death.

She was proud to have been a part of the great mass of humanity that had traveled from the corners of the earth to help in the cause. The International Brigades, disbanded in 1938, had suffered enormous losses, but they would be immortalized for their victories at Jarama, Guadalajara, Brunete, Belchite, Levante, and the Ebro. Nancy kept in touch with some who continued to fight to free prisoners in the concentration camps of southern France or who later joined the maquis or fought in North Africa and Italy or on the Eastern and Western Fronts. La Pasionaria's farewell address to the International Brigades, on November 1, 1938, remains a stirring tribute to all who went to Spain:

Mothers! Women! When the years pass, speak to your children. . . . Recount for them how, coming over seas and mountains, crossing frontiers bristling with bayonets, sought by raving dogs thirsting to tear their flesh, these men reached our country as crusaders for freedom, to fight and die for Spain's liberty. . . . They gave up everything—their loves, their countries, home and fortune, . . . and said to us, We are here. Your cause, Spain's cause is ours. It is the cause of all advanced and progressive mankind.

Some 300,000 refugees eventually returned to Spain after World War II. After D-Day, the Spanish, with the Allies, had liberated seventeen towns in France. One group of Spaniards, in Spanish tanks (named "Madrid," "Belchite," and "Guadalajara"), with the Spanish Republican flag flying high, entered Paris with General Philippe Leclerc.[46]

Those who knew Nancy in Spain extol her unselfish and heroic work. Charles Duff recalled:

The very first thing she did was to allocate her house in France, and the whole of her income, to refugees, . . . and she did this with a snap of her fingers and at a time when she had practically no other visible resources. . . . "It doesn't embarrass me in the least to do this, well knowing that it leaves me penniless," [adding] with a smile, . . . "I think I can make some kind of a living—a good enough one as I'm very ingenious at living on the smell of an oil-rag. You'll see!"

The painter Delia del Carril later described her saintly behavior: "Her profound love for humanity compelled her to participate body and soul in every drama that burst out in this, our sad world. She spent an inexhaustible heartful of energy in divine help. Help! The most exalted word in all languages. She also desperately needed a little dose for herself but there were always others to think of." Delia recalled the words of a simple Spanish woman who had later migrated to France, one of the 500,000 Spanish Republicans who had been defeated by Franco, Hitler, and Mussolini:

When the old folks and children were suffering intensely and often dying of hunger, cold weather and desolation and when all doors and even windows there around were hermetically closed, only one person, a tall, slender, pale lady dressed all in white had come to them with a smile and a tender gesture, bringing milk and bread and sweets for the children. As I listened, first my heart and then my mind were connecting a dear name to that mythical apparition in the shape of an archangel fighting the beast for the sake of the innocent. Only one angel, and what if it was Nancy? And so it was.[47]

Nan Green, in Spain with the British medical corps, believed that Nancy had inspired a new generation of writers. She recalled her introduction to Nancy:

> I *became aware* of Nancy, rather than becoming first acquainted with her, as one becomes aware of a particular instrument in an orchestra or a particular color in a tapestry—and the tapestry was Spain: the Spain of 1936–1939, . . . the Spain of the people who decided it was "better to die on our feet than live on our knees" and thereby aroused the hope and admiration of anti-fascists the world over.[48]

She also recalled her modesty, how Nancy mentioned only in passing such occasions as her "turning into an agent of Providence" by saving one of Picasso's friends from the camps. Nancy later helped Nan organize an exhibition on the Spanish Civil War "to raise a new consciousness of the war," especially in its exhibit of towns like Guernica, a tragedy few remembered. The exhibit inspired Nancy to begin her last great writing, in a long poem about Spain.[49]

I want to conclude this important period in Nancy's life with a section of her war poem "To Eat To-Day," printed in the *New Statesman and Nation* on October 1, 1938. Nancy provides a fitting depiction of the tragedy to which she bore witness:

> "Helmeted Nuremberg, nothing," said the people of Barcelona,
> The people of Spain—"Ya lo sabemos, we have suffered all."
> Gangrene of German cross, you sirs in the ether,
> Sons of Romulus, Wotan—is the mark worth the bomb?
> What was in it? salt and a half-pint of olive,
> Nothing else but the woman, she treasured it,
> Oil, for the day folks would come, refugees from Levante,
> Maybe with greens . . . one round meal—but you killed her,
> Killed four children outside, with the house, and the pregnant cat.
> Heil, hand of Rome, you passed—and that is all.
> I wonder—do you eat before you do these things,
>
> . . . .
>
> On the simple earth
> Five mouths less to feed to-night in Barcelona.
> On the simple earth
> Men trampling and raving on an edge of fear.
> Another country arming, another and another behind it—
> Europe's nerve strung like catapult, the cataclysm roaring and swelling . . .
> But in Spain no Perhaps, and To-morrow—in Spain, it is, Here.

A Passionate Cause and a Passionate Love

Nancy and Neruda had been, and would continue to be, more than friends. Although Neruda was thirty-two when they met and Nancy was forty, she had gained a reputation for independence and courage and was still strikingly attractive. Her hair was cut short and brushed back like a golden helmet, and in her tailored suits (with a carnation in her lapel) and colorful shirts, "she was slenderness's own self"; when she turned "her steady and uncompromising gaze, . . . her eyes, like those of some cats, were lucent among their dark lashes, a pale and precious enamel in which had been fused a suggestion of gold-dust—a sentient enamel." If she "moved to put a cigarette or cup or glass to her lips, attention was inevitably attracted to her thin, fine-boned arms," now bare since she had left her bracelets behind.[50]

Shortly after they met, Neruda began writing brief notes to Nancy: "Nancy Darling, Only a few words to tell you that you are the loveliest charmingest person in the world, dear. Pablo." He would write love letters to her until she died, often proposing a rendezvous: "Nancy Darling, Je t'embrasse. Pablo"; "Darling, I am alone here. Delia is gone to Buenos Aires. . . . Cerio (Edwin) has given me a house for two months. (Lo Studio, Capri). . . . Pablo"; "Te abrazo with love. Pablo."[51]

He had gone to Réanville in 1937, presumably to help with the *plaquettes*, the collection of poems on the war, even though, as he admitted, he knew little about printing: "I started setting type for the first time and I am sure there has never been a worse typesetter." (For years to come, Nancy teased him by addressing him with the nonsense word he created when he transposed *p*'s into *d*'s, printing *párpados* as *dárdapos*: "My dear Dárdapo," she would write). Neruda recalled in his memoirs (published posthumously in 1974) his arrival at Réanville as one of romantic disorientation:

> It was night and the moon was out. The snow and the moonlight fluttered like a curtain around the estate. I went for a walk, filled with excitement. On the way back, the snowflakes swirled around my head with chilly insistence. I lost my bearings completely and had to grope my way through the whiteness.

When he made the trip, his wife of five years, Maria Antoineta Hagenaar, and he separated. Later, after the war ended, "Nancy went off to Chile to be with Pablo Neruda."[52] She spent several months there; Neruda helped her get a visa by informing "the authorities that he had invited Nancy to stay with him in Santiago."[53]

When they first met in Madrid during 1936, Neruda had involved Nancy in the kind of intellectual coterie she had loved during her London and Paris years. He had been organizing these groups since his student days in Santiago, when he and his friends discussed Proust and Joyce, unknown at the time in Chile. For many years after this, "passion" had become a favorite topic, and he loved to recite his erotic poems at these meetings, particularly if the woman who had inspired him was present.[54]

Neruda was an exceptionally warm, gregarious, and sensual man, often describing himself in his memoirs as a devotee of women, wine, and song who dallied with several women simultaneously, whether he was married or not. He loved beautiful women, and if they were talented and politically active, he idolized them. If Nancy were ever going to meet her match, it would be Pablo Neruda. W. B. Yeats may have immortalized the distant Maud Gonne as the love goddess of his life, but Neruda's muses were considerably more numerous and earthy: (1) Albertina Azócar Soto; (2) Josie Bliss; (3) Maria Antonieta Hagenaar, whom he married; (4) the painter Delia del Carril, whom he married and separated from; and (5) his last wife, the singer Matilde Urrutia.

Nancy found Neruda fascinating. Despite their different social backgrounds, they had had similar early experiences. Both had begun writing at the age of ten, after surrogate parents had awakened in them a love of language and literature—G. M., in Nancy's case; in Neruda's, the local schoolmistress, the future Nobel laureate Gabriela Mistral. Their adolescence was also similar, for it was a time when their passion for literature was paralleled only by their precocious sexual feats. When Neruda was about eighteen, he discovered his own Corrupt Coterie. "We student poets led a wild life," he remarked, providing the kind of details Nancy always withheld: "The lovely widow had not yet peeled off her dark clothing for me, the black and purple silks that made her look like a snow-white fruit covered with a rind of mourning. That skin slipped off one afternoon in my room, . . . and I was able to fondle and explore all that fruit of fiery snow."[55] As adults, Nancy and Neruda were political idealists of such conviction that both risked their lives bringing refugees out of Spain.[56]

Since her youth, one of Nancy's favorite activities, with men or women, was reading poems aloud, particularly those of her friends. One can only imagine Neruda reading to her an erotically audacious poem such as "Body of a Woman," which, like the poems in the Song of Solomon, addresses a woman/deity about passionate yearning and fulfillment. She is a cosmic power, and she both subdues and elevates his spirit. It is more difficult to imagine Nancy reading to Neruda the love poems she was composing, such as "Aramanth of Sunset," about her fear of their inevitable separation:

Was this the man for me, the final man? . . .
I see my poet walking by the shore, . . .
You to your life, mijito ["my dear, my darling"], I to mine.

In "At Dawn," she writes:

> No! I will sit and let the iambics play,
>
> . . . .
>
> Hell and Eternity have met today
> . . . and . . . I defy them . . .
> A stranger in your land.[57]

Nancy told Neruda a great deal about her life, and he was touched by her painful recollections. He admired her fearlessness and courage, her standing up not just to her mother but also to the whole of English society:

> I recall that she said—I am quoting from memory, and her words were more eloquent: "Suppose you, your white ladyship, or rather your people, had been kidnapped, beaten, and chained by a more powerful tribe and then shipped far from England to be sold as slaves, displayed . . . as ludicrous specimens of human ugliness, forced to work under the whip and fed poorly. What would be left of your race?"

He believed that Nancy could never live in England after that.[58]

Nancy's later reflections regarding Neruda, like those recalling other men in her life, were positive—descriptive, flattering, and nonromantic. Her comments regarding her trip to Santiago in 1940 abound with fond memories of swimming in the Pacific Ocean at Neruda's private beach (and she took numerous photos of them sunning themselves). She recounts going with him to bars and restaurants and, despite her lifelong dislike of food, devouring platters of succulent mussels and huge crabs, along with very potent white wine. She also spent time by herself, traveling to the poor sections of the city and watching the children, as she had in Harlem and North Africa. She translated several of Neruda's poems—to some, faultlessly. Her rendition of "To the Mothers of the Dead Militia" has been described as "an act of true communion," capturing completely Neruda's personality, movement, tone, and, especially, his music.[59]

Nancy commented many years later: "Maybe my going to Chile . . . saved my life." An ambiguous remark, she may have been speaking literally, since she also said, "Maybe I should have stayed in France, been interned, possibly shot, or taken the humiliating but necessary road to Bordeaux"[60] More likely, she was alluding to her postwar despair and sense of renewal in seeing Neruda again, along with her highly gratifying political negotiations en route. She may have been referring to her delivery of (or plans to deliver) refugees to South America, which the realities of wartime would soon prohibit. She cryptically wrote about her voyage to Chile on the *Yasukuni Maru*: "It was 38 days on the sea, [a] hell of various kinds [and] near sinking at [the] start, adding, "Even if these cross-the-world-things are NOT for wartime, I did have the best of reasons, . . . saving lives."[61]

Once she arrived in Chile and took care of her business, she joined Neruda and met his friends—now, in the Intellectual Alliance of Chile. She was, at first, welcomed. They called her "el Alamo" (the national tree) because she was long and lean. Although she added a touch of welcome zaniness to their fiestas, once performing an extravagant dance "by the light of the moon and covered with flowers," on other occasions, her behavior upset the group's equilibrium. As Fernando Sáez indicates, these alliances had been organized to keep alive the ideals of the war and to discuss poetry, and they were formed to cultivate companionship and civility without emotional attachments. Conversations at Neruda's alliance with their new member, Nancy, and with wine flowing in excess, often became disagreeable and fiery. Neruda was obliged to ask her to regain control and at times had to act as her caretaker. Entirely different with Neruda than with any other man, Nancy never argued. She usually went away—and stayed away.[62] Neruda's obvious fascination with her caused Delia del Carril to leave the group and form her own organization.

Although Neruda had wooed Nancy at the same time he was involved with Delia (and perhaps other women), he deplored Nancy's pursuit of her own additional Latin lovers. Perhaps she was returning to her old self-protective ways so that Neruda would realize, like Louis Aragon and Henry Crowder, that he could not have her exclusively. Neruda writes in his memoirs: "She took a poet as her lover ["a slovenly vagrant"], a Chilean of Basque descent with some talent but no teeth. What's more, Nancy's new lover was a hopeless drunk and gave the aristocratic English woman nightly beatings that forced her to appear in public wearing enormous dark glasses."[63]

Of Neruda's writing about Nancy, one of his critics, Rafael Osuna, author of *Pablo Neruda y Nancy Cunard*, believes that if we read his "jumping and cascading" language describing this woman, "two figures emerge and converge, crossed in our conscious mind and unconscious: one is of a curious, picturesque foreigner; the other of a noble and passionate rebel." Osuna goes on to say that ultimately the two figures merge: "It's as if the two figures are like an eclipse of the sun and shadow." He believes that Neruda understood that he appealed to her because of the complex relationship she engendered with men, especially Latin men: she was submissive in idealizing the devastating, manly type and at the same time dazzled by their mythic Don Juan persona, defined by their promiscuity.[64]

Volodia Teitelboim, one of Neruda's biographers who saw them together in Chile, treats Nancy as a "femme fatale": "Nancy was one of the myths of that period, . . . the last of those exquisite faint-voiced women who were purveyors of damnation and the cause of men's agony." Highly critical of her ("[A] wicked halo . . . surrounded her. . . . [She had] an imperious walk and an extravagant way of dressing, which she exaggerated after nightfall, the time for hunting"), Teitelboim reminds us of Aragon's passion for Nancy and his futile demand for her fidelity. He repeats and dramatizes Aragon's despair, as though warning Neruda from afar: "In my life there was one woman, one who was very beautiful, with whom I lived several years and with whom I was not meant to live." He also strongly disapproves of Nancy's promiscuousness: "If she wanted a man—and this happened with extraordinary frequency—she had to satisfy her desire at once," and then disingenuously or naïvely describes Nancy and Neruda's interest in each other as one limited to friendship: "He struck her as a warm human being who loved friendship, . . . and immediately introduced her to his Spanish poet-friends." To Teitelboim, Neruda is always "pure and moral," whereas Nancy is not. We are chastened about extending any sympathy toward Nancy, who, as Teitelboim unkindly puts it, "would be sunk like the (Cunard) *Titanic*."[65]

Nancy left Chile when Neruda was reassigned as consul to Mexico. Although Anne Chisholm writes that Nancy was in Chile when France fell in June 1940, according to Sáez, she was in Mexico with Neruda. She had boarded Neruda's ship in Santiago.[66] For the next twenty-five years, Nancy and Neruda retained deep feelings for each other, as well as lifelong pride in having rescued Spanish refugees. But while Neruda was able to go on with his life after the Spanish Civil War, Nancy could never put aside Spain's defeat.

● ● ●

Neruda would be on her mind during her final moments of consciousness.

52. An invitation to authors to "Take Sides"

53. Nancy's snapshot of soldiers in Franco's army

54. Nancy's three snapshots of soldiers in the Republican forces

55. Pablo Neruda

56. Nancy, at fifty-two

57. Bracelets, a part of Nancy's everyday dress

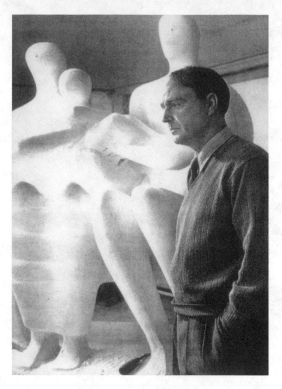

58. Henry Moore

59. Pablo Casals

60. Samuel Beckett

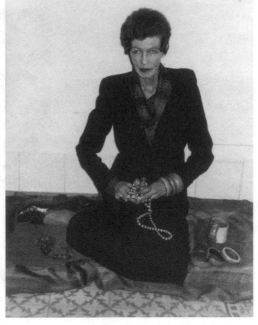

61. Nancy, ill, visiting friends

62. Nancy, flirting with a young Spanish boyfriend

63. S. C. Harrison, portrait of George Moore, Nancy's most cherished possession

13

Exile and Resistance in World War II

Pay attention, Hitler. . . . You must break them or be broken by them.
Therefore send your bombers, and more and more and more of them.
Spare no means. . . . Fling down fire. All is at stake.

But you must make haste: for hitherto they survive. Make haste. If
you leave them living it will be thought that there is something in the
world that the detonations do not shatter. Make haste, or their quietness
will echo round the world; their amusement will dissolve empires;
their ordinariness will become a flag; their kindness a rock, and their
courage an avalanche. Make haste. Blot them out, if you can.

—JOHN STRACHEY

In 1939, like many idealists during the Spanish Civil War, Nancy modified her
attitude toward the Western democracies, particularly England and France,
her two countries of residence. Russia, a former ally of the Republican forces,
signed its infamous nonaggression pact with Germany in June, and in the fall
Hitler invaded and rapidly overcame helpless Poland and divided the nation
with Russia. England and France finally accepted their treaty obligations and
declared war. The issue of democracy in Spain was eclipsed, as Britain and
France stood alone against the might of the Nazi war machine.

In 1940, when Nancy left Neruda and began her trip home, she knew she
could not return to Réanville because of the German occupation. She returned instead to London, where she spent most of the war years. She felt
compelled "to be of use" and "desperately" tried to maintain her position
with the *Manchester Guardian*: "Please do realize that I want to work for the
Guardian, really, anywhere in the future."[1] It had been her main resource
in aiding the Spanish refugees and if, in its wartime reduction to four pages,
the Spanish story was not of prominent interest, she would report on Hitler and the new war. In response to her many letters from September 1940
until the end of the war, Crozier replied that, to his "great regret," the "paper
[was] groaning under paper restrictions" and he could not offer her a regular
assignment. All the same, he did publish her articles periodically on a variety
of subjects.[2]

Nancy adjusted her sights and took on several jobs—all in the service of fighting fascism—even if they were less dramatic than they had been in Spain. Most of the time, she performed exhausting work around the clock as a file clerk, secretary, translator, news broadcaster—in whatever capacity she could be of use—for the Free French and SHAEF (Supreme Headquarters, Allied Expeditionary Forces). Although she barely had enough food or enough money to heat her one-room flat, she never complained. Typically, she found her work "sometimes rather hard because of rush—long but pleasant." She was always prepared to work six nightshifts in a row.[3]

Toward the end of the war, she worked on behalf of the maquis, as her letters to the diplomat-poet Edward Thompson reveal, although the specifics of her activities are unclear. Some speculated that it was Nancy who smuggled Aragon's poems out of Paris. Her comments in this regard were always vague: "I am going to the very core of the *maquis*. . . . Address c/o Triztan Tzara, Centre des Intellectuels, 5 Rue des Trois Journées, Toulouse." She had similarly told Thompson the nonspecific: "I [am] busy . . . with efforts for the French *maquis*."[4] She would also collect patriotic poems from well-known writers and send the proceeds to the maquis.

Nancy pursued a number of causes in her own distinctive way, and she took a spirited interest in issues both large and small. On hearing that the fascist Oswald Mosley and his wife might be released from jail, she organized protests against "Hitler's avowed friend and ally."[5] When a British traveler was detained for taking food to a family in France, she argued: "This is most outrageous. Sylvia Townsend Warner and Valentine Ackland [are] trying to agitate about such little help to France . . . in food and clothing. . . . Any ideas should be sent to them. . . . Letters to MPs, a campaign, in fact, IF it can be done."[6]

As the war proceeded, Nancy's appreciation of England and France grew. She extolled the stoicism of the English and grieved over the plight of the French. She was impatient when anyone complained about shortages or inconveniences. Near the end of the war, when her friend Norman Douglas grumbled about personal deprivations, she replied:

Too much fuss was made about the dreadful quality of the food, the scarcity or inexistence of many articles. What, in the fourth year of this monstrous war, what *could* be more natural? *I* never had any difficulty with the concept of "total war," which obviously, includes "total starvation"—if the enemy can manage as much. British rationing seemed to me very well organized and very fair—not at all the view of many![7]

While indifferent to the physical discomforts imposed by war, Nancy was angry and impatient with the pain she often felt from her worsening fibrositis (severe musculoskeletal pain). She also found the sounds and sights of war—blackouts and sirens—petrifying and lamented her lack of information about Réanville: "It seems incredible not to be able to know anything—all part of the hell." The loneliness that often prompted her need to travel had little outlet now. As a result, she had infrequent access to nature and the tranquility it provided her. "And I, here, alone very much; in fact, entirely so now," she wrote, adding: "Oh world that is too large . . . And life, too long."[8]

Her memoir of Norman Douglas, published after the war, reveals Nancy at a new stage in life—a woman in need of companionship, of friends to comfort her during the turmoil of war. Perhaps she had spent her portion of courage during the Great War and Spanish Civil War. World War II, and especially its aftermath, marked the beginning of Nancy's increasing loneliness, as well as the beginning of the physical breakdown that would finally take its psychological toll. Her close ties with people like Augustus John, Norman Douglas, and Louise Morgan continued, and she made new friends, but many in her old circle had vanished: she had been away too long and lost touch. Other old friends still disapproved of her political causes and lifestyle. In addition, she was not part of the literary groups flourishing in London, although she continued writing and publishing poems, many motivated by her hatred of war. She honored its heroes, as in "Sonnet Political," at the same time that she prayed for the day "humanity would be more intelligent" and plow the earth for fruit rather than for burial:

Maybe they yet will get their furrow straight,
Maybe some fact unborn will point the road.
Maybe the ox will amble half awake
. . . And grass proceed unhindered on war's grave.

In 1942, she began a lengthy affair with an American journalist, Morris Gilbert, whom she had known in Paris during the 1920s. He was working for the U.S. Office of War Information in numerous European cities and in North Africa. When he was in London, he and Nancy were inseparable, but during the long periods was on assignment, she saw other men. Her romantic life was no longer of public interest, and now, at forty-five, she began to enjoy the company of men at times barely half her age.

Return Home from Latin America

When France collapsed in 1940, Nancy was in Latin America, "desperate to return home." With her beloved France occupied by the Nazis, she felt driven to return to London. As one friend put it: "England was the country of her birth, after all. She admired its 'stand' and must offer her services." Despite enormous difficulties in returning to Europe, Nancy finally arranged to sail from one port to another—from Mexico to various islands in the West Indies to Cuba to New York and finally to Scotland (from which she traveled by train to London). It took "a year to get here from all those places in the New World," she commented, "but I was determined."[9] She reached London on August 23, 1941. During the months of waiting and on the long voyage home, she wrote poetry and articles for the ANP. Some reports were about the colonial oppression of blacks at the ports she had visited; others, compilations of war news she had collected from foreign newspapers. She also described conditions in Spain: more than 130,000 Spanish refugees had remained in French concentration camps. Many were forced to work in war factories or were sent to the "no man's land" between "the front lines of the French army and those of the Germans."[10]

The voyage back was unique, a period of triumph and notoriety, of unexpected affection and dreaded isolation. When her ship docked in Trinidad, to her great astonishment she was greeted as a celebrity. Honored for her work on *Negro* and her indefatigable concern with black causes, she was interviewed and feted. Calypso songs were even written to her:

"Black man and white woman," your masterpiece,
Created a sensation at its release.
Words are inadequate Miss Cunard dear
To say how we appreciate you and your career.

A handsome young policeman introduced her to Trinidad's beautiful beaches and exotic nightlife.

When she reached Cuba, she hand-printed on a pocket press *Psalm of the Palms and Sonnets*, an effort to capture her emotional experience of the West Indies. The poems are written like prayers for freedom learned under slavery, intended to be sung to colonial masters. "Psalm for Trinidad" begins with a voice from the living past: "I am Trinidad—Columbus discovered me" in a world of "palm-trees" and "humming birds." But the speaker, through time, has become part of the globally oppressed: "I am Africa, India now." As "brown bard of the people," he asks, "Slums of Empire—have you seen me?"

When Alfred Cruickshank, a well-known poet from Trinidad read this, he asked Nancy

What was it moved you to enlist
In our sad cause your all of heart and soul?

She replied in a poem addressed to him. "Why love the slave?" she begins, repeating his question, and then explains, reminiscent of her childhood dream of kinship with African blacks:

Cell of the conscious sphere, I, nature and men,
Answer you: Brother . . . instinct, knowledge . . .
and then,
Maybe I was an African one time.

In July 1941, Nancy sailed from Cuba to New York on the *Marqués de Comillas* and then arranged passage to Scotland. When the *Marqués* docked in Brooklyn, she was unable to disembark without a visa. When members of the press heard about her arrival, they tried to resuscitate her 1930s notoriety in Harlem. The *Daily News* rumored: "American Consular officials in Havana refused her a transit visa for reasons they kept to themselves"; the *New York Times* stated: "Nancy Cunard . . . was held aboard for deportation to Bermuda." Nancy railed at each report. To the *Times*, she wrote: "This is a complete fabrication and I am astounded that a serious paper like yours should venture to make it. The only reason I am not landing is because I had not the time in Cuba to wait the minimum three weeks for an in-transit visa. I am not sure that your misstatement does not come under the heading of libel." The *Times* followed up with "Nancy Cunard Wins Release from Ship" but still linked her "detention" to the State Department.[11]

Despite Nancy's frustration and anger, a wonderful interlude occurred. Kay Boyle, Sylvia Warner, Solita Solano, Louise Morgan, Otto Theis, and several Harlem friends traveled to Brooklyn to see her after reading about her in the newspapers. After they arrived, someone in authority, as Kay wrote, "turned his head the other way" as "Nancy came down the illicit gangplank, laughing softly at the sight of us there." They sat on packing boxes and crates, "drinking beer from cans, . . . and in time, as the gathering grew, a policeman or two joined us, and sat talking with us and listened, as we listened, to Nancy speaking with English gravity and Irish wit of the things that stir in all men's hearts, and speaking with such simplicity that one was pleased to be alive."[12]

Following this, Nancy spent five days on Ellis Island at her own request and saved the life of the Chinese author of a radical book called *Hanging on Union Square*. He was being held before deportation to Chiang Kai-shek's China where he faced death. Lawrence Gellert, who visited her there, recalls: "You enlisted my aid not in your own behalf, but rather . . . to see to it that the Chinese was permitted to remain in this country. . . . Through your influence and industry . . . forces were mobilized which eventually had Congress pass a special law to permit the Chinese (I forget his name) to stay here."[13]

At last, she boarded the ship, which, unbeknownst to its passengers, was to be part of a convoy carrying food and supplies to Britain. Not only was this a dangerous venture, with the British and Germans vying for control over the Atlantic, but it was the most famous convoy of the time: Winston Churchill, on the H.M.S. *Prince of Wales*, after secretly meeting with Franklin Delano Roosevelt off the coast of Newfoundland to plan the "Eight-Point World Democracy" program, stopped to review Nancy's ship, the flagship of the convoy. The world press covered the event.

Nancy kept a journal of the return, from July 31 until August 21, 1941,[14] on this "perfectly good boat" and delighted in "how British all this is!"; she had lived abroad for the better part of twenty years. "We are a lordly, if slow procession" of various nationalities, she observed, and she befriended a Korean nun, who told her "of the detestable imperialism" of the Japanese in Korea, where the Korean language and ways had been "abolished or replaced by Japanese." She noted the ship's wartime precautions: black-out wooden shutters inside the windows, portholes screwed shut, and rules prohibiting smoking on deck. Lifeboat drills began almost immediately (with Nancy "tumbling" into clothes and an ill-fitting life preserver); everyone listened to the news, to stories of the Blitz and of English heroism. No one knew what was happening. They heard that a destroyer would accompany them, but the approximate number of convoy ships remained a mystery. Nancy counted them daily. She soon counted forty-four. Word arrived that volunteers could sign up for gun watches; she was disappointed that only men could participate.

The monotony of the journey was interrupted when gas masks were distributed, and as they reached Newfoundland, planes flew above them with "a destroyer always on [the] left front." On August 10, with "mist and cold and cold and mist in a circle," they heard that a nest of submarines had been detected. A few days later when Nancy counted sixty-four ships, she wrote: "Tonight, for some unexplained reason I was intensely nervous"; soon there were seventy-two. On August 15, she looked out of a starboard porthole and saw

a *monumental* battleship with a full and stately flurry of spray at her prow, her guns pointing skyward, a great bridge between her two funnels. It is Churchill, returning from his talk with Roosevelt on the "Prince of Wales," six or seven cruisers accompanying them. This majesty passes us quickly, crosses in/out and comes by the right and the ship's other side—to see and be seen. Churchill's showmanship—a delight to all.

The next night, air raids and surface attacks returned; in the morning, there were "diverse gun practices, mainly anti-aircraft—sounds of machine guns and large guns from other ships. Kites shaped like double oblongs [were] used as an aerial barrage."

The trip from Iceland to Scotland was marked by rough storms, icebergs, the discovery of mines popped by an escort at the back of the convoy, and widespread illness on board. Arriving in Glasgow, she wrote, "How modest and even almost unimpressed are those who have charge of this great procession over the ocean. . . . Yes. Remarkable. . . . The *Might* of Britain. Inspiring." Nancy's final entry recorded a printed notice in the window of a Glasgow insurance company:

> Please understand: in this house there is no depression. Nor are we interested in any discussions about defeat. Such a thing is not possible.

The words were Queen Victoria's to Balfour when he announced a reverse in the Boer War.

Nancy returned to London the next day and remained there for three and a half years. This was the beginning of her perpetual search for a home, an almost impossible goal after the Blitz. She borrowed flat 126 in Clifford's Inn and later moved to single rooms on Queen Street, Half Moon Street, Rathbone Place, Hallam Street, and Jermyn Street—all of which she could barely afford, although she did have enough money to buy tea, sugar, milk, and biscuits. Nearly penniless throughout the war, she was forced to sell her six Tanguy drawings and Ascher and Tanguy paintings. She took most of her meals in and ate Spam and boiled potatoes, "cooked on that dear little old gas-ring" (which she fed 25 shillings a week). Later on, she was cheered to find a glut of tomatoes and green apples on street carts and some carrots, cabbage, and vegetable marrows, as well. She looked forward to "the onions . . . coming." Shortly after her return to London, she wrote "Black-Out Blues":

> I've got those black-out blues,
> I've got those BLACK-OUT blues
> . . . .
> And you tell me: that's hardly news.

Nancy moved to a furnished room on Half Moon Street before the end of the year; the diary of 1942 begins at this address.

Wartime London

England had survived the Blitz with extraordinary spirit, and as soon as Nancy returned she spoke to both friends and strangers to learn as much as she could about their experiences. Her notes after these interviews, along with other information about the time, provide an interesting chronicle of life during the war.[15]

London's war preparations, begun during the Munich crisis, were immediately apparent to Nancy: public shelters and trenches in royal parks and other open spaces; barrage balloons to protect against low-flying aircraft (she counted sixty-nine during her first night back); "impressive," gigantic water-tank traps for fire bombs; and "magnificent" searchlights and anti-aircraft guns and fighter squads. Hitler was determined to destroy British air power in preparation for a German invasion, but his Messerschmitt 109s were confronted by the RAF's Hurricane and Spitfire fighters ("Never have so many owed so much to so few," in Churchill's famous words). In his determination to destroy British morale, Hitler had also turned his focus from Britain's army to its industrial installations and the innocent civilian population. The Blitz (the British term for the German *Blitzkrieg*, or "lightning war") was his brutal effort to destroy the enemy's will to fight.

Fearing the return of German mustard gas, the government distributed gas masks to everyone. Also fearing mass panic, over 3.5 million people were evacuated, including a million children who left for unknown destinations with their schoolteachers rather than their parents. All the same, John Lehmann, the prolific poet, essayist, and publisher, reported that "in the beginning London was like two cities. During the day, people went about their business; at night . . . with blackouts, . . . people were floundering in the darkness." Even so, he continued, "the mood of London was calmer than one had imagined possible: a sense of tragic disaster was dominant, without the slightest trace of terror or patriotic hysteria."[16]

The first bomb on civilian targets had fallen, probably accidentally, on London on August 24/25, 1940. The frequency of the bombing was most intense from early September 1940 until May 1941, when, as it later became clear, Hitler was turning his attention to the east. Bombings continued for three more years when the buzz bombs appeared, and the intensity of bombardment reached new heights.

At the beginning of the Blitz, Hitler targeted factories and docks with daylight raids, beginning with a massive 400-bomber Blitz in the dock area, setting East London ablaze. On September 7, at least 430 civilians were killed; on the next day, 411, and the following, 370; there were raids for seventy-six nights.[17] Some like Virginia and Leonard Woolf secured poison so they and their friends could kill themselves not *if*, but *when*, the Germans arrived. Generally, however, most survived the terrible first months: indignation and stoicism had combined into a fierce sense of pride. One might say that Winston Churchill, who replaced Neville Chamberlain in May 1940, both inspired and echoed the British as they demonstrated their finest hour.

When Nancy returned, she felt much as she had in Madrid. It had become a way of life to experience the wail of sirens and rumble of bombs—and the intermittent silence before the bombs hit their target. She noticed on the day she returned, as she wrote in her diary,

> a place with a hole so big they had to build a special sort of bridge for the trams to go on. I was headed off but I could see where a tram had just gone so I followed it. A policeman came up "Where are you going?" "Following tram." "Stop right there. Get down, mind how you do, and have a look." Got down and saw about two feet of a very deep hole with nothing but the tram lines over it.[18]

She heard that on the night of "the Dorchester scare," where her mother lived, the "Grosvenor shook on its feet" and that "they got all but thirty of 500 buses in a depot." She walked to the East End and saw "a doctor [who] stood contemplating wreckage of an East End hospital saying, 'The five women I operated on yesterday to save their lives are under that now.'" Then she walked to Turner's Row, with "both sides of [the] street completely emptied of houses, roofs off, slates." She learned that in three weeks about 7,500 people had left a nearby district. She also heard, as she wrote in her diary, that "a new underground dissidents' parliament of over 100 deputies and senators, under [the] leadership of Herriot, [is] said to be formed in France—to oppose Pétain."

The destruction of homes had been so devastating that one in six people had to look for shelter, and homelessness became widespread. Nancy listed the various temporary emergency measures in place: government and charity organizations providing shelters and searching for family members, mobile canteens and soup kitchens, and yachtsmen forming river patrols. Although a variety of shelters had been built in basements, under railway arches, and in large buildings, the underground remained an extremely popular mass shelter, even though not all the stations were safe: 300 fatalities had occurred at the Marble Arch station on the same night the Royal Court Theatre was destroyed. Nancy took the Piccadilly Circus line and observed the "men, women, children, [and] babies" sleeping on "iron two-decker beds of lead."

The English spirit was, as she wrote, "invincible. . . . England is much as I knew it would be." There was little complaining about the commodities that had been cut to the core. Private cars bore signs for pedestrians caught out during an air raid: "Free Lifts at Your Own Risk." Home Intelligence reports indicated that during the heaviest attacks "steadiness and pragmatism" prevailed. On April 16, the raid had for lasted eight hours, with 100,000 tons of bombs dropped from 450 planes. More than 1,000 people were killed, and 148,000 houses were destroyed or damaged. The largest number for a single raid occurred on May 10: 1,436 were killed; 1,792 were injured; fire fighting followed for eleven days. By the end of 1941, over 40,000 Londoners had been killed or wounded.[19]

Shortly after Nancy's return, the all-day Blitz was succeeded by the horrific, if periodic, raids that some called the "Baby Blitz" or "Little Blitz." But even when the major raids stopped, the country maintained its precautions: compulsory blackouts after sunset (if someone left home with a light on, the police broke in and shot it out with air guns), a white stripe on vehicles (whose headlights were masked) for identification, the removal of street sign posts (in the event of parachute landings), and ladies of the night in Piccadilly with open coats into which they turned small flashlights. In 1943, the raids accelerated: "One or two extremely violent bursts of firing shook the house. . . . In the middle of the night it began again, with violent, house-shaking gunfire and the continuous, mosquito-persistent droning of aeroplanes. [The] two attacks [were] a gala warning display of the terrible new London barrage to come."[20]

Nancy said of the raids, "Increasingly troubling are the black-outs . . . tremendous, and, I see, every night a little different; the really dark nights have got to be accustomed to." She was acutely unnerved by the schizoid juxtaposition of "extreme quiet in the skies—mercifully—the impression that it is Sunday night because of silent streets" and the shocking reality of the vast destruction. "The City and the East End are terrific with their great gashes and absence of people," she wrote, adding, "I continue to be terribly moved and impressed by it all. . . . No one speaking of it with fear though: the stoical English."

The barrage of 1944 included German guided bombs. A forty-six-foot rocket, the A-4 or V-2, could carry a one-ton war head at 3,600 miles per hour for 220 miles ("V," an abbreviation for *Vergeltung* [vengeance]). Previously, the Luftwaffe had introduced the FZG.76 or V-1, a pilotless jet that could convey a one-ton warhead at 470 miles per hour for 250 miles. With this new weaponry, whole blocks disappeared; St. Paul's stood alone, miraculously, as the entire area around it was decimated. Nancy came upon the immaculate disappearance of her bank on Tottenham Court Road and saw just the wildflowers that had sprouted in its place—red clover, blue larkspur, and yellow-orange flaxweed.

The first night these planes were visible—"P-Planes," "Robot-Bombs," "Robots," or "Doodlebugs," as they were soon called—Nancy, like everyone else, was terribly confused:

[Our] guns then ceased shooting. . . . Many sirens, "ons" and "offs." At 9:20 a.m. I saw out of the window five or six of these (as yet "unpublished") engines, flying toward the house . . . in actual squadron-like formation. Guns opened fire, appeared to hit one, if not two. There was much quick drifting, vaporous cloud the while. Two of these engines began to fail, with clouds coming across really direct vision. The whole five or six then changed shape, became rounded and nebulous, disappeared. The whole thing was like a vision (No wonder some people see the whole crucifixion during an air raid; as happened in Norfolk this year); materially, it was exactly like a fade-out on the screen—. . . as the distinctly plane-shaped bodies turned into something more like balloons, then vanished.

On June 12, 1944, when ten V-1s were launched, six crashed; one reached London and killed six. On June 15, heavier raids occurred: 100 V-1s appeared that day. The government made plans to evacuate more people and built additional shelters. Nancy performed her own ritual to stay alive:

About the third day, . . . it really got on one's nerves. And, somehow, to "still" the nerves (which can't be done) I began to LIST my longing and proclaim my fate that "all would eventually come right" by mentally saying the name of . . . myriad villages in [France]—in a bus at Hyde Park Corner: Aillac/Cublac, Cubjac/Bénac/ Cressenssac/Cazennac/ . . . /Noirac/Vrérac/ Vitrac/ Vindrac/Vayrac.

The British stopped half the V-1s. The others fell during the workday when people were exposed, and casualties were very high. In two weeks, 1,600 Londoners were killed and 4,500 were badly injured. In one of its worst hits, 119 people were killed near St. James's Park. More than 20,000 houses were damaged each day in July 1944, and 200,000 required repair. Vere Hodgson, the legendary teacher, wrote in the summer of 1944:

One listens fascinated to the Doodle-Bugs Passing Over, holding one's breath, praying they will travel on, but feeling a wretched cad, because you know that means they will . . . explode on someone else. . . . The atmosphere in London has changed. Back into the Big Blitz. Apprehension is in the air. . . . Thousands . . . go early to the shelters. . . . Life seems to be one long air raid.[21]

The doodlebugs had been so named because they sputtered and moved across the sky like an inexpensive car, and when the rocket's fuel supply ran out, the engine stopped, and the behemoth plummeted from the skies.

Nancy wrote about the overhead "noise, the noise, all the appalling majesty of noise," night after night. She wondered, in addition, "Could one ever ignore the *distant sounds* of heavy artillery, like the hammering to pieces of

Boulogne? What was that gigantic bang? . . . somewhere in Chiswick?" And of the sirens, she said, "Faraway—[are] their scarves of sound waving about over some eastern stretch of Thames maybe."[22]

Nancy's spirit, like that of her compatriots, remained high, if apprehensive. Virtually everyone suffered the war disease of sleeplessness: "if only one could sleep four hours (the average) at night." Although few turned to the church for comfort, on her first evening back Nancy went to a service at St. Philip's Church, in Kensington. Afterward, she noticed how empty the streets were: only the adventurous went out. *Gone with the Wind* remained in the West End from April 1940 until the spring of 1944. The great pianist Myra Hess performed at the National Gallery to an audience in coats, mufflers, and mittens. On the occasions that raids occurred near restaurants, customers were given camp beds for the night and breakfast in the morning. Underground facilities were constructed—canteens, bars, restaurants (some with music and dancing). Underground first aid stations, chapels, and dormitories were also built.

In contempt of Goering, people started calling the bombs "screaming meemies." When Oxford Street and Piccadilly shop windows were damaged, customers boasted about touching merchandise through glassless windows. Cardboard in some of the open store frames were decorated with murals, and as holidays approached, people wrote one another salutations. It became a matter of pride to keep the shops open. Signs boasted "Business as Usual, Mr. Hitler," "Shattered but Not Shuttered," and the witty "They Can Smash Our Windows but They Can't Beat Our Furnishing Values." Effigies of a doomed Hitler filled the city. A sense of community developed: strangers told one another about bizarre survival events, such as how they had been in a w.c. when the building around them disappeared.

Work and Social Life

"That gentle glow of good whiskey and good conversation, that relief from day-long thoughts about war, that normal, hopeful feeling again! If one could only bottle *that*," said Nancy as the war droned on.

She looked for a job as soon as she returned. She filed the mandatory Registration for Employment Order 1941. ("British efficiency"—"the opposite of the bureaucracy of how many other countries": she also received her identity, ration, and clothing books with little ado.) She wanted to do something at which she could both fight and write for the good cause. She applied to the BBC and Ministry of Information; neither had openings. She tried for two years to get what she called "a reporterage book" contract from a London publisher; she continued to write to the *Guardian*.

She joined Le Français de Grande-Bretagne, an organization that defined itself as the only recognized body pledged to the British government and to General de Gaulle and the Free French forces. In the spring of 1942, she was offered a job with the Free French in Warrington as a radio monitor and translator. When she listened to broadcasts from France, she could actually hear the war, "aerial screechings on top of Vichy blasts." Her assignment was to recast typists' versions of enemy radio broadcasts in correct French: "enemy stuff from Paris, Berlin, Vichy, etc.—a good deal of it Jew-baiting." (Some of this included Pound's diatribes from Italy.) Her office produced fifty-five copies of a daily twenty-page bulletin that was sent to heads of governments in exile. The work was exhausting, and she often worked through the night, "those endless hours when ears and eyes give out, the spine turns to rubber, and nerves alternate between strung catgut and damp, flapping sails: dehumanization by exhaustion."[23] When Norman Douglas asked why she remained at the job, she replied, "I feel some compunction. We 'girls' there all do! And I have *got* to have war work." At the same time, she collected information about black troops in France and in Britain for the ANP; one of her articles was called "No Color Bar in the British Air Force."[24]

At about the time Nancy began working with the Free French, she collaborated with George Padmore on a long pamphlet on colonial matters, *The White Man's Duty* (1943). Their thesis was that the war should awaken the British toward race prejudice at home and lead to self-government for the colonies. It advocated, among other things, an act of Parliament to ban racial discrimination and ensure equal opportunities in every field; it sold nearly 20,000 copies. During this time Nancy also published poetry in the *New Statesman* and wrote reviews for *Our Time*, edited by her friend Edgell Rickwood. She maintained her ties with the International Brigade Association and Friends of Republican Spain, as well as the Colonial Center in Russell Square (which organized dances and lectures), the International Institute of African Languages and Culture, the Negro Welfare Center in Liverpool, and the West African Students Union; she also joined the Jazz Sociological Society. Although she had been unable to get a full-time job working directly for the Ministry of Information, the ministry welcomed her articles relating incidents of racial discrimination.[25]

In the autumn of 1943, Nancy found another opportunity to use poetry to further a moral cause. She edited an anthology of English poems to celebrate the French spirit of resistance. Following her methodology for *Negro* and *Authors Take Sides on the Spanish War*, she made her contacts ("I was writing all that autumn to every poet in England": 'Have you a poem to send me connected with France since the war began?'"), and she began with a statement of purpose, now linking France, which she called her "permanent home," and

England, in the "conviction that our two countries must ever march together." The seventy poems she collected included contributions from Vita Sackville-West, Hugh MacDiarmid, Alex Comfort, Herbert Read, Sylvia Townsend Warner, and Henry Treece, among others. Once again, Nancy retyped the poems, added explanatory footnotes, and wrote brief comments about each contributor. The project, an exhausting endeavor, was a sheer "labor of love." She worked on it in her tiny flat on Half Moon Street, where, always looking positively at her circumstances, she said that for just £1.5 every week, "the bed-sitter could be made warm and wonderful." *Poems for France* was published in 1944 by the Free French publishing house, La France Libre. As Nancy's papers reveal, she had an ulterior purpose in publishing this collection: she intended to auction books signed by the poets to raise funds for "the *maquis*, the partisans-patriots-guerrillas-secret army. They can do with help you know, and I have arranged how it is to go: as direct as it may be," adding the wistful, "Oh I wish I were the best poet that ever lived so as to write, once and for all, what tragedy is."[26]

Some of her postwar remarks, alongside the research of, for example, Douglas Porch in *The French Secret Services*, suggest that Nancy's jobs during the war were not as modest as she described them. "The quickest way to speed intelligence," Porch writes, "was via radio, and it was here that the battle between the Resistance and the Germans raged most fiercely."[27] Announcers (known as "operators" and "pianists") were trained in security, and two things remain clear: when Nancy worked for the Free French, she translated and rewrote material for a variety of purposes, including broadcasts; she also began training to be a "pianist," although she did not perform this work until she went to SHAEF. She spent several months translating and rewriting and then was told to spend the entire day reading English newspapers, marking and translating articles as items "of interest to France": "Weeks and months passed thus—the landings in North Africa, the stupendous battle of Stalingrad; the turn of the tide at last." Norman Douglas asked her once again not just why she remained at her job but why she had felt compelled to return to London in the first place. She replied that this war against fascism "is *my* war too" and again praised the fortitude of the English, adding: "I'm all for patriotism as I see it! To me it means fighting the common enemy in any way, in any country. I would like, preferably, to work in connection with France, within the scope of things here; but I have a real admiration for England in its dire ordeal."[28]

When in mid-1944 Nancy took a job at the newly opened Kingsway office of SHAEF, she was required to wear a uniform. The focus of all work here was propaganda and intelligence. Called the London Coordinating Committee for Political Welfare, the office had representatives from the Foreign

Office, State Department, Office of War Information, and U.S. Joint Chiefs of Staff. Its purpose was to issue broad directives for all the Allies' propaganda campaigns in northwestern Europe. The Psychological Warfare Section, developed to coordinate press and radio coverage, reported all British propaganda plans to Parliament; all outlines and intentions required agreement from Washington. This SHAEF division both conveyed coded messages on the news and spread propaganda. In its latter goal, it attempted to cultivate the Germans' acceptance of Allied unity and superiority, the inevitability of German defeat, and the kind treatment that would be given to prisoners. There was to be no suggestion that the Germans would be absolved of guilt as the aggressor or that the German military would continue after the war. It stressed Hitler's ineffective leadership, Germany's lack of equipment and manpower, and the weakness of the Luftwaffe. Germans were told they had done their duty and could surrender with honor.[29]

Nancy began her work at SHAEF as, in her words, "a translator of English [war reports] into French (with a good deal of military Americanese thrown in)," striving to comply with her orders to "make it all sound as much like proper French journalism as possible, such as 'Yesterday, at 17 hours, our troops advanced East by Northeast, taking one and a half kilometers of open ground.'" The coded material was subsequently added. Given the importance of the material that would be broadcast, she was meticulous in her translations: "'Choke-points' in American—did that mean 'bottle-necks,' 'traffic-jams,' or something to do with a throttle? . . . Not even the B.B.C., rung up at three a.m., could say." The job put her into a frenzy, and she began typing and working faster than anyone in the office. Working "all day or all night," "I now knew the . . . sameness of 'Tomorrow and tomorrow and tomorrow.'"[30] The shifts were grueling, and she wavered between a sense of gratification in assisting in the war effort and madness.

She finally became a "pianist," reading the *Resúmé des nouvelles* on the air. Her broadcasts gave the Allies important information, including German experimentation with bombs and their coastal defenses. Probably their most significant contributions were "in detecting and defeating the V-1 and V-2 attacks in Europe."[31] Yet, in spite of her enormous satisfaction in contributing to the war effort, she continued to miss her home in Réanville, particularly during holidays, often commenting: "How near is France, and how agonizingly far."

Still, she remained determined to use her free time for the cause: "And then Christmas itself—the frightful one of 1944! . . . freezing, heavy with the bad news of Arnheim (the end of the war thus delayed?). . . . Well, someone had to volunteer to do those two Christmas shifts—and why not I?" She spoke repeatedly of the "the criminal imbecility" of war and of her exhaustion—"I am at the penultimate night of the six nightshifts"; "such a rush is everything";

"always this awful haste"; "once again in tearing haste"—and her worry about France. She tried to retain her good spirits, in the "ice and snow over the city" and "the cold, cold, cold ." But she wrote to friends: "England's clothes rationing, etc., coincided with final penury for me at the *wrong* moment! But one gets along. . . . The SHAEF people eat well enough at Scribe and [the] canteens."[32]

One day Nancy saw Kay Boyle in London as the V-2 bombs were falling every twenty seconds, wiping out eight city blocks at a time. Kay had just arrived from the United States. The two women could barely believe their eyes: both were in uniform. Kay had been invited by the Army Air Forces to join writers touring American bases in Europe and North Africa and to write and lecture about her experiences. She was dressed as a "simulated captain"; she had even been taught to salute. "We were proud, . . . of the fight to which we were committed," said Kay. Nancy then asked, "How in the world did we get on the side of authority? . . . By what miracle? Are we really going to win in the end?"[33]

Nancy's fear of the blackouts and sirens increased and subjected her to what she called "a certain gloom": each winter seemed "a grimmer one than any in London annals." And she was not immune to the fear of her own mortality, writing in her diary: "One morning came the announcement from Goebbels that the whole of *this district* [Chelsea] was to be obliterated that night." Her letters reflected her increasing concern over the whereabouts of her friends. In one to Janet and Solita, who had been in the United States since the start of the war, she lamented: "Of Aragon we heard in Chile this: he was trapped in the Belgian defeat, got to England, crossed back to Brittany, nothing more. . . . Know nothing of Tzara. One day there may be peace, of a kind. Shall we ever be three again? Or under the trees at Réanville? . . . The ghastly fate, I think, of the Spanish." For the first time, she felt the need to "cling to" whomever she was walking with during "those dreadful blackouts": "How I wished," she said to the seventy-five-year-old Douglas, "we could have managed to live under the same roof!" Douglas was "the only person I saw . . . who soothed my exhausted nerves and took my mind off the horrible subjects we had to grapple with." Nevertheless, despite the efforts of "Hitler and the rest of that gang of criminals," she told Douglas how fortunate they were: "At least we're not occupied here as they are in France."[34]

Nancy had begun her affair with the American journalist Gilbert Morris at the beginning of 1942. When they met in Paris during the 1920s, he was a reporter for the *Herald*, chronicling the adventures of the Paris expatriates and traveling in diverse circles that included Hemingway, Josephine Baker, and Nancy and her friends. Gilbert had moved to Paris after actively engaging in Near East relief in Turkey. In 1925, when his funds ran short, he returned to

New York and joined the staff of the *New York Times*; he returned to Paris in 1929. When he had further financial woes, he again returned home and to the *Times*. During World War II, he was an attaché to the U.S. Army in Washington, London, Paris, Naples, and Algiers. This was the period during which Nancy and Gilbert began their affair. They were both equally obsessed with social equality and literature.

Nancy's papers contain Gilbert's letters through 1963, although their affair ended in 1947—a relationship that flourished, for the most part, through their correspondence. Gilbert called Nancy many terms of endearment—"darling," "my duck," "beautiful pet," and "baby musk rabbit"—and spoke of the "inhibitions in all these letters," counting on her to "uninhibit them in the reading." He offered her occasional words of wisdom, such as the "two inexorable things" he had learned in Naples about Vesuvius and war: "The one is hardly different in its inhumanity, its superhumanity, from the other. Humanity is incidental to these affairs." He was concerned with "how cold you have been, even with the green socks," and felt "miserable" at her "misery." Of her busy life, he wrote: "Your moves are a little dizzying," and in response to a poem she had sent him: "a passionate and glowing thing, deep, hard, somber, secret, and pure Nancy." He was also writing poems, at her encouragement. After three years passed and on a day he realized he had not heard from her for five weeks, he received her "urgent note of semi-starvation." He replied that he would like to provide for her as well as his wife and children. He returned to New York, separated from his wife, returned to the *Times*, felt "like a robot," complained to Nancy about his dull life, and found "so much love, warmth, tenderness, [and] understanding in your letters, it makes the heart crack." He admitted his uncertainties and need for financial security, concluding that as to "us as a team—there I have so felt the uncertainty, the strangeness which you would never admit, but which, now and then, I suffered, miserably, . . . that I was never in the tradition of the Nanciad." One of his earliest bits of advice to Nancy was about men: "Trust none. Men's oaths are wafer cakes."[35]

Throughout the war, on the infrequent occasions he was in London, Nancy spent every minute of her time with him. Otherwise, she met friends in the Shepherd Market area—John Davenport, Desmond Ryan, her cousin Victor Cunard, Walter Starkie, or Nell Hogg. They enjoyed dinner together, then read Shakespeare aloud and drank a great deal. Nancy often recalled a friend's remark: "No one yet, as far as I know, has written the great poem that should be made in praise of drink during war—how it has helped actions to be accomplished that would seem unbelievable."[36]

Sometimes she went to parties. Although she usually took Norman Douglas or Augustus John with her, after one that she attended by herself, she found herself leaving at the same time as an inebriated Dylan Thomas. He ordered her to introduce him to the great Norman Douglas, or, he said, he would destroy Douglas's hotel. Nancy had no intention of yielding to Thomas's bullying. Although she found him charming, his egocentric view of the war was irritating. He made no secret that his major concern with the war was that it would limit his chances of publishing: "I think a squirrel stumbling at least of equal importance as Hitler's invasions."[37]

Most often she saw old friends, particularly Douglas and John. They often distracted themselves from the gloom of daily events by listening to intelligent conversation on the BBC, by writers like George Orwell, E. M. Forster, John Connolly, and Louis MacNeice. They sometimes visited Otto Theis and Louise Morgan, who served them hot spicy sandwiches and precious old brandy. On occasion, they went to the countryside, which Nancy missed so much that she begged friends outside London to contact her if they came upon a room to let. And always fearful of being an imposition, she always added: "SOS from me to you. . . . Please realize that I could not bear to ask you if you felt it meant we had to meet!"[38]

Nancy's friendship with John dated back to the Corrupt Coterie days. Unlike Douglas, John shared Nancy's political views. With Henry Moore and Ben Nicholson, he formed the Artists' International Association Opposed to Fascism and War. John belonged to a number of causes like War Funds for German and Austrian Refugee Activity; he also supported the Voluntary Contraception League and the Campaign for the Abolition of Capital Punishment.

Nancy had always been interested in his painting. The horrors of World War I had destroyed his early visionary inclinations. Now, fearing the obliteration of the world, he retreated into a private world, seeking refuge in scenes of mountains and the sea, children and dancing; he also continued his portraits. Although not well disposed to military commanders, he agreed to do a portrait of Montgomery. Aware that he would view the general's sitting as an intrusion, he invited his friend George Bernard Shaw, who admired Montgomery, to have a conversation with them as he painted. Said Shaw: "Fancy a soldier being intelligent enough to want to be painted by you and to talk to me." When he later painted Churchill, the prime minister, finding it almost impossible to sit still, chattered on about his undistinguished school days. As John mumbled about official policies, Churchill became so uncomfortable that he remarked, "You can draw a man or you can punch him; you cannot do both." Nancy enjoyed these stories.[39]

Sometimes John and Douglas took her to the Pier Hotel at Battersea Bridge, and they listened to the doodlebugs; there, as Nancy put it, the "drink supply had generously expanded — to steady the clients' nerves." They had six favorite pubs that catered to a diverse clientele — from established artists and bohemians to firemen and military personnel of all nationalities. It seemed that London pubs had never been this stimulating. One could listen to "extraordinary revelations" and witness or make "unlikely encounters." The pervasive atmosphere of the pubs was one of carpe diem, an "almost tropical flowering of sexuality."[40]

After a pub or dinner, John often invited his friends back to his studio for a last drink, and he continued to amuse Nancy with his zany tales and humor. He recalled, for instance, the occasion he had been offered a knighthood, although the invitation was temporarily rescinded when an official learned that he was not legally married to the woman with whom he had lived for forty years and with whom he had four children. So John went home and knelt on one knee and proposed to his "wife," who turned him down. It was silly, she thought, to get married at this late date; furthermore, she had no wish to be a "Lady." John then received the Order of Merit, which required no declaration of marital status.

Nancy's room in Piccadilly was relatively close to her mother's new home. Maud had been in New York when the war began, and when she learned that Thomas Beecham was going to marry a much younger woman, a pianist from Seattle, she returned to London immediately.[41] Her house in London had been demolished, and she moved the salvageable furnishings into a three-room suite at the Dorchester. Although she was depressed over Beecham's abandonment, she licked her wounds, determined to reestablish her old way of life. Before long, she was entertaining politicians, diplomats, artists, and writers and finding herself the subject of London social buzz. She ended her crusade on behalf of opera.

Although mother and daughter had several mutual friends (John Strachey, one of Nancy's former lovers, said, "If Maud was aware of how well I had known Nancy in my pre-war Bloomsbury days, she never betrayed it"), they never saw or spoke of each other, and Nancy continued to protest against her mother's conservative friends, like Oswald and Diana Mosley. When their mutual friend Lady Diana Cooper asked Nancy to initiate a rapprochement, Nancy replied, "I think of Her Ladyship, when at all, with great objectivity," adding that her mother had never understood her: "She was at all times very far from me." Maud's attitude toward Nancy was also tepid. One evening returning from the theater, her driver swerved the car to avoid hitting a woman who had darted across the road. Maud gasped when she realized that it was Nancy but did not stop the car.[42]

Nancy continued to renew old acquaintances and make new ones. Her date books include a spectrum of well-known, talented people, such as "Sandy" Calder, Stephen Spender, and Herbert Read.[43] The novelist-poet Sylvia Townsend Warner became a close friend, although they had corresponded during the Spanish Civil War, seeing "eye to eye" on all the issues. Sylvia, three years older than Nancy, had an extraordinary mind. In addition to her literary skills, she had composed music in her teens and later edited a vast body of early sacred music for Oxford University Press. During her ten years at this endeavor, she also wrote poetry, novels, and a biography. She was both the partner of the poet Valentine Ackland and the secret lover of Percy Carter Buck, the director of the Harrow School.

Nancy finally met Sylvia and Valentine "in mid-war . . . —42 or 43," as Sylvia recalled. Nancy had walked into the lounge of the King's Arms holding a rare Spanish onion. "Inestimable treasure, 'your marvelous Dorch,'" exclaimed Sylvia. Her first impression of Nancy was as "a harsh breath of life, an embodied Resistance." She also noticed Nancy's light and mincing walk, "like the La Fontaine crane—her ivory bracelets slipped rigidly over her narrow hands, her leopard skin bonnet, and her pale sea-water eyes."[44] During the war, Nancy visited her new friends in Dorset whenever she could; her walks in the countryside were restorative. The three women spent long evenings talking about literature and war; they drank until late into the night. Sylvia recognized Nancy's "tormenting neuritis," although it neither prevented her from walking with great energy nor inhibited her evening ritual after returning to the house with loads of flints: she scrubbed them for an hour with a nailbrush, spread them on a towel, and admired, graded, and then repolished them: "This capacity for magpie delighting was one of her prettiest charms. She also used to collect beads (and sewed little bags containing them), shells, small nonsenses." When Valentine gave Nancy nineteen mother-of-pearl "fish counters," Nancy wrote the poem "A Nineteen of Pisces" (Nancy's astrological sign)—not entirely unlike the poems in T. S. Eliot's *Old Possum's Book of Practical Cats*:

> Nineteen little fishes
> (Never been so clean)
> Roach and dace
> And tench and plaice
> And dab and brill and bream.
> Skate and hake
> And a flounder's mate
> And spreckleback in stream.
> Herring, grayling,
> Whiting, spratling,
> All together for an outing . . .
> Cod and polk and carp and trout
> And all that's nineteen—no odd man out—

All in a horn—not on a dish—
19's *my* number: I'm a Fish.

Sylvia and Valentine were fascinated by Nancy's remarkable intelligence, her intensity in writing, and her elegance and delicacy of manner. Sylvia remarked that, although "her temper was notorious, [and] her life was willful and erratic—she was compellingly respect-worthy." Even when her language was bold and she had drunk too much,

> her manners were flawless. She always sat at meals, for example, upright and slightly formalized. . . . This frosting of social convention made her peculiarly entertaining, since it coexisted with a wide range of violent opinions and violent language. Even when she was drunk, it persisted, though allargando into solemnity and owlishness. "Nancy, you're tight," "Only a little, darling," flawlessly enunciated. And when an explosion of feeling broke through this habitual bel canto, the effect was formidable.

Sylvia also admired Nancy's gift "of nailing" a person in a phrase: when asked what General de Gaulle was like, she replied "in a flash": "froid, sec et cassant [cold, dry and brittle]." She had a "dash and dexterity in the spoken word" and was a poet's poet. She had been scrupulous in her translations for *Authors Take Sides*: if a word did not feel right, she studied dictionaries and phoned libraries, museums, and writer friends until she discovered the exact word. Of Nancy's writing, Sylvia believed that "her concern with poetry was carnal and passionate: she pursued the word, the phrase, with the patience of a weasel, the concentration of a falcon. When a poem happened to cost her no trouble, she was as pleased as if she'd stolen it out of the church collection."

Herman Schrijver became a close London friend. A Dutch interior designer for the rich and famous (Wallis Simpson, several Guinness families, one English king), Schrijver had met Nancy in 1931. She was, he thought, an "aristocratic rebel down to her slender fingertips and I fell completely under her spell." He respected her belief that poetry was central to a society's moral life, but what he most esteemed was her "passionate love of friendship—and this more than anyone I know."[45]

The offspring of an old and wealthy family, Schrijver was, like Nancy, a self-proclaimed anarchist who liked people from every station in life. Unlike Nancy, however, he was never active in social or political causes. He seemed to live vicariously through Nancy and was always intrigued by her rantings. He and Nancy shared a love of travel and often recalled pre–World War I days before passports were necessary. Schrijver was also a feminist before it became fashionable. During a broadcast in 1953, he asked his female audience:

Do you really believe that men are superior? . . . I'm afraid you do—and see what you have achieved? This effort of yours to make baby boys into "men" has produced millions of rather boring, pathetic, lazy, conceited, selfish brutes who lap up your adoration. They . . . are quite incapable of looking after themselves [and] have no idea how to look after you, or how to love you or cherish you.[46]

Schrijver appreciated Nancy's wit, and she loved his silly jokes. ("Custom officer to Englishman returning from the Continent: 'Are you bringing in any pornography?' Englishman: 'No, I didn't take my pornograph with me.'") Nancy's letters to him were filled with her own style of wit: "I see that Tuesday is the Immaculate Conception. How *can* that be? Unless, of course Jesus was as oddly gestated as conceived: seventeen days, or one year and seventeen days?"[47]

While Schrijver respected Nancy's political passion, his ardor lay in more hedonistic pleasures, in collecting Chippendales and gold snuff boxes, wearing meticulously tailored Savile Row clothing that flattered his plump body, and hosting gourmet dinner parties, renowned as serene rituals at which he balanced each course for color, texture, and smell. Nancy, who ate virtually nothing, admired his splendid cuisine, which "she would coo over and perhaps prod a little with her fork." Schrijver finally discovered that the only food she really liked was smoked salmon, and he delighted to see her finish one very thin slice. Nancy was always amused by Schrijver's dinner invitation policy, which he attributed to Louis XV, who would not invite husbands and wives together "because it does not make for glitter." He told her: "The older I get the more I like people by themselves and the more I hate them in couples; I might one day start an anti-couple move."[48]

One of her most unusual war acquaintances was the spiritualist-mystic Aleister Crowley, twenty years Nancy's senior, who, along with a group called the Thelemites, has retained a following to this day. A hedonist in his every endeavor, Crowley was a poet, philosopher, magician, yogi practitioner, athlete, and drug addict. Nancy first heard about his beautiful poetry in 1915, at the same time she was that told he was "a terrible and dangerous man." They finally met in 1933, and rumors circulated that Crowley was one of Hitler's admirers. Nancy's extensive recollections of their meetings, including their participation at anti-fascist rallies and his consistent "anger against the persecution of the Jews and other ghastly events," convinced her that he "felt deeply about human injustice and public danger." Her defense of him to all his critics was an example of her fundamental belief in human decency.[49]

They also enjoyed socializing, but when they drank whiskey, she "hoped he wouldn't start anything magical" with her. She was "fully prepared to believe that he had his own magic," adding, "but it wouldn't be 'mine.'" However, she realized, "I think he must have been a perceptive man," for the issue never materialized:

> So we just sat and slowly drank the whiskey and I remember he looked rather "deeply" at me. (Is that "occult"?) And then, having said something about "The Serpent's Kiss," [which I had heard about], he asked "Shall I give you the Serpent's Kiss?" This did slightly embarrass me. It seemed rude to say no, to ask ridiculous questions as to its meaning and, somehow, I felt no apprehension. So I said "yes." He applied his teeth very lightly to the inner edge of my right wrist and, after a few seconds, there it was: a tiny triangle of reddish dots—three of them—unfelt. How do you suppose he did that? There is certainly some kind of special process here! I knew him so little that I am quite unaware to this day if this was some kind of honor.

Once, when she visited him in Oxford,

> I told him I was almost speechless with fatigue and that may have caused him to think of a very special cocktail. . . . He took a small phial from his pocket and suddenly both glasses were filled with radiant aquamarine. He peered at me, murmuring "strychnine," then enquired slowly if I thought he was out to poison me. I told him: "Surely not! Why should you want to, for what would you gain? Are you not drinking the same too?" The cocktail . . . seemed to have no special effect beyond that of the non-aquamarine varieties.

At the end of one evening, he assured her that he was "working against Hitler on an '*astral* plane.'"

A totally different kind of person attractive to Nancy was the Oxford professor Edward Thompson, whom she grew to idolize through their correspondence. While collecting material for her *Poems for France*, Nancy began writing to Thompson—a moderately well known poet and longtime advocate for Indian political self-determination. As a young man, he had traveled to India and joined the literary circle of the Nobel laureate Rabindranath Tagore. He had long been a friend of Nehru, Gandhi, and other major Indian political leaders with whom the British had yet to gain contact, and he played an important role in India's movement toward independence in 1947.[50] His initial correspondence with Nancy involved an exchange of poems; he contributed to her *Poems for France* and included thirty of her poems in his collection *Augustan Poems*, writing to his publisher: "Nancy Cunard is my sole commitment for the future, and I have managed to get a really good and original and vigorous selection."[51]

Nancy and Thompson shared a zealous concern for the disenfranchised. "Nothing but total abolition will do," she wrote of both Indian and black people. "I am sick of these lovely lands and peoples being dubbed 'colored *personnel.*'" She anticipated, "of course, total freedom with the active aid of the governing whites for both India and the other colonies. (We'll never be able to make up, either, for all that's been), but . . . I know, I know, I know it will come, the real freeing . . ."[52]

Nancy's other good London friends and acquaintances included John Banting, Harold Acton, Geoffrey Hobson, and his son Anthony. Nancy fascinated Anthony, twenty-five years her junior. He would become a distinguished specialist in book collecting, as well as Italian, Dutch, and French bookbinding, and he would direct Sotheby's book department for twenty years. Even though she knew that "fibrositis and mental, physical, psychic, and intangible exhaustion had [become] my lot," the young man perceived her as the legend she had become. She was, he later said, "in my private mythology a lost Golden Age of happiness and licence":

> Nancy's appearance, bizarrely evocative of the Twenties, with her tall, thin figure, waistless dress, bandeau and long string of beads, would make everyone look up as she came into the room. She herself was unconscious of the stir her entrance caused, having learned long before to ignore those she thought boringly conventional. As she crossed the room one saw her for a moment from outside, noticing the superficial eccentricity, only to be captivated immediately by her warmth of greeting, her distinction of poise and manner, her beautifully modulated voice and magnificent wide set blue eyes. She always listened to one's doings with grave and courteous attention. Conversation was punctuated by the rhythmic clash of the rise and fall of her African ivory bracelets . . . worn seven or eight on each arm.[53]

They lunched frequently at the Savoy Grill or at small restaurants in Soho.

Despite her efforts to socialize with new and old friends, Nancy was often drawn to the past. One night when she was dining with friends, she recalled, with nostalgia, "the 'old' war, with Augustus John, Sybil Hart-Davis and Alvaro Guevara, when . . . that dear Augustus was dashing off exquisite sketches of everyone at the end of the tablecloth. Waiters in consternation were assured that each piece of napery would be paid for, cut up on the spot. . . . I still have the little head thus drawn of me." Then she added: "Let us not get sentimental! It's bad enough when one is in bed at night with one's thoughts. . . . As for people's voices—sometimes they go on and on in one's head, continuing the conversation when one wants to sleep, and can't."[54]

In the spring of 1944, when the new Blitz was launched and Nancy was forced to leave her room, Sylvia and Valentine welcomed her to Dorset. She seemed "in dire need of attention [and] was thin as a wraith and had a tormenting neuritis in her shoulder." The Powys sisters, Gertrude and Philippa, were visiting as well, along with Alyse Gregory, Llewelyn Powys's widow. Nancy was very relaxed in this house of six women and, despite her physical discomfort, she joined them in long walks and collected flora and fauna (concentrating on bees), trying to re-create a sense of prewar youthful innocence. Nancy walked with great speed and on one occasion even confessed that "with a sprained ankle, I climbed the superb and *real* earth to [a] high cliff." She had grown accustomed to walking at least eight miles a day, with or without pain. Sylvia and Valentine still marveled at her ability to lose herself in her intensely hard work when they returned.

Nancy was resigned when this visit to Dorset was cut short because new regulations for the southern coast had been issued. A second front was building—as Nancy put it, a "lengthy and well guarded prelude to the invasion of the continent." As a result, all nonresidents were prohibited from the area and sent thirty miles inland. Once again, Nancy packed, and, as Sylvia recalled, when she left, she "slid the heavy African ivory bracelets off her wrists and asked us to look after them. They would be safer in a Dorset village than in London. She looked sadly at her wrist when they were off. She would have felt much less denuded if she had stripped off her clothes." The bracelets remained hidden for a long time in Sylvia's staircase cupboard.[55]

Before she left Dorset, Nancy told Thompson about her longing for a home. Within the six-month period of their correspondence, she had had at least six different addresses and had often directed her mail in care of Lloyds Bank. She wrote: "By the end, Sisyphus had built something which became fixed to the mountain top thereby increasing its height so that it became a BEACON for all time and was seen from outside the land as well as from within the domain." While she was in Dorset, she wrote a poem to Thompson, "Man-Ship-Gun-Plane," evoking the terror of one's habitual responses during a raid from the air, sea, or ground:

Now the wild horses have it
Burst loose in the dizzy skies in their crazy mad gallopade,
Rearing-careering . . . roaring-careening,
. . . satellite steels, cascade of the shrapnel olive,
Casual flora of lead bloomed on street, iron spawn from the sky's black breast.

When Nancy left Dorset, she returned to London with bombs falling "like mad: all over and around London."

The Poetry Scene

Although groups of writers and artists met frequently after the Blitz, there is no allusion to Nancy's presence at their gatherings, just as there is no mention of these meetings in Nancy's papers. Perhaps the fact that Maud entertained the most celebrated artists of the period helps explain Nancy's absence; perhaps the envy of Edith Sitwell, a successful poet and another important patron of the arts, accounts for it as well.

Nancy had always been a vital member of artistic circles, from her London days to the post–Spanish Civil War period in Chile. However, during World War II—setting aside her relationship with Maud and Edith—it is fair to say that Nancy not only rejected the London literary scene but also was rejected by it. John Lehmann reports that, during the war, "the literary world of London became . . . something like a stable society. . . . We *needed* one another." Lehmann and Cyril Connolly frequently hosted lunch and dinner parties; on occasion, T. S. Eliot did as well; the Sitwells renewed their lavish entertainments of the 1920s; and on Sundays, Viva King held a "War Salon" at her house in Thurloe Square. When Louis Aragon, who had come to symbolize the suffering French, visited London, Connolly arranged a party with London's most distinguished people and Aragon's friends. Nancy was not invited. Lehmann suggested that a major cause of Nancy's isolation was that "the 'grand salons' were organized by 'skillful hostesses,' . . . the chief of them, the most famous and best frequented . . . by Lady Colefax and Lady Cunard."[56]

If Nancy was ignored by the writing establishment and their patrons, she also detached herself from the new writers. Having been a publisher, essayist, journalist, and poet—and having known the most exciting writers of her time—she did not hold the current generation in similar esteem. Scholars of the period, like Robert Hewison, Paul Fussell, and Adam Piette, agree that no significant new talent emerged between 1939 and 1945: poets failed to capture the fear of warfare; they believed they had no better cause for dying than had those in the Great War, and even if convinced of the clear-cut moral nature of the war, they found it difficult to fashion a verse that endorsed violence.[57]

J. B. Priestley, almost as popular as Winston Churchill in his regular radio speeches ("Postscripts" after the Sunday news), went so far as to state that "the war marked the end of literary society." Like Orwell, who considered the writer an anachronism, Symons, Connolly, Lehmann, and Priestley believed that the writer, disheartened if not disgusted by politics, could feel little but guilt or resignation. Auden and Isherwood, after all, had left England in 1939 to escape a "low dishonest decade." As Connolly put it, "Defeatism is their occupational disease." H. G. Wells (*The Fate of Homo Sapiens*), Virginia Woolf

(*Between the Acts*), and T. S. Eliot ("The Idea of a Christian Society") repeatedly associated the disintegration of civilization with contemporary events.[58]

There were exceptions, of course. Herbert Read, a veteran of World War I, was able to address the younger generation of soldiers in "To a Conscript of 1940." Other memorable British war poems include Louis MacNeice's "Brother Fire," C. D. Lewis's "World Over All," and Dylan Thomas's "A Refusal to Mourn" and "Ceremony After a Fire Raid," although Thomas's fame grew out of his poems about childhood and mortality.[59] Lesser-known war poets include the young soldiers Keith Douglas, Sidney Keyes, Alun Lewis, and Richard Hillary—all killed in action—and Henry Treece, Laurie Lee, and Roy Fuller.

Perhaps the best-known war poet, combining patriotism and despair, was Edith Sitwell. In "Still Falls the Rain," in *Street Songs*, she describes an air raid by relating the bombs to Christ's suffering:

> Still falls the Rain
> Dark as the work of man, black as our loss—
> Blind as the nineteen hundred and forty nails
> Upon the cross.

The rain is Christ's stigmata:

> See, see where Christ's blood streams in the firmament:
> It flows from the Brow we nailed upon the tree.

When Edith's reputation revived during the war, she also renewed her role as a patron of the arts, which she had initiated when she published the *Wheels* series (1916–1921) and *Façade* (1922). In the early days, she invited poets to her Bayswater home for tea and penny buns every Tuesday; now, she hosted by-invitation-only readings and elaborate parties. Nancy was no longer a regular guest at Edith's gatherings. In fact, Nancy was overlooked on most occasions by virtually everyone. It was her mother who was invited to all the prestigious readings at elite clubs, along with the literary and social celebrities of the time and, on occasion, with royalty.[60]

Several other factors, however, may explain Nancy's absence at these events—not the least of which was Edith's view of the war as a boring waste of time and talent. More compelling was her jealousy of Nancy. Victoria Glendinning, Edith's award-winning biographer, provides abundant details that portray her competitiveness, envy, and pettiness.[61] To begin, although Edith took credit for the *Wheels* project, many during the 1920s believed that it was Nancy who conceived of the series (and who wrote the title poem for the first collection) and Edith who just contributed to it. In addition, Edith, a six-foot-tall woman who dressed in an eccentric manner, lacked physical and personal charms equal to her creative talents. Nancy was "a new sort of friend for Edith, who was inexperienced and naive in areas in which [Nancy] was wise." "A Bacchante . . . with great aquamarine eyes," Nancy was "sexy, vital, [and] unpredictable."

Furthermore, since Edith at one time had been attracted to Aldous Huxley and at another was in love with the painter Alvaro "Chile" Guevara, "the spoke in Edith's wheel was Nancy Cunard." In 1927, seven years after Nancy moved to Paris, Edith wrote to Gertrude Stein to "watch out" for Guevara, who was planning to move to Paris: "It would be an awful thing if a man with a mind like his had to have it fretted away by the vulgar little clothes moths that sit drinking and pretending to be geniuses in the cafés." Glendinning adds the obvious, unspoken conclusion to the previous sentence: "like her erstwhile colleague, Nancy Cunard, presumably." The final blow was Edith's realization that her brother Osbert was in love with Nancy, "as much as he could be with any woman." In the end, Edith may have never forgiven Nancy for an early review in the *Manchester Guardian* that compared her *Troy Park* with Nancy's *Parallax*. It concluded: "This emotionalism is in danger in Miss Sitwell's new manner, as great as the verbal harlinquinade of the old. Her need is for very stringent criticism. . . . Miss Cunard has a very considerable expressive power. Her language is alive, free from the poetaster's time-worn turns of speech."[62]

Regardless of Nancy's isolation from the literary scene and readings, she published three small collections of war poetry and was invited to contribute to many anthologies; she also published poetry in numerous periodicals. "And Hate's Resistance," dedicated to Aragon and published by the *New Statesman* on January 15, 1942, received considerable attention. In 1944, Nancy published *Relève into Maquis*, about the Germans' failure to enlist the French into their labor force, despite their promises of either payment or a reprieve, or both, for a prisoner or family member. The poem begins with three generations of Frenchmen who see the mayors' orders and Laval's threats and reply:

"No. This Relève, this 'changing of the guard'
Is planned for dupes, by Vichy's fear of us;
They want a France unmanned. We shall not go."

Instead, the speaker "unearth[es] the rabbit gun" and "his old revolver, blessed by Spain," and goes to the maquis. She concludes that from every province they are called with only one gun for every twentieth man. Yet "Here is all

France . . . enlisted until war's end" to uphold France's sacred commandment to "hold your hand / Till it finds Death's hand responding as an ally."

Also before D-Day, Nancy translated a book on the French Resistance by Gabrielle Picabia, the wife of the painter. Months later, on September 9, she wrote in her diary, "The reign of the doodle bug was 80 days." She added a few calculations: "Robot P. Doodle (nickname was Buzz) made his first appearance in London on the 6th of June"; "his main grave, to the tune of 3,500—or more—was Kent and Sussex, and the Shaford, Tunbridge Wells and battle areas; as well as the parish of Wandsworth"; "a total of 8,070 flying bombs came over since the start—375 in the last week of all, which ended at 6 a.m. Sept. 4; some 2,000 got through (to London?) [sic]."

During the first days of the invasion, Nancy kept elaborate notes in her diary. A small portion is cited here:

June 6, 1944 INVASION—The moon was full 1 or 2 days earlier. It begins: Churchill in Commons. Eisenhower at about 11 a.m. spoke to all West European peoples. The Royal Flag flies on Buckingham Palace. June 6—4 years minus 2 days that Vernon, near my town, was bombed first during collapse of France. 2,000 (?) ships carried the invading forces. Parachutists were landed beyond the coast inland. Ships shelled coast. . . . I saw Charles Duff: "A very well-guarded surprise," he said. . . . A thunder of planes unseen in a cloud-rich sky.

5:30 p.m. BROADCAST— . . . Parachutes landed beyond German defenses. De Gaulle spoke from London: "Le Battaile Suprème est engagée [The supreme battle has begun]." . . .

6 p.m. CHURCHILL—"The battle now begun will grow in intensity for many weeks." First news was broadcast at 9.30 a.m. to world from S.H.A.E.F. headquarters. Beach head taken, dug in. There was blanket of cloud—Airborne troops were told "Raise all the hell possible" at the back of the Germans. . . . Over 1,300 bombers dropped 5,000 tons on coastal batteries. Sir Trafford Mallory, Air Chief Admiral, Admiral Sir Bertram Ramsey: "The greatest amphibious operation of all times." The naval bombardment began at dawn. Landings quickly followed: "It's not a question of keeping up the men's spirits. It's of keeping them back—so eager are they." The sun shone in the afternoon. The wind blew shoreward. French inhabitants were warned to leave towns, disperse in fields away from road and rail. We shall bomb heavily. However, do not rise prematurely. Be patient. Prepare—great battles lie ahead. We shall accept no less than full victory. . . . Montgomery to his men: "Good luck and good hunting. To us is given the honor to strike a blow that will live in history."

Correspondents—The ships stretched for miles across the horizon. The men were kept isolated for days before going. Board "security" has been unprecedented.

6:30 p.m. CHURCHILL—Landings have been successful all along line. Follow-ups proceeding with very much less loss than expected.

9 p.m. KING GEORGE VI—A chime of Big Ben. The light shone faintly on damask roses as the king spoke.

Religiously—as vague and general as a pause of utter silence between words.

Hesitant, conscientious, well-meant—full of meaning . . .

Trammeled—Even so taking it on the whole. Un-real in the light of the reality of the Continent Where It Is Going On. (Brit then, relativeness preserved. So was De Gaulle's.)

12 p.m. BBC—31,000 airmen in action, losses among airborne troops much less than feared might be. The attack put off 24 hours because of weather. . . . "You hardly see the sky for our planes," said a pilot. 640 guns battered coasts. . . . At dusk it rained.

WEDNESDAY, June 7— . . . *BBC 6 p.m.*—The Germans have said that they inflicted much damage but that the Allies hold 3 bridgeheads. . . .

THURSDAY, June 8— . . . Very little news. We are not told of how the French are reacting.

FRIDAY, June 9—Correspondents tell of the joy of the French and particularly stress the *efficiency* with which they have organized themselves, making small personal shelters. An old woman told one that the Germans fled with great fear from the force of the Landings. German prisoners have arrived in England. Paris reported short of light, gas, water. The French reveal they had been told by German military leaders that nothing could break the defense on the coast.

BBC 6 p.m.— . . . Lindsay Drummond told me a British ship equipped with radio and recording apparatus went off Calais, sent out a thick smokescreen, put on records and "noises" of "unmistakable British tars" shouting things like "Let the bloody anchor down" to draw German fire, and then left the "vessel." . . . The Germans stated they had repulsed an attempt off Calais.[63]

After the invasion "grandly progressed," Nancy wanted nothing more than to return to Réanville. With little information circulating between England and France—the shortest message to Réanville might take up to six months—Nancy had to summon great patience. All the same, she wrote one friend: "I am telling myself I KNOW the only thing left at Réanville will be the thyme bush there."[64] The London newspapers had been filled with stories about the devastation that followed the invasion, and Nancy heard "there was the hell of a bombardment in [nearby] Vernon," but she had no idea if it had reached her home. The Nazis were also routinely destroying houses as their last acts of war. The *Times* thoroughly covered the transformation of once-beautiful villages like Saint-Lô with breathtakingly grotesque images of inexpressible human despair.[65] Once lands of milk and apple scents, they were now funeral pyres with smoke coming out of the beaten earth.

Finally, and to her despair, she received news about her home. Her two friends watching over the house, Jean and Georgette Goasgüen, wrote: "Nothing, nothing is left." Gilbert, who had reported on the Allied advance for the *New York Times*, located a jeep, drove to her house, and returned with a tattered copy of one of her Hours Press books. He informed her that the "shambles of my Puits Carré" were due entirely to the animosity of the mayor, for no fighting ever occurred just around it. Gilbert said that "a mattress of ravaged books, six deep, now covers the whole of the bathroom floor." Nancy tried to maintain control: "Which books are down the well, and which ivories safe, I am much wondering. Vistas of great difficulties ahead, of need of tact, of still-suppressed wrath and disgust."[66]

With the new year upon her, she decided to start her "own campaign" to get back to France. Perhaps now she could receive commissions as a journalist. To her great satisfaction, she was visited one day by Tancred Borenius, editor of the *Burlington Magazine*, at her "rickety, bomb-shaken room in Jermyn Street." He commissioned her to look into the artworks in France that were missing after the German withdrawal. And

> there we sat. . . . How grim and cold was all this December; how symbolic—said he—of life nowadays. . . . Alas, nothing would ever be the same again. . . . We sat huddled over my small electric-heater. . . . No, nothing. And in process of sad talk and nostalgic memories, he thought he discerned a palm-tree in the concave curve. . . . It was but a tiny breath of grease from my solitary, clandestine cooking, yet it caused him to sigh for such far-away inaccessible strands.[67]

● ● ●

With the help of Peter Watson and Cyril Connolly of *Horizon* and other writers at *Our Time*, she received additional assignments. She also wrote for *Connoisseur* and the French magazine *Europe*. She continued her reports on black military troops for the ANP. Shortly thereafter, and sponsored by the British Council, she received permission to return to France.

14

Surviving Réanville

Can a miracle happen to whole countries . . . to all us of us everywhere,
so that the blasted weapons stacked up all round turn into ploughshares?

—NANCY CUNARD

Nancy returned to France on February 27, 1945. She felt like a displaced person, experiencing "an inexplicable sense of faltering," as if she had "risen from the dead . . . like Lazarus." "How bitter-bitter sweet," she wrote, "was th[e] exultation" of returning to Paris. She wandered from one end of the isolated city to the other, joyous when she heard that certain friends were alive, deeply saddened about those who were not. Paris was as beautiful as ever, but she felt disconnected from it. She was incredulous that the city had been virtually untouched by bombs. Georges Sadoul later told her that "every one of us, Aragon included, felt like this on returning to Paris from exile or from the Southern zone."[1] To force herself out of her "dreadful sense of strangeness," she visited Louis Parrot, editor of *Ce Soir*, one of the great Resistance newspapers. He described the efflorescence of great books and art now taking place by Aragon, Éluard, Sartre, Camus, and Malraux. Magazines were filled with the poetry of the Resistance, like Aragon's immensely patriotic lyrics in *Le Crève Coeur*, about France during the Nazi occupation. Even Cocteau, who had befriended the Germans, was enjoying widespread popularity.

Nancy's article for the June 1945 issue of *Horizon*, "Letter from Paris," recounted her return and how "with a surging tear I embraced the blue-bloused [train] porter, a hefty man, who said with emotion that it had been *trè dur* [very difficult] indeed during the horror of these years." At last, she wrote, she was home: "Paris at last, Paris, . . . twenty years my home." In the article,

Nancy tried to capture the lingering effects of "the misery of Occupation." She alluded to the city's unusual silence, how everyone still lived as if in a perpetual state of waiting. The Parisians had shown great integrity, she wrote, and the "Myth of the Maréchal [Pétain] never took in the great majority of the French." They had remained energetic and optimistic despite severe shortages. Paris would remain, for some time to come, a city of austerity, suffering, and want.[2]

She wrote about Camus, Sartre, Valéry, Aragon, and Éluard, as well as various art exhibitions; she predicted immortality for the new film *Les Enfants du paradis* and the new drama *No Exit*. Café de Flore, during the war "a perfect moral fortress against the Boches" and meeting place for Sartre, had now become a center for Resistance people. She was highly critical of any disparagement directed toward the Americans or British. Again and again, she applauded the indomitable French spirit: "The Germans have massacred, tortured, blackmailed, attacked psychologically and done much more, but they have emphatically NEVER dominated the spirit of the men, women and children of France. They have tried to make people as corrupt as themselves (and in some cases Vichy fascists could give the Germans lessons in baseness and vice)." One senses a personal note in her desire for a closer relationship between England, her birthplace, and France, her adopted home: "In the time, first, of amelioration, then of well-being that one hopes is on the way, friendship and a deeper feeling than ever for England will be evident. . . . Our countries need each other."

Nancy was grateful for her writing assignments, although they were not her métier: "What interests me is journalism. I am becoming a theater critic. Not my line but there you are," she wrote to a friend. Her major problem, and a critical one at that, was her lack of funds. She was nearly destitute: "A very difficult life is that in Paris. . . . Difficulties with money are dire. . . . Flore and Deux Magots open at about 9:30. Tea, white wine, filter 'beer' is what they serve. . . . Expensive. . . . [People travel in] little bicycle rickshaws. Not been in one ever as they charge hundreds of francs." Nancy refused financial help from her friends, confessing with amusement and vanity: "I can think of nothing I want save some DEPILATORY! (I want that fashion to change too!)."[3]

She had no home or future profession. She told Janet Flanner that she was living on £30 a month, in addition to a small income from writing. She would soon resort to selling a dress or blouse for a few francs and continue the Spartan lifestyle she had mastered in London—warming potatoes and food from tins on an electric heater, brewing tea in her room, and accepting jam and other provisions from the Red Cross and Americans. "If you can live in," she later wrote, "and combine hotel and 'in' (which I do with the long-lasting Red Cross and remains of the American staff), you eat for much less and you eat better. If you live IN, with French rations, and vegetables which can be bought, you save enormously. (How I go on writing about prices!)." Her next admission would recur more frequently in the years to come: "Loneliness is about the worst hell, and more so these times than ever before." During the first half of the next decade, she honed her survival techniques into an art, focusing on social and political causes, rather than material or emotional needs.

So Much . . . Gone Forever

Nancy had yet to see the shambles of her home in Réanville, an experience that deflated her exuberant faith in the French. She learned, as she later wrote, that

> one day during the war, a "woman gathering grass for her rabbits" observed the arrival of a black Citroen car, with two obvious German civilians ("cropped heads, squinty eyes, thin-rimmed gold specs") who went into my house, remained there two hours and issued laden with heavy, stuffed sacks (which, she noted, they had brought with them) which might have contained lots of ivory—judging by the noise they made—and with these, and many books, drove off.[4]

The mayor, a collaborator who had already confiscated several farms, then ordered Jean and Georgette Goasgüen, the friends who had watched over the house, to give him the keys. He opened the house to everyone in the vicinity to pillage at will. Le Puits Carré was looted by Nancy's neighbors; the Germans returned to finish the task, which included burning many items.

When Nancy saw the monumental wreckage, it was as though her past—her possessions and her friends and their experiences together—had been personally and savagely attacked:

> Invisible blood and tears of ravaged books and pictures! Here, a drawing by Wyndham Lewis under a tree. . . . There, among scattered pieces of type and shreds of African beading under the straw . . . some fragments of coral, hammered to smithereens. *Punch* . . . ceremoniously burned . . . on the grass, before stoning all my pieces of African sculpture . . . and blazing them up in the kitchen stove. Stabbed papers, wounds and mutilations everywhere.[5]

Doors and shutters had been ripped from their hinges; furniture, used as firewood. Nancy's precious ivories and oriental rugs had been stolen. Important documents and letters had been thrown into a deep well that was covered by excrement and a rotting animal carcass. Canvasses without frames hung on her pear trees. Her two Mirós and the Picabia had been torn apart. There were eleven bullet holes in her de Chirico. Her magnificent linden trees had been scorched by the fires that had burned her papers and books. The large thyme bush at the back of the house was gone. "The missing bush seemed to say," she wrote: "'No more, no more of any of this for you. Don't try to come back.'"[6]

When Nancy first saw the Goasgüens, she embraced them, "thanked them both from her heart," and gave them a sum of money that left them speechless. She tried to sue the fascist mayor, Bouret, and typed a fourteen-page inventory, modestly calculating a total loss of £3,600 pounds: £1,200 for damage to the house and land; £1,500 for the artworks; £900 for the pictures, books, and furniture. The case languished for several years. Nancy was accused of being a foreign subversive, and the suit was finally dismissed on grounds of insufficient evidence. During her subsequent spells of solitude, she stopped writing to her closest friends. Finally, she wrote to Janet/Solita: "France is DAMN different. . . . It is, to me, bitter and empty and entirely different in character." In a poem about Réanville, "my once-home, July 15, 1945," she wrote:

> "Death to the intellect!" was roared—
> Those Norman peasants heard the cry
> And oped their breeches and let fly.
> The Germans only burned the books
> And played their war and went away—
> The peasants shat another day.[7]

As Herman Schrijver put it, "Nancy's house had not been bombed. It was very carefully and very systematically broken up and looted by the Nazis, aided and abetted, I am afraid, by the villagers, for Nancy's name was high up on a list of intellectuals to be destroyed at all cost." Another friend was more specific: "The German commandant had declared that if he could lay hands on her he would hang her, because hers was one of the first names on the Führer's black list."[8]

She spent several days raking through the disarray, collecting whatever she could, including some ivory bracelets scattered in the fields. But all her precious letters—the remembrances of a lifetime—were gone "into the domain of what one now calls 'Before': gone were those letters of Arthur Symons, Aldous Huxley, Michael Arlen, Richard Aldington, Ezra Pound, T. S. Eliot, Wyndham Lewis, Robert Graves, Robert Nichols, Ronald Firbank, Roy Campbell, Osbert Sitwell, T. W. Earp, Sir John Hutchinson, Louise Morgan, . . . John Strachey, Iris Tree, Alvaro Guevara, Louis Aragon, Breton, Tzara, Crevel." Destroyed as well were three-quarters of the material for *Negro*— several hundred volumes of articles, photographs, and documents on race—

and most of her articles, books, poems, translations, and letters from the Spanish Civil War years. "How well, without benefit of bombs, may all the stuff of forty years be ravaged in a few days," she said. She mourned her "books, documents, paintings, letters—all *finis*. . . . So much was gone forever."[9]

Nancy repeated these words twenty-five years later in *These Were the Hours*, where she also recaptured the moment she realized that hers was the only targeted house in the area. It was an exquisite moment, for it gave her further insight into the power of the word: language was an even greater political weapon than she had thought when she published *Authors Take Sides* and *Poems for France*: "I cannot analyze my strange feeling. It was 'a discovery of something entirely new, bound up with something entirely past.'"[10]

The authorities had visited the house even before the Nazi occupation, when it was uninhabited. As she wrote:

> A press is very dangerous. It means the dissemination of ideas, obviously very bad ones in this case. . . . That would be the line taken in general at Réanville, I thought. . . . Yes, the French police had come to the house. It was in March 1940, before Hitler was on the move, during the phony-war period. They had made a thorough search, were particularly interested in books and papers. . . . [They] removed all the books for a time. . . . The rumor must have gone round that [I] was printing clandestine sheets of something or other that were somehow "dangerous."

Throughout, the venerable iron Mathieu press remained undamaged. She contemplated the "detestable permanent war-within-war of hatred in the village" with a measure of stoicism and, feeling once again like Lazarus emerging from the grave into life, explained:

> It was no sense of fatalism that made me accept the sack and loot, the ruin and end of Le Puits Carré. The very word "accept" is wrong, for one is not in a position to "accept" or to "refuse" a fact. Do either and nothing will be any different. . . . An absence of five years and more now led . . . to what? To a sort of voyage of discovery—of the *discovery* of *destruction*, and within it there was an element of "return after death."

Nancy discovered thirty letters of Caslon typeface in an old tin cigarette box. They seemed to symbolically repudiate the destruction: how well their survival defied "that famous cry 'Death to the intellect!' first shouted in Spain and later in Germany." Her subsequent meeting with Stuart Gilbert, the James Joyce scholar, at the British Embassy, also seemed prophetic. They spoke about the war and of return to France:

And then something he said made me start. . . . His voice had been as soft and remote as one imagines that of an oracle to be. But the roles were reversed, as if the oracle were questioning, the oracle making enquiry of the questioner, for what should come from his lips, so gently said, but "Are you going to start the Hours Press again?"

These are the last lines of *These Were the Hours*, and as the title reveals, this *was* the end of the Hours Press. Although Nancy would suffer a severe depression after returning to Réanville, she would soon thereafter reengage the enemies of freedom and equality through the written word.

First, she had to sell the house in Réanville. She lacked the money to repair it, but, more important, it was unthinkable to remain near her assailants. As she looked for a house during the next few years, she mourned everything that Réanville represented. Her friends tried to comfort her. Louise Morgan, frustrated and heartbroken for Nancy, wrote: "What I want to do, and what I would do, without conscience, is to rob the Victoria and Albert for you—Persian carpets, mandarin China. . . . But what about all the things I would not find at the V & A!"[11] For the next decade, Nancy would send inquiries and visit museums throughout the world in search of her lost treasures.

To add to her woes, she and Morris Gilbert separated. They had been moving from one hotel or borrowed flat to another and discussing a permanent relationship. But he had yet to separate from his wife, and they both knew that he would eventually return to the United States. Unsure about her future and inconsolable over the calamity at Réanville, Nancy again called this the "most incoherent time of my life. . . . Where, for one, where to live?"[12] The question would dominate her thoughts during the last days of her life.

When Gilbert left for America in 1946, Nancy went to Spain. She wrote a series of special reports for *Ce Soir*, urging a renewal of forces against Franco and reporting the conditions in his prisons and camps. She wrote letters to the *Nation* about Spanish Republicans arrested in the southwestern departments of France, brutally separated from their families and dispatched to Corsica and Algeria. She still wanted to be a correspondent for the *Guardian* and contacted A. P. Wadsworth, appointed to Crozier's position after his death in 1944. Aware that Nancy would need a visa to get into Spain, he and his associate J. M. Pringle exchanged memos, agreeing that she would be unable to go as long as Franco was in power. Even when she assured them that she could obtain a visa (and had been in Spain for two and a half months) and could supply firsthand information, they were reluctant: "Yes, when the time comes." She resumed her rescue activities. Writing from the foot of the Pyrenees, she modestly informed Janet/Solita that she had "liberat[ed] eighteen men condemned to death right in the jail itself." Then she added, "Thanks for the cigarettes for the Spanish," but "I need nothing, nothing at all."[13]

After five weeks in Andorra, she was forced to leave what she called the most expensive place in Europe, owing to "Franco's beastly money being the currency." Toulouse had been a welcome center for exiled anti-Franco Spaniards, and she returned to former battlegrounds like Bourg Madame. But after several weeks, she realized how "absolutely ghastly" the "Spanish situation is, . . . tragic beyond words. I have been very near to it, much closer than even before, including war days there and all." She vowed to be "WITH the Spanish workers for ever and AGAINST their enemies who are and always have been mine."

In leaving Spain, she wrote: "This has been most trying and MOST complicated, . . . and strange. That is because . . . Spain is as complex as the heart." She also wrote a number of poems in Spanish, pledging: "I shall write no more poems in English until something good come for Spain. That is the way I feel about it and that is all I can do."[14]

Carpe Diem and Tedium

In the spring of 1947, after one of her trips to Spain, Nancy returned to Paris and took both a room at the Hotel Montana and a new American lover, the wealthy and urbane William Le Page Finley. He was twenty-four; she was fifty-one. Good-looking, charming, and literate, he shared her political views regarding Spain and racial equality. When they first met, Nancy suggested they have lunch. He found that

> her looks and charm quite overpowered me. . . . She told me about the destruction of her house in Normandy by the Germans, that she intended to sell it and would I like to come with her to see it. We set off for Vernon where we stayed at a hotel and walked back and forth to the ruined house while she was negotiating the sale. The walks seemed endless to me but she never tired of walking all the time I knew her.[15]

Nancy was taken by Finley's background—he was American, Irish, and Native American—a combination of Henry Crowder and G. M., perhaps. She introduced him to her friends, unembarrassed about their age difference. They enjoyed traveling together, but when they went to Spain, now nearly ten years after the war, Nancy despaired: "My heart was dry and hard with hatred . . . and drier yet . . . at the increasing feeling that nothing will be done by 'the democracies' against Franco's detested regime." After a month in Portugal, Nancy and Finley went to Mexico, and when Finley was suddenly called back to New York, he left a depressed and near-penniless Nancy. She was about to suffer a number of debilitating mishaps.

First, she lost her footing while hiking and spiked the cornea of her eye on a cactus; her doctor was unsure if she would recover her sight. Then three teeth became abscessed and had to be removed; she drank tequila and, with one eye in bandages, wrote her articles. At one point, she remarked that her injuries would have been tolerable if they had been inflicted in battle. Trying, as usual, to emphasize the positive aspects of her life, she wrote Janet/Solita that all these problems were "now over and glad indeed am I of that. Pain finished and discomfort."

Her eye healed in two weeks, and she returned to Paris with a stopover in Barbados, where she hoped to see her cousin Edward. When she got stranded in Panama, the resourceful Nancy boarded "a tub," an uncomfortable, fetid, old troopship that took her back to France. After a young Jamaican stowaway was discovered on board, Nancy took up a collection so the girl could begin a new life in Europe. When Nancy returned home in the summer of 1948, she lamented: "Back again in France, [but] without any kind of 'house.'" Even though Finley had returned, she felt totally dislocated. She looked at "a tumble-down cottage" in southwestern France, in the area of Josephine Baker's château, and thought it would afford a measure of security. Nancy knew, in her own words, that "lack of a base is very bad for me. That is my trouble, my difficulty, my preoccupation. . . . God! for a house!" For Nancy, a "small house of my own" was an affirmation of her identity, as intimate and integral to survival as her physical well-being.

She traveled to Giverny with Finley after contracting what she called a "poisoned arm," an enormous swelling and fever perhaps following the sting of an insect; she had to remain in the hospital for a few days. She was most annoyed that the pain interfered with her assignments, "Londres Eté 48" for *Europe* magazine and an essay on Mexico for *Our Time*. After she was released, she and Finley checked into the Hotel de l'Arche de Noël; their nights of dissipated revelry were not unlike those Nancy had enjoyed in southern France in 1919. "It's divine here," she wrote; "Days in fields, nights with absolutely fantastic assortments of 'summerites': an ex-show girl Ziegfeld Follies style, Diaghilev's nephew, a broken-nosed British ex-Russian priest, a small brown irreducible French governess, and my own strange beautiful poetic Irish-Red Indian-American 'boy friend.' That was last night's lot."

"There are plenty more," she added, and the next night some English writers appeared: Malcolm Lowry and his wife, Margerie; Margaret Anderson (convicted in 1921 of publishing an episode of *Ulysses* in her *Little Review*) and her friend Dorothy Caruso (widow of the great tenor); and Sybille Bedford and Esther Murphy (once married to John Strachey, Nancy's former lover, in her words: "Indeed a very great friend at one time"). Nancy also found two old friends in town, Joan Black and Eda Lord. Although she thought the group was one where "girls like boys and boys like girls," she was about to learn otherwise about Finley.

One evening, Lowry and Finley, along with a bottle of gin, disappeared into an empty bedroom at Joan Black's house. When Nancy and the others located them, a nasty scene followed. The gin was removed, but the two men remained in the room. The next morning, they bought a bottle of cognac and locked themselves in a larger room, "stripped and went to bed with the cognac," as Finley recalls the event. By noon, Nancy and Lowry's wife were at the door, which Finley refused to open, pleading: "Can't you understand when two men want to be alone together?" Undeterred, Margerie got Malcolm dressed and took him away.

About this time, Maud became seriously ill. Her persistent sore throat turned into pneumonia, and just as she appeared to be recovering, she was diagnosed with throat cancer. A mutual friend kept Nancy informed about her mother's condition, and Nancy frequently corresponded with Janet and Solita about Maud's health. Shortly before her mother died, Nancy wanted to know if she had asked for her; after learning that she had not, Nancy did not go to her bedside. When Maud died on July 10, 1948, Nancy was in the Pyrenees on one of her clandestine trips. She returned and attended neither her mother's cremation nor the scattering of her ashes at Grosvenor Square. She wept, according to Finley, when she recalled Beecham's desertion of Maud to marry another woman.

Maud left an estate that was far smaller than one would have expected. After losing most of her fortune during the stock market crash, she had sold many of her paintings and jewels—substituting expensive imitations—in order to continue living in the style to which she had grown accustomed. Nancy had once taken an "emerald" bracelet her mother had given her to Cartier's for an evaluation: "They broke the news to me that the stones were one of the most remarkable imitations they had seen and were worth every penny of some derisory sum."[16]

Maud's estate was equally divided between Nancy and two close friends, Lady Diana Cooper and Sir Robert Abdy. In addition to £300 a year, Nancy was to receive S. C. Harrison's portrait of G. M. and G. M.'s *Étude pour le Linge* by Manet (after some litigation). Maud had inherited many of G. M.'s paintings, and most of them, along with her Poussin and Fragonard, Manuel Ortiz de Zárate's image of Nancy as a madonna, and Chile Guevara's magnificent portrait of Nancy (her most valuable painting), were auctioned at Christie's. G. M.'s love letters, which were to be published, had been left to

Sacheverell Sitwell, and this unsettled Nancy, who wanted to protect her mother's privacy. She paid Sitwell the £300 at which the letters were appraised and allowed Rupert Hart-Davis to publish them. The letters "read beautifully," she said afterward. Rupert "has edited them with the utmost taste [and] skill."

A month after Maud's death, Nancy changed her mind about buying the house in France: "I shall . . . get [a] hotel room [so] I can . . . be more in England too."[17] Perhaps her mother's death had left her free to return to London. Also about a month after Maud died, a reporter for the right-wing magazine *La Bataille* published a mean-spirited article about Nancy that only intensified her desire to leave France. In "Too Revolutionary to Be a Communist, the Rich Heiress Has Refused Millions and Nancy Cunard Lives by Her Pen in a French Village," he described Nancy as a physical disaster pitied by the local villagers:

> So who is this woman of uncertain age, with disheveled hair, dressed in old trousers and a cardigan? Her arms are as thin as those of the wretches returning from Ravensbrück, the feet she places on the steps of the village bus show a protruding vein, and her ankle bone looks as if it would pierce the skin. And yet there is a sparkle in the eye, a twitch of the mouth . . . yes, it is her. It is the Nancy Cunard, one of the curiosities of the interwar period, Aragon's egeria from the time.[18]

Nancy's ambivalence toward France increased. She became consumed with the destruction at Réanville. She sent "Death to the Intellect (For Hadley Mourer, Hemingway's first wife)" to her publisher-friend Roger Senhouse. The poem is also about Spain and World War II:

> Here is a bead, a mask, a hair
> I wore before the men were shot
> In Badajoz, Guernica bombed,
> And boys and girls freed, then entombed
> All in a day, now here, now there,
> Across the world, the roaring world.[19]

She agreed to return with Finley to the Dordogne, that bucolic region of France she associated with Pound and Crowder. She rented a cottage near Souillac, and, according to one observer, Finley ended the relationship, finding Nancy too possessive and tired of their drunken quarrels: "I adored her looks, her character, the stories she had to tell . . . [but] with her I had no life of my own." "Furthermore," he explained, "I preferred male companionship." Finley briefly reentered Nancy's life in the 1960s. He wrote, "My dear Nancy. . . . I don't quite know how to begin this but . . . the important thing is

I want to see you, if only for lunch or dinner in Souillac." Then he concocted a story about his mother's death and asked Nancy for some money. She replied by telegram, "Rencontre absolument impossible, Cunard."[20] Finley finis.

For the rest of 1948 and for several months in 1949, Nancy traveled through the Dordogne. Its beauty resuscitated her. The area, with its golden limestone villages and magnificent flowers, was rich in prehistoric artifacts and ruins and remnants of the Gauls, Romans, and Franks. The river had been the historic frontier between England and France during the Hundred Years' War. Nancy called the region the land of the caveman, the cradle of the race.[21]

She began the "Dordogne" manuscript in October 1948, adding beside the date, "ten years after the Munich peace" and "the pages that follow seem to me to belong to the arts of peace. . . . Do I dare think that we have entered the zones of peace again?"[22] "Dordogne" would include both poems and prose—elaborate descriptions of tiny villages and their antiquities: their history, architecture, uniqueness in population, local dialects, flowers, produce, and miscellanea. Since her diaries of 1948 and 1949 are a first draft of the prose section, they are interspersed with anecdotal material—her first visit to Cahors in 1920 in "Fred De Fenzo's white racing Bugatti; . . . Josephine Baker has a [Renaissance] chateau here. She looked superb in her white North African French uniform on the occasion of the anniversary of the liberation of Cahors." Nancy's writing becomes more trenchant when she speaks of twenty-two people shot nearby "in error" by the Germans in retaliation for a maquis raid: they had confused the name of the village Roufignac for Roufillhac.

A Second War Against Franco

Nancy traveled to Spain throughout the 1950s and, unallied to any political organization, pursued her various commitments, rescuing prisoners and smuggling them to France, delivering clothing and whatever money she could raise to friends with names like "El Segador" and "Aquesto," former Republican soldiers and Spanish maquisards. She rarely wrote friends about her activities, but when she did, she referred only to her rescue endeavors—tending women, children, and impoverished Republican soldiers still in hiding who "often arrived after five days on the mountain, in rags and with bleeding feet." One such soldier, Hidalgo, with Nancy's help, was eventually able to leave Spain and keep his family together. "I will send you snapshots," she wrote Janet/Solita—of María, Hidalgo's wife, and their child Antonita, "so sweet and very dark, Hidalgo being 'a blond' of exactly my colors."[23]

When Kay received letters like this, she praised Nancy for her courage, but Nancy replied,

I BEG you not to set me up so. That is sheer nonsense! There have always, and always, and always, been so many people in the world to protest against injustices. I am a grain of sand among them, yes, perhaps that. But what more?[24]

According to several commentators, it was said in the late 1940s that Nancy was literally waging war in Spain: "She took . . . lessons in dynamiting"; a second observer reported that she was "involved in smuggling arms from Toulouse across the border" and "was learning about explosives." A third described how she descended "for months at a time to pursue some complicated political plot with a community of exiled Spanish Republicans."[25] Although Nancy was arrested as a subversive on some of her trips, as the *Guardian* editors feared, she remained undaunted in her goals. She pursued her political agenda until she was physically incapable of traveling any longer.

Nancy liked the "virile" Spanish men (her frequent description): "There was love in Andorra, great love and much of it. Excitement, tragedy, danger, beauty, huge walks, climbing, dawns and nights, and WINE and TOBACCO." She felt most alive in Spain: "The heart, the mind, the days have all been full; good all-around eighteen-hour days (few, if any dawns) ploughing a way through *diurnal mischiefs*." Her scrapbooks are filled with unidentified attractive, younger men, as well as "Donald," the poet Neftali Bettram, and Tómas Canas Morales, with whom she was involved for several years.[26]

Since the end of World War II, Nancy had been consumed with the abhorrent chain of events that had made Spain the sacrificial lamb in the preservation of the free world. She had long remonstrated: "No one understands how Labour . . . can befriend Franco, not throw him out." Still hopeful that the righteous would prevail, she had urged her friends: "When people ask you what sort of thing is going on in Spain you can tell them: 'Thousands of guerrilleros [are] still and always working at the overthrow of Franco and the restoration of the Republic with NO compromise with any possible plan of the monarchy.'"[27] Nancy was one of many survivors involved, in a manner of speaking, in a second war against Franco—the guerrilla war that followed World War II, after which the seemingly indomitable ideals of a people would be once again defeated by the politics of nonintervention and opportunism.

The Spanish were to be victims of an appalling repetition of events. During World War II, international support of Franco among the Allies had fluctuated from one extreme to the other. But after the war and victory over fascism, Nancy, like a vast number of Spanish Republicans, assumed that the Allies would rid the world of Franco, as they had of Mussolini and Hitler. With the onset of the Cold War, however, with both Franco's continuing rancor toward Stalin and Spain's strategic geographical position in relation to the Soviet Union, Franco was permitted to remain in power. To Nancy and many others,

Franco was rewarded and even courted as an invaluable ally against Stalin. In fact, Franco's espousal of neutrality, alongside his explanation that Spain's policy was to be dictated by Spanish interests, allowed him to exploit both the Allies and the Axis powers at one time or another. As the leader of a neutral state, he felt "entitled to sell to the highest bidder"—first, his former ally, Germany, during its successes; later, the Allies during theirs. It would appear that Franco had come to believe the inscription on every Spanish coin—that he, the "Caudillo of Spain by the Grace of God," was responsible to only God and himself.

Franco's political nerve was remarkable. Although he had declared neutrality shortly after the beginning of World War II, his commitment to the Axis powers was blatant. In 1939, he had joined the Anti-Comintern pact and signed a secret treaty of friendship with Hitler. For the first three years of the war, with the Nazi war machine in the ascendancy, he was confident that Spain would have a place in Hitler's new world order. His state-controlled press praised every German victory and ignored, for as long as possible, every defeat. Franco allowed German submarines to occupy Spanish ports, German planes to use his landing strips, and German spies and saboteurs to roam his country. Furthermore, Hitler's invasion of the Soviet Union in 1941 allowed him an opportunity to actively avenge his enemies from the Spanish Civil War. He sent 18,700 of his Blue Division of Falangist volunteers to fight on the Eastern Front and developed his concept of "two wars": noninterventionist in the West; belligerent in the East. Hugh Thomas believes that Franco did not join Hitler in 1939 because Hitler refused to forgive Spain's Civil War debt of 400 million reichsmarks (saying it made him feel "almost like a jew [sic] who wants to make business out of the holiest possessions of mankind").[28]

With America's entrance into the war at the end of 1941, the tide began to turn. After the Allied landing in North Africa in 1942 and the fall of Stalingrad in 1943, the opportunistic Franco assumed a seemingly more genuine neutral position. At one and the same time, he smiled on the Allies (and "London, New York, and Washington—the strategists of economic warfare—[also] felt entitled to rub their hands"),[29] although he continued to send wolfram (tungsten) to Germany secretly. In 1944, Spain and the United States made several mutually beneficial agreements. Franco closed the German consulate in Tangier, expelled German spies and saboteurs from Spain, and stopped all wolfram shipments to Germany—in exchange for petroleum and other essential supplies. He allowed the Allies to use his landing fields, and Allied espionage agents were invited to begin their operations in Madrid.

In spite of this, in 1945, the United Nations, unforgiving of Franco's former collaborative activities with Hitler and Mussolini, repudiated Franco (with "incontrovertible evidence" of his "guilt") and denied Spain membership. In

1946, the U.N. General Assembly declared that Spain would be banned from the organization and all its special agencies as long as Franco remained in power. When the arrogant Franco heard about these proclamations, he uttered the famous response "Really?" adding that he had more important matters to consider that day, like his painting.

The period from 1944 to 1946 was a time of great hope for the Spanish anti-Francoists. Nancy recalled a visit at her London flat in 1944 by Spanish refugees now working in England, offering their skills as mechanics, as they put it, to serve "the machines of democracy." They had escaped from the camps and bore terrible scars on their bodies from the vicious police dogs guarding the Pyrenean frontiers. With changes in the war situation, the French, to some extent, had eased conditions in the camps, enabling more prisoners to escape, even though executions still continued. "The coming victory of the Allies is now plain," her guests explained, "and France must find some sort of conciliatory way out." They emphasized that their deep hatred of Franco and the Falange was shared by 95 percent of the Spanish people. They also emphasized their certainty that "Britain's victory over Fascism would mean theirs," repeating *"They wanted to work for that."*[30]

They spoke of many things, including the jubilation of the Spanish after the Allied victories in the Mediterranean and in North Africa. Of major concern was the future government in Spain. In the event of a restoration of the Republic, would the Republican leaders in exile return and assume their former positions? "No, they thought, or not at first. New leaders would come, men not identified with the Spanish war." They emphasized: "A democratic Republic is what Spain needs." Nancy's prescient last question to them was "Could Franco outlive the downfall of Nazism?" and they replied, "scornfully: *Can Spain exist as the only Fascist state after the democracy of the United Nations has triumphed?*"

She was to watch Spain's fate with increasing disbelief. At the U.N. meeting in San Francisco in 1945, the Junta Española de la Liberación felt assured that the government in exile would replace Franco. It assumed that after U.N. censure of Franco and an economic blockade, cessation of diplomatic relations would follow, and this would immediately end Franco's regime. However, the Western victors were generous only with their condemnation; they remained chary of any action, political or military, that might actually remove Franco. Although Franco was condemned by the civilized world—perhaps most vociferously by Charles de Gaulle and his government, whose proposal to the Security Council to end relations with Franco failed—the Spanish were once again to be left to their own resources.

At the Potsdam Conference in 1945, where Stalin alone argued for Allied intervention against Franco, Churchill, while clearly sympathetic to the

Republicans, repeated that the destiny of Spain remained in its own hands and that Britain would not interfere; nor did the British break relations with Franco. When Harry Truman said in passing that he "held no brief" for Franco, Churchill seized on the moment to convince him that any kind of interference might cause yet another civil war.

With the onset of the Cold War, the renewal of noninventionist policies signaled another betrayal of the Spanish Republicans. Franco's anti-Communist position was significant—for example, in America's dramatic revision of its policies. Between 1948 and 1950, and following the fall of Czechoslovakia, the Berlin blockade, and the outbreak of the Korean War, the United States normalized political and economic relations with Spain: the boycott of Franco's regime was lifted, full diplomatic relations were restored, cultural and educational exchange programs were established, and President Truman signed a $62.5 million appropriation bill for Spain.

Two other agreements, to be signed in 1953, strengthened Franco: the Pact of Madrid and the Concordat with the Vatican. The latter gave the Franco government full church recognition and barred the public practice of other religions. To many Spanish citizens, the Vatican had blessed Franco's rule. The Pact of Madrid with the United States provided mutual defense: the United States was granted full use of Spain's air and naval bases, thereby fortifying American defenses against the Soviet Union. In return, Spain received $226 million to modernize its economy and military. (Between 1953 and 1963, the United States provided Spain with $1.5 billion in aid.) In 1955, Spain was accepted into the United Nations. In 1959, President Dwight D. Eisenhower was the first head of state of a Western country to visit Franco, welcomed, in part, by the tune "The Yellow Rose of Texas." The nations of Europe were significantly less sanguine in their acceptance of Franco. The Western European members of NATO, like the European Community, vetoed Spain's membership in their organizations. Acceptance into both occurred only after Franco's death.

For Nancy's friends, the several thousand Republican soldiers who had escaped execution by remaining in France after the war, diplomacy had been catastrophic, and they pursued the only means left to them of taking back their country: guerrilla warfare. The Junta Suprema de Unión Fuerzas Democráticas Nacional, Allianza Nacional de Fuerzas Democráticas, and Partido Communista de España (PCE) organized the new resistance. The PCE, for instance, ordered one major attack, during which 4,000 people crossed the Pyrenees to invade Spain. With Franco's large counterforces stationed in key areas at the borders, the rebels were defeated, although the three organizations continued to coordinate insurgents in disparate parts of Spain. The reconstituted anti-fascist fighters retained the illusion that their activities would finally awaken the democratic nations of the world, which would then help them restore their republic. Not only did this not occur, but the anti-Francoists, running out of weapons and supplies, failed to gain a substantial following from a war-exhausted, terrified Spanish population. While many of the soldiers, most of whom had fought in France with the maquis, became Spanish household names—Juan Molina, José Mata, Cristino Gracia Grandas, and Francesco Sabato-Llopart ("El Quico"), as well as "El Bedoya" and "Caraquemada"—to Franco, they were all "bandits" and "the scum of the Spanish people."[31] By 1950, at least 22,000 were executed. By 1952, the "movement" was over, although hundreds remained in hiding, maintaining small independent groups ("El Piloto" did not surrender until 1965). These are the people Nancy visited on her dozens of trips to Spain.

In 1976, and after fifteen years in prison, Juan Molina said that more than 12,000 books had been written on the Spanish Civil War but none on the postwar guerrilla campaign. Even now, relatively few historians have pursued the subject.[32] Nancy indicates in her notes during 1950 two rare sources: Jesús Izcaray's "Spain Today," written for the monthly magazine of the British International Brigades after Izcaray's "long clandestine visit with the Guerrillos," and Isabel de Palencia's *Smouldering Freedom*. As a result, it remains difficult to comment on specific activities, since Franco's government released no such information and, one assumes, destroyed any enemy documentation that was discovered. Estimates of the number of people involved, including both Communists and anarchists, range widely, but 15,000 to 25,000 is the generally accepted estimate, along with 20,000 sympathizers like Nancy. According to Molina, their activities varied from writing and distributing propaganda and rescuing prisoners to assassinating officials and blowing up government offices, military installations, and factories. Since Franco possessed a virulent hatred of those against him,[33] when his enemies were located, they suffered terrible deaths like slow strangulation; to encourage their arrest, the local population was rewarded with 100 pesetas for delivering a living bandit; 50, for a dead one. But the fighters were doomed from the start because, unlike the maquis, they had no outside support—financial or otherwise. Louis Stern writes of those who persisted—the small and scattered, if always zealous, groups:

How can one evaluate the achievements of these isolated fighters? They did not succeed in stirring up a popular insurrection, to say nothing of bringing down Franco's regime. They were not effective in stimulating diplomatic action; in fact, their impact on the Western powers was negative and revived fears of social revolution. What, then, did they accomplish by their presence in the mountains, by their assaults on the Franco establishment, by their suffering, imprisonment, and death?

Were they Don Quixotes of the twentieth century, immersed in a fantastic dream and wearing tattered rags for armor? Were they simply zealots and revolutionaries who didn't know when to acknowledge defeat? Or were they heroes, anonymous idealists whose exploits, told and retold in the villages, would keep hope alive? The answers to these questions will not be known until the full story of the guerrillas is unearthed and written.[34]

Molina's final evaluation of their activities is grim: "The world, the democracies above all, had consummated the betrayal. . . . The democracies signed [Spain's] death sentence, provoking the people into the blackest era in Spanish history."[35]

Although Nancy never lost hope, she knew that she had to return to France and go on with her life. It was time to commit herself to new goals and the security of a new home.

La Mothe-Fénélon and the Promise of a Home

As the 1940s drew to an end, having sold Le Puits Carré and aware that her funds were shrinking, Nancy bought the tumbledown farmhouse she had looked at with Finley at La Mothe-Fénélon in the Dordogne. She was hopeful about the future. She had splendid associations with the village and, having traveled here many times over the years, felt at home in Sarlat (the home of Montaigne), Souillac, Cadouin, Moustier, and Lescaut—all with remarkable medieval castles, churches, and fortifications. Furthermore, her house was reasonably close to Toulouse and the Spanish border, which would enable her to continue her trips and remain involved with old and new friends still committed to restoring the Republic.

Nancy also planned to rebuild the house and pursue a life of cultural and intellectual satisfaction: she would travel in the region and to Paris, London (for up to three months, which the tax law allowed), Amsterdam, Leiden, and Toulouse, as well as the frontiers: "This is," she wrote, "a very stimulating and important time in my life and I want to keep it so!" But despite her persistent efforts to be optimistic, she knew she was making the best of a dire financial situation and rationalizing consuming questions: "Where to live, how to live, how not to live, what to try for? . . . Where will I be? . . . as the difficulties with money are dire, too dire to try and go anywhere else." For a time, she blamed herself for settling in so remote a location and for a lifetime of poor judgment: "I should not have a house at all, or at least it should be a house with two friends in it; they living there and I coming to it! How badly arranged all of my life has been."[36]

She regretted buying a "tiny shack"—"so tiny that I can't have anyone to stay save one person, accustomed to the roughest kind of living." The kitchen and guestroom were on the ground floor; Nancy's bedroom, in the attic. When she first bought the house, it was crude and primitive. There was no bathroom or electricity, and the old wood-burning stove had only one small opening on top to hold twigs; it took an hour to boil water. "I have been struggling long with the making of my own little new house," she wrote, "when the only thing in sight is patience." With growing frustration over her inability to lift the heavy beams necessary for the restoration, she wrote Janet/Solita: "Meanwhile I go on mending things and cleaning . . . and gazing at patience with great distaste."

After Nancy restored her "stone shanty," she filled it with the remnants of Puits Carré, along with inexpensive furniture and antiques that she bought on sale. George Moore's portrait was visible from the kitchen, and her gorgeous Manet was finally displayed over the fireplace. Beneath it, she placed a jam jar filled with pink, green, and gold wildflowers that complemented the pastels of the painting. The large table her father had made, which had miraculously survived Réanville, dominated the sitting room, along with paintings, books, and her special collections: her multivolume seventeenth-century French dictionary, G. M.'s books, and her two dozen Hours Press books, saved, if damaged, at Réanville. Similarly remarkable in its survival was her copy of *Ulysses*, number 569 of the original Sylvia Beach edition: "I have read every word of it, many passages several times. How well it stands up to the passing decades!" She had it bound in beautiful plain pigskin, with the title set in plain gold lettering. She pasted a photograph inside of Joyce posing with Sullivan, the tenor on whose behalf he had visited her twenty years before.

She scattered the rest of her books, most with her elaborate marginalia, around the house; decorated some walls with Moroccan tapestries; and put up velvet drapes, in her favorite color, green. Wildflowers, grasses, stones, and old bottles were again strewn throughout; the early Victorian photograph of her grandmother was reframed. Banting said that "the 'ambiance,'" as in Réanville, "was of her own creating and everything came under the Spell of the Muse."[37]

Transforming the house rejuvenated Nancy: "Ah but NOW I have a house: Incredibly small and elementary and I adore it and adore this region and know it and shall know it better in time. I have no desire for Paris . . . I wish I had NEVER seen bloody Normandy. Had I lived down here from the start the whole of my life would have been different and I should not have lost everything." She walked daily—often from early morning until evening—before returning to "my sweet darling own house."[38]

But the house was distant from her friends. Sylvia and Valentine made a few brief visits. Nancy often invited Kay, in Paris on assignment and busy with her husband, several children, and career: "How I wish you could fly to my funny little house and we [could] dig up the ruins." Increasingly lonely, Nancy befriended a woman she had met in Spain, the stylish writer-broadcaster Céraldine Balayé, an art historian and poet who had been active in the French Resistance. Nancy found in Géraldine those qualities she had valued in other women friends but rarely discovered in men: common goals, affection, and security. She hoped Géraldine would be a quasi-permanent guest. Géraldine watched Nancy the day she placed her few remaining treasures from Réanville on the grass: "Nancy was wearing her favorite red dress, and her eyes were bright with tears as she sorted out her things."[39] To Nancy's disappointment, Géraldine became progressively more busy with her broadcasts and parents, leaving her alone for long periods of time. Nancy now walked to Spain by herself, but the trips depressed her. After going to Sorède and discovering that the house she planned to visit had been demolished, she wrote Janet/Solita: "I feel stirrings of vagrancy, more and more." She wrote about the Spanish in Franco's Spain and in Latin America.[40]

Two or three other women visited La Mothe for extended periods, including Irene Rathbone, whom Nancy had met at a PEN meeting. A cousin of the actor Basil Rathbone and of a former member of the House of Lords, Eleanor Rathbone, Irene had remained actively in touch with exiled European writers during World War II. She wrote feature articles for numerous French newspapers, as well as a war novel. Irene was exquisitely empathetic to Nancy's situation.

On Nancy's nine- to twelve-mile hikes with Irene, as with her other guests (including Albert Betz, arrested during World War II as the publisher of a clandestine review), Nancy unveiled the magical diversity of the landscape — the forest trails that opened onto fabulous castle views, the ancient pilgrim tracks that passed through walnut groves and cornfields. They stopped at every grotto (Nancy was bewitched by the cave art at Lascaux and drew pictures of the animals in her diary), château, and museum, seeking local history and folklore. Sometimes they marched through clover fields in a burning sun to the coast of Spain, and nightingales sang during their return. Whenever they walked into Spain, Nancy left money for the political prisoners, many of whom she had known.

Regardless of their destination, with Nancy the navigator, walking was a mysterious adventure. They never took the same route twice and always avoided paths. Irene remarked: "I invariably see [her] moving behind crops, beside pastures, through woods, moving with that tall grace of hers, that elasticity." John Banting, a frequent visitor, felt reborn after their hikes. Always the artist, he loved to see Nancy "dart at some exquisite detail in the forests—moss, furred twig, [a] bee, [an] orchid . . . and proffer it with feather-light hands for my appreciation and possible . . . delineation." They also searched for fantastic beetles, insects, and the "changing pageantry of moths" and discovered a new species each day. To Banting, she was "Nancy of the laughing face."[41]

After their walks, Nancy and her friends read poetry aloud; they took turns selecting the readings. One night, the choice was Irene's: "I fetched from the house a poem of her own, . . . *Parallax*." Although it was long, "I made no haste over it. The light just lasted till I had finished." "Thank you," came Nancy's voice quietly. "You've made it sound—almost beautiful." Then she said, "But it's *young*, isn't it? I'd forgotten." To this Irene replied, "Young and bitter and life-loving and crazy and joyous and sad. Young in the manner of the 1920's, and in yours."[42]

Nancy wrote "LAMBENT (for Irène)," which captured their mood and the feel of the season. It begins:

See how the sun sits fast on the calm land!
Into the small birds' songs runs a new piping rhythm,
Fresh moss and tiny plants grow in the wooden table,
Yet it will come, the cold, after this lambent spread,
This odd profusion of sun-hot on placid earth.
Ay, they will come, wrecker autumn and raw November,
The ever-perennial need of rough log fires.

When Nancy bought La Mothe, she intended to live there from late spring until early autumn; since she could not afford to heat the house during winter, she would travel then and visit friends. She could write anywhere. At the beginning, her plan was successful. In 1951, she spent a great deal of time in London with Charles Burkhart, a new friend. The young American researching George Moore for his doctoral degree at Oxford had been eager to meet Nancy, and Beckett gave him her address. Burkhart was twenty-seven; she was nearly fifty-five.

Nancy's adoration of G. M. and her vivid and candid recollections of him created a strong bond between them, and Nancy came to believe that Burkhart was instrumental in her ultimately writing a memoir of G. M., "the brimming drop in *that* particular chalice that made it tip over into written words." She felt a mystical kinship with him; he was a gift from G. M.; she told him: "I love you, really I do. You have been a revelation, bless you. Ah— and it is G. M. who has brought us together—praise be!" Whatever the exact nature of their relationship, they appear to have had a few sexual encounters, after which Burkhart informed Nancy that he had an ongoing partnership with a man in America. Nancy was not embarrassed to admit her passion for him—"I am beginning to scream for you to be with me"—and she made clear that she wished most for his happiness: "Greetings to your most sympathetic friend"; "Be happy."[43]

Before and after their first meeting—and unique in her correspondence (except for a few letters to Pound)—she was seductive: "I am so very disappointed that you are [there] instead of being here, instead of 'having a drink with me,' the expression that covers so much else!" and "Dear dear Charles (And also OH dear dear me, for the wine was very much stronger than I had thought), . . . I should very much like to see you again. You are welcome at anytime—up the goat-track (but also into the hot-bath, let me add)."[44]

Nancy made frequent trips to London to see the handsome Burkhart. He had taken a flat on G. M.'s street, and they often walked from it to G. M.'s address, now home to a Finnish travel agency; it was a shrine to them. They also went to museums and antique sales within and outside the city. Nancy took Burkhart to Bath, Bristol, and Sylvia and Valentine's home in Dorset, her favorite part of England, to hunt for antiques. When they returned to London, they set their treasures out on the bed as if they were preparing a museum display. Burkhart loved to watch Nancy, in her bright red lipstick, her arms covered with African ivories waving drunkenly and gracefully; as he recalls: "We drank more whisky and the room grew muggier with smoke and the objects grew lovelier, and we congratulated ourselves on them at length and made plans for the morrow."[45]

Although to Nancy, these were romantic weekends, it was easy to convince Burkhart that she was not possessive.[46] She tried to help him understand his partner's point of view during a quarrel: "Oh how I understand. . . . I think the exacter must often not *realize* how much he exacts, but it is infuriating to the exactee." She was maternal in her sensitivity to his disappointments—amorous and otherwise. When Burkhart's dissertation was rejected because he had not followed university regulations, she addressed his despondency with confident encouragement: "PLEASE! If you are ever wild enough to think of tossing any of it away, let it come *straight* in my direction. [I] will put it away in a locked box until the time comes for it to be published." She told him to redirect his fury to the inane misjudgments "of them 'dons'": "Why should the enemy win? I cannot see how anything you write can be otherwise than good. You are a poet, you look like one, you act one, you write [like] one. . . . You feel [like] one. . . . I am sure the core—and how much else—must be good, and valuable."

After Nancy introduced Burkhart to Herman Schrijver at a party, they became romantically involved. Once, after hearing them "squabble," she recited her favorite Shakespeare line on friendship: "Grapple it to your heart ["soul"] with hooks of steel," adding, "I don't want [your] friendship to end."[47] Depressed before Burkhart left London for America, she wrote: "HOW I WISH you did not have to go to the U.S. at all. I can't imagine what Herman will do without you. Herman adores you; how rightly, too." In her last letter before he left England, Nancy said, "I too love you, really I do. You have been a revelation, bless you. . . . Those infernal dons in Oxford. . . . Write to me. Be as happy as you may. . . . Come back. Fond love, darling Charles."

• • •

Burkhart remained, undoubtedly, one of Nancy's most cherished friends for many years to come. In 1957, she wrote the long poem "Nada, Nada en la Nada" (Nothing, Nothing Within Nothing) to him. As early as January 2, 1952, she divulged to him her recurrent health problems ("this perennial cough and cold and nonsense of the sort which generally takes three weeks or even three months") and her anger at being ill ("Oh damn *the body*!), which she emphatically followed with "Enough of that!" She also acknowledged that her wish to travel was always "to be where she was not." It was clear to Burkhart "not so much that she traveled as that she was driven." At this point in her life, Nancy explained that she must leave La Mothe and reiterated her greatest problem: "the question of the ROOM. A thousand pities I have not one! . . . Herman will never get a house where I'll be able to rent a room in permanence."

15

Escaping La Mothe

Indeed, one should know how to live entirely alone from childhood —
to be absolutely self-dependent, physically and otherwise.

—NANCY CUNARD

Before one of her trips to Spain, Nancy visited Pablo Casals at his modest house in Prades, a small village in the south of France near the Spanish border. Casals was preparing to visit Puerto Rico, his mother's birthplace; he had about a hundred blood relatives there. He was nearly eighty and looked, in her words, "round and plump, without a line, and looking much younger than I who am not yet sixty." She noted, "He keeps very busy, . . . his walk is quick, his manner lovely." They sat in a small, pleasant room; two cellos lay, lightly wrapped, on a couch near a small piano and many books and photos. They spoke in French about the Spanish situation. Casals said "he often thought of me and of my goings and comings and doings in Spain." They agreed that things were worse now with Franco than ever.[1]

In addition to the guerrillas who were struggling to take back their country were the less pugnacious, if no less passionate, Republicans like Casals and Picasso, who doggedly raised money for the Republicans and refused to perform or have their work displayed in Spain until democracy was restored. Casals moved to Prades after Catalonia fell and spent the remainder of his life there in exile. In protest against any appeasement of Franco, he refused all engagements in noninterventionist countries. As Nancy explained: "In vain Franco sent emissaries, as did Hitler and Mussolini, to woo him to their countries. Intransigent, Pau (meaning 'peace' in Catalan, the language that Franco prohibited)" remained in Prades.[2]

Eternal Transit

Nancy despaired over Franco's growing power and repressive legislation, and whenever she returned to France her sense of isolation was intolerable. She pondered her options: she could entertain, although her guest lists had diminished; she could visit friends, but she worried about imposing. She decided to accept Sylvia and Valentine's open invitation but remained meticulous about not spending more than a weekend with them.

Sylvia's diaries describe Nancy in a state of eternal transit. She still "traveled light," as she had during the Spanish Civil War, with a few clothes neatly packed into a small sack and a typewriter slung across her shoulder. Once she settled in, she began to preen: to sew on a button, restitch a lining, devoutly polish her bracelets and nails, or do some washing. "On a desert island," wrote Sylvia, "in a jail cell, she would have kept herself spruced, well kept, clean as a cat." Sylvia's diaries often record Nancy's solitary ways on her short visits—usually hiking by herself. When Sylvia and Valentine joined her at a museum, she became their guide, an expert on the history and stylistic uniqueness of a remarkable number of pieces.[3]

But as always, Nancy most enjoyed their long, stimulating conversations that lasted well into the night. She remained intrigued by Sylvia's ruminations about logic: "It would be easier to believe in the divinity of Christ than in twice two making four. Somehow the very frequency of twice two etc. seems to invalidate it as a concept." Since she had long thought of divesting herself of all her possessions, she brought her jewelry on one visit, seeking her friends' help in selling it. After dinner, she reached into a variety of handbags, paper bags, and colored handkerchiefs and "unpacked the treasures of Africa, quantities of amber, and the few remaining valuables her mother had retained—pearls and some Cartier jewels."[4] She returned home, having sold none.

On one brief visit to Paris in 1952, Nancy saw Beckett (who still looked "like a magnificent Mexican sculpture"); she had not seen him since before the war. He was troubled to see how thin and nervous she had become. They talked about mutual friends, and Beckett touched Nancy when he told her he "still had *Negro* 'snug on my shelves, unlike most of what I once had, and even a few *Whoroscopes*.'"[5]

In the early 1950s, she met Henry Moore and his wife, Irina, and began a correspondence with them. Moore recalled his first impression of her: "Outwardly, Nancy Cunard did not correspond with the mental picture I had formed of her, [given] her many worthwhile and often unpopular causes. . . . I expected a more militant physical presence. Instead there was this elegant, sensitive woman whose very bone structure seemed finer and more delicate than anyone else's." Nancy captivated him with her nervous energy and burning enthusiasm—"a perpetual giving out, whatever subject (and her range was enormous) came under discussion." Moore immediately sensed her innate feeling for sculpture, "a rare appreciation of form-meaning, whether in man-made sculpture or in the kind of unusual objet trouvé she discovered." Nancy once sent him for his "lovely creative finger" an Avebury-shaped stone that she had found on the seashore near Saint-Jean-Cap-Ferrat. To Nancy, it looked like a ring perhaps from the Stonehenge period. It also reminded her not just of his bronze *Warrior's Head*, which she had seen in his studio, but of many other things—"of something to do with Denmark—of a *hood* in stone, of feudal wheels of iron, of Shakespeare and the sea; it seemed to urge itself out of the ground, rather than sink into it." She wrote him: "In all how much this stone sang to me OF YOU" and was overjoyed to receive "a delicious letter" saying "how much he liked the stone, with its many meanings, and that he might use it one day."[6]

Back at La Mothe, there were always mechanical problems. She told Richard Ellmann in 1955, after he interviewed her for his distinguished Joyce biography, "La Mothe is ruining my life." Yet Nancy struggled to improve her state of mind. She renewed old acquaintances. Allanah Harper, the former editor of the literary review *Echanges*, lived within traveling distance, and they visited each other regularly. Nancy was at her best, her friend was certain, in her own house when she entertained young men who aspired to be poets or were anti-fascist refugees. It was then that she lifted herself far out of the doldrums. Allanah vividly recalled an evening when, as two Spaniards played Flamenco music, Nancy began to dance, and, in Allanah's eyes, her "lightness and temperament turned her into a Spaniard," graceful, warm, delightful in manner.[7]

Nancy resumed inviting friends to La Mothe. If one was an aspiring writer like Walter Strachan, she helped him translate Resistance poets and tried to help him find a publisher. To Strachan, she looked as he remembered her at their first meeting ten years earlier, strikingly elegant, wearing clothing that emphasized her height and exotic rings that showed off her exquisitely tapered fingers. Today, as then, her smile and eyes were unforgettable, reflecting eternal youth, even if years of hectic activity and physical pain had taken their toll. Strachan also noticed how Nancy frequently sought escape in her favorite drink, "Romolo," rum and water. She told him, "The days go like small beads of the same color and I am alone [for] weeks." She conceded that the self-sufficiency she projected in her youth was not as complete as it had appeared: "I wish I had known you in the Scottsboro years. You would have helped terrifically."[8]

Over time, her guest lists dwindled. Anthony Hobson, now an authority in book-collecting and bookbinding history, visited with his wife: "We signed the visitors' book, almost the only signatures that year. Nancy's welcome was as warm as ever and she was quite unembittered by her relative loneliness." Another friend similarly remarked: "One cannot guess what happened when she was alone. It was a house that needed a guest always: and over those vast distances of middle France many of her friends did manage to arrive, but there were long gaps."[9]

The English novelist-screenwriter Anthony Thorne and his wife, Hume, also visited. Nancy had met Thorne at a PEN meeting in Venice in 1939, and they had a brief romance. He subsequently married but maintained the correspondence. Nancy had visited the Thornes in Berkshire, and although Hume was initially shy of the formidable Nancy legend, she was soon charmed by her wit and generosity. After the Thornes' son Simon was born, Nancy enchanted the child with stories of Lascaux and its 18,000-year-old bull drawings. They became pen pals, and Nancy mailed him stamps from all over the world. On more than one occasion, Thorne visited Nancy at La Mothe by himself, and they hiked down the terraced hillsides to the Dordogne River to watch its changing colors between the silver poplars in the morning mists. He continued to write to her in very affectionate terms: "Darling" and "Nancy, Most near, most dear, most lovèd and *most far* . . . (hélas)." He had never gotten over the experience of first hearing her name: "A girl once said to me, 'I come into a room and at the end of it there's the most beautiful woman I've ever seen. Then as I get near her I realize it's Nancy Cunard.' Yes, she was raddled and distressingly thin, but the fine bone was there and the fire-blue eyes of a warrior and a smile ready for a quip."[10]

He could still vividly recall their rendezvous when they stood on the balcony of the Palazzo Rezzonico in Venice. Nancy, in a black satin gown and her signature "barbaric jewelry" and forehead bandeau, had been suddenly overcome by a vision of the past. She poured a glass of champagne into the Grand Canal—"a libation" for her former beloved: "For Henry," she said in a soft voice. When they left the palace in the early morning, "both of us slightly drunk," they took a waiting gondola, which generated an unexpected future memory for Thorne: "I shall not forget that night," he wrote, "and to my perpetual amazement that same gondolier whom I ran into *eleven years later* still remembered Nancy. . . . How was it possible that a gondolier, who must have had thousands of clients a year, could still . . . recall Nancy?"

Thorne's letter to Nancy about the gondolier stirred Nancy's thoughts about the past. She sent Thorne a copy of *Henry-Music* with the inscription: "Dearest Henry authored this book," adding, a man you would have loved . . . who introduced an entire world to me in 1928, and two continents: Afro-America and Africa—plus Music, the music of the Negroes of the U.S.A. . . . A most wary and prudent man, who often said: "Opinion reserved!" Whereas to me, nothing nor opinion nor emotion nor love nor hate—could be "reserved," . . . on the score of . . . his race and the life of his race.

The villagers, curious about Nancy's simple life, asked her friends why she had no television or car. One explained: "What she cares about is foreign travel in winter, supporting at all times good causes, helping distressed friends, and buying, very occasionally, some small objét d'art." They were not aware, for example, that in 1950 she had taken several trips to Algiers, still in search of a home for exiled Spaniards. All the same, they worried about her safety and isolation: "Not a neighbor within hail . . . And her walks! She covers leagues of the country, companionless." Told that she had lost her way once and was forced to sleep on a hillside, Irene replied, "In Spain she underwent worse hardships." Hearing this, the townspeople spoke about Nancy's "courage in the neighborhood, standing up for someone unpopular, caring less for her own reputation than in making a point." Not surprisingly, Nancy was "adored and respected" by the villagers because of her generosity and modesty. Paying bills was continually difficult because she was supporting many crusades, but she always conserved a small sum. Then she could, as she did, pay the expenses for the oldest woman in town to visit her newly married daughter. She never turned anyone away from La Mothe in need of a meal, a haystack for the night, or a small amount of money.[11]

Since her political interests remained prominent, she and every guest discussed world affairs. One recalled how the "evils of the 1930s could still enrage us" and that Nancy remained spiritually attached to Franco's and Hitler's victims. Nancy took each friend to memorials to butchered maquisards—to Gabaudet, for example, where local maquisards had been shot or hanged: "We stood by the monument where their names were engraved," along with those words "Assassinés par les Boches, Juin 1944," and then "wandered between the black, broken walls of the barns and stable and listened to the silence."[12] Nancy also took everyone to Lampon to find the tall stone tablet with thirty names of the young "Victimes de la Barbarie allemande, Juin, 1944." They had been meeting in a barn when the Germans turned their guns on the barn before setting it on fire to ensure the death of everyone inside.

She was incapable of thinking about one political outrage without another coming to mind. One letter to Kay about Scottsboro concluded, "Imagine this [from] *Ce Soir*. . . . They are selling little sachets of remains of bones and ashes in DACHAU. . . . There is no news [yet] of the Spanish Republicans that have been deported to North America [and] no reasons for arrests."

Nancy's evaluation of old friends often depended on their stance toward war. Richard Aldington, who twenty-five years earlier had chastised her for her interest in blacks, was still a wretched man: "NO, [he is] not a friend. I loathe him! . . . On return from the safety of the war in the U.S., he insisted 'The maquis in France never existed and did nothing and was of no use.'"[13]

Nancy immersed herself in contemporary events and joined new organizations, like the Campaign for the Abolition of Capital Punishment. She remained active in several Spanish refugee aid organizations. Her major new concerns in the early to mid-1950s were the outbreak of McCarthyism in the United States, the execution of the Rosenbergs, and the possibility of atomic warfare. Kay remembered Nancy at a massive protest, "just before the execution of the Rosenbergs in the awful heat of Paris," adding, "and you were to be off to the States at once, to fight! Which you did, damn well too." Despite all her activities, Nancy continued to believe in the "likelihood that war-and-all will come again."[14] She mourned the monstrous irony that at the end of World War II, a weapon had been created that threatened the extermination of the human race. She joined numerous peace organizations, including the Committee for a Sane Nuclear Policy; she joined Albert Schweitzer and Pablo Casals in an appeal to the American and Russian governments to end the arms race and ban all future nuclear tests.

Kay Boyle, now writing for the *New Yorker* and always active in progressive causes, had been mailing her clippings about Joe McCarthy and the House Un-American Activities Committee. At one point, Kay became "nearly insane" because she and her husband, Joseph Franckenstein, an Austrian diplomat working in the U.S. Foreign Service, had been named by McCarthy. When in June 1953 Kay and her husband decided to return from an assignment abroad "to fight the damn thing *in* its own country," Nancy joined Janet and Solita to meet them in Paris. They spoke, as Kay later recalled, "about the madness that then possessed my country, . . . the dementia of McCarthyism." Although the accusations against them were dismissed, Kay and her husband were fired from their jobs, and his health subsequently deteriorated.

Nancy and Kay exchanged many letters about the hearings. Nancy wrote:

The case is stupefying, really stupefying. I am upwrought over it, and notice myself walking from room to room here alone, saying, almost without noticing I am saying it: "Good God all-mighty" out loud. . . . What ill faith has gone into it all: those "Charges"—on the exact level of gossip, and totally inconclusive and rather dull gossip at that. . . . NO proper Court or Board of Enquiry could take such charges seriously. And I see that the one that attended to your case did clear J[oseph]. And yet he is dismissed! . . . I cannot, as you see, write coherently of this.[15]

In a nineteen-page letter, Kay explained that she was charged as both a Communist and a sympathizer with the Spanish Republicans:

> I swore I . . . had never been at any time, a member of the C.P. . . . I was astonished at their insistence on the importance of where one's sympathies had been during the Spanish War. . . . [They asked if] I attended the Prado Exhibition of paintings in Geneva in 1936 and 1937, and I said I had indeed done so on more than one occasion in company with my husband and children. The consul general then asked me gravely if I had been aware of the fact that this exhibition was sponsored by the Republican Government.
>
> . . . Then [they] brought in Janet Flanner, who had come down from Paris to testify on our behalf. . . . When the panel asked her how she had stood on the matter of the Spanish Civil War, she said, "Why, naturally, I was against Franco. Weren't you?" . . . She made it clear that she was known throughout Europe as an anti-Communist writer, and had been blacklisted by the Soviets as a result. When the panel members asked her if she thought it possible that Kay Boyle had been living a double life during the past quarter of a century, she replied, "Yes, there could have been that possibility if Kay had had ten years of intense training with the Moscow Art Theatre, and had got hold of a big black beard and a moustache. Otherwise, no."
>
> When [they] pressed her on the question of my being a C.P. member she lost patience and cried out: "My dear friends, you don't seem to have the slightest idea what Communists are like! We who have lived in Europe for many years know about these things. Forgive me for saying so, but you do not. . . . We know Communists when we meet them. . . . We know them by their reaction to a certain book, a certain painting, a certain piece of music, a certain play. You don't have to ask them if they are party members. They have a certain flavor, a certain smell. When you become a member of the C.P. something absolutely final happens to you. A curtain falls across the mind and across the heart. A curtain has never fallen across Kay's mind or heart."[16]

After McCarthy's exposure, Nancy wrote Kay: "But splendid!—the brute who made so much trouble for you has been unveiled. I wish him all you think, but that isn't enough! Lord, when I think what you and Joseph have been through."[17] At the time of the hearings, Nancy attended anti-McCarthy demonstrations in London and Paris and tried to organize a protest at PEN.

Whenever she was alone at La Mothe, she was overcome by dread: the solitude of her surroundings made her inescapably aware of her declining health. Since her guest lists were diminishing and she continued to worry about imposing on friends, she decided that a highly ordered life might sustain her.

She had tried several strategies to rid herself of her loneliness. She would now do what she had done as a child: immerse herself in reading and learning.

The New Plan

To begin, she hired a woman to take charge of the heavy chores. Madame Achille took such control of the house and Nancy that visitors arrived forewarned about the virago's "ministrations at the end of a pitchfork." Then Nancy created a highly structured routine for disciplined writing. She usually worked on several projects simultaneously—the "Dordogne" manuscript, a new book on ivories, her diaries and correspondence—and she read a great deal, reviewed books, and translated poetry and fiction. Nancy knew that her major projects would never find a publisher:

> Naturally, my own subjects are Spain and slavery, and the big unfinished play for the screen on the transplantation of the Negroes to the New World (entirely historical), and there is a purely personal book in mind called "Départ à Zéro," factual, from 1940 to 1945, of wanderings through the Americas. . . . None of this is going to bring a smile to any publisher's face! . . . And my Poems, "The Lands that were Today"—all factual, all partisan.[18]

She was sparing with the amount of sleep she allowed herself, "a waste of time." She began each day with a light breakfast at 8:30 and a carafe of red wine at 11:00 and remained in her room—filled with books, albums of news clippings, African sculpture, a few photos, and some abstract decorations by John Banting—until lunch at 1:00. Then she replanted herself on her bed, neatly covered with papers, and typed—"the rattle-bang continu[ing]" for hours—sitting upright or lying on her stomach. After a light supper, she often worked through the night.

She read virtually everything written by most Spanish writers before and after the war and wrote the long essay "Decade of Exile: The Intellect of Spain Is Today in Other Lands" for *Arena* magazine.[19] Everyone knows, she began, the "weight" of fascism—"the enormous number of people in prison for 'disaffection with the regime,' the hunger, sickness, low wages, appalling cost of living and black market, and the utter lack of freedom of expression . . . save for the relatively few rich, the ostentatiously rich." Although she alluded to some of the clandestine activities still taking place in Spain, her main concern was the astonishing number of intellectuals living in exile. Her goal was to indicate the depth and breadth of intellectual vitality that had been snuffed out by Franco—either murdered (García Lorca), defeated by despair (Antonio Machado), or otherwise exiled (Casals). She made passing reference to other exiles, including philosophers (Vincente Gaos), historians (José Alborniz and Américo Castro), journalists (Jesús Izcaray), biochemists (the future Nobel laureate Severo Ochoa), sculptors (Alberto), architects (Segarra), painters (José Renau and Manuel Ángeles Ortiz), film and theater specialists, educators, lawyers, and scientists.

The bulk of the essay was given over to a detailed analysis of the work of some fifty Spanish writers, ranging from Rafael Alberti, Miguel Hernández, Jorge Guillén, and Juan Ramón Jiménez, each of whom achieved world fame, to others like Rafael Verdi, Ramos Oliveira, Quiroga Plá, and Juan-Miguel Roma, who were lesser known. Her assumption was that Spanish poets in exile produced "a quality, range, and quantity [unique] in the world today." The essay combined analysis of the trajectory of each poet's work, followed by illustrative verses and brief biographies. Nancy's translations and choice of poetry indicate her talent as poet, translator, and one-time publisher. The essay is also an extraordinary tour de force of poetic and political commentary evaluated through the eyes of a literary critic and historian. For example, Alberti's "Free Peoples—What of Spain?" expresses Spain's post–World War II cry for help from the democratic nations of the world:

> Peoples of the world who are free! Today the poet
> No longer sings but thunders aloud in his rage;
> No peace is there, no peace in the planet
> As long as the heart will not listen—O peoples,
> You who are free, behold: Spain is not voiceless,
> She bleeds, she flames in my words, she calls for your aid.

Nancy concluded the essay with the words of Antonio Machado: "'Un pueblo es siempre una empresa futura'—A people is for ever the task of the future."

Nancy made good on her new commitment. She worked all the time, allowing herself spare moments to answer every researcher's inquiry, to maintain her personal correspondence, and to read newspapers in several languages and follow the news about present and former friends. One of her many clippings was about street protests that forced the Italian government to reverse its expulsion of Pablo Neruda as an "undesirable." She saved several of Michael Arlen's obituaries. Because all of Nancy's prewar letters were destroyed at Réanville, it is fortunate that many to whom she wrote after the war saved her correspondence, available today in British and American archives. Although Nancy's correspondence, overall, included thousands of people, letters to the twenty or so friends she kept up with at any given period of time—while also writing dozens of acquaintances—are unique and intimate. They indicate an ongoing awareness of each friend's current concerns and mutual loyalty and affection.[20]

Some of the letters Nancy received during the 1950s are very moving because they are about aging and death, realities Nancy tenaciously tried to deny. The talented writer Louise Morgan (eleven years older, an editor, prolific author, and poet-Ph.D.) had been Nancy's friend since the 1920s. Her long letters had typically ranged from daily events to philosophical issues. Now, she addresses Nancy's concerns about growing older: "You express perfectly what is in my mind these days also. I no longer know myself, though I have intervals of being the same creature I was years ago. This feeling comes like an odd and quickly passing mood at fifty, and when you are like me, seventy-two (!!!), it is an actuality daily. Oh, *can* this be me! The only thing which utterly banishes it is friends and drink." One of Louise's later, most poignant letters begins: "Dearest Nancy, I keep forgetting to ask you something, in case I suddenly die and you by chance should be visiting the U.S.A., . . . please do visit Anne Hunter, my daughter. She and Tom are your cup of tea, and they would adore you. He is dean of the medical school at the University of Virginia."

Letters from Iris Tree echo Louise's mood. Children when they met and rebellious teens in the Corrupt Coterie, Nancy and Iris now write about love and the passage of time. Iris says: "I tussle with love and its subsidiaries [and] residues. Time blackens claims for happiness—for every promise"; "Yes Nancy, . . . life is thickly thinning out." Langston Hughes begins one letter: "It's always nice to get a letter from you, being one of my favorite folks in the world!" In another, he somewhat ironically marks the passage of time in their common cause: "Last week was funeral week in Harlem—Charlie Parker, the saxophonist, and Walter White. The wives and chief mourners (Charlie Parker had *two* wives) were all white at both—so you see, we're integreating [*sic*]!"[21]

Many of Nancy's letters from writers and artists reveal riveting details. Miró invites her to meet him in Majorca; Pavel Tchelichew describes his pleasure staying at her house during the winter of 1952/1953; Alexander Calder thanks her for a "beautiful and very understanding" review. "Sandy" later invites her to visit him in Roxbury, Connecticut.[22]

Samuel Beckett was a longtime admirer. Any Beckett devotee will realize that his letters to Nancy are unusually long and affectionate, even when he is writing about his plays (which he never refers to by name). "Bien chère Nancy," he begins, before thanking her for seeing the French production of *Waiting for Godot*, which was "more like what I wanted, nastier." Also modest although fluent in several languages, Beckett apologizes: "My translation is no great shakes either and I have a copy . . . for you, . . . if you would like it, though reading plays is a bore." He concludes: "I shall not fail to be in Paris round about the 20th and hope you will keep an evening free for me. The dog is duller than ever but its friends know it doesn't mind if they get up and go away. . . . Much love, dear Nancy."[23]

Later he writes about a new play (*Endgame*), "an entertaining ruffian": "I have taken on an ambitious job which will keep me quiet and . . . for the next couple of months in the writing." Once again, Beckett scholars, long pondering his writing habits, can be assured of his rapid composition: "And water is now pushing again through all ducts." He also reassures Nancy: "Your rain cistern will never again be dry in this world. Much love." Then, excited about a new form (in *All That Fall* and *Embers*), he admits: "Never thought about radio play technique but in the dead of t'other night got a nice gruesome idea full of cartwheels and dragging feet and puffing and panting which may or may not lead to something. . . . Back in the spinach after three tiring weeks in Paris and feel a little less pins screaming in an old cushion."[24]

After she mailed him her notes on Joyce, which he had requested, he teased her, "I loved your failed dinner with the Joyces at Fouquets," and then related the details Joyce had added. Nancy must have been pleased by his attempt to quote her poetry from memory ("the Battersea or thereabouts gulls skewered to the wind") before saying: "I want to read your *Parallax* again . . . but can't find it on my selves. If you have a spare copy, send it along." He ended: "Up to my palate in teeth misery myself at this moment, have been all my life. . . . Swing along happy in the south before the hydrogen and uranium get you and write as often as the spirit prompts to your ever affectionate Sam." Shortly thereafter, he reported: "Eating pineapple for the first time in my life with ferocious enjoyment." One of their last appointments mentioned in a letter begins: "I'll be in the queen's restaurant after the show on Wednesday, with a bottle of wine and the thought of seeing you. Love Sam."[25]

Nancy owned only two or three typewriters during her lifetime, and they were often in need of repair. As a result, she placed several unfinished letters—barely readable due to broken keys and an erratic ribbon—in her notebooks or diaries. One, to Kay, which she eventually retyped and mailed, was about their one-time friend:

Eliot is now . . . "purely a vestryman," not just generally a papist, but interested in VESTRY sorts of matters. I saw him at the PEN banquet, and he did look god awful—all dryness and stuffiness. . . . What is revolting is the way they are trying to whitewash [Pound's incarceration]. Ezra writes to me wild scrawls, which I can, and do, perfectly decipher. I cannot write to him. I do send him some literature now and then. I am very angry about it all, for there it is: one's rage at someone who WAS once a real value in the world—and that, I say, he was—becoming merely a bloody fascist. It's not more complicated than that. . . . How can a GOOD artist be a fascist? . . . Do you not think that the fact of accepting fascism must mean that a person is either a swine or quite demented? I mean, weak in the head, though I should say that fascism is invented by thugs for other thugs, and that's all.[26]

Whenever her friends mentioned Pound, she mailed them a copy of the scathing three-page letter she had sent him in 1946, a reply to his defense of the Fascist broadcasts he made during the war: "What the bluebuggering HELL are you talking about. I had 'freedom' of microphone to say what I liked—namely the truth that your shitten friends were afraid to hear." Nancy's letter had concluded:

> And now I will tell you of my life today. Réanville, my house, is in ruins, thanks to the Germans who lived in it, and to their friends, the French fascists. Among all the smashed windows there was one that held the wind still, for the reason that in lieu of glass someone had torn the pages out of Rodker's vellum edition of your *Cantos* and had crucified the cover against the window-frame. That is what I found in my house on return [from] the allies of your friends. [They also] destroyed all of my African things that you used to admire. . . . You will be glad to learn that, up till now, not all fascists have been punished [here.][27]

Although Anne Chisholm writes that Nancy abandoned most of her projects after the war,[28] the sheer number of her publications and of her manuscripts at the University of Texas at Austin and elsewhere reveal otherwise. In addition to numerous translations, articles, and poems published in a variety of magazines, she published several monographs, a volume of poems (*Nous Gens d'Espagne*), and the book-length memoirs of Norman Douglas and of G. M. Nancy translated into French Douglas's book on Tunisia, *Fountains in the Sand*, as well as plays by the early Absurdist Ramón del Valle-Inclán and poems by the former Surrealist and maquisard Albert Rémy. She received first prize at the Eighteenth Congress of Writers of France for French poetry translations in 1949; she also received its diploma of honor for services rendered to French letters. During the 1950s she gave poetry readings at PEN and collaborated with Géraldine Balayé on several radio programs (once, reading her poems about the French Resistance; another time, tracing the history of American black music).

She also began experimenting with a sonnet form in several languages simultaneously, inventing a form in which each line scanned and rhymed. One sonnet sequence consisted of eight poems, each in five different languages. Nancy believed that the universality of human needs should be reflected in multiple languages, despite the demands of the form, which called for specific rhyme patterns—in her case, in languages with different sounds.

Although still in draft form, "Spain" is a tour de force. Divided into several sections, the first surveys "present-day" Spain in 1957 and attitudes toward monarchy and the war; others describe the disparate sections of the country and each one's cultural history and uniqueness in terms of geography, products, population, and other demographics. It is an encyclopedia of the country. Nancy also wrote a long essay on the ancient stone ruins in Majorca and Minorca. Many of the antiwar poems of "Visions Experienced by the Bards of the Middle Ages," also in manuscript form, are an ambitious expansion of an earlier evocation of the modern era as "the crossroads of a violent world." There were numerous other projects she continued, including a book on Mexico and a history of African ivory sculpture ("The Ivory Road"). For each of these, Nancy did an enormous amount of research and wrote voluminous notes. She remained involved in all of them until her last days.[29]

As she told David Garnett, she was filled with ideas: from writing a book about literary reputations to the more interesting idea of "some sort of 'memoirs book,' about 'Writers and Artists [I have] known.'" With no lack of wit, she recalled the publisher Rupert Hart-Davis's clarification: "Chronologically, of course. . . . 'How else? said I.'" But she changed her mind almost immediately. She had been asked frequently to write her autobiography:

> Memories of people. The Surrealists would come into it—they used to meet every noon in the same Paris café in Montmartre, and Aragon would be telling them at lunch how Breton and Éluard and all the rest of them would be drinking four or five Pernods, the wonder being how they could possibly stand up afterwards. Fights, police; René's cry in the night to the filthy cops who were about to manhandle us: "Fumier!" And so on.

"Not for all the money in the world," she said finally: "A book of that kind would bring in too many people . . . who've let me down as well as loved me. [They] might be pleased to read what I'd made of them. . . . Others perhaps [might] bring libel actions! No! The choice lies between writing the thing fully, in detail, no holds barred—especially where I myself am concerned—or not writing at all. I choose *that*." Anthony Thorne was absolutely right when someone asked him to persuade Nancy to write her life story: "Well, I think she's doing so—as she prefers it—in writing the biography of others," an answer which Nancy highly approved.[30]

Some of her projects involved traveling. The ivories project was more difficult and lonely than she anticipated; she had to visit museums in Switzerland, Belgium, Holland, and finally Germany. ("Anger" and "disgust" had kept her from Germany all these years.) During the day, she spoke to curators and studied the ivories; at night, she sat alone at a bar or in her room and organized her massive notes. (She left only one blank page in her ledger, after her side trip to Dachau.) As she had once interviewed countless people for her various projects and news articles, she now spoke to anyone for companionship: young students, bartenders, businessmen. On December 25, 1955, in Utrecht, she wrote in her diary: "Christmas Day, and to constantly forget it was, [I spent] most of it in my room, sewing that leopard dress." She thought as she sewed: "It made me very indignant to hear [that woman] say how she had been hounded. . . . NOTHING is more vile than race theories and hatred. This persecution of the Jews makes me want to be a satrap with a flail of scorpions to torture the Nazis [and] fascists to death."[31]

With the trip ending, the idea of returning to La Mothe became so oppressive that Nancy decided to look for a room in London. After a considerable search, she wrote Burkhart a letter about her disappointment in not finding one. Nancy had come to call him her "second American" (Crowder being her "first") and had frequently asked him to seek out Crowder in the United States. It was then that she learned about Crowder's death. Now, of both Burkhart and Crowder, she said, "What America giveth, America taketh away." But Burkhart's return to America, to Germantown, near Philadelphia where he taught, also stirred Nancy's pride in her American roots. She wrote him about her father's connection to the Benjamin Franklin family and their antislavery stance, highly unusual at the time:

> Germantown was in part founded by one paternal ancestor, whose name is not quite known (end of 17th century [known] as Conrad, Kunders, or Cunard!). He (I think) was one of the first in the first signatories against slavery. Another ancestor (indirect as it was), his daughter married Benjamin Franklin's brother (or son?), . . . I think from Philly. I simply cannot remember these things properly in order.[32]

Burkhart now spent almost every summer in London, and he visited Nancy regularly. His memoir of her, written after she died, is particularly interesting because it describes Nancy during the mid-1950s when she still had what he called an "anachronistic" commitment to human justice. Her causes permeated her life ("Her art had become [her] weapon"), and nothing deterred her ("including imprisonment in eleven countries"). Such resolve, he continues, was a reminder of another era: "Nancy's heroic efforts, her ferocious commitment, now seem . . . dated. . . . She belongs to an earlier age of the rebel, the age of Shelley or Chénier. She belongs to history."[33]

That her manner of dressing dated back to the 1920s and 1930s—with "spit curls, white white skin and red lips, bedeckings of chunky amber or coral," a sweater, jacket, and long skirt—gave her a unique style: "getups" that sometimes embarrassed him. Perhaps Nancy dressed in memory of better times, but regardless of her style, now or in the 1920s, Burkhart avows, she always represented the vanguard of the future: "Nancy one thinks of not as a member of the *avant-garde*, rather, when not miles ahead of it, as the *avant-garde* itself." And "in some miraculous way," Burkhart adds, Nancy was always a lady, "irremediably, upper class," even "when she was assaulting a policeman with intent to kill, or, with other intent, an African exchange student in the back of a big black London taxi. . . . Drunk as the devil she could throw herself fully clothed into a bathtub full of water . . . with incomparable elegance"; with that same elegance she "grace[d] a reception for Tzara at the French Embassy." "She was the least vulgar person I have ever known," he repeats, adding, "Nancy picked up people indiscriminately by the score and was ready to know anyone, and did. . . . If ever she disliked or hated anyone, the cause was political." This keen interest in other people, in life itself, he thought, was at the core of her energy.

Going Another Round

As the years progressed, Nancy maintained her stoical bearing, even though her health was declining. Her long bouts with bronchitis and rheumatism were already frequent during the 1920s. Her chronic asthma eventually turned into emphysema, and anemia set in. Some of her complaints were attributed to "nerves." Advised repeatedly to stop smoking and drinking, she refused to acknowledge any bodily weakness ("One's body should not be felt") and was increasingly defiant of doctors who challenged her freedom. She scorned being told

> "No drink, no smokes, no coffee." . . . I have not given up anything and feel much better for all that. "No drink" indeed, "no smokes, no coffee"—fancy saying that! Nota bene the following: A Spanish friend told me that there is a man . . . who has NOT SLEPT for EIGHT YEARS. . . . Secondly, another Spanish friend told me his own father never consumed anything all of his life (died at over 90) but WINE and COGNAC.[34]

Nancy had always disliked food and, despite Madame Achille's culinary efforts, began to lose weight. Still, she refused to capitulate to the body's demands and retained her youthful disdain for any interference with her freedom. On the one hand, she admitted: "Something most peculiar that I had best call vaguely rheumatism is well with me in perpetuo," adding: "What is all this?" On the other, she was compelled to follow her rigorous schedule and complete her work on Spain: "All I seem able to do is write THAT

POEM." She knew, however, that she would never finish it—not because of her health but because the Spanish war had not ended, and this humiliated her: "I could never, somehow, get to finish the long epic poem on all that . . . and I feel ashamed: . . . [An] inner sense . . . arises within me that the war had not ended as it should and that was what stopped me, by cutting off the inspiration and the impetus."[35]

She had long equivocated about living in England and thought it ridiculous to worry about possessions, especially when they were in storage. The question of where to live remained. She wrote to Janet/Solita about all the things she hoped to keep in England: "some books, documents, writings, and all the few African ivories left me. How absurd . . . that these should have to live permanently in that trunk." Then she added, "It gets clearer and clearer to ME that I should own absolutely NOTHING, save the empty furnished shell of La Mothe, and even that, god knows, is an insufferable burden."[36]

Her anxiety about money exacerbated every other problem, as well as her fear of war: "The ever-rising cost of everything is now much more felt by me than two or three years ago. . . . This, coupled with the uneasiness about wars, often makes me troubled. Why own anything if it [is] in danger of destruction? I should live in a small hotel in warmth and write regularly six hours a day. I should like that." Although she had been earning small sums of money by writing essays and translating books for Editions Braun, it was becoming too expensive to stay with friends and in hotels during the long winters, even if she remained at the farm for the rest of the year. She thought about spending the winter at the Capoul, a small hotel in Toulouse, and traveling from time to time. Her letters are filled with solitary plans: "Am going tomorrow to Nîmes, thence Cannes-Vence, etc., on way to Italy." At the end of 1956 in Rome, Nancy ran into Iris, and they had a wonderful reunion, although Iris subsequently remarked: "I gathered that her days [at La Mothe] were lonely, somehow malevolent, bereft of surrounding sympathy or love."[37]

Good friends still lived in London and outside the city, and these would remain special trips. If her visits with friends seemed longer than she thought appropriate, she would check into an inexpensive hotel. Solitary trips to Spain became more difficult to negotiate, but there were always pleasures to enjoy in Spain. In one letter, she recalled an "odd moment in Andorra" when she came to recognize a former Republican soldier now also engaged in anti-Franco activities: "I suddenly found myself gazing straight into the eyes of EL TORO. . . . No sign of recognition on either side. He used to be a contrabandista. . . . But one minute later, the recognition was mutual, immediate and warm! We dined, and lunched next day. *Never* ask what anyone is doing when near the frontiers!"[38]

In 1957, she returned to La Mothe briefly. Her isolation ("I've been without mail since Jan. 4—from *anybody*"), compounded by her severe financial worries, had finally become unmanageable. She decided to return to England to sell everything. She took with her three Wyndham Lewis drawings, valued between £29 and £35, and her Arp painting, valued at £75. She had asked Burkhart if he might buy them, but he was noncommittal. She wrote him again: "Maybe if they are to be bought you could leave the money with Herman for me?"[39] She also wanted to sell two Malkine paintings.

With the idea of returning to La Mothe now "mortifying," she renewed her travels in order to support various causes. Fortunately, the Authors World Peace Appeal Against Nuclear War was meeting in London. After attending the conference, she turned to another of her major causes. She had long advised black organizations in London to work with white leaders to improve interracial relations. She now met London's black political leaders, including Una Marson, John Carter, Harold Moody, Learie Constantine, and Rudolph Dunbar, and offered similar advice. Then she went to Liverpool, where she had also worked with black communities trying to safeguard the African collections in the Liverpool Museum. She would now protest the city government's decision not to rebuild its great museum. She enlisted the help of Henry Moore and Augustus John and wrote a series of articles for the *Guardian*.[40]

In the summer of 1957, she became a tour guide of sorts to friends in Spain. She and Burkhart traveled to Toledo and went from one battle site to another, with Nancy pointing "behind *that* hill," to the spot at which she had stood during the fighting. The overwhelming heat forced her to stop frequently to rest. Burkhart saw that she was ill most of the time. All the same, later that year she joined Burkhart and his friend William Rose, an English professor at Vassar, on another trip and, while still infirm, gave them an exuberant tour and history lesson.[41] Nancy and Rose soon began an affair, and for about a year she felt reborn.

Twenty-five years younger than Nancy, Rose found her remarkable in lacking the "usual feminine concerns" about age, regarding herself or others. Initially overwhelmed by Nancy, Rose also saw her as a Romantic in the pursuit of high principles. He found her unique in every way, down to her "authentic" gestures: "One involved holding her elbow against her side, the arm going straight out in front, and at the end, the hand raised, palm outward, fingers slightly curved—like some Massenet heroine holding off the worst."[42] Nancy was as generous to him in his research on Wyndham Lewis as she had been to Burkhart in his work on G. M.

But once again, the young man left Nancy; and once again, Nancy said, "What America giveth, America taketh away." When she had first met him, Louise Morgan, a Vassar graduate, warned her that he "reminded me of

Vassar, which in my heart I hated. . . . There are very few men on the faculty, and those few are generally spoiled by massive female worship." After their breakup, Louise wrote:

> I can't bear it. If only I could throttle that foul man! I never heard anything like it. You're well rid of him. He'd torment you in other ways. I could cry with rage. . . . You don't realize your power and your uniqueness, Nancy. It's part of you that you don't. But I shall never cease willing myself toward recording your unique place in human development. You WERE. You ARE. Others display themselves, play to the gallery, put on masks, pretend, pretend, pretend. You WERE and ARE. This I know if I know nothing else about anybody. [You are] a great individual, representative of her time, shaping and changing her time by just being.[43]

In 1958 another man entered Nancy's life, a thirty-one-year-old Spanish photographer, mentioned in her correspondence but never by name. The details of her letters suggest that he had been arrested as an anti-Francoist. One to Banting begins with her dream of establishing an artists' center in Spain with the help of her new boyfriend, a center like Neruda's in Chile or like the Casa de España in Mexico, which many intellectuals from Argèles had joined after Nancy helped them gain release.[44] Of her plans for an artists' center—in her beloved Spain—she writes: "Without any drink at all, nor need of such, . . . [he] has shown me that my dream of 'A CASTLE IN RUINS IN SPAIN' . . . is no idle dream. . . . YOU my dear, shall come here, with Jim. And we will work and work and work. . . . Where shall it be? Perhaps in Aragon?"

She proceeds to describe the photographer, a model of the virility she had always liked:

> My man is a wild beast. . . . You want to know what he looks like, naturally. . . . Physique: toreador. (Very jealous indeed). Short, strong, dark of hair, determined (and how). Beautiful face, especially when seen in candlelight, or even in light of small, concentrated electric. . . . Is from deep south, Andalucian, very old fashioned ideas about dress, sex, women's knees showing etc. Otherwise of the most advanced kind of ideas.
>
> Not, thank god, an INTELLECTUAL. Very good photographer. . . . No money at all, of course. . . . Full of jokes, exquisite actor, . . . emeritus artist, . . . born actor. . . . Darling you'd love my man.[45]

Despite this enthusiasm, when Nancy returned to La Mothe, she was deeply troubled by the news that some of her best friends were ill or had died: "Darling, Padmore is dead," she wrote John Banting; "to me it seems unbelievable. He was 55 and ill (of liver) it seems."[46]

Her letters in the late 1950s also make clear that Nancy realized that she was too ill to divide her life between La Mothe and trips abroad. She began to work out an arrangement to spend part of the year with her old friend Jean Guérin, whose partner had recently died. Their tentative plan was that Nancy would stay at his home in Antibes during the winter, and Guérin would join her at La Mothe for the end of spring and summer, a felicitous resolution to their common loneliness.

Nancy's mental breakdown, which would occur in 1960, may have been linked to a series of trips begun in 1956, either to or associated with Spain. One night in Frascati, Italy, she emerged drunk and bull-like from a café with a cigarette inserted in each nostril and began pelting dogs with tomatoes. On another, after a row over a bill, she was hauled into a police station. When the authorities tried to arrest her, she resisted and was thrown to the ground and harshly kicked; she received severe injuries to her body.[47] She was beginning to react to anyone wearing a uniform in what some called a persecution mania, although according to Banting: "Anyone with her past activities would be a fool not to realize the possibility of persecution." He insisted that "a confusion of discreditable reports" characterized her every move; in a word, rumors about Nancy's behavior were rampant. After she bought a new dress and soaked it all night in a bathtub of water, she was called crazy. Banting, also her traveling companion both to Harlem and to Spain during the war, said of this: "From old, I knew her clever adaptation of ready-made dresses . . . [her] clever needlework—changing buttons, etc., so this was quite a rational act to me."[48]

Some accounts have her sitting on the floor of a train and eating her ticket; others, throwing her passport out the window. On her trip to Spain in 1958, when she met the thirty-one-year-old photographer who would help her build castles out of ruins, the two became entangled with the police and the man was imprisoned; Nancy was held for five hours. (After his release, and to no avail, he followed her to France.) In Barcelona, she got into bar brawls over politics. In Madrid, she was told by a Franco official that her visa would not be renewed; in a rage, she flew to Majorca and was placed in jail because she had apparently initiated a fistfight. Somewhere along the way, the *Daily Mail* heard about one of the incidents and dispatched a reporter to the scene. Nancy was portrayed as pale, frail, and indignant: "It's monstrous! How can they throw me out when all I did was try to get an innocent man released from prison?" Then her mood suddenly changed. "Let's forget the sordidness. I'll read you some of my poetry," she said, and for half an hour she recited her Spanish and English poems.[49]

When she returned to London, she was ill with food poisoning, serious bronchitis, and an infected toe. The Thornes took her in: "We did as much as we could for her but had to guard against too much solicitude, of which she would have been highly intolerant." Nancy admitted: "People jeered at me. 'Imagine taking Nancy on. . . . You'll regret that, won't you?'"[50] A physician diagnosed her as undernourished for years and overly nervous.

Sylvia saw Nancy in March 1959, looking "wan and worn, . . . with 'nervous asthma' and anemia, and aches. We talked about Africa, and mysterious Spain. . . . I was sad for her. She looked drained—and Lord knows what [a] hospital won't do to her." Nancy wrote to several friends on July 19 a version of the following: "Today's date has such a meaning for me: the beginning of the war in Spain, 23 years ago!"[51] Nancy had nowhere to go. Plans with Jean Guérin were still not finalized; she felt incapable of returning to La Mothe or to friends in London or abroad. She despaired of seeing yet another registration desk at another of the hundreds of hotels she had stayed in over the years.

In late 1959, she returned to Spain, aware that there were "almost two policemen or soldiers to every civilian, [and] a word of protest from her, after a couple of glasses of wine, would land her in jail."[52] All the same, she renewed her anti-Franco activities: most were clandestine; others, less so. Nancy's continued vigor, despite her physical decline, was remarkable. It was as though she knew this would be her last trip to Spain and had rallied all her energy both to fight Franco and to enjoy the kind of intellectual and social excitement of her earlier years.

She met Clyde Robinson in Majorca for New Year's Eve, where they joined a street festival before consuming "'the twelve grapes' at midnight [the Spanish tradition of eating one grape on each stroke of the clock], while dancing to 'Scheherezade.'" Nancy had met Robinson the year before when he recognized her from a Cecil Beaton photograph and introduced himself. After their reunion, they went daily to Llubí, an archaeological site they had visited before and began a month of intensive study. Nancy, who knew the Mallorquin dialect, could direct drivers to different sites. An expert on the Talayots—pre-Iberian Cyclopean stone constructions reminiscent of Stonehenge—when she returned to France she continued her work on the Talayot-Capacorps of Majorca; she had also written about the "Taula" stone edifices of Minorca.[53]

In addition to her political adventures and archaeological research, Nancy enjoyed the blue sea and sky of Majorca. Once, overlooking the harbor, she said to Robinson, with unexpected pride: "There's a Cunard ship—the orange smoke stacks, you know." In the evenings, they dropped in on "all the hole-in-the-wall cafés." Close to sixty-four, Nancy still "had a genius for ferreting out 'joints' and Gypsies!" according to Robinson. She also visited old friends—disabled veterans from the Spanish Civil War, waiters in bars, and a Spanish priest. And "from time to time," Robinson observed, "she would disappear in a taxi with Juan Blasco, their driver, on something very 'secret.'" After Majorca, Nancy went by herself to Valencia for two weeks to visit more of Franco's political prisoners; she had still been raising money to help them. Robinson went to Munich. In response to one of his letters, she recalled being told that "when the Nazis compiled the 'black list' of the British, under 'C' Nancy Cunard was next after Winston Churchill."[54]

• • •

In the spring of 1960, she was jailed in both Valencia and Majorca; and after yet another fiery, physically brutal scene with a Franco official, she was expelled from Spain. She left behind another boyfriend, a twenty-seven-year-old silversmith named Tomás Canas Morales.

16

The Last Great Glare

Let it be known in England that Nancy Cunard is not, as she believes, as "alone in the world as a new-born babe" and that there are men and women in France, Spain, and Italy, and in the whole of the Negro world of Africa and the United States of America, who have not forgotten her and who demand that she be fairly treated.

—LOUIS ARAGON

After her expulsion from Spain and return to London, rumors about Nancy's erratic behavior were legion: the former socialite had argued with a cabdriver and set his car ablaze with a flamethrower from the Spanish Civil War; the demented rebel had attempted to set a policeman on fire and then blow up a post office; the dilapidated siren had lifted her skirt in a restaurant to reveal her naked body. The facts hardly needed exaggeration. Nancy was drinking a great deal, raving about political persecution, and behaving erratically everywhere.

Involuntary Commitment

Soon after arriving in London, Nancy appeared at Anthony and Hume Thorne's house; it was past midnight, and Anthony was abroad. Nancy had lost her money and luggage and had just concluded a violent argument with a cabdriver, who remained at the door demanding his money; Hume had barely enough money to pay the fare. Nancy then began eating ham sandwiches from a paper bag, the only item she had not lost, throwing the bread crusts into the empty fireplace. When it seemed as if she was going to hurl an expensive ashtray after the crusts, Hume put her to bed, fearful that Nancy, clutching her cigarettes and matches, would burn down the house. (Not long afterward, she set her belongings on fire.)

Painfully thin yet fully adorned in her remaining African necklaces and bracelets, Nancy left the house the next day and began a crazed itinerary through the city streets. With the same determination that had marked her better expeditions, she made her way to Chelsea, where she had lived during the war, and was stopped for drunk and disorderly behavior. Once again, she resisted arrest and kicked a police officer. When she appeared in court, she took off her shoes and hurled them at the magistrate. She was detained for ten days before a friend or relative could be located.[1] In jail, she tore the buttons off the garment she was forced to wear before throwing it into a bathtub. Her cousin Victor finally agreed, on the advice of a doctor, to have her certified as insane and committed.

St. Clements Hospital, the dismal East End asylum to which she was temporarily referred, was located in the area Nancy had written about during World War II when she praised its heroic citizens. Now she was writing irrational letters to all her friends and to heads of government, including Nikita Khrushchev, to protest what she viewed as her politically driven, fascist-conspired commitment. After ten days, she was officially certified and transferred to Holloway Sanatorium, at Virginia Water, in Surrey.

She wrote her friends about the injustice and illegality of her commitment: "Drink has nothing to do with it. . . . Fascism does. . . . Damn Spain and all its doings. . . . It goes back, I suppose, to *Negro* and the Spanish War . . . [and] the Foreign Office." She told Janet/Solita:

> I am so sorry to mix you up in this particular chapter of my muck—all the fault of my authorities obeying your (bloodiest of all!) authorities, viz
>> Allen Dulles
>> Central Information Agency
>> U.S.A.—via British home office.
> Every single item is grossly illegal and could easily be proved so if I could only find a solicitor like MYSELF.

She told Clyde Robinson the history of her persecution and gave a local bank as her return address:

> I left Spain alone March 11, expelled! Went to Valencia. Returned to Palma three days later to look for Tomás in vain, was again fined 1,000 pesetas, and again jailed and expelled. This time from *all* of Spain. No fault or action of mine. On March 11 at 2:20 I had just finished lunch, alone, at the airport. I was then violently physically aggressed by four enormous men (Spaniards), one of whom called me appalling. . . . More I cannot say now. After that to . . . the South of France, surrounded by fascism, went twice to Geneva, . . . came to London April 20. Since then

impending law suits and rotten solicitors. . . . Damage to my left thigh which was x-rayed reported "slightly cracked" by Fascist aggression on March 21. England is cold, gray. I do not see many people at the moment.

Now, will you do something for me that may help me? Find out all you can about Allen Dulles (the swine) and his CIA. . . . These people are frightful enemies of us all and they seem to have heard of me. Should I say "again"? They indeed must be at the back of all my trouble with the Home Office . . .

Good God, how I wish we had a magnum of champagne and some hot caviar. I wish . . . we were in, on, by or under the bed TOGETHER, cursing and scheming and finally getting a bit high—'till dawn do us deliver.

Till dawn do us deliver.[2]

Without denying Nancy's break with reality, one can understand the origins of her paranoia. The Foreign Office, for no reason, had prohibited her from traveling with Henry Crowder to Africa in the 1930s; before that, her beloved G. M. had treated her with disdain when she planned to visit London with Crowder; her revered Norman Douglas, like many of her friends, was overtly derisive about her involvement with blacks, the Spanish Civil War, and World War II. The break with her mother and her society foreshadowed her isolation from many friends, as well as from the writing establishment during World War II. Authorities had investigated her Hours Press for subversive publications and searched her home in Normandy before the war. Afterward, Le Puits Carré became an unusual instance of official vandalism in collaborationist France. Nancy had been under surveillance for any number of activities: her anti-colonialist interests, which she reported for many years in the ANP, and her purported Communist links when she supported the Scottsboro boys, a free Ethiopia, and the Loyalists. She had been arrested and placed on the "wanted list" in Spain recently, as well as during the Spanish Civil War and World War II. From her earliest engagement in social-political causes, she had been the subject of newspaper gossip. Even now, in her sixties, she remained a target of scorn and ridicule for right-wing reporters.

Her second preoccupation at Holloway was Tomás Canas Morales, her twenty-seven-year-old Spanish boyfriend. She described him as a metalsmith of some standing and an aspiring writer. She implored her friends to help him travel to England because "I want him here, with me, as close as can be, FOR EVER." She explained that the hospital was holding her money (which it was), "save for a shilling a week." By the time Nancy and Morales saw each other after she returned to La Mothe, they discovered that they had little in common.[3]

As soon as she arrived at Holloway Sanatorium, Nancy was given a room of her own, with a view of trees. The door was adjusted to remain open. Nancy lay on top of her tidy bed, fully dressed and well groomed, with her usual bandeau stretched across her forehead. She was surrounded by people who were responding to their own internal stimuli: they shuffled through the halls, giggled sporadically, and stared at one another. One woman screamed repeatedly "Buggeress! You buggeress!"; another collected invisible fragments from the floor; several wandered aimlessly talking to themselves. Sometimes at night they banged on the doors and walls.[4] Her friends tried to rescue her; her family appeared to be indifferent.

For only a few days after her hospitalization, her handwriting was scratchy; her letters, irrational. She wrote to Janet/Solita:

> What your letter says about "drink" makes me roar with laughter. . . . Drink, the drink has *nothing to do with my case*, but fascism has—to have been more or less *wounded*, physically, by men and women later arrested for that—in France, Monaco, Geneva, here. . . . And as to have been eleven months in their grip I don't see where "drink" can come in. . . . Other people think I am demented! (to mean really and medically)! Others think I have had some collapse of nerves. None of these things are or were ever so—I am quite well and so furious and disgusted that I am leaving Europe for ever and changing my nationality *as soon as* I get out . . .
>
> I also think there will be war, don't you?
>
> So much love.[5]

It seems clear that whatever the causes of her paranoia, probably related to alcohol, the content of her delusions was connected to the triumph of fascism and its ongoing rule in Spain. Having combated this menace for the last twenty-five years, Nancy had taken the Loyalists' loss as both an intolerable human disaster and a personal defeat: "How VILELY all this has gone. . . . Spain and all its doings. It is because of that (I think) I am here. Fond love, N."[6]

Soon after her hospitalization, Nancy became distinctly more rational. Her rapid improvement clearly indicated the absence of severe psychosis. In addition to writing lucid letters, she distracted herself by writing poetry (with a pencil and paper; her typewriter had been confiscated). She cogently described what she would do after she was released; she complained that she had not been examined medically or given psychiatric treatment, apart from advice to rest and take tranquilizers and vitamins. But the tranquilizers made her feel empty: "How far seems Spain," she writes, "how 'lost' to me at the moment. They surely put something very dulling into their pills here, for I am without a thought in my head, and feel duller than I ever have in life. . . . That seems all wrong, does it not?"[7]

Nancy improved rapidly. She even found the food edible and gained weight. However, since the doctors would not tell her when she could leave, she wrote to Aragon for help. She may have been diagnosed as suffering from severe mental disorder complicated by alcohol, but, like many others, Aragon believed and was apparently correct that she was suffering only from alcoholism and would recover when she stopped drinking, which appears to have been the case. He wrote a lengthy article, "Pour la vie," and published it on the front page of the July 24, 1960, edition of *Les Lettres françaises*, alongside her new poem of that title. He spoke of her as Alice displaced from English society through the looking glass. He discussed her work with the Hours Press and her service to humanity during the Spanish Civil War and with the Free French in London. He quoted her poems on the Resistance and on the Loyalists. He indicated that for obscure reasons she had been certified insane, which, oddly enough in the land of habeas corpus, might mean she could be detained for the rest of her life. He emphasized that none of her letters or poetry revealed insanity and that the intellectual history of the first half of the century could not be told without discussing Nancy Cunard, a woman of great eminence.[8] Charles Burkhart, Georges Sadoul, and Walter Lowenfels (in the United States) issued similar statements. So did Pablo Neruda.

Nancy was embarrassed about her confinement:

Everything here continues to be *absolutely hellish*. A convicted prisoner has at least knowledge of the length of his sentence. Not so I. *I am accused of nothing.* . . . It will go down, falsely, that N.C. was a convicted lunatic from June something (ad infinitum, I expect). The stigma will remain. . . . I do not care what *anyone* thinks, but I *do* care if this gets in the way of whatever I may yet want to do before I die.

She was most frustrated about her lack of freedom to move about; she was not allowed to buy a stamp without an escort.[9]

Sylvia Townsend Warner also questioned why Nancy had been committed. Sylvia wrote in her diary, on July 4, 1960, that Nancy was "arrested on a drunkenness charge. . . . If she had had a house in London, this might not have happened. . . . But why certified, instead of being sent to jail? I wrote also to Roger Senhouse, Anthony Thorne, and Diana Cooper: waistcoats and diamonds seem the best allies to invoke."[10] Sylvia, like Aragon, was probably right: Nancy's bizarre behavior may have been as much an indication of alcohol abuse as paranoia. Still, the authorities may have served her well by committing her to an asylum rather than to prison, where her treatment would certainly have been less benevolent.

On July 9, 1960, less than a month after her confinement, Nancy wrote an unusually intimate letter to Janet/Solita, no doubt motivated by what she called a special anniversary, the start of the Spanish Civil War: "Dearest, . . . to think that 'it all' began today in 1936—in Spain." She cited the courageous acts of a Loyalist hero; he was the kind of man she could have "pledged herself to": "[He,] with his tiny old peasant cunning, understood me very well and with him was eaten (by me) the juiciest bit of meat roasted on the point of a stick in an Andorran cabin fire. Tell it to Solita again, the beautiful saying 'Contigo Pan y Cebolla' ("with thee bread and onion"). In its spare purity this means 'I want not more of life than these, *with thee*.'" Then she admitted:

> I don't think anyone has ever loved me save Louis, who did so, I think, entirely *all* the time we were together, two-and-a-half years (a long time). I, on the other hand, have truly and entirely loved many, Henry, and Morris, and Louis, and . . . several more. So much for love. As you remember Louis's line "Il n'y a pas d'amour sauf amour malheureux" [There is no love except unhappy love]. It seems incontrovertible for me—and perhaps for him. I don't know . . . [11]

Recovery

In the meantime, both new and old friends traveled to Surrey to see Nancy. John Banting visited regularly. A young man from Ghana arrived with flowers. He had long admired *Negro* and Nancy's work on behalf of blacks. Her former boyfriend William Rose also visited, incensed that her scorn for authority and "hectic behavior" in London should have landed her in a mental institution:

> Going to visit this elegant and sympathetic creature in that great Victorian brick madhouse, her room a pale green cubicle, I felt too poignantly the absurdity of her fate. Kafka or Brecht could not have designed a more grimly ironic situation. . . . She could not get at her money to hire a lawyer; she wanted to write and they would not permit her to have her typewriter. But she was her gallant self: "Look, darling, the door has no latch."[12]

Nancy's very good friend Louise Morgan wrote to the Holloway administrators on July 9, 1960, after visiting Nancy; her description is psychologically astute:

> Miss Nancy Cunard is a family friend . . . [of] nearly forty years. . . . She has never shown signs of insanity, . . . and when I visited her on Friday, yesterday, she was her usual self, except, as is natural with age, more individualistic and contemptuous of authority than ever. But NOT insane! She feels the world has been against her, as indeed it was throughout all her childhood and youth. She got the habit of rebellion in her cradle and nursery, and had an army of nannies and governesses,

one after the other, to "control" (not educate) her by a mother who knew nothing and cared nothing about children and was jealous of her as she grew up. . . . But [they] did not kill an innate gentleness, loyalty and utter sweetness of nature which overflows like a suddenly unfrozen fountain in the presence of understanding friends. . . . The sweetness in her never fails to respond to sweetness. I had a perfectly normal visit with her. I can tell you that it was one of the most hideous shocks of my life when I learned she had become a certified lunatic.[13]

Burkhart did not consider his visit to Nancy an unhappy one: "I never for a moment thought she was insane, though she did insane things; maddened, but not mad." He added: "And the gardens were lovely there, and Nancy was full of projects for when she was released—she usually had so much underway that it was rather funny, the busyness of it; she was grace itself—in offering us tea, and beautifully grateful for the fruit and chocolate and cigarettes we had brought her."[14]

Nancy's recovery was so rapid that within weeks she was allowed to go out for the day with friends. Raymond Mortimer and Roger Senhouse took her to Eton College. She seemed her old buoyant self, enjoying the details of the modern stained glass and medieval frescos in the school's chapel. In August, she was permitted to leave the hospital: "Now you can begin to go on weekend leaves of forty-eight hours. And then we'll see how you get on." She spent a weekend with Louise; then she stayed with Banting, who took her to a Picasso exhibit and the Ballets Africains; Nancy welcomed the renewed sense of freedom and aesthetic pleasure these weekends provided. She was depressed and lethargic when she returned to Holloway. She worried that no one else would invite her to visit: "At this moment I have had two weekends, but wonder about the third, for where to go? It has to be friends. I know so few people in London or near it who have a spare room."[15]

Most of her time at Holloway, Nancy not only continued her correspondence but also tried to help friends publish. Clyde Robinson mailed her his poems, which she read scrupulously and then sent to T. S. Eliot at Faber and Faber. He replied in a dictated letter that he would pass the manuscript on to a fellow director; at the same time, he informed her that the press published only already "esteemed" American poets, like Robert Lowell. Nancy put Robinson in touch with Roger Senhouse at Secker & Warburg.

On September 10, when Nancy was told she could leave permanently if a friend took her in, Louise guaranteed the authorities that she would be responsible for Nancy's mental rehabilitation. If Nancy "behaved," as the authorities put it, she could apply for a formal discharge and the return of her passport. Sylvia Townsend Warner was one of Nancy's last visitors. She recorded in her diary:

Today to see Nancy: . . . a long walk through corridors, then let into the ward, and locked in, and shown to a more social corridor where we sat at one of a row of little tables, while Nancy was told [we were there]. I was, I suppose, so surprised to see her still alive in this hygienic limbo that my heart rushed to her and was momentarily warmed. She was very affectionate, asked anxiously about [our] health; looked at us lovingly; but she is *ill, ill*. Something has died in her, perhaps her objective has died in her. Meanwhile she may be getting out on Thursday, to stay with Louise Morgan. She must stay under someone's roof. That is the terms of release.

Later, in recalling this visit, Sylvia spoke of Nancy's "courage, her invincible suavity as she walked towards us when we visited her in that intolerable place of detention. Oh!—as proud and detached as Lucifer, and with us—gently gay."[16]

Victor Cunard, Nancy's beloved cousin, died during her confinement. She wrote Robinson, "I am absolutely down . . . on the sudden death of my cousin Victor Cunard. . . . He was a little younger than I and we were so often together in childhood and later at difficult times. I can't believe it. Having been born (I suppose) melancholy, I have always asked *what is life for* since we have to die? Can you understand that as an instinct?"[17]

She tried to assume a positive outlook as she traveled to her caretakers: Louise, now seventy-five, and her husband, Otto, eighty. When she reached their tiny cottage in Sussex, she was wearing thick beige stockings, pale cream moccasins, and her red suit. She had taken in the side seams, and since the back slit of the skirt seemed too high, she wore an olive green chemise under the suit; the green patterned dress showed through the skirt. She brought a gift for Louise that she had made, several scarves of inexpensive red and white fabric sewn together with black thread. She arrived, as always, with books, letters, and her typewriter. One could see, Louise thought, that beneath her pain Nancy was "still brave and fearless," with "the capacity for endless friendship and loyalty." Louise took her on "refurbishing trips," and Nancy was overjoyed with her elegant new clothes, a coat and suit, a handmade dress, lined boots, and a new suitcase; she also had new dentures fit. Louise was pleased that during her several months with her she had slept well, been warm "and free and beloved here." She added: "She is the best possible guest—a miracle of guestmanship. . . . I don't think I could have done this for anybody but Nancy. She has been an angel of tact and understanding."[18]

After Nancy's release from Holloway, Aragon wrote a follow-up article for *Les Lettres françaises* about her discharge. In November, she received official certification that she was competent to handle her own affairs, and Louise later wrote the following to the Official Solicitor at the Royal Courts of Justice: "I have been meaning to tell you how grateful Nancy Cunard has been to you. You were the first official to treat her with kindness, and she was touched by it. . . . You may like to know that you helped her enormously in a very difficult effort. She lost her 'phobia' about officials."[19]

A New Life at La Mothe

Nancy left Holloway behind her, in mind as well as in body. Mechanical problems at the farm were inevitable, and her physical condition was deteriorating. But for now—and through most of her difficult last years—she maintained an optimistic outlook, excited about her writing, active in various causes, and free of self-pity. As soon as she returned to La Mothe, her feisty high spirit also returned, as though the bad days of the late 1950s had never occurred. Her letters to friends expressed her gratitude in finding the house (closed for a year) not as damp or cold as she feared. She was most relieved that her remaining treasures had been undisturbed. At Christmas, she sent greetings on postcards she had bought in Majorca: "All best New Year wishes to you all, dear friends, from this local 'talayot.' Love, Nancy."

Nancy heard from T. K. Utchay. He had contributed to *Negro* nearly thirty years earlier and, recently, in gratitude to her, had opened the first of several schools in Nigeria, calling the first one Cunardia. (He had also named his newborn child Nancy.) He was writing to describe his joy that Nigeria had achieved self-rule. Later he wrote:

> Although you have not told me much about it, I know you had sacrificed very much for the cause of the African race, and for that reason the people of your own race turned against you. We do not want you to continue to suffer. Africans will honor you. This is why we have named our school Cunardia. Some free-minded Europeans here call our school [the] Nancy Cunard School.[20]

Morales, Nancy's Spanish boyfriend, had been at La Mothe since her release from Holloway; he left, by mutual agreement, in July 1961. Then Nancy began to experience sleep problems: "I've got a new disease: I cannot get up in the morning (Not from 'late nights out'—oh, [but] reading till 2, 3, 4, or 5 in bed). . . . My worst trouble is too much sleep. . . . The trouble is probably that of the *SOUL!* What is *soul?* I suspect the word (in any language) is the moving pin of self."[21] Géraldine returned as often as her busy schedule allowed through 1964.

John Banting visited for five months in 1962. He painted and prepared exotic foods as Nancy worked at her poetry. In April, when he arrived, she was not well enough to go out for their customary walks. By July, she had gained weight and was joining him for afternoon strolls ("with breathless rests").

During the winter of 1962/1963 and in good spirits, Nancy returned to the Capoul hotel in Toulouse. She wrote a friend in February: "I've always had the feeling that everyone alive can [do] something that is worthwhile." She decorated her room, worked on several projects, and became enthusiastic about a previous idea: "Why not make a series of essays [on the] lives of the great before they were great?" She renewed some of her earlier habits, expressing an interest in local news, regularly sending stamps to Solita, and restoring some of her favorite catchwords in her letters: "Up and at 'em," "The facts, please! . . . without any hooly-gooly." Even though she was not sleeping or feeling well, she tried to make light of her condition: "Do you remember our little joke about getting thin? —Drink, fckng [sic], and worry. I have now another recipe: Just have what I've had. Can't eat, can't sleep—for a few days on end."[22]

She corresponded with old friends through the early 1960s: Gilbert, Neruda, Beckett, Robinson, Burkhart, Thorne, Guérin, Hiler, Kay, and Aragon (who wrote even more frequently than she); after mid-1963, she wrote Janet/Solita most often. Everyone wished her well—Beckett, for example, writing "I am so very sorry to hear you are not well—and that it has been long. Please get quite fit again soon and come to Paris for a gander on the old days when the world seemed one's oyster, in and out of season. Much love, Sam."[23]

In her responses, she commented on her current reading (of Proust and Dostoevsky: "Have you read 'Essai sur le Bourgeoise?'"; Chekhov's "brilliant" Seagull; and the "remarkable" Catcher in the Rye?). Two new poems by Stevie Smith captured the "purity of Chaucer" and indicated a new way of changing "from one meter into another." Art books recently published by Hachete had beautiful reproductions, but their essays were "irritating," with their "abstract French—I mean [with] too much of their goddamned rhetorical writing, . . . as if everyone knew everything already. That is their indescribable VAINGLORY." She returned to her idea of writing a single poem in several languages, respecting the uniqueness of each: one must know how to "get languages together, say I, and also know how to keep them apart. Remember Joyce's . . . Ulysses: 'When I makes tea I makes tea, and when I makes water I makes water?'"[24]

In one letter to Janet/Solita, she finally answered their question about her youthful affair with T. S. Eliot: "Yes I DID know Eliot. I knew him. AND HOW!" In others, she was nostalgic about past lovers, reminiscing in one about the huge hissing gray geese of the Dordogne, which she had first seen in 1923 with Pound. Some of the letters revealed intimate details. John Strachey "was one of mine in 1926 and a bit, in 1927"; Clifford Sharp, the first editor of the *New Statesman*, at "37 [was] tough, [with a] whiskey-leathered appearance, huge shoulders, bullying, mad crazy for women. . . . [He] got to love me once." Pound was frequently on her mind; she still found it incomprehensible that a great writer could renounce his writing (past and future):

> I WONDER if *Ezra* told [the *Daily Express*] that! It's *not true*. His beastly fascism cannot possibly cancel the extremely fine poems and poetry, he wrote before. . . .
> I know he is a very great poet. . . . Of course "THE CANTOS" are *hell* to follow. Too many "jumps" between subjects for one. But, if you have volume 1, read (I think it is Canto 42). It is the one on "LISURA"—straight all through. And then, in his hellish Italian time, the lines about "Pull down thy vanity." *Never such lovely lines*). . . .
> But I cannot write Ezra how wrong he is, because that might begin a rapprochement I don't want.[25]

Nor had Pound forgotten Nancy. When William Carlos Williams visited him before his release from St. Elizabeth's, they spoke "one day under the trees" of Nancy Cunard, her experiences during the occupation of France, and "many other such things."[26]

Nancy's letters also revealed new details about her activities on behalf of the Spanish Republican internees in the concentration camps:

> The young agronomist I knew . . . in 1936 had spent five years in jail. . . . I found him again, in Valencia, and how we embraced. Thin as a rail is he yet, but now a lawyer. Yes, it was perfectly possible . . . to pay the guards a little money wherewith to buy [the prisoners] a little food. So that was why . . . I collected [money] circulating [it to] less harsh guards and even more venal supervisors or whatever those devils are called. Naturally, it all had to be done pretty privately, but still it was, indeed, possible.

She remembered the French authorities in Perpignan trying to stop her from distributing food to the refugees: "Spain—Jan 1939. I got no farther than just inside the frontier [and] could not go any farther because of the French police. And so, then and there, I distributed ["the tins" and money] to the really starving women and children . . . into the frantic forest of fingers, . . . my hands already . . . slightly bleeding."[27]

Many letters addressed the health and whereabouts of former friends. She worried that Cocteau was dying. Despite their "antagonism (on account, mainly of Aragon)," she "liked him much." She mused on Shakespeare's "There is special providence in the fall of a sparrow":

On the whole, I suppose death should not matter to anybody—and the Hamlet words return: the sense of them being: ". . . If it's not for today, 'tis for tomorrow— and if not for tomorrow, 'tis for now. Well may we ponder this. 'Twill make no difference to our cries."

She continued to mourn the death of her second favorite cousin, Edward Cunard. At times, single sentences in her correspondence are cryptic ("I am tired of dreaming of impending climaxes").[28]

Nancy, concerned with finances for most of her life, now worried about her medical expenses. Having sold most of her art, family furniture, and jewelry, her only remaining objects of value were two silver cases and Manet's *Étude pour le linge*. (To sell S. C. Harrison's portrait of G. M. was "unthinkable.") Solita bought one of the jeweled cases, but Manet's painting, originally insured for £42,000, failed to reach her £21,000 reserve at Sotheby's. She gave it to Herman Schrijver for safekeeping after the Tate Gallery and various banks refused to store it; she was unable to continue paying for its insurance.

Nancy wrote a number of people about the civil rights movement in America. Langston Hughes replied that Arthur Spingarn, one of the founders of the NAACP,

at 86, is heading for Greenwood, Mississippi (where all the current voting trouble and riots are) next week—to prove he is with the Freedom Riders and other kids—one of whom . . . was just out of jail for teaching a voters' registration class. (Negroes have to learn to read the *whole* Constitution—and even then they've registered only ten in the past six months!) . . . There are only about three people I want to see in all of Europe—and you're one.[29]

She replied to Robinson's condemnation of southern racism:

Yes, those ghastly S.S. of Alabama and Mississippi and, now, as reported in French papers, of many other states. How I should like to machine-gun the evil whites. . . . "Nits breed lice," you know. It is a historic phrase to one who knows Negro history (revolt I think, of Nat Turner, about 1832; or it may have been that of Denmark Vesey, some years earlier). Hate does, indeed, *it does* breed hate. . . . Have just read Dr. Martin Luther King's book *Strive towards Freedom* (Ghandist, in that he believes in nonviolence). He must know his own S.S. best—not so I—so he must be right, but I rage with passion against them, the BAD whites. (Plenty of good whites by now, and more and more will come along.)[30]

She wrote Kay frequently. Their correspondence from early 1963 until October, when Kay's husband died, focused on the civil rights movement: Martin

Luther King's "I Have a Dream" speech, the Freedom Riders, riots, bombings and protests in Birmingham, as well as President Kennedy's interventions in Birmingham and at the University of Mississippi. One of Kay's early letters took Nancy back to the poem on Scottsboro that Kay had written to her (and Roger Sessions had set to music), "A Communication to Nancy Cunard." "I know it almost by heart," said Nancy, and "*now*, these hideous names arise again: Birmingham, Gadsden, Montgomery." But after 250,000 people marched in Washington, D.C., Nancy wrote: "I REJOICE!" and, addressing Kay's tentative optimism, she insisted: "'The marching children.' . . . I am sure these things DO count—if not at once (?). But yes, they must, THEY DO, in the States. I think THIS is a very big moment indeed for the Colored and Whites."[31]

In the spring of 1963, Nancy had considered moving to the United States, energized by the "multitude of masses" converging in the civil rights marches. (She reflected: "The Color question: how long since, how long ago.") She had received letters from American academics, including William A. Camfield at Yale, inviting her to visit their schools, and her first response was: "I could wish (not sure though!)—[I were] living at an American university" in order to debate with "many, many people." She had been keeping up with the civil rights movement through every available newspaper and magazine and was particularly impressed by James Baldwin's essays.[32]

Decline and Resistance

Given the vitality of Nancy's letters through the spring of 1963, one is surprised to learn about the extent of her physical debilitation: she had been bedridden for a considerable period: "By now, after the last three months in bed and the same condition of asthma, bronchitis, [and] nerves, the condition has become positively psychical I am sure, and probably what I could do, *without* staggering in the street from lack of balance, seems now impossible. To hell with it all." The winter had been unusually cold, and Nancy, again at the Capoul hotel in Toulouse, had begun struggling for air when she slept; waking had become a "torment." Walking, her favorite pastime, was nearly impossible. For a brief period, despite her efforts to make the best of things, she became despondent: "What CAN I say about myself? Nothing to the good. I cannot eat or sleep properly. I am all the time in this room. . . . To go out into the street alone would be awful . . . because of possibly falling down from 'le vertigo.' The room is nice enough . . . and so are the 'personnel.' But when will all this end?" Since Janet and Solita insisted on knowing more about Nancy's health, her reply was specific:

You are too kind—No darling, no monies, bless you. How can I explain what is the matter with me? (1) Total lack of energy—don't want to move. (2) Very much coughing and spitting out of the "products" produced by something in the lungs. . . . Thus Emphysema, Bronchitis, Asthma—which (the last) makes for frenetic heartbeat. (3) Loathing of any food—hence, weakness. (4) Sleep at night disturbed by sudden awakenings. (That does not matter so much!) (5) Dizziness at times to the point of falling down. *Who* will venture into street in *that* condition alone? (6) Doctors! Four came, prescribing things.[33]

None of Nancy's letters focused solely on her physical condition. In each, she asked detailed questions about her friends, discussed books and political issues, and was often witty and self-mocking.

She finally decided to remain at the Capoul through the spring of 1963 to avoid the "desolation" of La Mothe. She could tell Kay this ("I used not to mind being alone for weeks on end. Now I cannot bear being entirely so in the house"), but since Kay's husband was ill, she would not burden her with her own health problems. She had already written Janet/Solita, "Everything . . . is horrible, . . . the blank face of the future." When they offered financial help, Nancy replied, "Oh bless and thank you, . . . but NO." In response to their repeated offers, she invariably said, "Thank you so much, darlings. . . . One should learn to be independent from childhood."[34]

In the beginning of June, Nancy lost her balance and fell in her hotel room. She described her face with humor: "Sudden lack of balance and then crash everywhere. This [time], on the face. . . . It's a fair beauty (colors of Rouault) extending from upper right eyebrow, all that side of face, to neck, down to breast. I have now (4th day after) a thorough mustache of black over swollen lip, and a very convincing beard." When her friends requested more detail, she retained her sense of humor:

Indeed, [it is] more like a Rouault than anything I can think of—colors and outlines in-between. . . . I could maquiller [use makeup on] the other cheek and dark gray "mustache." . . . I mean you to laugh—but true, the right eye might have gone. . . . The doctor . . . and his tiny tube of (penicillate) "pate" has been applied . . . no doubt accelerating the passage of Rouault into Monet. . . .

. . . Enough of this! I love and bless you both.

She still had not answered to their satisfaction, and in yet another letter, she mixed humor and fond memories, describing the swelling on her forehead:

Darling,

Why does this ditty return to me NOW? The key-word is "Lump"! (And ain't it a honey?) The LUMP on face is slowly receding to crab-apple size (wild apples were so plentiful in Leicestershire—exquisite, small, ruby-red applets) that G. M. and I often gazed at, admiringly and wonderingly. You probably have them in the United States.

At last, she reported "the fading . . . continues," adding, "but I'm not worried at all about this, having been much knocked about in Spain—one of the last times by the sea on a rock."[35]

When Kay's husband, Joseph Franckenstein, became seriously ill, Kay and Nancy wrote frequently. Kay shared a note from Beckett in which he had "added such a lovely thing about Joseph's illness: 'It's a desperate feeling when the little light we live by goes dim.'"[36] Then she revealed to Nancy:

> Joseph is not going to get well, my darling Nancy . . . I am reading aloud to him "The Roots of Heaven" (Gary's "Les Racines du Ciel") and it is a strangely comforting book. I am sure you have read it, and in times of despair like this, it gives one another basis for hope—almost another concept of reality—I love the absolutely limitless freedom of the thought that the elephants, not us, are the roots of heaven—even their skins, their hides—more appropriate as roots than ours. I come back to my furnished room across from the hospital and know that the spirit cannot end if it has endured so long in species that are not man.

After Franckenstein died, Kay relied on Nancy to contact friends, admitting "I cannot write more. For once—perhaps the first time in my life, I have lost courage. I don't know how to go on." In response to Nancy's subsequent letter, unfortunately missing in the Boyle correspondence, Kay concluded: "I am grateful to you. . . . You make me aware of so many great and fundamental things that slip away, are lost—at least temporarily—when one loses hope" and "Nancy, I love you. And I am filled with admiration for you on this anniversary of Joseph's death—a month ago today. Thank you for having been, and for being, and for making all our lives a declaration."[37]

Nancy had despised Joe McCarthy, and she associated Franckenstein's decline with the terrifying hearings a decade earlier. She repeatedly expressed her joy that "the brute was unveiled, . . . GLAD INDEED, that that filthy, abominable slander against both of you was finally cleared up." At the same time, Nancy feared Communism as another kind of tyranny. She added to her political agenda her fears for Cuba under Castro.[38]

She continued to receive invitations from Americans now asking "'Why not come over and lecture? . . . Why not come and write filmscripts? . . . television, etc. Why not 'Memoirs?'" When she realized that once again she was being asked to discuss her personal relationships, she abandoned the fantasy of moving: "Not on your life, EVER!" In truth, Nancy was incapable of going anywhere, even if she wanted to: "La santé, 'c'est tout'! . . . WE damn well know it is NOT 'tout.' But, by hell and damn, it is more than I thought." At the same time, the "surge of wanting to write" remained "very great." She often told Janet/Solita: "You can imagine the kind of rage I am in. . . . "THE ONLY TIME I don't feel so ill . . . is when I get to this machine and compose, and correct, and copy.[39] Still afraid of leaving her room and walking alone, she reminded herself of her solitary, dangerous adventures in Spain and then moved slowly down the stairs.

Yet as much as Nancy wanted to live in her own house, La Mothe, with its magical trees and songs of the birds ("Chaucer called them Dryddes"), it was out of the question. Not only was she isolated at La Mothe, but she had no one to "collect" the basics: from the "blasted food" to the refuse. In the middle of 1963, she began writing as her return address "Temporary, til once somewhere else" and "Pro Tem." The question of where to live had returned. Then, in the summer of 1963, she was obliged to return to her house: Hugh and Thérèse Ford were arriving from America. During their six-week visit, her professor friend helped prepare the memoir of the Hours Press.[40] But even with the Fords there, Nancy knew that before long "I shall be entirely alone in this house and that (now) horrifies me."

Shortly after they left, she "was ready (at last)" to see about her health. On July 31, she entered the hospital in Gourdon for a thorough checkup, highly optimistic that she could be cured; instead, she was informed of the severity of her emphysema. She remained there for two weeks, writing Janet/Solita: "I am at last where I should have been nearly TWO YEARS ago." She wrote the same to Burkhart, adding that she could then have been "spared all those ghostly winters in bed most of the time in a Toulouse hotel."[41]

After Nancy was discharged, she moved into a hotel near the hospital with a suitcase filled with manuscripts and correspondence, as well as a bottle of rum. Once again, she wrote Burkhart: "Knowing you will come, . . . I am much better, can eat again, feel much less depressed. . . . Which day do you think you and Herman may come? . . . Come any time." In late August, Burkhart visited her in what he called the "ugliest hotel in the Dordogne or perhaps in the world: raw, white, and new." The first floor housed a café of pinball machines that attracted the local youth. On the second floor were tiny guest rooms paneled in an orange pine so fresh that the walls oozed with thick varnish. Noise from the pinball machines permeated the hotel.[42]

Until now, when Nancy felt able to leave her raw orange cubicle, she walked cautiously down the stairs and sat in a corner of the pinball area. She wrote letters and drank rough red. Occasionally, she asked one of the boys to have a drink with her; she was still smoking and catching her breath between Gauloises, "dazed and bemused with pain and with the drugs they [had given] her at the hospital." But with Burkhart at her side, she became her old self; Schrijver soon joined them. Burkhart had recently met Janet Flanner, who said it would be an errand of mercy to visit her. He found Nancy to be the same as always, angry at being ill and angry at the wrongs of the world:

> We arrived . . . to find the rain and the raw hotel and Nancy, able to walk five steps before she must stop to catch a little breath into her incredibly thin body, able to talk only a minute or two before rage overwhelmed her. . . . Like that of a puma encaged, an ocelot or a cheetah, [with] green eyes blazing, she pounded the table weakly and gasped in her fury, "If I could breathe!" Anger at everything, at the food she would not eat, she crumbled up bread and made little balls of it in her plate; at the doctors who were expensive and wrong; at Franco, fascism, and the world.

Burkhart and Schrijver drove her to La Mothe, only a few miles from Gourdon. They could hardly get to the front door, the grass had grown so thick by the gate. Once quite elegant, La Mothe was now crumbling. Books had mildewed; on the mantelpiece that once held the Manet painting were spiderwebs, a few old wine bottles, odd metal or wooden scraps, "*objets trouvés* from the [old] days when she could walk; musty sad debris of all that famous and brilliant and energetic life." The three of them sat on the floor going through Nancy's old trunk, where she had kept her remaining ivories. Burkhart said it was like "a nightmare: the cold and the rain and the mildew and the pointlessness." At one moment when Nancy held a favorite ancient bracelet to her cheek, she crooned something he could not hear, "with a look of dim, remote ecstasy, knowing I would understand." He thought,

> I did not understand any of it, nor do I yet, such suffering and such rage. One can call it rage against the coming of the night; this scarcely clarifies. The next day Herman and I left for Bordeaux, assured that Jean Guérin was coming to fetch Nancy. . . . I think that must have been the way she died, over a year later, in Paris, in such suffering and such rage. Not mad, but maddened.

Nancy returned to her noisy orange room with equanimity: "It is quite pleasant here," she said, "and I read much and try to write an essay on the Hours Press for *The Book Collector* of London," which Anthony Hobson had arranged. She also embarked on a rereading of Victor Hugo and kept up her correspondence. For a time, she tried to understand her illness scientifically: "Emphysema is a hardening of the lungs, lack of elasticity, sclerosis [and] shortness of breath; one does not get to the end of each respiration. The result is continuous ill-ease." Yet she could still laugh at herself and her daily efforts to strengthen her legs: "Now I must go and pant a little in the streets."[43]

Her resistance to the limitations imposed by her illness was admirable. She distracted herself by inquiring about and reading what was fashionable in literary circles. She was indignant if a writer she respected was publicly devalued:

> I am shocked at what you say has become the Hemingway de-fashion. How IDI-OTIC. Just because the man is dead now. . . . I don't suppose he would care, but I do. . . . He [was] a very good writer indeed, and nothing can take that away. I have not come across any of this befouling, which can only come from jealousy and "snobbery." The effects he achieves in his stories. Even the old man in the boat off Cuba fishing. . . . No Norman Mailers can take away a thing from Hem. (You remember *The Naked and the Dead?*)[44]

When Schrijver saw Nancy in the autumn, she "was a total wreck, bent double with emphysema, nevertheless smoking and coughing and drinking *sans cesse*. . . . Only the eyes, the beautiful 'star sapphire' eyes were the same, although dimmed, and her voice, to me always totally delicious—a tinkling voice—very high and girlish." At last, living arrangements with Jean Guérin were finalized, and Nancy went to his house, Villa Pomone in Saint-Jean-Cap-Ferrat, for the winter. She had known and liked him since her youth and most recently visited him in Majorca in 1958. Still mourning the death of his partner, Walter Shaw, Guérin had already begun painting a series of Nancy in portrait. He was a talented and intelligent man with no pretensions. As Nancy described him, he could look like "an old Breugel peasant"; at other times, "as if he were going to Longchamps."[45] In the tranquility of their relationship Nancy discovered the wonder of sleep without dreams. She played the piano, as she had as a child, and adopted a cat, which she loved holding in her lap.

With Guérin playing classical music most of the day on the phonograph, Nancy rediscovered a world of reliable transport. She believed she had located the inner resources G. M. once called the private lake in everyone's heart. Eventually, Guérin's health grew increasingly poor, as if in concert with hers, although he was as stoical as Nancy. On occasion, they would go to the theater or opera, both barely able to climb the stairs, and lose themselves in the performance. Dependence on alcohol and sedatives became a way of life.

"We are all rather ill," Nancy wrote her friends, at the same time that she and Guérin tried to live a normal life, dressing for dinner and inviting friends to join them. The classical music in the house inspired Nancy to pursue "one of the best poems I shall have written"—another revision of "The Vision." "Trying to . . . shape the whole, from memory," the new work would be a series of poems in which she expressed her moral vision of the Spanish Civil War and a protest against all wars. Her personae would still be the bards and troubadours who sang in the old baronial halls of pre-medieval times. Nancy began to regularly sign her poems "Nanción" (*canción* [song]), identifying herself as a troubadour. Since, as she repeated, "The only time I don't feel ill is when I get to this machine and compose,"[46] she also worked on her sonnets in five languages—Italian, English, Spanish, French, and German. She sent Janet/Solita "How Rich the Harvest When the Hour Comes," with notes. It begins:

> Adesso é altra sosta—ma dovè su Dante?
> If the fire burn low, it is the same, I see—
> Por mudo que vas tiras por adelante,
> Et tout ce qui fut avant peut renaître ici
> Noch gibt es einigen Moorsoldaten hier.

She included translations:

> (1) At this time comes another pause in history, but where is its Dante to chronicle it?
> (2) If the fire burn low (the spirit perforce be dim, inarticulate), it is the same fire.
> (3) Muted art thou (Spain), but strivest ever forward,
> (4) And all that happened before might well come here again.
> (5) Some of the "Moor-Soldiers" still live.

Additional notes explained relevant Spanish history.[47]

Periodically, news arrived about the death of a friend. She wrote Janet/Solita:

> And now, it seems that Tzara is dead.
> How well I remember your saying to me—some seven or eight years ago—in Paris: "Well, we have reached the age when one has to get accustomed to the thought of friends dying around us." Et voilà. What else could . . . possibly be said? It is final, and clean, and clear and incontrovertible. . . . My reaction is always anger at the death of anyone I have loved.[48]

Nancy still considered herself an imposition on others, even at Guérin's house, where she was contributing monthly to its maintenance. As a result, and despite her breathlessness and general body weakness, she forced herself to visit both friends and new acquaintances: Tony Gandarillas at Hyères; the art historian Douglas Cooper in the Languedoc; and Paul Hanbury and Bob

Schootemeijer near Lambesc. To this day, when she entered a restaurant, "All eyes would be spontaneously drawn toward her. . . . Conversations would stop in mid-sentence; then a total silence would ensue, broken only by the rattle of her few remaining African bracelets."[49]

For a very brief period, as her sixty-eighth birthday approached, her rage toward her physical ordeal returned: "I can hardly walk for dizziness. . . . If only I could walk or stand up properly." She told her friends how much their correspondence meant to her. She was deeply saddened that the trappings of her life, and her role in acquiring them, would be left to oblivion:

> Yours is A LOVELY letter . . . to be kept forever, though *to be left*, with so much else, *to whom?*

Writing would be her mainstay until death: "Oh Lor', MUST all this go on till death do come? I suppose so. Sitting and typing is, to me, like 'la sucette' shoved into baby's mouth to stop its howling."[50]

On her birthday, March 10, 1964, Nancy and Guérin went to see *Boris Godunov* in Monte Carlo. Nancy, barely able to stand, still had the power to draw all eyes to her: "Everyone looked up. . . . [She was] desperately thin . . . [but] her impact was unmistakable." The opera was so inspirational that she wrote a new sonnet sequence.

Her mood changed after her birthday; her correspondence became cheerful and at times exuberant. A line of poetry might come to mind—"Be bold, be bold, but not too bold," she began, "Lest thy heart's blood run cold"—and she would recall the first time she heard it, in this instance, from "the chaps of 1913–14 in the Corrupt Coterie." If she had forgotten a reference in the poem or its author, she asked friends about the "wonderful, strange piece that came to my young ears": "It was *Diana* and it was Duff [who] . . . would quote this to each other. It is, to me, extremely beautiful. HERE I hear the immortal, stone, ring of England. . . . It is, I think, very famous. . . . WHAT DOES IT REFER TO? Indeed I am MOST EXCITED that you might know it." (The lines are from "Mr. Fox," an English fairy tale.)

She recollected high moments of travel, like her visit to Sanguinetto, near Treviso: "I thought I should go mad when I saw it, for it seemed complete. Not a crag, not a gash in its superb walls." She was always happy to receive new books, particularly by writers she had first published and then befriended at the Hours Press. When the French version of Beckett's *Endgame* arrived, she had "re-read [it] sitting bolt upright on [the] edge of [the] bed here two nights ago till dawn. . . . How very lovely indeed." She had seen Beckett over the years but "nothing like enough." "We're getting on," she remarked, quoting from Beckett's "lovely" work. To another friend, she mused on her

Beckett: "[I] adore my Samivel. . . . My dear, *noir*, Samuel. . . . I should like to see him for once dressed in RED. As dressed he is, now, in pure BLACK. What a force—and what an artist. Let the drivellers have their say, babbling, in their criticisms, about 'Despair.' Sure, it's despair——but it is also a great, great deal more than that."[51]

As if suddenly at war with the enemy time, her typing could not keep pace with her ideas: "This mind is too QUICK, and so it forgets what it thought. Improvising is the only way for me . . . , and then work over and over as many a time as I can." She still tried to oppose sleep, more than ever a waste of time. "I think I shall be able to resist BED at this moment," she began one letter, ending it "P.S. Two hours later. That phenomenon, SLEEP did win. . . . Ooh, what a drug is the need of sleep."[52]

Nancy returned to La Mothe for the summer of 1964 and was visited by Irene and Géraldine. She tried to ignore the fact that she felt ill all the time. But still comfortable sitting, she pursued her projects. She sent Janet/Solita new and rewritten material from "The Vision," including her preamble, affirming the inevitable continuity of all natural processes. She asked if, "with flowers" and "new stars of effulgent colors," spring must be "the symbol of all hope" and replied that spring is undeserving of this "strange monopoly." "My faith," she affirms, is rather in continuity, "in the change of season to season, of day to night."

In July 1964, a doctor detailed the gravity of Nancy's condition, and she fell into another severe depression, similar to the one during the week of her birthday. On August 21, she wrote to Janet/Solita: "I can't write in this house. . . . My poem is not out of my head—but 'life' is." Although she fantasized about returning to London, she knew that any move was impossible, except to Guérin's villa. Géraldine visited La Mothe as Nancy was preparing to leave. She watched her with deep sadness as she embraced her portrait of George Moore and carefully wrapped it. Nancy asked if she might once more see the blue-green valley of walnut trees as the leaves were turning amber and gold, and Géraldine helped her make the walk. Nancy, struggling to breathe, climbed the hill and stopped once to pick up a golden pebble and branch. Géraldine was barely able to restrain her tears, for she now knew that "their usual 'au revoir' would be changed to 'adieu.'"[53]

Falling Down

Desperate for companionship, Nancy returned to Guérin's villa. The house was as damp and cold as she feared: "Cigarettes go out, envelopes get stuck, . . . a laughable sight, but hellish, [and we] suffer much pain." The stairs throughout the villa also frightened Nancy, "including seventeen . . . to the dining room." She vowed, yet again, to improve her mood. She would ignore the increasing bouts of exhaustion: "All my instinct . . . is to lie in bed, sleep colossally, [but I will] get to the typewriter [and] perhaps arrive at a final minus-one version."[54]

Then, the accidents began; after each, Nancy remained resilient. The first involved Guérin's Tibetan terriers, three of which had been born on her bed. "The brown one became my favorite," and from that point on, the "exquisite" puppy was frequently in her lap, often licking her face. Nancy delighted to watch it dance around her feet and bite her toes. One night a bookcase fell over and "killed the little baby." Nancy wrote Janet about how "sad, sad, sad" she was. She cursed "the BLOODY BOOKS!" To her horror, the first one she picked up was her own volume on George Moore.[55]

Later that winter, she fell on the slippery steps outside the villa and gashed her shin. She was taken to the Clinique Belvédère in Nice. The cut was eight inches long, and it extended to the bone and required several stitches. The doctor told her she might develop gangrene and the leg might have to be amputated. Again embarrassed and unaccustomed to being afraid, she said: "I am indeed ashamed of myself, as one generally is when ill." In one poem on the subject, she wrote about the exquisite, dizzying, symmetrical ecstasy of pain, its "mathematics and . . . calculations," and its synesthetic sensations— how it begins

> . . . alone, on the single string of a violin,
> Before the full chords . . . come mounting in
> On their majestic surge, their inexplicable wonder,
> Their strange plush colors.

From these chords arise the "thunder" that ascends "from bone to brain": such sensations transform the fiber of even the most exotic "strange Arab designs and Turkish fashions."

As she explained her surgery to Nan Green, her friend from the Spanish Civil War, her thoughts returned to Spain:

I have had to have my right leg cut open (to the bone or no?) to have two enormous cupfuls of 2- or 3-day old jelly extracted (with hardly any local anaesthetic), in Nice. . . . I will have to get up enough courage in a minute to turn on the light. . . . While the Nice doctor was cutting his 8 (?) inch slit in the leg, what should come back to me but the vision of the Spanish worker's forearm being lanced, without any anaesthetic at all, in the Escorial improvised hospital, in Sept. or Oct. 1936.

Looking for a "dum-dum" bullet was the surgeon, explaining to me as he probed on, that such "star shaped" wounds were due to [a] "dum-dum."

Louise Morgan wrote her:

> I am horrified to hear about your leg. Nancy's lovely legs are so much a part of her. I see you ALWAYS walking. Watching you from across a stream of traffic by the National Gallery—apart, intent, walking fast and effortlessly, as on air, head as ever high, atmosphere electric, people turning their heads after passing you, and you noticing nothing, intent, absorbed, creative. . . . I cannot imagine anything happening to your legs.[56]

During her stay in the hospital, Nancy was able to sit up; if she had sufficient rum and water and wine, she could "compose like mad." Back at Pomone, however, she realized that to avoid constant exhaustion she would have to curtail her drinking. Although alcohol numbed the pain, it interfered with polished writing: "*Correcting* one's writing . . . should not be done with drink . . . because the rhythms of composition get mixed up. . . . The 'final ear' should be ice, preferably marble-cold. A finality—not to be touched again ever."[57]

To buoy herself, she dressed "in the colors of Botticelli" but was distracted by the numerous arthritic bumps in her body. Although sleep remained anathema, she momentarily contemplated whether death, like sleep, was a restful oblivion: "Sleep is, indeed a [striking] phenomenon. . . . How it overtakes one at times! . . . When one issues from that, oh, from what another world—as complete as death. I hope death is as complete as that kind of sleep."[58]

On January 21, 1965, at 11:00 P.M., while trying to avoid stepping on one of the little dogs, Nancy tripped on the valance of her bed and broke her hip and cracked several ribs. She lay on the floor in severe pain all night. The next morning, an ambulance rushed her back to the Clinique Belvédère for emergency surgery; she was so weak that she required a blood transfusion. However, the surgeon was so pleased with her progress that he thought she could leave in a few days, although it would be "three months before 'normal' again." When she was moved into a private room, to the astonishment of the many nurses and her surgeon, she was cheerful and began writing.

She returned, "delighted, on a stretcher," to the villa on February 3, and two days later was diagnosed with "medical" or gastric poisoning. She was told to lie flat, but when her doctor thought she might develop pneumonia, she had to sit up, again warned not to stand or walk for three months. In her letters to Strachan, she made light of her pain "due to the enthusiastic, stubborn daily two-hours yankings of a masseuse." Although she had "one metal plate and several screws in the thigh," her vanity triumphed when she added that she had a "gorgeous vertical scar of twelve stitches and no flesh-bumps whatever. Wonderful surgeon."[59]

"In these grim conditions, did her morale collapse?" asked Irene in a rhetorical way. "On the contrary, [her] postcards . . . were spirited to the point of being humorous. [Her] pain in fact was bad and constant, but . . . she cursed it, she mocked it, she *worked*. . . . I thought about her . . . pain, her bravery." In a cheerful card to Janet/Solita, she brandished her battle scars: "*Stitches out?* Good God yes, painlessly . . . [and] no bumps"—except for "an illegible, rather beautiful" scar across the leg "in the shape of a Minoan brooch." She felt much better since Guérin's doctor had prescribed a blend of vitamin B-12 and two other ingredients. She celebrated the doctor's order that she consume absolutely "*no food* (hurrah!)." Shortly thereafter she wrote:

> So now I have at last all I want. Eau de riz (a sort of rice gruel) and tea with lemon. Books? to read? No. I don't *read*, I write—*all* the time. The same long poem you have some parts of. Radio by bed? Good God, NO. . . . [I have Jean's] beautiful, electric music.[60]

Nancy, discharged without medication, remained in severe pain but pursued her correspondence. Strachan described her mood, "not exactly stoical—that would be the wrong word—because she had to voice her protest—not against fate or death, but against being prevented by pain . . . from the tasks she had set herself to do." Strachan knew that "she could still muster the energy, born of a lifetime's habit—of concerning herself with other people's problems," both large and small. She would write him on February 14, 1965, a month before she died: "I see I missed answering a query of yours re: Yves Tanguy . . . " and even later, "I am uplifted at the thought of living in England again."[61]

She remained upbeat and wrote friends about many subjects. To David Garnett, she began: "What shall I write of? To write of PAIN again would be wearisome, and we must not weary our friends. Of poetry, and of its making, we may always write." She told him about her future projects, including three Negro sequences, a group of poems called "Animalitos," and another on the River Nene, and apologized for her handwriting, due, she said, to "wave after wave of sleep breathing over me." The letter, among the last she wrote, was dated two weeks before she died:

> Must a person believe in a "God" of some kind so as to try to get through life?— "Pie in the Sky" and all that? Why not *here* and *now*? Had I to choose a God, I

would opt for inter-kindliness—and not more. And THAT covers the end of all wars.[62]

Nancy's views regarding personal responsibility and divinity, as rarely as she discussed them, had been consistent through most of her life. To be sure, some of her poems addressed a deity—and the experiences she sought in nature were transcendental. But her life experiences, and everything she said about them, suggest her rejection of any traditional belief. "Who, do you suppose," she asked Kay at the end of 1963, "invented the figure of the Devil? I can understand, much better, the invention of the figure of 'GODS.' Neither helps us. Why should they?! I think that *fortitude* and decision are the things for people like us." She added: "I've always thought that jolly old Victorian rubbish 'Be good and you'll be happy' was one of the great poisons in the start of life to ANY child. All one can do is to TRY. Right?" In one of her memoirs, she recalled a conversation in 1946 with a priest in Andorra:

> I was a Protestant . . . and I told him I was not religious and did not consider myself a believer. . . . He looked at me thoughtfully, saying: "But, without a faith, do you not feel alone in life?" "I do not feel alone, or lonely."[63]

She also recalled a 1923 letter from G. M.: "The Christian says 'memento mori'; the pagan answers 'remember life,' which seems to me to express a finer spirituality, for do we not create ourselves, our bodies in some measure, our souls completely?" Perhaps only once, according to writings both about and by Nancy, did she suggest the desire, and particularly the comfort, of having religious conviction. She had "gently and with sad humility" asked her friend Allanah Harper: "Do you believe in God?" Allanah replied that she had always been attracted to religion, especially Vedanta, but had recently become a Roman Catholic and found fulfillment. "You are a good woman," Nancy replied and, looking at her with tenderness, added: "I wish I could believe in something."[64]

Nancy continued her orthopedic research and physical therapy during what she never suspected was the last month of her life. She was following her doctor's order that she not walk for three months: "Have been thoroughly studying 'Le Médecine pour tous' (à Larousse). I see what I have done is to badly break *my hip!* . . . Expert, confidence-giving, diplomaed masseuse now, daily, *and for months to come*." She even accepted her pain: "One gets accustomed to constant pain. . . . It's now a sort of frozen pain."[65] She continued her correspondence until days before she died.

A Frantic, Lonely Farewell

A young man and his pregnant wife visited Guérin's villa during Nancy's hospital stay, but their continuing presence intruded on the social equilibrium that Nancy and Guérin had established. In addition, Guérin began suffering badly from his various ailments at the same time that he was attending to his dying mother. He and Nancy began drinking more than usual. When Guérin became severely stricken with sciatica and arthritis, his physician advised that he leave the damp villa for a warmer climate. He announced this to Nancy two days before her sixty-ninth birthday, and she provoked a quarrel with such wounding words that he asked her to leave the house.[66] Perhaps in this way she did not have to deal with his "abandonment."

Feeling homeless and maddened with pain, loneliness, and rage, she left for Paris the next day. Barely able to stand or walk—"I'm held together by bolts and screws"—she threw some papers and ivory bracelets into a suitcase and called a cab. En route to the train station, she begged the driver to stay with her, which he did, and they drank rum together. When she pleaded further for him not to leave, he arranged for someone to place her on the train and rushed home; his wife was about to give birth. When the train arrived at the station, Nancy refused to board, lost her temper, hit one of the gendarmes who had been called to the scene, and was locked up in the police station for the night. The next morning, she could not find her money or ticket, and the police put her on the train. After she arrived in Paris, a porter carried her to a taxi, and she went to Orgeval to visit Solita. It was the eve of Nancy's birthday.

The cab driver carried her into the house. "Pay him, ducky," she said to Solita. "It's quite a lot. He's coming to fetch me tomorrow. May I stay here tonight?" Nancy drank several glasses of vodka and finished Solita's small supply of alcohol and wine. "I like this stuff, this vodka," she said, adding, "I'll sleep there" and pointed to a wheelbarrow in the garden. Solita phoned Janet, who said she would arrange to have a doctor in Paris the next morning; both she and the doctor would be waiting for Nancy.

Nancy did not sleep in the wheelbarrow. She remained in the same blue chair all night, writing and smoking. In the morning, pages filled with an illegible scrawl were scattered around the room. Although she seemed more calm than the night before, she refused to see a doctor. The cab driver returned and carried her to the car. Nancy said to Solita: "I don't expect we shall be seeing one another again."

During the next few days, she was driven by her own Furies on an odyssey that had no destination. Strachan agreed with Burkhart that her intention had been to return to London: "I could not help, from the evidence of Nancy's last messages to me, interpreting her last journey as a desperate attempt to get back to England via Paris." Burkhart later remarked: "She was too mad to know what she was going for. She was there, but why? Always in the past there had been a purpose for the innumerable expeditions—wall paintings in Altamira to be seen, . . . Spanish refugees who, to aid, the Pyrenees must again be stormed."[67]

Instead of meeting Janet and a physician, Nancy went to Raymond Michelet's apartment, where he was living with a woman. Nancy acted as though time had stopped, as if she and Michelet, her lover more than thirty years earlier, would return home together and collaborate on another book. Michelet phoned two doctors, but again Nancy refused to see them. She wanted to visit her old friends. Beckett was in the country and unreachable, but Michelet was able to contact Aragon and Sadoul. Aragon's wife, Elsa, said to him: "Do what you want, send her some money, go there if you want. I do not want her here." Although Aragon remained loyal to Elsa, he was, at the same time, self-accusatory and distraught over Nancy.[68]

When Sadoul and his wife arrived at Michelet's apartment, they discovered "a frightening spectacle":

[Nancy] had lost her reason and was delirious. She was thinner than a Buchenwald corpse. . . . With her broken thigh, she could no longer stand. Lying stretched out on a divan, half-naked, she spoke without pause. . . . [How had she traveled this far?] There was only one explanation. Her formidable energy had vanquished her infirmities. She *had* arrived. Her mind had cracked, her beautiful intelligence clouded over and she hardly knew she was insulting her best friends, present and absent.

Both Michelet and the Sadouls were fearful of taking on the responsibility of caring for Nancy, and when she mentioned a reservation at a hotel in the Latin Quarter, they took her there. They arrived after midnight, intent on seeing that she was safely in bed. They planned to have a physician there the next morning. However, as Sadoul reported:

The hotel didn't have a lift. [Nancy] allowed Michelet and me to support her as far as the base of the stairs, and she proclaimed her intention of climbing alone. . . . And she began to mount the stairs by herself. She would sit down on a step, find the strength to heave herself on to the next, then rest there long enough to gather her strength and breath, sometimes for as long as ten minutes. This slow ascent lasted ninety minutes, perhaps two hours. It seemed like the longest time of my life.

Nancy chatted calmly as she sat or climbed; guests stopped, astonished to see her, but Sadoul explained that she was ill and insistent on climbing to her room unaided. She asked if Neruda was going to win the Nobel Prize and if anyone knew Beckett's phone number; "He is very fond of me," she explained. She also announced, speaking in the third person, that "just today [she] had her 69th birthday."[69]

The next day, a psychiatrist tried to speak to her, but she was in a state of complete collapse. She phoned Michelet and accused him of being a fascist who had sent a spy to her room. When he returned to the hotel, he discovered that she had somehow managed to get downstairs and escape. Before leaving, she had piled up all her letters and papers in the middle of the room and set them on fire.

Her whereabouts for the next day or two are uncertain. On March 13, the police found her unconscious on the street. Her head was bruised as if she had fallen headfirst to the ground. After she was taken to the Hôpital Cochin, she recovered consciousness but was unable to remember her name. She requested wine (which they did not provide) and a pencil and paper; she spent hours writing poems and friends. When her condition deteriorated, she was forced to stop writing. She fell into a coma and died in an oxygen tent two days later, on March 16, almost a week after her sixty-ninth birthday. Visiting hours had just begun, and Nancy was, mercifully one must think, unconscious—alone on the public ward of the hospital.

Michelet was overcome by the agony of her last days. He believed that she was afraid to die, although he thought she had found a curious comfort in an African "animism" that promised something other than oblivion after death. He also thought that in her last days she had come to believe herself African and to think that her true life was no longer in Europe. At the same time, and using Beckett's words "Fin de Partie" (*Endgame*) three times, Michelet said that he witnessed no evidence of any form of solace in the frenzy of her final hours. She died in desperation, he said, at the same time she resisted and expired like fireworks: "And one wants to shield one's eyes from that last great glare."[70]

• • •

The British Embassy informed the Cunard family of Nancy's death. At the funeral service, at the British Embassy Church on rue du Faubourg Saint-Honoré, the pallbearers outnumbered the mourners. No one from her family attended. Her few friends present included Janet, Solita, Michelet, and the art critic Douglas Cooper. The reporter Sam White, in the *Evening Standard*, wrote about the "sad, lonely farewell to a toast of the Twenties." As the service was about to end, an enormous wreath arrived, with a banner and gold inscription: "With love from your cousins." Her ashes were placed in niche no. 9016 in the celebrated Columbarium Crypt of the Père Lachaise Cemetery, the last resting place for many great writers and historians. A few years later, a plaque identifying her was placed on the urn.

Epilogue

There was no memorial service for Nancy Cunard.

Her friends learned from one another the details of her sudden death and the last days of her life. At the same time, her incoherent letters and postcards continued to arrive in the mail.

In view of the many admiring comments made by her friends both before and after her death, I have selected a few that highlight what one had called "the Nanciad."[1]

Nancy Cunard was kind and good and catholic and cosmopolitan and sophisticated and simple all at the same time and a poet of no mean abilities and an appreciator of the rare and the off-beat from jazz to ivory bracelets and witch doctors to Cocteau but she did not like truffles at Maxim's or chitterlings in Harlem. She did not like bigots or brilliant bores or academicians who wore their honors, or scholars who wore their doctorates, like dog tags. But she had an infinite capacity to love peasants and children and great but simple causes across the board and a grace in giving that was itself gratitude and she had a body like sculpture in the thinnest of wire and a face made of a million mosaics in a gauze-web of cubes lighter than air and a piñata of a heart in the center of a mobile at fiesta time with bits of her soul swirling in the breeze in honor of life and love and Good Morning to you, *Bon Jour, Muy Buenos, Muy Buenos! Muy Buenos!*

—LANGSTON HUGHES

Gradually I watched the transformation of what the press might describe as "a popular society girl" into a militant propagandist for miscellaneous prickly causes, fighting in improbable surroundings, for the Scottsboro Negroes, the Spanish Republicans, refugees and down-and-outs of sorts, hardening her will to overcome exhaustion, courting physical discomfort, indifferent to calumny, smiling at risks. Her austerity was voluptuous. In the middle ages she would have become a mystic.

—HAROLD ACTON

As the years passed by . . . it became clear that to be in the presence of Nancy was more like coming to grips with a force of nature. . . . The weather was seldom calm and storm followed storm at various degrees of violence. . . . It was impossible for her to work quietly for the rights of man; Nancy functioned best in a state of fury in which, in order to defend, she attacked every windmill in a landscape of windmills.

The activities of her earliest causes—the right of a brilliant-minded child to study in her own way (not whacked by three governesses on the knuckles), the injustices of governments towards individuals, the discrimination against races, servants overworked and underpaid—all such activities were set into devastating motion by a word, a look, a memory. Then with her special battle cry, "Up and at 'em!" off she galloped to break still another lance. Sleep? Warmth? Food? No! Somewhere someone was suffering. . . .

The greatest efforts and disillusions of her life were in the catastrophe of Spain. Refusing to accept the inevitable, she worked on and waited thirty years for her side to recruit its conquered forces and to try again with its left-over heroes. . . . [Her] other [great] cause [black rights] . . . was not a lost one. In a poem one could ask: does the earth's halo hold enough gratitude for the fact that Nancy lived to see black become less black and white turn less white through shame?

. . . Her vast anger at injustice embraced the universe [and] her life's purpose was to use her universal anger for the moral evolution of mankind. It was her mania, her madness. It was the key that had turned her on from infancy to the hours when she sat writing her last illegible words.

—JANET FLANNER/SOLITA SOLANO

Heir to the Cunard Line, Nancy, daughter of Lady Cunard, had scandalized London in 1930 by running away with a black man. . . . When Lady Cunard found her daughter's bed empty, the noblewoman went to her lawyer and proceeded to cut her off without a cent. . . .

In December of the year in which her mother excommunicated her, the English aristocracy received as a Christmas present, a pamphlet bound in red, entitled "Negro Man and White Ladyship." . . . It is as trenchant as Swift, in some passages.

Her arguments in defense of blacks came down like clubs on the heads of Lady Cunard and English society—for thirty pages. . . . Nancy was never able to live in England after that, and from then on, she embraced the cause of the persecuted black race. During the invasion of Ethiopia she went to Addis Ababa. Then she traveled to the United States to make common cause with the black boys of Scottsboro who were accused of infamous crimes they had not committed. The young blacks were sentenced by racist U.S. Justice, and Nancy Cunard was deported by the democratic North American police.

My friend Nancy Cunard would die in 1965 in Paris. [There] she closed her lovely sky-blue eyes forever. . . . She was a mere skeleton. Her body had wasted away in a long battle against injustice in the world. Her reward was a life that had become progressively lonelier, and a godforsaken death.

—PABLO NERUDA

Many have asked me the meaning of Cunardia. The name belongs to Nancy Cunard of England. She is a woman who published a Negro anthology in 1934. . . . To hear that a white man or white woman was in true sympathy with the feelings of the Africans brought me peace, courage and sanity: and so I named the first school of the Education Missionary Society "Cunardia." . . . The Africans want to honor her for taking their side when the color war was raging fiercest. She suffered slander, ostracism and loneliness because of us. We simply want to honor her in so little a way. May she be blessed!

—T. K. UTCHAY

Nancy had a very advanced formulation of equity, ethics, and morals. It was as exceptional as it was different from the ideas usually held in connection with "proper" behavior and—in my opinion—of a much higher order. It was free from hypocrisy!

Once, when I needed friends very badly indeed I found that Nancy was the most steadfast, generous, and unselfish friend that I had. I'm not ashamed to say that her conduct was touching to the point of tears. If such qualities were not unique they were certainly most unhappily rare.

—HILAIRE HILER

Pale country of snow and shade, I shall never again leave your divine meanderings. Thus, having rediscovered the delightful inflection of your hip, or the bewitching detour of your arms, in myriad places to which I have been led by all the anxiety of existence and by this immense hope which has settled over me, I can no longer speak of anything but you; and do not believe my pretense—all my words are for you, and are your appearance. My images have acquired their glaze from your fingernails, my demented language heaves like your voice. Am I now going to pursue this lying description of a park which three friends infiltrated one evening? What for? You have arisen over this park, over the walkers, over thought.

Your trace and scent, that is what possesses me. I am evicted from myself, and from my development, and from whatever is not the possession of my self by you. You are the grasp of heaven on my formless clay. At last everything is divine for me because everything exists in your image, and I know above and beyond my reason and my heart what a sacred place is, I know what sacralizes it for me. I am the true idolator for whom temples have been sewed abroad like seeds of sickness. But here-after there is not a place which will not be hallowed ground for me, an altar. And I return to this arch where, in former times, people ardently sought death.

—LOUIS ARAGON

Dearest Nancy,

I am grateful to you for writing. You make me aware of so many great and funda-mental things that slip away, are lost—at least temporarily—when one loses hope. Your letters, because of these things they bring to life for me again, have given me a sort of vision of courage, a horizon of hope, although neither are quite realized, not reached, as yet.

. . . Yes, "fortitude and decision belong to us, and even when we are ailing, even when we die, the mark of them will be forever there."

I would not be writing to you now with the same admiration or love with which I wrote you the Scottsboro poem. I would not be making now the unchanging and unchangeable salutes to all you are, if you had not led your life with the decision and fortitude that made you uniquely you.

No, God and the Devil can be dispensed with, but not the unique God-head that is Nancy—who has vision, and her articulation of that vision, that lives in all of us who have understood the vision and who were moved and strengthened by the clarity of the articulation. You questioned, in your letters, the meaning of "good," and the reason for living at all—but because you have lived as you have you are forever uneraseable. You live in us who love and treasure you, as you live, in my instance anyway, in our children. They would not be what they are, my demon-strating, peace-marching children, if you had not shown the way.

You are, if you could but believe it, accept it, what made the Civil Rights march in Washington possible, and what has made James Baldwin all that he is. You are *indelible*, because you have never faltered and this demands that none of us falter. You have created this new world in which we can breathe more freely.

Nancy, I love you. And I am filled with admiration for you. . . . Thank you for having been, and for being, and for making all our lives a declaration.

—KAY BOYLE,
on the one-month anniversary of her husband's death

Notes

The following abbreviations refer to archival material most frequently cited.

BC Bodleian Library, Balliol College, Oxford University, Special Collections and Western Manuscripts
Correspondence with E. J. Thompson, 1943–1945. MSS Eng c 5285.

BRR Beineke Rare Book and Manuscript Library, Yale University
Miscellaneous correspondence, including letters to Ezra Pound. GEN MSS 438, folders 1–41.

HRC Harry Ransom Humanities Research Center Library, University of Texas at Austin
I draw on the following from this vast collection:

Series I. Works: manuscripts, newspaper articles, early poetry. Boxes 1–9.

Series II. Correspondence: outgoing, 1931–1965; incoming, 1909–1965; third-party correspondence, 1908–1965. Boxes 10–21.

Series III. Personal papers, "not creative works": legal and medical documents, 1920–1956; address and guest books, 1895–1956; commonplace books, diaries, scrapbooks, 1909–1959; lists, notes, 1911–1958; journals, notebooks, photographs, newspaper clippings, book reviews, travel notes. Boxes 21–31.

LC Library of Congress, Manuscript Division
Janet Flanner and Solita Solano Papers, 1870–1976. Box 2. Virtually all of Nancy's letters begin "Darlings" and are referred to in the notes as "to Janet/Solita"; many in the early years are undated, unique in Nancy's correspondence.

ML Morris Library, Southern Illinois University Library, Special Collections
Correspondence with Charles Burkhart, 1951–1965. Collection 57.

Correspondence with Walter Strachan, 1943–1965. Collection 58.

Kay Boyle Papers, 1935–1965. Collection 90.

TGA Tate Gallery Archive
Letters and postcards to John Banting, 1921–1960. 779/1/132–41.

UD University of Delaware, Special Collections
Letters to David Garnett, 1928–1965. 99 F580.

UM John Rylands University Library, University of Manchester
Guardian Archives, B/290A/1–125.

References to Nancy's newspaper articles are as complete as possible. There are no indexes of the American Negro Press (ANP) or of the individual newspapers in the consortium that date back to the 1930s. Items from some of the papers are available on microfilm or microfiche, but headlines and page numbers have not always been filmed. The Schomberg Center for Research in Black Culture of the New York Public Library has the largest holdings of the ANP collection in the United States. The Harry Ransom Humanities Research Center has many of her articles, some of which she clipped; among these, once again, dates and page numbers are often missing. Butler Library, Columbia University, has full holdings of some ANP newspapers such as the *Pittsburgh Courier* and *Norfolk Journal and Guide*.

1. Golden Girl

Epigraph. Quoted in Daphne Fielding, *Those Remarkable Cunards: Emerald and Nancy* (New York: Atheneum, 1968), 97.

1. "It seems fantastic now to think of the scale of our existence then, with its numerous servants, gardeners, horses and motor cars, now that all this has floated away for ever and time wears such a different dress" (Nancy Cunard, *G. M.: Memories of George Moore* [London: Rupert Hart-Davis, 1956], 22).
2. Morris Gilbert, "Nancy Cunard," in *Nancy Cunard: Brave Poet, Indomitable Rebel, 1896–1965*, ed. Hugh Ford (Philadelphia: Chilton, 1968), 201; NC to Charles Burkhart, 18 June 1963, folder 8, ML.
3. Anne Chisholm, *Nancy Cunard: A Biography* (New York: Knopf, 1979), 10.
4. Cunard, *G. M.*, 21.
5. Daphne Fielding, who knew both Maud and Nancy, writes: "It was commonly thought that Maud was O'Brien's daughter, not Burke's." She recalls one photo in particular where their facial similarities were obvious (*Remarkable Cunards*, 1, note 1).
6. Quoted in ibid., 2.
7. Ibid.
8. Cunard, *G. M.*, 114. See also George Moore, *Letters to Lady Cunard, 1895–1933*, ed. Rupert Hart-Davis (London: Rupert Hart-Davis, 1957), 10.
9. Fielding, *Remarkable Cunards*, 3–4. See also Moore, *Letters to Lady Cunard*, 13–14.
10. George Moore, *Memoirs of My Dead Life* (London: Heinemann, 1906), 12.
11. Quoted in Fielding, *Remarkable Cunards*, 4.

12. Quoted in Gilbert, "Nancy Cunard," 202; Anthony Thorne, "A Share of Nancy," in *Nancy Cunard*, ed. Ford, 304.

13. George Moore, *Conversations in Ebury Street* (New York: Boni and Liveright, 1924), 99.

14. Fielding, *Remarkable Cunards*, 8, 97. The HRC has 1,500 loose photos, as well as three large scrapbooks. Dozens of Nancy's notebooks and diaries, beginning in 1909, also include photos.

15. Cunard, G. M., 17–19.

16. Fielding, *Remarkable Cunards*, 16.

17. Diary, 1910, box 22, folder 7, HRC.

18. Diary, 1909, box 22, folder 6, HRC.

19. Cunard, G. M., 66.

20. Sometimes Nancy writes variations on these passages in the 1909 and 1910 diaries.

21. Fielding, *Remarkable Cunards*, 16.

22. Diary, 5 May 1909, box 22, folder 6, HRC.

23. Quoted in Fielding, *Remarkable Cunards*, 26.

24. The quotations in this and the following two paragraphs, including the poems, are from diaries, 1909–1910, box 22, folders 6 and 7, HRC.

25. Fielding, *Remarkable Cunards*, 12–13; Cunard, G. M., 34.

26. Cunard, G. M., 22.

27. Moore, *Letters to Lady Cunard*, 4 May 1894, 9 October 1904, 15 April 1908, 25 May 1908–19 January 1922, and 1 January 1929. Always using Maud as the model for the heroine in his fiction, Moore writes of Van Eyck's painting *Arnolfini and His Wife*: "The husband . . . speaks with an uplifted hand like one in a pulpit, . . . telling her that her condition—her pregnancy—is an act of the Divine Will" (*Memoirs of My Dead Life*, 59–60).

28. Elsa Maxwell, "The Perfect Hostess and Others," available at http://www.oldandsold.com/articles02/party4.shtml (accessed 26 November 2002); *New York American*, dated 13 September 1916 by Nancy, in scrapbook, box 26, folder 1, HRC.

29. Cunard, G. M., 32.

30. Ibid.

31. The image is in the visitor book, box 22, folder 1, HRC. Nancy comments on the caricature in G. M., 36.

32. Cunard, G. M., 33–34, 37; diary, 9 April 1910, box 22, folder 7, HRC.

33. Cunard, G. M., 39; Fielding, *Remarkable Cunards*, 26, 24.

34. Fielding, *Remarkable Cunards*, 23–24.

35. Diary, 20 July 1919, box 23, folder 1, HRC. Unless otherwise indicated, the material cited in the remainder of this chapter is from Cunard, G. M., 44–69.

36. Fielding, *Remarkable Cunards*, 20.

37. Cunard, G. M., 162.

38. Ibid., 101, 48.

39. Ibid., 116, 130–31.

40. Ibid. 81, 82.

2. Coming of Age During a Revolution in the Arts

Epigraph. Ewart Milne, "On Nancy Cunard," in *Nancy Cunard: Brave Poet, Indomitable Rebel, 1896–1965*, ed. Hugh Ford (Philadelphia: Chilton, 1968), 234–35.

1. J. Bryan III and Charles J. V. Murphy, *Windsor Story* (New York: Morrow, 1979), 119–22.
2. Quoted in Frances Donaldson, *Edward VIII* (Philadelphia: Lippincott, 1975), 178.
3. Quoted in Arthur Waley, "Three Nancy Cunards," in *Nancy Cunard*, ed. Ford, 13.
4. Diaries, 1909–1910, box 22, folders 6 and 7, HRC; Nancy Cunard, *G. M.: Memories of George Moore* (London: Rupert Hart-Davis, 1956), 101.
5. Cunard, *G. M.*, 112, 144.
6. Iris Tree, "We Shall Not Forget, for Nancy Cunard," in *Nancy Cunard*, ed. Ford, 21. Kenneth MacPherson writes: "Nancy's voice was then and remained, a miracle. And so was the way she walked" ("Ne Mai," in ibid., 345).
7. Quoted in Philip Ziegler, *King Edward VIII: The Official Biography* (London: Collins, 1990), 43.
8. Ibid., 32; quoted in Bryan and Murphy, *Windsor Story*, 118.
9. Donaldson, *Edward VIII*, 30–32. Ziegler writes that the prince neither acquired even a superficial knowledge of the English classics nor learned to read for pleasure (*King Edward VIII*, 16–17). In 1904, his skull was examined by a renowned phrenologist, who reported that Edward would develop his talents if he had "greater confidence." Michael Thornton discusses his childhood stammer, after his tutors tried to end his left-handedness, in *Royal Feud* (London: Michael Joseph, 1985), 69.
10. Ziegler, *King Edward VIII*, 166, 122, 96; Donaldson, *Edward VIII*, 86.
11. He "felt no sexual hunger," reports Ziegler in *King Edward VIII*, 88–89.
12. Cunard, *G. M.*, 102–3; Paul Fussell, *The Great War and Modern Memory* (Oxford: Oxford University Press, 1975), 24.
13. Daphne Fielding, *The Rainbow Picnic: A Portrait of Iris Tree* (London: Methuen, 1974), 35; Tree, "We Shall Not Forget," 18.
14. Quoted in *Anne Chisholm: A Biography* (New York: Knopf, 1979), 31.
15. Tree, "We Shall Not Forget," 21.
16. Ibid., 19.
17. Nancy Cunard, *These Were the Hours: Memories of My Hours Press, Réanville and Paris, 1928–1931* (Carbondale: Southern Illinois University Press, 1969), 32–33.
18. Ibid., 72.
19. Nancy Cunard, "Thoughts About Ronald Firbank," in *Ronald Firbank: Memoirs and Critiques*, ed. Mervyn Horder (London: Duckworth, 1977), 122–26. Stulik was a character in himself. He said he was the offspring of a famous ballerina who had been overwhelmed by an exalted, anonymous personage. On occasion, he identified that personage as Franz Josef, to whom he bore a distinct resemblance.
20. Quoted in Kevin Davey, *English Imaginaries: Six Studies in Anglo British Modernity* (London: Lawrence & Wishart, 1999), 29.
21. Ibid.
22. Tree, "We Shall Not Forget," 18.
23. Ibid., 20; David Garnett, "Nancy Cunard," in *Nancy Cunard*, ed. Ford, 27.
24. Tree, "We Shall Not Forget," 21.
25. Ibid., 20.

26. Cunard, *These Were the Hours*, 72, 66–67; after reading a passage about homosexuality among tramps, Nancy and Symons agreed: "What educated person, normally healthy in mind, is going to find 'salacious' or 'obscene' this matter?" (187).

27. *Times Literary Supplement*, 19 March 1914, 133–34; 2 April 1914, 137–58.

28. Janet Flanner, "Nancy Cunard," in *Nancy Cunard*, ed. Ford, 87–88.

29. In *New Age*, Hulme defined the objectives of modern poetry. Since the world had become a place of metaphysical desolation inhabited by hollow men, the artist was obliged to "clean the world of these sloppy dregs." Hulme, promulgating the moral-social imperatives of the artist (as an outgrowth of his belief in original sin), sought a new classicism in a formal, geometric art of sharp, precise images free of personal feeling or ideology. This would promote an orderly, disciplined society. Rejecting the post-Renaissance assumption that humanity has limitless potential for betterment, he spoke of the individual as animalistic and corrupt—as violent and destructive as a machine. And he himself had a gamy history. Infamous for his Cambridge dismissal for rowdyism, Hulme gathered around him young writers so he could brag about his sexual adventures. Once, after leaving them for five minutes, he returned to say that the emergency exit at the Piccadilly tube was the most uncomfortable place he had ever copulated. He was killed in World War I. See Julian Symons, *Makers of the New: The Revolution in Literature, 1912–1939* (London: Andre Deutsch, 1987), 32.

30. Cunard, *These Were the Hours*, 123. Nancy's close friend, the poet Edward Wyndham Tennant, was killed in the war, as was Pound's friend, the great French sculptor Henri Gaudier-Brzeska ("the most complete case of genius I've ever encountered").

31. The quotations in this and the following two paragraphs are from ibid., 123–24, 127, 156–58.

32. For his notation of these poems, I am indebted to James J. Wilhelm, "Nancy Cunard: A Sometime Flame, a Stalwart Friend," *Paideuma* 19 (1999): 201–21.

33. After Yeats showed him Joyce's poem "I Hear an Army," Pound immediately published it in *Des Imagistes*. Asking Joyce for additional work encouraged the completion of *A Portrait of the Artist as a Young Man*, which Joyce mailed to him, along with *Dubliners*. Pound published "The Dead" in the *Egoist* and arranged for *Portrait*'s serialization and then book form publication under the auspices of his magazine. He also persuaded Harriet Weaver to publish an English edition. Pound sent Joyce money that he had begged from friends and strangers alike (and old clothes as well). The money eventually allowed Joyce to rent an apartment, where he completed *Ulysses*, then published in installments in Pound's *Little Review*. Among the many magazines in which Pound publicized these writers were his own short-lived *Cerebralist* and his *Egoist*, as well as *New Age* and *Arts and Letters*, the forerunner of T. S. Eliot's prestigious *Criterion*. See Michael Reck, *Ezra Pound: A Close-Up* (New York: McGraw-Hill, 1967), 20.

See also Humphrey Carpenter, *A Serious Character: The Life of Ezra Pound* (London: Faber & Faber, 1988); Noel Stock, *The Life of Ezra Pound* (San Francisco: North Point Press, 1982); William M. Chace, *The Political Identities of Ezra Pound and T. S. Eliot* (Stanford, Calif.: Stanford University Press, 1973); C. David Heymann, *Ezra Pound* (New York: Viking, 1976); Hugh Kenner, *The Pound Era* (Berkeley: University of California Press, 1971); and Sister Bernadetta Quinn, *Ezra Pound* (New York: Columbia University Press, 1972).

34. Immediately after reading "The Love Song of J. Alfred Prufrock"—"the best poem I have yet had or seen from an American"—he mailed it to Harriet Monroe in Chicago who, while puzzled over its meaning, published it in the June 1915 issue of *Poetry*. Pound included "Prufrock" in the *Catholic Anthology, 1914–1915*, so that the poem could be published on both sides of the Atlantic. He then introduced Eliot to Harriet Weaver, who in 1917 published *Prufrock and Other Observations*. Pound had already introduced Eliot to Wyndham Lewis, who published his "Preludes" and "Rhapsody on a Windy Night" in the second issue of *Blast*. When he told Eliot about the gifted, needy James Joyce, Eliot took up his cause as well.

35. H. D. to NC, [illegible] 193[?], box 13, folder 5, HRC.

36. After the burlesque stripper incident, a career in academe seemed unlikely, so he traveled to Europe to further study French and Italian poetry, and with only £3 returned to London and was befriended by Ford Madox Ford, who introduced him to W. B. Yeats—to Pound, the greatest living poet. He was soon teaching Yeats how to fence and attending his Monday night poetry readings, where he served wine and cigarettes to guests and expostulated on modern poetry. When he was alone with Yeats, he encouraged him to reject abstract words for the definite and concrete statement. In 1914, Pound married Dorothy Shakespear and earned his highest income to date from his publications abroad—$1.85. He was in such acute financial straits that his overcoat functioned as his blanket. When Yeats won $250 for the best poem in *Poetry*, he asked Harriet Weaver to give the money to a "needy poet of talent"—Pound. And thus he continued his cause d'art. Although many people found him affected and conceited and greeted him with a mixture of resentment and admiration, certain qualities were undeniable: Pound was a person of exceptional intellect, a poetic virtuoso, and a servant of art. Even in the 1950s, at St. Elizabeth's Hospital, Hemingway greeted him by saying: "I have traveled 4,000 miles to see you." Then he showed him a manuscript, which Pound immediately began marking with a blue pencil.

37. G. M. to NC, 13 August 1929, LC; Cunard, G. M., 146, 188.

38. Ezra Pound to Harriet Monroe, 10 April 1915, quoted in Peter Ackroyd, *T. S. Eliot: A Life* (New York: Simon and Schuster, 1984), 84–85; Chisholm, *Nancy Cunard*, 49.

39. Eliot sought to bypass his readers' intellect and connect with them on a purely emotional level. He understood a reader would intuit, rather than discover through logic, that the footman referred to in "Prufrock"—"I have heard the eternal Footman hold my coat, and snicker, / And in short, I was afraid"—is death. His deliberate omission of transitions again forced the reader to intuitively or imaginatively fill in the missing links in his narratives. After Prufrock's "Let us go and make our visit," his reader inevitably asks "where?" and, without dropping a beat, he explains: "In the room the women come and go / Talking of Michelangelo." Eliot had also countered Romantic sentimentality by creating a persona that was both the sufferer and the satiric commentator, an ingenious device with which to veil personal feeling with impersonal irony: "Do I dare disturb the universe?" asks the self-conscious, timid, and self-mocking J. Alfred Prufrock. Eliot demanded that his audience become active in a radically new way, intuiting direction and meaning in a continuously evolving linear and vertical design (assimilating the primary poetic line with multiple literary references), akin to the interactions between space and planes in a Cubist collage. Ultimately, the reader in *The Waste Land* would become Tiresias, the seer-quester, who intellectually and emotionally is subjected to the trial of

reconstructing the great myths and literatures of the world. The reader-as-quester would ferret out and experience the most basic human experiences inherent in Eliot's encyclopedic allusions and thus take on the epic mission of sifting through Eliot's fragments to discern meaning and order in the flux of history.

40. For Nancy's letter and Hayward's reply, see box 6, folder 4, HRC. See also NC to Janet/Solita, 3 March 1965, LC.

41. Verified by the manuscripts librarian at the HRC.

42. Herbert Read, "T. S. Eliot: A Memoir," in *T. S. Eliot: The Man and His Work*, ed. Allen Tate (New York: Dell, 1966), 32. He had entered Harvard in the same class as John Reed and Walter Lippman and studied with Irving Babbitt, Josiah Royce, George Santayana, and the already retired William James and Charles Eliot Norton.

43. F. O. Matthiessen, *The Achievement of T. S. Eliot* (Oxford: Oxford University Press, 1958), xix.

44. Eliot's mother took a special interest in the punishment of juvenile delinquents (Ackroyd, *T. S. Eliot*, 20; T. S. Matthews, *Great Tom: Notes Towards the Definition of T. S. Eliot* [London: Weidenfeld & Nicolson, 1974], 13). Like Nancy, Eliot's earliest experiences at home were with nurses and housemaids. Regarding Eliot's father, see Lyndall Gordon, *Eliot's Early Years* (Oxford: Oxford University Press, 1977), 47.

45. Read, "T. S. Eliot," 23.

46. Gordon, *Eliot's Early Years*, 8. He also admitted that as a child he would pick the less perfect peaches in his grandfather's garden (89). Gordon also insists that Eliot enjoyed "a remarkably happy childhood" (14), but this is not incompatible with the conclusions that follow in this chapter. Quoted in Read, "T. S. Eliot," 15.

47. Wilhelm, "Nancy Cunard," 209; Read, "T. S. Eliot," 30. According to Gordon, neither Pound nor Eliot took the slightest interest in the other's religious or political inclinations (*Eliot's Early Years*, 68, 50). Poetry was their preoccupation. Regarding Eliot's anti-Semitism, see Anthony Julius, *T. S. Eliot: Anti-Semitism and Literary Form* (Cambridge: Cambridge University Press, 1995).

48. Eliot alludes to Maud:

Propelled by Lady Katzegg's guiding hand,
She knew the wealth and fashion of the land,
Among the fame and beauty of the stage,
She passed, the wonder of our little age;
She gave the turf her intellectual patronage. . . .

He sarcastically concludes: "Thus art ennobles even wealth and birth, / And breeding raises prostrate art from earth" (*The Waste Land: A Facsimile and Transcript of the Original Drafts, Including the Annotations of Ezra Pound*, ed. Valerie Eliot [New York: Harcourt Brace Jovanovich, 1971], 23–29).

49. In 1915, he impulsively married the pretty, vivacious, moody, and high-strung Vivienne Haigh-Wood, a ballet dancer. Vivienne was daring for the times in her provocative dress and uncensored opinions; she was also a fascist and an anti-Semite (Ackroyd, *T. S. Eliot*, 62; Gordon, *Eliot's Early Years*, 63).

For a discussion of Vivienne's subsequent membership in Oswald Mosley's British Union of Fascists and her belief in the conspiracy of international Jewry, see Matthews,

Great Tom, 118. See also Carole Seymour-Jones's study of Vivienne's papers, *Painted Shadow: A Life of Vivienne Eliot* (London: Constable & Robinson, 2001), 238, 519. The sexually inexperienced Eliot was attracted to her open manner, lavish temperament, and frank opinions—"frank to the point of what was then thought vulgar" (Gordon, *Eliot's Early Years*, 73). It was generally thought that although men found her attractive, she was not the sort of woman a gentleman would introduce to his mother. Bertrand Russell, Eliot's former mentor at Oxford, believed that Eliot was ashamed of the marriage (Ackroyd, *T. S. Eliot*, 65).

The marriage had shocked Eliot's parents, not only because of the couple's brief, two-month courtship but also because of Vivienne's emotional fragility. (They ordered him home to Gloucester for an explanation; he made the trip without his wife.) After a brief period, Vivienne became dependent on numerous drugs because of her blinding migraines and intestinal ailments. Even more debilitating were her increasingly bleak moods, and she was periodically and then permanently institutionalized. Frequently, before her hospitalizations, she was indisposed to receiving or visiting friends, and Eliot left her alone for long periods of time. *The Waste Land* clearly abounds with lovers in myth and in history who are incapable of relating to each other.

Before her mental problems became disabling, Vivienne and Eliot pursued an active social life with various intellectual communities. Bertrand Russell both introduced them to his friends and lent them a small bedroom in his flat, so small that Eliot slept in the sitting room or hallway. It was also widely known that while "Bertie" found Vivienne "a little vulgar" (Huxley did as well), he had an affair with her (Ackroyd, *T. S. Eliot*, 66; Bernard Bergonzi, *T. S. Eliot* [New York: Macmillan, 1978]). Russell remarked: "She married him to stimulate him but finds she cannot do it. Obviously he married to be stimulated. I think she will tire of him" (quoted in Ronald Bush, *T. S. Eliot: A Study in Character and Style* [Oxford: Oxford University Press, 1984], 54). Many of the parties the Eliots attended bored Vivienne, so she flirted outrageously and made scandalous statements. Stephen Spender recalls a lively dinner party at Mary Hutchinson's, with Nancy, Osbert Sitwell, and Duncan Grant that Vivienne found "very drunken and rowdy." She became such a chatterbox and so coquettish that Eliot became noticeably embarrassed (Gordon, *Eliot's Early Years*, 80). Osbert Sitwell also noted that her sharp wit verged on cruelty. Her behavior became a source of gossip (Ackroyd, *T. S. Eliot*, 62, 185).

Eliot's biographer Lyndall Gordon concludes that Eliot's problem with marriage in general was due to his "sexual failures": he "seems to have regarded a seductive woman not as a human being but as a man's ordeal." Eliot's sexual inhibition is amplified in Vivienne's diaries (Gordon, *Eliot's Early Years*, 73–74). For extended references to Eliot's repulsion toward the female body, see the more recent Seymour-Jones, *Painted Shadow*, esp. 45, 53, 74–75, 121, 161–62, 168.

50. T. S. Eliot, *Inventions of the March Hare Poems*, 1909–1917, ed., with commentary, Christopher Ricks (New York: Faber & Faber, 1996). Eliot writes of Columbus:

Now when they were three weeks at sea
Colombo he grew rooty.
He took his cock in both his hands
And swore it was a beauty.

Eliot's anti-Semitism in other poems is also blunt and coarse. One of his lines about a Jewish doctor is

The only doctor in his town
Was a bastard Jew named Benny . . . ,
And Benny filled Colombo's prick
With muratic acid.

On Lewis's rejecting these poems for *Blast*, see Symons, *Makers of the New*, 83.

51. B. Charles-Louis Philippe, *Bubu of Montparnasse* (New York: Berkley, 1957), 9, 24.

52. Then Eliot published a statement that Lewis was the most fascinating personality of the era (*Blast* 2, July 1915, 11). Eliot would continue to hold Lewis in the highest esteem, writing laudatory introductions to his prose work decades later. See, for example, Wyndham Lewis, *One Way Long* (London: Methuen, 1933).

53. Quoted in Paul Edwards, *Wyndham Lewis* (New Haven, Conn.: Yale University Press, 2000), 273.

54. Ezra Pound, in *Blast* 1, June 1914. Lewis defined his goals in more esoteric terms: "Vorticism design was . . . a mental-emotive impulse—by this is meant subjective intellection, like magic or religion—[and it] is let loose upon a lot of blocks and lines of various dimension, and encouraged to push them around" (*Caliph's Design: Where Is the Vortex?* [Glasgow: Wyndham Lewis Society, 1919], 38–39). To Lewis, Bergson had put "the hyphen between space and time," and, as Lewis believed, "as much as [we] enjoy the sight of things 'penetrating' and 'merging' do we enjoy the opposite picture of them standing apart—the wind blowing between them. . . . Much as we enjoy the 'indistinct,' the 'qualitative,' the 'misty, sensational and ecstatic,' very much more do we value the distinct, the geometric, the universal, non-quantified" (*Wyndham Lewis on Art: Collected Writings, 1913–1956*, ed. Walter Michel and C. J. Fox [New York: Funk & Wagnalls, 1969]; Edwards, *Wyndham Lewis*). Hugh Kenner refers to Lewis's "intensely primitive will" in his introduction to Walter Michel, *Wyndham Lewis, Paintings and Drawings* (Berkeley: University of California Press, 1971), 20. Henri Gaudier-Brzeska, in the second and last issue of *Blast*, wrote perhaps the most lucid explanation of Vorticism, which began: "We stand for the Reality of the Present. . . . We want to leave Nature and Man alone" (*Blast* 2, July 1915).

55. He would also, for example, blast the British climate "for its sins and infections, set round our bodies, of effeminate lout within" (quoted in Symons, *Makers of the New*, 46). The Vorticists included the painters William Roberts, Spencer Gore, and Edward Wadsworth and the sculptors Henri Gaudier-Brzeska and (peripherally) Jacob Epstein; their first manifesto was signed by seventeen artists. In very general terms, they developed an art appropriate to the new, scientific world, focusing on interacting fields of energy, much like Monet. Excellent early studies include Hugh Kenner, *Wyndham Lewis* (Norfolk, Conn.: New Directions, 1954), and Geoffrey Wagner, *Wyndham Lewis: A Portrait of the Artist as an Enemy* (New Haven, Conn.: Yale University Press, 1957).

56. Pound analogized Vorticism with "the spiral patterns that nineteenth-century astronomers found in star states, . . . the still point of maximum energy in the midst of conflicting forces" (*Blast* 1, June 1914, 63).

57. For Nancy's comments on Lewis, see Flanner, "Nancy Cunard," 87–88; notebooks, box 28, folder 5, HRC. "There was no one like her," he bragged of yet another woman to Nancy, adding that he "loved her unlike anyone else" (quoted in Paul O'Keefe, *Some Sort of Genius: A Life of Wyndham Lewis* [London: Jonathan Cape, 2000], 200). See also *The Letters of Wyndham Lewis*, ed. W. K. Rose (London: Methuen, 1963).

58. Preoccupied with his health, Lewis also reported on his erratic bowel movements to his mother. He survived numerous venereal diseases, which may have led to his eventual blindness and paranoia. Before that, he contracted trench fever during the lengthy Battle of Passchendale. Complications arising from his venereal diseases resulted in several major surgeries, with even further problems (Edwards, *Wyndham Lewis*, 167, 387, 538). His surgery seemed to have brought him to a state of benevolence toward humanity, but when the syphilis reached his brain, he became morbidly suspicious of almost everyone; his art changed again and was filled with sadistic images of torture and rape. See also Stanley Sultan, *Eliot, Joyce and Company* (Oxford: Oxford University Press, 1987), 208, 82, 46, 196; Timothy Materer, *Vortex: Pound, Eliot, and Lewis* (Ithaca, N.Y.: Cornell University Press, 1979); and Edwards, *Wyndham Lewis*, 6.

59. The group included the Woolfs; the economist John Maynard Keynes; the three Stracheys: James, Marjorie, and the biographer Lytton; the painters Vanessa Bell and Duncan Grant; the art critics Clive Bell and Roger Fry; the *Times* journalist Desmond MacCarthy; and Thosby and Adrian Stephen, who, with Vanessa Bell and Virginia Woolf, were Sir Leslie Stephen's four children; E. M. Forster was peripherally involved. For their full membership, see J. K. Johnstone, *The Bloomsbury Group: A Study of E. M. Forster, Lytton Strachey, Virginia Woolf, and Their Circle* (New York: Noonday Press, 1952). On various occasions, the group was visited by Arnold Bennett, George Bernard Shaw, W. B. Yeats, T. S. Eliot, Bertrand Russell, Alfred North Whitehead, Vita Sackville-West, and Aldous Huxley. It is alleged that Eliot gave the first reading of *The Waste Land* to the group.

60. Virginia Woolf to Vita Sackville-West, 16 November 1925, in *Conjured Spirits: The Selected Letters of Virginia Woolf*, ed. Joanne Trautmann Banks (London: Hogarth Press, 1989), 199.

61. Entries, 3 March 1926, in *The Diary of Virginia Woolf*, vol. 3, 1925–1930, ed. Anne Olivier Bell (New York: Harcourt Brace Jovanovich, 1980), 64, and 21 June 1924, in *The Diary of Virginia Woolf*, vol. 2, 1920–1924, ed. Anne Olivier Bell (New York: Harcourt Brace Jovanovich, 1978), 304.

62. Entry, 1 November 1924, in *Diary of Virginia Woolf*, 2:320.

63. Entries, 15 September 1924 and 15 October 1923, in ibid., 313, 270, describing the earlier experience where "the old devil has once more got his spine through the waves"; Leonard Woolf, "Nancy Cunard," in *Nancy Cunard*, ed. Ford, 58.

64. Leon Edel, *Bloomsbury: A House of Lions* (Philadelphia: Lippincott, 1979), 11. The Bloomsberries had different interests and commitments—Strachey studied Elizabethan and eighteenth-century literature, whereas Fry and Clive Bell were interested in modern painting—but Moore dominated their lives because his writing was stimulating and innovative in its inquiry into the relationship of logic and ethics and their relationship to "the good."

65. Entry, 12 July 1918, in *The Diary of Virginia Woolf*, vol. 1, 1915–1919, ed. Anne Olivier Bell (London: Hogarth Press, 1977), 166; Frank Swinnerton, *The Georgian Literary*

Scene (London: Heinemann, 1935), 109; entry, 7 November 1928, in *Diary of Virginia Woolf*, 3:202.

66. *Virginia Woolf: Moments of Being: Unpublished Autobiographical Writings*, ed. Jeanne Schulkind (New York: Harcourt Brace Jovanovich, 1976), 191–92.

67. Two books that address this in detail are Pamela Todd, *Bloomsbury at Home* (New York: Abrams, 1999), esp. 7–10, an excellent summary, and Alan Palmer and Veronica Palmer, *Who's Who in Bloomsbury* (Brighton, Eng.: Harvest Press, 1987).

68. David Garnett, "Bloomsbury Parties," in *The Bloomsbury Group: A Collection of Memoirs and Commentary*, ed. S. P. Rosenbaum (Toronto: University of Toronto Press, 1995), 39; David Gadd, *The Loving Friends: A Portrait of Bloomsbury* (London: Hogarth Press, 1974), 57; Edel, *Bloomsbury*, 151, 149.

69. David Garnett, *The Familiar Face*, vol. 3 of *The Golden Echo* (New York: Harcourt, Brace & World, 1962).

70. For a copy of "Soldiers Fallen," see box 26, folder 3, HRC; G. M. to NC, 2 December 1916, LC.

3. Counterpoint of War in London

Epigraph. A. J. P. Taylor, *The First World War, an Illustrated History* (London: Hamish Hamilton, 1963), 22.

1. Anne Chisholm writes, in 1979, that several of Nancy's friends "to this day" believe that Peter Broughton Adderly represented her only chance for a normal, happy life (*Nancy Cunard: A Biography* [New York: Knopf, 1979], 40).

2. *The Autobiography of William Carlos Williams* (New York: New Directions, 1951), 202–3, 221; Harold Acton, *Affairs of the Mind* (Washington, D.C.: New Republic Books, 1988), 183.

3. William Manchester, "The Great War: An Introduction," in David F. Burg and L. Edward Purcell, *Almanac of World War I* (Lexington: University Press of Kentucky, 1998), ix–xiv. See also Taylor, *First World War*; J. M. Winter, *The Experience of World War I* (London: Macmillan, 1988), and *The Great War and the British People* (London: Macmillan, 1985); Basil Liddell Hart, *The Real War, 1914–1918* (London: Faber & Faber, 1930); John Keegan, *The First World War* (New York: Knopf, 1999); Hew Strachan, *The First World War*, vol. 1, *To Arms* (Oxford: Oxford University Press, 2001); and Niall Ferguson, *The Pity of War* (New York: Basic Books, 1999). For their emphasis on daily life in wartime London, see Stephen Inwood, *A History of London* (London: Macmillan, 1998); Arthur Marwick, *The Deluge: British Society and the First World War* (Boston: Little, Brown, 1965); and the excellent Jay Winter and Jean-Louis Robert, eds., *Capital Cities at War: Paris, London, Berlin, 1914–1919* (Cambridge: Cambridge University Press, 1999).

4. Laurence D. Lafore, quoted in "The Prelude to Conflict," in Burg and Purcell, *Almanac of World War I*, 2. See also Lafore, *The Long Fuse: An Interpretation of the Origins of World War I* (Philadelphia: Lippincott, 1971).

5. Regarding this, and particularly the later casualty figures cited, Martin Gilbert speaks for many historians in stating that "figures . . . are conjectural, . . . almost certainly too low, but no accurate figures exist" (*Atlas of World War I* [New York: Oxford University Press,

1994], 158). Statistics cited in this chapter are compatible with Gilbert's findings: Winter, *Great War; Statistics of the Military Effort of the British Empire During the Great War, 1914–1920: The War Office, March 1922* (London: His Majesty's Stationery Office, 1922); Michael Clodfelter, *Warfare and Armed Conflicts: A Statistical Reference to Casualty and Other Figures, 1618–1991*, rev. ed. (Jefferson, N.C.: McFarland, 2002); and John Ellis and Michael Cox, *World War I Databook: The Essential Facts and Figures for All the Combatants* (London: Aurum Press, 2001).

6. Winter, *Great War*, 32; Thomas W. Davis, "Great Britain, Home Front," in *The European Powers in the First World War*, ed. Spencer C. Tucker (New York: Garland, 1996), 315. See, especially, Paul Fussell, *The Great War and Modern Memory* (New York: Oxford University Press, 1975), and Adrian Gregory, "Lost Generations," in *Capital Cities at War*, ed. Winter and Robert, 93–99.

7. Manchester, "Great War," xii–xiii.

8. Early in the war, the press ignored bad news or littered it with euphemisms. A retreat became a "rectification of the line"; deaths were "wastage" (Winter, *Experience of World War I*, 186; Reginald Pound, *The Lost Generation* [London: Constable, 1964], 13). For a good summary of popular culture during this period, see Jay Winter, "Popular Culture in Wartime Britain," in *European Culture in the Great War: The Arts, Entertainment and Propaganda, 1914–1918*, ed. Aviel Roshwald and Richard Stites (New York: Cambridge University Press, 1999), 330–48. See also J. G. Fuller, *Troop Morale and Popular Culture in the British and Dominion Armies* (Oxford: Oxford University Press, 1990), and Gregory, "Lost Generations."

9. Scrapbook, box 26, folder 1, HRC.

10. Manchester, "Great War," ix–x; K. B. Smellie, *Great Britain: A Modern History* (Ann Arbor: University of Michigan Press, 1962), 311; diary, 1919, box 22, folder 7, HRC.

11. Winter, *Great War*, 311; Smellie, *Great Britain*, 302; Manchester, "Great War," xi. Neil N. Heyman reports that the youngest suffered most severely; men of twenty faced the greatest danger of being killed in action (*Daily Life During World War I* [Westport, Conn.: Greenwood Press, 2002], 238). The statistic rose to one in seven after age twenty.

12. Manchester, "Great War," xvi.

13. Gilbert includes a range of statistical charts in *Atlas of World War I*, esp. 158–59. Regarding the consensus that all figures are conjectural, see note 5. See also the updated John Ellis and Michael Cox, *World War I Databook: The Essential Facts for All the Combatants* (London: Aurum Press, 2005), 209.

14. A. J. P. Taylor, *English History, 1914–1945* (Oxford: Oxford University Press, 1965), 1.

15. As reported by Alice Zinka Snyder and Milton Valentine Snyder, *Paris Days and London Nights* (New York: Dutton, 1921), 95. This is a fascinating chronicle told in the letters exchanged between Milton, stationed in Paris, and his wife, Alice, in London.

16. Fussell, *Great War and Modern Memory*, 155–90, and *Abroad: British Literary Traveling Between the Wars* (New York: Oxford University Press, 1980), 121–23, 166, 187; Winter, *Experience of World War I*, 226; Iris Tree, "We Shall Not Forget," in *Nancy Cunard: Brave Poet, Indomitable Rebel, 1896–1965*, ed. Hugh Ford (Philadelphia: Chilton, 1968), 19.

17. Manchester, "Great War," xi.

18. Clodfelter, *Warfare and Armed Conflicts*, 440.

19. Fussell, *Great War and Modern Memory*, 64–69. At rest camps, the subalterns were required to attend riding schools (Winter, *Experience of World War I*, 136).

20. Including the retreat at Mons, the first battle at Ypres, the ransacking of the majestic Louvain library, the tales of Germans' massacres in Belgium (when they murdered people, bayoneted babies to doors, raped young girls, and devastated entire villages), and the Zeppelin bombings (clippings, in scrapbook, box 26, folder 1, HRC).

21. Tree, "We Shall Not Forget," 21.

22. Snyder and Snyder, *Paris Days*, 27, 42–43.

23. Janet Flanner, "Nancy Cunard," in *Nancy Cunard*, ed. Ford, 87; Tree, "We Shall Not Forget," 22.

24. Winter, *Experience of World War I*, 206.

25. Nancy Cunard, G. M.: *Memories of George Moore* (London: Rupert Hart-Davis, 1956), 113.

26. Sir Douglas Haig, quoted in Snyder and Snyder, *Paris Days*, 95.

27. Davis, "Great Britain, Home Front," 83, 315–16; Heyman, *Daily Life During World War I*, 156, 190. See also Gregory, "Lost Generations."

28. Quoted in Daphne Fielding, *Those Remarkable Cunards: Emerald and Nancy* (New York: Atheneum, 1968), 59.

29. The date of their meeting has been controversial. Fielding placed it in 1916 (*Remarkable Cunards*, 59); Chisholm, in 1917 or 1918 (*Nancy Cunard*, 39–40).

30. *London Mail*, 6 September 1916, and undated articles, in scrapbook, box 26, folder 1, HRC.

31. *South Wales News*, 8 October 1916; *London Mail*, 16 September 1916; *Star*, 2 October 1916; *Sheffield Telegraph*, 10 October 1916, all in scrapbook, box 26, folder 1, HRC.

32. Unidentified clippings, in scrapbook, box 26, folder 1, HRC.

33. Ibid.

34. Chisholm adds that "it is hard to imagine any other specific reason for the violence of her reaction" (*Nancy Cunard*, 36). Yet in May 1917 (the item dated by Nancy), one reporter wrote, "Lady Cunard is being seen about a lot. She is always at the forefront at any war charity entertainment, and nowadays her daughter . . . goes everywhere with her" (unidentified clipping, in scrapbook, box 26, folder 1, HRC).

35. The quotations in this and the following three paragraphs, regarding Nancy and Sybil's friendship, are from Daphne Fielding, *The Rainbow Picnic: A Portrait of Iris Tree* (London: Methuen, 1974), 80–81, and Sir Rupert Hart-Davis, "The Girl at the Writing Table," in *Nancy Cunard*, ed. Ford, 29–30.

36. Snyder and Snyder, *Paris Days*; Pound, *Lost Generation*. For sixty narratives about life in London during this time, see C. B. Purdom, ed., *Everyone at War* (London: Dent, 1930).

37. For a discussion of the hospital situation, see Gregory, "Lost Generations," 93–98; for a graphic description of this period, see Snyder and Snyder, *Paris Days*, 86–88.

38. Quoted in Snyder and Snyder, *Paris Days*, 119.

39. Charles Repington, *The First World War, 1914–1918* (London: Constable, 1920), 291.

4. Postwar Breakdown

Epigraph. Diary, 1919, box 22, folder 1, HRC.

1. Diary, 1919, box 22, folders 7 and 8–box 23, folders 1 and 2, HRC.

2. Austin Harrison to NC, 17 and 20 September 1919, in scrapbooks, box 26, folders 1 and 2, HRC.

3. William Heinemann to NC, 15 and 17 March 1919, in scrapbooks, box 26, folders 1 and 2, HRC. Nancy had published poems in the *Oxford Chronicle* as early as February 3, 1917, and in the *Weekly Despatch* since November 17, 1917; her poems in the *Saturday Review* (London) appeared from May 11, 1919, until at least 1922; she also published regularly in the *Nation and Atheneum*, the *Observer*, the *Morning Post*, and the *New Statesman*, to name a few.

4. Quoted in Wyndham Lewis, *The Roaring Queen*, ed. Walter Allen (London: Secker & Warburg, 1973), 21.

5. Return to the World in Paris

Epigraph. Quoted in Brenda Wineapple, *Genêt: A Biography of Janet Flanner* (New York: Ticknor & Fields, 1989), 79.

1. *Negro, by Nancy Cunard*, ed., with an introduction, Hugh Ford (New York: Ungar, 1970), xiv. Ford again places Nancy's move to Paris in 1920, in his foreword to Nancy Cunard, *These Were the Hours: Memories of My Hours Press, Réanville and Paris, 1928–1931* (Cardondale: Southern Illinois University Press, 1969), ix; Anne Chisholm focuses on her travels from Paris to various sites until 1923, in *Nancy Cunard: A Biography* (New York: Knopf, 1979), 81–89.

2. Maurice Nadeau, *The History of Surrealism* (New York: Macmillan, 1965), 44.

3. William Wiser, *The Crazy Years: Paris in the Twenties* (New York: Atheneum, 1983), 160–61.

4. *Daily Express*, 26 and 27 July 1927, in scrapbooks, box 26, folders 2 and 3, HRC. For examples of fashion coverage in Germany, Ireland, France, Scotland, and the United States, see chapter 6, note 1.

5. Wiser, *Crazy Years*, 74.

6. Some, like Romaine Brooks, gave up their children for adoption; others, like H. D. and Colette, lived outside Paris and hired caretakers for their children. For an excellent discussion of lesbian society in Paris, see Andrea Weiss, *Paris Was a Woman: Portraits from the Left Bank* (San Francisco: HarperSan Francisco, 1995), 21. The new freedom from the "heterosexual imperative" is her term (20). See also the early study by Shari Benstock, *Women of the Left Bank* (Austin: University of Texas Press, 1986), and Wiser, *Crazy Years*.

7. Weiss, *Paris Was a Woman*, 111, 133; Janet Flanner, *Paris Was Yesterday, 1925–1939*, ed. Irving Drutman (New York: Viking, 1972), 123–36.

8. Weiss, *Paris Was a Woman*, 211.

9. Humphrey Carpenter, *Genuises Together* (Boston: Houghton Mifflin, 1988), 95; quoted in Sanford J. Smoller, *Adrift Among Geniuses: Robert McAlmon* (University Park: Pennsylvania State University Press, 1975), 216.

10. Smoller, *Adrift Among Geniuses*, 131. McAlmon had an unusual history, having negotiated a marriage of convenience with Bryher Ellerman, another British shipping-line heiress, who was in love with H. D. Since Bryher's parents refused to allow her to sail to Europe as a single woman, she married and traveled as McAlmon's bride but met H.

D. abroad. (Later Bryher, H. D., and Marianne Moore formed a "triumfeminate with an idiom of its own.") McAlmon benefited from the arrangement because the £14,000 divorce settlement allowed him to buy the Contact Press, which published Hemingway, Pound, Stein, and Nathanael West. He also acquired the nickname McAlimony. Bryher subsequently married the Scottish editor Kenneth Macpherson, at the time having an affair with her lover H. D., which protected Macpherson's affair with H. D.'s husband, Richard Aldington (Weiss, *Paris Was a Woman*, 208).

11. Robert McAlmon, *Being Geniuses Together, 1920–1930*, rev., with supplementary chapters, Kay Boyle (Garden City, N.Y.: Doubleday, 1968), 340.

12. Nancy Cunard, *G. M.: Memories of George Moore* (London: Rupert Hart-Davis, 1956), 164. She not only understood the effect of elliptical writing in broken-up syntax, but also was articulate in explaining the dynamics of Surrealist music and poetry.

13. In Eugène Jolas's view, the Surrealists had failed by retaining traditional language, instead of "the language of the nocturnal world," of "a-logical grammar" (*transition* 22 [1933]: 195). See also *transition* 15 (1929): 15, 11–16, and *transition* 16–17 (1929): 242–53, 268–71.

14. Nancy later writes that she first read *Ulysses* in 1922 (*G. M.*, 160). She marveled at Joyce's awareness that "no dream says: 'Thou shalt' or 'This is the truth'; it presents a picture, the way nature lets a plant grow" (*transition* 19–20 [1930]: 23–45). Nancy was also intrigued by the Surrealists' idealism, their faith in the connectedness of all experience, their wish to reconcile traditional contrarieties and dualities and to integrate the inner and outer worlds—their art of metamorphosis, like the dream, where images and feeling connect and separate, where a sense of transcendence or wholeness mingles with a sense of the fragile and tentative.

15. Wiser, *Crazy Years*, 158; McAlmon, *Being Genuises Together*, 310. A wide variety of dance styles became fads: some people learned classical dancing after the stunning successes of the Ballets Russes.

16. Quoted in Wiser, *Crazy Years*, 164.

17. McAlmon, *Being Geniuses Together*, 103.

18. Flanner, *Paris Was Yesterday*, xx. See also Jean-Claude Baker and Chris Chase, *Josephine Baker* (New York: Random House, 1993); Tyler Stovall, *Paris Noir: African Americans in the City of Light* (Boston: Houghton Mifflin, 1996); Philip Rose, *Jazz Cleopatra* (New York: Doubleday, 1989); and Ean Wood, *The Josephine Baker Story* (London: Sanctuary, 2000).

19. Wiser, *Crazy Years*, 157–58; Flanner, *Paris Was Yesterday*, xx–xxi.

20. Henry Lewis Gates Jr., "Harlem on Our Minds," in *Rhapsodies in Black: Art of the Harlem Renaissance*, ed. Richard J. Powell and David A. Bailey (Berkeley: University of California Press, 1997), 163.

21. Cunard, *These Were the Hours*, 79–80.

22. Chisholm, *Nancy Cunard*, 67.

23. Ruth Brandon, *Surreal Lives: The Surrealists, 1917–1945* (London: Macmillan, 1999), 240.

24. Medical records, box 21, folder 9; undated articles, in scrapbook, box 26, folder 3, HRC.

25. James J. Wilhelm, "Nancy Cunard: A Sometime Flame, a Stalwart Friend," *Paideuma* 19 (1999): 201. As Wilhelm indicates, the letters between Nancy and Pound (some of which are quoted here) from September 1922 to September 1923 are located at the Lilly

Library, Indiana University; from 1924 to 1946, at the Beinecke Rare Book and Manuscript Library, Yale University (220–21).

26. Wiser, *Crazy Years*, 32.

27. For the duration of the war, the three lived at Casa 60 in Sant' Ambroglio (David Heymann, *Ezra Pound: The Last Rower: A Political Profile* [New York: Viking, 1976], 152). Regarding the adoption of the child, see Sister Bernetta Quinn, *Ezra Pound* (New York: Columbia University Press, 1972). See also Michael Reck, *Ezra Pound: A Closeup* (New York: McGraw-Hill, 1967).

28. Cunard, *These Were the Hours*, 127.

29. Peter Buckley, *Ernest* (New York: Dial Press, 1978), 131.

30. Wilhelm, "Nancy Cunard," 210, 211.

31. Ezra Pound to NC, 26 April 1932, box 17, folder 10, HRC.

32. Wilhelm, "Nancy Cunard," 219; Cunard, *These Were the Hours*, 27.

33. Cunard, *These Were the Hours*, 128–29.

34. NC to Pound [a three-page, single-spaced letter], 11 June 1946, box 10, folder 6, HRC.

35. Quoted in Helena Davis, *Dada Turns Red: The Politics of Surrealism* (Edinburgh: Edinburgh University Press, 1990), 2–3. Regarding the repetition of syllables ("boomboom," "dodododo"), intended to evoke the reality of the void, see Mary Ann Caws, *Tristan Tzara: "Approximate Man" and Other Writings* (Detroit: Wayne State University Press, 1973), and Lee Elmer Peterson, *Tristan Tzara* (Rutgers, N.J.: Rutgers University Press, 1971).

36. Brandon, *Surreal Lives*, 99.

37. Quoted in Wiser, *Crazy Years*, 135; see, esp., 132–42.

38. Quoted in Jean-Michel Palmier, "Expressionist Reviews and the First World War," in *Passion and Rebellion*, ed. Stephen Eric Bronner and Douglas Keller (New York: Columbia University Press, 1983), 5.

39. Brandon, *Surreal Lives*, 240.

40. Undated articles from *Ce Soir*, *Daily Express*, and unnamed newspapers, box 26, folder 3, HRC; Morrill Cody, with Hugh Ford, *The Women of Montparnasse* (New York: Cornwall Books, 1984), 89; John Banting, "Nancy Cunard," in *Nancy Cunard: Brave Poet, Indomitable Rebel, 1896–1965*, ed. Hugh Ford (Philadelphia: Chilton, 1968), 179–80.

41. Another example was his *Traité du style*, "a book of medium length, which he planned and completed during the single month of September" (Cunard, *These Were the Hours*, 44–45, 8).

42. Her presence was at times a source of Aragon's embarrassment or discomfort: the Surrealists were notoriously inhospitable to women, if not misogynous (Wiser, *Crazy Years*, 163).

43. Cunard, *These Were the Hours*, 42. The artistic goals of the Surrealists were becoming common parlance: "pure psychic automatism, . . . the real process of thought [with] . . . all exercise of reason and every esthetic or moral preoccupation being absent" (André Breton, "What Is Surrealism," in *The Modern Tradition*, ed. Richard Ellmann and Charles Feidelson Jr. [New York: Oxford University Press, 1965], 602). Breton's *Surrealism and Painting* and *Nadja* would conclude with a demand for "convulsive beauty" born out of the automatic image—a reiteration of Lautréamont's description of beauty as something "shivering" and "trembling," like the "chance encounter of a sewing machine and an umbrella on a dissecting table."

44. Cunard, *These Were the Hours*, 41.

45. Quoted from *Paris Peasant*, in Jerrold Seigel, *Bohemian Paris: Culture, Politics, and the Boundaries of Bourgeois Life, 1830–1930* (New York: Viking, 1986), 109, 111, 377.

46. Cunard, *These Were the Hours*, 41.

47. Paul Webster and Nicholas Powell, *Saint-Germain-des-Prés* (London: Constable, 1984); Paul Max Adereth, *Elsa Triolet and Louis Aragon: An Introduction to Their Interwoven Lives and Works*, Studies in French Literature, vol. 17 (Lewiston, N.Y.: Mellen, 1994), 123–29. See also Dominique Desanti, *Elsa–Aragon: Le couple ambigu* (Paris: Belford, 1994), 75.

48. Brandon, *Surreal Lives*, 249. Additional fragments of the manuscript survived; since they were not tainted as part of "a novel," sections were published by friends in various journals (Dan Franck, *Bohemian Paris: Picasso, Modigliani, Matisse, and the Birth of Modern Art* [New York: Grove Press, 1998], 400; Adereth, *Elsa Triolet and Louis Aragon*, 38).

49. Cunard, *G. M.*, 181–82; see also 165–67.

50. Brandon, *Surreal Lives*, 246–47.

51. Quoted in Daphne Fielding, *Those Remarkable Cunards: Emerald and Nancy* (New York: Atheneum, 1968), 75.

52. Regarding their engagement, see, for example, *Liverpool Post*, 20 January 1927; *Bulletin* (Glasgow), 21 January 1927; and *Daily Express*, 19 January 1927. Regarding Nancy's denial, see *Liverpool Post*, 3 February 1927; *Bulletin* (Glasgow), 3 February 1927; and *Daily Express*, 3 February 1927, all in personal papers, box 26, folder 3, HRC.

53. Quoted in Chisholm, *Nancy Cunard*, 114.

54. Lachlan MacKinnon, *The Lives of Elsa Triolet* (London: Chatto & Windus, 1992), 76, 115, 120. Only when Nancy was near death was "the man of letters [finally] tied and trussed, [and] taken away from . . . his friends who were a bad influence [and he was] distanced from everyone who could have played the go-between for him with Nancy Cunard" (Franck, *Bohemian Paris*, 405–6).

55. Webster and Powell, *Saint-Germain*, 62; McAlmon, *Being Geniuses Together*, 219.

56. Raymond Mortimer, "Nancy Cunard," in *Nancy Cunard*, ed. Ford, 48.

57. Lewis's drawing, in *Sketch*, 3 January 1923; photo with Tzara, in *Sketch*, 15 April 1925; photo at mirror, in *Frankfurter Zeitung*, 19 June 1927, all in personal papers, box 26, folder 3, HRC.

58. NC to Walter Strachan, undated, ML; Sir Bache's letter, 9 April 1917, HRC.

59. Fielding, *Remarkable Cunards*, 73, 84.

60. Kay Boyle, "Nancy Cunard," in *Nancy Cunard*, ed. Ford , 78.

61. Wineapple, *Gênet*, 78–79. We are fortunate that Janet changed her 1923 will, which had instructed that her papers be destroyed. The 1974 revision allowed Solita to dispose of them as she saw fit. Nancy's early letters frequently and atypically lack specific dating.

62. Flanner, *Paris Was Yesterday*, 51; Janet Flanner, introduction to *London Was Yesterday, 1934–1939*, ed. Irving Drutman (New York: Viking, 1975), 8.

63. Weiss, *Paris Was a Woman*, 213. For Janet's comparison, see Wineapple, *Gênet*, 78–80.

64. Weiss, *Paris Was a Woman*, 180.

65. NC to Janet/Solita, undated, LC. She invited Marie Beerbohm, the witty niece of Max Beerbohm; Dolly Wilde, the niece of Oscar Wilde and a brilliant talker; and Mary Reynolds. Nancy seated G. M. beside two magnificent women dressed expressly for him: one, like a Manet; the other, "a Renoir come to life."

66. Solano, quoted in Boyle, "Nancy Cunard," 78; Flanner, in Wineapple, *Genêt*, 262.

67. *Daily Chronicle*, 2 January 1926; article, [?] 1924; *London Mail*, 17 September 1921, all in scrapbook, box 26, folder 3, HRC.

68. *Saturday Review* editor to NC, 11 May 1919, in scrapbook, box 26, folder 3, HRC; G. M.'s review, in *Observer*, 27 February 1921, and G. M. to NC, 13 August 1921, LC.

69. *Daily Chronicle*, 2 January 1925; *Guardian*, 6 July 1923; *London Mail*, 17 September 1921, all in scrapbook, box 26, folder 3, HRC. Some quotations are from clippings that lack both dates and sources.

70. Undated articles; for Sydney's marriage to Angela Fane, see *New York Herald*, 2 August 1926, all in scrapbook, box 26, folder 3, HRC.

71. Clippings, in scrapbook, box 26, folder 3, HRC.

72. Leonard Woolf, "Nancy Cunard," in *Nancy Cunard*, ed. Ford, 58.

73. The letters quoted in the remainder of this chapter are NC to Janet/Solita, mid-1926, LC.

6. Reluctant Icon

Epigraph. Harold Acton, "Nancy Cunard: Romantic Rebel," in *Nancy Cunard: Brave Poet, Indomitable Rebel, 1896–1965*, ed. Hugh Ford (Philadelphia: Chilton, 1968), 73.

1. For example, she was photographed as a model of contemporary dress in *Frankfurter Zeitung*, 19 June 1927, and, again, with Tristan Tzara, in *Sketch*, 15 April 1925; Wyndham Lewis's drawing appeared in *Sketch*, 3 January 1923. On occasion, she is grouped with other "models" of the time: Olivia Wyndham, Iris Tree, Lady Cynthia Asquith, Marchioness Townshend, and Lady Diana Cooper. Reports were typically: "That night Miss Cunard looked very charming in black, with a wonderful coral red hat" (*Daily Express*, undated), and "The fashion of wearing a black ring round the eyes seems to be growing. . . . Nancy Cunard had a rather mild version of it . . . and was also wearing a remarkable black velvet evening dress" (*Daily Sketch*, 27 January 1927). See also *Daily Chronicle*, 14 July 1926; *Harrogate Herald*, 8 February 1927; and *Dublin Evening Herald*, 22 and 27 January 1927, as well as her photo and an article clipped from the International Press-Cutting Bureau, 24 August 1927: "Miss Nancy Cunard, in a beige jumper suit and quaint little silver tissue hat, was at the Casino the other evening, and had added a barbaric touch to her simple costume by a necklace and bracelet of jagged coral" (all in scrapbooks, box 26, folders 2 and 3, HRC).

2. Quoted in Brenda Wineapple, *Genêt: A Biography of Janet Flanner* (New York: Ticknor & Fields, 1989), 79, 65; Mary Hutchinson, "Nancy: An Impression," in *Nancy Cunard*, ed. Ford, 97.

3. Nancy Cunard, *Grand Man: Memories of Norman Douglas* (London: Secker & Warburg, 1954), 70–71. "Those hellish twenties," those "years of pain and struggle," Nancy frequently wrote to Janet/Solita (9 July 1960 and 14 April 1965, LC).

4. Kevin Daley, *English Imaginaries* (London: Lawrence & Wishart, 1999), 9, 29.

5. G. M. had said, "I am an old man. . . . Oh! Let me at least see your naked back!" She faced away from him. "Oh, what a beautiful back you have, Nancy! It is as long as a weasel's." In *Ulich and Soracha*, Moore describes his Irish woman's "back like a weasel

with a dip in the middle." Nancy deleted this entire event from her memoir. See Janet/ Solita correspondence, LC.

6. For example, Kay Boyle's "Scottsboro" and "A Communication to Nancy Cunard," as well as her memoirs: *Primer of Combat* (New York: Simon and Schuster, 1942) and *365 Days* (New York: Harcourt, Brace, 1936); Richard Aldington, "Now Lies She There: An Elegy," in *Soft Answers* (London: Chatto & Windus, 1932), 61.

7. NC to Charles Burkhart, 10 August 1955, ML.

8. Harold Acton, *Memoirs of an Aesthete* (London: Methuen, 1948), 223–24.

9. Anne Chisholm, *Nancy Cunard: A Biography* (New York: Knopf, 1979), 152.

10. *The Autobiography of William Carlos Williams* (New York: New Directions, 1951), 202–3.

11. Ibid., 221.

12. Williams writes as though he has an adolescent's crush on them: "I felt a strong affection for them. Either of them . . . was powerfully desirable to me. . . . There was nothing I wanted to do about it, and I was happy to know that if there had been a possibility of raising a love from such stuff, it would be quite impossible to describe. . . . It is an experience, remote, childish, like the very first feelings of love, unassociated with sex" (ibid., 220–22).

13. Harry Ahern, *William Carlos Williams and Alterity: The Early Poetry* (Cambridge: Cambridge University Press, 1994), 3, 26, 102. This division is apparent at the beginning of the autobiography: "Only yesterday, reading Chapman's *The Iliad of Homer*, did I realize for the first time that the derivation of the adjective venereal is from Venus! And I a physician practicing medicine for the past 40 years!" (Williams, *Autobiography*, 3).

14. He explained, "I love my senses in the morning. Unclouded by drunkenness, unfucked out—undesirous, still as a rock—springing within themselves with strength, the fountain of everything" (William Carlos Williams, "Rome," *Iowa Review* 9 [1978]: 1–65). He adds that after his abstinence and composition, he christened his writing with "champagne and semen" (14). See also, for example, Paul Mariani, *William Carlos Williams: A New World Naked* (New York: McGraw-Hill, 1981), 227, and Ahern, *William Carlos Williams and Alterity*.

15. Mariani, *William Carlos Williams*, 228–29, 239; Ahearn, *William Carlos Williams and Alterity*, 26–27.

16. See Williams's other recollections, such as the suppers with Nancy's cousin Victor and the conversations about cummings's *Tulips and Chimneys* and Gaudier-Brzeska's magnificent sculpture, in *Autobiography*, 227.

17. Quoted in John Banting, "Nancy Cunard," in *Nancy Cunard*, ed. Ford, 180.

18. See, especially, Michael Arlen, "An Appeal to Sense," *Ararat* 4 (1916): 180. Of additional interest, see Arlen, "The Young Armenian," *Ararat* 4 (1916): 89–91, among several essays cited in Harry Keyishian, *Michael Arlen* (Boston: Twayne, 1975), 18.

19. Quoted in Chisholm, *Nancy Cunard*, 66; Michael Arlen, *The Green Hat* (New York: Collins, 1924), 32.

20. The quotations in this and the following two paragraphs are from Arlen, *Green Hat*, 58–59, 104, 80–81, 224.

21. Quoted in Chisholm, *Nancy Cunard*, 66.

22. "Civilized Emotion," *New York Times Book Review*, 21 September 1924, 9; "An Audacious Author," *Saturday Review of Literature*, 4 October 1924, 159.

23. The quotations in this and the following three paragraphs are from Arlen, *Green Hat*, 58, 29–30, 31, 285.

24. In the novel, Iris Storm is a "shameless, shameful" woman, married to a virtuous man who commits suicide on their wedding night. She allows everyone to believe that his recent discovery of her reckless life has driven him to this. At the end of the novel, it becomes clear that the young husband had syphilis, and the ruthless woman remained silent to save his reputation, at the greater cost of her own.

   The silent film begins with the gallant woman speaking to another man whom she deeply loves. He says, in the caption: "There's something more important than love. I'm proud you're rich. I'm not." Prodded by his meddling father, he goes off to Egypt to earn his fortune. "Wait," she is told; "what are a few years more or less?" She marries an old friend, a man who "always stood for decency," and remains devoted to him. One day he says to her, "You've never said you love me. You're fine," and jumps out of a window. Although many people question her role in his suicide and she becomes socially chastised, everyone finally agrees that he "died for decency. Bravo." For the next two years, she lives recklessly (in the film, we see Garbo moving from one glamorous hotel to another and flashing her beautiful smile to a number of handsome men). She is "a gallant lady trying to forget." She finally returns to London; the man she has always loved also returns, married. (He tells his wife that she wears "too much lip rouge.") Reporters "cook up a good story," but the lovers reunite, separate, and reunite once again, after which the gallant lady is killed in a car crash. It becomes clear that her "decent" husband's suicide was motivated by his embezzlement, which the gallant lady kept as their secret by making secret restitution for his thefts.

25. Louis Kronenberger wrote, typically, "No other author . . . has gathered around him so large an army of enthusiasts who quickly became turncoats" (*New York Times Book Review*, 19 May 1917, 27); Michael Arlen, *May Fair* (London: Collins, 1925), and *Young Men in Love* (New York: Doran, 1927), 20.

26. Michael Arlen, *Lily Christine: A Romance* (Garden City, N.Y.: Doubleday Doran, 1928), 192–93.

27. Quoted in Sybille Bedford, *Aldous Huxley: A Biography*, vol. 1, 1894–1939 (London: Chatto & Windus, 1973), 132.

28. Alexander Henderson, *Aldous Huxley* (New York: Russell and Russell, 1964), 190.

29. Aldous Huxley, *Antic Hay* (Normal, Ill.: Dalkey Archive Press, 1997), 50. Of her eyes he writes: "Her eyes had a formidable capacity for looking and expressing; . . . they were like the pale blue eyes which peer out of the Siamese cat's black-velvet mask." Sometimes biographical details are highly amusing. In *Eyeless in Gaza*, a dead dog falls from an airplane onto a couple making love out of doors; this apparently happened to Nancy (William Wiser, *The Crazy Years: Paris in the Twenties* [New York: Atheneum, 1983], 161).

30. The quotations in this and the following two paragraphs are from Huxley, *Antic Hay*, 52, 137–39, 131–32.

31. Aldous Huxley, *Those Barren Leaves* (New York: Doran, 1925), 150–51, 200.

32. The quotations in this and the following paragraph are from Aldous Huxley, *Point Counter Point* (New York: Library Guild of America, 1928), 5, 170, 172–73.

33. Aldous Huxley, *The Gioconda Smile: A Play from the Short Story in "Mortal Coils"* (London: Chatto & Windus, 1948).

34. Evelyn Waugh, *Unconditional Surrender* (Boston: Little, Brown, 1966). Waugh creates another cast of characters who have become detached and scarred by war, although the book eludes any resemblance to *The Sun Also Rises* or *Antic Hay*, when, at the end, religion becomes a source of comfort in the face of war. At the same time, Waugh would seem to be rejecting traditional notions of honor, country, and romance. According to Cyril Connolly, Waugh's Virginia figure served as the last embodiment of the Fitzgerald-Hemingway-Arlen "ghost of Romance who walked between two wars" (quoted in Calvin Lane, *Evelyn Waugh* [Boston: Hall, 1981], 134).
35. Wyndham Lewis, *The Roaring Queen*, ed. Walter Allen (London: Secker & Warburg, 1973), 36.
36. Robert McAlmon, *Being Geniuses Together, 1920–1930*, rev., with supplementary chapters, Kay Boyle (Garden City, N.Y.: Doubleday, 1963), 328, and "You Cannot Stay Forever in One Place," *transition* 15 (1929).

7. Nancy as Publisher

Epigraph. Daily Chronicle, 14 July 1927, in scrapbook, box 26, folder 2, HRC.
1. Nancy Cunard, *These Were the Hours: Memories of My Hours Press, Réanville and Paris, 1928–1931* (Carbondale: Southern Illinois University Press, 1969), 6–7.
2. *Paris Tribune*, 10 January 1930, in scrapbook, box 26, folder 2, HRC.
3. Cunard, *These Were the Hours*, 15. See also note 9.
4. Cunard, *These Were the Hours*, 82; the well-known Spanish poet Manuel Altolaguirre told her that her books were an inspiration, and he had tried to copy her style: "Did you not know?" (197).
5. Ibid., 47, 9.
6. Ibid., 14, 9, 51–52; *Paris Tribune*, 6 January 1930, in scrapbook, box 26, folder 3, HRC.
7. Daphne Fielding, *Those Remarkable Cunards: Emerald and Nancy* (New York: Atheneum, 1968), 90; Harold Acton, "Nancy Cunard: Romantic Rebel," in *Nancy Cunard: Brave Poet, Indomitable Rebel, 1896–1965*, ed. Hugh Ford (Philadelphia: Chilton, 1968), 75.
8. Cunard, *These Were the Hours*, 17.
9. Ibid., 115. On yet another occasion when she was at the Hotel Crystal in Paris and suffering from a throat abscess so painful that she could barely speak, Joyce knocked at her door. Again she recalled: "The stupefaction at seeing James Joyce . . . was great and greater yet my confusion and difficulty in uttering words of welcome and . . . of the honor of his visit. Groping in near-blindness he made for a chair, and I remember my consternation at the thought of him thus, alone in the streets, in shops and on staircases, tackling all the business of an ordinary day."

"'I am James Joyce,' he announced once again"; Nancy's immediate response was: "My immense admiration for *Ulysses*, my love, even. . . . Here now was the great man himself, taut, aloof—and inexplicably. The courage of him was terrific, and the formality of his manner was terrible." Once again, he asked her to encourage Lady Cunard to have Beecham "realize that Sullivan must be engaged forthwith." He continued: "Had Beecham even heard of HIM?" And once more, Nancy told him that she had little influence with her mother. Joyce would do best asking Lady Cunard himself. "Sullivan *must* be engaged," he insisted. Nancy later thought, "I did not feel like recalling to him that she had been very instrumental indeed in 1917 or so in obtaining public recognition for his [Joyce's] great talent as a writer." But Nancy did talk to her mother, who "did not listen much," commenting that "it was a matter for Thomas Beecham, and he was extremely busy."

Joyce suddenly appeared yet again, now at her bookstore in Paris: "Several of us were there. . . . We ran forward to greet him: would he not take a drink with us in our local bistro, perhaps even have dinner?" She told him about Maud's response, and Joyce said that if Sullivan were engaged, he would give her something for her press. "How peculiar is this episode," Nancy remarked; "I suppose it throws one of a million lights on Joyce, on the sincerity of his friendship for the singer, on his brooking no denial."

Later in the decade, Nancy had further contact with Joyce when he, his wife, and Nancy were to have dinner at Fouquet's. Nancy was unavoidably late because it was the night of a student festival, and the streets were filled with people. The skies suddenly opened, and Nancy was caught in the storm, unable to find a taxi. Although she phoned the restaurant several times, the Joyces were nowhere to be found, and she was told on each occasion that "his name meant nothing to them." She wrote and telephoned him to apologize. In 1937, during the Spanish Civil War, when she was forced to leave Spain because her three-month permit as a journalist had expired, she received a letter from Joyce in Paris. "How did he know where she was?" she wondered. He mailed her an "8 to 10 page" protest against the pirating of *Ulysses*; he would allow her to publish it. She had to inform him that she was no longer publishing books. See Nancy Cunard, "On James Joyce: For Professor Ellmann," in *Joyce at Texas: Essays on the James Joyce Materials at the Humanities Research Center*, ed. Dave Oliphant and Thomas Zigal (Austin: Humanities Research Center, University of Texas, 1983), 83–89.

10. Cunard, *These Were the Hours*, 84–86.

11. Ibid., 161.

12. Ibid., 187, 190.

13. Ibid., 111.

14. Ibid., 112, 117.

15. Deirdre Bair, *Samuel Beckett: A Biography* (New York: Harcourt Brace Jovanovich, 1978), 110.

16. Cunard, *These Were the Hours*, 59. In her memoir of Douglas, Nancy details a man of "radiant humanism," "a great individualist," "a free spirit," "a salubrious iconoclast . . . of profound and perfect taste." She continues to say that his critical reasoning was the aspect of him that impressed her most: "The innate feeling in him for things fine and true was always expressed with magnificent and arresting lucidity" (*Grand Man: Memories of Norman Douglas* [London: Secker & Warburg, 1954], x).

17. Cunard, *Grand Man*, 83.

18. Robert MacAlmon, *Being Geniuses Together*, 1920–1930, rev., with supplementary chapters, Kay Boyle (Garden City, N.Y.: Doubleday, 1968), 81.

19. Ibid., 132; Sanford J. Smoller, *Adrift Among Geniuses: Robert McAlmon* (University Park: Pennsylvania State University Press), 83. Nancy later said to Douglas: "How could anyone who had been through the collapse of France not have a good deal to say?" (*Grand Man*, 167, 116).

20. McAlmon, *Being Geniuses Together*, 132, 146.

21. Henry Crowder, with the assistance of Hugo Speck, *As Wonderful As All That? Henry Crowder's Memoir of His Affair with Nancy Cunard, 1928–1935* (Navarro, Calif.: Wild Trees Press, 1987), 68.

22. Ronald Bush, "Modernism, Fascism, and the Composition of Ezra Pound's *Pisan Cantos*," *Modernism/Modernity* 2 (1995): 70. Mussolini's statements, such as the following, were cited regularly in the American press: "Men nowadays are tired of liberty. . . . These masses like rule by the few. [Fascism] will pass again without the slightest hesitation over the more or less decomposed body of the goddess of liberty" (quoted in Lois Gordon and Alan Gordon, *American Chronicle: Year by Year Through the Twentieth Century* [New Haven, Conn.: Yale University Press, 1999], 128).

23. Cunard, *Grand Man*, 81–82.

24. Ibid., 83.

25. Nancy Cunard, "Does Anyone Know Any Negroes?" *Crisis*, September 1931, 300–301.

26. The quotations in this and the following three paragraphs are from Crowder, *As Wonderful As All That?* 21–53.

27. Cunard, "Does Anyone Know Any Negroes?" 301.

28. Cunard, *These Were the Hours*, 26, 53.

29. NC to David Garnett, undated and 22 December 1956, UD.

30. Cunard, *These Were the Hours*, 148, 54.

31. Quoted in ibid., 89.

8. Prelude to *Negro*

Epigraph. Nancy Cunard, untitled poems, box 1, folder 1, HRC.

1. Nancy Cunard, *These Were the Hours: Memories of My Hours Press, Réanville and Paris, 1928–1931* (Carbondale: Southern Illinois University Press, 1969), 26–29. Throughout this chapter, all citations to *Negro* refer to Nancy Cunard, *Negro* (London: Wishart, 1934); on occasion, reference is made to the abridged *Negro, by Nancy Cunard*, ed., with an introduction, Hugh Ford (New York: Ungar, 1970), which is cited as *Negro*, abridged ed.

2. Alluding to George Moore's remark, in Nancy Cunard, *G. M.: Memories of George Moore* (London: Rupert Hart-Davis, 1956), 81.

3. Nancy Cunard, *Grand Man: Memories of Norman Douglas* (London: Secker & Warburg, 1954), 93.

4. Quoted in Daphne Fielding, *Those Remarkable Cunards: Emerald and Nancy* (New York: Atheneum, 1968), 104.

5. Ibid., 105; quoted in Anne Chisholm, *Nancy Cunard: A Biography* (New York: Knopf, 1979), 158.

6. Nancy Cunard, "Does Anyone Know Any Negroes?" *Crisis*, September 1931, 301.

7. Fielding, *Remarkable Cunards*, 106; Henry Crowder, with the assistance of Hugo Speck, *As Wonderful As All That? Henry Crowder's Memoir of His Affair with Nancy Cunard, 1928–1935* (Navarro, Calif.: Wild Trees Press, 1987), 122–24.

8. Quoted in Chisholm, *Nancy Cunard*, 165, 166.

9. Crowder, *As Wonderful As All That?* 127–28.

10. Fielding, *Remarkable Cunards*, 110. Chisholm believes that Maud continued Nancy's allowance (*Nancy Cunard*, 169); Fielding (like most others, including Ford, in *Negro*, abridged ed., xviii) reports that it "was cut off" (*Remarkable Cunards*, 110).

11. Cunard, "Does Anyone Know Any Negroes?" 301; Nancy Cunard, *Black Man and White Ladyship: An Anniversary* (London: Utopia Press, 1931), reprinted in *New Review*, April 1932, 2; Brian Howard, "Nancy Cunard," in *Nancy Cunard: Brave Poet, Indomitable Rebel, 1896–1965*, ed. Hugh Ford (Philadelphia: Chilton, 1968), 101.

12. Sybille Bedford expresses a unique opinion regarding Nancy's allowance: "Most people felt that Maud cut Nancy off. Not so. Money accumulated in the bank in Nancy's name over the decades untouched. Nancy lived in poverty, often squalid poverty. What moneys she had she gave away. She spent the rest of her life in cheap hotels, . . . and bought her clothes at thrift shops and street fairs" (*Aldous Huxley: A Biography*, vol. 1, 1894–1939 [London: Chatto & Windus], 134). Crowder did not approve of behaving this way toward a parent and so did not mail the letter (*As Wonderful As All That?* 118).

13. Raymond Michelet, "Nancy Cunard," in *Nancy Cunard*, ed. Ford, 127–32 [my translation].

14. Cunard, *Grand Man*, 140.

15. "Suddenly," Nancy wrote, recalling April 1, 1931, "I was possessed of a new idea, . . . the making of an anthology on the Negro race and its afflictions . . . [where] in England . . . one point of view was even 'Why make such a book—aren't Negroes like ourselves?' . . . I could assure [the questioner] that if Negroes be like us their lives are mighty different!" (ibid., 97).

16. Lawrence Gellert, "Remembering Nancy Cunard," and Walter Lowenfels, "Nancy Cunard," in *Nancy Cunard*, ed. Ford, 141, 92.

17. Nancy's flier read as follows:

The new book on COLOUR here described comprises what is Negro and descended from Negro. . . .

1. The contemporary Negro in America, S. America, West Indies, Europe. (Writers, painters, musicians and other artists and personalities). With photographs.
2. Musical section. Last century and modern American Negro compositions. (Spirituals, Jazz, Blues, etc.)—Reproduced. As much African tribal music as obtainable—Reproduced. This section is in charge of the composer George Antheil.
3. African. Ethnological. Reproductions of African Art. Sculpture, Ivory carvings, etc. Explorers' data. Recent African photographs.
4. Political and sociological (the colonial system, Liberia, etc.) by French, English and American writers—the French translated beside the original text. Accounts of lynchings, persecutions and race prejudice.

The book is also to contain—Poems by Negroes, Poems addressed to them. A list of museums containing African art. Reproductions of Colored Advertisements. Many English and American authors will write articles, essays, and give documentary facts on Africa and question of color in U.S.A. and in Europe.

I want outspoken criticism, comment and comparison from the Negro on the present-day civilizations of Europe, America, South America, the West Indians, African Colonies, etc.— where conditions are best for Colored people—individual documents, letters, photographs from those that have traveled and can judge the attitude of diverse countries and races.

Nancy was correct in concluding: "This is the first time such a book has been compiled in this manner."

18. Langston Hughes to NC, 30 September 1931, box 15, folder 11; Claude McKay to NC, undated, box 17, folder 1, HRC.

19. Quoted from John Banting to Hugh Ford, 1 December 1969, in *Negro*, abridged ed., xxi; Nancy Cunard, "Harlem Reviewed," in *Negro*, 67–74.

20. Nancy Cunard, "Black Man and White Ladyship," in *Nancy Cunard*, ed. Ford, 108.

21. Cunard, *These Were the Hours*, 183; Crowder, *As Wonderful As All That?* 184, 138, 137.

22. Crowder, *As Wonderful As All That?* 137, 138, 130.

23. Nancy summarized the trips: the first was "no trouble, but great disgust"; the second was "much trouble, little disgust" (*Negro*, abridged ed., xix).

24. *Daily News*, 2 May 1932; *Daily Mirror*, 2 May 1932. I am indebted to Pat O'Haire, reporter for the *News*, for photocopying these and many of the following items. Dates, pages, and titles are as complete as they appear on microfilm. Some items were clarified on microfilm at the Schomberg Center for Research in Black Culture, New York Public Library.

25. NC to press, 2 May 1932, in scrapbook, box 28, folder 2, HRC.

26. Ibid.; *Daily News*, 3 May 1932.

27. *Sunday News*, 25 June 1932; *New York Herald Tribune*, 3 July 1932, both in personal papers, box 28, folder 2, HRC.

28. Personal papers, box 28, folder 2, HRC.

29. Quoted in Gellert, "Remembering Nancy Cunard," 142, and in Nancy Cunard, "The American Moron and the American of Sense," in *Negro*, 197–200.

30. *Daily Mirror*, undated.

31. Gellert, "Remembering Nancy Cunard," 142.

32. Eugene Gordon, "The Green Hat Comes to Chamber Street," in *Nancy Cunard*, ed. Ford, 134–36, 139.

33. *Daily News*, undated; *Boston Post*, 16 July 1932; undated clippings, all in personal papers, box 28, folder 2, HRC.

34. Nancy Cunard, "Jamaica, the Negro Island," in *Negro*, 437.

35. Undated clippings, in personal papers, box 28, folder 2, HRC. The libel suit was reported in the *Times* (London), 15 July 1934, 4.

36. Quoted in William Plomer, "In the Early Thirties," in *Nancy Cunard*, ed. Ford, 124–25; *Negro*, abridged ed., xxiii.

37. Quoted in Chisholm, *Nancy Cunard*, 208.

38. Crowder, *As Wonderful As All That?* 158, 185, 174.

39. NC to Charles Burkhart, 10 August 1956, ML.

40. *New York Times*, 17 February 1934, 5; *New York Amsterdam News*, 7 October 1934; Janet Flanner, "Nancy Cunard," in *Nancy Cunard*, ed. Ford, 88.

41. Hughes to NC, 14 April 1934, box 15, folder 11; Alain Locke to NC, 14 April 1934, box 16, folder 4; the other letters are undated, box 20, folder 10, HRC; *Negro*, abridged ed., xii. David Levering Lewis writes that Nancy "captured [the Harlem Renaissance's] essence in the manner of expert taxidermy" (introduction to *The Portable Harlem Renaissance Reader*, ed. David Levering Lewis [New York: Penguin, 1995], xxxix).

42. *Times* (London), 5 May 1934, 15, 156; 22 February 1934, 21; 15 December 1934, 17. For the bracelet item, see *Times*, 5 February 1934, 10; for the Cunard Line, *Times*, 7 and 15 March 1934.

43. Crowder, *As Wonderful As All That?* 53.

44. Ibid., 61–62, 65, 68.

45. Ibid., 10, 72, 92.

46. Ibid., 72, 98.

47. Ibid., 180, 185.

48. Ibid., 104, 155.

49. The material cited in the remainder of this chapter is from ibid., 183–97.

9. *Negro*

Epigraph. Nancy Cunard, *Negro* (London: Wishart, 1934), 644.

1. Brent Hayes Edwards remarks that, noting in detail the difference in the political and social traditions to which all blacks were exposed across the world, her work advanced black internationalism (*The Practice of Diaspora: Literature, Translation, and the Rise of Black Internationalism* [Cambridge, Mass.: Harvard University Press, 2004], 242, 317–18). See also *Essays on Race and Empire: Nancy Cunard*, ed. Maureen Moynagh (Peterborough, Ont.: Broadview Press), 2002.

2. These divisions consist of "America," the longest section, with eleven subheadings; "Negro Stars"; "Music," including American, Creole, West Indian, and African expressions; "Poetry" by Negro, West Indian, and white poets (on Negro themes); "West Indies and South America"; "Europe"; and "Africa," in three subsections, including thirty-seven plates of West African sculpture, forty-seven of Congolese sculpture, and drawings of Congolese masks.

3. *Negro, by Nancy Cunard*, ed., with an introduction, Hugh Ford (New York: Ungar, 1970). All the articles discussed in this chapter are cited from Cunard, *Negro*.

4. Edward A. Johnson, "A Brief Outline of Negro History in the U.S. Until Abolition," 3–9.

5. Wendell P. Dabney, "Slave Risings and Race Riots," 9–13.

6. Sarah Frances Chenault, "The Ku Klux Clan in Indiana," 170–72.

7. William Pickens, "The American Congo: Burning of Henry Lowry," 21–31.

8. William Pickens, "A Roman Holiday" and "Aftermath of a Lynching," 32–38.

9. "Facts from the American Press," 181–97.

10. Nancy Cunard, "Harlem Reviewed," 67–74.

11. Zora Neale Hurston, "Characteristics of Negro Expression," 39–62, 359.

12. Josephine Herbst, "Lynching in the Quiet Manner," 269–71.

13. Nancy Cunard, "The American Moron and the American of Sense: Letters on the Negro," 197–200.

14. George Antheil, "The Negro on the Spiral, or A Method of Negro Music," 346–51.

15. Robert Goffin, "Hot Jazz," 378.

16. Robert Goffin, "The Best Negro Jazz Orchestras," 291–93.

17. Clarence Cameron White, "The Musical Genius of the American Negro," 351–55.

18. For other essayists who address African-American music, see 356–93, such as Edward G. Perry, "Negro Creative Musicians," 356–59.

19. Robert Lewis, "Rose McClendon," 317–19.

20. U. S. Thompson, "Florence Mills," 320–21.

21. Ralph Matthews, "The Negro Theatre: A Dodo Bird," 312–16.
22. Nancy Cunard, "Southern Sheriff," 181–97.
23. Raymond Michelet, "African Empires and Civilizations," 585–603.
24. A. V. Lester, "'Clicking' in the Zulu Tongue," 647–48.
25. R. C. Nathaniels, "Eue Proverbs and Riddles, Alaga and Zagbeto," 640–41.
26. E. Kohn, "A Zulu Wedding at a Zulu Kraal near Durban, Natal," 648–49.
27. Nancy Cunard, "Negro Sculpture and Ethnology," 684–86, 687–93.
28. Ladislas Szecsi, "The Term 'Negro Art' Is Essentially a Non-African Concept," 679.
29. Raymond Michelet, "The White Man Is Killing Africa," 820–55.
30. *Negro*, abridged ed., xii.

10. Nancy as Journalist

Epigraph. Langston Hughes, "Ballad of Ethiopia," Langston Hughes Poems, box 33, folder 7, HRC.
1. Nancy Cunard, "Scottsboro and Other Scottsboros," in *Negro* (London: Wishart, 1934), 245–69. See also, for example, "Scottsboro Boys Due Damages," *Atlantic Daily*, 30 July 1937.
2. Cunard, "Scottsboro and Other Scottsboros," 251.
3. Ibid., 252.
4. Ibid., 247.
5. Quoted in ibid., 257.
6. Ibid., 248–50.
7. Lawrence Gellert, "Remembering Nancy Cunard," in *Nancy Cunard: Brave Poet, Indomitable Rebel, 1896–1965*, ed. Hugh Ford (Philadelphia: Chilton, 1968), 143.
8. For example, "Nancy Cunard Aids Prisoners," *New York Evening Journal*, 8 July 1933, and "Party Given by Miss Cunard at London Hotel," *Daily Express*, 5 July 1933, quoted in *Gaily Gleaner*, 22 July 1933. See also *New York Evening Journal*, 22 July 1933.
9. "Nancy Cunard's Exotic Party to Champion the 'Martyred Negroes,'" *West Indian Overseas Granada*, 28 August 1933.
10. Roland Wolseley, *The Black Press, U.S.A.* (Ames: Iowa State University Press, 1971), 29. For a history of the ANP, see Todd Vogel, ed., *The Black Press: New Literary and Historical Essays* (New Brunswick, N.J.: Rutgers University Press, 2001); Frederick Detweiler, *The Negro Press in the U.S.* (Chicago: University of Chicago Press, 1992); and Lawrence D. Hogan, *A Black National News Service* (Rutherford, N.J.: Fairleigh Dickinson University Press, 1984). Among the ANP's subscribers in the United States were the *Afro-American*, to which Langston Hughes contributed, and *Negro World*, Marcus Garvey's forum about the Organization of Negro Improvement Association. William Pickens used the ANP as an outlet for publishing information about the NAACP. Other ANP subscribers included the *Atlanta Daily World, New York Amsterdam News, Norfolk Journal and Guide, Philadelphia Tribune*, and *Pittsburgh Courier*, all of which are still publishing. See Nancy's articles on Scottsboro in the *Norfolk Journal and Guide*, 30 January 1936, 1, 10, and *Atlanta Daily World*, 30 July 1937, 1.
11. Quoted in Hogan, *Black National News Service*, 121.

12. "Europeans in African Colony Clamoring for 'Home Rule,'" *Norfolk Journal and Guide*, 1 February 1936, 1; "Protest Against French Actions in North Africa," *Pittsburgh Courier*, 7 December 1935; "Nancy Cunard Pays Tribute to Famous Dutch Anthropologist," *New York Age*, 4 August 1934.

13. According to Joseph Whitaker, ed., *An Almanac: 1934* (London: Clowes, 1935). Of the British who did have jobs, 74 percent earned £4 a week; the official dole allowed a married couple with three children was 29s, 3d. See Alan Hutt, introduction to *The Condition of the Working Class in England* (London: Lawrence, 1933), xii. For detailed charts and analyses, see Keith Laybourn, *Britain on the Breadline: A Social and Political History of Britain Between the Wars* (Wolfeboro Falls, N.H.: Sutton, 1990). See also Martin Green, *The Children of the Sun* (New York: Basic Books, 1976), 259.

14. NC to Janet/Solita, 12 [?] 1964, LC.

15. George Orwell, *The Road to Wigan Pier*, quoted in Ronald Blythe, *The Age of Illusion: Glimpses of Britain Between the Wars* (Oxford: Oxford University Press, 1964), 161.

16. Blythe, *Age of Illusion*, 161. See also Julian Symons, *The Angry 30s* (London: Eyre Methuen, 1976), 41, and items in the daily press. On the Jarrow hunger march, see Ellen Wilkinson, *The Town That Was Murdered* (London: Gollancz, 1939), 236, 246. See also Laybourn, *Britain on the Breadline*, 140–42.

17. Robert Skidelsky, *Oswald Mosley* (New York: Holt, Rinehart and Winston, 1975), 309–10, 440. See also Blythe, *Age of Illusion*, 174–87.

18. Richard Griffiths, *Fellow Travellers of the Right* (London: Constable, 1980). See also A. J. P. Taylor, *English History, 1914–1945* (New York: Oxford University Press, 1965), 33–35, 170.

19. Arthur Marwick, *The Expansion of British Society and Britain in Our Century* (London: Thames & Hudson, 1984), 87; Green, *Children of the Sun*, 279.

20. Anne Chisholm, *Nancy Cunard: A Biography* (New York: Knopf, 1979), 225. Anthony Thorne, like many others, reports that Nancy was never part of any political movement; she "was against any government you could mention, being impassioned for her own liberty, for everybody's liberty" ("A Share of Nancy," in *Nancy Cunard*, ed. Ford, 297). See also Solita Solano, "Nancy Cunard: Brave Poet, Indomitable Rebel," in ibid., 77.

21. Quoted in Chisholm, *Nancy Cunard*, 224; *New York Amsterdam News*, 23 December 1934. She wrote after her trip to Russia that "the bureaucracy appalled me" (quoted in Thorne, "Share of Nancy," 297).

22. Norman, her most witty character, is an elderly but "hale individualist." Once aboard the ship, he meets a cultured young music critic, a salesman, as well as a taxi driver ("a natural-born comrade") and a Jewish woman and her daughter. Although they are all seated in the third-class dining room, several have paid for first-class passage. "Wonder why they have first class," says one; "I thought it would all be one-class under Socialism." The sage Norman answers, "Russians are clever people, logical people," and a steward completes his explanation: "International business-men . . . do not like the sound of third-class or tourist, . . . so we give them first and they pay more. Everybody is happy so." There is some discussion about the Soviets' acceptance of women as sailors and more liberal sex, as well as banal lines like "there's always been Fascism in the world." At one point, Nancy makes a prescient reference to Paris, as one character speaks of "Hitler youth parading on the right bank. They are such pure Aryans and pale that you

can almost see through them"—perhaps the only funny line in the piece ("Untitled Play Concerning a Trip to the USSR in 1935," box 1, folder 1, HRC).

23. Lengthy manuscript, 5 August 1935, for the ANP and *Crisis*, box 2, folder 8, HRC.

24. Addendum to ibid.; Nancy Cunard, *G. M.: Memories of George Moore* (London: Rupert Hart-Davis, 1956), 106; Jacqueline Hurtley and Elizabeth Russell, "Women Against Fascism," *Barcelona English Language and Literature Studies* 7 (1996): 47.

25. For example, *Pittsburgh Courier*, 2 July 1936, one of the newspapers distributed through the ANP. For a history of this monumental event and the Ethiopian crisis, see Gebru Tereke, *Ethiopia: Power and Protest* (Cambridge: Cambridge University Press, 1991); Richard Pankhurst, *The Ethiopians: A History* (London: Blackwell, 2001); and Harold G. Marcus, *A History of Ethiopia* (Berkeley: University of California Press, 2002), and *The Politics of Empire* (Berkeley: University of California Press, 1983).

26. Among the high-profile journalists present were Sisley Huddleston, *Christian Science Monitor*; Vernon Bartlett, *News Chronicle* (London); and Sir Norman Ewer, *Daily Herald*. More than forty nations sent reporters. For this report, see typed manuscript of the ANP article, 1 July 1936, box 1, folder 4, HRC.

27. Nancy Cunard, *Grand Man: Memories of Norman Douglas* (London: Secker & Warburg, 1954), 106. Among her most interesting stories are "Nancy Cunard Writes Inside Story of Selassie's Plea Before League of Nations," *Philadelphia Tribune*, 16 July 1936; "Haile Selassie Will Retain His Claim to the Throne," *Atlanta Daily World*, 11 August 1937; and "Haile Selassie's Personal Fortune Is Gone," *Pittsburgh Courier*, 20 November 1937.

28. "Haitians Would Aid Ethiopians," *Norfolk Journal and Guide*, 8 July 1936, 3.

29. *Pittsburgh Courier*, 31 October 1936, 1, 12.

30. "Il Duce Will Take Boys of Eight to Make Fascist Soldiers," *Pittsburgh Courier*, 12 February 1936, 12.

31. "Blacks in Spanish Revolution Fighting on Side of Royalists," *Pittsburgh Courier*, 22 August 1936.

32. J. Bryan III and Charles J. V. Murphy, *Windsor Story* (New York: Morrow, 1979), 119–20.

33. Army friends had introduced him to an Amiens prostitute who "did her job with tact and skill." After this, he became preoccupied with sex, although whether or not he gave women pleasure has been the subject of an amazing amount of speculation. See Michael Thornton, *Royal Feud: The Queen Mother and Duchess of Windsor* (London: Michael Joseph, 1985), 78, and Philip Ziegler, *Edward VIII: The Official Biography* (London: Collins, 1990), 88.

34. "A sort of hopelessly lost feeling has come over me, and I think I'm going mad, he said of Freda" (Ziegler, *Edward VIII*, 122). Freda Ward was not the first married woman he had loved: he had pursued a three-year affair with Lady Coke, twelve years older, as well.

35. Thornton, *Royal Feud*, 123, 78.

36. Ziegler, *Edward VIII*, 208.

37. Frances Lonsdale Donaldson, *Edward VIII* (Philadelphia: Lippincott, 1975), 208. Mosley writes of how Maud attracted people of "money as well as wit and intelligence—like a magnet," with her wit and effrontery. She had honed her social stratagems into an art: "She would wake the company up with a direct frontal attack," for example, by saying to the most devoted member of the Church of England: "Lord Hugh, I cannot

believe you are really a Christian." This "would require a face of brass to stand up to the barrage of badinage and comment, but it was all enormous fun" (*My Life: Sir Oswald Mosley* [New Rochelle, N.Y.: Arlington House, 1968], 75–76). The brightest woman after Maud, both Mosley and Maud believed, was his wife, Diana, whom Maud hoped would be her successor in London society.

38. Thornton, *Royal Feud*, 76.

39. Ziegler, *Edward VIII*, 142. See also Owen Bowcatt and Stephen Bates, "Car Dealer Was Wallace Simpson's Secret Lover," available at http://www.politics.guardian.co.uk/ politicspast/story/0,9061,88526?oohtml (accessed June 2002).

40. Daphne Fielding, *Those Remarkable Cunards: Emerald and Nancy* (New York: Atheneum, 1968), 119–20; Ziegler, *Edward VIII*, 250, 208; Bryan and Murphy, *Windsor Story*, 536.

41. With a policy dictated by Lord Rothermere, the *Daily Mail* had paid homage to Hitler's "magnetic influence" in retrieving Germany from "Israelites of international attachments" (10 July 1933). Among many excellent press histories, see John C. Merrill, *The Elite Press* (New York: Pitman, 1960); John C. Merrill and Harold A. Fisher, *The World's Great Dailies* (New York: Hastings House, 1980); Franklin Reid Gannon, *The British Press and Germany, 1936–1939* (Oxford: Clarendon Press, 1971); and John Hohenberg, *Free Press/Free People* (New York: Columbia University Press, 1971). See also *A King's Story: The Memoirs of H.R.H. The Duke of Windsor* (London: Cassell, 1951), and S. J. Taylor, *The Reluctant Press Lord: Esmond Rothermere and the Daily Mail* (London: Weidenfeld & Nicolson, 1998), 48–49.

42. In 1996, suspicions about Edward's loyalty resurfaced, suggesting that he and Wallis had advocated Germany's victory during World War II as the means of regaining the throne—as both king and queen. Investigations were curtailed because his sister-in-law, the Queen Mother, was still alive. At the end of June 2002, three months after she died, a member of Parliament asked the United States and British Naval Intelligence for the release of papers that might shed light on Edward's links with Nazism. Among them was a file from 1941, when Franklin Roosevelt ordered the FBI to watch Edward and Wallis during their visit to Florida. Wallis was believed to have passed secrets to her former lover Ribbentrop in 1936 and to have given him information around the time of the German invasion of France in 1940. See "New Clues to Edward VIII's Nazi Links," *BBC News*, 29 June 2002, available at http:www.//bbc.co.uk/2/ hi/uk_news/2074100.stm (accessed 9 July 2003). See also Emma Simpson, "Simpson's Nazi Past Led to Abdication," 9 January 2003, available at http://bbc.co.uk/2/hi/uk_/ news/12644123.stm (accessed 9 June 2003). In early 2003, the *Guardian* reported on the 234-page document released by the FBI under the U.S. Freedom of Information Act, revealing Edward as "a friend to the Germans"—not just a guest of the Führer but the man who would be returned to the throne when Hitler defeated Britain. The file also revealed that Hitler believed that Edward was "the only Englishman" who could negotiate peace or armistice terms when the time came ("Friend to the Germans," *Guardian*, 13 February 2003). See also the first article to even question Edward's allegiance before a silence that lasted until the Queen Mother's death: Margaret Lowrie, "60 Years Later in Britain, King Edward's Loyalty Is Debated," *CNN Interactive*, 11 December 1996, available at http://www./cnn.com/WORLD/961211/edward.abdication (accessed 12 December 2003).

43. Chris Burford, "Edward VIII's Nazi Sympathies," available at http://www.archives. econ.utah/edu/archives/Penl/2003w04/msg0076.htm (accessed 16 January 2004). See also "New Clues," available at http://www.guardian.uk/freedom/Story/0,2763,885183,00. html; "Would Windsors 'Flit' to Germany?" available at http://bbc.co.uk/2/hi/uk_ news/2074100.stm; and Stephen Bates, "Royal News," available at http://bbc.co.uk/2/hi/ uk_/news/12644123.stm (all accessed 16 January 2004). Martin Allen cites an OSS document describing how Hitler, Göring, and Ribbentrop, at a dinner party in Montoire four months after the occupation, expressed their gratitude to the Duke and Duchess of Windsor by standing in front of their portrait and saluting "in the Nazi fashion" (*Hidden Agenda: How the Duke of Windsor Betrayed the Allies* [London: Macmillan, 2000], 296).

44. More than 15,000 books have been written on the complex nature of the war and its causes, events, and outcome. On one side, those like Paul Preston, in *The Concise History of the Spanish Civil War* (London: Fantana, 1996) and in personal correspondence, emphasize the failure of Western democracies to fulfill their legal obligations to the elected government of Spain; on the other side, those like Stanley G. Payne, in *The Spanish Civil War, the Soviet Union, and Communism* (New Haven, Conn.: Yale University Press, 2004) and in personal correspondence, emphasize Soviet machinations.

45. Stanley Weintraub, *The Last Great Cause: The Intellectuals and the Spanish Civil War* (New York: Weybright and Talley, 1968), 9. See also Preston, *Concise History*.

46. For his discussion of the historical causes of the war as the result of more than 100 years of conflict between liberalizing and antireformist movements, see Preston, *Concise History*, chap. 2. Payne emphasizes, in correspondence, that the revolution was the culmination of a long-standing revolutionary process.

47. Quoted in Hugh Thomas, *The Spanish Civil War*, rev. ed. (New York: Modern Library, 2001), 7.

48. Ibid., 8. Many scholars believe that this story is a fantasy.

49. Total deaths in the war are estimated at between 500,000 and 1 million.

50. See, especially, the more recent Stanley G. Payne, *The Collapse of the Spanish Republic, 1933–1936: Origins of the Civil War* (New Haven, Conn.: Yale University Press, 2006), and Ronald Radosh, *Spain Betrayed: The Soviet Union in the Spanish Civil War* (New Haven, Conn.: Yale University Press, 2001). On March 28, 2000, the Hoover Institution sponsored a relevant symposium, "For Whom the Bell Tolls: The Spanish Civil War," with participants Christopher Hitchens and Radosh. For more classic discussions of the war, in addition to George Orwell's *Homage to Catalonia* (New York: Harvest, 1952), see Paul Preston, *Concise History*, and *Franco: A Biography* (London: HarperCollins, 1993); Raymond Carr, *The Spanish Tragedy: The Civil War in Retrospect* (London: Weidenfeld & Nicolson, 1977), and *Spain, 1808–1975* (Oxford: Clarendon Press, 1982); Thomas, *Spanish Civil War*; Gabriel Jackson, *A Concise History of the Spanish Civil War* (London: Thames & Hudson, 1980), and *The Spanish Republic and Civil War, 1931–1939* (Princeton, N.J.: Princeton University Press, 1967); Gerald Brenan, *Spanish Labyrinth* (Cambridge: Cambridge University Press, 1976); Richard Bernack and Peter Carroll, *Front Lines of Social Change: Veterans of the Abraham Lincoln Brigade* (Berkeley, Calif.: Heyday Books, 2005); George Esenwein, *Anarchist Ideology and the Working-Class Movement in Spain* (Berkeley: University of California Press, 1989), and, with Adrian Shubert, *Spain at War* (New York: Longman, 1995); and Sebastiaan Faber, *Exile*

and Cultural Hegemony: Spanish Intellectuals in Mexico, 1939–1975 (Nashville, Tenn.: Vanderbilt University Press, 2002).

51. Hugh Thomas, like Orwell many years earlier, believed that Stalin, fearing that revolutionary activity would alienate Britain and France, which he courted as allies against Hitler, ordered Communist agents in Spain to lead a counterrevolution by attacking various Republican organizations and leaders.

52. George Orwell, "Spilling the Spanish Beans I," *New English Weekly*, 29 July 1937, 307–8.

53. Payne, *Spanish Civil War*, 290–93, 295–98; Paul Preston, e-mail to author, 28 December 2005.

11. On the Front Lines in the Spanish Civil War

Epigraph. Nancy Cunard, "Enquête" to *Authors Take Sides on the Spanish War*, in miscellaneous articles on Spain, box 8, folder 7, HRC.

1. Nancy Cunard, *Grand Man: Memories of Norman Douglas* (London: Secker & Warburg, 1954), 107.

2. George Orwell, *Homage to Catalonia* (New York: Harvest, 1952), 48.

3. Robert Capa, *Death in the Making* (New York: Covici-Friede, 1938), *Heart of Spain: Robert Capa's Photographs of the Spanish Civil War* (New York: Aperture, 1999), and *Fotográfo de guerra* (Hondarribia: Argitaletxe, 2000). See also Laurie Lee, *The Sun My Monument* (London: Hogarth Press, 1944); Gustav Regler, *The Owl of Minerva: The Autobiography of Gustav Regler,* trans. Norman Denny (London: Rupert Hart-Davis, 1959); Antoine de Saint-Exupéry, *Wind, Sand, and Stars,* trans. Lewis Galantière (London: Constable, 1955); and John Sommerfield, *Volunteer in Spain* (London: Lawrence & Wishart, 1937).

4. Orwell, *Homage*, 4–5.

5. Ibid., 6.

6. Cunard, *Grand Man*, 107.

7. "Blacks in Spanish Revolution Fighting on Side of Royalists," *Pittsburgh Courier*, 22 August 1936.

8. For Nancy's notes, see, for example, box 1, folders 1 and 3; box 2, folder 8; box 6, folder 4; and box 27, folder 1, HRC. See also NC to Walter Strachan, early 1945, ML.

9. Orwell, *Homage*, 5–16.

10. NC to Walter Lowenfels, 3 October 1959, ML.

11. Orwell, *Homage*, 8–10, 105. For striking images of the militias, see Capa, *Death in the Making, Heart of Spain*, and *Fotográfo de guerra*.

12. Stanley Weintraub, *The Last Great Cause: The Intellectuals and the Spanish Civil War* (New York: Weybright and Talley, 1968), 14; Orwell, *Homage*, 19.

13. See, especially, Capa, *Death in the Making*; Orwell, *Homage*, 13–14.

14. Sommerfield, *Volunteer in Spain*, 97–98.

15. Weintraub, *Last Great Cause*, 10; Luis Buñuel, "The Civil War," in *Voices Against Tyranny: Writing of the Spanish Civil War*, ed. Jonathan Miller (New York: Scribner, 1986), 164.

16. John Dos Passos, "Room and Bath at the Hotel Florida," in *Voices Against Tyranny*, ed. Miller, 21–22.

17. Hugh Thomas, *The Spanish Civil War*, rev. ed. (New York: Modern Library, 2001), 423–24.

18. The following details are from pages inserted in notebooks, box 28, folder 4, HRC.

19. Antoine de Saint-Exupéry, "Barcelona and Madrid," in *Voices Against Tyranny*, ed. Miller, 69–70.

20. For Nancy's explanation during her first trip to North Africa, see Cunard, *Grand Man*, 107–11.

21. Pablo Neruda, *Memoirs*, trans. Hardie St. Martin (New York: Farrar, Straus and Giroux, 1976), 128. See also Fernando Sáez, *Todo debe ser demasiado: Biografía de Delia del Carril, La Hormiga* (Providencia, Chile: Sudamericana, 1997); Volodia Teitelboim, *Neruda: An Intimate Biography*, trans. Beverly J. Delong-Tonelli (Austin: University of Texas Press, 1991); and Rafael Osuna, *Pablo Neruda y Nancy Cunard* (Madrid: Orígenes, l987).

22. Nancy Cunard, "Decade of Exile: The Intellect of Spain Is Today in Other Lands," 1949, box 2, folder 5, HRC.

23. Stephen Spender's analysis is in "Poems About the Spanish Civil War," in *Voices Against Tyranny*, ed. Miller, 11. For an interesting history of the poem, see Weintraub, *Last Great Cause*, 67–70.

24. Donald Ogden Stewart, *Writers Take Sides: Letters About the War in Spain from 418 American Authors* (New York: League of American Writers, 1938). Faulkner stated: "I most sincerely want to go on record as being unalterably opposed to Franco and Fascism, to all violations of the legal government and outrages against the people of Republican Spain"; Steinbeck: "Your question . . . is rather insulting. Have you seen anyone not actuated by greed who was for Franco? . . . I am treasonable enough not to believe in the liberty of a man or a group to exploit, torment, or slaughter other men or groups. I believe in the despotism of human life and happiness against the liberty of money and possessions"; Anderson: "Sure I am against all the damn Fascists or any other kind of dictator"; Jeffers: "You ask what I am for and what I am against in Spain. I would give my right hand, of course, to prevent the agony; I would not give a flick of my finger to help either side win."

25. For example, Cecil Woolf and John Bagguley, eds., *Authors Take Sides on Vietnam: Two Questions on the War in Vietnam Answered by the Authors of Several Nations* (New York: Simon and Schuster, 1967), and Jean Moorcroft Wilson and Cecil Woolf, eds., *Authors Take Sides: Iraq and the Gulf War* (Carlton: Melbourne University Press, 2004).

26. Cunard, *Grand Man*, 109; John Banting, "Nancy Cunard," in *Nancy Cunard: Brave Poet, Indomitable Rebel, 1896–1965*, ed. Hugh Ford (Philadelphia: Chilton, 1968), 182–83.

27. Theodore Dreiser, "Barcelona in August," in *Voices Against Tyranny*, ed. Miller, 198.

28. Pablo Casals, *Joys and Sorrows: Reflections*, as told to Albert E. Kahn (New York: Simon and Schuster, 1970), 224–25. On one occasion in Barcelona, a bomb fell and everyone fled the concert hall. Casals began to play a Bach suite, and the entire audience returned. He remarked: "The miracle was with what courage and dignity [the people] went about their lives!" At a moment of gravest crisis, they still expressed their "love of art and beauty"—"an affirmation of the indomitable spirit of man" (227).

29. Cunard, *Grand Man*, 110.

30. *Atlanta Daily World*, 27 September 1937, 1, 3; "Black Moors, Fighting for Spanish Fascists, Given Demoralizing Treatment," *Atlanta Daily World*, 15 July 1937, 1, 6.

31. Daphne Fielding, *Those Remarkable Cunards: Emerald and Nancy* (New York: Atheneum, 1968), 122.

32. She reported any indication of support—for example, a sign that France might formally support the Spanish: "Last night there was a meeting of solidarity with Spain, of 30,000 people . . . in Paris. . . . Tonight there is another gigantic meeting of Spanish-French solidarity in the mammoth stadium" (*Pittsburgh Courier*, 22 August 1936).

33. *Atlanta Daily World*, 27 September 1937, 3.

34. See, for example, "African Negroes Fighting in Spain Against Their Will," *St. Louis Argus*, 11 December 1936. Nancy wrote both "the war, becoming more and more international, is going to last a long time" and "I still think Madrid may be able to drive [the rebels] off" ("Europeans in African Colony Clamoring for 'Home Rule,'" *Norfolk Journal and Guide*, 1 February 1936, 1).

35. "Il Duce Will Take Boys of Eight to Make Fascist Soldiers," *Pittsburgh Courier*, 12 February 1936, 12.

36. "A Negro Girl Is Spain's Hero," *St. Louis Argus*, 11 September 1936; "African Negroes Fighting in Spain Against Their Will," *Atlanta Daily World*, 15 July 1937, 1, 6.

37. "Blacks in Spanish Revolution Fighting on Side of Royalists." See also *Philadelphia Tribune*, 13 August 1937, and, for the article on Oliver Law, *Atlanta Daily World*, 19 December 1937.

38. Casals, *Joys and Sorrows*, 226.

39. "Black Moors, Fighting for Spanish Fascists, Given Demoralizing Treatment."

40. *Atlanta Daily World*, 27 September 1937, 3.

41. Ibid., 1. See also "Discontent Among Military Forces: Many Desertions," *Pittsburgh Courier*, 19 November 1937.

42. Anne Chisholm, *Nancy Cunard: A Biography* (New York: Knopf, 1979), 243; Banting, "Nancy Cunard," 183.

43. Weintraub, *Last Great Cause*, 57–59; Pablo Picasso, "Address to the American Artists' Congress," in *Voices Against Tyranny*, ed. Miller, 50. Auden and Spender managed to get to Spain on their own. Spender spent most of his first year observing experts catalogue the Prado's works (Robert A. Stradling, *History and Legend: Writing the International Brigades* [Cardiff: University of Wales Press, 2003], 19).

44. Ernest Hemingway, "Notes for the Next War: A Serious Topical Letter," *Esquire*, September 1935, 19, 156; Dos Passos, "Room and Bath," 30.

45. In his articles during 1937 and 1938 for the *New York Times*, Hemingway reported on France's closing of borders ("Hemingway Finds France Is Neutral," 17 March 1937), praised the courage of youths in battle ("Bruhuega Likened by Hemingway to Victory on World War Scale," 29 March 1937), and described Madrid during war ("Heavy Shell-Fire in Madrid Advance," 10 April 1937, and "War Is Reflected Vividly in Madrid," 25 April 1937). He wrote that Franco would never take Madrid because of the heroism of the man in the street ("Spanish Fatalism Typified by Driver," 23 May 1937) and described the Americans still alive in Spain and enumerated the challenges Franco faced ("Americans in Spain Veteran Soldiers," 14 September 1937). See also "Main Rebel Threat Is Deemed in North," 11 April 1938; "Loyalists Await Tortosa Assault," 19 April 1938; and "Lerida Is Divided by Warring Forces," 30 April 1938.

46. Cunard, *Grand Man*, 244.

47. Ernest Hemingway, "On the American Dead in Spain," *New Masses*, 14 February 1939, 3.

48. Danny Duncan Collum, ed., with Victor A. Berch, *African Americans in the Spanish Civil War: This Ain't Ethiopia, but It'll Do* (New York: Hall, 1992). This is a much-needed and enormously interesting book on this subject.

49. Canute Frankson, who wrote this in July 1937, became an icon of the Abraham Lincoln Brigade (available at http://www.english.uiuc.edu/maps/scw/letters.htm [accessed 13 April 2004]). Also in the United States, newspapers, churches, and professional groups raised sufficient funds to buy a fully equipped ambulance for use in the war. Harlem hosted concerts by Count Basie, W. C. Handy, Fats Waller, Cab Calloway, Eubie Blake, and Noble Sissle. James Baldwin, then only twelve years old, published his first essay, "Negroes in Spain." Josephine Baker danced in Paris to raise money. Writers from Cuba, Africa, and the West Indies wrote and read for Spain. Black nurses from every corner of the earth went to Spain to work in the medical corps.

50. Wright underscored Hughes's and Nancy's awareness of the irony of Franco's sending Muslim troops on a crusade to rid Christian Spain of Communism. For two excellent studies of this, see Vogel, *Black Press*, and Collum and Berch, eds., *African Americans in the Spanish Civil War*. See also "Hughes Finds Moors Being Used as Pawns by Fascists in Spain," *Baltimore Afro-American*, 30 October 1937, 3. Hughes also wrote, "They die in Spain, . . . victims of fascism . . . under a banner that holds only terror and segregation for all the darker peoples of the earth" ("Negroes in Spain," in *Good Morning Revolution: Uncollected Writings of Langston Hughes*, ed. Faith Berry [New York: Citadel, 1991], 106).

51. On the ride from Madrid to Barcelona, the driver frequently went off the road and almost hit several buildings. After she rebuffed his flirtations, he sobered up (Banting, "Nancy Cunard," 183); Chisholm, *Nancy Cunard*, 250. Chisholm also quotes Beckett's remark: "Nancy Cunard bounced in the other evening from Spain. I was very glad to see her" (245).

52. Cunard, *Grand Man*, 111.

53. Buñuel, "Civil War," 167–68.

54. Cunard, *Grand Man*, 155–56.

55. Ibid., 156–57; NC to W. C. Crozier, 31 December 1938, UM.

56. There were, for example, photos of "Spanish refugees . . . able to take their cattle and household goods" into France and of "Spanish Government troops waiting to be repatriated" (*Manchester Guardian*, 3 February 1930, 9).

57. NC to Crozier, 31 January 1939; Crozier to NC, 1 February 1939, UM.

12. Exposing the Concentration Camps After Franco's Victory

Epigraph. Cited in Bertrand Russell, preface to *Einstein on Peace*, ed. Otto Nathan and Heinz Norden (New York: Simon and Schuster, 1960), x.

1. Pierre Vidal-Naquet, "A Paper Eichmann: Anatomy of a Lie," in *Assassins of Memory: Essays on the Denial of the Holocaust*, trans. Jeffrey Mehlman (New York: Columbia University Press, 1992), 1–64. Speaking of the "whole of the Second World War," he

writes: "The camps established at Perpignan by the Third Republic and the French state [were] as much a part of it as Auschwitz and Treblinka" (15).

2. David Wingeate Pike, *Spaniards in the Holocaust: Mauthausen, the Horror on the Danube* (New York: Routledge, 2000). See also Martin Gilbert, *The Holocaust: A History of the Jews of Europe During the Second World War* (New York: Holt, Rinehart and Winston, 1985), and Herbert L. Matthews, *Half of Spain Died: A Reappraisal of the Spanish Civil War* (New York: Scribner, 1973), 218, who writes that during the occupation, the Nazis, with Franco's agreement, hastened their death in Dachau, Mauthausen, and Buchenwald.

3. *Manchester Guardian*, 27 January 1939, 11. Hereafter in this chapter, *Manchester Guardian* is abbreviated *MG*.

4. Reported in ibid.

5. For a retrospective and thoughtful evaluation of this, see the excellent Louis Stern, *Beyond Death and Exile: The Spanish Republicans in France, 1939–1955* (Cambridge, Mass.: Harvard University Press, 1979), 9–11.

6. Quoted in David Mitchell, *The Spanish Civil War* (London: Granada, 1982), 185.

7. William Pickens, "What I Saw in Spain," in *African Americans in the Spanish Civil War: This Ain't Ethiopia but It'll Do*, ed. Danny Duncan Collum, with Victor A. Berch (New York: Hall, 1992), 114.

8. Nancy Cunard, *Grand Man: Memories of Norman Douglas* (London: Secker & Warburg, 1954), 158. At the time, she wrote: "We are all half demented here, trying to cover the news" (NC to W. C. Crozier, 31 January 1939, UM).

9. NC to Crozier, 29 January 1939, UM.

10. "300,000: Growing Tragedy of Refugees" and "A Welter of Wretched Faces, Despairing and Patient," *MG*, 1 February 1939, 14, 10.

11. Quoted in "The Exodus from Spain," *MG*, 8 February 1939, 12.

12. 9 February 1939, UM.

13. "Exodus from Spain," 18.

14. NC to Crozier, 3 February 1939; Crozier to NC, 7 February 1939, UM.

15. Daphne Fielding, *Those Remarkable Cunards: Emerald and Nancy* (New York: Atheneum, 1968), 122; NC to Crozier, 30 or 31 January 1939; Crozier to NC, 31 January 1939, UM.

16. For Nancy's additional requests, see Crozier to NC, 31 January 1939; NC to Crozier, 3 February 1939; and appeals in *MG* and other newspapers, UM. For example, on February 5, 1939, she wrote, "It will be magnificent if the *Guardian* will open the fund. HOW they need it. . . . I wish you would see all of this tragedy for yourself. Forgive my bad composition and untidiness; if only there were more time." See also Nancy's letter on the Centro, in *MG*, 16 February 1939, 20. In addition to her appeals, she expressed gratitude for the funds (*MG*, 17 February 1939, 20; 18 February 1939, 15). Her ads had begun: "This is an appeal . . . to all those compassionate and generous readers of the *Manchester Guardian* who may want to help alleviate the indescribable suffering of scores of thousands of refugees pouring in during the past week. . . . 55,000 . . . [and] 10,000, 20,000 [arriving]."

17. NC to Crozier, 8 February 1939, UM. See also Gustav Regler, *The Owl of Minerva: The Autobiography of Gustav Regler*, trans. Norman Denny (London: Rupert Hart-Davis, 1959).

18. 9 February 1939, UM.

19. "An Army Crossing the Frontier" and "The Soldiers Leave Their Battlefield Behind: Great Shortage of Medical Help and Supplies," MG, 9 February 1939.

20. 11 February 1939, UM.

21. She wrote of seeing men hopelessly trying to build a shelter with cane, pine branches, and strips of cloth and corrugated iron (MG, 6 and 12–17 February 1939).

22. MG, 13 February 1939, 8; [?] March 1939, 7.

23. Stern, Beyond Death and Exile, 29, 19, 46.

24. Needless to say, there was no medication, such as quinine or aspirin (MG, 16 February 1939). First, she reports the increase to 78,000 prisoners at Argèles; 70,000 at Saint-Cyprien; 25,000 at Arles-sur Tech; 20,000 at Amélie-les-Bains; and 10,000 each at Prats de Mollo and Le Boulou. Death statistics of soldiers and civilian males over five days include 25 from hunger, cold, and sickness at Saint-Cyprien; 10 in one night at Argèles; 3 children and 7 adults from consumption, as well as 8,500 soldiers freezing in the rain, with 140 ill, at Arles-sur-Tech. Then she lists several rampant diseases in the camp (MG, 18 February 1939, 15). Other horrors, such as 20,000 living in the snow and mud at Bourg Madame, resulted in 8,000 returning to Spain.

25. 16 February 1939, UM. In 1949, Nancy wrote that Aragon, Eluard, Casson, Bloch, Tzara, and Pozner, among many others, "extended an unexpected hand of friendship" to these prisoners, as did the British Joint Aid Committee. Many were able to go to Mexico, Chile, Santo Domingo, Cuba, and other Latin American republics ("Decade of Exile: The Intellect of Spain Is Today in Other Lands," box 2, folder 5, HRC).

26. Matthews, Half of Spain Died, 218, 46; NC to Crozier, 3 February 1939, UM.

27. Crozier to NC, 16 February 1939; NC to Crozier, 11 February 1939; Crozier to NC, undated, UM, in reference to MG, 17 February 1939, 15.

28. NC to Crozier, 13 February 1939, UM. Referring to "the one," he adds that it "had mainly to do with the indictment of the French authorities"; he had, he thought, already done enough "on that score" (Crozier to NC, 17 February 1939).

29. NC to Crozier, undated, UM.

30. C. H. H. to Crozier, 20 February 1939; Crozier correspondence, 21 February 1939, UM.

31. The ships were set up for the seriously wounded and those afflicted with tuberculosis and typhus (MG, 18 February 1939, 15); MG, 20 April 1939, 15; 2 March 1939, 15; 8 April 1939.

32. Cunard, "Decade of Exile."

33. Carl Geiser, Prisoners of the Good Fight: The Spanish Civil War, 1936–1939 (Westport, Conn.: Hill, 1986), 200.

34. Ibid., 220.

35. MG, 3 March 1939, 10.

36. MG, 9 March 1939, 6; 3 April 1939, 7; 15 April 1939, 12.

37. MG, 10 March 1939, 15.

38. When the French complained about their expenses in "housing" their Spanish guests, they claimed 8 francs per refugee (more than they spent on each French soldier). To further defray costs, the authorities confiscated several Spanish trucks carrying jewels and precious metals; the government withheld 41.8 million francs from the Bank of Spain, held on deposit with the Bank of France (Stern, Beyond Death and Exile, 46); MG, 22 March 1939, 17.

39. *MG*, 13 March 1939, 12, 39; 15 March 1939, 6.

40. Stern, *Beyond Death and Exile*, 39, 53, 42.

41. See, for example, *Gringoire*, 23 February 1939; *L'Action française*, 3 January 1939; and *Le Figaro*, 3 January 1939; Stern, *Beyond Death and Exile*, 40.

42. NC to Crozier, 22 March 1939, UM.

43. NC to Crozier, 30 March 1939, UM.

44. NC to Crozier, 6 July 1939, UM.

45. Nan Green, "Nancy Cunard and Spain," in *Nancy Cunard: Brave Poet, Indomitable Rebel, 1896–1965*, ed. Hugh Ford (Philadelphia: Chilton, 1968), 171.

46. Matthews, *Half of Spain Died*, 218.

47. Charles Duff, "Nancy Cunard," and Delia del Carril, "Nancy Cunard," in *Nancy Cunard*, ed. Ford, 187, 198.

48. Green, "Nancy Cunard and Spain," 171.

49. "My meters must be perfect. . . . Oh Lord! Yet it has to be done. Disciplina, Señora! Se acaba! POR FIN! I bid you farewell," she ended her letter to Nan, signing it "'Nanción, a fancy which pleased and amused us both" (ibid., 176).

50. Fielding, *Those Remarkable Cunards*, 122; William Plomer, *At Home: Memoirs* (New York: Noonday, 1958), 101–2.

51. Pablo Neruda to NC, 10 April 1937, [from Capri] 3 May 1949, [from Dardapa] 13 February 1952, and 23 February 1965, all in box 17, folder 5, HRC.

52. Pablo Neruda, *Memoirs*, trans. Hardie St. Martin (New York: Farrar, Straus and Giroux, 1976), 128, 356; Jacqueline Hurtley and Elizabeth Russell, "Women Against Fascism," *Barcelona English Language and Literature Studies* 7 (1996): 48.

53. The length of her stay there is uncertain. Volodia Teitelboim (*Neruda: An Intimate Biography* [Austin: University of Texas Press, 1991], 214) and Anne Chisholm (*Nancy Cunard: A Biography* [New York: Knopf, 1979], 257) believe that she was in Chile for twenty months. See also Fernando Sáez, *Todo debe ser demasiado: Biografía de Delia del Carril, La Hormiga* (Providencia, Chile: Sudamericana, 1997), 135.

54. Teitelboim writes that Albertina Azócar Soto was always in the room when he read "Body of a Woman" (*Neruda*, 76–77). Neruda said that Proust had greatly influenced him; he also translated some of Joyce's poems as a student (55).

55. Neruda, *Memoirs*, 33.

56. Compelled to speak out against the fascists, Neruda's words were taken as Chile's official position, which violated the neutrality of his government. In 1939, he was recalled from Madrid and transferred to Paris, where he continued to denounce the atrocities occurring in Spain and to beg the French government to intervene. Nancy reports that he was responsible for 5,000 refugees arriving in Chile ("Decade of Exile").

57. Nancy Cunard, "Sonnets in Chile," box 8, folder 7, HRC.

58. Neruda, *Memoirs*, 126–29.

59. Hugh Ford, *A Poet's War: British Poets and the Spanish Civil War* (Philadelphia: University of Pennsylvania Press, 1965), 81.

60. Cunard, *Grand Man*, 160.

61. Notebook, 1942, box 23, folder 3a, HRC.

62. Sáez, *Todo debe ser demasiado*, 135; Walter Strachan, "Nancy Cunard," in *Nancy Cunard*, ed. Ford, 277.

63. Neruda, *Memoirs*, 128.

64. Rafael Osuna, *Pablo Neruda y Nancy Cunard* (Madrid: Origenes, 1987), 48–49, speaking of Neruda's prose [my translation]. See also Morris E. Carson, *Pablo Neruda: Regresó el caminante* (Madrid: Playor, 1973), 56–59.

65. Teitelboim, *Neruda*, 212–16.

66. Sáez says that she was with the poet-boyfriend whom Neruda had described, a former bullfighter, who had decided he would rather leave the bulls and Nancy in order to open a grocery store and sell sausages (*Todo debe ser demasiado*, 136). And Neruda's recollection was correct: the poet replacement did give Nancy such beatings that both of them were detained by the police in Manzanillo (Osuna, *Pablo Neruda y Nancy Cunard*, 48).

13. Exile and Resistance in World War II

Epigraph. John Strachey, *Digging for Mrs. Miller: Some Experiences of an Air-Raid Warden in London* (New York: Random House, 1941), 150.

1. NC to W. C. Crozier, 20 October 1941, UM. Nancy wrote to Crozier as soon as she returned from Spain. As early as March 1939, she expressed her plans to visit "Mexico, Central and South America, West Indies," and he provided letters of introduction. See, for example, ca. March 1939.

2. She bombarded Crozier with requests; he responded in cordial terms until the end of the war. See, for example, Crozier to NC, 31 July 1945, UM. He did publish a number of Nancy's articles during the war on South America, Mexico, and Spain.

3. NC to Edward Thompson, 14 October 1944, BC.

4. NC to Thompson, 28 February and 2 March 1945, BC.

5. Nancy's handwritten comment about Oswald Mosley is attached to the clipping "Mosley's Prison Life," *Star Telegram*, dated 23 December 1943 by Nancy, in diary, 1942, box 23, folder 3, HRC.

6. NC to Walter Strachan, 11 February 1945, ML.

7. Nancy Cunard, *Grand Man: Memories of Norman Douglas* (London: Secker & Warburg, 1954), 192.

8. She writes almost identically to Strachan, 16 November and 12 December 1944, ML.

9. Cunard, *Grand Man*, 169; Irene Rathbone, "Nancy Cunard," in *Nancy Cunard: Brave Poet, Indomitable Rebel, 1896–1965*, ed. Hugh Ford (Philadelphia: Chilton, 1968), 243.

10. The quotations in the following three paragraphs, regarding her trip from Latin America to New York, are from an untitled manuscript, box 1, folder 1, HRC.

11. *Daily News*, 23 July 1941, 45; *New York Times*, 23 July 1941, 8; 26 July 1941, 17; Nancy's responses to the press, box 1, folder 1, HRC.

12. Untitled essay, Kay Boyle Papers, ML.

13. Lawrence Gellert, "Remembering Nancy," in *Nancy Cunard*, ed. Ford, 143.

14. The quotations in this and the following two paragraphs, regarding her trip from New York to Glasgow, are from an untitled manuscript, box 1, folder 1, HRC.

15. The quotations in this and the following paragraphs, regarding the war in London, are from diaries, 1942, box 23, folder 3, and date books, 1942, boxes 24 and 25, HRC. For excellent summaries of this period, see *The Blitz: The Photography of George Rodger* (New York: Penguin, 1990); Stephen Inwood, *A History of London* (New York: Carroll

and Graf, 1998); Leonard Mosley, *Backs to the Wall: The Heroic Story of the People of London During World War II* (New York: Random House, 1971); Constantine FitzGibbon, *The Blitz* (London: Allan Wingate, 1957); William Sansom, *Westminster in War* (London: Faber & Faber, 1947); and David Johnson V-1, V-2: *Hitler's Vengeance on London* (New York: Stein and Day, 1981).

16. John Lehmann, *I Am My Brother: Autobiography II* (New York: Reynal, 1960), 23, 25.

17. For details on the Blitz and the period that followed, see, especially, Rodger, *Blitz*; Inwood, *History of London*; and Johnson, V-1, V-2.

18. Unless otherwise indicated, the quotations here and to the end of this section are from Nancy Cunard, "A Doodle-bug Book," box 28, folder 1, and date books, 1942–1944, boxes 24 and 25, HRC.

19. For statistics during the Blitz, see Robert Hewison, *Under Siege: Literary Life in London, 1939–1945* (London: Weidenfeld & Nicolson, 1977); for a discussion of social life, see Rodger, *Blitz*.

20. Paul Fussell, *Wartime: Understanding and Behavior in the Second World War* (Oxford: Oxford University Press, 1989), 200; Lehmann, *I Am My Brother*, 155.

21. Quoted in Mosley, *Backs to the Wall*, 380. Harold Nicolson wrote: "Every morning one is pleased to see one's friends appearing again!" (diary, 19 September 1944).

22. Cunard, *Grand Man*, 193, 199, 169.

23. Ibid., 182.

24. Ibid.; Nancy Cunard, "No Color Bar in the British Air Force," box 7, folder 1, HRC.

25. Anne Chisholm, *Nancy Cunard: A Biography* (New York: Knopf, 1979), 266.

26. Cunard, *Grand Man*, 190; NC to Thompson, 14 January 1944, BC.

27. Douglas Porch, *The French Secret Services: From the Dreyfus Affair to the Gulf War* (New York: Farrar, Straus and Giroux, 1995), 240.

28. Cunard, *Grand Man*, 183, 169. See also, for example, NC to Strachan, 15 November 1945, ML.

29. Forest C. Pogue, *The Supreme Command* (Washington, D.C.: Center of Military History, United States Army, 1996), 84–144 (esp. 131–32), 336–37, 344. See also other publications, such as Paul M. A. Linebarger, *Allied Forces: Supreme Headquarters—Psychological Warfare Division (SHAEF): An Account of its Operations in the Western European Campaign, 1944–45* (Bad Homburg, Germany: SHAEF, 1945), 13–20.

30. NC to Thompson, 14 October 1944, BC; Cunard, *Grand Man*, 200–202.

31. NC to Thompson, 24 October 1944, BC.

32. Cunard, *Grand Man*, 202–4; NC to Janet/Solita, 25 August 1941, 9 and 16 October 1944, and 15 January 1945, LC.

33. Undated, Kay Boyle Papers, ML.

34. Cunard, *Grand Man*, 169, 183, 180; NC to Janet/Solita, 1 September 1944, LC.

35. Morris Gilbert to NC, box 14, folders 8 and 9, and box 15, folder 1, HRC.

36. Cunard, *Grand Man*, 175.

37. Paul Ferris, *Dylan Thomas: The Biography* (Washington, D.C.: Counterpoint, 2000), 191.

38. Cunard, *Grand Man*, 171; NC to Thompson, 1 June 1944, BC.

39. For example, NC to Strachan, 13 January 1945, ML; Augustus John, *Finishing Touches* (London: Jonathan Cape, 1966), 103, 105; and Michael Holroyd, *Augustus John: The New Biography* (London: Chatto & Windus, 1966), 559–60.

40. Lehmann, *I Am My Brother*, 191–94; Hewison describes the "strange *mélanges*" that flourished throughout London (*Under Siege*, 63).

41. Daphne Fielding, *Those Remarkable Cunards: Emerald and Nancy* (New York: Atheneum, 1968), 131.

42. Ibid., 268.

43. Other acquaintances included Brian Howard, Raymond Mortimer, Roger Senhouse, David Gascogye, John Lehmann, Roger Penrose, and Charles Duff.

44. Sylvia Warner's comments about Nancy in this and the following paragraph are from entry, 18 March 1965, in *The Diaries of Sylvia Townsend Warner*, ed. Claire Harman (New York: Random House, 1996), 296; "Nancy Cunard," in *Nancy Cunard*, ed. Ford, 226–228; and quoted in Chisholm, *Nancy Cunard*, 271.

45. Charles Burkhart, *Herman and Nancy and Ivy: Three Lives in Art* (London: Gollancz, 1977), 41, 27, and "About Nancy," in *Nancy Cunard*, ed. Ford, 342.

46. Quoted in Burkhart, *Herman and Nancy and Ivy*, 47–48.

47. Ibid., 12–13, 119; NC to Charles Burkhart, 14 December 1953, ML.

48. Burkhart, *Herman and Nancy and Ivy*, 25, 26, 44.

49. The quotations in this and the following paragraph are from Nancy's notes on Aleister Crowley, box 13, folder 2, HRC.

50. Edward Thompson to Whitehall and 11 Downing Street, especially letters to and from his closest military contact, Major General R. Jack Collins, BC. See also Mary Lago, *India's Prisoner: A Biography of Edward John Thompson, 1886–1946* (Columbia: University of Missouri Press, 2001).

51. Thompson to NC, 21 July 1944, BC.

52. NC to Thompson, 3 January 1944, BC.

53. Anthony Hobson, "Nancy Cunard," in *Nancy Cunard*, ed. Ford, 230.

54. Cunard, *Grand Man*, 190.

55. Ibid., 195; Warner, "Nancy Cunard," 226–27; entry, 18 March 1965, in *Diaries of Sylvia Townsend Warner*, 296.

56. Lehmann, *I Am My Brother*, 165, 181.

57. Hewison, *Under Siege*; Paul Fussell, *The Great War and Modern Memory* (Oxford: Oxford University Press, 1975); Adam Piette, *Imagination at War: British Fiction and Poetry, 1939–1945* (London: Macmillan, 1995).

58. All quoted in Hewison's excellent chapter "Barbarians at the Gate," in *Under Siege*, 5–26.

59. I refer to a poem like "Fern Hill," a work of passion and physicality, of juxtapositions of sexual and Christian imagery in gorgeous lyrics of intricately braided rhymes. During the war, Thomas inspired a new school of Apocalyptic and Neo-Romantic poets who also preferred to write about childhood innocence, transcendence, mortality and the organic, the irrational and mythic. See the poetry of Drummond Allison, Keith Douglas, John Heath-Stubbs, Michael Meyer, Alan Ross, John Wain, David Gascoygne, Norman MacCaig, Nicholas Moore, and Henry Read.

60. Edith once gathered leading British poets to read before the queen and Princesses Elizabeth and Margaret. At another, Eliot read "What the Thunder Said" from *The Waste Land*. Maud often hosted the parties that followed. After such events, it was difficult for Cyril Connolly and Spender to criticize Edith's writing. Spender admitted: "Her kindness was a completely redeeming side of her nature" (quoted in Geoffrey Elborn, *Edith*

Sitwell: A Biography [Garden City, N.Y.: Doubleday, 1981], 171). For interesting biographies of Sitwell, see Victoria Glendinning, *Edith Sitwell: A Unicorn Among Lions* (New York, Knopf, 1981), and G. A. C. Cevasco, *The Sitwells: Edith, Osbert, and Sacheverell* (Boston: Hall, 1987).

61. Glendinning won the prestigious James T. Block Award. Glendinning, *Edith Sitwell*, 56–57, 61, 107, where she adds that when Nancy was invited to contribute to a new magazine, Sitwell replied: "I regret that"; Glendinning continues: "Edith never let up over Nancy Cunard." In agreement are Nina Hamnet, *Laughing Torso: Reminiscences of Nina Hamnett* (London: Constable, 1932), 87, and Cevasco, *Sitwells*, 13–14, 24, 244.

62. *Manchester Guardian*, 6 July 1925, in scrapbook, box 26, folder 2, HRC.

63. Cunard, "Doodle-bug Book."

64. NC to Thompson, 2 February 1943, BC.

65. *Times* (London), 4–20 and 24–26 July 1944, particularly the photos of 14 July l944.

66. NC to Strachan, 15 January 1945, ML ; Cunard, *Grand Man*, 204–5.

67. Cunard, *Grand Man*, 204–5.

14. Surviving Réanville

Epigraph. NC to Charles Burkhart, 27 November 1951, ML.

1. Nancy Cunard, *Grand Man: Memories of Norman Douglas* (London: Secker & Warburg, 1954), 206; Georges Sadoul to NC, undated, box 28, folder 4, HRC.

2. Unless otherwise indicated, the quotations in the remainder of this section are from Nancy Cunard, "Letter from Paris" [*Horizon*, June 1945], in *Nancy Cunard: Brave Poet, Indomitable Rebel, 1896–1965*, ed. Hugh Ford (Philadelphia: Chilton), 217–21.

3. NC to Janet/Solita, undated, LC.

4. NC to Burkhart, 2 January 1951, ML.

5. Cunard, *Grand Man*, 207.

6. Quoted in Anne Chisholm, *Nancy Cunard: A Biography* (New York: Knopf, 1979), 277.

7. Irene Rathbone, "Nancy Cunard," in *Nancy Cunard*, ed. Ford, 244. Comments on the mayor are in NC to Kay Boyle, 11 November 1948, ML; NC to Janet/Solita, undated, LC.

8. Herman Schrijver, "About Nancy," in *Nancy Cunard*, ed. Ford, 270; quoted in Daphne Fielding, *Those Remarkable Cunards: Emerald and Nancy* (New York: Atheneum, 1968), 143.

9. Cunard, *Grand Man*, 206–7.

10. The quotations in this and the following two paragraphs are from Nancy Cunard, *These Were the Hours: Memories of My Hours Press, Réanville and Paris, 1928–1931* (Carbondale: Southern Illinois University Press, 1969), 201, 205, 208.

11. Louise Morgan to NC, undated, box 17, folder 4, HRC.

12. Cunard, *Grand Man*, 209. Nancy continued to lament Gilbert's departure, and he continued to write about his poor financial and emotional state.

13. Memoranda between A. P. Wadsworth and J. M. Pringle, 9–14 January 1946, UM; NC to Janet/Solita, 12 April 1946, LC.

14. NC to Walter Strachan, 26 September 1946, ML.

15. The quotations in this and the following five paragraphs, regarding Nancy and Finley's relationship, are from Fielding, *Remarkable Cunards*, 153–54; Chisholm, *Nancy*

Cunard, 281, 283; Cunard, *Grand Man*, 216; and NC to Janet/Solita, 21 September 1957, LC.

16. The quotations in this and the following paragraph, regarding Maud's estate, are from William Plomer, "In the Early Thirties," in *Nancy Cunard*, ed. Ford, 124. Borrowing Joyce's spelling, Nancy first describes the three-hour "exagmination" of G. M.'s will regarding his love letters to Maud, on January 7, 1949, at the offices of Messrs. Hastie. For her subsequent negotiations with attorneys O. Parsons and Guiness, Mahon, see box 21, folder 7, HRC. Nancy worries that she cannot afford the £300 necessary to acquire the G. M.–Maud letters, in NC to Burkhart, 7 December 1951–12 May 1953, ML.

17. NC to Strachan, 26 April, 1948, ML, with the return address in care of National-Provincial Bank, London.

18. Quoted in Chisholm, *Nancy Cunard*, 285.

19. Included in NC to Roger Senhouse, 2 September 1949, LC.

20. Quoted in Chisholm, *Nancy Cunard*, 286; William Finley to NC, 23 September 1962, box 14, folder 3, HRC. Nancy later met the poet Clyde Robinson, whom Finley had first written for the money. Robinson wrote to Nancy: "Imagine: after fourteen years that he [Finley] dare to try to get in touch again! . . . Of all the lousy adventurers. Now his mother is dead for the second time" (22 August 1962, box 14, folder 3, HRC).

21. NC to Burkhart, 12 May 1953, ML.

22. Nancy Cunard, "Dordogne" [a 100-page manuscript], box 2, folder 4, HRC.

23. NC to Janet/Solita, 10 December 1946, LC.

24. NC to Kay, 18 November 1963, ML.

25. Fielding, *Remarkable Cunards*, 153; Chisholm, *Nancy Cunard*, 280; Cecily Mackworth, "Nancy Cunard," in *Nancy Cunard*, ed. Ford, 290.

26. Scrapbooks, 1948, box 23, folder 4, HRC.

27. NC to Strachan, 26 September 1946, ML. Until the end of the war, she usually spoke of replacing Franco with the Giral government in exile; NC to Janet/Solita, [illegible] 1948, LC.

28. Hugh Thomas, *The Spanish Civil War*, rev. ed. (New York: Modern Library, 2001), 922.

29. Brian Crozier, *Franco: A Biographical History* (London: Eyre & Spottiswoode, 1967), 38. See also Raymond Carr, *Spain, 1808–1975* (Oxford: Clarendon Press, 1982), 697.

30. The quotations in this and the following paragraph are from Nancy Cunard, "The Future of Spain After World War II," box 1, folder 1, HRC.

31. Carr, *Spain*, 719.

32. Juan M. Molina, *El movimiento clandestine en España, 1939–1949* (Mexico City: Editores Méxicanos Unidos, 1976), 5–7, cited in Louis Stern, *Beyond Death and Exile: The Spanish Republicans in France, 1939–1945* (Cambridge, Mass.: Harvard University Press, 1979), 223. See also, for example, Rogelio Martínez, comp., *Crónica del exilio español* (Montevideo: Editorial Bergamin, 2001); *Who Are the Spanish Refugees?* (New York: Spanish Information Bureau, Spanish Republican Government in Exile, 1947); Lois Elwyn Smith, *Mexico and the Spanish Republicans* (Berkeley: University of California Press, 1965); and David W. Pike, *In the Service of Stalin: The Spanish Refugees in Exile, 1939–1945* (Oxford: Oxford University Press, 1993).

33. Jesús Izcaray, "Spain Today"; Isabel de Palencia concentrates on the war of 1936 to 1939, with the hope that a continuing insurgency will eventually be victorious; she quotes Romain Rolland: "All people will in the future envy the sufferings and the glory of

Republican Spain" (*Smouldering Freedom: The Story of the Spanish Republicans in Exile* [New York: Longmans, Green, 1945]). See also Carr, *Spain*, 690.

34. Stern, *Beyond Death and Exile*, 228.

35. Quoted in ibid., 229.

36. The quotations in this and the following two paragraphs are from NC to Burkhart, 2 January 1951 and 9 July 1953, ML, and NC to Janet/Solita, [?] August 1949, LC. See also Nancy Cunard, "On James Joyce," in *Joyce at Texas: Essays on the James Joyce Materials at the Humanities Research Center*, ed. Dave Oliphant and Thomas Zigal (Austin: Humanities Research Center, University of Texas, 1983), 89.

37. John Banting, "Nancy Cunard," in *Nancy Cunard*, ed. Ford, 181.

38. Quoted in Mackworth, "Nancy Cunard," 291.

39. NC to Kay, 17 September 195[?], ML; Fielding, *Remarkable Cunards*, 152.

40. For example, Nancy Cunard, "Andorra" and "Articles Regarding a Spanish Family in Franco's Spain," box 1, folder 3; "Mexico" and "Mexico-and-More," box 6, folder 5; "Mexican Perspective—Notes," box 6, folder 7; "Notes de L'Amérique du Sud," box 7, folder 1; and "The Worst Case of Injustice in This Century," box 9, folder 7, HRC.

41. Irene Rathbone, "Nancy Cunard," and Banting, "Nancy Cunard," in *Nancy Cunard*, ed. Ford, 253, 181.

42. Rathbone, "Nancy Cunard," 249–50.

43. NC to Burkhart, 27 February 1956, 1 August 1954, July–August 1955, 17 June 1957, and 9 July 1952, ML.

44. NC to Burkhart, 7 and 27 November 1951, ML.

45. Charles Burkhart, "Letters from Nancy," in *Nancy Cunard*, ed. Ford, 324.

46. With former lovers, Nancy had turned to other men in order to establish her independence and protect herself from rejection. She wrote to Burkhart: "What sort of wishes do you want for New Year? Mere writing? The termination of the G. M. book? To be able to turn to others of your own? In which countries? To be left in peace? To all of these please find me a sincere subscriber" (30 December 1951, ML).

47. The quotations in this and the following paragraph are from NC to Burkhart, 24 April 1955, 3 June and 1 August 1954, 4 April 1957, and 2 March and 30 December 1959, ML.

15. Escaping La Mothe

Epigraph. NC to Janet/Solita, undated, LC.

1. Diary, 6 November 1955, box 23, folder 6, HRC. See also NC to Pablo Casals, 1946–1949, box 13, folder 1, HRC.

2. Nancy Cunard, "Decade of Exile: The Intellect of Spain Is Today in Other Lands," 1949, box 2, folder 5, HRC. In his memoir, Casals tells of one exception: he performed at the White House because "in my heart I felt that [John F. Kennedy] would do all he could for my people" (*Joys and Sorrows: Reflections*, as told to Albert E. Kahn [New York: Simon and Schuster, 1970], 291).

3. Entries, 23 and 24 February 1952, in *The Diaries of Sylvia Townsend Warner*, ed. Claire Harman (New York: Random House, 1996), 186–87. See also entry, 21 March 1956, about their visit to the village of Saintage to see its Romanesque churches and local "Suffolk-like convolvulous major, yuccas, oleanders, etc." (225).

4. Entry, 6 December 1953, in ibid., 17. See also entry, 27 February 1952, where she remarks about Ash Wednesday: "Waking early, and hearing the cocks crowing, [I] thought of Jesus setting out early in the morning, leaving the cockcrows and the villages behind, bound for temptation in the wilderness I daresay, but also the amplitude of self-sufficiency. This turned into a dream of notable color, in which I first saw him in a desert of fired rock and sand, the rock a little crumbling, and both of the pigeon and breast colors of pale reddest lilac, pale gray, snuff brown, thence into another scene where he got into a small boat and floated down a very narrow salt stream, of the most brilliant emerald green, fringed with scarlet alder stakes and enameled windows. The water had a saline brilliancy, sleekness and tranquility" (187). Her jewelry included "an inch-long mat of turquoise matrix, . . . in minute bands of black enamel and diamonds" (entry, 10 December 1953, 204).

5. Deirdre Bair, *Samuel Beckett: A Biography* (New York: Harcourt Brace Jovanovich, 1978), 470; Samuel Beckett to NC, 5 May 1956, box 12, folder 1, HRC.

6. Henry Moore, "Postscript to the Preceding Account," in *Nancy Cunard: Brave Poet, Indomitable Rebel, 1896–1965*, ed. Hugh Ford (Philadelphia: Chilton, 1968), 287–88. See also Walter Strachan, "Nancy Cunard," in ibid., 271, 280.

7. Diary, 17 October 1955, box 23, folder 6, HRC; Allanah Harper, "A Few Memories of Nancy Cunard," in *Nancy Cunard*, ed. Ford, 343.

8. Quoted in Strachan, "Nancy Cunard," 278. He was very grateful for her extensive help in the translations. Always fastidious about philosophical and political inferences, she had once written Kay Boyle, while translating her work into French, "I reach the word 'wilderness' and it springs back at me not in French but in German, 'Wüste.' . . . It is but a step to think of your poem in German. This is a world-poem, look you, 1937 is 1948, *et al*. . . . In German, say, 'Come now, all you new Germans, . . . all you dis-poisoned men, there must be amongst you one . . . sign of [a] change of heart'" (11 November 1948, ML).

9. Anthony Hobson, "Nancy Cunard," and Anthony Thorne, "A Share of Nancy," in *Nancy Cunard*, ed. Ford, 231, 302.

10. The quotations in this and the following two paragraphs are from Anthony Thorne to NC, undated, box 19, folders 9 and 10, HRC, and "Share of Nancy," 294, 296.

11. Irene Rathbone, "Nancy Cunard," in *Nancy Cunard*, ed. Ford, 253, 246–47. According to Daphne Fielding, "Nancy, the eccentric, the incomprehensible who, when she journeyed about the country, went third class among peasants and baskets of live hens, whose clothes were of no known style yet somehow became her, . . . though springing from 'la class dirigeante [high],' was taken a sort of pride in locally, taken perhaps advantage of and treated at once as chatelaine [a "Lady"] and friend" (*Those Remarkable Cunards: Emerald and Nancy* [New York: Atheneum, 1968], 161).

12. Rathbone, "Nancy Cunard," 248.

13. NC to Kay, 17 September [?], ML.

14. She hoped that her house, close to the beginnings of civilization and far from a large city, would protect her. She states many of these concerns in NC to Charles Burkhart, 7 and 27 December 1951 and 23 September 1952, ML. See also Kay to NC, 15 August 1963, ML, and undated, box 12, folder 8, HRC. I have been unable to find additional information about Nancy's interest in the Rosenberg trial.

15. NC to Kay, 28 May [?], ML.

16. Kay to NC, 16 September 1959, ML. See also Kay to NC, 29 October 1952.
17. NC to Kay, 22 September 1963, ML.
18. NC to Walter Strachan, 12 November 1953, ML.
19. The quotations in this and the following paragraph are from Nancy Cunard, "Decade of Exile: The Intellect of Spain Is Today in Other Lands," *Arena*, no. 3 (n.d.): 4–26. Neruda gave a brief interview for the same issue.
20. To get an idea of the extent of her correspondence, the inventory of outgoing correspondence at the HRC is eleven pages long, with approximately seventy-five names on each page; certain friends received more than 100 letters.
21. Louise Morgan to NC, undated and 11 and 20 January 1959, box 12, folder 1; Iris Tree to NC, 30 January 1956 and 11 January 1957, box 20, folder 1; Langston Hughes to NC, 2 June 1954 and 30 March 1955, box 15, folder 11, HRC.
22. Joan Miró to NC, 19 July 1957, box 16, folder 8; Pavel Tchelichew to NC, winter 1952, box 19, folder 4; Alexander Calder to NC, 25 September 1947 and 21 January 1948, box 13, folder 1, HRC.
23. Beckett to NC, 5 May 1956, box 12, folder 1, HRC.
24. Beckett to NC, 11 November and 6 December 1956, box 12, folder 1, HRC. Beckett is avidly reading her books on Norman Douglas and G. M., "more I confess for what it tells of you" than of them. Beckett to NC, 23 September 1956.
25. Beckett to NC, 21 May 1956 and [?] October 1958, box 12, folder 1, HRC.
26. NC to Kay, 8 August 1949, in notebook, box 23, folder 6, HRC.
27. Ezra Pound to NC, 1 August 1946. Part of Nancy's letter, dated 11 June 1946, is quoted in chapter 5. Copies of the entire letter can be found in the Kay Boyle Papers, ML, and in the Janet Flanner and Solita Solano Papers, LC. See also some of the Pound–Cunard correspondence, box 10, folder 6; box 17, folder 10; and box 21, folder 4, HRC.
28. Anne Chisholm, *Nancy Cunard: A Biography* (New York: Knopf, 1979), 291. The inventory at the HRC includes 335 separate works not divided into genres or dated. A cursory glance at these include, from this period, "Various Articles Regarding Spanish Families in Franco's Spain," "Bugs and Franco," "Dordogne," "Pariahs—en El Nuevo Mundo, Londres," "Gabaudet," "Haywood Patterson Jail," "Pablo Casals," and "When Can We Stop Being Refuges," in addition to the works already mentioned. Not listed are a series of poems, "In Time of Waiting," and another series, "Trees," published in *Colony* (1954); *Oradour*, one of her many pamphlets, on the German massacre in that region; "Decade of Exile: The Intellect of Spain Is Today in Other Lands," *Arena*, no. 3 (n.d.): 4–26; and "Musique Noire des États-Unis," *L'Europe*, April 1949. She wrote in French for *Europe*; in English for *Horizon* and *Connoisseur*; in Spanish for dozens of Spanish magazines. Nancy had used an ingenious format for *Grand Man*—a series of "Letters to Norman," which allowed her both to concentrate on his intellectual gifts and to avoid his personal life. G. M. portrays the life of a surrogate father through the eyes of a loving and grateful admirer. Both memoirs received excellent reviews.
29. The ivories project was "a promise to self," after Réanville—in her words, "out of destruction, one of creation." Her plan was to duplicate her preparation for *Negro* by traveling extensively after studying at the British Museum. A curator at the British Museum had already contacted her to catalog its inventory of African ivories (diary, box 23, folder 6, HRC).

30. NC to David Garnett, 22 December 1956, UD. She added: "The thought of settling down to 'A Life' is unthinkable." She repeats this in NC to Burkhart, 10 August and 3 November 1956, ML. See also Thorne, "Share of Nancy," 304.

31. NC to Kay, 11 November 1948, ML; diary, 25 December 1955, box 23, folder 6, HRC.

32. NC to Burkhart, 18 June 1963, ML.

33. The quotations in this and the following paragraph are from Charles Burkhart, *Herman and Nancy and Ivy: Three Lives in Art* (London: Gollancz, 1977), 16–18, 114, 20.

34. NC to Clyde Robinson, 15 February [?], box 18, folder 3, HRC.

35. Quoted in Fielding, *Remarkable Cunards*, 167. See also Miriam J. Benkovitz, "A Memoir: Nancy Cunard," in *Nancy Cunard*, ed. Ford, 323.

36. NC to Janet/Solita, 15 November 1956, LC.

37. NC to Burkhart, 5 November 1956, ML; quoted in Chisholm, *Nancy Cunard*, 453.

38. NC to Janet/Solita, 23 October 1956, LC.

39. NC to Burkhart, 2 April, 17 June, and 15 August 1957, ML.

40. Maroula Joannou, "Nancy Cunard's English Journey," *Feminist Review* 78 (2004): 141–63.

41. Charles Burkhart, "Letters from Nancy," in *Nancy Cunard*, ed. Ford, 330–31.

42. W. K. Rose, "Remembering Nancy," in ibid., 319.

43. Morgan to NC, undated, box 17, folder 4, HRC.

44. One of the few books on the Spanish refugees and their intellectual circles in Mexico is Patricia W. Fagen, *Exiles and Citizens: Spanish Republicans in Mexico* (Austin: University of Texas Press, 1973).

45. NC to John Banting, 9 February 1958, TGA.

46. NC to John Banting, 7 November 1959, TGA.

47. For an account of these events, see Fielding, *Remarkable Cunards*, 162. See also Chisholm, *Nancy Cunard*, 311, and Thorne, "Share of Nancy," 304–5.

48. John Banting, "Nancy Cunard," in *Nancy Cunard*, ed. Ford, 184. Fielding speaks of her "personal apocrypha" (*Remarkable Cunards*, 167, 184).

49. Quoted in Chisholm, *Nancy Cunard*, 310.

50. Thorne, "Share of Nancy," 304.

51. Entry, 10 March 1959, in *Diaries of Sylvia Townsend Warner*, 255; Benkovitz, "Memoir," 323. Nancy refers to July and the "anniversary of the OLD one" (NC to Kay, 11 November 1948, UD).

52. Thorne, "Share of Nancy," 305.

53. Manuscripts and her lengthy work on the ivories, box 5, folder 6–box 6, folder 2, HRC.

54. Clyde Robinson, "Nancy Cunard in Mallorca," in *Nancy Cunard*, ed. Ford, 323–34.

16. The Last Great Glare

Epigraph. Louis Aragon, "Pour la vie," *Les Lettres françaises*, 24 July 1960, 1, written after Nancy's commitment to a mental institution.

1. Daphne Fielding, *Those Remarkable Cunards: Emerald and Nancy* (New York: Atheneum, 1968), 167–68.

2. NC to Janet/Solita, 14 and 16 July 1960, LC; NC to Clyde Robinson, 10 July 1960, box 10, folders 7 and 8, HRC.
3. NC to Janet/Solita, undated, LC.
4. Fielding, *Remarkable Cunards*, 168.
5. NC to Janet/Solita, 16 July 1960, LC.
6. NC to Janet/Solita, 19 July 1960, LC.
7. NC to Robinson, 10 August 1960, box 18, folders 3–5, HRC.
8. Reported in Fielding, *Remarkable Cunards*, 169.
9. NC to Janet/Solita, 9 July 1960, LC.
10. Entry, 4 July 1960, in *The Diaries of Sylvia Townsend Warner*, ed. Claire Harman (London: Chatto & Windus, 1994), 265.
11. NC to Janet/Solita, 9 July 1960, LC. She also assesses her life accomplishments: "NEGRO"; her liberation of Spanish soldiers; her fine collection of African ivory bracelets; her modest pride in the Hours Press; her poetry, particularly her recent work; her writing the truth about the exodus into France from Spain in 1939; and her wish to finish a book about African ivories.
12. W. K. Rose, "Remembering Nancy," in *Nancy Cunard: Brave Poet, Indomitable Rebel, 1896–1965*, ed. Hugh Ford (Philadelphia: Chilton, 1968), 318.
13. Louise Morgan, "My Nancy," in ibid., 312.
14. Charles Burkhart, *Herman and Nancy and Ivy: Three Lives in Art* (London: Gollancz, 1977), 120.
15. NC to Janet/Solita, 23 August 1960, LC.
16. Entries, 5 September 1960 and 18 March 1965 (two days after Nancy's death), in *Diaries of Sylvia Townsend Warner*, 266–67, 296.
17. NC to Robinson, 3 September 1960, box 18, folders 3–5, HRC.
18. Morgan, "My Nancy," 313, 314.
19. Louise Morgan to Official Solicitor, 13 January 1961, quoted in ibid., 314–15.
20. Quoted in Anne Chisholm, *Nancy Cunard: A Biography* (New York: Knopf, 1979), 325–26.
21. "Tomás was beastly here, utterly different! [I hear you laugh], and bored to death, although less so than I" (NC to Janet/Solita, 3 March 1961, LC). On her health, NC to Robinson, 14 June 1961, box 18, folders 3–5, HRC.
22. NC to Janet/Solita, 2 February 1962, [from Toulouse] undated and 14 March 1963, and [from Souillac] undated, LC.
23. Samuel Beckett to NC, 17 July 1963, box 12, folder 1, HRC.
24. NC to Janet/Solita, 15 March and 20 April 1963, LC. See also NC to Janet/Solita, 16 and 22 January 1964. In such letters as those of 8 September and 10 December 1963 and 9 January 1964, she writes: "The really FINAL version! . . . for me, anyway, is a real difficulty. RHYTHMS— . . . I hear them (the various ones) so clearly, but, day by day, they sometimes change, and my difficulty is mixing them. . . . There should be no rough shocks in the change of one rhythm to another, ever."
25. NC to Janet/Solita, 15 March, 7 April, 8 September, and 23 June 1963, LC.
26. Quoted in Paul L. Mariani, *William Carlos Williams: A New World Naked* (New York: McGraw-Hill, 1981), 337.
27. NC to Janet/Solita, 1 October 196[?], LC.

28. NC to Janet/Solita, 4 and 7 April 1963, LC. At other times, they are both provocative and baffling: "About drink . . . who's ashamed of drinking alone? It is best—perhaps purest—but then it's so important to me. . . . The bottle = tower = phallic symbol = (finally landscape; a tree, the skeleton and from that the erect coffin presumably): the mark at the end of the plain. Always visible. Honorable. Never touches. Bless!" (NC to Janet/Solita, 8 September and 23 June 1963).

29. Langston Hughes to NC, 28 April 1963, box 15, folder 11, HRC.

30. NC to Robinson, 15 or 16 June 1963, box 10, folder 7, HRC.

31. NC to Kay Boyle, 22 August 1963, ML.

32. NC to Kay, 5 March, 23 June, and 18 and 29 December 1963, ML; NC to Janet/Solita, 14 and 24 April 1963, LC.

33. NC to Janet/Solita, 14 and 20 April, 15 May[?], and 2 June 1963, LC.

34. NC to Kay, undated, ML; NC to Janet/Solita, 3 June 1963, LC.

35. NC to Janet/Solita, 6, 10, and 22 June and 1 July 1963, LC.

36. Samuel Beckett, quoted in Kay to NC, 6 September 1963, ML.

37. Kay to NC, 25 October and 7 December 1963, ML. For some time after Franckenstein's death, Nancy continued to express such sentiments as "I am most, most upset by Joseph's death. I think of you constantly" and "Darling, my furious tears, . . . in rage and fury and love" (NC to Kay, 20 November 1963). See also Sandra Whipple Spanier, *Kay Boyle, Artist and Activist* (Carbondale: Southern Illinois University Press, 1986), 11–18.

38. NC to Kay, 22 September 1963, ML.

39. NC to Janet/Solita, 11 and 18 June 1963, LC.

40. NC to Janet/Solita, 11 June 1963, LC. See also NC to Kay, 2 and 18 November 1963, ML. Nancy had been unable to find an English publisher—the subject was too specialized—but Ford placed it with Southern Illinois University Press, which published *These Were the Hours* in 1969.

41. NC to Janet/Solita, 5 August 1963, LC. See also NC to Charles Burkhart, 9 August 1963, ML. She would also have been spared the "gloom when I [had to] put up the newspapers over all the books at La Mothe [and] . . . , put up those dreadfully heavy wooden shutters—all for winter and its ravages."

42. The quotations in this and the following two paragraphs are from NC to Burkhart, 18 August 1963, ML; Burkhart, *Herman and Nancy and Ivy*, 112, 113; Charles Burkhart, "Letters from Nancy," in *Nancy Cunard*, ed. Ford, 325; and Chisholm, *Nancy Cunard*, 329.

43. NC to Janet/Solita, 21 and 25 August 1963, LC.

44. NC to Janet/Solita, 24 August 1963, LC.

45. Herman Schrijver, "About Nancy," in *Nancy Cunard*, ed. Ford, 269; NC to Janet/Solita, [?] February 1964, LC.

46. NC to Janet/Solita, 9 and 22 January 1964, LC.

47. NC to Janet/Solita, 2 January 1963, LC; NC to Walter Strachan, 21 December 1963, ML.

48. NC to Janet/Solita, 3 January 1964, ML.

49. Fielding, *Remarkable Cunards*, 173–74.

50. The quotations in this and the following two paragraphs are from NC to Janet/Solita, 6 and 8 March 1964, LC; Chisholm, *Nancy Cunard*, 330; and NC to Janet/Solita, 7 April 1964.

51. NC to Janet/Solita, 7 and 23 April 1964, LC. Nancy, who saw the play some years earlier, says, "To read, I think, it is even much finer" (NC to Janet/Solita, 6 or 7 May 1964; NC to David Garnett, 20 March 1964, UD).

52. The quotations in this and the following two paragraphs are from NC to Janet/Solita, 23 May, 23 June, and 21 August 1964, LC.

53. Quoted in Fielding, *Remarkable Cunards*, 174.

54. NC to Janet/Solita, 2 January 1965, LC; NC to Strachan, undated, ML.

55. NC to Janet/Solita, undated, LC.

56. Nan Green, "Nancy Cunard and Spain," in *Nancy Cunard*, ed. Ford, 174; Louise Morgan to NC, undated, box 17, folder 4, HRC.

57. Walter Strachan, "Nancy Cunard," in *Nancy Cunard*, ed. Ford, 283.

58. NC to Janet/Solita, 1 and 2 January 1965, LC.

59. NC to Strachan, 30 January and 9 February 1965, ML. Told that her stomach was full of bacteria—"real poison"—she was not allowed to ingest anything but pills and powders, and she had to endure a "pipe" every two hours and bedpan every three, which she found both painful and embarrassing.

60. Irene Rathbone, "Nancy Cunard," in *Nancy Cunard*, ed. Ford, 258; NC to Janet/Solita, 12 February 1965, LC.

61. Strachan, "Nancy Cunard," 285.

62. NC to Garnett, 24 February 1965, UD.

63. NC to Kay, 2 November 1963, ML; Nancy Cunard, *G. M.: Memories of George Moore* (London: Rupert Hart-Davis, 1956), 197.

64. Quoted in Allanah Harper, "A Few Memories of Nancy Cunard," in *Nancy Cunard*, ed. Ford, 343.

65. NC to Janet/Solita, 17 February and 2 March 1965, LC.

66. Fielding, *Remarkable Cunards*, 177.

67. Chisholm, *Nancy Cunard*, 333; Strachan, "Nancy Cunard," 286; Burkhart, *Herman and Nancy and Ivy*, 60.

68. Lachlan MacKinnon, *The Lives of Elsa Triolet* (London: Chatto & Windus, 1992), 191–92.

69. Georges Sadoul, "The Fighting Lady," in *Nancy Cunard*, ed. Ford, 154–55 [my translation].

70. Raymond Michelet, "Nancy Cunard," in ibid., 131 [my translation].

Epilogue

1. The quotations are from Langston Hughes, "Nancy: A Piñata in Memoriam," and Hilaire Hiler, "Nancy Cunard," in *Nancy Cunard: Brave Poet, Indomitable Rebel, 1896–1965*, ed. Hugh Ford (Philadelphia: Chilton, 1968), xxi, 35; Harold Acton, *Memoirs of an Aesthete* (London: Methuen, 1948), 223–25; Janet Flanner and Solita Solano, typescript, LC; Pablo Neruda, *Memoirs*, trans. Hardie St. Martin (New York: Farrar, Straus and Giroux, 1976), 126–29; T. K. Utchay, quoted in Anne Chisholm, *Nancy Cunard: A Biography* (New York: Knopf, 1979), 325–26; Louis Aragon, *Nightwalker*, trans. Frederick Brown (Englewood Cliffs, N.J.: Prentice-Hall, 1970), 139–40; and Kay Boyle to NC, 7 December 1963, ML.

Illustration Credits

• • •

By permission of the Houghton Library, Harvard University *AC9.el464.Zzx: 13
Cecil Beaton Archive, Sotheby's: 31
Curtis Moffat Estate: 28, 39
Der Quer Schmitt, Dusseldorf: 41
Estate of Constantin Brancusi: © 2006 Artists Rights Society (ARS), New York/ADAGP, Paris: 33
Estate of Man Ray: © 2006 Man Ray Trust/Artists Rights Society (ARS), New York/ADAGP, Paris: 20
Estate of Nancy Cunard: 46, 50, 51, 52
Estate of Oskar Kokoshka: © 2006 Artists Rights Society (ARS), New York/ProLitteris, Zürich: 34
Harry Ransom Humanities Research Center, The University of Texas at Austin: frontispiece, 1, 4, 5, 7, 15, 16, 18, 19, 35, 36, 40, 42, 43, 44, 45, 53, 54, 56, 57, 61, 62
Irish Times: 60
Library of Congress: 3, 8, 9, 10, 11, 12, 14, 22, 23, 25, 27, 29, 30, 49, 58, 59

Morris Library, University of Southern Illinois, Carbondale: 24
National Gallery of Melbourne: 37
New Directions: 26
Schomberg Center for Research in Black Culture, New York Public Library: 47, 48
The Wyndham Lewis Memorial Trust: 38

Index

Bloomsbury group, 27, 29, 31, 44–47, 51. *See also specific individuals*

Blunden, Edmund, 231

Boas, Franz, 196, 256

"Body of a Woman" (Neruda), 265

Boer War, 17, 275

Le Boeuf sur le Toit (restaurant), 98, 108, 153, 154, 167

Bontemps, Arna, 181, 183, 193

Borenius, Tancred, 299

Boston Post, 170

Bow, Clara, 14

Bowen, Stella, 96

Boyle, Kay: correspondence of, 310–11, 326–28, 332–33, 354–55, 421n.8; memoirs and poems by, 126; and Nancy, 94, 97, 117, 126, 139, 144, 273, 318, 332–33, 375; and World War II, 284

Brancusi, Constantin, 96, 97, 100, 108, 119, 126, 182

Braque, Georges, 108

Brave New World (Huxley), 134

Breton, André, 110, 112, 303, 392n.43

Bridges, Robert, 54

Bridgetower, George Augustus, 182–83, 192

"Brief Outline of Negro History in the U.S. Until Abolition, A" (Edward Johnson), 184

British Council, 299

British Museum, 157, 163, 422n.29

Brooke, Rupert, 31, 54, 148

"Brother Fire" (MacNeice), 295

Broun, Heywood, 196

Browder, Earl, 205

Brown, Bob, 126, 141

Brown, Sterling, 164, 169, 181, 193

Die Brücke, 91

Bubu of Montparnasse (Philippe), 41

Buckingham Palace, 24, 70, 203

Buñuel, Luis, 109, 157, 220, 226

Burkhart, Charles, 319–21, 335–36, 338; and G. M., 319, 338; and Nancy's illness, 347, 349, 358–59, 368–69

Café Royal, 29, 30, 58, 60, 130, 132, 134

Calder, Alexander ("Sandy"), 98, 287, 331

Campaign for the Abolition of Capital Punishment, 327

Camus, Albert, 300, 301

Cantos (Pound), 33, 101, 103, 126

Capa, Robert, 222

Cape, Jonathan, 172

Capoul (hotel), 337, 352, 355–56

Carpentier, Horace, 3–4, 5, 6

Carrington, Dora, 46

Caruso, Dorothy, 307

La Casa de las Flores, 228–30

Casals, Pablo, 233, 322, 327, 330, 409n.28

Cassirer, Ernst, 93

Cathay (Pound), 32–33

Ce Soir (newspaper), 257, 300, 305

Central America, refugees in, 221

Chaliapin, Fyodor, 13

Chamberlain, Neville, 202, 277

Chanel, Coco, 108

Channon, Chips, 213

Chaplin, Charlie, 111

"Characteristics of Negro Expression" (Hurston), 188–89

Chile, 264–68

Chisholm, Anne, 64, 99, 180, 268, 333

Chopin, Kate, 72

Churchill, Lady Randolph, 12, 14, 85. *See also* Cornwallis-West, Jennie

Churchill, Sir Winston, 21, 342; at Potsdam Conference, 313–14; and Roosevelt, 274; and World War II, 274, 277, 286, 294

Clinique Belvédère, 364–65

Cocteau, Jean, 100, 108, 129, 140, 353

Cold War, 311, 314

Colebrooke, A. A., 170–71

Colefax, Lady Sybil, 212

Coleridge-Taylor, Samuel, 183, 193

Colonial Center, 281

Comfort, Alex, 282

Communism, 91, 111, 151, 183, 345, 357; and fascism, 214–15, 256; Hitler, Franco, Mussolini, and, 256; and Russia, 204–5; and Spain, 214–15, 218, 222, 230, 238, 243, 251, 257–59, 315, 408n.51; and Stalin, 218, 222, 408n.51. *See also* McCarthy, Joseph

Con d'Irène, Le (Aragon), 145–46

concentration camps: in France, xii, 221, 242–63, 272, 411n.1, 412n.2; after Franco's victory, 242–68, 305; in Germany, 242, 253, 412n.2; intellectuals in, 253–55, 260, 413n.25; in Lipari Islands, 151; military, 248–53; Republicans in, xii, 242–43, 248–58, 353; and Spanish Civil War, 151, 221, 272

Connoisseur (magazine), 299

Connolly, Cyril, 294, 299

Conrad, Joseph, 31

Contact, 127

Contact Press, 140, 390n.10

Cooper, Douglas, 361, 370

Cooper, Duff, 21, 30, 64, 85

Cooper, Lady Diana, 21, 115, 287, 308, 347

Corey, Mabel, 85

"Coriolanus" (Eliot), 50

Cornell, Katharine, xii, 133

Cornwallis-West, Jennie, 12, 14. *See also* Churchill, Lady Randolph

Corrupt Coterie, 23, 27–30, 46, 129; members of, 27–29, 38, 134, 286, 331; during World War I, 51, 60

Coughlin, Charles E., 256

Cowley, Malcolm, 94

Craigie, Marjorie, 28

Crane, Hart, 119, 140

Crève Coeur, Le (Aragon), 300

Crevel, René, 107, 118, 303

Crisis (magazine), 159, 206

Criterion (magazine), 50

Crowder, Henry, 149–55, 205; death of, 173, 335; and Nancy, 129, 142, 149–55, 156–66, 172–73, 174–80, 345; and *Negro*, 156–66, 172–73, 174–80, 182; and racism, 152–55, 156–66, 174–80; at Réanville, 154, 172; in United States, 129, 142, 149–55, 156–66, 157, 162–73, 172–73, 174–80, 335; works of, 142, 152, 154, 157, 174–78, 325

Crowley, Aleister, 290–91

Crozier, W. P., 240–41, 243, 245, 247, 415nn.1–2. See also *Manchester Guardian*

Cruickshank, Alfred, 272

Cuba, 170, 272, 357

Cubism, 91, 95, 107

Cullen, Countee, 140, 163, 181, 183, 193

Cunard, Bache: death of, 116; at Haycock Inn, 10, 26, 87, 116; and Maud's parties, 14, 65; Maud's relationship with, 1–2, 6, 11–12; money left to Nancy by, 116, 140; Nancy's relationship with, 3, 10–11, 13–14, 22, 26, 87, 116, 178; at Nancy's wedding, 63

Cunard, Edward, 9, 85, 149, 307, 354

Cunard, Maud Alice Burke ("Emerald"): affairs/lovers of, 3–5, 13–14, 20–21; Bache's relationship with, 1–2, 6, 11–12; and Beecham, 3, 20–21, 26, 71, 145, 159, 287, 308, 397n.9; and Carpentier, 3–4, 5, 6; as conversationalist, 21; death/estate of, 308–9, 419n.16; and Eliot, 39; and geopolitics, 211–14; and G. M., 3–5, 11–14, 18, 132, 379n.27; identity of father of, 3, 5; and Joyce, 13, 32, 88, 145; in London, 10, 20–21, 22, 71, 88, 287; and motherhood, 6, 24; name change of, 116–17; Nancy's allowance from, 86, 159, 160, 400nn.10,12; on Nancy's presentation as debutante, 23–24; Nancy's relationship with, 6, 9–13, 15, 29, 88–89, 116, 140, 145, 156–57, 159–61, 166, 170, 178–79, 178–80, 294; at Nancy's wedding, 63; on Nancy's worthless life and sickly appearance, 75; parties of, 11–14, 21, 25, 65, 138, 417n.60; and Pound, 31–32, 35; press on, 12, 174; and Prince of Wales, xii, 20, 21, 88, 97, 211–14; racism of, 156–57, 159–61, 170; and Virginia Woolf, 46

Cunard, Nancy: and Acton, 52, 125, 138, 141, 144, 154, 292, 373; and Adderly, 51, 62–63, 65, 70, 72, 85, 88–89, 387n.1; allowance of, from Maud, 86, 159, 160, 400nn.10,12; and Aragon, xii, 94, 95, 98, 103, 109–14, 123–24, 126, 141, 144, 145–46, 268, 270, 300, 301, 375; and Arlen, 126, 129–34, 137, 176; Bache's relationship with, 3, 10–11, 13–14, 22, 26, 87, 116, 178; at balls, 23–24, 29, 84, 108, 149; beauty

Edel, Leon, 45, 47
Eden, Anthony, 21
Editions Braun, 337
Edward, Prince of Wales, 380n.9,
    405nn.33–34; and Germany/Hitler,
    211–14, 416n.42; and Maud Cunard, xii,
    20, 21, 88, 97, 211–14; and Nancy, 21,
    24–25, 200
Edward VII (king of England), 20
Edward VIII (king of England), 211, 213–14
Edwards, Brent Hayes, 181, 402n.1
Eiffel Tower (restaurant), 28–29, 30, 42, 82,
    87, 134, 158
Eighteenth Congress of Writers of France,
    333
Einstein, Albert, 107, 196, 200, 204
Eisenhower, Dwight D., 314
Eliot, T. S., xii, 146; anti-Semitism of,
    39, 384n.50; childhood of, 37–39,
    383nn.44,46; death of, 36; as Imagist,
    31; and Maud Cunard, 39, 383n.48;
    and Nancy, 35–41, 69, 126, 176, 352; and
    Pound, 33, 35; and publishing, 140, 349;
    on religion, 37, 39; and sexuality, 39–41,
    383n.49; and Spanish Civil War, 231;
    and Symbolism, 37; in United States,
    38–39; and World War II, 294, 295; and
    Wyndham Lewis, 41, 385n.52
Eliot, Vivienne, 35, 383n.49
Ellerman, Bryher (Winifred), 93, 94, 129,
    390n.10
Ellington, Edward ("Duke"), 182, 190–92
Ellis, Havelock, 30–31, 65, 118, 141, 146–47
Ellmann, Richard, 324
Éluard, Paul, 300, 301, 413n.25
Emmet, Robert, 3, 156, 165
Empire News, 171
Endgame (Beckett), 332, 362, 370
English Review, 86
Epstein, Jacob, 28, 385n.55
España en el corazón (*Spain in the Heart*;
    Neruda), 228
Ethiopia, 55, 138; and African Americans,
    210, 238; Hitler, Locarno treaties, and,
    214; and Italy, 201, 206–11; and Musso-
    lini, 138; Nancy's reporting on, 55, 201,

206–11, 223, 238, 345. *See also* Abyssinia,
    crisis in
Ethiopian News, 207
Europe (magazine), 299, 307

Fairbairn, Sydney, 63–64, 81, 88, 120
Fairbanks, Douglas, 47
Falange/Falangists, 216, 246–47, 249, 312–13
Farewell to Arms, A (Hemingway), 66–67,
    68, 215
Farquhar, Earl, 88
fascism, 104; in Africa, 202; in Britain,
    202–4; colors for, 225; and Commu-
    nism, 214–15, 256; and Ethiopia, 209;
    and France, 254; and Italy, 90, 103, 149,
    151, 209, 217; and Mosley, 203–4, 212,
    270; and politics, xiii, 151; and Pound,
    34, 231–32; and Spanish Civil War, 34,
    39, 114, 202, 214–19, 221–22, 225, 229–30,
    234, 236, 238, 409n.24; and Stalin, 205,
    214–15, 218; and World War II, xiii, 34,
    114, 270, 282, 311, 313, 314; writers op-
    posed to, 256
Faulkner, William, 220, 232, 409n.24
Faure, Elie, 226
Fauvism, 95
Fenollosa, Ernest, 33
Ferdinand, Archduke, assassination of, 52
Ferdinand of Romania (king), 108
Fielding, Daphne, 63, 234, 247, 421n.11
Figaro, Le (newspaper), 258
Finley, William Le Page, 306–10, 316,
    419n.20
Finnegans Wake (Joyce), 96
Firbank, Ronald, 138, 303
"First Sonnet, The" (Cunard), 17
Fitzgerald, F. Scott, 97, 119, 125, 140
Fitzgerald, Zelda, 92, 97, 119, 125
Flanner, Janet: letters to, 303, 305–6, 308,
    310, 317–18, 337, 344, 346, 347–48, 352–
    53, 355–56, 358, 361, 363, 366, 424n.24;
    and Nancy, 31, 96, 117–20, 123, 126, 284,
    301, 373, 393n.61; on *Negro*, 173; and
    New Yorker, 93, 117–18; in Paris, 90, 92,
    93, 96, 327, 368; at Réanville, 144; on
    refugees, 246

Flint, F. S., 31
Ford, Ford Maddox, 13, 31, 35, 100, 382n.36
Ford, Hugh, 174, 184
Ford, Thérèse, 358
Forster, E. M., 44, 286, 386n.59
Le Français de Grande-Bretagne, 281
France: concentration camps in, xii, 221,
    242–63, 272, 411n.1, 412n.2; and fascism,
    254; Janet Flanner and Solita Solano
    in, 117; occupation of, 114, 129, 203, 269,
    271, 298–99, 300–301, 304; racism in,
    156, 157, 166; refugees in, xii, 221, 240,
    242–63, 413n.38; and Spanish Civil War,
    239–40, 410nn.32,45; and World War I,
    52, 55, 57, 61; and World War II, 269–70,
    281–82, 301. See also specific cities
Franckenstein, Joseph, 327, 357, 425n.37
Franco, Francisco: concentration camps
    after victory of, 242–68, 305; death of,
    314; and Hitler, 242, 256–57, 312, 326;
    Hitler, Mussolini, and, 256, 262, 312,
    322; neutrality of, during World War II,
    218, 312; second war against, 310–16; and
    Spain, 305–6, 310–16, 330; and Spanish
    Civil War, 138, 216–19, 221, 223, 229, 231,
    232, 234–36, 238, 240, 409n.24, 410n.45,
    411n.50; and Spanish refugees, xiii, 221,
    242–63; and Stalin, 311–12, 313
Franklin, Benjamin, 1, 335
Frazier, E. Franklin, 181
Free French, 270, 281, 282
"Free peoples—What of Spain?" (Alberti),
    330
French Secret Services, The (Porch), 282
Freud, Sigmund, 34, 44, 85, 91, 93
Freund, Gisèle, 93
Friends of Republican Spain, 281
"From the Train" (Cunard), 49–50
Fry, Roger, 31, 44, 46
Fussell, Paul, 25, 57, 294
Futurism, 91

G. M. See Moore, George
G. M.: Memories of George Moore (Cu-
    nard), 319, 333
Galsworthy, John, 31

Gandarillas, Tony, 361
Gaos, Vincente, 330
Garbo, Greta, xii, 93, 133
Garçonne, La (Margueritte), 92
Garnett, David, 29–30, 46–47, 140, 154,
    200, 366
Garvey, Marcus, 154, 171; wife of, 206–7, 210
Gates, Henry Louis, Jr., 98
Gaudier-Brzeska, Henri, 115, 381n.30,
    385nn.54–55, 395n.16
Gellert, Lawrence, 169–70, 200, 273–74
Gellhorn, Martha, 237
geopolitics, and Maud Cunard, 211–14
George V (king of England), 24, 61, 88, 211
Germany: concentration camps in, 242,
    253, 412n.2; after Franco's victory, 242,
    244, 412n.2; Nancy in, 22, 51; nonaggres-
    sion pact of, with Russia, 217, 269; and
    Prince of Wales, 211–14, 416n.42; and
    Spanish Civil War, 232, 233, 234, 236,
    242; in World War I, 52, 61; in World
    War II, 269–71, 275–84, 290, 297–99,
    301–5, 312. See also Hitler, Adolf; Nazis
"Gerontion" (Eliot), 37
Gide, André, 140, 200, 204
Gilbert, Morris, 271, 284–85, 299, 305,
    418n.12
Gilbert, Stuart, 304, 305
"Gioconda Smile, The" (Huxley), 138
Glendinning, Victoria, 295–96, 418n.61
Glyn, Elinor, 14
Goasgüen, Jean and Georgette, 299, 302,
    303
Goded, Angel, 223, 259
Gödel, Kurt, 93
Goffin, Robert, 191–92
Gollancz, Victor, 204
Gordon, Eugene, 169, 206
Gordon, Lyndall, 383n.49
Gordon, Taylor, 166, 168, 173
Gough, Sylvia, 97
governesses, 6, 7–9, 178
Goya, Francisco de, 215
Grampion Hotel, 166–69
Grand Man: Memories of Norman Douglas
    (Cunard), 148, 208, 422n.28

Milhaud, Darius, 98, 107, 108
Mills, Florence, 98, 190, 193
Ministry of Information, 280, 281
Miró, Joan, 95, 96, 220, 303, 331
Mirror (newspaper), 168, 169
Modigliani, Amedeo, 114
Moens, Bernelot, 202
Moerman, Ernest, 191
Moffat, Curtis, 28, 30, 115, 116, 126
Mola, Emilio, 216
Molina, Juan, 315, 316
Mondrian, Piet, 95, 96, 220, 236
Monnier, Adrienne, 93, 96, 129
Monroe, Harriet, 31, 33, 35
Montgomery, Bernard, 286
Moore, George (G. M.): and Aragon, 112;
    and Bloomsbury group, 45, 386n.64;
    and Burkhart, 319, 338; on friends of
    color, 157; on homosexuality, 35; and
    Irish Revival, 17, 18–19, 156; and Maud
    Cunard, 3–5, 11–14, 18, 132, 379n.27;
    memoir of, 88, 319, 333; and Nancy, 4,
    5, 6–7, 8–9, 11–19, 22–23, 35, 47, 60, 72,
    75, 87, 88, 120, 126, 141, 145, 161, 178, 345,
    394n.5; and poetry, 16–17, 48; portrait of,
    308, 317, 354, 363; and sexuality, 18, 60;
    and Yeats, 12, 18–19
Moore, Henry, 220, 236, 286, 323–24, 338
Moore, Irina, 323
Moore, Marianne, 31, 390n.10
Morales, Tómas Canas, 311, 342, 345, 351
Morgan, Evan, 27, 30
Morgan, Louise, 271, 273, 286; correspon-
    dence of, 303, 305, 331, 338–39, 365; and
    Nancy's illness, 348–51
Morgan, Otto, 350
Morning Post, 189
Mortimer, Raymond, 44–45, 115, 349,
    417n.43
Mosley, Lady Diana, 287, 405n.37
Mosley, Sir Oswald, 137, 287, 405n.37; and
    fascism, 203–4, 212, 270
La Mothe-Fénélon, 316–42, 345, 351–55,
    358–59, 363
Moynagh, Maureen, 181
Moyses, Louis, 98

Murphy, Esther, 308
Mussolini, Benito: and Abyssinian crisis,
    138, 202, 206–10; and Hitler, Franco,
    and gaining power, 256, 262, 312, 322; in
    Italy, 150–51; Matteoti's murder by, 151;
    and Pound, 102; and Spanish Civil War,
    216, 221, 235

NAACP, 182, 198, 354
"Nada, Nada en la Nada" ("Nothing, Noth-
    ing Within Nothing"; Cunard), 321
Nadeau, Maurice, 90–91
Narcisa (refugee), 240
Nathaniels, R. C., 194
Nation, 223, 263, 305
NATO, 314
Negro (Cunard), 98, 181–95, 204; "Africa"
    section of, 194–95; art in, 182, 183, 195,
    402n.2; and Beckett, xii, 182, 191, 192,
    323; birth of, 173–74; colonial exploi-
    tation in, 195; copies of, destroyed
    in Blitz, 174; and Crowder, 156–66,
    172–73, 174–80, 182; "Europe" section
    of, 183, 402n.2; flier on, 163, 400n.17;
    Harlem in, 182, 187, 189; histories in,
    165, 181, 182; imperialism in, 182, 183,
    195; Jamaica essay in, 171, 172, 182, 194;
    material for, at Réanville, 303; "Music"
    section of, 182–83, 189–93, 400n.17,
    402n.2; "Negro Stars," 402n.2; organiz-
    ing/methodology for, 231, 281, 422n.29;
    poetry in, 182, 183, 184, 193–94, 402n.2;
    prelude to, 156–80; and press, 173–74,
    186–87, 189; religion in, 185, 187–88;
    and Russia, 205, 206; Scottsboro boys
    in, 182, 196–202; slavery in, 183–86, 189;
    and social justice, 19; "West Indies and
    South America" section of, 402n.2; Wis-
    hart as publisher of, 172, 173, 174. *See
    also specific individuals*
"Negro on the Spiral, or a Method of
    Negro Music, The" (Antheil), 189–90
Negro Welfare Center, 281
Negro Worker (magazine), 205
Neruda, Pablo, xii, 103, 330, 414n.54; and
    Nancy, 126, 228–30, 264–68, 330, 347,

Sitwell, Osbert, 21, 27, 67, 102, 115, 149, 296, 303, 383n.49
Sitwell, Sacheverell, 28, 115, 309
Sketch (magazine), 116, 394n.1
Slade School, 26
"Slave Risings and Race Riots" (Dabney), 185
Smith, Ada ("Bricktop"), 97
Smoller, Sanford J., 95
Smouldering Freedom (Palencia), 315
Snyder, Milton and Alice, 388n.15
"So You May Nail Your Sorrow to My Name's Cross" (Cunard), 105
Soir, Le (newspaper), 240
Solano, Solita, 117–19, 273, 284, 393n.61; letters to, 303, 305–6, 308, 310, 317–18, 337, 344, 346, 347–48, 352–53, 355–56, 358, 361, 363, 366, 424n.24; and Nancy, 117–19, 284, 373, 393n.61; in Paris, 327, 368; at Réanville, 144
"Soldiers Fallen in Battle" (Cunard), 47–48
"Sonnet" (Cunard), 48
"Sonnet Political " (Cunard), 271
Sonnets to Aurelia (Nichols), 88
Sorley, Charles S., 67
Sotelo, José Calvo, 216
Soto, Albertina Azócar, 414n.54
South, Eddie, 152, 153
South Wind (Douglas), 65
"Southern Sheriff" (Cunard), 193–94
Soviet Union. *See* Russia
Spain: Barcelona, 210, 216–17, 220–22, 225–26, 232–34, 239–40, 242–44, 247, 340, 409n.28, 411n.51; and Communism, 214–15, 218, 222, 230, 238, 243, 251, 257–59, 315, 408n.51; and Franco, 305–6, 310–16, 330; Loyalists in, 129, 345, 346; Madrid, 111, 216–17, 220, 225–27, 233–34, 239, 242, 340, 410n.45, 411n.51; Nancy in, 115, 210–11, 305–6, 310–16, 318–19, 337, 338–43; refugees from, xii–xiii, 221, 227, 240, 242–63, 268, 272, 327, 414n.56, 423n.44; and Russia, 311–12; and United Nations, 312–13; and United States, 312–14; after World War II, 262, 311–16.

See also Spanish Civil War; *specific individuals*
"Spain" (Auden), 230–31
"Spain" (Cunard), 334
Spain at War (newspaper), 223
"Spain Today" (Izcaray), 315
Spanish Civil War, xii; and arts, 230, 236–37; and blacks, 210, 221, 223, 235–38, 411n.49; causes of, 215, 407n.46; deaths in, 218, 234; "Enquête" (questionnaire) about, 231–32; and fascism, 34, 39, 114, 202, 214–19, 221–22, 225, 229–30, 234, 236, 238, 409n.24; and France, 239–40, 410nn.32,45; and Franco, 138, 216–19, 221, 223, 229, 231, 232, 234–36, 238, 240, 409n.24, 410n.45, 411n.50; and Germany, 232, 233, 234, 236, 242; and Hitler, 214–17, 221, 233, 239, 260, 312, 408n.51; International Brigades in, 210, 215, 217–18, 221, 225–26, 235–36, 238, 281; Lincoln Brigade/Battalion in, 210, 217–18, 237–38, 256, 411n.49; and Moors, 221, 233, 235–36, 239; and Mussolini, 216, 221, 235; Nancy's reporting on, 55, 201–2, 210–11, 214–19, 220–41, 304, 323, 397n.9; and Neruda, 126, 220, 228–30; neutrality/nonintervention during, 220–21, 239–40, 243; *plaquettes* about, 230–31, 264; and poets, intellectuals, and idealists, 214–19; and Pound, 108, 231–32; and Republicans, 103, 202, 215–19, 226–27, 228, 230, 231, 233, 236, 237, 408n.51; revisionist interpretations of, 218–19, 220, 407n.50; and Russia, 205, 214–19, 226; sequelae of, 223. *See also specific individuals*
Spanish Earth, The (film), 226
Spanish Newsletter (newspaper), 223
Speck, Hugo, 180
Spender, Stephen, 103, 220, 230, 287, 383n.49, 410n.43
"Spiders Weave, The" (Cunard), 105–6
"Spilling the Spanish Beans" (Orwell), 218–19
Spingarn, Arthur, 354